Contemporary Tibet

Contemporary Tibet

Politics, Development, and Society in a Disputed Region

Barry Sautman and June Teufel Dreyer, Editors

An East Gate Book

M.E.Sharpe
Armonk, New York
London, England

An East Gate Book

The EuroSlavic fonts used to create this work are © 1986–2002 Payne Loving Trust.
EuroSlavic is available from Linguist's Software, Inc.,
www.linguistsoftware.com, P.O. Box 580, Edmonds, WA 98020-0580 USA
tel (425) 775-1130.

While every effort was made to contact the
owners of the materials printed herein,
we apologize for any omissions.

Library of Congress Cataloging-in-Publication Data

Contemporary Tibet : politics, development, and society in a disputed region / edited by
Barry Sautman and June Teufel Dreyer.
    p. cm.
"An East Gate book."
Includes bibliographical references and index.
ISBN-0-7656-1354-9 (hardcover : alk. paper)
    1. Tibet (China) I. Dreyer, June Teufel, 1939– II. Sautman, Barry, 1949–

DS7686.C64 2005
951'506—dc22   2004022523

Printed in the United States of America

The paper used in this publication meets the minimum requirements of
American National Standard for Information Sciences
Permanence of Paper for Printed Library Materials,
ANSI Z 39.48-1984.

∞

BM (c)   10   9   8   7   6   5   4   3   2   1

Contents

List of Tables

Contemporary Tibet

1

Introduction

The Tibet Question in Contemporary Perspective

Barry Sautman and June Teufel Dreyer

Contemporary Tibet[1] is the subject of one of the world's longest running ethno-territorial conflicts, dating from just after the People's Republic of China (PRC) was founded in 1949. Virtually every aspect of state–society interaction in Tibet has been contested by the principal parties—the Tibetan exiles led by the Dalai Lama and the PRC government led by the Chinese Communist Party (CCP).[2] It is this "Tibet Question" that links the essays in the present volume, most of which are revised and updated versions of papers presented on panels at international conferences on Asian studies or political science held in North America from 1999 to 2001.

There have been intermittent expectations of formal negotiations between the principal parties to the Tibet Question, but their zero-sum view of Tibet's political status, harsh recriminations, and mutual suspicion have been persistent obstacles. The participation of other actors has also had an effect. Foreign states acknowledge that Tibet is part of China and none formally recognizes the Tibet government-in-exile (TGIE), yet a number of states sustain the exile cause in other ways. Thousands of "Tibet supporters" have also rallied to it, including members of parliaments, rights activists, actors, musicians, and ordinary converts to Tibetan Buddhism in the West. Scholars have also begun to influence debates about the Tibet Question. The present volume is a contribution to that trend, one that will likely continue for some time because, as the Dalai Lama has observed, a political solution to the Tibet Question is still far off.[3]

The conflict over Tibet has above all been about its political status. As with many sovereignty disputes, the seas of ink spilled in polemics over historic claims have not formed an ocean of wisdom. That is because, as our contributor Wang Lixiong often argues, it is anachronistic to use modern political and legal standards to judge pre-modern Tibet's relationship with China.[4] As with other disputes, moreover, Tibet's status cannot be resolved mainly through assertions of priority of possession or rule, which is seldom straightforward. Exercises of actual and symbolic authority and the attitude of the international community have proved to be more relevant to framing and settling the sovereignty aspects of such conflicts.[5]

Many of our contributors have previously produced works on salient historical issues,[6] allowing us to focus on matters of contemporary concern. In the present volume, several contributors (Dibyesh Anand, Robbie Barnett, He Baogang, Wang Lixiong) deal with the status and governing of Tibet. Other contested areas examined by chapters herein include economic development (June Teufel Dreyer, Melvyn Goldstein, Hu Xiaojiang and Manuel Salazar, Dawa Norbu), population (Barry Sautman), religion (Yu Changjiang), the role of external powers (A. Tom Grunfeld, Xu Mingxu and Yuan Feng), and representations of the Tibet Question itself (Christiaan Klieger, Amy Mountcastle).

The Issues: Binaries and Beyond

The debate about Tibet is often framed in binaries, but varied views do exist within the two camps on key issues, such as how Tibet relates to China's prospective political development. Many exiles argue that independence is attainable because China, like the former Soviet Union, will disintegrate due to economic and social problems.[7] Among advocates of independence are some who "propose the use of all means, violent if necessary" to achieve it.[8] From the early to late 1990s, the Dalai Lama also foresaw the PRC's collapse,[9] but did not support violence to hasten this result. He no longer speaks of the possibility of collapse,[10] hoping instead that "China will become more open and eventually more democratic" and that this change will lead to an offer of expanded autonomy for Tibet.[11] By the same token, some PRC officials contend that the exile cause will recede when the Dalai Lama passes on and development transforms Tibetan society,[12] while others hold that these changes will not end the dispute.[13]

The two sides' judgments of each other's staying power affect not only their "negotiations about negotiations," but also a range of PRC policies and the exiles' reactions to them. For example, the PRC would not likely invest the billions of dollars it has put into building a railway into central Tibet, across hundreds of kilometers of the world's most difficult terrain,[14] if it believed its hold on the region were shaky; nor would the exiles criticize the railroad as sharply as they have if they were convinced that Tibet (and the railroad with it) were soon to be theirs.[15] Internal disaccord thus often determines policy as much as do the differences between the two sides. That being said, the principal parties have evinced sharp and longstanding—although not necessarily unbridgeable—differences on many matters. As one of our contributors, Melvyn Goldstein, has said elsewhere, "Both sides have expended an enormous amount of time and effort to spread their representations of past history and contemporary politics, the result being diametrically opposed constructions of reality."[16] The contrasting positions of the parties as to the most significant issues can be briefly introduced as background to the chapters that follow.

Status and Governance

Tibetan exiles maintain that for the past 2,000 years Tibet has always been an independent political entity,[17] while the PRC contends that Tibet has been part of China since the Yuan dynasty of the thirteenth century.[18] The two sides have quarreled over this historical issue more than any other matter, with the debate aiming at mobilizing support, rather than arriving at a common ground. A resolution of the historical dispute is not, however, the make or break matter it is often portrayed to be: neither side explicitly demands that the other accept its view of history as a precondition to negotiations. Some exiled leaders, such as the Dalai Lama's eldest brother, do hold that the consequence of asserting the past independence of Tibet is not only that Tibet is an occupied state, but also that its independence must be regained.[19] The Dalai Lama also holds that Tibet was independent before 1951, but argues that the matter of its past status should be left "up to historians and up to legal experts" and that "We accept Tibet as part of the People's Republic of China."[20] The PRC has accused the Dalai Lama of "mak[ing] false propaganda of Tibetan history" and sometimes cites his claim that Tibet has always been sovereign as evidence that he has not abandoned the goal of independence. It does not, however, require that he renounce his view of Tibet's history in order for negotiations to begin.[21]

If the Tibet Question's principal parties were to set aside their dispute about Tibet's historical relationship with China and agree, in some fashion, that Tibet is part of China, it would not mean that they concur on the consequences this has for governance in Tibet. The Dalai Lama seeks "genuine autonomy" for Tibet in cultural, religious, economic, environmental, and educational affairs.[22] He has also proposed a "one country, two systems" relation with the PRC,[23] based on a high degree of political autonomy, with a multiparty system and direct elections. Because it would obviate the CCP's leading role,[24] the PRC opposes for Tibet the model it supports for Hong Kong and Macao[25] and maintains that the Tibetan exiles want this arrangement as "a disguised independence of Tibet, a gradual progression to independence."[26]

Development

While the Dalai Lama has stated that "all Tibetans want more prosperity, more material development,"[27] Tibetan exiles and Tibet support organizations criticize development in Tibet as primarily benefiting the Chinese state and Han migrants, whether permanent or temporary, to the region.[28] At the same time, Tibetans are impoverished[29] even as their environment is irreparably damaged.[30] They argue that the PRC government carries out development in Tibet with little regard for the views of Tibetans, and that the PRC treasury profits from Tibet through state enterprises, such as in mining and timber, that operate in Tibet. Infrastructure in Tibet, it is argued, is constructed to facilitate military operations and the central government's exploitation of resources, while most Tibetans, who are peasants and herders, are shut out of development or at least have benefited from it much less than Han Chinese migrants to Tibetan areas.

The PRC government contends that it sustains a net loss from Tibetan areas because it heavily subsidizes infrastructure development and government services, including more than 90 percent of the annual budget of the Tibet Autonomous Region (TAR).[31] It argues that Tibetans are the principal beneficiaries of Tibet's development, which provides opportunities and facilities open to all, including elements of preferential policies for Tibetans. Government statements emphasize that most Han Chinese in Tibet are temporary migrants engaged in small trade and thus should not be the most significant elements in any assessment of who, among long-term residents of Tibet, benefits from development. While urban areas, where non-Tibetans concentrate, are at the level of other PRC towns and thus much more prosperous than the countryside, urban–rural disparities are a universal phenomenon, while most rural Tibetans have experienced significant increases in income levels, education, health care, transport, and communications over the past half-century. The environment, it is argued, is the best preserved in China and pristine by world standards.[32]

Population

Demographic issues in the Tibet Question have been about the effects of conflict, migration, and family planning. Both the TGIE and Tibetan Youth Congress have compared China's actions in Tibet to the Nazi extermination of Jews.[33] Exile leaders contend that the Tibetan population was 6 million in 1950 and the same a half-century later, because the PRC government killed at least 1.2 million Tibetans through war, imprisonment, execution, or famine.[34] The figure is cited in Western media,[35] but has been challenged by demographers[36] and a prominent British writer, who, while leader of the main UK Tibet support group, examined and found useless the documents on which the figure is based.[37]

The Dalai Lama has accused China of "demographic aggression."[38] Exile leaders contend that as a result of migration and family planning restrictions, Tibetans in Tibet are outnumbered by 7.5 million non-Tibetans.[39] The geographical basis of the figure is not clear, but seems to take in all contiguous territories in which some Tibetans live. Wang Lixiong has pointed out that the 1982 census (China's first actual enumeration) showed 1.541 million Han in all the officially designated Tibetan areas, which cover almost the entire Tibet Plateau, an area comprising about one-fourth of the territory of the PRC, and most, but not all, territories the exiles claim for Tibet. The 1990 census showed Han in these areas dropping to 1.521 million.[40] By the 2000 census, the number had fallen to 1.470 million. Tibetans in the PRC numbered 3.870 million in 1982—about 99 percent in the Tibetan areas—and increased to 5.416 million by 2000.[41]

Tibetan exiles and supporters argue that family planning restrictions contribute to "cultural genocide" and assert that coercive birth control is applied, if not in Tibet as a whole, at least in its northeast.[42] Government sources counter that, particularly in ecologically fragile areas such as Tibet, there is a delicate balance of population to land area that should not be exceeded. Arguing along a different line, regional Family Planning Commission head Purbu Zhoima asserts that "Tibet has no policy that sets a quota for the number of children Tibetan women may have, nor does it force women to have abortions or undergo sterilization procedures."[43] The U.S. government concluded in 2002 that "Family planning policies permitted Tibetans, like members of other minority groups, to have more children than Han Chinese. Urban Tibetans, including Communist Party members, were generally permitted to have two children. Rural Tibetans were encouraged, but not required, to limit births to three children. These guidelines were not strictly enforced."[44]

Religion

Spirituality and sovereignty are linked in the Tibet Question through Tibet's traditional system of governance in which politics and religion were tightly intertwined.[45] Many exile officials continue to regard this system as ideal for Tibet, and the two top leaders of the exile administration, the Dalai Lama and his prime minister Samdhong Rinpoche, are indeed religious figures. Ten of the forty-six seats in the Tibetan parliament-in-exile are reserved for representatives of the four Tibetan Buddhist "sects" and a pre-Buddhist Tibetan religion. Religion expressly underpins Tibetan nationalism.[46] The Dalai Lama may not view this arrangement as ideal, however. He has stated that "Religious institutions and politics should stay apart."[47]

Religion is also linked to governance in Tibet by the CCP's hostility to believers playing a leading political role. The (Han Chinese) CCP secretary in Tibet, Chen Kuiyuan, from 1992 to 2000 stated that Communists are not allowed to have any religious belief, that high-level officials cannot participate in religious activities, and that interest in religion should fade as Tibet becomes more prosperous.[48] Other disputes concern religious freedom, contested in terms of whether there are enough monks and nuns in Tibetan areas (there are about 150,000),[49] the right of Tibetans to engage in ordinary religious practices,[50] and the monasteries' relationship with the state, especially in terms of political surveillance.[51] Exile leaders maintain there is no religious freedom in Tibet;[52] PRC officials claim that there are no restrictions on religious belief.[53]

The Role of External Powers

Among the states involved in the Tibet Question, India and the United States stand out, the former as the exiles' primary host and the latter as their main source of pressure on China.[54] This support has been reciprocated by exile leaders. The Dalai Lama has stated that he has never lost an opportunity to express gratitude to India. He endorses India's position on Kashmir (including its view that the region's accession to India was unproblematic), as well as its development of nuclear weapons, self-image of "strong democratic traditions" and "nonviolence and tolerance," and bid to become a UN Security Council permanent member. In 2002, the International Campaign for Tibet (ICT) presented its annual Light of Truth Award to India.[55]

The Dalai Lama has found U.S. leaders "all very supportive of the Tibetan cause" and has said that visiting George W. Bush was like encountering an old friend. He generally refrains from criticizing U.S. foreign policy and has stated that "The social freedom you Americans instituted has proved immensely valuable to all people around the world."[56] He remarked in 1990 that it was unfair for the United States not to do for Tibet what it had done for Kuwait,[57] and regards the outcome of the war in Afghanistan as "perhaps some kind of liberation." He has stated that it would take some years to judge whether the war in Iraq was justified, but has praised past U.S. military efforts, averring that the Korean War "protected South Korea's prosperity and freedom" and that in Vietnam the United States had "the same aim, the same motivation" as in Korea, but had failed.[58]

China, while not happy with the Dalai Lama's presence in India, has reached a modus vivendi on the issue with the Indian government. India provides financial, but little direct political, aid to the exile cause, while China has promised to stay out of India's internal and foreign affairs.[59] In contrast, China decries the more outspoken U.S. expressions of support for the exiles.[60] The CCP secretary in Tibet very likely had not only imperial Britain, but also the contemporary United States in mind when he stated that "So called 'Tibetan independence' is the outcome of imperialist aggression against China in modern history, in a vain attempt to divide the Chinese nation. It is the outcome of class struggle on an international scale."[61] China also contends with criticisms by other external actors, especially Tibet caucuses in the European, Canadian, and Japanese parliaments, which demand the PRC unconditionally begin negotiations with the Dalai Lama's representatives.[62]

Representations of Tibet and the Tibet Question

Representations of Tibet by the exiles and PRC government are almost wholly at odds. Exile leaders, it is said, have adopted the Western Shangri-La myth of pre-1951 Tibet[63] and now see the West as a surrogate Shangri-La,[64] with both places foils for negative representations of contemporary Tibet. The PRC government in contrast portrays pre-1951 Tibet as a house of horrors.[65] Former premier Li Peng has stated that "old Tibet was one of the darkest and most backward regions in the world, and one of the regions where the violation of human rights was most serious";[66] a National People's Congress official has said that in pre-1951 Tibet, "the cruelty and misery suffered by the Tibetan people were even harsher than that of medieval Europe,"[67] while contemporary Tibet is said to be experiencing "the best period" in its history.[68] The Dalai Lama, however, counters that "Three generations of Tibetans have lived through this darkest period of history, undergoing tremendous hardship and suffering."[69] The TGIE asserts that "Tibet today is in the throes of a second Cultural Revolution as the Chinese authorities step up their long-term strategy to exterminate Tibet's distinct cultural and ethnic identity."[70]

The PRC government represents the Tibet Question as provoked only by forces external to China, arguing it manifests continuing support by Western states for Tibetan separatists.[71] The exiles contend that the question arises only from PRC policy. The Dalai Lama has stated that "It is an issue of colonial rule: the repression of Tibet by the [PRC] and the resistance to that rule by the people of Tibet."[72] Both sides maintain that negotiations require meeting conditions, with the PRC having conditions for initiating negotiations and the exiles having conditions for conducting them. As affirmed by Premier Wen Jiabao in 2003, the PRC preconditions are that the Dalai Lama renounce independence, abjure separatist activity, and recognize that Tibet and Taiwan are inalienable parts of China.[73] The TGIE has said that negotiations should be started without pre-conditions,[74] but its prime minister has added that as to the negotiations themselves, "[W]e have two conditions. First, the whole of Tibet should be considered as one and second, the political system of Tibet should be a democratic one."[75]

The Chapters

Contributors writing on the status and governance of Tibet view concepts such as sovereignty and autonomy in ways that the major contenders in the Tibet Question generally do not. They see notions related to Tibet's status as modern impositions whose rigidity admits few opportunities for shaping mutual accommodation. The contributors also recognize that issues of governance in Tibet cannot be reduced to such dichotomies as whether autonomy is "genuine" or "meaningless," whether individuals or policies serve "Chinese" or "Tibetan" interests, or whether Tibet should or should not have a liberal democratic system. They believe that status and governance questions have proved to be too complicated for such binary analysis.

Dibyesh Anand underscores the West's role in the discursive constructions of Tibet's status and of Tibetanness. Sovereignty, viewed as exclusive national jurisdiction, is an aspect of modernity: indeed, the West supplies the very categories and vocabulary that the Tibet Question parties employ in the discourse of sovereignty, even though an absolute understanding of sovereignty and independence was alien to both Chinese and Tibetans before the twentieth century and even though both peoples identify themselves as politically and culturally non-Western. While the parties marshal their historical "facts" as resources in a highly statist debate over sovereignty, they fail to question the concept of sovereignty itself, as well as related concepts such as autonomy and self-determination. Their accep-

tance of these concepts in simplest form amounts to an unquestioning acquiescence to the hegemony of Western ideas. Yet alternatives to this realist conception
of sovereignty can and should be imagined.

Because of the need for Western support and the significant role played by
externally based Tibet support groups in the Tibet Question, Western hegemony is
accepted as well in diasporic discourses concerning Tibet and Tibetanness. A neo-
orientalist strategic essentialism that simplifies Tibetan identities in translating Tibet
for Westerners also impacts the self-identities of diasporic Tibetans, many of whom
accept Westernized notions of Tibetanness. Thus, although a modern sense of nationhood was absent in pre-1951 Tibet, exile representations cast Tibetan nationhood as an historical reality. To gain legitimacy in the West, democratizing elements
have been added to exile self-governance, and the vocabulary of human rights,
development, environmental protection, and so forth has been deployed. Representations that directly fulfill the established Western image of Tibetans as inherently spiritual and peaceful have been especially prominent.

Robbie Barnett argues that everyone but the Tibetans in Tibet are in one way or
another external to the Tibet Question, or that at least it can be said that those
Tibetans play a much greater role in determining events in the region than is commonly imagined. The Tibetan exiles and their supporters tend to represent Tibetans in Tibet as either collaborators or martyrs, while the Chinese state advances a
dichotomy of patriots and reactionaries. There have indeed been political actors
who clearly opted for one side or the other, but also Tibetans who engage in ambiguous political activities that do not fit easily into such simplistic classifica-
tions. At present, some who take this path have sought to utilize such PRC united
front institutions, such as the Chinese People's Political Consultative Conference
(*zhengxie*), to advance their efforts to secure cultural autonomy. Other Tibetans in
Tibet may involve themselves directly in cultural activities, or they may become
entrepreneurs. Some who participate in these activities practice strategic concealment, not in the sense of being agents of exile forces, but in wanting to promote
Tibetan culture, education, or development in ways that may not be in full accord
with the current thinking of state leaders. Such concealment feeds suspicion of
Tibetan officials that intersects with Han chauvinist conceptions. These suspicions
are likely to grow if Chinese nationalism is reinforced, diminishing the possibilities for Tibetan officials working with the state for reasons other than personal
advancement.

He Baogang inquires whether the concept of autonomy, particularly as conceived by the Dalai Lama, provides a solution to the Tibet Question. He notes
that the PRC government's idea of autonomy is different from liberal theories of
autonomy in not being conceived as fulfilling a right to self-determination and
in not being grounded in electoral politics. The Chinese state's conception of
"ethnic regional autonomy" is derived from Marxism, which favors a unitary,
centralized political system and the multi-ethnic solidarity of workers and peasants, as well as from a pragmatic assessment of what sort of system facilitates

stability and economic development. Political autonomy—a sort of "one country, two systems"—existed in Tibet after the People's Liberation Army entered the region in 1951, but came to an end with the Lhasa uprising of 1959. Elements of this autonomy were restored at the beginning of the 1980s, but trimmed back after demonstrations in Lhasa in the late 1980s and the collapse of the Soviet Union and Yugoslavia in the early 1990s. In practice, there is little political and legal autonomy, the system in those respects being a fair representation of the national approach. More, but far from complete, autonomy is provided as to religion, culture, and education. The Dalai Lama's notion of genuine autonomy is grounded in liberal principles, and hence is dismissive of the present autonomy in Tibet, but there have actually been some limited achievements in the practice of autonomy there. Recognition of these may provide grounds for compromise between the two sides on the autonomy issue.

Wang Lixiong proposes a system of government that, he argues, can simultaneously uphold China's unitary state while creating more autonomy for Tibet. Wang notes that newly democratized states have by no means ended ethnic conflict. Abrupt democratization has led to instigation of ethnic passions, as opinion leaders and media both incite and take advantage of imprudent popular sentiment. A democratic system in Tibet will not, he believes, guarantee that the region will remain part of China, since competition among nationalists will tend to exclude the expression of other, more moderate, opinions. The Dalai Lama seeks a political structure with directly elected representatives, whom he sees as providing a buffer against public irrationality. In an abruptly democratized Tibet, however, Wang predicts that representatives will not have administrative responsibilities. In order to secure election, they will act irresponsibly in following public opinion. Under the Dalai Lama's plan, moreover, representatives will empower the executive branch. The resulting lack of countervailing power will mean continued conflict between Tibet and China, with the parliament bent on separating Tibet from China and, once the Dalai Lama, with his pacifist message of nonviolence, is gone, that may lead to violence. Even a democratic Chinese government would therefore reject the Dalai Lama's proposal.

By contrast, Wang envisions an indirect representation system, where powerholders at a given level are elected by those at the level just below them and each level carries out administrative functions, as assuring China's unity and Tibet's autonomy. Independence drives typically come from above, but indirect representational power comes from the bottom. Lower-ranking officials will have no incentive to support higher-ranking ones in a pursuit of independence. The former will exercise partial control over the actions of the latter, and religion will be excluded from politics. Indirect representation will provide Tibetans with self-governing bodies—each exercising a high degree of autonomy—that together constitute a self-supporting greater Tibet. If the Dalai Lama adopts this approach, a dialogue between the two sides is possible.

Barry Sautman questions the Tibetan exile claim of demographic annihilation.

He argues that the idea is advanced to paint Tibet as China's colony and thus entitled to self-determination, including independence. Sautman reviews in detail the depopulations carried out by classic colonial regimes from the sixteenth through twentieth centuries, but finds no credible evidence for it in the case of Tibet.

In the last two decades, a statistical table of unnatural deaths among Tibetans from the 1950s through the 1970s has been widely circulated by Tibetan exiles and their supporters. Its total of 1.2 million is based solely on unconfirmed refugee estimates, but is cited often by Western politicians and media. Sautman points out that even the Dalai Lama, in a 1998 interview with a dissident Chinese journal, stated that there was "overlap" present in the statistics. Patrick French, head of the Free Tibet Campaign in Britain, examined the refugee interview documents and found large-scale duplications, unsubstantiated assertions, and improbabilities; for example, the number of men they claimed to have died would have amounted to 85 percent of the total Tibetan male population. A study by a demographer of the sex ratio in 1960 among young adult Tibetans also found that the number of Tibetans who may have died of famine was a small percentage of that claimed in exile statistics. As claimed, battle deaths would have been several times the ratio for the main belligerents in the two world wars. As claimed, prison deaths would have required that one-tenth of all Tibetans were imprisoned during each year of a three-decade-long period. While there certainly were unnatural deaths in Tibet, the spread of misleading statistics will ultimately alienate those concerned for Tibetans' welfare, as well as the PRC officials with whom the exiles will have to deal.

Contributors of chapters on the TAR economy agree that the average Tibetan's material well-being has improved since the decollectivization of agriculture in the 1980s, but Hu and Salazar are more sanguine about sustaining gains made since then than other contributors, including Dawa Norbu, Dreyer, and Goldstein and his co-authors. Shortcomings in the PRC government's level of sensitivity toward Tibetan culture and traditions, and their negative effect on its plans for modernization of the region, figure in Dawa Norbu's, Yu Changjiang's, and Dreyer's papers.

Hu Xiaojiang and Miguel Salazar analyze the development of the private business sector in Lhasa and its relation to migration from other provinces. They argue that labor flows into the TAR have been seen almost exclusively in the context of the ongoing political struggle over the status of the TAR, with little reference to lines of analysis of economic development and migration theory, which they believe to be more meaningful. While aggregate statistics from the Lhasa Industrial and Commercial Bureau show a clear advantage of migrants in absolute numbers, even in traditional fields such as crafts, the authors dispute the conclusion that local Tibetans are at a clear and consistent disadvantage vis-à-vis migrants. Breaking down the aggregate data, they find a more complex picture: while traditional products such as Tibetan food, sweetened tea, brick tea, and the like are still firmly in the hands of Tibetans, migrants tend to dominate the fast-growing nontraditional fields instead. In enterprises related to the trade and distribution of consumer goods produced elsewhere, it is likely that the dominance of migrant entrepreneurs will remain so long as intermediary markets and distribution channels are dependent on personal connections and informal contacts based on kinship and in-group trust.

Hu and Salazar suggest that ethnic Tibetans may be able to improve their relative position in the consumer goods trade if they can exploit their existing connections with South Asia. As markets mature and new forms of consumer demand emerge, the authors expect that new opportunities will open up and there will be more ethnic and regional diversity. While factors such as initial capital, skills, and knowledge may give a significant first-mover advantage, facilitating the formation of an ethnic niche, these factors have limited force as barriers to entry for second-wave entrepreneurs, including locals. The authors conclude that only when migration to Lhasa is seen as migration rather than just another development in a political conflict can we effectively assess its social consequences.

Dawa Norbu asserts that the Chinese population transfer to Tibet has had devastating effects on the indigenous population, as Han settlers and their children take away the better homes, jobs, schools, businesses, and hospitals from indigenous people, who are displaced to the peripheries of the new economy as tourist curios. He argues that in the post-communist era, tradition need not be consigned to the dustbin of history: if judiciously used, it can facilitate an industrial revolution in Tibet. It is, the author believes, unfair and incorrect to dismiss Tibetans as unfit for or incapable of modernization. The experience of Tibetan refugees in India, Nepal, and Canada indicate that, given favorable conditions of freedom and fair opportunity, they can modernize in their own ways, which are by no means unique or eccentric. The experiences of exiled Tibetans conform to a general Asian pattern of modernization modified by culture. For example, in a 1995 pilot project, Tibetan students in a Tibetan-language school passed graduation exams with an average of 80 percent, while Tibetan students studying in a Chinese-language school scored an average of only 39 percent. In what Dawa Norbu sees as a hidden agenda, the party/government ignored such evidence of the advantages of instruction in Tibetan, opting instead for teaching in Chinese.

Yu Changjiang's study of Lara Village supports Dawa Norbu's contention that Tibetan tradition is not antithetical to modernization and economic progress. Yu finds no hard evidence of inevitable conflict between Buddhism and socialism in either development goals or personal self-cultivation. During his residence in Lara, he observed that its citizens were wont to absorb certain Han cultural norms and retain traditional ways as they deemed convenient. For example, locals happily gathered around the radio to listen to traditional Tibetan New Year's greetings. And particularly among younger males, so-called Mao suits are popular for everyday wear. Women, feeling that they look more attractive in traditional clothing, prefer to wear it, as does the older generation in general; robes continue to be worn for ceremonial occasions. Yu does, however, urge the government to have more consideration for local concerns in such areas as investment, in order to strengthen the trust of the local people in the motives and outcomes of these investments.

On the basis of fieldwork conducted in rural Tibet from 1997 to 2000, Melvyn

Goldstein and co-authors Ben Jiao, Cynthia M. Beall, and Phuntsog Tsering dispute the frequent reports of extreme poverty in rural Tibet. Their data reveal that the majority of inhabitants have made marked progress since decollectivization; when compared to traditional Tibetan standards, they have attained basic subsistence in the sense of good food and housing. However, despite recouping the losses sustained during the period of communes in Tibet, the current level of development and the standard of living in rural Tibet remain low, even in better-off areas. For example, none of the thirteen villages they studied had improved dirt roads or running water in houses; only one village, near a county seat, had electricity and water—a single tap—for its inhabitants. Overall, two and a half times as many houses were considered to be in poor condition as were considered in good condition. In the poorest area, nearly half the households were unable to produce enough grain to meet their own needs. Education also lags behind, with only 7.1 percent of young people having gone beyond primary school, meaning that rural Tibetans are not getting adequate education to enable them to compete effectively in the modernizing economy of the TAR.

While nearly all those interviewed agreed that material life has improved since decollectivization, the authors link further improvement to two other factors: population and nonfarm income. Because of political sensitivity, party and government have not actively pushed family planning, and the combination of high population growth with fixed land resources has led to a decrease of nearly 20 percent in per capita land holdings since decollectivization. One coping strategy has been to engage in nonfarm labor: the authors discovered that nearly half the households they studied had one or more member engaged in some form of nonfarm labor, including construction work; craft labor; private business; ritual work such as mantra specialist; or government employment such as official, teacher, or health aid. However, villagers complained that there were not enough jobs for them and that because of low skills, those who found jobs got only the lowest-paying ones. They found themselves competing with non-Tibetans, a situation the authors predict will increase. As the new Invest in the West development policy pumps more funds into infrastructural projects in Tibet, Tibet's economy is likely to shift further into the hands of Chinese firms and laborers. Despite these serious structural problems, there is no sign that the government is considering ameliorative measures such as job preferences or set-asides to citizens of the autonomous region in the government-funded construction sector, or providing tax rebate programs for hiring Tibetans on construction projects. Unless major changes like these are adopted, the progress rural Tibetans have made since decollectivization may not continue, and will certainly not increase, in the future.

June Teufel Dreyer takes note of the fact that the central government's large and increasing subsidies to Tibet have not resulted in a substantially more comfortable life for the majority of Tibetans, and that they have come at considerable cost to the cultural values of the society. Urban Tibetans perceive themselves as disadvantaged by the ingress of Han from other areas of the PRC, while rural Tibetans, though better off than during the period of collectivization, have not improved their lifestyles much beyond that. Discrimination against Tibetans is a part of the problem, as is the central government's inadvertent creation of a welfare mentality through its subsidies. These infusions of capital, rather than fostering self-sustaining development, are the reason for Tibet's impressive growth rates over the past two decades: money invested in the region actually has a negative multiplier effect. Since modernization is perceived as forced on the area from outside rather than generated from within, there is resentment and distrust of projects espoused by Beijing. Many locals view the railroads, water control schemes, and educational plans that the central government portrays as motivated by its desire for economic development in the area to be actually motivated by a desire to enhance the central government's control over Tibet. Outside Tibet, there is resentment over the favorable economic treatment accorded to an ungrateful minority, and less reluctance to say that Tibetans themselves should be held responsible for their poverty.

Contributors to the question of Tibet's place in the international configuration accord a major role to the United States. Both Xu Mingxu and A. Tom Grunfeld argue that Washington's interference in the Tibet Question has deleterious effects in terms of Sino-American relations and on Beijing's attitude toward Tibetans.

Xu Mingxu and Yuan Feng indict the Western powers for their double standard on human rights, pointing out that they do not allow the Bosnian Serbs to exercise self-determination or the Turks of Cyprus to become independent. The government of Spain will never allow the Basques to become independent, and the Lincoln Memorial eulogizes the president who preserved the union. Xu Mingxu and Yuan Feng ask why, then, China is not accorded the same right when confronted by rebellious Tibetans. While the United States has formally agreed that Tibet is an integral part of China, its Congress has nonetheless supported the Tibetan independence movement. So did the Nobel Prize Committee when it presented the peace award to the Dalai Lama in 1989. In contrast with the contributors of the economics chapters, Xu Mingxu and Yuan Feng believe that the welfare policy adopted by the central government since the 1980s has markedly improved the life of the average Tibetan, and that religious freedom has been restored. Instead of praising the efforts of the Chinese government, the U.S. Congress has criticized its efforts as attempts at erasing Tibetan culture. They believe that if the PRC government did not make these efforts, Congress would have condemned it for allowing the TAR to languish in poverty. By such actions, Washington has insulted the entire Chinese people, and particularly the 90 percent who are Han. This has produced a backlash of Chinese nationalism directed against the United States. Therefore, if Washington desires to overthrow the CCP and promote democracy, it should cease encouraging separatist movements in Tibet and elsewhere.

Tom Grunfeld argues that Tibet became a pawn in the Cold War for an America that heretofore had little interest in the area. Because many Tibetans were also anti-communist, U.S. officials began to engage them in a dialogue. However, the two sides had different objectives, and ultimately this would be detrimental to

Tibetans who wished to extricate themselves from Chinese rule. Each time the U.S. Congress held a hearing on Tibet or issued a resolution pertaining thereto, it had the effect of strengthening the position of Chinese leaders who took a hard line on Tibet. Grunfeld sees commonalities in the aims of the exiled Dalai Lama and the Beijing government: stability and economic development for the area. A settlement in which the Dalai Lama would be allowed to return to Lhasa and preserve his people's culture would, Grunfeld believes, attract considerable foreign investment to the area, concomitantly easing the need for Beijing's huge subsidies to the region. It would also burnish the Chinese government's international image. However, twenty years of abortive attempts at negotiation have left a residue of distrust on both the Tibetan and the Chinese sides. And the internationalization of the Tibet issue has left Beijing defensive while curbing the power of the officials who are most willing to negotiate with the Dalai Lama. In the end, Grunfeld asserts, the United States has done more to betray the Tibetan exile community than to help it.

The contributors on representations of Tibet and the Tibet Question challenge the idea that there is a "real" version of either. The real interests of the parties to the Tibet Question cannot be disconnected from the discourse of human rights that has been constructed by the exiles and their supporters and that has a close fit with a rising tide of similar concerns in international politics generally. Modern Tibet cannot be found exclusively in the "reality" of the Chinese emperor's subordination of Tibetan hierarchs, nor in an equality between the two, nor in orientalist and post-orientalist notions of Tibet as Shangri-La.

Amy Mountcastle notes that criticisms of framing the Tibet Question as a discourse of human rights come from the PRC government, parts of the exile community, and Western scholars alike. While exile critics see a human rights strategy as detracting from a focus on Tibet's lack of independence, PRC officials regard it as the heart of the exile campaign to internationalize the Tibet Question. Meanwhile, Western scholars view the human rights discourse as a diversion from understanding the issues of key importance to the parties and what divides them. Human rights appear secondary to the "real" interests of those connected to the Tibet Question, but this is not so if one considers the context of international politics, where rights issues enjoy a growing profile and are counterposed to the hegemony of state interests and statist discourse. The representation of the Tibet Question as a human rights problem, as the centerpiece of the exiles' strategy since the mid-1980s, has garnered support from across the political spectrum and provides the exiles and their supporters with a participation in global politics they would not otherwise have. It stands, moreover, as a challenge to the forced dichotomy of the real versus the ideal and the hegemony of realism in politics generally.

Christiaan Klieger finds that the concept of a Tibetan nation is treated in contradictory ways, through Western notions of sovereign performance, Chinese policies toward national minorities, and popular, local histories. There are three prominent paradigms of modern Tibetan history: (1) Tibet as represented in PRC ideology, based on a combination of Confucian imagery and Marxist, secular national self-determination: contemporary Tibet is seen as fulfilling a long-term civilizing mission; (2) Tibet as constructed by Tibetan historians: Chinese and Mongol rulers are portrayed as patrons of Tibetan theocrats, from whom the rulers gain legitimacy and to whom they pay obeisance rather than control; (3) Tibet as Shangri-La: a frequent characterization of Western literature that serves to limit Tibet's claim for sovereignty in the international community.

Modern Tibet can be viewed in relation to the priest–patron nexus (*mchod-yon*) that began in the Yuan dynasty and saw China's emperors elevate first the hierarchs of the Sakyapa school and then those of the Gelukpa school of Tibetan Buddhism as temporal and spiritual rulers of Tibet. Reincarnating lineages of Buddhist hierarchs were used to forge a state that combined religion and politics for both Tibetans and their patrons. Under the "Chinese" centrist ruler–subject view, the emperors' patronage effect of subjecting Tibetan hierarchs to their wills is paramount, while Tibetan historians stress priest–patron equality. The paradigm of Tibet as Shangri-La, based on a Western colonial view that exiles have adopted as the construct most acceptable to contemporary Westerners, represents Tibet as an historically sacred land with a unique culture, independent of China, and entitled to self-determination. Tibet can actually be located in all three paradigms.

The essays in the present collection reflect the wide range of disciplinary perspectives and political viewpoints found in the academic discourse of contemporary Tibet. A grand synthesis of the Tibet Question is unlikely to emerge from this discourse and, even if it did, it would not likely change the relationship among the question's primary actors. There is evidence, however, that the uneven and incremental contributions of scholars to understanding the plethora of Tibet-related issues have already led to a rethinking by the principal parties of several contentious matters, disturbing the widely held conviction that a solution to the Tibet Question is improbable. If the present work disturbs this conviction further, we will judge it a success.

Notes

1. The Chinese government reserves the term "Tibet" (Xizang) for the Tibet Autonomous Region (TAR), the central-western Tibet Plateau areas, traditionally referred to as U-Tsang, that were under the Dalai Lamas' administration until the mid-twentieth century. Tibetan exiles refer to the whole plateau as Tibet. Many Western scholars distinguish "political" (central-western) and "ethnographic" (eastern) Tibet. Melvyn Goldstein, "The Dalai Lama's Dilemma," *Foreign Affairs* 77, no. 1 (1998): 83–90. The eastern Tibetan areas contain ten Tibetan prefectures and two Tibetan counties in Qinghai, Gansu, Sichuan, and Yunnan provinces, where more than half of PRC Tibetans live.

2. Tibetan exile leaders accuse China of physical and cultural genocide and of being a "terrorist state." "Exiled Tibetan Official Slams 'Cultural Genocide,'" *Globe & Mail* (Toronto), July 8, 2002; "China Is a Terrorist State: Rimpoche," *Times of India*, September 24, 2001. PRC media have stated that "The Dalai Lama wants to return Tibet to the dark ages, when it was a cruel, feudal and semi-colonial society" and call into question his

leadership of Tibetan Buddhism. "China Launches Verbal Assault on Dalai Lama," Agence France-Presse (AFP), November 25, 1995; "Tibetan Eminent Monks Doubt Dalai Lama's Status as 'Religious Leader,'" Xinhua, May 15, 2001.

3. "Dalai Lama Says Envoys Could Return to China Soon," Reuters, April 23, 2004.

4. Wang Lixiong, *Tian Zang: Xizang de mingyun* (Sky burial: The fate of Tibet) (Brampton, Ontario: Mirror Books, 1998).

5. See *Sovereignty over Pulau Ligitan and Pulau Sipadan* (Indonesia/Malaysia) (International Court of Justice, 2002), www.icj-cij.org, Nonrecognition by states and international organizations renders an entity that otherwise satisfies the criteria for statehood unable to exercise the associated sovereign rights, particularly the right to freely conduct its own foreign relations. Brad Roth, *Government Illegitimacy in International Law* (Oxford: Clarendon Press, 2000): 129.

6. See, for example, Melvyn Goldstein, *A History of Modern Tibet, 1913–1951: The Decline of the Lamaist State* (Berkeley: University of California Press, 1989), and *The Snow Lion and the Dragon* (Berkeley: University of California Press, 1997); A. Tom Grunfeld, *The Making of Modern Tibet* (Armonk, NY: M.E. Sharpe, 1996); Dawa Norbu, *China's Tibet Policy* (London: Curzon Press, 2001); Xu Mingxu, *Yinmo yu qiancheng: Xizang saoluan de lailong qumai* (Intrigues and devoutness: The origin and development of the Tibet riots) (Brampton, Ontario: Mirror Books, 1999).

7. Suthichai Yoon, "The Young Show Signs of Impatience and Frustration," *The Nation* (Bangkok), June 19, 1999. In 2004, Khedroob Thondup, the Dalai Lama's nephew and a member of the pro-independence Tibetan parliament-in-exile, joined with Lee Teng-hui to launch the Chinese edition of Ross Terrill's *The New Chinese Empire and Its Meaning for the United States* (New York: Basic Books, 2003), which predicts the collapse of China, in part through revolts in Tibet and Xinjiang. "Lee: China's 'Empire' Will Deteriorate," *Taipei Times*, March 11, 2004, 4.

8. Ann Frechette, *Tibetans in Nepal: The Dynamics of International Assistance Among a Community in Exile* (New York: Berghahn Books, 2002): 166.

9. "China to 'Go the Russian Way' Dalai Lama Says," Japan Economic Newswire (JEN), August 1, 1992; Tony Walker, "Believer in a Middle Way," *Financial Times*, March 29, 1997, 7.

10. The Dalai Lama stopped predicting the PRC's collapse more or less at the time the U.S. government began to view a collapse as unlikely and undesirable. "Transcript of Clinton interview by Radio Free Europe," U.S. Newswire, June 24, 1998.

11. "Statement of the Dalai Lama on the 45th Anniversary of the Tibetan Uprising," www.unpo.org/news_detail.php?arg=52&par=463.

12. "Chen Kuiyuan in Qamdo Says Prosperity Will Drive Out Religion," Tibet People's Broadcasting Station (TPBS), November 28, 1994, in British Broadcasting Corp./Survey of World Broadcasts (BBC/SWB), December 5, 1994; "Brooking No Dalai," *Economist*, December 16, 2000.

13. "The Dalai Lama Visits Taiwan," CNN, March 29, 2001. The TGIE prime minister has been quoted as stating that "the number of Chinese politicians supporting autonomy [for Tibet is] growing compared to past times." Tsering Dhondup, "Prof. Samdhong Rinpoche Speaks at the National," World Tibet Network (WTN), April 27, 2004.

14. "More Funds for Qinghai–Tibet Railway," Xinhua, April 8, 2004.

15. *Crossing the Line: China's Railway to Lhasa, Tibet* (Washington, DC: International Campaign for Tibet, 2003).

16. Melvyn Goldstein, "Tibet and China in the Twentieth Century," in *Governing China's Multi-Ethnic Frontiers*, ed. Morris Rossabi (Seattle: University of Washington Press, 2004): 186–229.

17. "N.Y. Governor Sets March 10 as State's Tibetan Day," Central News Agency (CNA) (Taiwan), March 11, 2001; "The Heart of Tibetan Resistance," *Peace Magazine* 14, no. 2 (1998): 8–19 (quoting the Dalai Lama as stating "Tibet has always historically been an independent country").

18. "Chinese Embassy in Ottawa Celebrates 50 Years of Tibet Achievements," Xinhua, June 1, 2001. Occasionally, a PRC official will assert that Tibet has always been part of China, "Speech at All-Tibet Conference on Ideological and Political Work," *Xizang ribao*, October 18, 2000 (TAR CCP Secretary Guo Jinlong), BBC/SWB, October 27, 2000.

19. "Takster Rinpoche Speaks in Washington DC," WTN, September 8, 1995.

20. "His Holiness the Dalai Lama Explains His Position on China's Preconditions," *Tibetan Bulletin* 7, no. 4 (September–October 2003), www.tibet.net/tibbul/2003/0903/focus1.html; "Vatican Keeps Dalai Lama Meeting Low Key," *South China Morning Post* (SCMP), November 29, 2003, A8. The Dalai Lama has said that there is "some historical basis" to "the idea that Tibet is an autonomous region of the [PRC], not a part of China itself." The implication is that Tibet became part of China only after the PRC was founded. Robert Thurman, "The Realpolitik of Spirituality: An Interview with HH the 14th Dalai Lama," www.shambalasun.com/Archives/Features/1996/Nov96/DalaiLama.htm.

21. "China Lays Down the Law to Dalai Lama Over Possible Return," AFP, November 13, 2003; "China Reasserts Negotiations Offer to Dalai Lama If He Abandons 'Trickery,'" Xinhua, April 17, 1997.

22. "China Has Sent Positive Signals for Talks, Says Dalai Lama," Press Trust India (PTI), October 28, 2002; "China in Mind, Joshi Keeps Off Dalai Meet," *Indian Express* (New Delhi), January 22, 2004. The Dalai Lama told a press conference at the Vatican that "Tibet will not separate itself from mainland China. If Tibet is given greater autonomy, its people will be very happy." Deutsche Presse Agentur (DPA), November 26, 2003.

23. DY, November 4, 2003.

24. "Dalai Lama Leaves Taiwan After 10–Day Visit," JEN, April 8, 2002.

25. AFP, November 13, 2003.

26. Catherine Armitage, "Tibetan Snub to Dalai Lama," *The Australian*, September 17, 2002, 6 (quoting Legqog, governor of Tibet). A PRC commentator has claimed that the idea of securing a high degree of autonomy to eventually attain independence for Tibet originated with U.S. vice president Al Gore in 1993, who "advocated realizing 'Tibet independence' in two steps." Hua Zi, "What is the Real Intention of the United States?" Xinhua, June 9, 2003.

27. "Dalai Lama's Tibet Hopes: It Should Stay Part of China, Exiled Leaders Says," *Toronto Star*, April 23, 2004.

28. *Tibet 2000: Environment and Development Issues* (Dharamsala: Department of Information and International Relations [DIIR], 2000); Tibetan Youth Congress (TYC), *Development for Whom? A Report on the Chinese Development Strategies in Tibet and Their Impacts* (Dharamsala, 1995). The Dalai Lama has stated that in Tibet "all profits and gain go to China," and that "The Chinese have been exploiting Tibet's natural resources." "Dalai Lama Urges Beijing to Address Tibetan Issue Realistically," CNA, September 11, 2003.

29. Andrew Fischer, *Poverty by Design: The Economics of Discrimination in Tibet* (Montreal: Canada Tibet Committee, 2002); Commission on Human Rights and Democracy, *Impoverishing Tibetans* (Dharamsala: TCHRD, 2000).

30. *Tibet 2003: State of the Environment* (Dharamsala: DIIR, 2003), passim.

31. Jampa Phuntsok, chair of the TAR, has stated that the region received subsidies of US$4.9 billion from 1995 to 2001 and will have an additional $8.5 billion in subsidies in 2001–2005. "Official Says President Hu Jintao Behind Tibetan Development Push," AFP, August 25, 2003.

32. "Who has Benefited Most in Tibet?" *China's Tibet*, no. 2 (2004): 2–9. In the TAR, over 85 percent of the population of residents with household registration in the region engage in agriculture. Zhongguo minzu gongzuo nianjian bianji weiyuanhui, *Zhongguo minzu gongzuo nianjian* (Yearbook of Chinese ethnic work) (Beijing: Minzu chubanshe, 2003), 581. There are comparable percentages in most other Tibetan areas.

33. "Nazis of Asia Set Out to Hoodwink the Free World," DIIR, October 10, 1997,

www.ibiblio.org/obl/reg.burma/archives/199710/msg00147.html (stating that "it is the Communist leaders of China who are indisputable Nazis of Asia, their actions in Tibet and China evoking a painful reminiscence of Jews' holocaust nightmare"); "Tibetan Groups in India Protest Lhasa Arrests," United Press International (UPI), May 23, 1993 (demanding that the International Olympics Committee reject Beijing's bid for the games because the PRC government "resembles the Nazi regime in every respect, including . . . the intended extermination of the Tibetans like the Jews and the maintaining of large concentration camps throughout Tibet").

34. See the TGIE website, www.tibet.com/Govt/Intro-tib.html. Exile mass organizations, Tibet support groups, and Western newspapers use the figure as well. "Tibetans Observe Anniversary of National Uprising Day," *The Hindu* (Delhi), March 11, 2004; "Scientist Defends Tibet Expedition," *Guardian* (London), November 15, 2002, 11; "Jigme Phuntsok," *The Times* (London) (editorial), January 12, 2004.

35. See, for example, "The Distance Between Tibet and Quebec," *Globe & Mail* (Toronto) (editorial), April 15, 2004.

36. Yan Hao, "Tibetan Population in China: Myths and Facts Re-examined," *Asian Ethnicity* 1, no. 1 (2000): 11–36.

37. Patrick French, *Tibet, Tibet: A Personal History of a Lost Land* (London: HarperCollins, 2003): 289–292.

38. "Dalai Lama Commits to Tibetan Integration, Not Independence," AFP, October 18, 2003.

39. See DIIR, www.tibet.net/eng/diir/enviro/wssd/intro.html. The Dalai Lama has at times been more cautious than his officials in stating that Han migrants outnumber Tibetans in "some areas" or in "Tibet's largest cities." "Tibetans Becoming Minority in Some Tibet Areas," PTI, January 7, 2004; "Dalai Lama Warns of 'Cultural Genocide' in Tibet," Associated Press (AP), September 26, 2000. He has also said, however, that "ethnic Chinese" probably outnumber Tibetans "overall in the Tibet Autonomous Region." "Tibet Facing 'Cultural Genocide,'" *The Australian*, October 10, 2002, 10. China terms the 7.5 million figure a "monstrous lie." "China Steps Up War of Words Against Dalai Lama," AFP, November 27, 1995.

40. Wang Lixiong, "Xizang: ershiyi shiji Zhongguo de ruan lei" (Tibet: China's 21st century soft rib), *Zhanlue yu guanli* (January 1999): 21–33.

41. Barry Sautman, "'Demographic Aggression' and Tibet" (paper presented at the University of North Carolina, March 14, 2004).

42. David Murphy, "Tibet: Mother and Child," *Far Eastern Economic Review*, December 23, 2001.

43. "No Mandate for Sterilization in Tibet: Official," *People's Daily*, March 1, 2000, http://fpeng.peopledaily.com.cn/2000003/01/eng/20000301Z111.html.

44. U.S. Department of State, "Human Rights Practices in Tibet—2003," www.asianresearch.org/articles/1934.html.

45. Phuntsog Wangyal, "The Influence of Religion on Tibetan Politics," *Tibet Journal* 1, no. 1 (1975): 78–86; Bina Roy Burman, *Religion and Politics in Tibet* (New Delhi: Vikas Publishing House, 1979).

46. Rebecca French, "A Conversation with Tibetans? Reconsidering the Relationship Between Religious Beliefs and Secular Legal Discourse," *Law & Social Inquiry* 26, no. 1 (2001): 95–114; Ashild Kolas, "Tibetan Nationalism: The Politics of Religion," *Journal of Peace Research* 33, no. 1 (1996): 51–66; "Tibetan Parliament in Exile," www.tibet.com/Govt/aptd.html.

47. Alexander Norman, "Lama of God," *Sydney Morning Herald*, April 9, 1988, 70. The Dalai Lama has stated moreover that "Whether or not a person is a religious believer does not matter much" because "We humans can live quite well without recourse to religious faith." Dalai Lama, *Ethics for a New Millennium* (New York: Riverhead Books, 1999): 19–20, and "If the words of the Buddha and the findings of modern science contradict each other, then the former have to go." Jeffrey Paine, *Re-enchantment: Tibetan Buddhism Comes to the West* (New York: W.W. Norton, 2004): 12.

48. TPBS, November 28, 1994. Tibet University students have also been barred from religious activities. Philip Pan, "In the Name of the Panchen Lama," *Washington Post*, September 19, 2003, A17.

49. The TAR has 47,500 officially registered monks and nuns and many more who are unregistered. John Gittings, "Cultural Clash on Land on the Roof of the World," *Guardian*, February 17, 2002, 17. The TAR government has stated that this number "satisfies Tibet's religious needs," but Tibetan exiles often contrast that number with the 114,000 monks in the area in 1951. Henry Chu, "Pin Tibet, Dalai Lama Remains the People's Choice," *Los Angeles Times*, August 28, 1999, A1. The U.S. government estimates that the eastern Tibetan areas have over 100,000 monks and nuns. U.S. Department of State, *International Religious Freedom Report 2003: China*, http://Hongkong.usconsulate.gov/uscn/hr/2003/121801.htm. The estimate coincides with that of Matthew Kapstein, "A Thorn in the Dragon's Side: Tibetan Buddhist Culture in China," in *Governing China's Multi-Ethnic Frontiers*, ed. Rossabi, 230–269. The quota on "clergy" is subject to change. In 1994, the TAR government stated that 34,000 monks and nuns were "sufficient for Tibet," but the quota was subsequently increased to 46,000. "China: Restricts Number of Monks and Monasteries in Tibet," Inter Press Service (IPS), January 5, 1995.

50. An exile leader has claimed that Tibetans who carry a picture of the Dalai Lama, pray, or burn incense will be arrested. "North American Tibetan Representative and Students for a Free Tibet Join the People's March for Economic Justice in Santa Barbara," WTN, April 28, 2002. Other sources deplore alleged bans on monks teaching laypersons outside religious sites and performing life-cycle rites. International Fellowship of Reconciliation, "Violations of Human Rights in Tibet: A Social and Cultural Perspective," in United Nations, *Secretary-General's Report: Situation in Tibet*, E/CN.4/1992/37. The Tibetan head of the TAR Ethnic and Religious Commission has stated that Tibetans are "free to practice their faith, visit the temples and make offerings. The public can invite lamas to their homes for funeral rites." *Channel News Asia*, August 18, 2003.

51. TAR officials justify surveillance on the ground that "Monasteries must maintain a correct quality." Seth Faison, "Icy Wind from Beijing Chills the Monks of Tibet," *New York Times*, November 18, 1998, A3.

52. Government of Tibet in Exile, "China to Set Up Rival Panchen Lama," www.tibet.com/PL/oct21.html.

53. "Xinjiang, Tibet Deputies Assert Religious Freedom Protected," Xinhua, March 7, 2000. Note that it is faith, not practice, that is said to be wholly unrestricted. A U.S. official put it to Congress that in Tibet "The authorities permit many traditional religious practices, but not those seen as a vehicle for political dissent." "Prepared Testimony of Jeffrey Bader, Deputy Assistant Secretary for East Asian and Pacific Affairs Before the Senate Foreign Relations Committee," Federal News Service, May 13, 1997.

54. U.S. actions to support the exiles have included military (from the mid-1950s to mid-1970s), financial, political, and media support; see Barry Sautman, "The Tibet Issue in Post-Summit Sino-American Relations," *Pacific Affairs* 72, no. 1 (1999): 7–21; Xu Guangqiu, "The United States and the Tibet Issue," *Asian Survey* 37, no. 11 (1997): 1062–1077; Kenneth Knaus, "Official Policies and Covert Programs: The U.S. State Department, the CIA, and the Tibetan Resistance," *Journal of Cold War Studies* 5, no. 3 (2003): 54–79. India provided "military aid" also through its creation of substantially ethnic Tibetan paramilitary forces, such as the Indo-Tibet Border Police and the Special Frontier Force, financial aid through grants of land and subsidies for development of Tibetan exile communities, and political backing of varying degrees. John Garver, "The Security Dilemma in Sino-Indian Relations," *India Review* 1, no. 4 (2002): 1–38; Dawa Norbu, "Tibet in Sino-Indian Relations," *Asian Survey* 37, no. 11 (1997): 1078–1095.

55. "Dalai Lama Clarifies on Kashmir Again," *Times of India*, August 8, 2001; "Buddhists Want Democratic Government in Afghanistan: Dalai Lama," PTI, November 7, 2002;

Ranjit Devraj, "Compassion Must be the New Religion, Dalai Lama Says," IPS, December 18, 2002.

56. "America Honors Dalai Lama," UPI, April 17, 1991.

57. "Dalai Lama Compares Chinese in Tibet to Iraqis in Kuwait," AP, September 22, 1990.

58. "US Supportive of Our Cause: Dalai Lama," *Times of India*, October 6, 2003; "Blair Provokes Outrage over Refusal to Meet with Dalai Lama," *Independent* (London), January 10, 2004; "Dalai Lama Warns War on Terrorism Could Backfire," AAP Newsfeed, May 21, 2002; "Tibetan Leader Reserves Judgment on Whether Iraq War Was Justified," AP, September 11, 2003.

59. Peter Kammerer, "Focus on Trade Can Build Trust and Help Neighbours Settle Thornier Issues," SCMP, June 25, 2003, 6.

60. "China Objects to Dalai Lama's White House Visit," *Canberra Times* (Australia), September 12, 2003.

61. *Xizang Ribao*, October 18, 2000, 1.

62. "Chinese Assembly Responds to EU Resolution on China," Xinhua, April 18, 2002.

63. Donald Lopez, *Prisoners of Shangri-La: Tibetan Buddhism and the West* (Chicago: University of Chicago Press, 1998); Robert Barnett, "Violated Specialness: Western Political Representations of Tibet," in *Imagining Tibet: Perceptions, Projections and Fantasies*, ed. Thierry Dodin and Heinz Rather (Boston: Wisdom Publications, 2001). The Dalai Lama has characterized pre-1951 Tibet as "feudal," but also as a "a society of peace and harmony [where] we enjoyed freedom and contentment," where peasants and herders had a light work load, with ample land and food, and where people were generally happy. "Idealized, Trivialized, Distorted Hollywood Celebrates the Dalai Lama," *Panorama*, no. 553, in WTN, December 6, 1997 (quoting Dalai Lama); Robert Thurman, "The Rolling Stone Interview: The Dalai Lama," in WTN, May 8, 2001; Dalai Lama, in Steve Lehman, *Tibetans: A Struggle to Survive* (New York: Umbrage, 1998) (flyleaf comment).

64. Keila Diehl, *Echoes from Dharamsala: Music in the Life of a Tibetan Refugee Community* (Berkeley: University of California Press, 2002).

65. Thomas Heberer, "Old Tibet a Hell on Earth? The Myth of Tibet and Tibetans in Chinese Art and Propaganda," in *Imagining Tibet*, ed. Dodin and Heinz, 111–150.

66. "Li Peng Says Human Rights Best Ever, Tibet Liberated," Xinhua, June 14, 2000, in BBC/SWB, June 16, 2000.

67. "Official Condemns European Parliament Resolutions on Taiwan, Tibet," Xinhua, April 19, 2000.

68. "Tibet Receives 90 Million US Dollars in Grants," Xinhua, June 25, 2002.

69. Dalai Lama, speech on the 42nd anniversary of the Lhasa uprising, March 10, 2001, excerpted in "China's Leadership Should Honor Long Overdue Promises to Tibet," *New Perspectives Quarterly* 21, no. 1 (Winter 2004).

70. TGIE, "China's Current Policy in Tibet," www.tibet.com/Eco/Introduction.html. Lodi Gyari, the Dalai Lama's representative in North America, has stated, however, that "The current Chinese political structure is . . . being run by professional career politicians with an understanding of democratic processes"; "The Happy People," *The Witness* (South Africa), February 11, 2004, in WTN, February 17, 2004.

71. Hua Zi, "Secrets of 20–Year Central Government—Dalai Lama Contacts," *Tzu Ching* (Hong Kong), no. 105 (July 5, 1999): 4–8.

72. "Address by His Holiness the Dalai Lama at the Palace of Westminster, London, July 16, 1996," http://hhdl.dharmakara.net/westminstewr.html.

73. WP, November 23, 2003.

74. "Exiled Government Again Proposes Autonomy, Not Independence for Tibet," PTI, May 22, 2001.

75. "Interview with Tibet Prime Minister-in-Exile Sandhong Rinpoche," *The Day After* (India), July 16, 2003, in WTN, July 19, 2003.

PART I

Politics and Representation

2

Beyond the Collaborator–Martyr Model

Strategies of Compliance, Opportunism, and Opposition Within Tibet

Robert Barnett

> A man who betrays his culture should not preach about its ways. There was a time when I would have wished you dead. But your shame will be your torture, and your torture will be your life. I wish it to be long.

Thus spoke the American actor Brad Pitt, 1998, addressing a Tibetan official of the Chinese government in Lhasa in the Hollywood film *Seven Years in Tibet*.[1] Pitt was playing the part of Heinrich Harrer, a European émigré in 1950s Lhasa who opposes China's takeover of Tibet. His words are directed at Ngapö Ngawang Jigme, the Tibetan aristocrat who was in charge of the Tibetan border troops at the time of the Chinese invasion and who later became the first governor of Tibet after the Chinese annexation. In the film Ngapö is shown blowing up the Tibetan arsenal before fleeing alone and in disguise, rather than organizing resistance to the Chinese troops then crossing the border. Pitt later comes across him wearing splendid clothes as an official in the new administration, beneath a picture of Mao and with a Chinese military escort; unable to contain his indignation at Ngapö's infamy, he knocks the Tibetan official to the ground.[2]

The encounter between Ngapö and the Austrian exile is fictional,[3] and seems to be a sort of parable by the filmmaker of what a Western hero, intent on defending the Tibetan people, should have done to those Tibetan leaders who did not openly resist the Chinese encroachment on their land. Perhaps it also expresses the filmmakers' view as to how Tibetans should have treated their traitors.

This chapter comes out of a sense that the role of Tibetans in the Chinese–Tibetan issue is often seen in the Western or foreign imagination as a drama of collaboration and resistance, in which the leading Tibetan players are offered only these options. This is a paradigm which seems to me inappropriate as a description of the present situation, even if it might possibly have represented some local views concerning the Tibetan elite forty or fifty years ago. In this chapter I therefore suggest an alternative way of viewing the efforts of Tibetan officials[4] and others working within the Chinese system in Tibet. I look at the activity of these officials in terms of what is sometimes called "public space," having assumed that there must be a great range of complex and varied aspirations among the different social classes and regional groupings in Tibet, as well as the various groupings of Tibetan officials within the elite. Regrettably, I am not able to identify these in any detail, since our knowledge as foreigners of such questions is at so primitive a stage and is anyway so greatly constrained by the intensely secretive nature of the Chinese political system.[5] But I can suggest briefly some of the ways in which certain groups of Tibetans express aspects of these agendas. After making some comments about the notion of resistance and the perception of high officials in Western culture, I outline the use of public space by Tibetan officials such as the Panchen Lama, and discuss the expansion of that space in Tibet in the 1980s and its contraction in the 1990s. Finally, I try to describe something of the response of Chinese leaders in Tibet to the initiatives of their Tibetan counterparts, and the indications of a growing gulf between these two groups.

Resistance, Concealment, and Newton

In many Western cultures the notion of resistance is often associated with heroism and virtue, and its absence regarded as collaboration or betrayal, both of which are seen as inherently pernicious. This view is not, however, a description of Western practice on such issues. For one thing, such heroization of resistance is often a view of those who do not have to suffer the costs of undertaking it, and, for another, in practice we often condone or even admire quite different behavior by officials. Scholars have in recent years expressed doubt about the intrusion of "the romance of resistance" in academic study, where "instead of taking these [sorts of resistance] as signs of human freedom," Lila Abu-Lughod wrote, we would be better using them to "tell us more about forms of power and how people are caught up in them."[6] The Mongolian anthropologist Uradyn Bulag has likewise criticized the Western penchant for glorifying those it sees as oppressed, practices that claim to represent them and which deny them agency.

In the Tibet case, the honoring by foreigners of open resistance by Tibetans is fraught with problems. For one thing, this option is more or less indistinguishable from martyrdom, since the balance of power in Tibet is overwhelmingly tilted toward a government that does not tolerate opposition; it is fine for us to admire martyrdom, but quite another thing to encourage others to undertake it.[7] For another thing, it is not at all clear that martyrdom is effective. The 1959 rebellion, in which thousands of Tibetans (including many high officials) openly opposed the

Chinese state, led immediately to a crackdown that included thousands of deaths and that in one form or another lasted for up to two decades. The series of street demonstrations that began in Lhasa in September 1987 led to hundreds of arrests and attracted major world interest, but have been criticized by some Tibetans and others as counterproductive, since they led to increased repression and controls, many of which are still in place.[8]

The perception of collaboration raises similar problems. When Ngapö blew up the Tibetan arsenal in 1950 after the Chinese had overrun his troops, he was following standard military practice by denying the incoming troops access to additional arms. In any case, it is not true that, as claimed in the Hollywood film, he tried to flee alone. His decision to accept the terms of surrender presented to him by the Chinese authorities in Beijing a year later has to be seen in the light of historical research and his own claims, which suggest that his orders from Lhasa left him no room for maneuver.[9] The fact that he and some other leaders chose not to go into exile but to accept posts under the new government could even be seen now as responsible and brave, since it gave them an opportunity at least to moderate some of the policies that ensued, which the exiles were powerless to do. One of the most important comments on this issue was made by Ngapö's son, Jigme, now living in the United States, in an interview about his father published in the Hong Kong paper, the *South China Morning Post:* "In fact the Chinese government has never trusted him. My father has been a figurehead. He never really had any power."[10] If that is true, the adjudication as to whether these decisions should be seen as infamous or noble is clearly complex and is perhaps best left to the participants to decide, rather than to outsiders. The assessment of such issues is in any case peculiarly volatile, and can change overnight even among those with close knowledge of the case.

Nevertheless, the image of the traitor is a more persistent and perhaps attractive version of history. At a public meeting in Paris in 2001 a number of Westerners said that contemporary officials in Tibet should be condemned as collaborators.[11] It appeared that for them this was a matter of principle rather than of empirical inquiry, which followed necessarily from their view of the Chinese regime. This branding of a person as a collaborator is not merely an act of fiction, since it can have real-world effects way beyond the individual concerned: for one thing, it structures the way foreign diplomats and analysts conceive of political solutions, decide who should be consulted, assess which opinions are to be believed, and so on—thus Ngapö, for example, now in his nineties and living in Beijing, and apparently all senior Tibetan officials in Tibet or China, seem never to have been considered by outside parties as potential participants or advisers in the process of negotiations, despite their experience in the day-to-day running (or observing of the running) of their country. We are not therefore dealing with idle fictions of no consequence, but with constructs that might well have impact on and even damage other people's lives.

The admiration of open resistance and the condemnation of collaboration have a long history in Western thought, but it has not always been a glorious one. One of the difficulties with this notion in contemporary thought is that open resistance is often seen as a form of virtue, because it appears to resemble honesty and courage. In fact, the choice of resistance or collaboration is not strictly speaking a moral question: it is a political question, a question of strategy. It involves for the participants the taking of crucial decisions about what strategy might best ensure their survival, and the survival of their family and in some cases their nation, in a situation where these are under significant threat. This moralization of the issue in Western thought is therefore something of a luxury or an ideal that ignores the real strains that such choices represent.

This might be attributable to the fact that after the Reformation the debate over this question in the West moved primarily from the area of politics to the sphere of religion. As the Protestant movement gained momentum, the issue of strategic deceit versus open resistance became part of an aggressive debate in Western society as to whether religious believers should openly confess their faith even in situations where it might mean danger or death for them. The history of this question has been studied in great depth by Perez Zagorin in his book *Ways of Lying*.[12] By the late middle ages, the Catholic Church had developed a theory of "mental reservation" that allowed believers to assent falsely to views in situations of great risk;[13] among some persecuted Protestant communities a similar practice came to be justified by reference to a biblical figure named Nicodemus, who "came to Jesus by night" (John 3:2) rather than reveal his conversion. This led Calvin, and later John Knox in Britain, to launch vociferous campaigns against "Nicodemism," calling instead for public martyrdom in the name of the new faith and as a confrontation to Catholic orthodoxy. In their diatribes, the decision about whether a Protestant believer should reveal his true views even if this means risking death was a purely religious issue, and to hide one's views was immoral and sinful.

Since then the argument against strategic concealment in cases of great danger has continued to be put to highly sectarian uses. A 1997 review of Zagorin's book in an American Presbyterian magazine, for example, claimed that "Zagorin's account clearly demonstrates the insidious nature of Jesuitical reasoning [and shows that] many contemporary 'evangelicals' are quite naive in their dealings with Papists, taking at face value the statements of popish apologists."[14] The claim that others should be prepared to sacrifice their lives or freedom for a cause has, therefore, a checkered history, at least in the Christian tradition, and has to be regarded with some caution.

The modern Western tradition does, however, have models for the opposite practice—that of officials who chose to conceal their beliefs and to collaborate with the state. In these cases, these officials are not often seen as lacking in virtue at all, but are instead regarded as showing good sense and pragmatism.[15] These can be found even among radical, sectarian Protestants: Sir Isaac Newton was not only an iconic figure in modern science and philosophy, but an adamant nonconformist who hid from the public and from the state his total opposition to belief in the Trinity and to the immortality of the soul. Denial of these dogmas could have led to imprisonment or ostracism in late-seventeenth-century England.[16] Newton was more than an outstanding world scientist of his time: he was also a knight of the realm, a university professor, and a member of Parliament, and the latter two bodies required all their members to take oaths accepting belief in the Trinity. The complexities of Newton's position led to strange contortions of belief and action:

> While serving in Parliament as an MP for Cambridge University in 1689, Newton was appointed to sit . . . on 15 May 1689 on a parliamentary committee for considering the 'Bill for Liberty and Indulgence to Protestant Dissenters.' This was none other than the 1689 Toleration Act. The committee members, all of whom were to have a voice in the deliberations, were to meet on 16 May 1689. When they reported back to Parliament the next day, they included among their recommended additions the requirement that dissenters 'profess Faith in God the Father, and in Jesus Christ his Eternal Son, the true God, and in the Holy Spirit, One God blessed for evermore.' What could Newton—by this time a fierce antitrinitarian—do in these pressing circumstances? He dare not raise suspicion by speaking out against the amendment. . . . On the other hand, involvement (intentional or otherwise) in an Act that extended no tolerance to heresy would serve as the ultimate cover for a secret heretic.[17]

Newton offers, therefore, a model within Western culture of the senior state official who resorts to self-serving concealment and to public cooperation with injustice in order to maintain his social position and freedom. The reasons for this decision are strategic, not moral: although openness might be morally admirable (and Newton specifically insisted on the virtue of public religious declaration),[18] such declaration most likely seemed to Newton to have been futile and counter-productive at his time. How should we consider him? He certainly collaborated with an unjust regime, and gained greatly by doing so, but to ostracize him as a collaborator, with all the condemnatory and moral force of that word, would be to add largely religious and moral complications to an issue that would probably only confuse and hinder our understanding of both the person and the situation. In addition, it would tend to divert us from pragmatic issues, such as whether or not he did good for his circle and society. Today, few besides strident Calvinists would criticize him for his decision to pursue a lifelong policy of public silence. It is therefore hard to see why Tibetan or other officials in extremely pressing situations should be judged by different standards.

The Monolithic Cadre View

The perception of state functionaries in China as collaborators and the perception of them as incapable of divergent thought is not a purely Western construction: it is actively fueled by the Chinese Communist Party's traditional presentation of itself as enjoying wholly unified leadership and total consensus. Such statements are not descriptions of fact in any real world, but are rhetorical constructions or lies that are part of the larger set of myths which officials and others in China (as in most states) are required to maintain—the Party represents the wishes of the people, it pursues socialism, it practices democracy, the liberation of Tibet represented popular wishes, the state allows freedom of religion, and so on. Lying in China is, therefore, especially for cadres, mandatory.

As a result, outsiders see much of official discourse as an appearance of total conformity and of repetitive mimicry, and this encourages the perception of the cadre in China as a clone or puppet of the state, unable or unwilling to have idiosyncratic views. Since we are aware that this presentation is coerced, our impression of conformity among Chinese officials is contradicted by our sense that these people may be lying about their beliefs in order to protect themselves.[19] This makes an assessment of this situation confusing and uncertain, perhaps leaving even some policymakers to abandon the attempt to include the thinking of the actor-dissemblers in their considerations and concentrating instead on the thinking of the topmost leader or leaders alone.

Among China analysts and those who are familiar with the situation and the people involved, the view of China as enjoying a real-world unity of opinion among its officials and citizens would, I think, be unlikely: they are all aware of other levels of discourse within China that include difference, and that these days are anyway often public, at least in the inland areas. There are in any case sound historical reasons for assuming that such contradictions exist, even if we cannot see them, quite apart from our personal experience of difference among Chinese people we have met. The history of the Chinese Communist Party is, after all, one of repeated internal divergence, which is why it constantly resorted to rectification campaigns. The story of hidden disunity within the Party reached its peak with the five-year campaign against Lin Biao that followed his mysterious death in 1971— Lin Biao had until then been Mao's heir apparent, but was abruptly accused of planning secretly to overthrow him. Overnight, the Party found that it was having to admit openly that its leadership had been anything but united, and that at least some of its dogmas had been lies.

That there is a recognition among many foreigners of a significant degree of hidden divergence or uncertainty among cadres in China has not, however, carried over to outsiders' discussions of Tibet. There, the image of total conformity among cadres seems to have remained in place. There is, of course, evidence that the situation in Tibet is more coercive than conditions in most of China—for example, a 1993 study estimated that the majority of political arrests throughout China that year involved Tibetans.[20] And it is also the case that Tibetan cadres in practice have less power and influence than their counterparts in inland China.[21] But this is not a reason for assuming that Tibetan cadres are different from their Chinese counterparts in their capacity for divergent thought. Perhaps it is because there is less knowledge of Tibet among scholars, and because it still is so extensively "othered," that the Tibetan situation is seen in a way that is rather different from the "informed" or "expert" view of China. Whatever the reason, Tibetans inside

Tibet are frequently perceived as bifurcated along these lines: the populace are victims and the officials are collaborators.

Of course there are historical episodes that support this image. We know of many cases of popular opposition in Tibet, such as the rebellion of the Chushigangdruk in the 1950s, the Lhasa Uprising of 1959, the revolt by Nyemo Ani in 1969, or the street demonstrations of the late 1980s. And there are also accounts of Tibetans who at the opposite extreme cooperated closely with the Chinese authorities.[22] But not very much fits into models that position Tibetans in this way, as persecuted people versus compliant cadres.

First, there is in China a very extensive tradition of debate within the Party that is not made public, or of which only slight traces emerge. Particularly during the period after 1980, before the arrival in Tibet of Chen Kuiyuan as Party secretary in 1992, such debates quite frequently showed eventual signs of their existence. Even as late as 1991 an article appeared in the official newspaper *Xizang Ribao* saying that Tibetans in the TAR Branch of the Party should be allowed to be Buddhist, clearly indicating an important division of opinion on that issue within the Tibet Branch of the CCP at that time.[23] In 1997 the official radio station in Lhasa broadcast a statement denying "a rumor that the leading group in Tibet Autonomous Region will be changed and that leading members of the regional party committee will leave Tibet. . . . All comrades of our leading group," it continued, "are determined to unite as one, dedicate ourselves heart and soul to the same cause, firmly follow the instructions of the party Central Committee, Deng Xiaoping Theory and the party's basic line, and improve construction work in Tibet together with comrades of the party and non-party friends."[24] This unusual announcement probably indicated the opposite, namely that there had recently been some dissension within the Tibet Party Committee. Public silence does not therefore indicate private silence, and there may be fierce antagonisms openly declared within Party meetings behind the public mask of conformity.

Second, the collaboration image is an ahistorical view in the sense that the situation was and is changing constantly. The death of Lin Biao, for example, is crucial to any description of Tibetan cadres, because, as far as I can tell, it was the campaign against him (and not the Cultural Revolution) that led many of them to question their belief in the unity of the Party and their admiration for its views. For some it was at this moment that what had been cooperation with the Party changed to a simulacrum of cooperation. Such changes were not, of course, perceptible to others, but the widespread and constant phenomenon of radically shifting but fabricated cooperation makes it difficult to apply the notion of collaboration to this situation.

Third, some political movements or initiatives looked like compliance with the Chinese state at one time, but were seen as resistance at another. This is famously true of the Panchen Lama, the seniormost Tibetan dignitary in China after the Dalai Lama went into exile in 1959. The Panchen Lama worked closely with Ngapö Ngawang Jigme both in the early 1960s and again in the 1980s, and at both times was reviled in foreign opinion and sometimes even locally as a collaborator, since he had not gone into exile and had remained in high office in Tibet. This view retained currency even though the Chinese state openly declared in 1964 that he had been detained on accusations of treason and conspiracy; in fact, he remained in custody of one sort or another for some fourteen years. In the early 1980s, when he returned to the ranks of officialdom and made strenuous efforts to encourage the Tibetanization of the administration and the economy in Tibet, he was mocked by many observers, including Tibetans, as a collaborator, and given the derisory epithet "the fat lama." When he died in 1989 the Chinese leadership praised him as a hero who had patriotically supported the Chinese state. But he was described at the same time by the exiled Dalai Lama as a hero who had opposed the PRC. He had retained his ambiguity, without which his efforts to improve the lot of the Tibetan community would have been futile.

Lastly, as we have seen, the various postures of collaboration with the state and the expression of compliant opinions are often reflections of pragmatic concerns about safety, danger, and survival that require deception. For most people, for example, the radical change in the perception of the Panchen Lama came about rapidly after his death, and, like most historical changes, passed almost unnoticed, as if things had always been this way.[25] But in choosing to praise the Panchen Lama only after his death, the Dalai Lama had other considerations. He would have known, for one thing, that any hint of such praise from him during the Panchen Lama's lifetime would have been disastrous, because it would have instantly destroyed the latter's relative freedom to operate in Tibet; indeed, there are people who believe that the Panchen Lama's death was in fact an assassination by those who regarded his support for the Party as suspect.[26]

Concern about the huge dangers that could follow exposure or doubt is one of the most prominent issues expressed by cadres and others in any conversation on this topic with foreigners in Tibet: there are constant reminders of the risks that could follow any casual remark by a foreigner suggesting that an official might not be sincere in his or her support for the state. Most frequently, this danger is expressed by citing a famous remark made by Mao on the apparently unrelated theme of distinguishing enemies from allies. It is no coincidence that Ngapö, when interviewed about his depiction as a traitor in *Seven Years in Tibet,* refers to the same saying:

> Ngapoi expressed little concern about the film's vicious attacks on him person-
> ally. He pointed to Mao's viewpoint that whatever the enemy opposes is good.
> "We will support whatever the enemy opposes," said Ngapoi, "and thus I'm not
> bothered by the slanderous remarks."[27]

It has often been noted that Chinese Communist texts should be read in reverse, not merely those that concern Tibet, and Ngapö's text is no different—it belongs to a universe of opposite and ambiguous discourse. Thus we could also read Ngapö's reference to Mao's slogan as meaning conversely that "we" (meaning here the Party or the state, not the speaker) will oppose whatever the enemy supports, or, in other words, that to be praised by foreigners would be an automatic reason for ostracism within the Party. For practical reasons, therefore, apart from any other concerns, it would be self-destructive if Ngapö were to have welcomed foreign admiration and contested slander. The remark could therefore be read as conveying nothing about Ngapö's own views other than noting the rather lethal implications of such questions being answered directly by Tibetans and other cadres working within present-day China. Whether it is so intended or not, and if so, for what reasons, we cannot know: its strength is its ambiguity.

There is in fact one statement by a leading official that openly describes the pragmatic imperative behind official deception within the Communist system, namely the fear of punishment and in some cases of death. It was provided by the Panchen Lama himself in an internal speech given in Beijing in 1987, speaking of detentions in eastern Tibetan areas (Qinghai province) in the period 1959–1962:

> Almost half of the prison population [in Qinghai] perished. Last year, we discovered that only a handful of people had participated in the rebellion. Most of these people were completely innocent. In my 70,000 character petition [of 1962], I mentioned that about 5 percent of the population had been imprisoned. According to my information at that time, it was between 10 to 15 percent. But I did not have the courage to state such a huge figure. I would have died under *thamzing* [struggle session] if I had stated the real figure. These are serious matters as far as Tibet is concerned.[28]

In context, this statement is even more poignant than might at first appear. Although the Panchen Lama concealed the true extent of the then problems in Tibet in his 1962 petition, it was the writing of that deliberately understated petition that led to his spending fourteen years in detention.[29] In addition, it is possible that the "truth statement" he gives here, of 10 to 15 percent of the Qinghai population being imprisoned, may again have been a politic understatement. And, perhaps it is also for reasons of safety that the argument in this case is historicized, such that it appears to be true of an earlier political generation and not of the then, post-Mao era; in fact the imprisonments of those Chinese intellectuals and journalists who contested the number of deaths in Tiananmen Square eighteen months later, or the detention in 1995 of the abbot of the Panchen Lama's monastery for sending letters abroad to the exiles concerning his master, are testimony that such concerns were still appropriate then and subsequently. We can therefore assume that Tibetan officials have remained concerned about the risks in recent times of even understating the truth in their reports and statements, let alone of stating their views directly.

In Tibet the Panchen Lama, more than a decade after his death, is popularly revered as an iconic example not of ambiguity but of self-sacrifice, albeit his self-sacrifice took the form in the last ten years of his life of submission to the demands of compliance that are imposed on high officials within the Chinese administration. At the time of writing, his portrait can be seen in thousands of Tibetan shops and tea stalls; the fact that it, one of the few images of modern Tibetan leaders of which display is allowed, is still permitted within Tibet is a strikingly eloquent demonstration of his extraordinary mastery of political ambiguity. When he is spoken about, it is as the ideal official who strove to extract the maximum possible concessions from the state for the people he represented—a plaudit that is sufficiently ambiguous for it to be safely made in public. It is sometimes implied that he suffered immensely for this effort, not least because of the indignity of having constantly to lavish praise on the state in order to retain his position and influence.[30] Even the fact that he married, and thus broke his vows as a monk, is often seen, rightly or wrongly, as a sacrifice he undertook in order to retain high office and thus the option to intervene on behalf of the Tibetan people.

In this single case, which is certainly the paradigm in the Tibetan imagination of the modern Tibetan official, we can see both that the external perception of collaboration is liable to utter misjudgment and to rapid alteration, and that among Tibetans in Tibet the moral question of deceit or honesty is irrelevant: for an honest official in modern Tibet concealment is seen as a requirement for survival and, in this case, for bringing benefit to the wider community. The moral question, and perhaps the only question, is whether the official does indeed bring benefit to the community, not whether he uses direct or indirect methods to achieve this.[31]

Having introduced the possibility of strategic deception, we must at the same time be extremely cautious in assuming that this entitles us to take a binary or opposite view. It does not do so: deceiving the state or concealing opinions does not in most cases in any way represent rebellion or even necessarily protest. When the Panchen Lama wrote his 70,000–character petition in 1962, it was not to foment rebellion or plot independence, but to correct local policy abuses in Tibetan areas, which he described as the result of malfeasance by minor officials. As such, it was legitimate criticism, in Party terms, and the then premier, Zhou Enlai, indeed seems to have viewed it in this way; it was only Mao's extremist interpretation of the text that led to the Panchen Lama being removed from office and vehemently abused. In other words, divergence does not necessarily mean total opposition to a regime. It may represent sectoral interests or demands that are important to the actor and his constituency but are marginal or irrelevant to the state at one time or another. The hidden and dissenting views of apparently compliant cadres are therefore not necessarily in any way conflicts with the state or with its wider claims to power and territory.

This becomes somewhat clearer if one considers the range of other initiatives currently reported from Tibet, which are not necessarily oppositional, but which allow Tibetans to express identity or to comment indirectly on political conditions. For complex political and historical reasons, such aspirations are usually not formally enunciated in such terms: they are described and justified by their proponents according to whichever formal dictums cadres are at the time being exhorted by the Chinese leaders to use. The Chinese state legitimizes the use of only a certain range of policy objectives and aims at any one time, and it would be unwise for officials, and especially "minority" officials, to go beyond the defined lexicon of purposes. It is such nonoppositional initiatives that I would now like briefly to discuss.

The Varying Uses of Public Space

Initiatives of this kind are those where there is active intervention by Tibetan officials in one or another area of policy that is particularly advantageous to the Tibetan community but which at the same time is not necessarily threatening to, or critical of, the state. In Tibet the quintessential model for such efforts again can be found in the work of the Panchen Lama to promote a Tibetanization of the economy and the administration during the early 1980s, and there were no doubt earlier examples of such practices by Tibetan officials like him before the Cultural Revolution. Bulag has demonstrated in his work that the Mongolian Communist leader Ulanhu had used similar principles (for somewhat different reasons) to moderate local CCP policies in Inner Mongolia during the late 1940s, when the Panchen Lama's strategy encouraged the Party leadership to replace its "universalizing" policy stance—submitting all policies to a single global principle such as class struggle—with "a politics of difference," if only for tactical purposes:

> Taking advantage of conflict between class theory and practice with regard to ethnicity, Inner Mongolian Communist officialdom succeeded in framing a signifying strategy in which Mongols, especially pastoral Mongols, the symbolic center of Mongol identity, were recognized as a distinctive culture that warranted a boundary. This continued as a valid argument which Chinese leaders were prepared to accept not only because their universalized land reform and class struggle had produced great "deviations," which Mao and other leaders came to deplore, but also because Inner Mongols, as a role model for soliciting support from other ethnic minorities in China and/or incorporation in a future "unified China," had to be treated leniently.[32]

This experience reshaped Chinese nationality policy and must have contributed to Mao's decision to allow extensive cultural and political autonomy in Tibet for the years from 1950 to 1959.[33] By the mid-1960s, however—indeed, several years earlier in Tibet—the politics of difference was once again subjected to a universalist reading, according to which calls for the acceptance of ethnic difference were seen as stratagems by nationality leaders to conceal plots for independence. It is this apparent detail of ideology, this proclivity in CCP thought, which is one of the crucial reasons why the depredations of the Cultural Revolution were so much worse in Inner Mongolia and Tibet than in any ethnically Chinese areas, and why minority nationality officials in China still remain far more cautious in their statements and decisions than their Chinese counterparts. The most important shift to have taken place in recent Chinese politics, the decision by Deng Xiaoping to allow "liberalization and opening-up" in 1979, can thus be seen as a return to the 1949 decisions arising out of the Party's experiences in Inner Mongolia, at least in terms of nationality policy. By the same token, for nationality leaders, this return might well have carried strong associations of risk and contingency, since the Party's earlier experiments in tolerating difference had backfired so dramatically. But the new policy allowed Chinese people to discuss, consider, and even to criticize their rulers in a number of areas that had previously been banned or confined to debate within the Party. In addition, large areas of cultural and economic practice that had previously been outlawed were allowed for the first time in some ten or twenty years. For the nationalities, this was perhaps the most important of all aspects of the new, post-Mao, regime.

It was these newly enlarged areas of policy that created the opportunities for nonoppositional initiatives by nationality leaders. I have found it helpful to think of these areas in terms of what is sometimes called "public space," by which I mean those areas of discourse that are for a time regarded by the state as acceptable for open public discussion and participation. This term seems to me particularly useful here, first because it is value-neutral—it does not carry any of the dangerously binary associations of notions such as criticism, resistance, or collaboration—and second because it describes a sphere of action which by definition is regarded by the state as legitimate, so it has no connotations of subversion or resistance. In addition, it is a term that includes an implicit sense of its own mutability, since we are all familiar with the phenomenon of changing public space, whether it be (to give uncontentious examples) in the extent of our urban parks or the tolerance of erotic literature.

The chief point that I would like to make about the expansion of this public space after 1979 is that it was at that time the result of deliberate policies of the state. In metropolitan centers like Beijing, as Geremie Barmé and others have suggested, this process of expansion may have since become less susceptible to close management, but even now this is not the case in areas like Tibet.[34] That it was not coincidental or unconsidered by the leadership and their theorists can be seen from some of Hu Yaobang's own initiatives: during his historic visit to Tibet in May 1980, when he famously announced a six-point program of reform and liberalizations,[35] he himself told Tibetan leaders that they should resume wearing *chupas*, the traditional Tibetan robe or gown.[36] The wearing of local dress and the pursuit of ethnic customs had thus not only become again acceptable, but was an explicit request made by the top leadership, presumably as part of its desire to celebrate and publicize China's new image as a multinational state with a politics of regional variation and local consultation. Twenty years later it is still almost impossible to find in the official Chinese press any film or photograph of Tibetan university students who are not wearing a *chupa,* even though no students normally wear these clothes at the university. The assistance of fiction is required to construct China's image of tolerance and difference, just as it is to maintain the claim of Party unity.[37]

Tibetans, like most groups in China, were quick to take advantage of the opportunities that came after Hu's 1980 visit, whether these were in the form of accepting honorary positions in political bodies such as the Chinese People's Political Consultative Conference (CPPCC), or guarantees offered by the Chinese constitution for cultural autonomy. There was an extraordinary proliferation of revitalization in the areas of religion, literature, education, and the arts: in Amdo the literary innovator Dondrub Gyal was writing modern poetry in Tibetan, while the composer Chowpatthar wrote music to accompany "Tsho Ngonpo" (Blue Lake), the most famous of these poems; in Beijing Dungkar Lobsang Thrinley was teaching classical Tibetan poetics at the Nationalities Institute; in Drepung Monastery Geshe Lamrin was giving religious instruction and replacing the married monks with celibate applicants for the monkhood.[38] Throughout areas inhabited by Tibetans, hundreds of monasteries were being reconstructed and thousands of men and women were taking monastic vows. In Lhasa, commercial cooperatives were formed by Tibetans who opened The Banakshol (the Black Tent Place) and The Snowlands, backpacker hotels housed in buildings decorated in "traditional" style. Publishing houses were producing books in Tibetan containing folktales, religious texts, and even history; young Tibetan painters were following Han Zhuli's experiments with new ways of using traditional Tibetan *thangka* motifs in modern art. In such ways, and in countless others, Tibetans rapidly took advantage of the opening up of public space.

In a Western society these activities might well be seen as expressions of individual culture and creativity. In Communist China, however, while they are also that, they are primarily signs that the Party has allowed such expressions: without policies permitting these activities they would not take place. Each one of these initiatives—each book that was published and each painting that was exhibited—required one or more officials to sanction its public display. This was, of course, also the case with larger projects such as the reconstruction of monasteries and the alteration of school syllabi. Practices involving the expansion not just of cultural but also of physical space represented major changes in policy: for example, travel from one area inhabited by Tibetans to another was again allowed, with appropriate permissions, with the result that the Jokhang in Lhasa became once again a focus of national pilgrimage; Tibetans who could produce proof of relatives living abroad were allowed to travel to visit them in Nepal and India, and in 1985 perhaps 10,000 were given permission to go to India to attend the Dalai Lama's teachings that year in Bodh Gaya. Almost immediately, some lamas and other Tibetans, including some exiles, were allowed to set up schools and clinics in rural areas.[39] In 1986 the Mönlam festival was held in the Lhasa Jokhang for the first time in twenty-seven years.

Each of these acts represents decisions by several officials to reverse some twenty years of previous policy. Of course, these officials had the example of Hu Yaobang to encourage them—otherwise these micro-permissions could not have been successfully negotiated at the local level. But he was a long way away in Beijing, and, as we shall see, there was intense opposition to his policies among Chinese and other officials in Lhasa, so that the local cadres who argued for and obtained these permits were often taking considerable risks. We can get a rare insight into the creativity and the bravery of official decision makers at this time from a little-known initiative taken by a small group of Tibetan cadres in Gansu in November 1980, in what is perhaps the most remarkable of all the early-1980s initiatives taken by officials: they wrote a petition to the Party center proposing that all Tibetan-inhabited areas be united into a single autonomous region. They were quite explicit about the risks that they faced in doing so, but at the time considered themselves to have a reasonable hope of success:

> The Central Secretary People's Congress and the State Council opinions as noted above are very popular sentiments which are often discussed among the mass of Tibetan people and intellectuals. Because of the Han chauvinists' repressions in a long series of historical turmoil, those [Tibetans] who have no power are afraid to say anything and those who hold the power, practice nationality nihilism and they don't speak the truth. Consequently the Central Government can hardly understand the people's hearts. Having been for a long time educated by the Party and as young workers for the government, we have taken a risk and hope that we will not be accused as "local nationalists" and at the same time, we have been emboldened by the Party's Third Plenary emphasis on the principle of openmindedness and on the policy of seeking the truth and we therefore respectfully submit this petition. We hope the Central Government will grant us forgiveness for pointing out these faults.[40]

The petition was rejected, and the petitioners are said to have been punished by demotion and similar sanctions. Another group of Tibetan cadres petitioned the center to allow Kham, including the Tibetan areas now part of western Sichuan, to be upgraded to the level of an autonomous region; this was also rejected. No doubt many other official, internal petitions of which we do not know led to similar results at this time.

Unlike the 1980 petition, most of these initiatives were not categorically labeled within the Party at the time as oppositional, as far as I can tell, partly because for this brief period in the early and mid-1980s, everything was so new and so tentative that no one was quite sure where the limits of permissibility lay—the Chinese state and many Tibetans had converging interests in this period, for different reasons: the state itself wanted to demonstrate its tolerance of difference, and in these cases for once did not need to resort to either force or fiction for this difference to be displayed. Tibetan officials were thus able to embark upon and facilitate new initiatives that involved specifically Tibetan cultural expression. But the specific negotiation and enactment of these initiatives at the local level required enormous effort and risk on the part of Tibetan cadres in order to get the rest of the bureaucracy to accept that they lay within the guidelines of the new, centrally authorized policies. In 1987 the Panchen Lama and Ngapö were, for example, working hard to get local legislation passed that mandated Tibetan-medium education, so that the core of these concessional policies would be enshrined in law and would have a chance of surviving even if the politicians changed their views on these issues. The law was passed that year; it defined itself as celebrating China's enlightened policy toward nationalities by encouraging local cultures and it would not have been enacted if it had been seen as oppositional by the center at the time, although many local Party members may already have seen it in that way.[41]

Even up until the mid-1990s private individuals (and some cadres as well) were still publishing essays and academic studies arguing about the importance of education being available in the Tibetan language, and at the time there were no indications that this was seen as unacceptable by the central authorities.[42] Indeed, at this time, the fact that some of these educational appeals were not adopted as policy might have had as much to do with lack of funding as with ideological objections. As we shall see, however, to support and guide these initiatives was high risk, because there was deep local resentment within the cadre force toward those Tibetan officials who insisted on taking full advantage of the central policy concessions offered at this time.

These initiatives had one element in common: they had what are called in Party phraseology "Tibetan nationality *khyad chos*" ("characteristics" or "features") or *dmigs gsal khyad chos* ("special characteristics"), meaning that they had aspects that were recognizably Tibetan, the display of which was sanctioned by Party policy. This was a phrase borrowed from the official lexicon of the Party, which had specifically ordained that the various minority nationalities of China should carry out activities displaying their local characteristics. Such initiatives implied a degree of compliance with the Party's wishes, while at the same time celebrating Tibetan identity and capacity.

There were, of course, cases where Tibetans developed initiatives that did not have any local nationality features: some artists painted in a wholly Western style; one Tibetan businessman sought permission to open a branch of McDonald's in Lhasa, and another built a house in Lhasa in a Western modernist style.[43] But these cases were happening all over China, and if they occurred in Tibetan areas, the local officials who gave approval for them were less likely to face opposition or criticism: it was the taking up of the option to include extensive "nationality features" in some of these initiatives, or the privileging of Tibetans in these projects, that invited suspicion and potential criticism within the Party in the post-1979 era.

"Tibetanizing" practices in themselves, however, have no inherent purity of purpose or origin, and it is easy to find examples of economically driven and government-mandated fabrications of the celebration of Tibetan identity. Because tourists will pay much more money for a Tibetan-style product, Chinese and foreign entrepreneurs, as well as Tibetans, have been quick to cash in on this trend and to colonize this space for the accumulation of profit, so that many of the most Tibetanized restaurants or products in Tibet (or anywhere) are made or owned by non-Tibetans. The only Tibetan-style restaurant located in a genuine, reconstructed Tibetan aristocrat's house in Lhasa is owned and run by a Chinese businesswoman,[44] and so is the gallery of modern art sporting the legend "[Tibetans] as We Want to Be Seen," although the employees seen by the customers are mostly Tibetan.

This is not just entrepreneurial initiative, but an imitation of the Party's own practice: the Tibetan decor on the windows and doorframes of the houses around the Jokhang, for example, are required by law, in order to preserve the "nationality character" of the area, presumably to attract tourists and to convey the government's concern for the preservation of Tibetan culture.[45] Chinese culture—the culture produced by the state or by Chinese individuals—is so addicted to demonstrating its tolerance of and admiration for its minority nationalities that it is almost impossible to find examples of Chinese pop videos, television programs, books, paintings, music, and costume that do not include Tibetan or other nationality features.[46] Perhaps the outstanding example of gratuitous difference is the design of Chinese banknotes, all of which in the 1980s included the faces of stereotyped members of the minorities.

Why should these practices, when carried out by Tibetans (or members of other non-Chinese nationalities), invite suspicion and danger for their proponents, given that they are authorized and frequently required by the Party leadership itself? The reasons are the same as those elucidated by Bulag in his study of 1940s policy in Inner Mongolia: a deep and irreconcilable contradiction within the Party (or, some would say, within Chinese thinking) between its views of class and its views of ethnicity, and between its universalizing and differentiating tendencies. This is the same tension as that between the conviction of racial superiority and the ideal of equality, or between the use of force and display of tolerance.[47] A theory that requires belief in the progressiveness of its most advanced members cannot avoid also implying and eventually acting out the backwardness of others. In the Chinese case, it leads to the further perception that efforts at advancement by the backward "others" are potential conspiracies. In other words, any initiative encouraging difference, except those carried out by the Chinese themselves, is liable to be perceived by the Party and the state as a veiled attempt at separation or independence. The Tibetans and other nationalities in China are thus caught in a dilemma in which they are required to exhibit their nationality, but their efforts at self-expression are liable to be read as insurrection. Their only guarantee of tolerance is the performance of backwardness, and even that can be interpreted as concealed nationalism.

The Contracting Spaces of Public Discourse

Since at least 1986, if not earlier, the space for political discourse that had been made available to Tibetans at the beginning of that decade began to be closed down. For one thing, Hu Yaobang's insistence during his 1980 visit to Lhasa on replacing most of the Chinese cadres in Tibet had been extremely unpopular among those cadres, and may have contributed to his fall from power seven years later.[48] The officially sanctioned increase in religious activity antagonized significant sections within the Party, including certain groups of Tibetan cadres who saw their positions threatened by these developments.[49] The efflorescence of Tibetan language and culture, and of a Tibetan-oriented economy, and the rapid rise of newly appointed Tibetan cadres whose fathers had been aristocrats or traditional leaders, apparently also led to fierce conflicts and power struggles. There was a series of extremely important moves within the higher reaches of the Party indicating that further restrictions were likely to follow in the public sphere: Hu Yaobang had been deposed from his positions in Beijing in 1987, and the following year the first and only Party secretary of Tibet who was not Chinese—Wu Jinghua, a member of the Yi nationality—was removed from his position on the grounds of "right deviationism," ironically largely because he had exhibited too much sympathy with the Tibetans by wearing a Tibetan *chupa*.[50] Other moves only came to light much later, all of them involving the outstanding Tibetan cadres who had been prominent in the early 1950s when the CCP had first allowed a liberalization policy in Tibet: In 1982 the famous Tibetan Communist Baba Phuntsog Wangyal was criticized within the Party for unacceptable views on nationality issues, and was not given the position of Tibet Party secretary when it became available in 1985. The famous Tibetan cadre Yangling Dorje, deputy Party secretary of Tibet from 1980, had been moved from Tibet to a less contentious position in Sichuan in 1985, reportedly because of his objections to an increase in Chinese immigration into Tibet; Phuntsog Tashi, a leading cadre who had translated for the Dalai Lama during negotiations with the Chinese in Yadong in 1950,[51] had been moved to Beijing and rapidly retired immediately after giving a strong speech in support of the Panchen Lama's language law in 1987. These were indicators of major retrenchment, but the cultural and religious practices among ordinary people were not shut down, and continued even after the outbreak of popular unrest in the streets of Lhasa in 1987.

The emergence of unrest, and of open calls for independence, brought a major change to the situation in Tibet, yet it was not in the security sphere, but rather the cultural sphere. The authorities moved into what we might call security mode—that is, besides using the police force, the paramilitary, and, from March 1989, the PLA to stop these protests and detain or shoot their proponents, they also used security arguments to close down any debate around independence demands. Strictly speaking, however, this was not a contraction of public space, since arguments for independence had never been allowed. But it meant that those Tibetans operating in public space—building schools and monasteries, developing businesses, writing books, passing regulations on Tibetan language use, and so on—were vulnerable to attack if their opponents could suggest that these initiatives were connected to the independence movement, and they had to go to much greater lengths to declare their commitment to defending China's territory. This was not new—it was an intensification of a situation Tibetans had already faced for some years, particularly as a result of the 1985 decision to allow many

Tibetans to travel to India for the Dalai Lama's teachings in Bodh Gaya that year (these Tibetans were said to have returned with more nationalist sentiments). But the faction opposed to these cultural practices was gaining ascendancy, and in August 1989 a definitive article appeared in the Party newspaper in Tibet, signed by a group called "The Tibet Youth Association for Theory." The article was a leftist attack on proponents of liberalization policies in the TAR. It implied that there had been strong factional debates on this issue in the region since 1979:

> The movement to "Redeem Wrongs" started in Tibet between 1979–1980, when there were two main events. The first was the major discussion on "Practice Is the only Yardstick for Truth" during March–April 1979; the other was the First Symposium on Work in Tibet held by the Central Government in March 1980. After the ten year disaster of the Cultural Revolution and the errors of "leftism," the priority in politics was to make practical theoretical decisions both to negate leftist ideology and [the theme] of "taking class struggle as the key link."

Each section of the article argued that the various theoretical positions taken by the moderates in these debates since 1979 were in fact not only anti-socialist, but were basically attacks on the Chinese people:

> The debates on "Practice is the Yardstick" and "Proceeding from Tibet's Reality" were to eliminate and oppose "leftism." These turned into discussions on the chauvinism of Han people. . . . So too with the issue of nationalism. The argument for a special regional and national character became so popular it was as if Tibet could move along a path diametrically opposite to that of the modernization of the rest of the world. . . . It seemed as if in the problems of relations between nationalities there was only a Han Chauvinism, but no local national differences. It seemed as if it was right to put sole and heavy emphasis on the so-called "inequality in relations between nationalities" [then] simplified to "Han Oppression" and to deny or reduce the importance of the common efforts of all nationalities, and especially the backward nationalities themselves, in eliminating the [material] differences left by history. [. . .] Those who hold these views often quoted from Marx, Lenin, Stalin and Mao, but they never paid any attention to the integrity of their thoughts.

Behind this argument are two assumptions: one is that the Chinese are more advanced than the other nationalities (it suggests that the ethnic Chinese do not have nationalism: "As some knowledgeable people have already pointed out in examining the errors of our Party, Han people have only political sentiments, not national sentiments; but with some national minorities it is the opposite"). The other is that all aspects of policy presented by the liberalizers are forms of strategic concealment: the true purpose behind the notion of "prudence" in development in Tibet is "to adopt the traditional Tibetan culture left by the backward serf system as a whole"; among these liberals are people "who discreetly introduced the idea of self-determination" so that they could argue for independence. Tibet *appears* to be carrying out the same policies as the rest of China but

Tibet, while it has the same atmosphere as the rest of the country . . . , here it has taken its own form. Its character is to counter the interests of the whole country with national interests, to deny Marxism and Maoism's guiding position with religious national consciousness, and to take crude, bourgeois ethnology as the basis for the study of social science.

The article concluded by warning that the efforts at liberalization in Tibet are part of "a strategy used by foreign reactionary forces to fight against the Soviet Union and the socialist countries" by using "religion and nationalism as a pressure on socialist countries: 'splittism' both inside and outside Tibet flaunts the flag of religion and nationalism, dividing the country." These are the same universalist arguments that were used by the CCP to suppress the Inner Mongolians' "politics of difference" and to launch the Cultural Revolution in 1965. Those Tibetan and other leaders who had predicted a return to the witch-hunt mentality of earlier phases of Communist policy were shown to be right. What was different about this phase of suppressing difference in China, and what was confusing for outside observers, was that the 1980s reversion to universalism, unlike its predecessors, was able to coexist with economic pluralism. This was unprecedented: it was not evident before then that two apparently opposite policies could be operated in parallel spheres at the same time. In fact, this apparent contradiction rests on a misapprehension about economic diversity, which appears to be pluralistic but in fact, at least in the Chinese case, is the opposite, as we shall see.

While the universalizers were reestablishing their predominance within the Tibet Communist Party, and the space for cultural and political liberalization was shrinking, it was still not wholly shut down. Limits already existed on the number of monks in each monastery, for example, but these were still not actively enforced. The 1991 article in the *Xizang Ribao* that argued for allowing Tibetan Party members to remain Buddhist was an extraordinarily liberal proposal that was outlawed by the Party center some two years later. Significantly, that article appears to have been written by Chinese cadres, judging from their names, a reminder that the category "Tibetan cadres" and the category "Chinese cadres" were not single entities containing individuals with identical views whose thinking can be essentialized as either collaborationist or persecuting.[52]

From the time of Chen Kuiyuan's arrival in Tibet to take over the post of Party secretary in Tibet in March 1992,[53] however, a pattern begins to become clear in the closing down of tolerated areas of debate.[54] The first stages of this pattern emerged in April 1992 when a public furor developed in the Chinese press in response to Deng Xiaoping's "Southern Tour," which led to the "Spring Tide" campaign and the call for rapidly accelerated marketization of the economy. In the TAR (and no doubt in other nationality areas as well) extreme conservatives like Chen were able to use the rhetoric of the economic reformers to shut down available political space by arguing that since marketization required uniform and unhindered reform of the economy, policies of difference were counter to progress, and were disguised forms of opposition to reform; these moves became explicit in articles that appeared in the official press in 1994.[55] These conservative leaders had a political objective rather than an economic one: they saw the reform policy as an opportunity to denounce any objections to the immigration of non-Tibetans into the TAR as an attack on Deng Xiaoping's reform policy.[56] From this time on, public discussion over Tibet's economic path was effectively closed down, at least insofar as it reflected ideas such as the Panchen Lama's principle that a form of economic development could be devised that was in some way oriented toward Tibetans. Of course, there was still economic development—Tibetans could still do business, and were encouraged to do so, but they were not entitled to economic advantage or priority because they were Tibetan. Unexpected though it might seem, the closing down of public space thus began with restrictions on economic debate.[57] The imagery of the market economy as a site of diversity was thus used for exactly the opposite purpose in the Tibet political landscape: it was used to impose economic uniformity on Tibetan traders so that they would be obliged to accept a Chinese-dominated economic system.

The subsequent phases of contraction are much easier to identify. In April 1994 a series of public speeches and official newspaper articles appeared indicating again that the discussion based on "special characteristics" had been shut down and was no longer tolerable.[58] This removed the ideological basis for other arguments celebrating local difference, besides the economic arguments that had been disallowed two years earlier. In July 1994, at a meeting known as "The Third Forum on Work in Tibet," which set the center's policies for Tibet for the next ten years or more, it became rapidly clear that these involved a contraction of public space in terms of religion. At first this applied principally to the person of the Dalai Lama—until then, it had been tolerable since 1980 for Tibetans to express religious but not political respect for him; after 1994 it was ruled that he could not be shown religious respect either. The justification for this shift, which contradicts the Chinese constitution, has never been clear: it simply represents the ascendancy of the argument that religious policies are concealed forms of "splittism." Within a year the public display of photographs of the Dalai Lama had been banned, and in 1996 a campaign began that required all monks and nuns to denounce the Dalai Lama in writing. At around this time it was announced that the number of reconstructed monasteries and temples, and the number of monks and nuns, was "sufficient" for the needs of the people, and other restrictions were introduced to limit these practices from further expansion. The religious area was contracting: it was no longer acceptable for Tibetans to argue that they were entitled to more religious freedoms or privileges.

In 1997 came the first public signs of the closing down of cultural space.[59] This was marked by an infamous speech that July by Chen Kuiyuan that for the first time named Desi Sangye Gyatso, a seventeenth-century prime minister of Tibet, as a reactionary figure who could no longer be written about or praised.[60] The speech also said that Buddhism was a "foreign culture" and not an essential part of Tibetan culture, meaning that it should not be included in courses of study at the

University of Tibet.[61] This followed the downgrading of translation committees, the closing of middle-school Tibetan-medium education, the rewriting of history textbooks at the University of Tibet, and the suspension of admissions to the university's Tibetan department.[62] The principal provisions of the landmark Language Law of 1987, which had only been partially implemented, were now in effect withdrawn.[63]

Significant moves were also taking place within the Party, where Chen had overturned previous policies (and perhaps national regulations) regarding regional autonomy by appointing in 1995 the ethnic Chinese cadre Hu Chunhua as the leader of the Lhokha prefectural administration. Previously, Chinese officials had frequently held positions as leaders in the Party in Tibet, but in the administrations of prefectures and counties had only been appointed as deputy leaders. Later, Chinese cadres were appointed to head the administration in Shigatse prefecture and in several counties in Tibet, and in September 2000 a class of some seventy ethnic Chinese was opened at Tibet University specifically to train future Chinese officials so they could take up leadership positions in Tibetan counties and townships.[64] The closing of public space is thus paralleled by the closing down of space within the political apparatus, so that the opportunities for Tibetan officials to take up leadership positions have become increasingly limited. At the same time it became more and more dangerous for Tibetan officials to sanction or support public initiatives by fellow Tibetans.

In November 1997, Chen went on to identify in a public speech a new form of enemy within Tibetan society, which he defined as "the hidden reactionary." As examples he referred to unnamed individuals among the few great Tibetan intellectuals remaining in the universities and among the educated Tibetans who had secured relatively senior positions in the administration during the reform period of the early 1980s.[65] In internal speeches, Chen is said to have referred to three important Tibetan officials who had defected as further evidence of the unreliability of Tibetan cadres—the hotel director Jamyang Choegyal, the television journalist Ngawang Choephel, and the famous singer Dadron. They were all from areas of cultural or economic activity (tourism, state journalism, and pop music) that were part of officially tolerated public space, and none of them had openly defied or challenged the system before their defections.[66] The specter of Newtonian deception among high Tibetan officials had thus been openly stated to be a major policy concern and a threat to security.

As areas of public space were restricted, closed down, or redefined, initiatives for peculiarly Tibetan expression appeared in other areas. Among these we might include Tibetan literary publications, pop music, Tibetan music halls, and the study of the English language, all of which flourished well into the 1990s. The emergence of nangmas, or Tibetan music halls, dating from the mid-1990s, arose in response to the government's efforts after 1992 to encourage the setting up of bars and karaokes in Tibet in order to accelerate the development of the private economy. This had led to a proliferation of Chinese nightclubs in Tibetan towns—in other words, as cultural space was being closed down, economic space was being opened up. The *nangma*s were one of the few specifically Tibetan responses to this shift of public space from the cultural to the economic zone: they are also commercial dance halls, but the singers, musicians, and clientele are almost exclusively Tibetan, as are almost all of their songs and videos. The expansion of trading in Tibetan medicine was another Tibetan response to the new economic opportunities emerging at this time—it could be safely pursued by Tibetans because it could be presented as an effort to enter the new market economy, as required by Deng's "Spring Tide" reforms, and at the same time it could be presented as an example of Tibetan secular traditions rather than of its religious culture.[67] It is now being pursued by Tibetans as a commercial opportunity, and a group of Tibetan officials has been trying to reach a deal with a major Western multinational pharmaceutical company to market Tibetan herbs.

It is, of course, impossible to tell which Tibetans are taking part in business opportunities to make money and which (if any) are doing it to make a statement about their identity and their cultural objectives; no doubt these issues are often mixed. But the fact that it is becoming harder for Tibetans to find state-condoned opportunities to articulate views does not mean that those views are diminishing in significance or intensity. The evidence is that Tibetans continue to seek out ways to pursue or communicate a number of political and personal objectives. These initiatives also face difficulties of various kinds. Although business enterprise in general remains an allowed area, Tibetans can no longer claim special advantage in this field as they had in the 1980s, and the Tibetan medicine producers are likely to be rapidly bought out by Chinese and other competitors. The *nangma* operators face constant political suspicion from the authorities, and shortly after they emerged, they were all closed down for two days while officials worked out rules to determine which songs could be played. A number of songs were banned, on the grounds that they were politically inflammatory, among them (according to some reports) Yadong's song "Mchod-rten Dkar-po" (White Stupa), and Dadron's "Nga yi Dongrub Tshe-ring" (My Dondrup Tsering), which are seen as paeons to the Dalai Lama.[68] Yadong's song is still available in Chinese, however, as is his "Shengqing de Didi" (Magnificent Little Brother) regarded by some as an ode to the missing Panchen Lama child. Perhaps the words of these songs are so ambiguous that to ban them outright would be to invite ridicule, or they are seen as dangerous only if in Tibetan rather than Chinese.

Even activities that have no Tibetan characteristics at all and appear to be purely commercial can arouse the same political suspicions when carried out by Tibetans; studying English, for example, and education in general is encouraged throughout China, but the private and adult evening schools established by Tibetans in Lhasa during the 1990s have come under pressure from the authorities, apparently on the grounds that they might be designed secretly to facilitate the learning of foreign political ideas.[69] Entrepreneurial activity can thus be viewed alternatively as the modernist pursuit of profit, as an assertion of identity, as veiled nationalist plots, or as an indirect indigenous response to political restrictions on cultural expression.[70] It is thus not at all clear whether these social activities are oppositional or not—they might, for example, be only opportunist attempts to make money, to gain promotion, or to promote personal or group interests. The Tibetanization of public space is therefore partly fiction, partly economic opportunism, and partly a display by the state (and often by individual Chinese people also, especially artists) of the preferred self-image as tolerant of ethnic difference. But primarily these activities are forms of cultural and ethnic expression, and as such the Tibetan officials who have fought within the Party for these initiatives to be allowed remain at constant risk of attack by their counterparts for condoning hidden vehicles of nationalist thought. For most Tibetan cadres, the reality of this risk was finally made concrete by the abrupt demotion in September 2001 of Tenzin, the deputy Party secretary in Tibet who had been most closely associated with Tibetan cultural initiatives in the previous two decades. No public reference was made to his removal and no reasons were given; moreover, he had never publicly contravened Party policy. His removal is almost certain to have been a result of fear among Chinese officials of Newtonian concealment among even the highest levels of the Tibetan cadre force.

The Cadres and the Ethnic Divide

It is not possible to define the agendas of the various groupings among the Tibetan cadre elite, given that so much is concealed.[71] Evidently, there are Tibetan cadres of all political persuasions, including some who fully support China's policies, but to identify individuals as belonging to one faction or another would be to place many of them in danger. Much can, however, be seen by looking not for explicit statements of cadres' views and objectives, but what we might call their negative image—the official Chinese responses to those views. Again, in this universe of strategic concealment, where all levels of the state are involved in deception, it is not possible to read these responses in any categorical way—for one thing, ethnic Chinese officials in Tibet (and in Inner Mongolia) frequently distort and exaggerate the extent of local opposition and nationalism in order to bolster their own positions and to extract more funds from the center. The descriptions by leading Chinese officials tell us much more, however, than the official view of Tibetan cadres: they demonstrate the increasing fissure between the Tibetan and Chinese cadres, and provoke its deepening even where it had not preexisted.

The key to these responses lies, it seems to me, in a statement published in the official Party newspaper in Tibet in October 1991, which quoted a leading Chinese official as saying that "some party cadres, including some leading cadres, no longer believe in Marxism and socialism . . . and regard the Dalai Lama, a political exile, as their spiritual support."[72] It was an unusually open declaration that a significant cohort of cadres in Tibet were politically unreliable, and it raises deep questions about the legitimacy of the Chinese project in Tibet, not because it revealed opposition at the highest levels—Marxism predicts contradictions within society in the primary stage of socialism, because of the unextinguished remnants of the class system—but because many of the cadres in Tibet were too young to have experienced the Dalai Lama's rule and could only be reacting to their experience of Chinese life, not their recollection of the earlier regime.

This statement in itself refutes the perception of Tibetan cadres as collaborators: clearly, the Chinese authorities by the early 1990s did not view the Tibetan cadre force in this way. In fact, if we compare this statement to Brad Pitt's orotund condemnation of Ngapö, it would seem that the truth is exactly the opposite, just as Ngapö's son indicated to the *South China Morning Post* at the time—it is not the would-be Western defenders of Tibet but the Chinese leaders themselves who seem now to curse the Tibetan officials for their perfidy.

After 1991 a number of policy mechanisms were put in place in the TAR that have been perceived by many outsiders in terms of restrictions on personal freedoms and abuses of individual rights. Viewed from the perspective of cadre policy, and in light of the 1991 statement, however, many of these policies can be seen as having served a very different and much more practical function: to test the political loyalty of officials, and to identify those who are disloyal. In the Appendix to this chapter I have reproduced a number of official statements describing a dozen or so of these policies during the 1990s, including those banning people from sending their children to schools in exile, displaying Dalai Lama photographs, supporting the exile choice of Panchen Lama, having shrines in their rooms, owning more than one private property without permission, and (in the case of university teachers) encouraging the inclusion of religion in the teaching syllabus. The chief targets of these prohibitions were Tibetan officials, and for them, whether or not these policies countered various individual or collective rights would have been secondary to the fact that they were almost certainly veiled mechanisms for identifying cadres with links to the exiles, with religious beliefs, or with attachments to the Dalai Lama.

Other political campaigns in this period do not appear to outsiders at first glance to be related to testing cadre loyalty. But in practice they are. The 1996 patriotic education campaign in monasteries, for example, involved teams of cadres staying in monasteries for up to three months to lecture and investigate monks. Since the cadres were in teams, the pressure on each official to carry out the reeducation and interrogation of monks would have been rigorous, and it is likely that these operations functioned as intensive tests of the loyalty and dedication of the cadres to the Party's orders as much as that of the monks. The current drive to introduce competitive entrance exams for government positions, to lower the age of retirement, and to downsize the administration is a pan-Chinese policy with a sound economic basis, but the examinations include directly political questions, and in the TAR this mechanism is used by the leadership to remove Tibetan cadres who are regarded as politically unreliable, particularly those with extensive knowledge of Tibetan culture and language.

These official statements about the risks posed to China by Tibetan cadres in themselves destroy any simplistic perception of that group as co-optees of the state. But there are other significances to be drawn here, not least of which is the fact that this interpretation suggests that to a considerable extent Chinese policy in Tibet is being driven by Tibetan cadres, if only through the specter of their envisaged dissent. For this reason alone, we cannot say that Tibetan politicians in Tibet are wholly without power or influence, albeit in an inverted way.

The major significance of these moves, however, lies again in a detail of ideology. Cadres in the Party are being subjected to scrutiny all the time throughout China—in the 2000–2001 period, for example, they had to go through the Three Stresses Campaign and the Three Representatives drive—so this is not in itself unusual: divergence within the elite is in fact normal in the CCP, notwithstanding official presentations of a unified leadership. But those divergences are almost always ideological or ethical—they involve officials whose political views are incorrect or (more commonly) those who are involved in corruption. The mechanisms of cadre assessment in Tibet are entirely different because the scrutiny there is based on ethnicity, not ideology or ethics. This racial differentiation is never stated explicitly, but it can be demonstrated by asking of each practice, is this rule in practice likely to apply to ethnic Chinese officials? Chinese people are not, for example, likely to have Dalai Lama photographs, nor to have sent their children to school in India. Neither are they likely to have a view on the Panchen Lama's incarnation, or to have difficulties telling monks to denounce the Dalai Lama.[73] The various campaigns of rectification and improvement that appear to apply to all cadres are therefore in fact directed against Tibetan cadres on the basis of their ethnicity first, and their views or performance only second; they would not apply, or would do so only very marginally, to ethnically Chinese cadres working in the TAR. In other words, these campaigns indicate that Tibetans are seen by the Party and perhaps the state as intrinsically unreliable because of their nationality.

Ethnic labeling was taboo in Maoist days, and it contradicts previous incarnations of Communist theory. On paper it is still unacceptable in terms of the Party's commitment to equality of the nationalities. The fact that operating in public space remains perilous for Tibetans where it would be trivial for Chinese, and the fact that the Party's disciplinary campaigns in contemporary Tibet target Tibetan cadres, therefore represents an important shift in Chinese ethnopolitics: it indicates that the discourse of national unity has been replaced by a theory of vertical distinction according to ethnicity. The basing of political theory and practice on a universal or absolutist notion, that of class struggle, had been brought to an end by Deng Xiaoping in 1979 and replaced by a pragmatic politics based on a project of national construction, which included the celebration of difference. In Tibet it now appears that at a basic level of discourse, a form of universalist politics has in effect been reinstated, although this time it is a politics of ethnic superiority rather than of class.[74] Paradoxically, even the more aggressive forms taken by Chinese communism in its earlier incarnations had offered ideological space in which ethnic equality was guaranteed and could at least in theory be pursued. Chinese nationalism, however, offers no such guarantees—it sanctions and endorses notions of ethnic Chinese superiority and reliability. Thus the current shape of policy in Tibet communicates two messages: first, that the Party's offers of equality are false, and second, that the distrust of the Chinese toward Tibetans is endemic, irreversible, and intrinsic. Evidence of Tibetan disloyalty to the Party is not required for the Chinese to perceive it, and evidence of Tibetan loyalty does not mitigate the state's distrust of its Tibetan cadres. In this situation, the contempt of Chinese officialdom for their Tibetan colleagues is self-fulfilling, and is likely to deepen the gulf between them.

Conclusion

We can now answer the Newtonian question—whether or not Tibetan officials practice strategic concealment. From the evidence declared by Chinese leaders in their speeches, and from the extent of those leaders' efforts to identify such concealment, it is likely that many do. Indeed, the extent of secret opposition may be very significant, even though it might take the form of facilitating local education and religious practice. That does not necessarily mean that any of these leaders are martyrs, heroes, separatists, or resistance fighters acting under deep cover as operatives for the Dalai Lama: they may disagree strongly with the exiles, and there are many other, less extreme ideals to which they might secretly aspire, of which by far the most important are the promotion of Tibetan culture, education, and economy. In fact, we can safely presume that as in any other society, there is a range of interest groups and constituencies, each with competing interests and imperatives. And we can also presume that there will still be Tibetans of various groups and affiliations who will conclude that even in these conditions their interests may lie with the state, or in some parallel space of cooperation that it offers.

But the question of strategic concealment among officials has been eclipsed in significance by another question, which arises from the response we have seen by the Chinese leadership to the possibility of that concealment: is the relationship between the Tibetan cadre force and the modern Chinese state structurally and endemically flawed? It does seem that at a fundamental level the issue of public space and the constant suspicion toward Tibetan access to it has opened up a deep cleavage along ethnic lines within the leadership in Tibet. It has revealed within the Chinese state a residual and apparently growing belief in ethnic superiority that is contrary to Communist dogma and to the Party's own rhetoric. If so, fewer and fewer Tibetans are likely to see their purposes served by committing themselves to the Party other than for expedient reasons. The rift that the current Chinese leadership already sees between itself and its Tibetan cadres is therefore likely to deepen over time, especially as Chinese nationalism is in the ascendant. In this context, the notion of collaboration is redundant, and the more urgent questions for Tibetan officials will increasingly be those that focus on the remaining possibilities of developing a specifically Tibetan culture and economy in Tibet.

Appendix: Examples of Official Criticisms and Campaigns Targeting Tibetan Cadres in the TAR, 1991–2001

October 1991: "Some Party cadres, including some leading cadres, have mixed in among the local people and no longer believe in Marxism and socialism. . . . They openly believe in Buddhism and regard the Dalai Lama, a political exile, as their spiritual support. . . . In our region there are some Party comrades, especially some leading Party cadres, who have ignored class struggle and the people's democratic dictatorship."[75]

July 1994: "A few Party members and cadres at grass-roots levels do not even have a clear attitude toward separatists."[76]

September 1994: "Some cadres of our region don't have a firm standpoint and the cadre force is not pure. Although the Party Committee of the TAR has carried out some internal consolidation this year [1994] the achievement was not even. . . . The purification of our cadre force and our region's development have a direct connection with the fight against separatism, and the size of the victory relies on them. . . . All Party members, especially leading members, are not allowed to put up religious symbols, Dalai photos, and altars in their house, and should not have prayer rooms."[77]

October 15, 1994: TAR Government Document Number 15 (1994) was issued. It required all government cadres to fill in a questionnaire stating whether or not their children were attending exile schools in India.[78]

October 1995: Chen Kuiyuan, Tibet's Party secretary, declared at an internal meeting that the pro-independence movement had been found to be based on Tibetan religion, which was linked in turn to Tibetan culture. In the following months the experimental project in Tibetan-language secondary education was abandoned, several Tibetan-language courses at the University of Tibet were canceled, new students in Tibetan studies were rejected, and university staff were ordered to rewrite textbooks for Tibetan-related courses and to reduce their religious content.[79]

November 4, 1995: Chadrel Rinpoche is denounced, the first high Tibetan leader to be publicly purged since the Cultural Revolution. He and his supporters are described as "reactionaries" and as "the scum of this holy place of Buddhism," a reference to Tashilhunpo.[80]

November 24, 1995: "The struggle to expose and criticise the Dalai is a serious political struggle. The Chinese People's Political Consultative Conference [CPPCC] at all levels in Tibet must follow the instructions of the Party Central Committee and the Regional Party Committee and boldly call on and organize CPPCC members to relentlessly expose and criticize the Dalai's schemes and crimes of splitting the motherland. All CPPCC members should participate in condemning the Dalai both orally and in writing. No matter what their rank, they must maintain a firm, clear stand. That is because their stand regarding the issue of exposing and criticizing the Dalai is a major political question that serves as the main basis for determining whether the political orientation, stand, and viewpoint of CPPCC cadres, particularly high-ranking cadres, including CPPCC members, is correct; whether cadres can distinguish between right and wrong; and whether their political acumen is strong or weak. At the same time it also serves as the main basis for determining whether patriots are worthy of the name. The people will judge your practical performance in this serious political struggle; they will judge whether you side with the Party and the people and play a positive role in matters of great importance at a critical juncture."[81]

May 1996: "The regional party committee and the regional people's government in May 1996 decided to conduct patriotic education in temples and lamaseries throughout the region and to experiment on establishing normal order in them. The autonomous region, as well as various prefectures and cities, organized strong work groups and sent them to some temples and lamaseries to carry out education among the monks in patriotism, state law, and regulations, and the party's policies toward nationalities and religion. By so doing, we educated and united most monks, dealt blows to a small number of ethnic separatists, and enhanced the monks' conscientiousness in safeguarding the unification of the motherland, opposing separatism, loving the country, and cherishing their religion."[82]

July 11, 1997: "What is strange is that a very small number of people in Tibet and other parts of the country have made the same statements as the Dalai clique's. There are several representative views that should be exposed. When you encounter such views, you should be vigilant. The first such view is to equate Tibetan national culture with Tibetan religion, alleging that the Tibetan national culture is actually a Buddhist culture and that there would be no Tibetan national culture without a Buddhist culture. Some people say that the Tibetan national culture is connected to religion in form and essence. Some others say that college teaching material will be void of substance if religion is not included and that in that case, colleges would not be real colleges. If what such people talked about were a Buddhist college, I would have no comment. But what they refer to is a Tibet University, so they have no reason whatsoever to make such an allegation. . . . The view of equating Buddhist culture with Tibetan culture not only does not conform to reality but also belittles the ancestors of the Tibetan nationality and the Tibetan nationality itself. I just cannot understand that. Some people, claiming to be authorities, have made such shameless statements confusing truth and falsehood. Comrades who are engaged in research on Tibetan culture should be indignant at such statements. Making use of religion in the political field, separatists now go all out to put religion above the Tibetan culture and attempt to use the spoken language and culture to cause disputes and antagonism between nationalities, and this is the crux of the matter."[83]

July 31, 1997: "Response to the letter to Jiang Zemin: the document issued by the Centre is dated 31st July 1997. And as a result of that there was a specific document by the TAR government which just came out. And it is entitled document 106. So the document specifically states that Party members and cadres are misusing state funds for private purposes such as housing and cars. Therefore investigations and inspections must be launched. This is specifically aimed at the Tibetan cadres, because the Chinese cadres build their houses or have cars in their home areas, and so these things are less obvious than for the Tibetans. These investigations are now being carried out. Another point in the document is dealing with the Party members' strong religious beliefs and having faith in the Dalai Lama, having photos and altars at home. Not only the cadres, even the ordinary people, are being ordered to remove their altars and photos at home."[84]

November 7, 1997: "We must pay particular attention to a small handful of dangerous elements who have passed themselves off as upright persons with an ulterior motive and have mingled among us. For example, Qiazha [Chadrel Rimpoche, former abbot of Tashilhunpo Monastery, arrested for cooperating with the Dalai Lama in the search for the reincarnation of the Panchen Lama], who secretly worked for the Dalai clique to the detriment of our interests, is not an isolated case among our ranks. However, reactionaries, regardless of whether they were dispatched from outside the region or they have long hidden inside the region, are incapable of toppling our socialist system and separating Tibet from the big family of the motherland."[85]

November 17, 1997: "Adjustments [have been made] to reinforce a number of leading groups at prefecture and county levels. . . . We should further strengthen Party building with the improvement of leading groups at various levels as the main content."[86]

May 2000: "Southwest China's Tibet Autonomous Region has started to significantly reduce its staff of regional government employees as part of the national effort to downsize local governments. Sources from the regional government said that the number of regional government departments in Tibet will drop from the current 29 to 23, and their staff will be cut by 25 percent, from 2,618 to 1,963 employees."[87]

September 2001: The *Xizang Ribao* announces the names of the Party leaders who attended the five-yearly congresses of the Tibet Branch of the CCP, and the composition of its new Standing Committee, with no reference to Deputy Secretary Tenzin.[88]

Notes

I would like to thank the East Asian Institute of Columbia University and the Oesterreichischen Fonds zur Foerderung der Wissenchaftlichen Forschung for their assistance and support during the research and preparation for this chapter.

1. The film *Seven Years in Tibet* was directed by Jean Jacques Annaud and released by Tristar Pictures in December 1997. For a Chinese semi-official response, see He (1998).

2. *Asiaweek* published a brief interview with Ngapö with the display quote "The Traitor? Ngapö Ngawang Jigme, 80, Is Content" (see Hsieh 2000). The historian Tsering Shakya noted of Ngapö that "most Tibetans in Tibet despise him as a traitor" (Becker 1998); Shakya (1999, 198, 300) describes the prevalence of this view in Tibet in 1959 and 1964.

3. "The 'Ngawang' in the film, with Ngapö Ngawang Jigme as his prototype, is described as a 'hidden traitor,' and the film hints at his having secret communication with the Chinese Communists. He is even denounced to his face as 'betraying Tibet' through Harrer's mouth. This is a complete fabrication on the part of the screenwriter and director of the film" (He 1998). Some of Ngapö's claims in these articles are also false, as argued in Becker (1998) and TIN (1998).

4. In this chapter when speaking of Tibetan officials I am using the term "Tibetan" in its ethnic sense. In China the words "official" or "cadre" mean literally anyone employed by the state, but I am referring primarily to the 24,000 or so who hold office in the administration (which I use to mean the government) or in the Communist Party of the Tibet Autonomous Region. For a fuller discussion of these cadres, the reader may wish to consult Conner and Barnett (1997).

5. I have attempted to describe a number of different groups among officials in Tibet, and in some cases the interests with which these groups are associated, in Barnett (2002).

6. See Abu-Lughod (1990), and Bulag (1999). Bulag's paper argues "that resistance should, instead of being romanticized, be seen as a diagnostic of power within the society concerned."

7. Martyrdom has taken on an iconic role recently in the exile community, following the self-immolation of Thubten Ngodrup, presumably in part because of the influence of such practices in Indian politics, but some hints of doubt were expressed about its effects. See, for example, Karma Yeshe Wangmo's poem "in memory of Thubten Ngodrup, the Tibetan who burned himself for the sake of all beings" which says "May that sacrifice be seen as an act of patience rather than one of impatience . . . May it be seen as a perfect act rather than one of weakness" (Karma 1998).

8. This view was expressed by a group of young Tibetans at a panel discussion held at the Tibet Foundation, London, September 2, 1998.

9. "There were fewer than one million people in Tibet at that time. Tibetan troops were neither well trained nor well equipped. How (could they) fight with the PLA? How (could they) win victory?" Ngapö told Jasper Becker (see Xinhua 1998 and Becker 1998). Ngapö had good reasons for believing that resistance at that stage was not only futile but might be counterproductive, and in any case many of his colleagues in the Tibetan cabinet and elite preferred a negotiated settlement to a bloody conflict that was almost sure to end in defeat, especially since they had no international support at the time. Furthermore, the surrender Ngapö negotiated in Beijing a year later was exceptionally generous in the terms it pledged to the Tibetans, apart from the fact that it removed absolutely their right to sovereignty, a term which Shakya shows Ngapö was not instructed by his Tibetan superiors to concede. See Shakya (1999). Becker's 1998 article on Ngapö includes succinctly many of the major arguments put forward by Shakya. Robert Ford, who was Ngapö's radio operator in Chamdo at the time of the invasion (October 1950), accuses Ngapö of incompetence in not allowing him to send the one spare radio set to Riwoche to give the defenders advance warning of a

Chinese troop movement that would cut off their line of retreat, but Ford (1958) does not refer to treachery. *Asiaweek* noted that Ngapö "was depicted in Hollywood's *Seven Years in Tibet* as a traitor to Tibet, though arguably he was a minor official with little choice but to co-operate" (Hsieh 2000).

10. "Ngapö Jigme adds that despite their differences, his father has tried his best for Tibet 'When things go wrong, people always look for a scapegoat but it is more complicated than that,' the son said" (Becker 1998).

11. Arianne Mnouchkine, a distinguished theater director, and others suggested this at a public discussion in the Théatre du Soleil, Paris, April 2001.

12. Zagorin (1990 and 1996) notes that Islam and Marranic Judaism permitted outward lies about inward faith to avoid religious persecution.

13. The sixteenth century Catholic authority Martín de Azpilcueta (called Dr. Navarrus) urged that the doctrine of mental reservation permit lying when responding to questioning by judges and other superiors. See also Slater (1913), explaining that Catholicism permits lying to thwart serious harm to others. These references are from Allen (1999), which gives a useful refutation of critiques of President Clinton's use of deception to protect sexual privacy. "I am suggesting that the conclusion that . . . to agree that trust is vital, but to disagree that trust in government hinges crucially on officials never lying to protect privacy."

14. "These 'evangelicals' are willing to accept Romish assurances about common beliefs, values, and social goals; they are oblivious to the subtleties of popish sophistry in respect to inter-church relations" (Reed 1997).

15. Oskar Schindler can be seen as Hollywood's own model for this kind of official, in the heroic mode. Of course, he is redeemed by the evidence of secret resistance, but in principle this is a model of tolerated collaboration.

16. Snobelen (1999) shows that the probable punishment in Newton's later years would have more likely been social ostracism and loss of legal rights, but the official punishment was three years in prison, and one anti-trinitarian died in an English prison in 1662, while in Scotland another such heretic was hanged in 1697 (p. 395). Newton's disciples Whiston and Clarke did speak out openly about their nonconformist views after 1710, but managed to avoid imprisonment. Newton kept his strongly held views secret for some forty-five years (p. 396).

17. Snobelen (1999, 399, n135) notes that "all of this assumes that Newton actually attended on the day the committee met. Unfortunately, the record is silent on this detail. It is certain, however, that Newton was both asked and expected to attend." Snobelen speculates that these pressures might have contributed "to the psychological stresses that eventually led to his 1693 breakdown."

18. "Wherefore when thou art convinced be not ashamed of ye truth but profess it openly . . . rejoyce if thou art counted worthy to suffer in thy reputation or in any other way for ye sake of ye Gospel," Newton wrote in the 1670s (Snobelen 1999, 399).

19. I am using the term "Chinese officials" here in the sense of ethnically Chinese officials, since I think this is the generally understood meaning of this term among English speakers; I use it instead of using the term "Han," which has complex political connotations. When referring to institutions such as the Chinese government, the army, or the system, I am using the term to denote that these belong to China.

20. An Asiawatch report in 1994 found that over 80 percent of the political arrests made by the government of the People's Republic of China since 1989 had involved Tibetans. The study was based on partial figures, and was an estimate only—it is possible, for example, that a higher proportion of politically related arrests was taking place in Xinjiang than in the various areas of Tibet, but few details were available from that area; however, it still indicated an increased degree of coercion in the Tibetan areas of China.

21. See Shakya (1997) and Barnett (1997).

22. Some journalistic reports point to the involvement of ordinary Tibetans in the sacking of the monasteries in the early stages of the Cultural Revolution as if this were a revelation or an exposé (see, for example, Wong 1994), but this only reveals that the journalists had adopted the binary collaborator–martyr model. Condemnations by Tibetans inside Tibet of collaborators are rare, and since the 1980s tend to be chiefly of Tibetan lamas who made anti–Dalai Lama statements unnecessarily when they (unlike cadres) could have used their positions to avoid such statements. Dedrug Rinpoche attracted popular criticism for a public statement he made after the March 1988 demonstration, and Sengchen Rinpoche was despised for his attempts to unseat the Panchen Lama in 1964 and again in 1995, when he was given the nominal leadership of Tashilhunpo; a bomb was detonated outside his house in Lhasa in January 1996 (see *Sunday Morning Post*, Hong Kong, January 28, 1995). The house of a lama named Druk-khang in Nagchu was bombed or burnt down in 1996 (see DIIR 1996, and TIN 1997d). Among officials, Ragti and the *arriviste* Jinzhong (Tsedrung) Gyaltsen Phuntsog are often described as extreme opportunists. Goranangpa, writing of the Maoist era, is quoted as saying that "the Han nationalism of certain leaders of minority nationalities who enjoy high positions and handsome salaries, or desire to climb the ladder in their official career, is even worse than that of some of the Han cadres. In a socialist country, under the direction of fanatical leftist opportunism purporting class struggle, a few minority leaders went so far as to brazenly desert their precious traditional culture, language and customs in order to exhibit their so called 'progressive' and 'revolutionary' zeal" (Zla ba'i shes rab 1999).

23. Zhang and Guo (1991). See also TIN (1991).

24. Tibet People's Broadcasting Station (1997). See also TIN (1997c).

25. However, newspaper obituaries of the Panchen Lama did describe this shift. See, for example, those by John Gittings, Andy Higgins, and Graham Hutchins in the *Guardian*, the *Independent,* and the *Daily Telegraph*, respectively, shortly after the lama's death on January 28, 1989. See also Hilton (1999).

26. See, for example, *The Guardian* (London), March 10, 1989, for a report of a demonstration in Shigatse sparked by rumors of his death. See also Hilton (1996), or Forney (1996).

27. Xinhua (1998).

28. Panchen Lama (1987). Note that even in this internal speech the Panchen Lama added a saving clause specifically to this remark, apparently as a form of exoneration: "People may not like what I am saying. But I am saying this out of my love for the motherland."

29. See Barnett (1998).

30. "'The late Panchen Lama was a great Tibetan patriot gifted with an unsurpassable conviction to help alleviate the suffering of the Tibetan people,' His Holiness the Dalai Lama said to a gathering of 700 representatives from Tibetan communities, both monastic and lay, all around the world. 'While he was alive, he devoted all his energies toward preserving and promoting Tibetan Buddhism and culture.'" (DIIR 1999). The Chinese authorities held a celebration to commemorate the Panchen Lama, whom they declared to have been a Chinese patriot: "Wang Zhaoguo, vice-chairman of the National Committee of the Chinese People's Political Consultative Conference (CPPCC), . . . highly praised the 10th Bainqen Erdini for his patriotic spirit and his dedication to national unity" (Xinhua 1999).

31. Even Heinrich Harrer, who had strong views on collaboration, concedes of Ngapö in his second book that "one should not conceal some positive aspects of the activity of collaborators" and, speaking of Sholkhang, that "it was better if a genuine Tibetan looked after the young people than someone whose feelings and thoughts were entirely Chinese" (Harrer 1984, 19, 75).

32. Bulag (2000).

33. I have used the word "nationality" in the sense often used by the Chinese state until recently, namely to refer to the fifty-five *minzu*, or peoples, recognized as minorities. Officials in China are now required to use the word "ethnicity" for this use.

34. See, for example, Barmé (1999).

35. These included freedom of religious practice, tax amnesty for farmers, and increasing the proportion of Tibetan cadres. See TIN (1999); also Goldstein (1995) for a useful summary. About 20,000 Chinese cadres were sent back to China in the following five years, although the net number after allowing for new cadre transfers in those years was around 11,000. See Huang Yasheng (1995).

36. Interview with Tibetan leader, name withheld, 1999. This has turned into a highly gendered practice now, so that among Tibetan officials and leaders it is only the women who are expected to wear Tibetan dress on official occasions. In October 2001 a Tibetan male official, speaking anonymously, said that male officials would be "at risk" if they wore *chupa*s at an official event. Students (and television newsreaders), however, are expected to wear *chupa*s for photo opportunities, even if they are male; so are Tibetans living in the countryside, other than male officials.

37. Julie Brittain, a foreign teacher at the university in 1987, made this point in an article in the *Independent* (London), 1988, and it was still the case some ten years later.

38. See Palden and Shakya (1997) for a description of the reconstruction of the monastic community at Drepung in the early 1980s.

39. The most important initiatives of this kind were those organized by a development project called Rokpa, set up by Akong Tarap Rinpoche, a Tibetan lama based in Scotland. Namkhai Norbu, a lama and a historian based in Italy, also set up a number of aid projects inside Tibet. In both cases these were mainly in Tibetan areas outside the TAR. The scholar and writer Tashi Tsering, who had returned from exile in 1964, set up an important chain of primary schools in Ngamring in the TAR after 1991 (see "Man Devoted to Improving Education" 1997 and Brauchli 1997, as well as Goldstein, Siebenschuh, and Tsering 1997).

40. Kesang et al. (1980). There were, of course, many other attempts that clearly exceeded acceptable limits, such as the reintroduction of the Gesar of Ling cult (as opposed to the Gesar epic), which was "eliminated" in Nagchu in 1982 (see Anon. 1992).

41. The "Regulations on the Study, Use and Development of the Tibetan Language" were passed by the TAR Congress in 1987 and promulgated in March 1989.

42. See, for example, Derong (1995). *Wo de Xinyuan* was circulated as "reference material" in a print run of 1,000 copies, which were not available for sale to foreigners, so it was regarded with a certain degree of sensitivity, but this may have been because it was written in the form of petitions to the Party leadership, which would have made it internal Party correspondence. See also Bass (1999).

43. The prominent Tibetan businessman Tenpa Targye is said to have approached McDonald's unsuccessfully for the Tibet franchise.

44. The Ganglha Metok is a bar and gallery in Dekyi Shar Lam (now called Beijing Donglu). The art gallery is below the Barkor Café on the southwest corner of the Barkor Square.

45. These limits on architectural reconstruction were demonstrated when the Tibet Heritage Fund was banned from Tibet in 2000 (see AFP 2000). The organization was based in Lhasa using Tibetan craftsmen, but was run by two Westerners. It worked on the reconstruction of old Tibetan houses rather than on the construction of modern imitations (see Alexander and Azevedo 1998). This suggests that Tibetanization is seen as a government pursuit that should not be in the hands of foreigners, or perhaps not even the private sector.

46. The question of China's representation of its minority nationalities has been studied in some detail by Gladney, Harrell, Schein, and others. See, for example, Gladney (1994); Harrell (1995); Schein (1997); and Chiao and Tapp (1989).

47. Sautman (1997b) gives a helpful description of similar shifts in Chinese views on ethnicity. See also Sautman (1997a).

48. See Yang (1988).

49. A major factor in this tension is said to have been the retention in the cadre force of Tibetan cadres (notably Ragti and Pasang) who had been promoted during the Cultural Revolution and who were from "serf" backgrounds and were "leftist" in outlook. See Sharlho (1992); Goldstein (1995); Smith (1996); Shakya (1999); and Barnett (2002). New appointments after Hu Yaobang's visit included the reinstatement of a significant number of former aristocrats and traditional leaders, including the Panchen Lama, and the appointment of their children. There was also ideological conflict between the former serf and former aristocratic groups.

50. See Wang Xiaoqiang (1994).

51. Phuntsog Tashi (Pengcuozhaxi in pinyin) "became at various times in his career the Director of Publications for the Tibetan Administration, the vice-Chairman of the Tibetan People's Congress and the vice-Chairman of the Social Science Academy." See Wang Yao (1994). Phuntsog Tashi was mentioned by name in Hu Yaobang's famous six-points speech of 1980 and thus was identified as one of the three most prominent 1950s Tibetan cadres (apart from Phunstog Wangyal in Beijing) to have been rehabilitated after the Cultural Revolution.

52. See Zhang and Guo (1991).

53. Chen took up this position officially in December 1992, but he had been in effective control since arriving in the region as a deputy Party secretary in March of that year. The previous Party secretary, Hu Jintao, had been absent from his post since October 1990, having supposedly returned to Beijing on the grounds of ill health. Later it became clear that Hu had been recalled in order to be groomed for promotion as Jiang's heir apparent.

54. The origins of this shift in policy, and of the decision to appoint Chen, are probably connected to Jiang Zemin's visit to Lhasa in July 1990, two months after the lifting of martial law, but so far I have not been able to find material demonstrating this connection. Generally it is assumed that these ideas were developed by Hu Jintao during his brief period as Party secretary in Tibet from December 1988 to October 1990, during most of which it was under military rule, and then expedited once he returned to Beijing. This suggests that Chen Kuiyuan's appointment, and his policies, were carried out under Hu's patronage.

55. "Some people, motivated by a conservative desire to maintain the status quo and by certain selfish interests, exploit or misinterpret the principle of stability and unity and find fault with some reform and opening measures" (Tibet TV 1992), said one statement attacking critics of economic reform. In the 1994 articles, opponents of these reforms were attacked as leftists, although in fact the opposite was probably the case: "Chen Kuiyuan said: A major obstacle to socialist economic construction and the implementation of profound reforms in Tibet is leftist ideas and outmoded ways of thinking. By leftist ideas we mean sticking to an economic mode that is outdated, runs counter to the conditions in China and stands in the way of the development of productive forces" (Tibet People's Broadcasting Station 1994).

56. The migration-related aspects of this policy were indicated by the fact that checkpoints between the TAR and inland provinces were removed on December 30, 1992, presumably in part as a kind of public statement to encourage migrants or traders to move into the TAR, as was happening throughout China.

57. This was a reversal of the process by which Hu Yaobang and other 1980s reformers had operated: they had introduced the discussion of political reforms in China by initiating a discussion of economic reforms. See, for example, Fewsmith (1994), and the discussion in Keyser (1995).

58. The term "special characteristics," and the exemptions from conformity to central policy that it legitimated, disappeared from public official discourse following the success of the "Spring Tide" campaign of 1992. "Is Tibet willing to accept the label of being special and stand at the rear of reform and opening up? . . . Backwardness is not terrifying. Being geographically closed is not terrifying. What is terrifying is rigid and conservative thinking

and the psychology of idleness" (Liu and He 1994). See TIN (1994b). The same argument attacking "special characteristics" claims was restated six years later in "Chinese Scholar Wants Accelerated Urbanization in Tibet, End to Fossilization" (Xinhua 2000a). A milder form of this argument against local exceptionalism had been given in 1993: "A one-sided, inaccurate, superficial, and even distorted understanding of the theory with special charac- teristics can also affect the cause of our reform and opening up, and can slow down the speed of the economic construction" (Chen 1993).

59. See, for example, "China Fights Tibet" (1997), citing myself.

60. "There are also a small number of literary and artistic works which, by turning things upside down, extol what should not be extolled, and even go all out to sing the praises of the separatist chieftain Desi Sangay Gyamtso and the 14th [present] Dalai" (Chen 1997a).

61. Chen's speech states that this issue—claiming Buddhism is intrinsic to Tibetan cul- ture—is a strategy used by hidden separatists to promote political disunity. This means that he recognizes (to use my terms) the use being made by Tibetans up till then of that area of public space, and is closing it down by identifying it as a concealed threat to the state. He said: "Is only Buddhism Tibetan culture? It is utterly absurd. Buddhism is a foreign culture. . . . The view of equating Buddhist culture with Tibetan culture not only does not conform to reality . . . I just cannot understand that. Some people, claiming to be authorities, have made such shameless statements confusing truth and falsehood. Comrades who are en- gaged in research on Tibetan culture should be indignant at such statements. Making use of religion in the political field, separatists now go all out to put religion above the Tibetan culture and attempt to use the spoken language and culture to cause disputes and antago- nism between nationalities, and this is the crux of the matter" (Chen 1997a).

62. There were wide variations in different Tibetan areas about which spaces in public and political life were considered open for public use at various times. For example, in Amdo (Qinghai), Tibetan-medium secondary education has not been a contentious issue and can still be promoted. This was also true in Kham (western Sichuan) for some years, but in March 2000 the governor, Zhou Yongkang, questioned its value for the state: "It is such a heavy burden to promote minority education. You have to teach Han language and Tibetan language. There are also Yi minority people in the province, too," he said. "The whole world is learning English. Why bother so much?" (Ma 2000).

63. In May 1997 a senior TAR official said that the 1987 decision to "allow grade 1–3 boys and girls to be taught only in the Tibetan language will do no good to their children's growth. . . . Thus the regional government has reversed its decision made in 1987" (Xinhua 1997). See also TIN (1997a). The 1987 legislation undertook the setting up of Tibetan- medium junior secondary schools in the TAR by 1993 and to have "most" university courses available in Tibetan shortly after the year 2000; these never happened. See also AFP (1997), and, for a detailed discussion, Bass (1999).

64. TIN (1997e). In April 1992 Renmin Ribao (People's Daily) announced that at least 111 Chinese cadres, some as young as twenty-two years old, had taken up posts in Tibet, mainly as leaders at the county level in remote areas (Renmin Ribao 1992).

65. "For example, Qiazha [Chadrel Rinpoche, former abbot of Tashilhunpo Monastery], who secretly worked for the Dalai clique to the detriment of our interests, is not an isolated case among our ranks. However, reactionaries, regardless of whether they were dispatched from outside the region or they have long hidden inside the region, are incapable of top- pling our socialist system and separating Tibet from the big family of the motherland" (Chen 1997b).

66. The "treachery" of Chadrel Rinpoche, as well as the later defections of Agya Rinpoche from Kumbum Monastery to the United States in 1998 and the flight of the Karmapa and his retinue to India in January 2000, had much higher profile than these cases, but those were religious leaders who had always been regarded with suspicion and

who could not be members of the Party. The three lesser cases were all government employees with no known religious or nationalist affiliations (in fact, Jamyang Choegyal's father, Kashöpa, a government minister along with Ngapö, had been viewed since the 1950s as the classic Tibetan collaborator), and so their defections were in a sense more threatening since they implied that any official could be concealing anti-Chinese thoughts, irrespective of his outward loyalty.

67. The same is true of Gesar stories, which since at least 1979 had been presented by Tibetan scholars and writers as examples of Tibetan folk culture rather than as aspects of the religious tradition, and so had been republished in profusion. The claims that the traditions of Gesar and Tibetan medicine are not part of Tibetan religion are debatable.

68. "Mchod-rten Dkar-po" describes a Buddhist monument that inspires peace in the world, and "Nga yi Don-grub Tshe-ring" describes the singer's wish to meet a long-lost friend and spiritual guide (I am indebted to Isabel Henrion-Dourcy for her work on this subject). "Shengqing de Didi" refers to love for an absent younger brother. Dadron had also released the equally ambiguous song "*Blue Cuckoo*": "Oh, blue cuckoo/Do not return to Eastern India/Take this into your turquoise thoughts/And stay firm . . . Sing sweetly and stay firm" (from the cassette *Melody of Tanglha* by the Tibetan singer Chamba Tsering, issued with a Chinese-Tibetan cover on tape CY-9102 by the Chengdu Tape and Video Publishing House, probably in 1990) (see Chamba 1992). Dadron left Tibet to go into exile in August 1992.

69. See, for example, the closing of the "Cool-Land School" (TIN 1994a). In 1997 Dragpa Wangdu, the famous headmaster of the Shol Primary School, was detained despite having been publicly praised at length in the official press less than two months earlier in *Xizang Ribao* (1997a) and Jia (1997). In August 1999 the Gyatso Orphanage School in Lhasa was shut down by the authorities (see TCHRD 2000), and its two directors, Bangdu Jigme and Nyima Choedron, were detained and sentenced to fifteen and ten years in prison respectively. The reasons for these arrests are not known, but the last two apparently involved receiving money from foreign supporters and were probably perceived by the authorities as receiving secret political funding.

70. This can be compared with views that see trends like alcoholism or drug abuse in minority communities as representing an "allowed" form of celebrating group identity, albeit in a self-destructive form; Behan, for example, argued that Irish drinking was an indirect response to the history of British repression, and specifically the British ban on Irish language (author's personal conversation ca. 1976). Alcoholism is prevalent in Tibetan towns, where it is said to have increased since the early 1990s.

71. There is one remarkably unveiled statement by Ngapö that appears in an internal document and shows that among the objectives of senior Tibetan cadres was the attempt to create a more genuine form of autonomy for the TAR: "In my view, at present, the Tibet Autonomous Region has relatively less power of autonomy compared with other autonomous regions, let alone compared with provinces. Therefore Tibet must have some special treatment and have more autonomy like those special economic zones. We must employ special policies to resolve the special characteristics which have pertained throughout history" (Ngapö 1988). Ngapö has also shown his capacity for significant dissent by publishing an important article in *Xizang Ribao* in August 1989 in which he categorically rejected the Chinese claim that Chinese officials had officiated at the 1940 enthronement of the present Dalai Lama, an important part of China's claim to sovereignty (see also DIIR 1995, which quotes Ngapö on this issue).

72. Zhaxi Pingcuo, director of Tibet's Department of Civil Affairs, in *Xizang Ribao* (1991), cited in *South China Morning Post*, October 17, 1991.

73. Ethnically Chinese cadres are also not likely to have a second house within the TAR, even if they are involved in corruption, a point that was often made by Tibetans (privately) during the 1997 campaign to check on cadres' property holdings. The survey did not in-

clude property holdings outside the TAR. See below for details of the questionnaire and accompanying documents.

74. Sautman (1997b) gives a useful description of similar shifts in Chinese views on ethnicity. See also Sautman (1997a).

75. Zhaxi Pingcuo, *Tibet Daily,* October 7, 1991.

76. TAR Communist Party Propaganda Committee (1994). This is the published summary of the decisions of the "Third National Forum on Work in Tibet," which was held in Beijing in July 1994.

77. Ragti (Raidi) (1994). The ban on religious symbols and Dalai Lama photographs initially could only be applied to Party members, but by the autumn of 1994 it was being applied also to most government officials as well.

78. See *TIN Doc 1* (WH) for the questionnaire, plus TIN (1995a).

79. The information regarding Chen's internal speech was provided by a source within the leadership. See TIN (1997b).

80. See Questions 13 and 54 in *Xizang Ribao* (1995). See also TIN (1995b.)

81. Pagpalha Gelek Namgyal (1995).

82. Tibet government Work Report (1997).

83. Chen Kuiyuan (1997a).

84. Private communication from Tibetan cadre in Lhasa, describing new campaign to search all apartments and residences of government cadres for signs of religious practices. Communication received September 3, 1998 (ref 54rb3). The questionnaires were distributed to each government cadre in September 1998 requiring them to give details of their possessions. See *"Krung gung lha sa grong khyer grong khyer drong gseb gor yug srung skyobs 'dzugs skrun au yon lhan khang tang tsu'u yi yig cha"* (1998).

85. Chen Kuiyuan (1997b).

86. TAR Executive Deputy Party Secretary Raidi (Ragti 1997).

87. Xinhua (2000b). The process is accompanied by opening all appointments to open competition, which is assumed by many Tibetans to give advantage to Chinese candidates and to increase the pressure on Tibetans to be politically compliant.

88. *Xizang Ribao*, September 15, 2001.

References

Abu-Lughod, Lila. 1990. "The Romance of Resistance: Tracing Transformations of Power Through Bedouin Women." *American Ethnologist* 17, no. 1: 41–55.

AFP. 1997. "China Denies Education Clampdown in Tibet." Agence France-Presse (AFP), Beijing, May 7.

———. 2000. "Une portugaise et un allemand expulsés du Tibet." Beijing, August 16.

Alexander, A., and P. de Azevedo. 1998. *The Old City of Lhasa—Report from a Conservation Project.* Berlin and Kathmandu: Tibet Heritage Fund.

Allen, Anita L. 1999. "Reuschlein Lecture: Lying to Protect Privacy." *Villanova Law Review* 44, no. 8: 161.

Anon. 1992. "Nang khul gyi dus deb yin bas nyar chags bya rgyud do snang byed dgos." In *Bod sjongs 'phrin deb* (Tibet Information Book), vol. 9, pp. 39ff. Partially published in translation as "The Heroes of Ling: Elimination of a Sect" (including postscript by John Hillary), in "Background Papers on Tibet—September 1992," Part 2, *TIN News Review,* pp. 30–33. London: Tibet Information Network,

Asiawatch. 1994. *Detained in China and Tibet.* New York: Asiawatch.

Barmé, Geremie R. 1999. *In the Red: On Contemporary Chinese Culture.* New York: Columbia University Press.

Barnett, Robert. 1997. "Towards an Analysis of the Tibetan Cadre Force." *Leaders in*

Tibet: A Directory, ed. Victoria Conner and Robert Barnett. London: Tibet Information Network.

———, ed. 1998. *A Poisoned Arrow: The Secret Petition of the 10th Panchen Lama.* London: Tibet Information Network.

Barnett, Robert. 2002. "The Babas Are Dead: Street Talk and Contemporary Views of Leaders in Tibet." In *Proceedings of the International Association of Tibetan Studies*, ed. E. Sperling. Bloomington: University of Indiana.

Bass, Catriona. 1999. *Education in Tibet: Policy and Practice Since 1950*. London: Zed Books.

Becker, Jasper. 1998. "Interview with Ngapoi Ngawang Jigme." *South China Morning Post*, Hong Kong, April 4.

Brauchli, Marcus W. 1997. "To Integrate Tibet, China Tries Economic Lures." *Wall Street Journal*, July 14.

Bulag, Uradyn E. 1999. "Models and Moralities: The Parable of the Two 'Heroic Little Sisters of the Grassland.'" *China Journal*, no. 42 (July).

———. 2000. "From Inequality to Difference: Colonial Contradictions of Class and Ethnicity in 'Socialist' China." In *Post-Colonialism and Its Discontents*, special issue of *Cultural Studies*.

Chamba Tsering. 1992. "Blue Cuckoo." See *Background Papers on Tibet: September 1992 Part 2*. London: Tibet Information Network, September.

Chen Hanchang. 1993. "Further Deepen the Study of the Theory on Building Socialism with Chinese Characteristics." *Xizang Ribao* (Tibet Daily), November 12. Published in translation in the BBC *Summary of World Broadcasts* OWO512142193.

Chen Kuiyuan. 1997a. "Tibet Celebrates Hong Kong Reversion." *Xizang Ribao* (Tibet Daily), in Chinese, July 16. Published in translation as "Tibet Party Secretary Criticizes Erroneous Views of Literature, Art," in the BBC *Summary of World Broadcasts*, August 4.

———. 1997b. "Study the Spirit of the 15th National Party Congress, Reinforce the Patriotic Front; and Strive for Tibet's Stability, Reform, and Development." Tibet People's Broadcasting Station, Lhasa, November 9. Published in translation in BBC *Summary of World Broadcasts*, November 17 in FE/D3078/CNS 171197 as "Tibet Party Leader Justifies Religious Policies, Denies Rumors of Personnel Changes."

Chiao Chien and Nicholas Tapp, eds. 1989. *Ethnicity and Ethnic Groups in China*. Hong Kong: Chinese University of Hong Kong.

"China Fights Tibet on Cultural Battlefield—Government Has Changed Policy to Target Buddhism, Observer Says." 1997. *Globe and Mail* (Toronto), August 12.

Conner, Victoria, and Robert Barnett. 1997. *Leaders in Tibet: A Directory*. London: Tibet Information Network.

Derong Tsering Dondrup. 1995. *Wo de Xinyuan* (Tibetan: *Bdag gi re smon*). Ganzi baoshe yinshuachang (Ganzi Newspaper Office Printing Press), November.

DIIR. 1995. "The Dalai Lama." Press Release, Department of Information and International Relations, Dharamsala, India, November 29.

———. 1996. "Bomb Blast in Nagchu—Eighth Reported Incident." Exile Government Department of Information, Dharamsala, India, April 30.

———. 1999. "Dharamsala Commemorates the 10th Death Anniversary of the 10th Panchen Lama." Department of Information and International Relations, Dharamsala, India, January 31.

Fewsmith, Joseph. 1994. *Dilemmas of Reform in China*. Armonk, NY: M.E. Sharpe.

Ford, Robert. 1958. *Captured in Tibet*. London: Pan Books.

Forney, Matt. 1996. "That's My Boy—Beijing Uses Panchen Lama, Police Against Tibetans." *Far Eastern Economic Review*, June 20, 26.

Gladney, Dru. 1994. "Representing Nationality in China: Refiguring Majority/Minority Identities." *Journal of Asian Studies* 53, no. 1: 92–123.

Goldstein, Melvyn C. 1995. *Tibet, China and the United States: Reflections on the Tibet Question.* The Atlantic Council of the United States Occasional Paper.

Goldstein, Melvyn C., William Siebenschuh, and Tashi Tsering. 1997. *The Struggle for Modern Tibet: The Autobiography of Tashi Tsering.* Armonk, NY: M.E. Sharpe.

The Guardian. 1989. March 10.

Harrell, Stevan. 1995. "Civilizing Projects and the Reaction to Them." In *Cultural Encounters on China's Ethnic Frontiers*, ed. Stevan Harrell, pp. 3–36. Seattle: University of Washington Press.

Harrer, Heinrich. 1984. *Return to Tibet—Tibet After the Chinese Occupation.* London: Weidenfeld and Nicolson.

He Chong. 1998. "The Film 'Seven Years in Tibet' Grossly Fabricates History." Zhongguo Tongxun She, Hong Kong, April 17, republished in translation by the BBC *Summary of World Broadcasts* 0714240498 as "Chinese Commentary Says Film 'Seven Years in Tibet' Distorts History," April 21, 1998.

Hilton, Isabel. 1996. "The Boys Who Would Be Lama." *Independent on Sunday*, London, April 21.

————. 1999. *The Search for the Panchen Lama.* London: Viking.

Hsieh, David. 2000. "'Nothing Will Change'—An Insider Looks Back—and Ahead." *Asiaweek*, October 20.

Huang Yasheng. 1995. "China's Cadre Transfer Policy Toward Tibet in the 1980s." *Modern China* 21, no. 2 (April): 184–204.

Jia Lijuan. 1997. "One Day in the Life of an Old Headmaster." *Xizang Ribao*, April 13.

Karma Yeshe Wangmo. 1998. "Torch of Victory? A Poem in Memory of Thubten Ngodrup, the Tibetan Who Burned Himself for the Sake of All Beings." World Tibet News (www.tibet.ca), May 1.

Kesang Tseten, Jamyang Lota, Ula Tsering, and five others. 1980. "Letter Addressed to the CCP Central Secretariat, the National People's Congress, and the State Council." *Gannan*, November 27.

Keyser, Catherine. 1995. "Elite Conflict and the Emergence of the Young Reformers." *China Information* 9, no. 4 (Spring): 106–109.

Krung gung lha sa grong khyer grong khyer drong gseb gor yug srung skyobs 'dzugs skrun au yon lhan khang tang tsu'u yi yig cha" (Document of the Leading Party Group of the Lhasa City [Branch of the] Chinese Communist Party's Committee for City, Neighbourhood, and Village Environmental Protection and Construction), Document No. 21 (1998), September 6, 1998 (Document Nos. 65rb3 and 66rb3 in my collection).

Liu Wei and He Guanghua. 1994. "Backwardness Is Not Terrifying, What Is Terrifying Is Rigid and Conservative Thinking." In *Renmin Ribao* (People's Daily), Beijing, May 16, p. 1, published in translation in the BBC *Summary of World Broadcasts*, May 31, 1994.

Ma, Josephine. 2000. "Tibetans 'Wasting Money' on Donations to Monasteries." *South China Morning Post* (Hong Kong), March 14.

"Man Devoted to Improving Education." 1997. *China Daily*, Beijing, August 1.

Ngapö Ngawang Jigme. 1988. "Apei Awang Jinmei on the Relationship Between Tibet and the Motherland—When Did Tibet Come Within the Sovereignty of China?" *Tibet Information Network News Compilation.* London: Tibet Information Network. October 1992, p. 81 (an English translation of an article published as an internal document in Chinese in *The Bulletin of Tibet Party History*, Vol. 3, 1988 [Number 21 of the General Series], published by the Committee for the Collection of Historical Materials on the Tibet Committee of the Chinese Communist Party, Lhasa).

Pagpalha Gelek Namgyal. 1995. Tibet TV, November 24; published in translation in the BBC *Summary of World Broadcasts* on November 28.

Palden Gyatso and Tsering Shakya. 1997. *Fire Under the Snow.* London: Harvill.

Panchen Lama. 1987. "Panchen Lama's Speech to the TAR Standing Committee Meeting of the National People's Congress, Beijing, 28 March 1987." Republished in "The Panchen Lama Speaks," Department of Information and International Affairs, Dharamsala, India, 1991.

Ragti (Raidi). 1994. "Seize This Good Opportunity of Having 'The Third Forum,' Achieve in an All-Round Way a New Aspect on Works in Tibet," September 5. Published as an internal document called "The 5th Document of the 7th Plenary of the 6th Standing Committee Session of the Tibet Autonomous Regional Branch of the Chinese Communist Party." An official public summary of the speech was printed in the Party newspaper *Xizang Ribao* (Tibet Daily) on September 6 and published in an English translation by the BBC *Summary of World Broadcasts,* September 26, 1994 (FE/2110 G/7–10).

———. 1997. *Xixang Ribao,* November 18.

Reed, Kevin. 1997. "Religious Dissemblers and Theological Liars." Dallas: Presbyterian Heritage Publications.

Renmin Ribao (People's Daily). 1992. April 13.

Sautman, Barry. 1997a. "Myths of Descent, Racial Nationalism and Ethnic Minorities in the People's Republic of China." In *The Construction of Racial Identities in China and Japan,* ed. Frank Dikötter, pp. 75–95. Honolulu: University of Hawaii Press.

———. 1997b. "Racial Nationalism and China's External Behavior," *World Affairs* (Fall): 78ff.

Schein, Louisa. 1997. "Performing Modernity." *Cultural Anthropology* 14, no. 3: 361–395

Shakya, Tsering. 1997. "Historical Introduction." In *Leaders in Tibet: A Directory,* ed. Victoria Conner and Robert Barnett, pp. 1–14. London: Tibet Information Network.

———. 1999. *Dragon in the Land of Snows—A History of Modern Tibet Since 1947.* London: Pimlico.

Sharlho, Tseten Wangchuk. 1992. "China's Reforms in Tibet: Issues and Dilemmas." *Journal of Contemporary China* 1, no. 1: 38.

Slater, T. 1913. "Mental Reservation." In *The Catholic Encyclopaedia,* ed. Charles G. Herbermann, p. 195.

Smith, Warren. 1996. *Tibetan Nation: A History of Tibetan Nationalism and Sino-Tibetan Relations.* Boulder, CO: Westview.

Snobelen, Stephen D. 1999. "Isaac Newton, Heretic: The Strategies of a Nicodemite." *British Journal of the History of Science* 32: 381–419.

South China Morning Post (Hong Kong). 1991. October 17.

TAR Communist Party Propaganda Committee. 1994. "A Golden Bridge Leading into a New Era" (*Dus rabs gsar par skyod-pa'i gser zam*), or "Reference Materials to Publicize the Spirit of the Third Forum on Work in Tibet." Tibetan People's Publishing House, October 1.

TCHRD. 2000. "Private Tibetan School Closed, Teachers Arrested." In *January 2000 Human Rights Update.* Dharamsala: Tibetan Centre For Human Rights and Democracy. India, February 9.

Tibet People's Broadcasting Station. 1997. Published in translation in the BBC *Summary of World Broadcasts* (FE/D3078/CNS 171197) as "Tibet Party Leader Justifies Religious Policies, Denies "Rumors" of Personnel Changes." November 9.

Tibet People's Broadcasting Station, Lhasa, 1994. April 18. Published in translation in BBC *Summary of World Broadcasts,* April 20.

Tibet TV. 1992. May 10. Republished in translation in BBC *Summary of World Broadcasts,* May 13.

TIN (Tibet Information Network). 1991. "Communist Party in Tibet: Nearly 20% Illiterate." *TIN News Update.* London: TIN, August 31.

———. 1994a. "Tibetan School Closed, Director Arrested." *TIN News Update.* London: TIN, April 19.

———. 1994b. "Top Tibetan Cadre Not Seen for 8 weeks." *TIN News Update.* London: TIN, July 15.

———. 1995a. "Ban on Tibetan Children Going to India Extended." In "Reports from Tibet November 1994–March 1995." *TIN News Review No. 23*, London, March.

———. 1995b. "Anti-Abbot Campaign Begins, Aims to Eliminate Dalai Lama Influence." *TIN News Update.* London: TIN, December 5.

———. 1997a. "Policy Shift in Teaching in Tibet." *TIN News Update.* London: TIN, May 6.

———. 1997b. "Leading Scholar Dies, Cultural Criticism Stepped Up." *TIN News Update.* London: TIN, August 4.

———. 1997c. "Power Struggle in Tibet Party; "Hidden" Enemy Targetted." *TIN News Update.* London: TIN, November 16.

———. 1997d. "Tibet Leaders to Visit Europe; Drubkhang Rinpoche Criticised, House Burnt Down." *TIN News Update.* London: TIN, November 23.

———. 1997e. "New Party Chief in Lhasa; Chinese Heads Lhokha Government." *TIN News Update.* London: TIN, December 7.

———. 1998. "China's Top Tibetan Official Criticises Panchen Lama Report." *TIN News Update.* London: TIN, April 6.

———. 1999. "The Chinese Leader Who Apologised to Tibet: Hu Yaobang's 1980 Speech." *TIN News Update.* London: TIN, April 12.

Wang Xiaoqiang. 1994. "The Dispute Between the Tibetans and the Han: When Will It Be Solved?" In *Resistance and Reform in Tibet*, ed. Robert Barnett, pp. 290–295. Bloomington: University of Indiana Press.

Wang Yao. 1994. "An Account of Hu Yaobang's Visit to Tibet, 22–31st May 1980." In *Resistance and Reform in Tibet*, ed. Robert Barnett, pp. 285–289. Bloomington: University of Indiana Press.

Wong, Jan. 1994. "Tibet—Life at the Top of the World." *Globe and Mail* (Toronto), December 10.

Xinhua. 1997. Beijing, in English 1443 GMT, April 17. Republished in BBC *Summary of World Broadcasts* FE/D2897/CNS 190497 as "Tibet Leader Danzim Meets US Envoy, Welcomes Investment, Justifies Ethnic Policy."

———. 1998. "Senior Tibetan Official Ngapoi Ngawang Jigme Has Accused the Makers of the Hollywood Film Seven Years in Tibet of Sheer Fabrication and a Vicious Personal Attack." Beijing, 0650 GMT, April 8. Republished in BBC *Summary of World Broadcasts* 0843080498 under the title "China: Tibetan Official Details Fabrications in Hollywood Film."

———. 1999. "China Holds Forum to Mark 10th Death Anniversary of Panchen Lama." Beijing, January 28. Published in BBC *Summary of World Broadcasts,* same day.

———. 2000a. Beijing, April 19. Published in BBC *Summary of World Broadcasts,* same day.

———. 2000b. "Tibet Downsizes Regional Government Divisions, Employees." Lhasa, May 18. Republished in the BBC *Summary of World Broadcasts,* May 18.

Xizang Ribao (Tibet Daily). 1995. "Questions and Answers Regarding the Reincarnated Child of the 10th Panchen." November 10. Published in translation in FBIS, November 30, and in the BBC *Summary of World Broadcasts*, November 28.

———. 1997a. "Sacrificing One's Family and One's Own Interests to Educating Pupils—Tapa Wangdu—the Headmaster of Shol School." April 4.

———. 1997b. "Tibet Government Work Report 1997." Lhasa, in Chinese, May 29. Published in translation in the BBC *Summary of World Broadcasts*, June 28.

Yang Zhongmei. 1998. *Hu Yaobang: A Chinese Biography.* Armonk, NY: M.E. Sharpe.

Zagorin, Perez. 1990. *Ways of Lying: Dissimulation, Persecution, and Conformity in Early Modern Europe.* Cambridge, MA: Harvard University Press.

Zhang Shirong and Guo Wutian. 1991. "On the Regional Characteristics of Party Construction in Tibet." *Xizang Ribao* (Tibet Daily, Chinese language edition), January 7.

Zla ba'i shes rab. 1999. *Sgor ra nang pa phun tshogs dbang rgyal (phun dbang) gyi mdzad rnam mtor bsdus* (A Brief Biography of Phuntsog Wanggyal Goranangpa), undated ms., c.1999.

3

The Dalai Lama's Autonomy Proposal

A One-Sided Wish?

He Baogang

In 1987 and 1988 the Fourteenth Dalai Lama proposed that the government of the People's Republic of China remain responsible for Tibet's foreign policy while Tibet is governed by its own constitution or basic law, and that the Tibetan government should comprise a popularly elected chief executive, a bicameral legislature, and an independent legal system. Ten years later, in 1998, the Dalai Lama expressed his great disappointment. "Sadly, the Chinese government has not responded positively to my proposals and initiatives over the past 18 years for a negotiated resolution of our problem within the framework [apart from the question of total independence of Tibet all other issues could be discussed and resolved] stated by Mr. Deng Xiaoping."[1]

Presidents Bill Clinton and George W. Bush have pressed the Chinese leadership to talk with the Dalai Lama. In October 2001 the U.S. Congress passed the Tibetan Policy Act initiated by Dianne Feinstein, the U.S. senator from San Francisco, and Tom Lantos, representative of San Mateo County. EU External Affairs commissioner Chris Patten and Indian defense minister George Fernandes also called on China to begin dialogue with the Dalai Lama in March 2002.[2] A twenty-strong European delegation to China in July 2002 urged dialogue between Beijing and the exiled government of the Dalai Lama, but was told by China's parliamentary head Li Peng and Vice Premier Qian Qichen that Beijing was not ready for talks with the Tibetan leader.[3]

So far Beijing has not accepted the Dalai Lama's proposal, and only allowed two visits to China led by the Dalai Lama's special envoy, Lodi Gyari. Gyari led the first delegation to China and Tibet in September 2002. A year later Lodi Gyari and Kelsang Gyaltsen, accompanied by Sonam N. Dagpo and Bhuchung K. Tsering, visited the provinces of Jiangsu, Zhejiang, and Yunnan from May 25 to June 8, 2003. This second visit followed the changes in leadership of the Chinese Communist Party as well as of the Chinese government.[4] The local leaders in the Tibet Autonomous Region regarded the first visit as purely private in nature. Beijing acknowledged the second visit and the existence of the "official" contact between the two sides.

These two visits have given Tibetans in exile the opportunity to reestablish contacts and to engage extensively with the new Chinese leaders and officials responsible for Tibet and China's relationship. They aimed to build mutual trust but touched little on the real question of autonomy. The fact that the Chinese host institution for these two visits was the Department of the United Front indicates that the Chinese leadership was interested in winning the hearts of the Tibetan people in order to oppose separatism, rather than in coming to the negotiating table to discuss the Dalai Lama's autonomy proposal.[5] Recently, on August 20, 2003, Chinese authorities rejected a visit request from the Tibetan government in exile for a group of prominent exiled Tibetans, including former Tibetan exile government ministers Sonam Topgyal, Tenzin Namgyal Tenthong, and Alak Jigme, the former head of the Tibet Fund in New York, Rinchen Dharlo, and former head of the Office of Tibet in Tokyo, Pema Gyalpo.[6]

In Western communities, people tend to think that the Dalai Lama's autonomy proposal provides a sound solution to the Tibet question, that the Dalai Lama has already met China's precondition for dialogue,[7] and that the real problem lies in the Chinese leadership's negative perception of the Dalai Lama. In this view, if the Beijing leadership changes its view on the Dalai Lama, the Tibet problem can be solved easily. For example, Professor Orville Schell, dean of the Graduate School of Journalism at the University of California, Berkeley, in his letter to the Standing Committee of the Politburo of the Central Committee of the Chinese Communist Party in June 2001, advised Beijing to view the Dalai Lama as an asset who could serve the interests of Han Chinese and Tibetans alike rather than a die-hard "splittist," to experiment with new ways of solving old problems, to begin a dialogue with the Dalai Lama, and to find a mutually agreeable way for him to return to Lhasa as a religious and cultural avatar.[8]

Schell argues that it is in China's interest to settle the Tibet issue and to implement full autonomy in Tibet because "China's impasse with His Holiness significantly harms China's acceptance as a great and respected power." The Tibet problem has become a hotbed of instability, threatening the unity of China. It has implications for China's other burning issues concerning Taiwan and Xinjiang. The question is, however, why did Jiang Zemin fail to take Schell's advice, thus losing an opportunity to leave a "political legacy . . . [of] a Tibet at peace and a more unified China"?[9] Is it the case that some Western commentators are too naive to understand the complexity of the issue?

This chapter aims to address the following essential questions: To what degree can the Dalai Lama's autonomy proposal provide a solution to the Tibet question? How does Beijing react to the Dalai Lama's autonomy proposal? Why does Beijing reject the autonomy proposal? To address these specific questions, I will examine in detail Chinese official documents and academic articles in Chinese journals. Chinese documents and articles are often dismissed by Western commentators as "propaganda," and indeed they are. Nevertheless, to understand Beijing's refusal of the Dalai Lama's autonomy proposal, it is essential to examine the Chinese theory and practice of autonomy. Chinese cadres in charge of the autonomy matter are informed by the official Chinese theory of autonomy. Indeed, on his two visits to China, Lodi Gyari has confronted a substantial question, that is, Chinese officials always stress that China has already developed a sound system of autonomy, implying that China does not need the Dalai Lama's autonomy proposal.[10] My detailed presentation of the official Chinese theory of autonomy and Beijing's view on the actual status of autonomy in Tibet can help us to understand the substantial difference between Beijing and Dharamsala and the obstacles to implementing the Dalai Lama's autonomy proposal. It should be noted that my presentation and summary do not suggest that I share and accept the official Chinese theory and view.[11]

The Dalai Lama's Proposal for Autonomy and the Chinese Response

A Competing Model of Autonomy in Tibet

The Dalai Lama's proposal was first presented on Capitol Hill during his visit to Washington in 1987 and was presented a year later at the European Parliament. Under the proposal, the government of the People's Republic of China would remain responsible for Tibet's foreign policy while Tibet would be governed by is own constitution or basic law, and the Tibetan government would comprise a popularly elected chief executive, a bicameral legislature, and an independent legal system.[12] Because religion constitutes the source of Tibet's national identity, and spiritual values lie at the very heart of Tibet's rich culture, it would be the special duty of the government of Tibet to safeguard and develop its practice.[13] The government of Tibet would also develop and maintain relations, through its own Foreign Affairs Bureau, in the fields of religion, commerce, education, culture, tourism, science, sports, and other nonpolitical activities. Tibet would join international organizations concerned with such activities.[14] The proposal contains what the Dalai Lama regards as "maximum" concessions by the Tibetans, which provide that Tibet would not be fully independent of China.[15]

Beijing has rejected the Dalai Lama's proposal for fear it would create an internal boundary and an "independent kingdom." For Beijing, Chinese autonomy is characterized by a combination of political "self-rule," economic integration, cultural exchange, and ethnic intermingling. Beijing is also reluctant to accept the idea of the chief executive in Tibet being elected rather than appointed. With regard to the return of the Dalai Lama to Tibet, China has said that the Dalai Lama may return as spiritual head of the Lamaist faith, but not as a secular leader.[16]

Beijing also has different views on the issue of federalism. While the Dalai

Lama advocates a loose federal system, Beijing is reluctant to adopt the idea of federalism. Both Mao Zedong and Deng Xiaoping rejected federalism. Even if Beijing were to adopt any vague form of federalism, China would still be more inclined to go for the stronger, centralized U.S.-style federalism rather than the weaker, Indian-style federalism.[17]

The Borders of an Autonomous Tibet

The location of Tibet's border is one of the most sensitive and highly controversial issues contained in the Dalai Lama's proposal. According to the Dalai Lama, Tibet comprises some areas now in Qinghai, Gansu, Sichuan, and Ningxia. Under the Dalai Lama's proposal, the whole of Tibet, which is known as Cholka-Sum (U-Tsang, Kham, and Amdo), would become a self-governing democratic political entity, founded on laws by agreements of the people for the common good and the protection of themselves and their environment, in association with the People's Republic of China.[18] The conceived Greater Tibet includes most of Qinghai, parts of Gansu, Ningxia, Sichuan, and Yunnan, where the remaining 51 percent of the Tibetan population lives with Han Chinese and other ethnic groups.[19] The idea of a Greater Tibet constitutes the core of modern Tibetan nationalism, which has been committed to a pan-Tibetan identity since 1959 and will continue to be on a collision course with Chinese nationalists over the sensitive internal boundary question. In 2003, the Dalai Lama no longer uses the concepts of "Greater Tibet," or "smaller Tibet." Instead, he emphasizes the protection of Tibetan culture within a Tibetan cultural zone.[20]

For Beijing, however, Tibet is confined to today's Tibet Autonomous Region (TAR). Even Chinese dissidents, such as Yan Jiaqi, who are sympathetic to the Dalai Lama, share this view. According to Yan, in a future federal China, the border of the Tibetan member-state would encompass what it does now within the TAR.[21] By contrast, the Dalai Lama does not recognize the border of the TAR. When Beijing celebrated the twentieth anniversary of the creation of the autonomous region of Tibet, the Dalai Lama commented, "it is a very bitter anniversary. . . . It is the beginning of enslavement."[22]

It is interesting to observe that when the Dalai Lama talks about the domination of the Han Chinese in Tibet, he refers to the Chinese population not only in today's TAR, but also in the eastern parts of Qinghai and the western parts of Sichuan. For example, Samdhong Rinpoche, the former spokesman of the Tibetan parliament in exile, states that Chinese statistics show 2.5 million Chinese in Amdo province, but only 750,000 Tibetans. Yet when Beijing denies the charge that the Chinese population dominates, it refers only to today's TAR. By 1982, for example, more than 20,000 Han Chinese had been transferred out of the region, reducing the percentage of Han Chinese in Tibet from 7.6 percent in 1979 to 4.8 percent. The percentage of Han Chinese further dropped to 3.7 percent when the fourth national census was conducted in 1990.[23]

Conditions for Negotiation

The Dalai Lama's proposal for autonomy sets up some preconditions for any negotiations. First, it demands the withdrawal of Chinese troops before a genuine process of reconciliation could commence.[24] China can have the right to maintain a restricted number of military installations in Tibet solely for defense purposes until a peace conference is convened and demilitarization and neutralization achieved. Second, for the Tibetans to survive as a people, it is imperative that Chinese immigration to Tibet should stop and Chinese settlers be repatriated.[25] In 2003, the Dalai Lama stated that the numbers of the People's Armed Police should be reduced in Tibetan cities, implying his acceptance of the stationing of Chinese troops.[26]

Chinese president Jiang Zemin stated firmly in 1998 that before a dialogue could begin, the Dalai Lama must "publicly make a statement and a commitment that Tibet is an inalienable part of China" and "must also recognize Taiwan as a province of China."[27] Per Gahrton, a Swedish parliamentarian, thought that the Dalai Lama met these conditions when he gave a speech to the European Parliament in Strasbourg on October 24, 2001.[28] Beijing did not agree. This is because the Dalai Lama stated, "Tibet was an independent country before its occupation by China. It had its own government, now in exile. . . . There is no justification claiming that Tibet was 'part of China' as Peking claims today."[29] In 2002, in reacting to the latest Chinese offer to the Dalai Lama—that he is welcome to return to Tibet if he meets two conditions—Mr. Sonam Dagpo, the secretary in the Department of Information and International Relations, said the preconditions laid down by China, including accepting Tibet as part of China and accepting Taiwan as its province, were just not acceptable, since Tibet had always been an independent nation until China occupied it forcibly.[30]

Beijing sees the Dalai Lama's public advocacy of autonomy for Tibet as little more than a smoke screen for an independence bid, because he failed to stop all independence activities. The Tibetan Youth Congress (TYC) is one example. The TYC clearly stated that its mission is to build an independent state of Tibet whose head is the Dalai Lama. The size of an independent state of Tibet would be 2.5 million square kilometers with 6 million people, and the three provinces of U-tsang (central), Dhotoe (eastern), and Dhome (northeastern). The national flag of Tibet would be twelve red-and-blue rays with two snow lions in the lower center. The TYC promotes and protects Tibetan national unity and integrity by giving up all distinctions based on religion, regionalism, or status; works for the preservation and promotion of religion and Tibet's unique culture and traditions; and struggles for the total independence of Tibet even at the cost of one's life. It has launched campaigns like Boycott Made in China and No Olympics 2008 in Beijing.[31]

On December 7, 2002, Tibetan youth organizations and their supporters launched an international Boycott Made in China campaign designed to create economic pressure on the Chinese government to end its occupation of Tibet. Simultaneous demonstrations in front of toy stores and shopping malls in cities across Canada, the United States, New Zealand, Europe, and India marked the beginning of long-term and coordinated efforts to urge people to stop buying goods made in China. The Dalai Lama's oldest brother, Professor Thupten Norbu, sent a blessing message: "I am confident that the campaign to boycott Chinese products will gain the support of freedom loving people around the world, and will eventually succeed in forcing China to respect the rights of its own people and acknowledge Tibetan independence."[32]

Can the Hong Kong Model of Autonomy Be Applied to Tibet?

The Dalai Lama and many Western commentators have raised the question of whether China should apply the Hong Kong model of autonomy to resolve the Tibet question.[33] It has been suggested that, following the Hong Kong model, Beijing would be responsible for Tibet's foreign affairs and defense; but in other areas, including issues of religion and culture, the Tibetans would be free to make their own decisions. Hong Kong commentator Frank Ching argued in 1998: "It will take an act of statesmanship for China to offer this special status to an area already under its control. But such an offer, at a time when China is basking in the world's approval for its handling of Hong Kong, will be welcomed by the international community as a genuine attempt to resolve an issue that has proven to be intractable for almost four decades."[34] In 1992, the president of Qinghua University in Taiwan raised the issue to President Jiang Zemin, citing his "layman's viewpoint" in asking if the "one-country-two-systems could be applied to Tibet." Jiang Zemin answered, "It is right to say this, but we have gone so far already, and cannot go back to apply one-country-two-systems in Tibet."[35]

It should be pointed out that Beijing adopts a pragmatic attitude toward Taiwan and Tibet. While Beijing offers Taiwan a Hong Kong model of autonomy and, in fact, a much higher degree of autonomy than Hong Kong's because Taiwan can maintain its own army, it rejects the Dalai Lama's proposal. Apparently, the Chinese practice of autonomy is largely dependent on the power relations in each situation. Beijing thinks that the Hong Kong model of autonomy characterized by judicial independence, Hong Kong's own currency, an internal border with China, and representatives in international organizations with regard to economic and cultural matters would be offering too much to Tibet.

It should be stressed that Beijing has in mind several models of autonomy to meet the needs of different circumstances. While Hong Kong enjoys a higher form of autonomy, Tibet should enjoy much less autonomous power than Hong Kong but greater autonomous power than that for Xinjiang and Inner Mongolia. The Hong Kong model of autonomy could not be applied to Tibet because Hong Kong had to be united with the mainland while Tibet has already been under China's control. In the eyes of Beijing, a "one country, one system" relationship between the PRC and Tibet has already been in place for several decades, thus rendering the "one country, two systems" inapplicable.[36]

Chinese Concepts of Autonomy

Both Mao's and Deng's concepts of autonomy are different from, and contrary to, current liberal theories of autonomy.[37] Chinese concepts of autonomy play down the role of local elections and see autonomy as a product of political expediency (thus it can be changed when situations change) rather than as an inviolable right. In the view of the Chinese, autonomy does not involve an ontologically privileged right to self-determination.

The debates over what kind of autonomy should be implemented in Tibet stem from different theoretical sources and positions. While the Dalai Lama's *genuine* autonomy proposal draws on liberal principles of autonomy, the official Chinese conception of *regional* autonomy derives from Marxist principles. These theoretical bases are difficult to reconcile, and this may make it very difficult to resolve the question of autonomy in Tibet.

Take the example of self-determination. Orville Schell asserted: "After all, this is an era of self-determination. Most colonies and territories have been granted independence. Quebec is regularly allowed to vote on secession from Canada. Scotland holds referendums on autonomy from Great Britain. Why should Tibet not have the right to determine its future relationship to China?"[38] By contrast, the Beijing leadership holds a different view of self-determination.

The Maoist Concept of Autonomy

Mao Zedong went through an ideological transformation from his early idea of federalism and self-determination to that of regional autonomy as a solution to China's nationality question.[39] Mao initially supported the right of self-determination (in the 1920s and 1930s), but quickly abandoned it on the following grounds: (1) Lenin's theory of self-determination was used by Japan to support the independence of Mongolia; (2) the right to self-determination should be denied except in the case of oppressed nations casting off the rule of imperialism and colonialism to fight for independence; (3) the right to self-determination is not feasible in China where different nationalities overlap and are interdependent;[40] (4) the self-determination of China's nationalities had been decided, once and for all, by their common revolutionary struggle and voluntary incorporation into the PRC.[41]

Mao also thought that federalism was not applicable in China because: (1) Marx, Engels, and Lenin all supported a unitary centralized system; and (2) China, as a unitary country in which many nationalities have lived together for centuries, is different from Europe in general, and Russia in particular, where federalism was adopted in the wake of the Communist revolution.[42]

Following Marxism, Mao Zedong maintained the view that the nationality question is by nature a question of class, and that nationality and ethnicity will wither away after the end of class conflict. Mao also held that class division is much more important than ethnic division, that the majority of any nationality are peasants and workers, and that working classes across different nationalities could and should be unified against their common enemy, the exploiting class.

Deng Xiaoping's Concept of Autonomy and the Nationality Question

To a large extent, Deng continued to follow Mao's theory and practice in relation to the nationality question.[43] Like Mao, Deng asserted that the autonomous nationality system is suited to the Chinese situation, and works much better than federalism. He claimed that this system could not be given up, for it has many advantages.[44] In Deng's view, a unitary system with autonomous regions for nationalities is the best system to defend the unity of the nation-state against secessionism, and therefore works best for China.

Deng emphasized the implementation of "genuine autonomy" in terms of the rule of law. He stated clearly that genuine autonomy involves putting into effect all self-governing rights according to laws, that is, all the autonomous rights to be defined by the Constitution and the Autonomy Law.[45]

Mao's class analysis of the nationality question, and his idea of the "vanishing" of nationalities, have no place in Deng's pragmatism. In fact, Deng repudiated the importance of class background, and turned his attention to the market and economic development as a way of dealing with the nationality question. For him, without economic development, autonomy is an empty word.[46] Deng stressed the economic prosperity of ethnic nationalities. For Deng, economic development is the way to prosperity, and prosperity will erode antagonism among nationalities. Deng said that "Tibet is so big but has a small population. Developing Tibet only by Tibetans is not enough. It is not bad for Han Chinese to help them to speed up economic development."[47] Accordingly, the influx of Han Chinese into Tibet's minority areas is a necessary step in economic development.[48]

Deng's theory of modernization requires economic development to override any consideration of ethnic identities. Deng therefore highlighted the centrality of the stability of the autonomous regions. For him, the maintenance of stability is a precondition for economic development and improvement of the autonomy system.[49] Deng's concern with stability may override the need to protect some rights of autonomy.[50]

The Practice of Autonomy in Tibet

A Brief History of Tibet's Autonomy (1950s–1990s)

From the CCP's perspective, the treaty concerning the peaceful "liberation" of Tibet, reached in 1951 between the central government and the Tibetan government, established the sovereignty of China over Tibet. For example, it established that China was to be responsible for the foreign affairs and national defense of Tibet. However, the Dalai Lama offers a different interpretation. His view is that Tibet was an independent state when the Communist Chinese army invaded in 1950–51, in direct violation of international law. It was the newly installed Communist government in Beijing that forced the Tibetans to sign a treaty for the "peaceful liberation of Tibet" and which then proceeded to occupy Tibet.[51]

Article 3 of the agreement stipulated that the Tibetan people have the right to establish regional autonomy under the guidance of the central government. The agreement gave Tibet a high degree of autonomy: the position and authority of the Dalai Lama and Panchen Lama would be maintained, and the existing political system (the unity of politics and religion) would not be changed. This political accommodation in Tibet was different from the so-called "new democratic system" established in other areas of China at that time. Such an arrangement can be seen as a kind of "one country, two systems." However, in 1959, the People's Liberation Army (PLA) clashed with what the CCP called a rebellion led by the Dalai Lama, and the one country, two systems for Tibet became one country, one system. In September 1965, the Tibet Autonomous Region was formally founded.

During the Cultural Revolution (1966–1976), autonomy existed in name only. The 1975 Constitution even deleted the provisions concerning nationalities' rights to develop their languages and maintain their cultural customs and traditions.[52]

Since 1978, the Chinese government had been trying to reestablish and improve regional autonomy. In the 1980s, the State Council abolished the people's commune system and admitted that its policy of forcing Tibetans to raise wheat rather than the barley they preferred had not only been a cultural mistake, but an ecological disaster as well.[53] With the arrival of Wu Jinghua as regional Party secretary of the TAR, and with Dorje Tsering as regional government leader, a limited cultural liberalization took place between 1985 and 1988.[54] This provided, for example, increased freedom of speech for the Panchen Lama.[55] Wu Jinghua dressed in Tibetan clothing for his first speech as Party secretary, and Dorje Tsering promoted the training of more minority cadres and an end to "leftist" mistakes.[56]

However, since 1989, the CCP has adopted a tough policy toward Tibetan secessionism that has undermined efforts to implement true autonomy. The breakup of the Soviet Union and "peaceful evolution" in Eastern Europe were alarming precedents for China. Chen Kuiyuan, Party secretary of the TAR, explained changes in China's policies toward Tibet by referring to international changes in the post–Cold War era: "Especially under the influence of the international macro-environment, separatist activities have intensified in Tibet and the situation of the anti-separatist struggle has sharpened. These factors are causing political instability."[57] China's official press also claimed that the Dalai Lama's supporters harbored "a hidden motive": "They want to take advantage of (turmoil) to split China. To be frank, they want to bring about another 'Bosnia-Herzegovina' in China! But China is not Yugoslavia."[58]

Areas of Autonomy in Practice

We will examine briefly Chinese practice of autonomy in the four areas: politics, law, culture, and the economy. First, in the area of political autonomy, according to Chinese sources, the growing ranks of minority nationality cadres constitute an important milestone.[59] A large number of ex-serfs and their children have taken up leading posts at various levels of government in Tibet, including chief leaders of the people's congresses, governments, courts, and procuratorates at various levels.[60] In 1994, there were 37,000 Tibetan cadres, or 66.6 percent of the total number of cadres in the region. In September 1994, Tibetan cadres were reported to account for 71.7 percent of all cadres at the regional level, 69.9 percent at the prefectural level, and 74.8 percent at the county level.[61] By 1982, all Party first secretaries and government leaders at prefectural and city levels were members of ethnic minorities; and at county levels, minorities accounted for 86 percent of first secretaries, county chiefs, and people's congress standing committee chairmen. By September 1994, Tibetan women accounted for 10.2 percent of officials at the county level and above.[62]

In June 1956, only seven Tibetans were admitted into the CCP. In 1963, the CCP had about 3,000 ethnic Tibetan members. The number increased to 40,000 by 1988. By 1991, the CCP had over 57,000 Tibetan and other minority members. By the end of 1989, it is reported that there were about 1,000 Tibetan officers in leadership posts in the PLA, of whom 16 were commanders and 164 held the rank of major.[63]

There are at least two interpretations of the above figures. The first is that they show a level of power sharing and limited autonomy. The second interpretation, the official one, is that the data demonstrate self-rule by Tibetans. This is highly problematic as most high-ranking Tibetan cadres wield only titular power. Candidates for the chairpersons of the TAR are chosen by central leaders, while TAR Party secretaries are appointed by central Party leaders and are non-Tibetans, such as Wu Jinghua (Yi nationality) (1985–88), Hu Jintao (Han Chinese), and Chen Kuiyuan (Han Chinese). Only regional government leaders are Tibetans, such as Dorje Tsering (1985–88) and Gyaincain Norbu.[64]

Table 3.1 demonstrates how the percentage of Tibetan cadres varies in different areas. The percentage of Tibetans is lower in the most powerful institutions such as Party and government, but higher in those with the least power such as culture and religion.

In the area of legal autonomy, Tibet had enacted seventy-two special sets of rules and regulations, local laws, and legal resolutions as of the end of June 1999.[65] They involve such areas as the structure of political power, social and economic development, marriage, education, written language, the legal system, natural resources, and environmental protection. The government issued regulations banning the presence of outsiders at the traditional Tibetan sky burial ritual when the Tibetans took offense at groups of intrusive tourists.[66] Nevertheless, most local laws passed by local people's parliaments are, as in the rest of China, formalistic in that they basically repeat national laws. Local laws can modify national laws but cannot override the authority of national law, which emanates from the center.

In the area of cultural autonomy, it became possible for Lamaist Buddhists to

Table 3.1

The Percentage of Tibetan Cadres in Different Areas

Institution	Tibetan cadres (N)	Total cadres (N)	Tibetan cadres (%)
Tibetan Party Committee	43	195	22
Tibetan People's Congress	53	98	54
Tibetan Government	88	216	40
Tibetan Political Consultation Committee	139	164	85
Tibetan Nationality and Religion Committee	36	60	60
Tibetan Buddhist Association	51	52	98
Tibetan Institute of Social Science	100	122	82
People's Bank	69	146	47

Source: Statistical Bureau of the Tibet Autonomous Region, *Xizang shehui jingji tongji nianjian, 1990* (1990 Year Book of Social and Economic Statistics in Tibet) (Beijing: State Statistical Bureau, 1990), 189–190; the table has been shortened by the author.

make the pilgrimage to Lhasa again beginning in the 1980s. Monasteries and temples destroyed during the Cultural Revolution were rebuilt and expanded,[67] and young men were again permitted to become monks if they so desired.[68]

In September 1988, a committee established under the leadership of the late Panchen Lama called for "self-government of religion" in Tibet in order to preclude administrative interference in the religious affairs of all Tibetans in China.[69] Ironically, when the Panchen Lama died, Beijing initiated its own search for his reincarnation while denying the Dalai Lama's findings.

The central government has placed limits on the number of people who may become monks.[70] This is not only to limit the spread of the faith, but also to relieve the state's financial burden, for lamas enjoy state subsidies for food just like any local urban residents.[71]

The government also controls pilgrimage through the regulation that one has to receive permission to travel from one's work unit. Sometimes permission is denied for purely economic reasons: the absence of a large number of people at the same time could affect production. Other times, the motivation for refusal is connected with social control,[72] as pilgrims have raised banners calling for independence, hoisted Tibet's "snow mountain and lion" flag (banned by government authorities), and distributed anti-Chinese leaflets in the past.[73]

In 1987, the Tibet Autonomous Region's People's Congress adopted the Regulations on the Study, Use, and Development of the Written Tibetan Language for trial implementation. At the same time, it articulated the principle of attaching equal importance to both written Chinese and Tibetan languages (with the emphasis laid mainly on the latter), and established a committee in charge of the use and development of the written Tibetan language. The people's government of the

TAR promulgated, in October 1988, rules for the implementation of these regulations. These rules clearly stipulate that all conferences of the autonomous regional government and all official documents should use both Tibetan and Chinese languages; all newspapers, radio, TV, and other mass media should use the two languages; all units, streets, roads, and public facilities should be written in both Tibetan and Chinese languages; schools should gradually establish an educational system centered around Tibetan language education; and the judicial organs, while examining and trying cases, must guarantee that Tibetan citizens have the right to legal proceedings in their own language.[74]

By 1993, middle school texts had to be written entirely in Tibetan, and by 1997, most subjects in senior middle and technical schools were to be taught in Tibetan. After 2000, institutes of higher learning were to gradually start to use Tibetan as well.[75] However, this plan has been abandoned and almost all subjects are taught in Chinese, starting in junior high school. By 1994, 7 newspapers, 11 magazines, and 231 books were produced in Tibetan,[76] and every year, 25 Tibetan language films are made.[77]

The Beijing government had issued repeated directives to Chinese residents of Tibet to learn the language, but in most cases these directives had been ignored.[78] Officials and factory managers who spoke only Chinese tended to prefer employees who could speak Chinese, and this excluded many Tibetans.[79]

By 1990, college-educated students in Tibet comprised 5.7 per thousand of the population, compared to 4.2 per thousand in 1982. The figures for high school education were 21.2 per thousand in 1990 and 12.1 per thousand in 1982. The proportion of illiterates and semi-literates in the Tibetan population dropped from more than 90 percent in the 1950s to 46 percent in 1982, and further to 44 percent at the end of 1994.[80]

In the area of economic autonomy, Tibet has been permitted to make its own decisions concerning the development and exploitation of resources, which are to be used to benefit the local population.[81] However, the economic powers of minority nationalities, as one Chinese scholar acknowledges, are very limited because the center does not want to give up its power. There is no legally defined boundary of economic power between Beijing and the autonomous regions. In all existing laws there is no provision for the financial aspect of autonomy rights.[82]

The Law on National Regional Autonomy stipulates that localities may, in accordance with state stipulations, carry out foreign trade activities and, with the approval of the State Council, they may open foreign trade ports. At the Second Session of the Fourth People's Congress of the TAR in July 1985, Tibetan government leaders issued a series of preferential policies on Tibet's foreign trade activities. Tibet opened the Zham Port, abutting Nepal, for the development of border trade. In order to promote the development of Tibet's foreign trade activities, the central government has adopted special policies that specify lower rates for import and export duties, and has allowed the autonomous region to retain all of its export earnings (100 percent for Tibet, 50 percent for other autonomous regions).[83] However, presently, Tibetan exports to Nepal, Bhutan, and India are increasing at a snail's pace. Total exports from the TAR amounted to a paltry US$20 million in 1994, with imports at US$337 million.[84]

To encourage economic development in Tibet, Beijing had exempted Tibet from the general rule that one must be a permanent resident of a given area to start a business there. The result was that Tibetan cities, Lhasa in particular, were inundated with a so-called "floating population" of Han Chinese from other provinces.[85] Typically possessing better linguistic and technical skills than the locals, the Han Chinese tended to take business away from native Tibetans.[86] There was also a widespread feeling that it was the Han Chinese, and not the local people, who profited from tourism.[87]

Evaluation of the Chinese Practice of Autonomy

We are now entering into a subjective and biased area. Beijing emphasizes the sacrifices made by a significant number of Chinese aid cadres who come to Tibet to provide their selfless services to Tibetan economic and cultural lives. By contrast, Kalon T.C. Tethong, the kalon for the Department of Information and International Relations, regards the increasing number of these "aid cadres" as a move "to rule Tibet directly from Beijing" because these cadres are directly appointed to sensitive and important posts in Tibet and are accountable to Beijing and not to the TAR authorities in Lhasa.[88]

Chinese theories and their criteria present an official picture of the "great achievement" of Chinese autonomy. The record, however, has been unimpressive indeed, if Chinese practice were to be compared with the practice of autonomy in other parts of the world.[89] Nevertheless, a due recognition of the *limited* achievement of Chinese autonomy is needed. A liberal criterion and its judgment of Chinese autonomy as "virtually meaningless"[90] do not do the Chinese any justice.

It is difficult to fully confirm the claim that the record of the Chinese practice of autonomy in Tibet is merely a "paper autonomy." "Cultural genocide" is not an intellectually appropriate conceptual framework for assessing PRC state policy.[91] Clearly, minority rights are exercised and protected much more in the "soft" areas such as the economy, health, and culture than in the "hard" area of political rights. Certainly, autonomy in culture and economy has often been undermined whenever the Party/state sees some practices threatening the unity of the Chinese nation-state.

Generally speaking, around the world, autonomy can exist independently from federalism. But autonomy would be limited without a functional federalism. Indeed, the limited practice of Chinese autonomy operates under a unitary state. Chinese autonomy lacks an internal boundary and an independent local judiciary with full responsibility for interpreting local laws and whose exercise of power is generally not subject to veto by the central government.

When a perceived stability question arises, autonomy is restricted or reduced.

In 1994, Beijing circulated a resolution reaffirming the leading position of Han Chinese cadres in the Tibetan government and Party organization, and demanding Tibetan cadres cut off their links with the Dalai Lama.[92] In China, the concept of a unitary multinational state is underpinned by a consensus that stability overrides all other considerations.

Conclusion

Beijing rejects the Dalai Lama's autonomy proposal as a solution to the Tibet question on the ground that the Dalai Lama has "internationalized" the Tibet Question, and for the following reasons:

1. Beijing thinks that the acceptance of the proposal would create an internal boundary and an "independent kingdom," which would eventually lead to Tibet's full independence.
2. Beijing is reluctant to accept the idea of the chief executive in Tibet being elected rather than appointed.
3. The Dalai Lama's demands that the territories of Tibet's autonomy should comprise some areas now in Gansu, Sichuan, and Ningxia are totally unacceptable to Beijing.
4. Beijing will not accept the Dalai Lama's precondition for negotiation: a withdrawal of Chinese troops from Tibet. At the same time, the Dalai Lama refuses to satisfy Beijing's demand that the Dalai Lama should "publicly make a statement and a commitment that Tibet is an inalienable part of China."
5. Chinese leaders reject the proposal because it entails the right to self-determination. While the Dalai Lama's *genuine* autonomy proposal draws on liberal principles of autonomy, Chinese theories of *regional* autonomy, derived from Marxist principles, reject the right of self-determination being applied to Chinese minorities. Chinese theories of autonomy are not based on rights, but on pragmatism and a combination of Marxism and Confucianism.
6. According to the Chinese leadership, China has already established the Chinese system of regional autonomy for minority nationalities, which comprises three elements: a constitutional framework, laws governing autonomy, and government policies. The Chinese style of autonomy can be characterized as a sort of limited autonomy with plural models in practice. Chinese autonomy can also be characterized by a combination of political "self-rule," economic integration, cultural exchanges, and ethnic intermingling. Above all, Hu Jintao, the new general secretary and the president of China, stated clearly that "it is essential to fight unequivocally against the separatist activities by the Dalai clique and anti-China forces in the world, vigorously develop a good situation of stability and unity in Tibet and firmly safeguard national unity and state security."[93]

Notes

An earlier version of this chapter was published in *Review of Asian and Pacific Studies* (Seikei University, Japan), no. 22 (2001): 57–72. The current version has been substantially revised and updated. The author would like to express his sincere thanks to Professor Barry Sautman and Mr. Eric Zhang for their comments, suggestions, and criticisms.

1. *The Political Philosophy of His Holiness the XIV Dalai Lama: Selected Speeches and Writings*, ed. A.A. Shiromany (New Delhi: Tibetan Parliamentary and Policy Research Center, 1998), 144.

2. *Tibetan Bulletin*, January–April 2002, 9.

3. www.tibet.ca/wtnarchive/2002/7/15_2.html.

4. www.tibet.com/NewsRoom/delegation2.htm.

5. For China's attempt to adhere to the popular United Front in the new century, see http://fpeng.peopledaily.com.cn/200012/04/eng20001204_56813.html.

6. www.tibet.ca/wtnarchive/2003/8/21_1.html.

7. www.tibet.ca/wtnarchive/2002/7/15_2.html.

8. Orville Schell, "Chinese Puzzle—Why Won't Beijing Make Peace with the Dalai Lama?" *San Francisco Chronicle*, June 24, 2001; www.tibet.ca/wtnarchive/2001/6/26_3.html.

9. Ibid.

10. From the author's interview with Lodi Gyari on August 31, 2003, in Washington, DC.

11. For my personal view on self-determination and democracy, see Baogang He, "Referenda as a Solution to the National Identity/Boundary Question: An Empirical Critique of the Theoretical Literature," *Alternatives: Global, Local, Political* 27, no. 1: 67–97; "Democracy and Civil Society," in *Democratic Theory Today: Challenge for the 21st Century*, ed. April Carter and Geoffrey Stokes (Cambridge: Polity Press, 2002), 203–227.

12. June Teufel Dreyer, "Unrest in Tibet," *Current History* 88, no. 539 (September 1989): 284.

13. Ibid., 48.

14. S. Rinpoche, *Tibet: A Future Vision* (New Delhi: Tibetan Parliamentary and Policy Research Centre, 1996), 47.

15. "Statement by His Holiness the XIV Dalai Lama on His September 1995 Visit to the United States," *Tibet Press Watch* 7, no. 5 (October 1995): 5.

16. Dreyer, "Unrest in Tibet," 284.

17. China would be more likely to adopt a congruent federalism than an incongruent federalism. In a congruent form of federalism, such as that in Australia, Austria, Germany, and the United States, the political boundaries between the component units cut across the social boundaries between religious or ethnic groups. Such a system has not been challenged by any serious secessionist movements. In the incongruent form of federalism such as those of Belgium, Canada, and Switzerland, political and social boundaries tend to coincide, and strong secessionist movements can occur as in Belgium and Canada, and even in Switzerland. Indeed, Canada's decentralized federalism seems to be dysfunctional.

18. Rinpoche, *Tibet: A Future Vision*, 47.

19. The idea of Greater Tibet may have a selling point. For example, World Bank directors rejected a US$40 million loan to China to resettle 58,000 farmers in Qinghai province where the Tibetan spiritual leader, the Dalai Lama, was born. See Reuters, July 7, 2000.

20. *Open Magazine*, August 2003; www.open.com.hk/4j.html.

21. But Yan concedes that the federal parliament would ultimately decide on the scope of the Tibetan border and other border changes. Yan also argues that the concept of Greater Tibet has yet to take shape among Tibetans in Qinghai, Gansu, Ningxia, Sichuan, and other provinces, and the influence of the concept of "Tibetan independence" among them is extremely limited. See Yan Jiaqi, "Federalism and the Future of Tibet," *Tibet News*, no. 19

(Autumn): 14–16. On this matter, Sautman and Lo suggest a solution to this dispute: "While present administrative borders might be kept in place during a trial period of enlarged TAR autonomy, there could be negotiations over issues affecting Tibetans outside the TAR, and rights provided within the TAR for all ethnic Tibetans, irrespective of their residency." See Barry Sautman and Shiu-hing Lo, *The Tibet Question and the Hong Kong Experience*, Occasional Papers/Reprints Series in Contemporary Asian Studies, no. 2, 1995, School of Law, University of Maryland, 48–49.

22. *The Spirit of Tibet, Vision for Human Liberation: Selected Speeches and Writings of His Holiness the XIV Dalai Lama*, ed. A.A. Shiromany (New Delhi: Tibetan Parliamentary and Policy Research Center, 1996), 81.

23. Hollis S. Liao, "The Recruitment and Training of Ethnic Minority Cadres in Tibet," *Issues and Studies* (December 1995): 59.

24. Rinpoche, *Tibet: A Future Vision*, 52.

25. Ibid., 53.

26. *Open Magazine*, August 2003; www.open.com.hk/4j.html.

27. Frank Ching, "Hong Kong Solution for Tibet?" *Far Eastern Economic Review* 161, no. 31 (July 30): 37.

28. www.tibet.ca/wtnarchive/2002/7/15_2.html.

29. *The Political Philosophy*, 60.

30. *Tibetan Bulletin*, January–April 2002, 10.

31. www.tibetanyouthcongress.org/homepage.htm.

32. www.tibet.org/sft/action/boycott_mic.html.

33. For a good discussion of this question, see Sautman and Lo, *The Tibet Question and the Hong Kong Experience*.

34. Ching, "Hong Kong Solution for Tibet?" 37.

35. Song Liming, "Minzu zhuyi yu Xizang wenti" (Nationalism and the Tibet Problem), *Modern China Studies*, no. 2 (1997): 159–167.

36. Sautman and Lo, *The Tibet Question and the Hong Kong Experience*, 17.

37. For example, W. Kymlicka's neoliberal theory of minority rights emphasizes the inviolable rights, in particular the right to self-government. The international campaigners for Tibet and the international human rights law group, for example, adopt Hurst Hannum's *liberal* definition of autonomy, which denotes a locally elected legislative body, a locally elected chief executive, an independent local judiciary, and joint authority over matters of common concern. See the International Campaign for Tibet and the International Human Rights Law Group's report, *The Myth of Tibetan Autonomy: A Legal Analysis of the State of Tibet* (Washington, DC: 1994), 6–7.

38. Schell, "Chinese Puzzle."

39. See Chen Yanbin, Liu Jianzhong, and Qiao Li, "Mao Zedong sixiang minzu lilun yanjiu huigu" (Review of the Studies on Mao Zedong Thought about Nationalities), *Heilongjiang minzu congkan* (Heilongjiang Nationality Series Collection) (Harbin), no. 4 (1998): 33–38; Yang Jingchu and Wang Geliu, "Woguo de minzu quyu zizhi: Mao Zedong dui Ma ke si zhuyi minzu lilun de gongxian" (National Regional Autonomy in China: Mao Zedong's Contribution to Marxist Theory of Nationality), *Minzu yanjiu* (Nationality Research), no. 1 (1994): 1–8.

40. Yang Jingchu and Wang Geliu, "Woguo de minzu quyu zizhi," 1–2.

41. Warren W. Smith, "China's Tibetan Dilemma," *The Fletcher Forum of World Affairs* 14, no. 1 (Winter 1990): 78.

42. Ma Xing and Zhong He, "Minzu quyu zizhi yanjiu huigu" (Review of the Studies on National Regional Autonomy), *Heilongjiang minzu congkan* (Heilongjiang Nationality Collection) (Harbin), March 1998, 29–38.

43. See Chen Qinghua and Wei Yingxue, "Deng Xiaoping minzu lilun yanjiu huigu" (Review of the Studies on Deng Xiaoping's Theory About Nationalities), *Heilongjiang minzu congkan* (Heilongjiang Nationality Series) (Harbin), no. 4 (1998): 39–44; also see

Sun Yi, "1996–1997 nian minzu wenti lilun yanjiu zongshu" (A Summary of the Theoretical Studies on Nationalities Between 1996 and 1997), *Heilongjiang minzu congkan* (Heilongjiang Nationality Collection) (Harbin), no. 3 (1998): 43–48.

44. Deng Xiaoping, *Deng Xiaoping wenxuan: Volume 3* (Beijing: People's Press, 1993), 257. It has also been argued by many scholars that the Chinese unitary system, comprising many autonomous nationality regions, is better than a federal system. This is demonstrated by the fact that the federal system of the former Soviet Union and Yugoslavia promoted localism and ethno-nationalism and finally led to the collapse of the socialist system. See Chen Tianyu and Xu Liyun, "Lun woguo minzu quyu zizhi zhidu de jiben tese" (On the Basic Characteristics of the Regional Autonomy System in China), *Zhongyang minzu daxue xuebao (Shehui kexue ban)* (Journal of Central Nationality University [Social Sciences]), no. 2 (1997): 49.

45. Guojia minwei zhengce yanjiushi (Nationalities Commission Policy Research Division), "Jiaqiang minzu quyu zizhi lilun yanjiu, jianchi he wanshan minzu quyu zizhi zhidu" (Enhance the Theoretical Study on Regional National Autonomy, Uphold and Improve the System of Regional National Autonomy), *Dangdai Zhongguo shi yanjiu* (Studies in Contemporary Chinese History), no. 5 (1997): 83.

46. Deng Xiaoping, *Deng Xiaoping wenxuan*, 167.

47. Cited in Wang Dewen and Huang Xiaohong, "Minzu quyu zizhi zhengce zai Xizang de weida shijian" (Great Practice of the Regional Autonomy Policy in Tibet), *Xizang ribao* (Tibet Daily), August 11, 1995, 3.

48. For example, Deng told former President Carter that "it is not a bad thing if the number of Han population increases in minority areas; the key issue is whether the economy has developed there." Certainly, Carter could not fully understand Deng's remark in terms of Confucian culture. See Deng Xiaoping, *Deng Xiaoping wenxuan*, 246–247.

49. Guojia minwei zhengce yanjiushi, "Jiaqiang minzu quyu zizhi lilun yanjiu," 83.

50. Some Tibetans, however, hold a different view of economic development. As Lobsang Sangay, a Tibetan exile and later a Ph.D. candidate at Harvard, put it: "Tibetans have felt increasingly marginalized in their own territory and see themselves as mere observers of an economic development benefiting others. This has made the ethnic 'us vs. them' sentiment all the more concrete, since it is usually the Han Chinese who reap the profits of change." See Lobsang Sangay, "China in Tibet: Forty Years of Liberation or Occupation," *Harvard Asia Quarterly* (Summer 1999): 27.

51. "Statement by His Holiness the XIV Dalai Lama on His September 1995 Visit to the United States," 4.

52. Yao Junkai, "Shixing minzu quyu zizhi, cujin Xizang fanrong changsheng" (Implement Regional Autonomy, Promote Tibet's Prosperity), *Xizang minzu xueyuan xuebao (Shehui kexue ban)* (Journal of the Tibetan Nationality Institute [Social Sciences]), no. 3 (1995): 18.

53. Dreyer, "Unrest in Tibet," 281.

54. Solomon Karmel, "Ethnic Tension and the Struggle for Order: China's Policies in Tibet," *Pacific Affairs* 68, no. 4 (1995): 486.

55. Ibid., 488.

56. Ibid., 489.

57. Cited in ibid., 494.

58. Cited in ibid., 494.

59. Luo Qun, "The Autonomous Rights of Tibet," *Beijing Review* 34, no. 21 (May 27–June 2, 1991): 21.

60. Ibid.

61. Liao, "The Recruitment," 56–57.

62. Ibid.

63. Ibid.

64. Karmel, "Ethnic Tension and the Struggle for Order," 494.

65. *People's Daily* (Overseas edition), June 21, 1999, 4.

66. Dreyer, "Unrest in Tibet," 281.

67. Ibid.

68. Ibid.

69. T. Heberer, *China and Its National Minorities–Autonomy or Assimilation?* (Armonk, NY: M.E. Sharpe, 1989), 125–126.

70. Dreyer, "Unrest in Tibet," 283.

71. Ibid., 284.

72. Ibid., 283.

73. Ibid.

74. Luo Qun, "The Autonomous Rights of Tibet," 20.

75. Dreyer, "Unrest in Tibet," 284.

76. *China's Ethnic Statistical Yearbook 1995* (Beijing: Ethnic Publishing House, 1995), 376–382.

77. Zhang Lei, "Fanrong xingwang de kekao baozheng: Minzu quyu zizhi zhidu zai Xizang de chenggong shijian" (Reliable Guarantee to Prosperity: Successful Practice of Regional Autonomy Policy in Tibet), *Xizang ribao* (Tibet Daily), September 15, 1995, 5–6. Nevertheless, there are no data available on this in *China's Ethnic Statistical Yearbook 1995,* 369.

78. Dreyer, "Unrest in Tibet," 282.

79. Ibid.

80. Liao, "The Recruitment," 60–61; and Luo Qun, "The Autonomous Rights of Tibet," 20–22.

81. Heberer, *China and Its National Minorities,* 46.

82. Dai Xiaoming, "Guanyu minzu zizhi difang caizheng zizhi jiqi falu wenti" (On Financial Autonomy of National Autonomous Regions and Related Legal Issues), *Minzu yanjiu* (Nationality Studies), no. 6 (1997): 8–17.

83. Luo Qun, "The Autonomous Rights of Tibet," 22; also see Li Jianhui, "Luelun Zhongguo minzu zhengce tixi" (On the System of Nationalities Policies in China), *Dangdai Zhongguo shi yanjiu* (Contemporary Chinese History Studies), no. 5 (1997): 91.

84. Karmel, "Ethnic Tension and the Struggle for Order," 495.

85. Dreyer, "Unrest in Tibet," 282.

86. Ibid.

87. Ibid.

88. *Tibetan Bulletin* (July–August 2001): 10; www.tibet.net/eng/diir/tibbul/0107/jintao.html.

89. Eva Herzer, "The Practice of Autonomous and Self-government Arrangements," paper presented at International Workshop on Tibetan Autonomy and Self-Government: Myth and Reality, Heritage Village, India, November 10–12, 1999.

90. The International Campaign for Tibet and the International Human Rights Law Group's report, *The Myth of Tibetan Autonomy,* 4.

91. Barry Sautman, "'Cultural Genocide' and Tibet," *Texas International Law Journal* 38, no. 173 (2003): 177.

92. Liao, "The Recruitment," 59–60.

93. *Tibetan Bulletin* (July–August 2001): 10; www.tibet.net/eng/diir/tibbul/0107/jintao.html.

4

The Question of Tibet and the Politics of the "Real"

Amy Mountcastle

This chapter considers the question of Tibet, how the debate is defined, and who sets its parameters. In recent years a considerable amount of ink has been spent attempting to sort through the issues: the history, controversies, exaggerations, charges, and countercharges (e.g., Barnett 2001; Dodin and Rather 2001; Goldstein 1997, 1995, 1994, 1989; Grunfeld 2000, 1996, 1987; Sautman 2003; Sautman and Eng 2001; Shakya 1999; Smith 1996). One strategy is to reduce the question down to its essential elements: to free it of the emotions that cloud it and the propaganda that shrouds it, and especially to retrieve it from its expropriation as a human rights and populist issue (e.g., Goldstein 1997; Sautman 2003).

The criticism of the human rights strategy, a centerpiece of the Tibetan Government in Exile's international campaign for the last decade and a half, comes from virtually every quarter—from supporters of the Tibetan cause, backers of the exile government, critics of it, from the People's Republic of China, from Western and Tibetan academics and scholars, and even casual observers.

The specific arguments and their relative merits differ, but what is interesting is that they are frequently linked by a curious structural similarity, namely that human rights considerations are seen as oppositional to some purported "real" issue. This, then, is the starting point of the present discussion. What is the real issue, how is it defined, by whom, and why? What are the implications of labeling something "real," and how does this frame the subsequent discussion?

Questioning Reality: Defining the Tibet Question

To the first question: What is the real issue? There seems to be a plurality of opinion. It is defined in sometimes contradictory and sometimes overlapping ways, depending upon who does the defining, and when it occurs. For some, focusing on human rights detracts from the root causes of oppression of Tibetans and the lack of viable options for their ethnocultural survival. The real issue is "independence" (Lazar 1994), while human rights connotes other, more fundamental, problems. Some Western scholars take a pragmatic position, arguing that the human rights strategy has been ineffectual, and some seem to suggest that human rights and the Tibetan cause serve as little more than a repository for the displacement of Western fantasies and New Age spiritual aspirations (Bishop 1993, 1989; Dodin and Rather 2001; Lopez 1998, 1994).[1] Rallying for human rights may make people feel good, but in the end, little of political value seems to result. Western scholars point to the dangers of the Western enchantment with, and popularization of, the Tibet issue, much of it hinging on the wave of interest in human rights as well as becoming a cause célèbre among Hollywood and rock stars (Barnett 2001, 1998; Bishop 1993, 1989; Feigon 1996; French 2003; Goldstein 1997; Grunfeld 2000, 1996; Lopez 1998, 1994; Norbu 1989; Schell 2000).[2] Some are concerned that there is much to be lost, including lives in Tibet, political headway for the cause of Tibet, or for Tibetan culture (Barnett 1998; French 2003; Goldstein 1997).

From the perspective of the Chinese state, raising the human rights question represents interference, an affront to its national sovereignty, and imperialist "splittism" on the part of the West, especially the United States. China reacts with counteraccusations that the United States habitually ignores its own human rights problems and practices a double standard in its human rights diplomacy (Weil 1994). Other perspectives define the real issue as one of classic nationalism or ethnonationalist struggle (Goldstein 1997); about historical continuity to the Mongol period (Information Office, PRC State Council 1992; Grunfeld 2000); as a question of colonial invasion and occupation (Gyari cited in Barnett 2001, fn. 60; van Walt van Praag 1987);[3] as concerning self-determination of indigenous peoples (Thonden 1994 in Lazar 1994); as about cultural survival and ethnocide; and as about universal ideals and saving an endangered and unique cultural legacy.[4]

Historically, definitions of the Tibet Question have not been any more consistent than the complex and varied fortunes of the Tibetan State. For example, during parts of the Qing Dynasty, Tibet seemed to be more of an irritant than anything else, and the Qing ruler, according to one rendition, intervened in the internal squabbles of the Tibetans mainly to prevent them from harming the dynasty (Goldstein 1997, esp. 14; 1994; also Smith 1996, 146–149). The Tibet Question as a *national* question arises at the earliest during the Guomindang, as China began to assert itself and define itself in the idiom of nationalism (Norbu 1992; Smith 1996, esp. 151). As for who was doing the defining, the etic viewpoint certainly differed from the emic viewpoint (Smith 1996, 148), as we see when the Fourteenth Dalai Lama says,

> When we won our complete independence, in 1912, we were quite content to retire into isolation. It never occurred to us that our independence, so obvious a fact to us, needed any legal proof to the outside world. If only we had applied to

join the League of Nations or the United Nations, or even appointed ambassadors to a few of the leading powers, before our crisis came, I am sure these signs of sovereignty would have been accepted without any question, and the plain justice of our cause would not have been clouded, as it was, by subtle legal discussions based on ancient treaties which had been made under quite different circumstances. (Dalai Lama 1997 [1962], 65–66)

But here our purpose is not to analyze or debate the finer points of history. Instead, I would like to explore the *idea* of the *real issue* and how it is dichotomized, in many instances, with other issues that have been raised concerning the Tibet Question; namely, human rights. Each of the ways of defining the Tibet Question draws upon particular schemas, sets of ideas and images that direct attention to some features over others and that are component parts of a given reality.[5] Clearly, there is no consensus about what the real issue of Tibet is; in fact, quite the contrary: the "real" issue is a contested one.

Among the most prominent voices in the contest to define the real issue are academic ones. Scholarly work is presumed to be the valid arbiter in a controversy where truth is protean and elusive. Sometimes scholars view themselves as standing outside of the contested field of representational politics, particularly when employing rhetorical and discursive strategies that have the resonance of objectivity.[6] For example, statistical data and economic indicators may be used to paint a picture of the PRC's success in its policies of economic development in Tibet (Sautman and Eng 2001). These and other data have been used in attempting to discredit the exile government's assertions concerning the dismal state of Tibetans in Tibet and the serious human rights charges levied by the exile government, its allies, and others (see Sautman 2003, for example). Presumably, the alleged material well-being of Tibetan beneficiaries of this state benevolence signifies satisfaction in, acceptance of, or at least acquiescence to, the social, political, and cultural conditions under PRC domination. Lacking in this kind of material/realist assessment is the acknowledgment of cultural and political alienation, or the importance of this in evaluating the legitimacy or wisdom of the continued implementation of the policy of development, much less the continued occupation of Tibet (e.g., Misra 2000; International Commission of Jurists [ICJ] 1997; FlorCruz et al. 2000). Similarly, while legalistic analysis of the use of terms such as *cultural genocide* (Sautman 2003) may be beneficial in clarifying points of law and sharpening definitions of legal terminology, it fails to recognize or acknowledge the catastrophic humanitarian crisis of cultural and social deterioration and neglect (see, for example, Liu and Mahakian 2001 on the closure of Serthar Monastery).[7] Statistical and legalistic analyses have their place and they certainly appeal to policymakers and politicians, sometimes because they offer justification for decisions that may be unpopular or even morally reprehensible.

Scholars, even as they set out to clarify the issues, make no small contribution to the confusion surrounding the Tibet Question, sometimes because the "facts" themselves may (intentionally or unintentionally) serve a political agenda cloaked in the mantle of academic and scholarly objectivity. Statistics, factoids, and legalisms have a long history of being used as smoke screens for other agendas. At other times, despite what are sincere attempts to present a dispassionate assessment and illumination of the dynamics surrounding the controversy, clarity does not prevail because an enumeration of facts (which are also contested) or a display of quantitative data does not adequately illuminate or convey the historical and ideological complexities of the Tibet Question. In other words, facts, in their singular dimensionality, cannot account for or represent the multidimensionality of the Tibet Question in either its historical or contemporary complexities. This is why these kinds of data often seem reductionistic.

Academic discourse has, of course, its own way of defining questions and issues, and uses specific representational tools. To assume that particular kinds of academic discourse stand apart from other representations of the Tibet Question, and that these are therefore more apt to convey, in some essential sense, "the real issue" of Tibet is to reify and support a particular view of the world, one that privileges certain values over others and upholds a particular constellation of power, privilege, and domination that structures knowledge and reality. Academic discourse, rather than standing apart from representational politics, is constitutive of it—and to no incidental degree—a fact that many scholars, especially since Edward Said's seminal works, have recognized.[8] In this context, academic discourse on Tibet cannot be seen as neutral, unbiased, or objective, but is itself programmatic. Part of the problem in sorting out the Tibet Question has been that the act of defining the question is constitutive of the question.[9]

Image and reality are inexorably linked. If we take seriously Benedict Anderson's notion that the nation is an imagined community, then image, and the production, control, and management of image, is not at all tangential, not epistemologically or ontologically irrelevant, but indeed at the root of existence.[10] In the case of Tibet, its reality and existence are in question,[11] notwithstanding the critique that this position may inflame of the essentialization of culture.[12] The definition of the Tibet Question is fundamentally predicated on which images are given precedence; thus who controls the images, controls the question. From the mid-twentieth-century Communist rhetoric of liberation and democratization to the late twentieth/early twenty-first-century rhetoric of development and democratization, from images of feudalism and slavery to visions of a moral and environmental oasis, the contest and control of images of Tibet are very much a part of the "real" question, of defining the terms of a debate that includes the question of who the legitimate spokespersons for Tibet and Tibetans are or will be.

The Tibet Question has been in many respects an extra-Tibetan issue, most recently in the imperial contests and Great Game politics of the early twentieth century (Goldstein 1997), and in the postcolonial global restructuring that brought about the current order of nation-state politics (see Norbu 1992). Tibetans have been historically marginalized, in large part, from setting the agenda and defining the terms of the debate, since at least the early 1900s.[13] Aside from the failed Simla

Convention in 1913 and the ambiguous recognition of Britain and the United States throughout the period of Tibetan de facto independence (from 1913 to 1949)[14] (Goldstein 1997, 36–40), Tibetans have not been given full say in addressing the question of the status of Tibet.[15] Ultimately, they were not allowed to play in the high-stakes game of territorial acquisition and distribution after the Second World War (Goldstein 1997, 40). To summarize, the importance of the matter of defining the Tibet Question should not be underestimated. Implicated in this debate are questions of who has the right to define the question and the terms of the debate and why. Who is granting that right? Who is speaking for whom? These are political questions with moral/ethical dimensions that are of no small consequence, especially to Tibetans.

Similarly, in the postwar period and in the present game of power politics, Tibetans do not have access to the main political channels and halls of power. Virtually all nation-states have asserted a one-China policy (Great Britain is the exception).[16] After 1971, when the People's Republic of China was admitted to the United Nations, there was little international interest in Tibet and few opportunities for Tibetans to gain an audience either in the political foreground or behind the scenes.[17] Tibetan voices, then, were largely absent from the mainstream political scene. In Tibet, those voices were and continue to be effectively silenced by a totalitarian state. Tibetans, therefore, have been for many years at a severe disadvantage in advancing any explicit *political* agenda.

Among the alternatives for staging a viable resistance movement, especially for people who are shut off from official political forums,[18] is to internationalize a cause. Two important means of achieving this are terrorism[19] and to a lesser extent guerrilla warfare, and using the international forum on global issues and concerns—such as human rights, environmental issues, women's issues. As has been the case for a number of other groups that have built resistance movements on global issues, linking the Tibetan cause to human rights has allowed a level of participation in the global political arena in the last decade and a half that would otherwise have been unlikely. Human rights as political strategy, therefore, can be viewed not only from the conventional realist perspective of efficacy, but also as a means of challenging the overwhelming realist political ideology that restricts access and participation. If we view it in this way, as ideology, and we question the reified standing the realist approach has been enjoying for the last half-century, then we are led to consider what lies behind the critique of alternative positions, or versions of reality. To de-legitimate the human rights platform and agendas by locating them outside of the privileged realm of "the real" is, then, a political act[20] about advancing particular versions of the truth, attempting to control the narrative (of truth), and quelling competing versions of it. One way of doing this is to cast "real" political issues in opposition to "ideal" human rights issues. The realist framework not only sets up a dichotomy between "the real" and "the ideal," but the elites who may legitimately participate in the discourse are set apart from popular spokespersons and other nonexperts who might attempt to enter into the debate.

The devaluation of the human rights strategy thus may go hand in hand with the fact that the Tibetan cause has a popular resonance and appeal.

To reiterate, the human rights impetus of the Tibetan exile government is dismissed easily by friend and foe alike because to do so reflects the ideology of realism that structures mainstream national and global politics. It is part of a broader pattern in global politics that privileges realism over what are viewed as idealist notions. It also privileges the state over the stateless. The point for our purposes here is not to question the validity of arguments regarding the efficacy and wisdom of the human rights approach, but rather that the consideration of the human rights focus has been, in a sense, short-circuited because of the structural framework within which it is being considered. As a structuring paradigm, realist politics dichotomizes itself with "idealism" and therefore precludes, from the outset, certain kinds of debate and discussion, and forecloses possibilities that would challenge its validity.[21] The Tibetan case, therefore, not only raises some important questions regarding the place and role of human rights in global politics more generally, but also, perhaps more significantly, it raises questions about the implications of this realist/idealist dichotomy for framing political debate and participation. I will further explore these matters in a later section.

For the moment, we should note that the historical charge of the human rights platform has evolved from a rather weak articulation of the bounds of acceptable behavior for state entities on or against their own people, to a challenge to extant regimes of power and as an alternative means of conceiving of the political universe.[22] This evolution of the role of human rights in the global arena is the topic of the next section, where I also take a further look at the view that the human rights approach is ineffectual and tangential to real politics and at the criticisms of the Tibetan exile government for using it.

Refracting Reality: Tibet, Global Politics, and the Evolution of Human Rights

The linking of the Tibet issue to human rights has been traced to the Dalai Lama's and exile government's decision to "internationalize" the Tibet Question in the late 1980s (Barnett 1998; Goldstein 1997, 75–78; Grunfeld 1996, 231–233; McGlagan 1996; Shakya 1999, 412–416). The springboard of the human rights position is the principle of nonviolence, an important aspect of the public face of the exile government as well as fundamental to its policies. This has facilitated a seamless incorporation of a human rights consciousness into existing exile government approaches, while simultaneously making it plausible and credible to popular audiences, especially perhaps to non-Tibetan observers and supporters (Mountcastle 1997a, 1997b).

This is not the first time, of course, that Tibetans have sought intervention from the international community. Shakya (1999) and others have detailed the attempts to get the international community involved via the United Nations throughout the first decade of the Chinese occupation. For a variety of reasons, some related to Cold War politics, the self-interest of protecting the colonial establishment, and worries about giving China leverage for admission into the UN, member-states were, for the most part, ambivalent about raising the Tibet issue in the General Assembly (Shakya 1999, 212–228). There was a modicum of success in that three resolutions were passed (in 1959, 1961, and 1965)[23] raising the problem of human rights violations in Tibet.

Some scholars suggest, however, that the current campaign differs from the earlier one in that now the Dalai Lama himself delivers the message directly to the United States and the West, seeking governmental, rather than purely religious, forums. The current campaign would also, according to Goldstein, "redirect the significance of the Tibet Question from the arena of geopolitical national interests to the sphere of core U.S. values—to the U.S. ideological commitment to freedom and human rights" (Goldstein 1997, 76). However, this is not entirely accurate because it suggests that prior to the late 1980s Tibetans were not invoking the human rights platform to any significant degree. This is not the case. The use of the human rights platform and the emphasis on nonviolent struggle have been part of the exile government's "strategy" since at least the mid-1970s. In 1977, Tibetan hunger strikers in Delhi, members of the Tibetan Youth Congress, asked the United Nations to support their nonviolent struggle, lest Tibetans turn to other (violent) methods of resistance (*Tibetan Review* 1977b, 7). Also in 1977, a Tibetan student wrote a letter to Congressman Donald M. Fraser, chair of the Committee on International Relations' Subcommittee on International Organization, referencing House legislation signed by President Gerald Ford in 1976 that denies security assistance to countries whose governments "engage in a consistent pattern of gross violation of . . . human rights" (*Tibetan Review* 1977a, 4).[24] In 1979, the representative in the New York Office of Tibet sent a letter to the *Christian Science Monitor* suggesting that the United States was easing up on the question of human rights at the United Nations and appealing to the General Assembly to take a fresh look at the human rights situation in Tibet (*Tibetan Review* 1979, 26–27). In 1983, a news report discusses the fourteen-page report promulgated by the government in exile entitled "Chinese Human Rights Abuses in Tibet, 1959–1982" (*Tibetan Review* 1983, 4).

It is clear from a review of reports that refer to human rights and nonviolence in the *Tibetan Review* over the years, that exile government policy reflects continuity, and that rather than Tibetans jumping onto some human rights bandwagon of recent years, the case is more likely that their message has begun to be heard by a Western audience that has become receptive to human rights issues. It is perhaps the case that as human rights again rose to a higher level of visibility in the late 1980s and through the 1990s, Tibetan strategists reinvigorated their campaign to capitalize on its new salience. This explicit linking of the Tibet issue to the emerging concerns in Western popular politics of human rights, democracy, environment, indigenous peoples and self-determination, and women's issues was an astute and timely move (Shakya 1999, 413; see also McGlagan 1996; Mountcastle 1997a, 1997b).

Another important difference between the early attempt to internationalize the Tibet issue in the 1950s and 1960s and the current campaign is the fact that in the latter case, Tibetans are able to be direct participants in the staging of the debate about themselves and their homeland. Earlier efforts centered upon getting recognized UN member-states to raise the Tibet issue on behalf of an exiled Dalai Lama. Now, the force of the idea of human rights, its global diffusion and popular support, gives Tibetans a public presence and greater leverage in trying to impact those whom they seek to speak on their behalf. It is *their* voices that are being heard, notwithstanding the fact that it is yet the voices of the great powers that continue to matter the most (see Barnett 2001).

The late 1980s was a time ripe for this kind of campaign. Various sea-changes were occurring or were imminent across Latin America, South Africa, in the Soviet world, and also in China. The implementation of truth commissions, the rise of democracy movements, and organizations such as the Madres de Plaza de Mayo, suggest that something was happening across the globe that would give hope to people everywhere who suffered under the oppression and brutality of dictatorial regimes.[25] In the Soviet Union, *perestroika* and *glasnost* were implemented. Democracy movements sprang up in China.[26] Protests in Tibet in 1987 were preceded by protests in 1986 across Chinese college campuses. The crackdown in Tibet was matched by a crackdown on the democracy movement in China. The declaration of martial law in Tibet came a few months before martial law in China and the Tiananmen Square democracy movement.[27] Since the mid-1980s, the political complexion of a number of states dramatically changed and popular movements for democracy, human rights, and indigenous rights became more visible in the global media. Human rights scholars have documented that the role of human rights and the development of a global human rights agenda over the course of the last fifty odd years has made steady, if sometimes hesitant, gains. Its role has expanded enormously since the fall of the Soviet Union in 1991 (Hurrell 1999). While it is evident that human rights are not often the centerpiece of foreign policy, a number of indicators suggest a growing role for them, such as an expanding discourse of human rights, a broadened participation in that discourse, a growing institutional network of human rights–centered organizations, a growing challenge to the principle of state sovereignty, and the continued evolution of international human rights law.

Numerous critiques (which have arisen since the 1960s) of the Western-centric nature of universal human rights have given rise to an expansion of definitions and priorities incorporated into the human rights agenda and to the expansion of the discourse itself (An-Na'im 1992; Van Ness 1999). For example, the cultural relativist/universalist debate, so fundamental to the Cold War East–West contest over defining human rights, has been replaced by efforts to build consensus and incorporate multiple perspectives from diverse cultural traditions.[28] Similarly, the dichotomy between first- and second-generation rights has given way to the recognition (by some) of the interdependent nature of civil/political and economic, social, and cultural rights (Pollis 2000). Furthermore, the rise of the so-called third generation rights of self-determination and environmental safety, as yet controversial and ill defined, also attests to the idea that the International Bill of Rights is a living document that is continually taking shape in response to real world events. While Western states continue to dominate the playing field, no longer is the human rights discourse solely their purview (An-Na'im 1992; Pollis 2000; Van Ness 1999).[29] Few state actors deny the legitimacy of human rights initiatives, although there is disagreement about which human rights should take precedence. This is the crux of the current difference of opinion between the Chinese state and some Western states. The former emphasizes social and economic rights, while the latter continues to emphasize political and civil rights. China produced nine White Papers addressing human rights between 1991 and 1998 (Wan 1998). The human rights scholar Jack Donnelly notes, "Human rights have become a central, perhaps even defining, element of the social and political reality of the late-twentieth-century world" (Donnelly 1998b, 85). Evidence to support this suggestion is not scarce. The responsiveness of state entities, including China (as the publication of several White Papers on Human Rights in Tibet attest), and their sensitivity to charges and to international pressure for accountability on human rights matters, suggests that human rights are being viewed as a serious component of social and political reality (see Sautman 2003 and Schell 1998 concerning Tibet).

A key feature of the expanding role of human rights is the rise over the last fifty-two years of the institutional infrastructure to support it. This includes multilateral treaties and supporting organizational infrastructure, regional regimes, and a proliferation of nongovernmental organizations. Some scholars argue that the establishment of sustainable "networks among domestic and transnational actors who link up with international regimes" is crucial for the spread of human rights norms (Risse, Ropp, and Sikkink 1999, 5). In other words, the human rights agenda cannot be expanded without these networks in place. This can be seen clearly in the case of the new republics of the former Yugoslavia, where local human rights organizations have been able to support and sustain efforts (although not unproblematically) to rebuild multiethnic communities despite the ethnonationalist policies deployed by state regimes (Mountcastle and Tot 2000). Regional human rights organizations—the Asian Human Rights Commission (est. 1981), the African Commission on Human and People's Rights (1981), the Inter-American Commission on Human Rights (1959), and the Council of Europe (1949)—play an increasingly important role in propagating human rights values and encouraging compliance of member and nonmember countries.

The expanding human rights agenda, with its growing visibility at the global level, has opened up the social and political space that enables people to challenge the domestic status quo and to challenge the state. While official political channels, meaning recognition and membership in governmental and intergovernmental organizations, are closed to peoples who are not represented by nation-states, specific issues of transnational and popular interest, such as human rights, provide the forum for representation. An example of this is the increased visibility of indigenous peoples that has resulted from placement of the rights of indigenous peoples on the human rights agenda. Many of these groups (such as the Kayapo) are able to gain international support by joining the transnational environmental movement. People are suddenly finding that they have rights, or becoming aware of having rights, because there is a forum for exercising, practicing, or claiming them. Using the Argentinian example of the election of Radical Party candidate Raúl Alfonsín in 1983, Owen M. Fiss points out that human rights, as social ideals, "can move the law toward the creation or recognition of certain claims as a matter of positive law, both international and domestic" (Fiss 1999, 267). Human rights were never meant to be "merely" ideals. They comprise an idealistic vision, but those who drafted the United Nations' Universal Declaration of Human Rights intended that these ideals would be applied and put into practice and the impact of the Declaration in the years after its promulgation was not insignificant (Lauren 1998, 241).

One of the first areas challenged by the Universal Declaration was state sovereignty (Claude and Weston 1992, 4–5). The primacy and sacrality of the state was dealt a significant blow with its promulgation. The Westphalian principle of the equality of sovereigns and the sanctity of the right to govern a territory unhindered continues to be one of the most contentious issues in international politics, especially given the NATO war in Kosovo in 1999 and the U.S. and British attack of Iraq in 2003. "Internationalizing" an issue shifts it from the "sacred" domain of the state. It is a kind of political "tattle-taling" and breaks the implicit code of silence and complicity that sovereigns have had with one another. Perhaps this is why we regard "internationalizing" an issue, such as the Tibet Question, like a dirty word or an accusation. The challenge to the sovereignty principle, however, has not been unambiguous, and scholars dispute the extent of the impact made by the mid-twentieth-century human rights initiatives (Falk 1992; Donnelly 1998a, 1998b). Human rights principles were placed on the back burner shortly after the onset of the Cold War, and progress was measurably slowed and viewed as irrelevant to the *realpolitik* of a newly nuclearized bi-polar world (Donnelly 1998a). It would not be until the 1960s that the International Human Rights Covenants, the treaties that would make the Universal Declaration of Human Rights legally binding to its signatories, would be completed (Donnelly 1998a, 4–9). Since the Charter of the UN reiterates the principle of state sovereignty in Article 2, section 7, as well as in a variety of other places, it was, arguably, primarily a symbolic blow. But the symbolic act in 1948 cleared the way for a host of other actions of a more substantive type in the decades to follow. Despite the inherent conservativism of UN bodies, especially with respect to issues of state sovereignty, the development of the human rights framework and the supranational bodies and treaties that support it has continued, if sometimes fitfully over the last fifty years. The most obvious example, other than the ones just mentioned, is the case of South Africa.

International pressure on South Africa, led by the UN and in conjunction with nongovernmental organizations, would eventually provide the impetus for the ending of apartheid. Similarly, the attempt by Spain recently to extradite Augusto Pinochet from the U.K., where the former dictator of Chile was seeking medical treatment, serves as another example, as do the two tribunals that are currently trying individuals suspected of crimes against humanity in the tragedies of Rwanda and the former Yugoslavia.[30] The literature abounds with recent cases that reflect the ongoing human rights–based challenges to state sovereignty.[31]

Human rights in the diplomacy of the United States have typically been viewed as a weak foreign policy instrument, and during some periods as hostile to U.S. foreign policy interests, such as in the case the Southern Cone during the Nixon presidency.[32] The Reagan administration, in keeping with what were viewed as the dictates of Cold War *realpolitik,* followed in the model of its Republican predecessors, supporting the Pinochet government in Chile, participating in the training of death squads across Latin America, conducting joint military exercises, and permitting loans from the InterAmerican Development Bank (Donnelly 1998b, 102). During the Carter presidency, human rights played a more robust role in foreign policy and included public mention of human rights violations in the Southern Cone as well as the cessation of military aid to Southern Cone countries and the reduction of development aid (Donnelly 1998b, 100; Lauren 1998, 271–272). However, overall, regardless of the political predispositions of the administration in power, human rights have been viewed as largely secondary considerations to other state interests, although there are exceptions, such as Norway and the Netherlands, which have integrated human rights directly into their foreign policy objectives and have a history of acting on those objectives (Donnelly 1998b, 107–110).

Human rights and other transnational issues (such as the environment) have proved a boon for marginalized identity groups across the globe, popularizing their political concerns and aspirations. Not only do popular movements that hinge on "rights" challenge state authority, but more recently, the authority of multinational corporations as well.[33] Still, given the unevenness with which state entities have applied human rights leveraging, when they do invoke human rights to justify policy they are met with cynicism by oppositional political actors or by the public. The concept of human rights *diplomacy* itself implies the contamination of human rights as ideals; it is a flawed concept from the standpoint of idealists, because it reflects the imperfect fit between their goals and national interests. It also reflects the gap between popular and state interests. In the ideal world, rights should be above interests, but in the "real" world, they are merely ideals. Note the charges of hypocrisy that greet purportedly humanitarian missions such as intervention in Kosovo most recently and the Gulf Wars of 1991 and 2003.[34] The critique of the human rights tact from the standpoint of "real" politics says that little actually changes for groups that make human rights their primary strategy. What are gained are mostly symbolic victories: some otherwise silenced people get a chance to make a little noise about their situation—they are literally given voice and, it is argued, not much else.

But this kind of criticism ignores or discounts the fact that these groups have gained a real popular audience and it also discounts subtle shifts in the tenor and context of international diplomacy that may have been achieved by these symbolic, and/or what are sometimes viewed as Pyrrhic, victories. The symbolic and substantive are not mutually exclusive domains of meaning and reality. In the symbolic domain, power is also challenged and negotiated. While symbolic acts may not bring about substantive change directly, as noted earlier, they nevertheless create a space in which changes may take root. Thus High Commissioner for Human Rights Mary Robinson noted on a BBC News report in the spring of 2001 concerning China's acceptance of the International Covenant on Economic, Social, and Cultural Rights, that while this might not have signaled any immediate changes in state policy, it does create an opening for potential changes in Tibet, the Xinjiang Uyghur Autonomous Region, and other areas where marginalized groups reside. Acts that start out as symbolic or that are instrumental and self-serving can sometimes lead to unintended consequences. The case of the Soviet Union comes to mind. When Mikhail Gorbachev introduced economic reforms under the policy of *perestroika* in 1985, it was not his intention to bring down the Communist state. When *glasnost* was introduced as a means of putting public pressure on intransigent bureaucrats, again, it was not with the intention of jeopardizing the state; quite to the contrary, these were moves made to save the state.

What often seems to be overlooked in assessments of the efficacy of using human rights agendas to challenge and shape foreign policy, at least in the Tibetan case, is the fact that global politics are in a state of flux, change, and transformation. While we should not overstate the role of human rights, if international relations and human rights scholars are correct, then rights have become a "new standard of civilization" (Donnelly 1998a) which nation-states will be less and less able to ignore. Even a scholar like Donnelly, who is conservative about the impact of human rights, does not hesitate to say that "the infusion of human rights into the mainstream of international relations . . . has subtly reshaped national and international political space" (1998a, 19).[35] Having a say where none was before possible, then, is not merely a symbolic victory, but also a political one after all. The enabling and empowering effect of being able to participate in a dialogue, through the human rights platform, should not be so readily discounted. Attempts to do so need to be challenged. What are the political and ideological reasons behind wanting to restrict the number or kinds of voices that are allowed to be heard about a given issue?

In the case of Tibet, much of what has been achieved by exiled Tibetans in engaging the human rights agenda and discourse is also written off as merely symbolic. As noted earlier, to some, it appears that the human rights approach is just another overlay on the already existing multi-layered complex of images and emotions associated with Tibet—part of the Tibet of Western fantasy.[36] In the first place, it is difficult to argue with these charges because of the nature of the West's long imaginative engagement with Tibet and because there seems to be little to show in the way of substantive political results from this policy. But another reason that it is difficult to challenge this view of the human rights approach is that to do so is to also challenge the ideology of realism. It is to this task, and to the framing power of the dominant concept of the real, that I now turn.

Reframing Reality: Ideology and Opposition

The Tibet issue reflects, I believe, the larger ideological contest in the global political arena, a contest over political culture and about the nature of political and social reality. The term *ideology* here is intended to convey several related properties: It refers to a dominant frame of reference in the political culture, "a more focused dimension of political culture," according to Aronoff (1980, 7). Political culture is "manifest in the meanings which political actors ascribe to and explain to justify their behavior" (ibid., 8). Part of this ideology is the taken-for-granted nature of realist goals and perspectives, in other words, the tautology that realist goals "make sense" in some objective fashion, and thereby become their own justification. Realism makes sense because of the nature of reality. There is very little questioning of the "sense" that is made, nor of the reality that is upheld. In the ideology of realism, it is the nation-state reality, and statism more generally, that is privileged. I use the term *ideology* also in one of the senses described by Geertz (1973, esp. 198) as a selective perception of reality—a distortion, in effect. This is related to the assumed naturalness of the position. A number of distortions arise out of this particular view of the universe. One is the idea that there is basically one valid way of defining social and political reality. As a cultural system, ideologies are self-perpetuating. One thing that is accomplished in setting up a dichotomy is a kind of cognitive shorthand, a convenient system of labeling and value judgment. Anything that challenges the system is automatically assigned a pejorative label, such as "irrational" or "irrelevant" or, in this case, simply "idealistic." Ideals are associated with sentiments, not with "hard" realities; they are based on "soft" humanitarian aspirations. This provides an easy means of discounting the position and of excising any unwanted challenges. For example, the fact that the human rights approach inhabits the realms of the idealist and the popular makes it easy to dismiss as not very serious or worthy of consideration. Idealists are notoriously, well, idealistic and unable or unwilling to ground themselves in the harsh realities of the real world and real political life. The populist position is unsophisticated and unreliable, based on popular sentiments that are easily manipulated and misled.

Up to now, the preeminent definition of reality in the global political sphere has been based on the Hobbesian model whereby power and self-interest are the foundation of human interactions and, therefore, the basis of political decision making. Ideals, on the other hand, are rooted in the philosophical and moral domain, and stand in structural opposition and subordinate to the "real."[37] These two spheres are conceived of as mutually exclusive, isolated domains. Thus idealist goals are viewed as antithetical to realist goals, but also *as not being of the same discourse*. As I alluded to earlier, idealists also participate in dichotomizing "real" and "ideal" and are thereby contributors to the ideology of realism. The expropriation by states of the human rights discourse to promote their own, often antithetical, agendas has led to cynicism and charges of hypocrisy. There is a reluctance, then, to wed human rights as ideals with political, and as is often the case, military action. The use of human rights by state actors is viewed by human rights proponents as a kind of contamination and abomination of the ideal. Idealists in this way participate in the de-legitimation of human rights as a political strategy.

The realist ideology subordinates other possible versions of social and political reality, and contradictory realities are submerged. The defining of the Tibet issue, I have argued, occurs within this context: as "real issue" vs. idealistic, or extraneous, or irrelevant, human rights. Yet, as noted earlier, we need not look far into the fields of international law, international relations, human rights scholarship, and into the last five decades of history to see the extent to which human rights have come to be inserted into the sphere of real politics.

It would appear, then, that the dichotomy between real and ideal is a false dichotomy. Viewing the debate between "real issue" and "human rights" as one between ideological competitors enables us to see some of the underlying tensions between the two, and to view the debate as a struggle over power and interests, rather than as two mutually exclusive realms of meaning. Human rights are actually not separate from the paradigm of power and interests associated with the real, but in competition for how, where, and by whom power and interests are to be reckoned and reckoned with. The dominance of the ideology of realism is a dominance based not on some objective claim to a better definition of reality (more real), but on a monopoly on power.

Richard Falk's depiction of the global political universe as consisting of competing ordering logics is illuminating for the argument in a number of ways. First, these ordering logics exist simultaneously and within the same political sphere, and second, we see some reasons of a *realpolitik* nature for the subordination of ideals to this particular notion of "real." Falk refers to these "normative logics" as ordering principles in the world political system that accordingly "determine[s] the relationship of human rights to the world legal order" (Falk 1992, 32).[38] The dominant normative logics tend to be those that give preference to the state, either upholding the notion of juridical equality ("statist logic") or that reflect geopolitical inequality and the purported "leadership" role of some states ("hegemonial logic"). Among the weakest of normative logics is "naturalist logic," the idea that human rights "rest on a moral imperative" and are therefore prior to politics and "independent of their formal acceptance by a government" (Falk 1992, 35). Naturalist logic does play a part in foreign policy decisions to intervene in another state's matters in some of the more extreme cases (Falk 1992 cites Uganda and Cambodia, 36), but policy decisions are usually couched in goals tied to statist or hegemonial logic because "disembodied naturalism (that which is right) is disregarded by policymakers and leaders as sentimental and moralistic" (ibid., 36). Populist logic is the weakest form, but also "potentially most subversive" (ibid., 39). It draws on naturalist logic, denies the legitimacy of the state, and emphasizes the role of popular sovereignty.

The hostility between the state/official discourses and popular discourses is not surprising. According to this view of global order, the popular is in direct competition with state interests and those who uphold them. At base, the matter centers on who has representational authority.[39] With respect to the Tibet Question, the popular draws on the naturalist logic, a combination that, in democratic societies, can make a potent political cocktail. The imprecision of the popular logic, the tendency to galvanize supporters from different parts of political and social spectra, the amorphousness of popular sentiments, can be an irritant to those who prefer tidier modes of constructing and dispensing political and cultural knowledge, values, and facts. The out-of-hand dismissal of the popular must be viewed, from this perspective, as an attempt to control political discourse. Human rights, as a people's issue, provide an avenue for contesting the preeminence of the state, its interests, and its spokespeople. Nevertheless, in most cases, popular power is no match for state power. The problem I have with Falk's model is that it does not clearly show the disproportionate amounts of power and access to power of the various proponents of these "logics." This power variance results in the silencing of some and the foregrounding of the viewpoints of others.

Conclusion

I have tried to situate the issue of Tibet within the context of the ongoing dynamics of a global political stage. I have focused on human rights, the centerpiece of the exiled Tibetans' strategy for nearly a decade and a half, as a component of this global dynamic. I argue that Tibetans are using a political avenue open to them, as any marginalized, dispossessed identity group might, and that in light of the dynamics of the last two decades, it is becoming an increasingly viable avenue. Human rights policy may or may not be the most effective course of action. But its role should not be summarily dismissed because of a false dichotomy between "real" politics and social and political ideals. There is an increasing body of evidence that suggests that internationalized political action through global issues such as human rights, environmentalism, and women's issues can be an effective strategy for resistance movements of politically marginalized and disenfranchised groups. Furthermore, with respect to political action based on human rights issues, there is mounting evidence that it is making an impact on how politics is done both intra- and inter-nationally.

The realist framework by which the human rights strategy is evaluated is paradigmatic and consequently constrains thinking about human rights both as a part of real politics and as a legitimate political tool. Criticisms of human rights policy, in the Tibetan case and in general, should themselves be scrutinized. In a world that seeks to uphold a global political order that privileges state actors, state sovereignty, corporate interests, and that has a bias toward expediency and to being self-serving, attempts to de-legitimate (or expropriate) one of the few viable options available to marginalized and brutalized peoples must be critically examined, and not accepted with blind allegiance to and stock reverence for the rhetoric of realism. The ideology of realism sets up a false dichotomy between itself and the "ideal," which is used to then discount or discredit popular outlets for political expression. The effect of this in terms of the Tibet issue is that the exile government's human rights emphasis and the popular support it has garnered are made peripheral to the central political argument, and the position is thereby trivialized. This threatens the participation of Tibetans in the Tibet Question.

If human rights scholars are correct, the human rights platform and network are an integral part of and force in a rapidly changing field of international politics. The debate surrounding how the problem of Tibet should be handled, as well as defined, is an example of the growing challenge to the ideology of realism. But in the "real world" of politics, human rights are as yet a weak basis for making policy decisions, and some of the events of the last several years provide little scope for optimism. The idea of human rights, however, should be viewed not so much as a *set of ideals* that were envisioned more than fifty years ago when the Charter of the United Nations and the Universal Declaration of Human Rights were set to paper, but rather as evidence of the recognition by world leaders that what had allowed much of the horrendous carnage of the first half of the twentieth century was the evasion of responsibility under the Westphalian system that promoted the view of citizens as the sole property of the sovereign state. As put by Tom Farer:

> For the first time in history, states assumed obligations to their own citizens as precisely and formally defined in many cases as the legal obligations they had hitherto owed to each other under international law. Both through formal treaties and informal practice, they bound themselves not to torture or summarily execute their citizens, or to convict them without due process of law or to dissolve their trade unions or to discriminate among them on the basis of religion or to do a great number of other things that in earlier ages were matters entirely at the discretion of sovereigns. (1981, xv)

To dismiss human rights by relegating them to some unattainable, pie-in-the-sky, idealistic fantasy land, and to thus depoliticize the issues represented by the human rights discourse, or to criticize those who engage in the human rights discourse for the unseemly politicization of a set of ideals (two sides of the same realist paradigm), is to deny political agency to people. It is to forget that for many people, human rights are not ideals, but a matter of survival. It is to allow political discourse to be controlled by state authorities and members of privileged groups. It is to forget that states do not need protecting, people do.

Notes

1. See Neilson (2000) for a unique perspective on the New Age appropriation of the myth of Shambhala and its political implications for the Tibet movement as well as for a politics of resistance to global capitalism.

2. The validity of these viewpoints is not being addressed here. I merely wish to point out the variety of viewpoints that have been expressed.

3. See Craig (1992, 223), citing Hu Yaobang, for an unusual Chinese perspective.

4. The Dalai Lama has articulated this in a number of forums, including a recent public audience with the Tibetans and Himalayan peoples in New York City (September 20, 2003, St. John the Divine Cathedral), as has the current Ganden Tripa and former presiding officer of the Tibetan Assembly of People's Deputies, Professor S. Rinpoche.

5. See Klieger (1992) for a discussion of the differences between Chinese and Tibetan historiography and the framing of reality.

6. See Katz (1983) for a discussion of the concept of academic neutrality in relation to the Tibet issue.

7. We are reminded of the inability of the United Nations to agree that what was occurring in Rwanda in 1994 constituted "genocide." To use the term would have meant that the UN would have had a moral imperative to take decisive action. The legalistic hair-splitting was painfully apparent in a press conference with a Clinton administration spokesperson who was unable to speak coherently in reply to a reporter's question about whether the administration considered the massacres in Rwanda as genocide (PBS 1999). More importantly, the massacre of some 800,000 people in a few month's time is an indictment of hyperlegalism and a moral travesty.

8. See Anand (2002) for an interesting discussion of the case of Tibet and postcolonial analysis in international relations.

9. See Kvaerne, "Tibet Images Among Researchers on Tibet" (2001), and McKay, "Truth, Perception, and Politics: The British Construction of an Image of Tibet" (2001), as well as other entries in the same volume (Dodin and Rather 2001).

10. Some excellent literature and commentary takes this premise as its starting point. See especially, for example, Lopez (1996) on the relationship of the appropriation and manipulation of concepts and ideas and the symbolic and literal erasure of the geographical reality of Tibet. See also Lopez (1998, 1994); Bishop (1993, 1989). See McGlagan's discussion of mass media and the link between images and legitimacy in politics (2002) and Anand (2000) on Tibetan identity and representation.

11. One telling example has to do with the politics of mapping. We recently installed a wall map mural in one of our classrooms at SUNY–Plattsburgh. Published under the direction of the Department of Defense, Defense Mapping Agency, and the U.S. Naval Oceanographic Office, by Environmental Graphics Inc. (2002), "The World" map makes no mention of the Tibet Autonomous Region at all.

12. I am not discounting this perspective; however, there are few who would disagree about the unprecedented rapid cultural change that is presently occurring within Tibet and in the exile Tibetan community, albeit for different reasons, and the peril this poses for the survival of cultural and linguistic communities.

13. It is important to note that Tibetans excluded themselves from participating in international politics to a large extent, and in retrospect they realize that this was a mistake (see Dalai Lama 1997 [1962]). When they attempted to rise and be counted, however, they were not. See Anand (2000) for a look at Western hegemony and its effects on the framing of the Tibet issue in international politics.

14. Goldstein is ambiguous about this period, suggesting that it lasted from 1913 until the death of the Thirteenth Dalai Lama in 1933, after which a Chinese delegation was

allowed into Tibet. But because China became preoccupied with the Japanese in the late 1930s and later World War II, the issue of Tibet's status was put on hold until the Communist invasion.

15. Klieger (1992) notes this as well.

16. Robert Barnett notes the ironic fact that states that had not previously asserted a one-China policy in explicit terms have done so on the insistence of China after it began receiving widespread criticism for human rights abuses. See Lehman (1998, 193–194).

17. U.S. CIA support of Tibetan rebels ceased at about that time as well.

18. Grunfeld (1996, 232–233) notes that the U.S. government's rejection of the Dalai Lama's "Five Point Peace Plan," introduced in 1987 was because no government recognized the exile government that had submitted the plan.

19. Jamyang Norbu subtly suggests this as an alternative for Tibetans at the end of his essay, "Moulting of the Peking Duck" (1989, 22–31). Goldstein also outlines this option (1997, 113–117).

20. When it is not political action, then at least it should be recognized that there are political consequences for defining a problem within the realist paradigm.

21. I suggest that not only is the realist framework paradigmatic (in the sense of Thomas Kuhn), but also hegemonic (in the Gramscian sense).

22. Falk (2000) outlines the trajectory of human rights and its political salience in his Introduction.

23. Resolution 1353 (XIV); Resolution 1723 (XVI); and Resolution 2079 (XX).

24. See also Lekhi (1975).

25. The events since the 1980s have been of particular interest to human rights scholars, representing a watershed in the evolution of human rights norms.

26. Goldstein (1997, 61–99) and Grunfeld (1996, 220–239) provide succinct accounts of this period of regionally specific Sino-Tibetan history. Donnelly (1998b, 115–120) provides a summary of events taking place in China during this period.

27. There is some discrepancy about when martial law was declared. Grunfeld says March 1988 (1996, 235); Goldstein (1997, 90–91) and Schwartz (1994) say 1989.

28. See and compare, for example, "Human Rights: A Western Construct with Limited Applicability" (Pollis and Schwab 1979), with "A New Universalism" (Pollis 2000).

29. See also Rapport's (1998) review of Wilson's edited volume, *Human Rights, Culture and Context* (1997).

30. Falk (2000) discusses some of the complexities of these cases in his Introduction. They are by no means unproblematic examples of the changing guidelines for international intervention. Also, for a critique of these developments and the attendant problems of world criminal courts and human rights interventions, see Rieff (2000).

31. See, for example, Li (2000) on the PRC reaction to challenges to the sovereignty principle. Also, for perspectives on sovereignty challenges in other contexts see: McCorquodale and Fairbrother (1999); Hawthorn (1999); Manasian (1998); Lauren (1998); Rosas (1995); Pease and Forsythe (1993); Walther (1999); Webber (2000).

32. National Security Adviser Henry Kissinger in 1976 publicly reprimanded the U.S. ambassador to Chile for using "quiet diplomacy" (see Donnelly 1998b, 100).

33. The case of the civil action brought against Shell Oil by the Ogoni people of Nigeria is an example. Protests in the West against the arrest and execution of Ogoni dissident Ken Saro Wiwa is an example of the human rights–based challenge to multinational corporations (in collaboration with a state government).

34. Not that the charge isn't warranted. I am referring to the structural element that these charges represent.

35. How the new campaigns against terrorism will impact this "infusion" is yet to be seen. There is some evidence to suggest that concerns about terrorism are replacing (and displacing) concerns about human rights, as the human rights scholar (and former president

of the Inter-American Commission on Human Rights) warned in 1981 (Farer 1981).

36. Barnett (2001) explores the reappropriation of these images by Tibetans. See also my doctoral dissertation (Mountcastle 1997a).

37. This is not to suggest that the domain of morality or the definition of human rights are unproblematic or uncontested.

38. These "normative logics" are: statist, hegemonial, naturalist, supranationalist, transnational, populist. Human rights occupies a specific place in each. As a basis of action, these "logics" are not mutually exclusive, although they may be contradictory at some levels, creating tensions in the global order (see Falk in Claude and Weston 1992, 31–41 for a condensed synopsis of his argument).

39. Here I do not address the competing discourses of the scholarly and the popular. Lopez (1998) examines the question of the production of knowledge about Tibet from this perspective.

References

Anand, Dibyesh. 2000. "(Re)Imagining Nationalism: Identity and Representation in Tibetan Diaspora in South Asia." *Contemporary South Asia* 9, no. 3: 270–287.

———. 2002. "A Story to Be Told: IR, Postcolonialism, and the Discourse of Tibetan (Trans)national Identity." In *Power in a Postcolonial World: Race, Gender and Class in IR*, ed. Geeta Chowdhry and Sheila Nair, 209–224. London and New York: Routledge.

An-Na'im, Abdullahi Ahmed, ed. 1992. *Human Rights in Cross-Cultural Perspectives: A Quest for Consensus*. Philadelphia: University of Pennsylvania Press.

Aronoff, Myron J. 1980. "Ideology and Interest: The Dialectics of Politics." In *Political Anthropology Yearbook I*, ed. Myron J. Aronoff, 1–29. New Brunswick, NJ: Transaction Books.

Barnett, Robert. 1998. "Essay." In *The Tibetans: A Struggle to Survive*, ed. Steve Lehman, pp. 178–196. New York: Umbrage.

———. 2001. "'Violated Specialness': Western Political Representations of Tibet." In *Imagining Tibet: Perceptions, Projections, and Fantasies*, ed. Thierry Dodin and Heinz Rather, 269–316. Boston: Wisdom Publications.

Bishop, Peter. 1989. *The Myth of Shangri-La*. London: Athlone Press.

———. 1993. *Dreams of Power*. London: Athlone Press.

Claude, Richard Pierre, and Burns H. Weston, eds. 1992. *Human Rights in the World Community: Issues and Action*. 2d ed. Philadelphia: University of Pennsylvania Press.

Craig, Mary. 1992. *Tears of Blood: A Cry for Tibet*. New Delhi: HarperCollins.

Dalai Lama. 1997 [1962]. *My Land and My People*. New York: Warner Books.

Dodin, Thierry, and Heinz Rather, eds. 2001. *Imagining Tibet: Perceptions, Projections, and Fantasies*. Boston: Wisdom Publications.

Donnelly, Jack. 1998a. "Human Rights: A New Standard of Civilization?" *International Affairs* 74, no. 1: 1–23.

———. 1998b. *International Human Rights*. Boulder, CO: Westview Press.

Environmental Graphics, Inc. 2002. "The World" World Map (mural). Hopkins, MN.

Falk, Richard A. 1992. "Theoretical Foundations of Human Rights." In *Human Rights in the World Community: Issues and Action*. 2d ed., ed. Claude and Weston, 31–41. Philadelphia: University of Pennsylvania Press.

———. 2000. *Human Rights Horizons: The Pursuit of Justice in a Globalized World*. New York: Routledge.

Farer, Tom J. 1981. "Introduction." *International Bill of Human Rights*, xiii–xxi. Glen Ellen, CA: Entwhistle Books.

Feigon, Lee. 1996. *Demystifying Tibet*. Chicago: Elephant Paperbacks.

Fiss, Owen, M. 1999. "Human Rights as Social Ideals." In *Human Rights in Political Transitions: Gettysburg to Bosnia*, ed. Carla Hesse and Robert Post, 76–111. New York: Zone Books.

FlorCruz, Jaime A., Mia Turner et al. 2000. "Tibetan Tragedy." *Time International* 156, no. 2 (July 17): 18ff.

French, Patrick. 2003. *Tibet, Tibet: A Personal History of a Lost Land.* New York: Knopf.

Geertz, Clifford. 1973. "Ideology as a Cultural System." In *Interpretation of Cultures*, ed. Clifford Geertz, 193–233. New York: Basic Books.

Goldstein, Melvyn. 1989. *A History of Modern Tibet: 1913–1951.* Berkeley: University of California Press.

———. 1994. "Change, Conflict and Continuity Among a Community of Nomadic Pastoralists: A Case Study from Western Tibet, 1950–1990." In *Resistance and Reform in Tibet*, ed. Robert Barnett and Shirin Akiner, 76–111. London: C. Hurst; Delhi: Motilal Banarsidass.

———. 1995. "China, Tibet and the United States: Reflections on the Tibet Question." Occasional Paper, The Atlantic Council of the United States.

———. 1997. *The Snow Lion and the Dragon.* Berkeley: University of California Press.

Grunfeld, A. Tom. 1987. *The Making of Modern Tibet.* Armonk, NY: M.E. Sharpe.

———. 1996. *The Making of Modern Tibet*, 2d ed. Armonk, NY: M.E. Sharpe.

———. 2000. "Reassessing Tibet Policy." *Foreign Policy in Focus* 5, no. 9 (April): 1.

Hawthorn, Geoffrey. 1999. "Pinochet: The Politics." *International Affairs* 75, no. 2 (April): 253–258.

Hurrell, Andrew. 1999. "Power, Principles and Prudence: Protecting Human Rights in a Deeply Divided World." In *Human Rights in Global Politics*, ed. Tim Dunne and Nicholas J. Wheeler, 277–302. Cambridge: Cambridge University Press.

Information Office of the State Council of the People's Republic of China. 1992. "Tibet—Its Ownership and Human Rights Situation." September, Beijing.

International Commission of Jurists. 1997. "Tibet: Human Rights and the Rule of Law." Geneva: International Court of Justice.

Katz, Nathan. 1983. "'Academic Neutrality' and Contemporary Tibetan Studies." *Tibet Journal* 8, no. 4 (Winter): 6–9.

Klieger, P. Christiaan. 1992. *Tibetan Nationalism: The Role of Patronage in the Accomplishment of a National Identity.* Berkeley: Folklore Institute.

Kvaerne, Per. 2001. "Tibet Images Among Researchers on Tibet." In *Imagining Tibet: Perceptions, Projections, and Fantasies*, ed. Thierry Dodin and Heinz Rather. Boston, MA: Wisdom Publications.

Lauren, Paul Gordon. 1998. *The Evolution of International Human Rights: Visions Seen.* Philadelphia: University of Pennsylvania Press.

Lazar, Edward, ed. 1994. *Tibet: The Issue Is Independence.* Berkeley: Parallax Press.

Lehman, Steve. 1998. *The Tibetans: A Struggle to Survive.* New York: Umbrage.

Lekhi, Pran Nath. 1975. "Human Rights of Tibetans in and Outside of Tibet." *Tibetan Review* 10, no. 1 (January): 20–27.

Li, Bin. 2000. "China's Security Environment in the Early 2000s." *Beijing Review* 43, no. 2 (January 10): 17–20.

Liu, Melinda, and Rusty Mahakian. 2001. "Trouble in Shangri La." *Newsweek International* (September 17): 28.

Lopez, Donald S. Jr. 1994. "New Age Orientalism: The Case of Tibet." *Tibetan Review* (May): 16–20.

———. 1996. "'Lamaism' and the Disappearance of Tibet." *Comparative Studies in Society and History* 8, no. 1: 3–26.

———. 1998. *Prisoners of Shangri-La.* Chicago: University of Chicago Press.

Manasian, David. 1998. "The World Is Watching: A Survey of Human Rights Law." *The Economist* 359, no. 8097.

McCorquodale, Robert, and Richard Fairbrother. 1999. "Globalization and Human Rights." *Human Rights Quarterly* 21, no. 3: 735–766.

McGlagan, Meg. 1996. "Mobilizing for Tibet: Transnational Politics and Diaspora Culture in the Post–Cold War Era." Ph.D. diss., Department of Anthropology, New York University.

———. 2002. "Spectacles of Difference: Cultural Activism and the Mass Mediation of Tibet." In *Media Worlds*, ed. Faye D. Ginsburg, Lila Abu-Lughod, and Brian Larkin, 90–111. Berkeley: University of California Press.

McKay, Alex. 2001. "'Truth,' Perception, and Politics: The British Construction of an Image of Tibet." In *Imagining Tibet: Perceptions, Projections, and Fantasies*, ed. Thierry Dodin and Heinz Rather. Boston, MA: Wisdom Publications.

Misra, Amalendu. 2000. "Tibet: In Search of a Resolution." *Central Asian Survey* 19, no. 1: 79–93.

Mountcastle, Amy. 1997a. "Tibetans in Exile: The Construction of Global Identities." Ph.D. diss., Rutgers University.

———. 1997b. "The Construction of a Tibetan Identity: Women's Practice and Global Process." *Inner Asia* 2, no. 1 (May): 128–142.

Mountcastle, Amy, and Ljubomir Tot. 2000. "Nongovernmental Projects 'Return and Trust Rebuilding—Pakrac' and 'The Bench We Share.'" In *Managing Multiethnic Local Communities in the Countries of the Former Yugoslavia*, ed. Nenad Dimitrijevic, 293–307. Budapest: Local Government and Public Service Reform Initiative, Open Society Institute.

Neilson, Brett. 2000. "Inside Shangri La/Outside Globalization: Remapping Orientalist Visions of Tibet." *Communal/Plural* 8, no. 1: 95–112.

Norbu, Dawa. 1992. "Imperialism and Inner Asia 1775–1907: How British India and Imperial China Redefined the Status of Tibet." In *Ethnicity and Politics in Central Asia*, ed. K. Warikoo and Dawa Norbu, 21–59. New Delhi: South Asian Publisher.

———. 2001. *China's Tibet Policy*. Richmond, Surrey: Curzon Press.

Norbu, Jamyang. 1989. "Moulting of the Peking Duck." In *Illusion and Reality*, ed. Jamyang Nosbur, 22–31. New Delhi: TYC Books.

———. 1994. "The Tibetan Resistance Movement and the Role of the CIA." In *Resistance and Reform in Tibet*, ed. Robert Barnett and Shirin Akiner, 186–196. Bloomington: Indiana University Press.

PBS. 1999. "The Triumph of Evil" (video). *Frontline*. See: www.pbs.org/wgbh/pages/front-line/shows/evil.

Pease, Kelly Kate, and David P. Forsythe. 1993. "Human Rights, Humanitarian Intervention, and World Politics." *Human Rights Quarterly* 15: 290–314.

Pollis, Adamantia. 2000. "A New Universalism." In *Human Rights: New Perspectives, New Realities*, ed. Adamantia Pollis and Peter Schwab, 9–30. Boulder, CO: Lynne Rienner.

Pollis, Adamantia, and Peter Schwab. 1979. "Human Rights: A Western Construct with Limited Applicability." In *Human Rights: Cultural and Ideological Perspectives*, ed. Pollis and Schwab, 1–18. New York: Praeger.

Rapport, Nigel. 1998. "The Potential of Human Rights in a Post-Cultural World." *Social Anthropology* 6, no. 3: 381–388.

Rieff, David. 2000. "A New Age of Imperialism?" In *Human Rights and Revolutions*, ed. Jeffrey N. Wasserstrom, Lynn Hunt, and Marilyn B. Young, 177–190. Lanham, MD: Rowman and Littlefield.

Risse, Thomas, Stephen C. Ropp, and Kathryn Sikkink. 1999. *The Power of Human Rights: International Norms and Domestic Change*. Cambridge: Cambridge University Press.

Rosas, Allan. 1995. "State Sovereignty and Human Rights: Towards a Global Constitutional Project." *Political Studies* 43 (Special Issue): 61–78.

Sautman, Barry. 2003. "'Cultural Genocide' and Tibet." *Texas International Law Journal* 38, no. 2: 173–246.

Sautman, Barry, and Irene Eng. 2001. "Tibet: Development for Whom?" *China Information* 15, no. 2: 20–75.

Schell, Orville. 1998. "Softening the Intractable: Tibet, China and Ethical Pressure." *Whole Earth* (Winter): 28.

———. 2000. *Virtual Tibet: Searching for Shangri-La from the Himalayas to Hollywood.* New York: Metropolitan Books.

Schwartz, Ronald D. 1994. *Circle of Protest: Political Ritual in the Tibetan Uprising.* New York: Columbia University Press.

Shakya, Tsering. 1999. *The Dragon in the Land of Snows: A History of Modern Tibet Since 1947.* London: Pimlico.

Smith Jr., Warren W. 1996. *Tibetan Nation: A History of Tibetan Nationalism and Sino-Tibetan Relations.* Boulder, CO: Westview.

Thonden, Yoden. 1994. "The Indigenous Route: A Path Not Yet Taken." In *Tibet: The Issue Is Independence*, ed. Edward Lazar, passim. Berkeley: Parallax Press.

Tibetan Review. 1977a. "Influential US Congressman Against Military Assistance to China." XII, no. 2, 3 (March): 4.

———. 1977b. "Hunger Strike Unto Death." XII, nos. 2, 3 (March): 7.

———. 1979. "China's Human Rights Record." XIV, no. 1 (January): 26–27.

———. 1983. " 'hinese Human Rights Abuses in Tibet, 1959–1982." XVIII, no. 1 (January): 4.

Van Ness, Peter. 1999. *Debating Human Rights: Critical Essays from the United States and Asia.* London and New York: Routledge.

van Walt van Praag, Michael C. 1987. *The Status of Tibet.* London: Wisdom.

Walther, Steven T. 1999. "The Globalization of the Rule of Law and Human Rights." *Futures* 31, nos. 9, 10: 993–1003.

Wan, Ming. 1998. "Chinese Opinion on Human Rights." *Orbis* 42, no. 3 (Summer): 361–377.

Webber, Frances. 2000. "Justice and the General: People vs. Pinochet." *Race & Class* 41, no. 4 (April–June): 43–57.

Weil, Robert. 1994. "Of Human Rights and Wrongs: China and the United States." *Monthly Review* 46 (July–August): 101–103.

Wilson, Richard, ed. 1997. *Human Rights, Culture and Context.* London and Chicago: Pluto Press.

5

Indirect Representation Versus a Democratic System

Relative Advantages for Resolving the Tibet Question

Wang Lixiong

Premise: The Highest Priority in Resolving Ethnic Problems Is to Avoid War

As China continues to develop, it is possible that ethnic problems will pose its foremost challenge. Members of ethnic minorities frequently remind Han nationality advocates of democracy that self-determination is their democratic right. When the People's Republic of China becomes a democratic nation, it will be time for minority peoples themselves to determine their political affiliations. Concerning the debate on independence versus unification, minority people emphasize respect and understanding; they argue against forcible inclusion in a Han-dominated state. However, can the problem be resolved by asking the Han to understand the desire for independence of the minority? If the Han, conversely, request that minority peoples understand their desire for unification and not to dismantle the territorial integrity of their nation, whose will should prevail?

In my opinion, understanding and respect cannot be the foundation for ethnic relationships. If a huge gap exists between two parties and one party receives understanding and respect, the other party may consider itself in the position of not having understanding and respect. Since people change, conditions will change and understanding will also change. I agree with the ideology of the global village, in which nations are not separate, and ideology is based on the harmony of human beings. The problem is, how many of the Han, out of a population of 1.3 billion, will agree with this point? Even in the future, with complete democracy, it is possible that most voters will want the government to fight against separatist minorities. Democracy does not imply resolution of the ethnic problems.

If a minority is strong enough to fight the Han, it may achieve independence. But this is unlikely in the PRC, where all fifty-five minorities together make up barely one-tenth the numbers of Han, and there is a great disparity between their economic and military power as well. Therefore, war is not a realistic choice for the minority.

The Dalai Lama's realization of the futility of war led him to abandon the idea of the autonomy of Tibet. Autonomy could be a means, but it is not the objective, which should be the peace and happiness of the people. Independence might not bring people happiness. Many nations have become self-governed in this century, but their people continue to starve and suffer. Rule by those of one's own ethnicity is not necessarily better than colonial rule.

People's happiness should first be built on avoiding warfare. People should not be asked to make sacrifices that cannot lead to victory. With this in mind, I subscribe to the ideal of China as a unified nation. The idea of unification has existed in China for thousands of years. The nineteenth century brought insults and humiliation to the Chinese. The Communist Party then championed the cause of nationalism and burned its flame for fifty years. Several generations have absorbed its message since birth. People with no other ties have only the symbol of "nation" as a commonality. It is the only symbol that can initiate the movement of the Han. "Unification" has thus become the baseline; it is believed that any kind of stimulation would result in chaos. Of course, while I believe most wars are irresponsible, they often originate from chaos. Should a democratic system emerge suddenly in China, the danger of war would be greater than ever.

I absolutely do not view the above-mentioned Han baseline and view of chaos as reasonable but, distasteful or not, this is the reality. It is just like a doctor with a giant patient; if you touch sensitive points on his body, the patient will react enormously. You can only see him as sick, but not scold him as unreasonable with anger. If you do not have the ability to stop him, he might actually hurt you. The wise approach is not to touch the sensitive points intentionally: at least wait until his illness is cured.

If you are not touching the Han baseline, can the freedom and happiness of other ethnicities be fulfilled? In fact, there is a wide area within that baseline. With China undergoing social transformation, it is time to build up a new social system and new ethnic relationships. In the past, "continuous revolution" caused the Han to own nothing at all: their ideology, religion, and traditional culture all disintegrated to a certain extent. The majority of Chinese still consider the mature democratic system of the West to be impractical. But, facing the problem of independence created by China's own history and reality, they see no suitable system and have no clear thoughts. The problems are enormous. A society with 1.3 billion people is unique in history. If we do not use this opportunity to build a society with ethnic equality and harmony, it may lead to warfare. Although strident statements on China's uniqueness are laudable, it does not solve the problem and does a disservice to its people.

In my view, the issue of unification versus independence is not the real problem. When the happiness of the people receives top priority, it is actually unimportant whether there is unification or independence. We should follow the approach that is more beneficial to the people, so, from the viewpoint of avoiding throwing people into disaster, what should be done right now is not to stand independent. This must be guaranteed with a system. Of course, this system must, at the same time, satisfy both sides. First it must entirely fulfill the freedom and autonomy of every ethnicity. Second, it must guarantee the unification of China. Neither of these can be ignored. The democratic system cannot do this.

Tibet as an Example: The Democratic System Sharpens Ethnic Conflicts

Even Britain, the oldest democracy, has ethnic problems. In the United States, which is seen as a model for democracy, the ethnic problem continues without end. In societies that democratize rapidly, ethnic breakups and conflicts follow. Democracy has, to a great extent, become a catalyst for the outbreak of ethnic problems.

To solve the ethnic problem in China, the "Middle Way" as proposed by the Dalai Lama, is relatively complete. Put simply, for Tibet the Middle Way involves staying in China and using a democratic system to ensure meaningful autonomy for the whole of Tibet, sometimes called Greater Tibet.[1] Therefore, whether the Middle Way can be achieved or not, remaining in China should be the first principle.

In the view of the Dalai Lama, a democratic system is the device for developing meaningful autonomy in Tibetan areas. But can a democratic system guarantee that Tibetans will wish to stay in the PRC, or is the promise no more than a ploy? For a problem of this magnitude, a promise will not suffice. What effect will a democratic system have on the Tibetan Question? If there are no guarantees, or if there are adverse effects, the Middle Way would lose its priority, not to mention its other aims. Therefore, we should first discuss the Dalai Lama's thoughts on a democratic system in the context of the problem of remaining in China.

In 1992, the Dalai Lama delivered a speech on Tibet's future political way and its constitution.[2] There were concrete comments and discussions on his thoughts about the democratic system, and a foundation was established for the discussion of the relationship between the democratic system and ethnic problems. The key ideas of the Dalai Lama on a democratic system included the election of representatives to the country's representative body, and giving them power to enact legislation and choose an executive committee and the chief executive.

It can be seen that the councilors and representatives have influential roles in this political design. In addition to their legislative powers, they elect the president and authorize the executive powers. This kind of arrangement obviously takes into account the fact of the wide dispersion in Tibet's population, its low education levels, and its lack of training in democracy. When compared to the format of other democratic systems, it is more suitable to the situation in Tibet. But can this format guarantee that Tibet will stay in China? This democratic society has disconnects between opinion leaders, the media, the public, councilors, and government. How will that affect Tibet in the future, and how will the elements of society affect each other?

Opinion Leaders

A democratic system is a competitive system of selection. Therefore, it encourages conflicts in the political culture. This is why the democratic system is superior to the autocratic system. However, we must also look at the negative aspect of these conflicts. Politicians who do not hold an official position, including thinkers, scholars, and authors, play an important part in influencing public opinion. They and political decision makers are part of the elite stratum, although opinion leaders have word power rather than political power. They are people of ideas but not actions. They approach problems by asking how they *should* be solved instead of how they *can* be solved. Since they need not deal with reality, they can hold high the flag of ethnic rights. Additionally, members of the elite who have no official position often covet political power, and feel that the best way to gain support for themselves is by emphasizing ethnic issues. Sudden democratization will mean that many elites compete among themselves for power. Hence, their incentive to attack the existing power elite is often very strong. Mature democracies still experience this kind of drama, and a society experiencing abrupt democratization will find it still more difficult to avoid pernicious competition. The relationship between Tibet and China will suffer from opinion leaders inciting the public's ethnic passions.

We cannot expect opinion leaders to speak for China at that time. When one goes from being restricted to being free, it is natural to release the hatred that has been built up for years. At the same time, a democratized society will unveil the wickedness of the autocratic rule, uncovering offenses that occurred over many years. These revelations will intensify hatreds still more.

The public can also influence opinion leaders in an inflammatory manner. In this case, if they wish to continue to be opinion leaders, they must chase after public opinion and even stay ahead of it. Especially for those elites who are not in official positions but would like to be, they must respond to public opinion.

The Media

A basic feature of democratization is freedom of speech and, more concretely, the dominance of the privately owned or unofficial media. Abrupt democratization will bring a vast array of media into existence. Those who hope to survive must compete intensely in order to attract the attention of the public. Only then will people pay money for their output and become loyal followers of their messages. Hence the competitors will exploit hot topics to stir up social passions. If Tibet should democratize abruptly, the hottest topic and most motivating material would be persecution by Han China, the tragedy of the Tibetan people, and the alleged secret agenda of the Han. This kind of incitement could quickly get out of hand, resulting in the promulgation of irresponsible exaggerations. Insisting on inspection would lengthen the publication cycle, increase costs, and in general worsen the position of the media. Even in the West, with its more mature liberated media, sensationalist small papers exist. The criteria for developing responsible media are lacking when a society democratizes abruptly.

The Public

In the period since the Cultural Revolution, there has been no organized people's movement in Tibet. This does not mean that Tibet can never have a people's movement again. Autocracy devastates, breaks up, and limits any power outside the political system. Society, as distinct from the autocratic government, is disunited. Lacking a medium for expression and release, people in this environment often feel lonely and helpless. Twisted psychologically and intensely depressed, they look for ways to overcome these feelings. Until a way appears, they often feign indifference. When, however, a possibility appears, they tend to behave in an explosive and extreme manner in order to compensate. At this moment, those who are used to being disunited are actually easier to stir up, since they have intense emotions but lack channels for buffering and restructuring. They communicate directly with the macro stratum, but do not have the ability to make judgments on macro affairs. Because their message and their ardor come from the media, they magnify its provocations. This will not be the voice of prudence.

Another feature of the public is that they like looking back. At least in theory, it is possible to understand and reach a consensus on events that have already happened, but the future is filled with uncertainties. There are many different opinions, creating an unfavorable climate for the public to affect the state of affairs. Even dwelling too much on the past will lead only to the continuation of the quarrels in history, thereby creating new conflicts and hatred. There have been so many disasters and agonies in Tibet that once there is possibility for release the explosive power is not difficult to imagine.

Apart from the ever stronger sense of nationalism, other opinions can hardly dare to be expressed in the media. Any attitude other than opposing China will be seen as weakness and cowardice. The media will become the amplifier of the people's voices. Prudent voices will not be tolerated. The public will only have one kind of judgment, and the entire Tibetan group will become extremist.

Representatives and Councilors

The above represents the likely situation in Tibet if it is abruptly democratized. This is the foundation on which the Dalai Lama depends in order to build up and control the political system. The key point of the social and political structure he envisions will be the election of councilors (representatives) by the public. The electors determine the councilors, so the councilors must satisfy the opinions of the electors. Therefore, the Dalai Lama's political design is first to empower the parliament under the restriction of the public's emotion.[3] His initial objective was to expect the parliament to buffer the irrationality of the public. A similar democracy in the West did fulfill this function. But the difference is that if there is no target to motivate Tibet's entire people, if there is no target to hate, and without a milieu that pushes the society toward extremity, the parliament may play the role of buffer. Even the existence of functioning parliaments in the West cannot always avoid public disturbances. In a suddenly democratized Tibet, these conditions would be extreme, and would furthermore lack the buffering quality that political parties and the profit motive provide in the West. Councilors will not be able to avoid following public opinion.

Not daring to betray the public is a kind of passivity. In the competitive system of democratic politics, councilors face competitors who want to displace them. Typically, the competitors will attack the real or perceived weaknesses of the councilors, forcing them to take more extreme positions. This strategy often succeeds quite easily. The public loves heroes and they like seeing feats and hearing grandiloquence. Facing such competition, the councilors have no choice but to run hard. On a running track, the one who runs in front will receive cheers and win the prize. Therefore, councilors will not be able to buffer the emotion of the public prudently. Instead, in order to stabilize their own positions, they have to run ahead of their competitors.

Even in a mature democratic society, councilors put considerable effort into showing off. A democratic political system breeds politicians who are good at performing in the media rather than trying to impress the public with their intellect and integrity. However, in a suddenly democratized society that lacks democratic training, voters are easily puzzled by the vows and promises of irresponsible politicians.

Meanwhile, the councilors sit and criticize: They do not have administrative responsibilities and are not, therefore, responsible for the outcomes of decisions. Therefore, their motivation for dealing with concrete matters is far less important than their motivation for moral matters. Autocratic societies are bureaucratized and the final decision of authority belongs to the regime instead of the councilors. However, under the Dalai Lama's political system, the parliament is responsible for enacting legislation, for the election of the top leader, and to empower the executive branch. It therefore has decisive authority, and there is no power that can oppose it. Under this system, therefore, the conflict between Tibet and China will have to continue.

Leaders and Government

According to the Dalai Lama's plan, the leader of Tibet will be elected by parliament rather than the public. He has arranged special authority for this leader, who can, for example, directly appoint some state councilors and must approve legislation that the parliament has passed. However, if the highest leader is elected by parliament, she or he need only please the parliament and cannot act as a check against its excesses. Although he is theoretically the chief leader, he must follow the parliament's will.

With regard to the relationship between Tibet and China, the extreme tendencies of the parties in this parliament compete, thus polarizing the debate. On foreign problems, the parties will show the same attitude, opposing enemies and showing their affection for the nation. This kind of behavior is uncommon in other countries.

Conversely, if the public elects the highest leader, it will be possible for him or her to contest the parliament. The Dalai Lama's plan will lead to the narrowing of the leader's political stance, meaning that there will be little flexibility. It is equivalent to hanging a sword above the chief leader's head. The Dalai Lama's proposed political structure does not effectively separate the administrative and discussion functions.

The tacit encouragement of extremism that is built into this system means that it is likely that the parliament will try to separate Tibet from China.

Can the Dalai Lama Guarantee that Tibet Will Stay in China?

The unique special characteristic of Tibet is the Dalai Lama himself. He has the power to lead Tibetans spiritually, though this power is far from democratic in nature. But can he guarantee that Tibet will stay in China? Tibetans generally believe that as long as the Dalai Lama lives, no one will dispute his ideas. However, the system he designed has, to a certain extent, weakened his political purpose. The Dalai Lama has stated that, after the introduction of democracy in Tibet, he will not take part in politics.[4] However, in a democratic Tibet, there would be no one except the Dalai Lama who could lead the parliament. Therefore, only if the Dalai Lama does not act as the political leader will the Tibetan government be led by its parliament. If the system allows the public to elect the chief leader, the Dalai Lama can use his influence: when he expresses his support for someone, the public will vote for that person. However, under his system, the public is to elect the councilors and representatives so that he will not be able to instruct the voters in every voting region whom to vote for. This, of course, should not be done, since it violates the principle of democracy. On the other hand, if the elected councilors and representatives vote for the chief leader, they are unlikely to follow the Dalai Lama as blindly as the common people. His political influence will therefore be limited.

Can Time Solve the Problem?

Chinese democrats in exile drafted a constitution of a United Chinese Federation,[5] partly because of the attention that the Tibet problem has received. Under this proposal, Tibet will be given the position of an autonomous state, with the high degree of autonomy demanded by the Dalai Lama. Two of the five entities currently designated as autonomous regions, Xinjiang and Inner Mongolia, would have to have their designation as autonomous states approved by two-thirds of the parliament.[6] Tibet alone would be allowed to decide on its identity of staying in China or becoming independent after twenty-five years.[7]

I believe that the drafters of the constitution wish to have Tibet stay in China. Since twenty-five years constitutes a generation, it may be sufficiently long that historical antagonisms will fade and persuade Tibetans to abandon the pursuit of independence. However, it can also be argued that, in historical terms, twenty-five years is just a snapshot, and will not be able to erase Sino-Tibetan hatred. As a case in point, the Cultural Revolution has been over for twenty-five years, but has certainly not been forgotten. World War II has been over for fifty-five years, but Jews have certainly not forgotten about it.

While old hatreds may fade, new conflicts will arise. For example, the problem of Greater Tibet—that is inclusion of ethnically Tibetan areas that the Beijing government excluded from the Tibet Autonomous Region it created—was avoided in the draft constitution. Tibetans cannot be expected to have the same attitude as the drafters. If in the future China is composed of linked states, will those areas originally given the designation autonomous, including the Zhuang and others, be willing to give up territory to the Tibetan state? Will the expanding Han population move into the Tibetan region? If so, their suppression of the Tibetans and sense of nationalism may create new problems. In a democratic society, even tiny conflicts can be twisted and amplified by the media, not to mention the presence of those people who intentionally motivate the ethnic group to which they belong. If the constitution of the United Chinese Federation is enacted in its current form, I believe that Tibetan leaders will wait out the twenty-five-year time period without abandoning their goal of independence, and that they will use the intervening quarter-century to motivate the public and prepare to establish a separate nation. They will be thankful to the people who drafted the constitution of the United Chinese Federation for assisting Tibet's independence without the need for violence. They are confident that, at the end of the twenty-five-year period, the majority of Tibetans will vote for independence. By that time, the Dalai Lama will have passed away, with his vows having followed him to another world.

Difference Between Scalar Addition and Vector Addition

I mentioned that wars must be avoided for the happiness of the people. Is there a contradiction between the Han people's strong desire to fight against those who would divide the state and the Tibetan people's fight for their independence? It may be argued that if warfare is truly the choice of both sides, and they are willing to pay the price of warfare in order to achieve an objective they consider higher, then it is not for other people to judge whether war is to be avoided or not. But in fact, the nationalistic feelings on both sides are not inherent but have been nurtured and motivated by their respective ethnic elites. Ordinary Han people do not care whether Tibet and China separate from each other or not: it is not related to their lives. Also, the average Tibetan does not care whether Tibet should be independent or not: the concept of sovereignty has no meaning to her or him. People of both sides want only to see that their families have a comfortable life. Seeking the vector addition of the will of thousands of people, there would not be warfare for independence.

However, things would be different if we carried out scalar addition. This addition is from the top down; it needs preparatory problems and measures, and also an expression and explanation for the results. Elites equate their own will with the will of their ethnic group. Elites have a stronger sense of nationalism and are more sensitive to the suppression of ethnic groups. It is widely recognized that there is a hierarchy in nationalism. But there is another reason for the nationalism of ethnic elites: their desire for authority. Most ethnic elites stick to unification; they oppose the independence and autonomy of the minority because they do not want to give up power. But minority elites also want independence and power. To them, independence will confer the greatest resource—new authority. Under the current international system, once Tibet becomes independent, it will receive equal status with other nations. Therefore, this option is extremely attractive to the ethnic elites.

Of course, these motivations are not spoken of publicly: elites always talk of opposition to disintegration and the pursuit of independence as being necessary for the well-being of the ethnic group. They also claim that they represent the will of the people. However, in a binary society, ethnicity is little more than a slogan. In reality, it indicates little more than the will of the ethnic elites. Ideas, principles, targets, determination—these will not be spontaneously generated in the public's mind, but are created and spread by minority elites. Even votes purporting to indicate the support of the majority do not truly represent the will of the people, because there are several sides of the problem:

1. A complete personal will represents the integration of multiple factors. When a person agrees with a single solution to a problem, this might reflect only one of these factors, and the agreement might be cancelled out if all factors are considered. For example, if the question is solely whether people are willing to become independent, they may say yes. However, if the question becomes whether in addition they are willing to have their families broken up and people die, they may not. One of the ways that ethnic elites mislead is that they ask people only the former question and then declare that response as the people's will. The latter question is either concealed or avoided.

2. The general public is inexperienced and finds it difficult to grasp macro affairs. They have inadequate channels for communication and therefore can only passively react to the opinion of the ethnic elites in terms of "yes" or "no" choices. Hence, what they appear to eagerly support is in fact no more than the will of the ethnic elites, who alone have the right to speak.

3. Absolutism can make use of national institutions and religious beliefs and behavior to influence the minds of the people. Democratic politicians can also make use of the mass media and trick their people. Hence, what people express may not be their own will, but is in reality a reflection of the deceit of their leaders.

4. Typically, there are inadequate channels through which those with different opinions can express themselves, since they are monitored and controlled by the elites. Some little people are able to express themselves privately, but most of those who disagree must keep their views to themselves. Hence, the minority who do express opinions are mistakenly believed to represent the whole.

In a binary society, most things cannot be done without authority and elites. Even in a democratic society that enjoys freedom to vote and to express one's opinion, there must be a certain degree of control by the elites, who therefore lead while the public must follow. The Han elites express their will of nationalism; there is no public acknowledgment of the fact that the Han common people do not care whether or not Tibet is a separate political entity. Similarly, Tibetan elites express their will of nationalism, and it cannot be seen that the Tibetan common people do not care about independence. Since the elites of the two ethnic groups oppose each other, it appears as though the Tibetan people and the Han people oppose each other.

Therefore, in a scalar society, the ethnic problem cannot be solved smoothly. Only in a vector society can people free themselves from elite guidance, giving expression to the will of the society and making decisions. And at that moment, the aversion to war and the pursuit of peace will become major trends, while the contest for authority will fade. An indirect representation system will become the structure of addition of vectors.[8]

An Indirect Representation System Reassures China

As previously mentioned, there are two prerequisites for solving China's ethnic problems. The first is to fully accomplish the freedom and autonomy of all ethnic groups. The second is to guarantee the unification of China. With respect to Tibet specifically, this amounts to what the Dalai Lama has termed a "double reassurance": "reassure the Chinese, reassure Tibetans . . . China does not have to worry about the separation of Tibet, Tibetans do not have to worry about the disappearance of temples in Tibet."[9]

Let us examine whether the indirect representation system can achieve this double reassurance. As discussed above, a democratic system cannot guarantee that Tibet will remain in China, and might actually push Tibet and China into conflict or even war. In recognition of this, the Chinese government rejects negotiation with the Dalai Lama, claiming that his proposals are "half-independence" or "independence in another way." Hence they believe that negotiation will be in vain. Even a democratic Chinese government would reject the Dalai

Lama's proposals. Only if his plan can be modified to ensure that the separation of Tibet from China is impossible will the government be sufficiently reassured that it will be willing to negotiate.

Lack of Independence Motivation in the Indirect Representation System

From the viewpoint of Tibetans, it is enough to have the Dalai Lama's promise to have Tibet stay in China. This is because the Dalai Lama is their divinity and it is unreasonable to doubt him. However, for politicians outside Tibet, this reason is not enough. Even if the Dalai Lama is trustworthy and reliable, he is not immortal. Given the level of mutual distrust between the two groups, it is plausible that each ethnic group would hurt the other ethnic group for its own benefit. Therefore, there should be safeguards against every unfavorable possibility and a system constructed that would not depend on a particular leader or leaders remaining in charge. Such a guarantee is more reliable than trust in creating harmonious ethnic relationships.

The system of indirect representation is such a system. It can guarantee that Tibet will not separate from China, and it will not stimulate the pursuit of independence. The origin of power in the indirect representative system is the bottom, not the top. Since the motivation for independence comes from above, from elites seeking to enhance their power, the indirect representative system will dampen such tendencies. Should independence come about, the common people will bear the risk and sacrifice it entails; they will also have additional expenses for defense and foreign affairs, which are now borne by the Beijing government. But they receive nothing in return. Ethnic leaders of the lower ranks will not attain glory through independence, since authority does not belong to them. The difference is that there will be one less rank in the hierarchy above them, but that will have no practical consequences in enhancing their status. Therefore, under the indirect representative system, lower-ranking officials will not be motivated to support higher-ranking leaders in their pursuit of independence, and the lower their rank, the lower their motivation. Under this system, since the higher rank is elected by the rank below it, the lower rank exercises at least partial control over significant events above it. Lacking support from the lower ranks, those in the higher ranks will have reduced incentive for independence and a lesser capacity for trying to bring it about.

A situation in which all the people, including the lower ranks, are willing to fight for independence will occur only when a region is strongly suppressed by a foreign ethnic group and the whole group of oppressed comes to the conclusion that death will be preferable to living without freedom. At that moment independence becomes a must. However, if the indirect representation system is in place, that situation will not occur. Since the organizational structure of the ethnic group is produced by indirect representation, foreign ethnic suppressors will not be elected.

Suppression can occur in only one way—through invasion and occupation. Given a state of occupation, the invaders cannot acknowledge the indirect representative system of the invaded ethnic group because they intend to build their own authority so as to suppress that ethnic group. Therefore, it can be said that if an indirect representation system exists, there will never be ethnic suppression.

In a suddenly democratized society, the motivation for independence also comes from the "effect of the public square," which results from the gap among opinion leaders acting on mass media, which acts on the public who make demands on their councilors and ultimately influence the government's decisions. However, in an indirect representation system, opinion leaders must try to lower the fury of the public. This is because the path for obtaining power has changed. In the past, leaders obtained votes by inciting the public; now they must return to reality. Counseling and administration must be unified, with counseling bearing the responsibility.

The reasoning of opinion leaders will directly influence the media because these leaders are the origin of the media's views. If opinion leaders display disparate opinions, this will be beneficial in producing a balance of views and so reduce the thrust of the media toward the public. In addition, the rationalization and diversification in viewpoints of the opinion leaders will bring more choices to the public and reduce the likelihood that they will instigate violence. In contrast, that would alleviate the market pressure faced by the opinion leaders and the media and create a positive recycling effect.

Most importantly, the indirect representative system will do away with the link of public → councilor, and the links remaining in the chain—opinion leader → media → public—will create a shared emotional vigor. Additionally, the elimination of the public → councilor link will remove it from the decision-making process. The public electing the councilors will mean that the public will constrain the councilors, who will have to cope with public opinion when they elect the top leaders and appoint the government. This increases restraint and applies it to the government. Indirect election is sensible and will restrict violent emotions; it will coach and condense electoral responsibility. There will be realization of the harm and potential danger brought about by independence. Therefore, the electorate will remain responsible and demand that their top leader be responsible as well. The top leader does not need to appeal to nationalist emotion, since the lower ranks will absorb the pressure for him. Therefore, he can act in the most beneficial way without worrying about his future at the polls. This is extremely important for a society's long-term well-being.

Indirect Representation and Greater Tibet

China remains anxious about another goal advocated by the Dalai Lama: unification of the whole area of Tibet. As mentioned above, Greater Tibet totals more than 2.4 million square miles; this constitutes one-fourth of China's total land area. The Chinese government intentionally divided ethnic Tibet into two sections, with one-half under the control of four contiguous provinces with large Han populations. Since this arrangement has been in place for over two centuries, it will be difficult to convince China to change it.

Given the existence of separatist feelings in Tibet, for the Beijing government to accede to demands for the creation of a Greater Tibetan administrative unit puts a much larger area at risk. A Greater Tibet would have greatly enhanced territory and its loss would double the land area taken from the PRC. Only if demands for independence cease will it be possible for China to yield to demands to unify all areas of Tibet. The introduction of the indirect representation system will reduce Tibetans' motivation for independence. The nature of autonomy is, to a substantial degree, to seek personal benefits and to prevent outsiders from gaining control of the area's resources. Therefore, the introduction of the system of indirect representation will not lead to the unification of Tibetan areas into a single body. On the contrary, Tibet will be divided into a number of self-governing bodies, each of them exercising a high degree of autonomy. Even if a Greater Tibet were to be created, this nature will not change.

Conversely, the integration of Tibetan-populated areas into a Greater Tibet should be beneficial to China. According to the 1990 census, Tibetans in the Tibet Autonomous Region comprise 96.46 percent of the TAR's total population. If autonomy is carried out alone in the absence of a Greater Tibet, that will create a single Tibetan self-governed body. In the contiguous areas of Sichuan, Qinghai, Gansu, and Yunnan, Tibetans account for only 57.93 percent of the total population. Should a Greater Tibet be created by merging the TAR with contiguous Tibetan areas, its Tibetan population would be 70.84 percent.[10] The increased ratio of Han to Tibetans in Greater Tibet would be beneficial to maintaining China's sovereignty in the area. The integration of different Tibetan areas would also avoid the problem of diverse treatment of Tibetans in different provinces, which has had disastrous consequences in the past. For example, in the 1950s, Tibetans in the area now known as the TAR did not have to carry out the so-called democratic reforms, whereas Tibetans who lived in other provinces did. Many of those who were dissatisfied with the reforms fled to Lhasa and surrounding areas, where they spread rumors and were instrumental in the 1959 revolt.

The establishment of a Greater Tibet with meaningful autonomy would have another advantage for the Chinese government: it would not have to worry about the Tibetan area. Tibetans themselves would have to deal with their problems and bear the responsibilities that are part of autonomy. Even if the Chinese government continued to provide assistance, it would receive a measure of gratitude for doing so.

Another factor to be considered is that Beijing is more likely to accept an indirect representation system. The Communist Party's single-party rule and the democratic system are recognized to be antithetical, so for the Communist Party to acquiesce in the institution of a democratic system would imply the failure of the Communist system. If democracy is institutionalized in Tibet, it is certain that the

Dalai Lama's side will be on stage and the Communist officials will be off. The two sides have contested for forty years and the Communist Party cannot accept such a consequence. The system of indirect representation avoids this win/lose format: it does not favor either side. Even currently exiled Tibetans who return to Tibet cannot be involved in sovereignty issues, since they are identified with the exile organization. Because the system of indirect representation is not affected by macro factors and is not controlled by the mass media, there will be no foundation on which to establish a political alliance. Those who want to be elected must face the reality that, in the new Tibet, formerly exiled persons and pro-Communists are completely equal.

Dare we hope that, if the Dalai Lama should change his demand for autonomy for Greater Tibet within a democratic system in China into autonomy for Greater Tibet within an indirect representative system in China, a dialogue between the Dalai Lama and Beijing government could be facilitated?

A System of Indirect Representation Will Make Tibet Better

The Advantages of Both Unification and Independence

I keep reminding people who insist that Tibet be independent of China that they should think not only about the advantages of independence, but also about the difficulties. If one day Tibet should become independent, after the joy of victory its people would have to face everything independently, starting with daily necessities like rice, oil, and salt. Tibet would also have to face the issues of frontier defense and immigration. The countries that surround Tibet include China, India, and Pakistan, which have among the highest population densities in the world. Inevitably, large numbers of people would seek to enter relatively sparsely populated Tibet. In order to protect its frontiers, Tibet would have to rely on a big country—either China or India. China would definitely not accept Tibet relinquishing its frontier defense to India: such an eventuality would only result in more serious conflicts. Tibet would thus become the battlefield for these two Asian giants, and the adverse effects would be greatest on Tibet itself. Hence, for Tibet to remain unified with China, with China continuing to be responsible for its frontier defense, is most beneficial to Tibet itself as well as to the avoidance of conflict.

In its fifty-year rule of Tibet, the PRC has nurtured a substantial modernized sector there whose continued existence is dependent on Chinese help. In 1997, the TAR had an income of $295,370,000 and expenditures of $3,819,520,000.[11] The deficit, which was twelve times the TAR's income, was paid by Beijing. If Tibet became independent, these subsidies would end, and with them, the modernization of Tibet. Some Tibetans hope that foreign countries will make up the shortfall. Although there might be support from abroad, it cannot be as reliable as that from China. There are Tibetans who believe that modernization is not necessary. But, one's personal views of modernization notwithstanding, a modernized sector already exists. In 1994, there were 160,000 employees of state-owned enterprises in the TAR, of whom 108,900 were Tibetans.[12] Even if we assume that these people alone constitute the modernized part of Tibet, would not adverse effects on these 15 percent of the population create shock waves in the larger society? They are the most energetic representatives of Tibetan society; if their problems are not solved, Tibetan society will be unstable.

Therefore, Tibet must stay within China based on its own need for safety and stability. And if the indirect representation system is carried out, many of the benefits of independence can come about without a formal declaration thereof.

Some people wonder, given the huge difference between the Tibetan population and that of the Han, whether the Tibetan people's will would be reduced to irrelevance by the Han under a China-wide system of indirect representation. Here, bear in mind that every province and autonomous entity will consider its own benefits first and foremost. If Tibet is one of thirty provinces in the PRC, although provinces with a Han majority will dominate, this does not mean that the Han will unite to oppose the Tibetans. If there are differences of opinion among them, they are likely to reflect differences in the benefits to their individual problems rather than differences in ethnicity. Some Han provinces might not agree with the opinions of the Tibetans, while others would. This could be beneficial to Tibet, which could engage itself as one of the provinces in China rather than in terms of a Tibetan versus Han dichotomy. The leadership under the system of indirect representation in the whole of China is composed of the leaders in the thirty provinces. They would form a committee to manage China,[13] carry out legislation, discuss administrative issues, establish the scope of political discourse, and elect the top leader for the nation. The top leader of Tibet will be one of thirty such leaders, giving him or her added authority. Even in Greater Tibet, the whole population is just 7 to 8 million (the 1990 census showed 6.4567 million),[14] but the authority of Tibet's top leader would be equal to that of provincial leaders in Henan and Shandong, which have populations of 100 million or more. This system will function much as do parliaments in Western democratic systems.

In terms of ethnicity problems, Tibet will not be isolated under an indirect representation system. There is the potential for alliance with Xinjiang, Inner Mongolia, Guangxi, Ningxia, and even Yunnan, where there are high concentrations of ethnic minorities. This kind of alliance could play a significant role in voting.

Finally, it should be noted that the process of decision making by committee involves protracted negotiations, mutual delayed compensation, and arrangements for how members are to be selected.[15] There will be long-term interactions among the actors, with everyone understanding that today's majority can become tomorrow's minority and today's concession can lead to tomorrow's quid pro quo. Therefore, decision making by committee is not characterized by suppression and autocracy, but by bargaining, compromise, and mutual adjustment. Particularly when the minority has a strongly assertive attitude, the majority will make concessions. Such a system will provide better protection for the rights of minority peoples.

Addressing the Alliance of Politics and Religion

Tibet has had a theocratic tradition for several hundred years. The current Dalai Lama, who is the fourteenth incarnation, exercises both temporal and spiritual power in Tibet's exile society. Even in the TAR, religion has a great impact on everyday issues. The spirit of democracy, however, involves individual decision making on multiple issues as well as multiple candidates for office. If the majority of people follow the command of one, or a small number, of living Buddhas, this is not a true democracy.

Some people believe that in a democratic Tibet, the majority of those elected will be lamas. This is indeed possible. Even if there are laws on the separation of politics and religion (as the Dalai Lama has promised), and clerics may not run for office, many common people will follow the Dalai Lama's advice when they vote. Laws cannot control people's minds, and if the mind of the average person is controlled by religion, religion will intrude into politics through other channels.

Religious faith is, of course, a personal choice. But ceding political judgment and the right to govern society to clerics is already an extension of the divine into the secular sphere. Although religion exists in Western democratic societies, it plays a very minor role in their citizens' political lives—far less than is the case in Tibet. Therefore, establishing a democratic system in Tibet will not guarantee that democratic objectives are achieved. If, unfortunately, decision making is under the control of an absolute ruler or small group of rulers, this will subvert the spirit of democracy. By analogy, the Cultural Revolution in China was also a great democracy under the will of Mao.

I do not oppose religion, but I believe that it is necessary to consider how to sustain the significant position of religion in Tibet while at the same time preventing its intrusion into politics—as the Dalai Lama himself has stressed. The system of indirect representation can accomplish this. Under it, religion cannot provide specific instructions for politics, but can serve only as an ethical background for making choices. For example, when ordinary people elect councilors, they might not understand whom they should vote for and might refer to the instructions given by the living Buddha. However, they will have sufficient understanding to elect their own village leaders. Elections will be based on the people's perceptions of benefits to the voters, and religion will play a decisive role in their choices. At higher levels in the electoral hierarchy, voters will use the political body rather than religion as the starting point for consideration. Hence, the people in power will not have to worry about the attitudes of the clergy.

The system of indirect representation would serve two directional functions. First, it would group heretofore disunited people together and, second, it would separate the sacred from the secular. These two functions are important. Only the system of indirect representation can exclude religion from politics without doing harm to religion itself. This system will not have to bear the consequences of challenging religion, and therefore will help avoid conflicts and pressures for separatism. This is important for Tibetans in terms of facilitating modernization without confronting their religious faith.

The System of Indirect Representation Is Most Suitable for Elections in Tibet

The United States has two centuries of experience with elections, and its people begin their education in the electoral process very early in life. Even so, problems remain: a survey conducted during the 2000 presidential campaign showed that 40 percent of the voters confused Bush and Gore. In the state of Florida, one county used a so-called butterfly ballot that some voters found so confusing that they inadvertently voted for the wrong candidate. Actually, there were arrows clearly instructing the voters, but mistakes occurred nevertheless. The chaos that would occur in a Tibetan election is scarcely imaginable.

A local-level official in Tibet told me of his experience in an election of an agricultural organization that was only electing representatives: Although he spent three days in the village, the common people still did not understand how to put a tick on the ballot. Most of their votes were redundant. If Tibet should adopt Western-style democracy, it is possible that half or more of the ballots would be spoiled. The consequences could be even more serious than the 2000 Florida election. The majority of the people are agricultural and nomadic, and they tend to be illiterate and/or lacking in political experience. Hence, there are serious concerns about how well they would respond to Western-style democracy.

Another serious problem in Tibet relates to the region's large size and the fact that its population is dispersed over a wide area. This would cause difficulties for political participation in a regionwide election. The common people do not know for whom they should vote and would therefore be indifferent to the election; they would not be motivated to travel long distances to vote, either. Even in the United States, where most adults own cars, as many as half of those eligible to vote do not do so. In some elections, nonvoters may be larger in number than either the Democratic or Republican voters. This phenomenon is apt to be even more prevalent in Tibet. If only a small proportion of the population votes and votes are cast by those who have little knowledge of the issues involved, democracy becomes meaningless.

In a system of indirect representation, peasants dispersed across a wide area need elect only the village leaders, reducing the time they must travel to vote as well as the complications of not knowing the individuals for whom they are voting. Illiteracy and lack of training in democracy also matter less. All voters are on roughly comparable levels. Those contending for office do not need television and newspapers for communication; they can communicate with the peasants directly. The voters are unlikely to be confused by tricky wordings and empty promises because they know the candidates personally. They will understand the background of each of the candidates and have a clear idea of whom they choose. If basic-level elections can be concluded successfully, upper-level elections will follow. This will guarantee motivation and have positive effects for future elections.

Indirect Representation Will Prevent the Disintegration of Tibetan Society

The autonomy created in Tibet by a democratic system would not be true autonomy, but rather a form of self-management against the Chinese government. The Chinese government itself is still ruled by elites. Tibetan autonomy and democracy is just a change from the Han elite's rule over Tibetans to the Tibetan elite's rule over Tibetans. Since this is simply exchanging one such elitist structure for another, it is not appropriate for Tibet. One small group will continue to decide everything. Further, if a society bifurcates into two opposing parties, no matter which one wins, the other party will be ruled, and this opens up the potential for conflict between them. Even though democracy is theoretically more tolerant than absolutism, the basic expression of people's will—voting—implies by nature winner-take-all: if one belongs to a minority, one's own vote is irrelevant. In mature democratic societies, there are protective measures for the minorities. However, in a suddenly democratized society, absolutism tends to become dominant, suppressing and even harming minorities. If those minorities constitute a substantial proportion of the population and their power is relatively large, they may choose to oppose or condemn the ruling organization, thus bringing about disintegration and instability in the society.

China's half-century intrusive presence in Tibet brought a lot of structural changes to the society and created numerous problems. Tibet has to deal with these, however averse it may be to do so. When Tibet is ruled by China, it is easy for Tibetans to unite against the foreign presence. However, if Tibetans rule themselves, internal rifts will quickly become apparent. One of the first problems will be how to deal with those who held positions of power under Communist Party rule. Another will be the disposition of the state-owned enterprises, which are currently heavily subsidized by Beijing because of their unprofitable nature. Should the new Tibetan government continue to subsidize them? If yes, can it afford to do so? If not, workers at the enterprises, who are used to being fed by the government and will be suddenly forced to fend for themselves, will soon be yearning for the Communist Party. Eastern Europe has already shown us such a phenomenon. If the people's needs are not met, they will hate their new ruler, Tibetan or not, even if he is the Dalai Lama. There are numerous other problems, just as Mao Zedong found when he tried to reform the peasants. Tibetans, no matter who rules them, will encounter problems. This cannot be overlooked.

The transformation from pseudo-autonomy to actual autonomy may provide a solution. Actual autonomy is the kind of "full-scale autonomy" that will be brought about by the system of indirect representation. If this autonomy is realized, there will not be a ruling organization from bottom to top or one side that is able to suppress the other. Hence, each side can maintain a tolerant and peaceful mind. At the same time, this kind of autonomy will allow each side to form groups within itself. Exiled Tibetans, for example, can have their own bodies, as can those Tibetans who are Communist officials. Each body can function according to its principles, maintain its culture, and protect its members. The principle of interaction among the autonomous bodies is decided by the top level under the system of indirect representation. This top level is characterized by common sense and is good at reaching compromises. By the time the transition to the new system takes place, the root causes of disintegration and feelings of differentness will also have faded away and society will be ready for integration.

Apart from that, this kind of "full-cell autonomy" has another advantage: every level of the autonomous body can deal with its own internal contradictions. Since autonomy refers to the "import and export" relationship between the autonomous body and the outside, its internal processes are decided within itself, making the autonomous unit responsible for the consequences of its own behavior as well as unable to avoid its responsibilities. Under pseudo autonomy, authority runs from top to bottom. Since everything is under the ruler's control, he must therefore bear all the responsibility. Those who are being ruled will express their discontent to the ruler. For a democratic ruler in particular, since his or her power is circumscribed, he or she must endure criticism from all sides in the society. It is difficult to lead, and leadership has many potential hazards.

In the system of indirect representation, every autonomous level from the lowest to highest has a self-management committee. Big issues are decided together, directions are set by it, the leader is elected by everyone, and the work is done by all the people. Therefore, people cannot blame others. What they can do is to improve the management body itself, or change the leaders they have selected. Even in state-owned enterprises, if allowed to manage themselves through the system of indirect representation, the staff will stay with the enterprise to help transform it rather than lose their jobs. This is a fair system and one that is conducive to the self-transformation of the enterprise. It is certainly an improvement over management by, and assistance from, the government. Of course, this is an extremely complicated matter that requires detailed and specific planning.

The system of indirect representation can bring despair to the winning elites in the competition for power, since no person or organization will be the winner no matter how they struggled in the past. For example, the Tibetan Government in Exile has been campaigning for Tibet's freedom for forty years. If Tibet obtains its freedom and a democratic system, they will undoubtedly claim sovereignty as the just reward for their prolonged struggles. However, if Tibet's freedom is obtained through an indirect system of representation, the exile government can return to Tibet only as ordinary citizens, with no special leadership roles despite their prolonged struggles. Those who aspire to political leadership must start at the bottom.

All the benefits will belong to the citizens, and the people will have everything. From the past until the present, there have been innumerable offenses that originated from the desire for authority. If the elimination of offenses can start with abolishing authority, then we should not feel regretful about doing it. This is something to be proud of; it is glorious.

Notes

1. What is regarded as the Tibet Autonomous Region (TAR) by the Chinese government includes an area of 1,228,400 square kilometers and, in 1994, a population of 2,300,430, of whom 2,235,900 are Tibetans. However, Greater Tibet also includes most of Qinghai province, southern Gansu, western Sichuan, and northeastern Yunnan. This is approximately twice the size of the TAR and had a Tibetan population of 4,573,800 in 1990. More than 2 million Han and other ethnic groups live within the borders of Greater Tibet.

2. At that time, the June 4th disturbances were not yet settled, and the content of the "Middle Road" referred to by the Dalai Lama is still unclear, so there were voices of independence, including "China must return freedom to Tibet," "China should retreat from Tibet," and "Tibet will become an internationally neutral nation forever." However, such slogans are standard propaganda. Our focus is on producing a design for democratization in Tibet.

3. The Dalai Lama, "Tibet's Future Political Way and Constitutional Elites," document published by the Tibetan Government in Exile, May 1993, 19–20.

4. Ibid., 15.

5. Yan Jiaqi, a political scholar, and Yang Jianli, chair of the Twenty-first Century China Provident Fund Committee, were the major initiators of these proposals.

6. "The Constitution of a United Chinese Federation (draft proposal)," no. 36.

7. "The Constitution of a United Chinese Federation (draft proposal)," no. 39.

8. A simple description of the system of indirect representation is that those holding political power at any given level are elected by those in the level immediately below them. Specific details can be found in "The Indirect System of Representation: Principles and Methods," *Chinese Social Science Quarterly* (Fall 2000); see also *Dissolving Power: The System of Indirect Representation* (Hong Kong: Mingjing Publishing Company, 1998).

9. Lin Zhaozhen, "Independence Is Far Away, Exiled Tibetans Fervently Desire to Return Home," *Chung-kuo Jih-pao* (China Daily, Taipei), November 9, 1998.

10. *Tibetan Population in Modern China* (Beijing: Chinese Studies of Tibet Publishing Company, 1992).

11. *Annual Statistics of Tibet, 1998* (Beijing: Chinese Statistical Publishing Company, 1999), 99.

12. *Annual Statistics of Tibet, 1995* (Beijing: Chinese Statistical Publishing Company, 1996), 56.

13. Committee here is defined according to the following features: (1) an interactive face-to-face organization; (2) a systematic organization that exists for a long time; (3) a decisive organization that faces a series of problems. See Joe Stanley, *Democracy Theory* (Hong Kong: Oriental Publishing Company, 1993), 231–232.

14. Yu Zheng, *The Modernization of Tibet* (Beijing: Nationalities University Publishing Company, 1999), 38.

15. Specific comments on this statement can be found in Stanley, *Democracy Theory*, 231–235.

PART II

Economic Development

6

Economic Development in Tibet Under the People's Republic of China

June Teufel Dreyer

Today, on the "roof of the world," home appliances such as TV sets, telephones, and refrigerators are as commonplace as they are in the developed eastern parts of China. . . . Since [1994], the average annual growth rate of Tibet's gross domestic product has reached 12.9 percent, higher than the national average. . . . In the past, most Tibetan farmers and herdsmen wore one woolen robe all year round, having no other clothes to change into . . . but today, young Tibetans not only have enough clothes to wear, they also want to follow the latest fashions, even in the farming and pastoral areas. . . . [They] did not have any choice for food and had to rely on beef and mutton, and farmers lived on a simple diet of potatoes and radishes in winter. But nowadays, more and more Tibetans can afford to buy seafood air-freighted from inland provinces. And greenhouse vegetables and fruits are now common sights on Tibetans' dinner tables.

—Xinhua, March 2002

The above quote[1] is typical of official descriptions of life in contemporary Tibet, thanking the Chinese Communist Party (CCP) and government of the People's Republic of China (PRC) for the prosperity they have brought to the region. In other venues, however, neither party nor government would deny that accomplishments have fallen far short of aspirations. Although the Chinese name for Tibet, Xizang, means "western storehouse," it is by far the poorest area under the jurisdiction of the PRC. Even a cursory glance at the *Statistical Yearbook of China* will confirm that the Tibet Autonomous Region (TAR) ranks last on virtually every indicator: total revenue, taxes remitted, per capita income, joint ventures, literacy, and even life expectancy at birth. Notwithstanding Tibet's daunting climate, which includes extreme cold and wind as well as aridity and thin air, the region does not lack natural resources. The gold-bearing sands of cultural Tibet have been renowned for centuries. Less well known are the area's other rare metals, including lithium, lead, antimony, and, it is rumored, uranium. There are also coal deposits and an abundance of salt. Additionally, the region has received generous subsidies from the central government, exceeding those given to any other province or autonomous region.

Difficult to approach geographically because of its location in the Himalayas, Tibet's unique culture and seeming isolation have given it an aura of romantic mystery and spiritual enlightenment that lured a number of hardy adventurers from the West. In fact, though detached from the rest of the world in many ways, pre-1949 Tibet had a thriving export trade in wool—its principal export—and salt. Tea was imported from China, and other goods from India and Nepal. Exiles remember this as a golden age, when granaries were stocked against lean years and Tibetans ruled their own land.

Phase I: "One Country, Two Systems," 1951–1958

The arrival of the People's Liberation Army (PLA) in October 1950 was traumatic in many ways, particularly in the capital of Lhasa and other large cities, but did not initially have a major impact on traditional economic patterns. According to the agreement signed between the "local" government of Tibet and the People's Republic of China in 1951, the area would retain internal autonomy. The Beijing government promised to improve the people's livelihood, though it did not specify how this was to be done, and also promised that it would not use compulsion to implement reforms.[2] Cultural Tibet was divided among Sichuan, Yunnan, Qinghai, and the Tibet Autonomous Region. Technically, the last did not attain the formal status of an autonomous region until 1965. Roads were built so as to ease the integration of Tibetan areas with Han China. While potentially of great value to the economies of these areas, the construction process caused a disruptive inflation. Soldiers who were building the roads needed local supplies, thereby bidding up prices and leading to shortages of many commodities. The indigenous population had been informed that the Chinese Communist Party had graciously liberated them from the practice of corvée labor, known as *ula*, from their feudal lords. Not surprisingly, they sometimes failed to see the difference between the *ula* imposed by feudal lords and the road construction and maintenance duties exacted by the party. Moreover, the economic advantages conferred by the roads had to be weighed against the possibility that they represented the entering wedge of Han Chinese dominance: armies and immigrants could move across them as easily as trade caravans.

Economic data were released only rarely from the period 1950–1959; those figures that exist must often be calculated backward from numbers released later—

that is, "grain production in 1982 was more than three times the 1952 figure."[3] It is likely that the central government had only the vaguest idea of what production figures were in this period, and that comparisons with later years are really guesstimates, at least some of which were designed to enhance the gains later-day officials claimed had been made under their administration. Production for Tibetan areas outside the TAR was included in the data of provinces to which they now belonged.

Phase II: Democratic Reforms, 1959–1969

The failure of a rebellion against Chinese rule in March 1959 began the second stage of economic development under the PRC. The uprising caused an estimated 80,000 Tibetans, out of a total population of little more than a million, to flee with their spiritual and temporal leader, the Dalai Lama, to India. This exodus, plus the mopping-up operation by the PLA, must have adversely affected production, although this cannot be confirmed, since no statistics were released for the period. The Chinese government declared that, since the local government of Tibet had broken the 1951 agreement, Beijing was no longer obliged to postpone reforms. It proceeded to enact them. According to official sources, the institution of what it described as democratic reforms led to huge increases in the production of virtually all goods. The exact amounts were not specified—a typical statement was, for example, "in 1961, there was a big increase over 1960, despite natural disasters."[4] China as a whole was at that time suffering from a major famine brought on by the misguided policies of the Great Leap Forward. It was later admitted that party and government did not in fact know what the production figures for Han China were. Hence, it is unlikely that the figures for Tibet are any more reliable. The Tibetan economy after democratic reforms, as before, rested on animal husbandry and agriculture.

Phase III: The Communes, 1970–1980

A third phase in Tibet's post-liberation economic development began with the institution of communes. As in many other sectors of development, this happened later in the TAR than in other areas of the PRC, where they were introduced in 1958. A 1965 source alluded to communes in unspecified "selected places" in the TAR;[5] the party Central Committee's newspaper, *Renmin Ribao*, stated that experimental communes began to be introduced in the Lhasa area in 1965. Resistance from Liu Shaoqi and other recently discredited leaders was blamed for the long delay.[6] Not until 1970, however, were communes formed in Tibet in any numbers. The official Xinhua news agency announced that a total of 666 communes had been established in 34 percent of the TAR's townships in that year,[7] and that communes existed in 70 percent of townships in 1973.[8] By 1974, 90 percent of townships were reported to have communes,[9] a figure that rose to 93 percent in 1975.[10]

No details of their organization were provided. It is likely that the TAR's communes took a form very different from those in the rest of China, where the great age of commune-founding was 1958. The communes of 1958 confiscated all private property, including livestock and even wristwatches and cooking pots, and featured large dormitories and even larger communal dining facilities. These would have been impossible arrangements for the TAR's many nomadic herders. Tent-dwellers, they live at great distances from one another in order to pasture herds. Moreover, the economic disaster that followed the establishment of the 1958 communes led to many of their more objectionable features being eliminated. The fact that communes were established at all in the TAR, long after their deficiencies were well known, seems to indicate that there was considerable influence from ideological radicals. A mid-1970s description of a "model commune" in the TAR speaks of a two-level organization—commune and production team—rather than the three-tier structure—commune, brigade, and production team—of the communes founded elsewhere in China during the late 1950s.[11] Another source disclosed that agricultural taxes in Tibet were collected on an individual rather than a collective basis.[12] Consonant with the area's sparse population, fewer people were contained in each commune.

The formation of communes was accompanied by large-scale efforts at crop diversification. In 1973, 1974, and 1975, successive delegations of scientists from China's most prestigious research institutes investigated the area's climate and terrain to ascertain, among other things, what sorts of crops and animals could survive at high altitudes. Their findings were introduced experimentally on selected communes under the assumption that, if successful, the reforms would be extended elsewhere in Tibet. Hog raising was one of these innovations, in contrast to the sheep and yaks that had been the area's traditional staples. In the first half of 1976, 290,000 hogs were raised, or 5.2 times the number in 1959 and 2.5 times that of 1965.

The cultivation of winter wheat was also heavily promoted, whereas the staple food of the area had been barley. Also frequently mentioned was a wide variety of fruits and vegetables, including tomatoes, peppers, apples, peaches, and pears. Though it was claimed that the success of these crops was due to the Han Chinese bringing the benefits of advanced science to grateful Tibetans, Charles Bell, writing in the 1920s, noted that all of these were cultivated on a small scale—mainly for resident Chinese, since most Tibetans did not care for pork or vegetables.[13] The cultivation of wheat was a particular irritant, since local people preferred barley and felt that, in addition to being ruled by the Han, they were now being forced to raise food for them.

Production figures for livestock and wheat reportedly increased by large amounts. However, by the end of the decade there was ecological disaster and widespread hunger. Emergency price controls were put into effect.[14] Airplanes were sent to evacuate Han Chinese administrators who were deemed nonessential.[15] Two separate groups of Western scientists who visited reported seeing barely a plant or animal in their travels.[16] Wheat cultivation, which according to official figures had increased by an average annual rate of 18.1 percent from 1972 to 1975, dropped precipitously. The 1979 harvest was a disaster.[17] Intensive cultivation techniques and inappropriate choice of fields had exhausted the soil. With virtually no grain at all for a period, residents killed animals to keep from starvation, reducing the total number thereof. Lhasa Radio referred to "economic dislocation," with numbers of livestock allowed to increase beyond the capacity of grassland to provide food for them.[18] Refugees blamed the Chinese military for another component of the ecological tragedy: soldiers had killed thousands of animals for amusement, for their hides—which were subsequently sold, with the proceeds going to the units involved—and for target practice. This behavior reminded Westerners uncomfortably of their own ancestors, who slaughtered buffalo for similar reasons. The PLA had also denuded forests for fuel and to manufacture and sell furniture for the profit of its members.

Phase IV: Hu Yaobang's Reforms, 1980–1987

A fourth stage of economic development began in 1980, when a central government delegation led by then–party head Hu Yaobang visited Tibet. Hu was, by all accounts, appalled by what he saw. A high-level work meeting on Tibet was called to decide how to cope with the difficulties there. The TAR's communes were ordered disbanded, as was happening elsewhere in China as well. The disaster was blamed on the leftist influence of Lin Biao and the Gang of Four. There was no explanation of why the misguided policies had outlived their perpetrators: Lin had died in 1971, and the Gang of Four had been in prison since 1976. One can hypothesize that bureaucrats who had been appointed while leftist influence permeated the top levels of government continued to implement leftist policies at this outpost of empire even after their mentors had been removed. A new first party secretary, Yin Fatang, was installed, presumably to indicate a break with these leftist influences. According to his biographical sketch, Yin had worked in the TAR for many years and, in contrast to many Han administrators, spoke Tibetan.[19] What it did not mention was that, like many long-term Han administrators in Tibet at the time, Yin was a military officer.

Party and government pledged to make amends through a policy of rest and rehabilitation. In order to lessen the masses' burden, agricultural, pastoral, industrial, and commercial taxes would be remitted "for a few years." Animals were returned to private ownership, and farmers freed to return to barley cultivation. Hog raising disappeared from mention. The practice of producing farm, animal, and sideline products under unified plans or through assignment was officially rescinded, as were all forms of apportionment. The state would subsidize agriculture and animal husbandry, and satisfy "the urgent needs of the Tibetan people in their daily living."

In this difficult situation, regional and local governments were to be flexible in their policies and respect the right of production teams, work groups, and individuals to make their own decisions on production. Collectives and individuals were to be encouraged to engage in sideline and handicraft endeavors, to hold rural trade fairs, and to trade across borders. At celebrations held in May 1981 to commemorate the thirtieth anniversary of the agreement between the Lhasa government and Beijing, the mood was upbeat. A major speech by the chief Tibetan representative at the signing of the 1951 compact set the goal of ending poverty in the TAR within the next two to three years, topping the region's highest known living standards within the next five to six years, and "bring[ing] about massive development in Xizang's economy within ten years."[20]

A *New York Times* reporter who visited the TAR in 1983 reported that the population was beginning to emerge from the brink of starvation; 37,800 acres of land had been taken out of winter wheat and returned to grazing or barley cultivation. Lhasa's Han population, which had been 50 percent, or 60,000 people, was now only 30 percent, or 36,000. However, Beijing was already rethinking this policy in light of concerns about stability should too many Han leave.[21]

The optimistic predictions of 1981 notwithstanding, poverty had not ended after two to three years. This is clear from the records of a second high-level conference on work in Tibet that was held in 1984. Three hundred cadres were summoned from Tibet to Beijing, and Hu Yaobang himself officiated at the sessions. Delegates were informed that, despite the reforms, economic indicators had dropped. Additional reforms were announced. The exemption from taxes was extended; workers were to be brought in from outside the TAR to help develop its industries, and tourism would be encouraged. Although the reforms introduced by the 1984 conference were later credited with beginning a sharp increase in living standards,[22] this was not immediately obvious in the years following. In 1986, regional First Party Secretary Yin Fatang revealed that cadres had to grow their own vegetables and acknowledged the irony that, in a pastoral area, there were shortages of milk and other dairy products.[23] Others complained that, while taxes had theoretically been abolished, they reappeared in the guise of government charges for services rendered to the populace. In order to encourage Han to come to Tibet to contribute their skills to its development, the government paid them salary supplements. This created a two-tier wage scale that disadvantaged local people, creating jealousy. Tibetans also complained that Han received preferential treatment in hiring and promotions. The official media spoke of problems of internal order in factories and offices, adding that these problems frequently had important consequences that included serious harm to both the disputants and production.[24]

Yin Fatang was replaced as first party secretary by Wu Jinghua, a member of the Yi minority from neighboring Sichuan province. How this choice was made is a mystery. Tibetan leaders construed the appointment of someone of another minority—and, moreover, a minority group viewed as being exceptionally backward—as a denigration of their own capabilities. Another important constituency, the PLA, was annoyed because Wu had no military background. Despite this inauspicious start, Wu did a number of things that endeared him to at least some Tibetans: returning streets in Lhasa to their original Tibetan names, appearing at religious ceremonies, and making donations to monks. Still, he never acquired a power base. Wu did not long survive the ouster in 1987 of Hu Yaobang, under whose tenure he had been appointed. And problems, though scarcely of Wu's making, continued to accumulate. He was replaced by Hu Jintao, beginning a bright career that would culminate in the latter's appointment as party general secretary and president of all of China.

In an exceptionally frank article published in 1985 in a Shanghai newspaper that was later closed for being too outspoken, an unnamed commentator argued that the reported increases in the TAR's total industrial and agricultural output were entirely attributable to state subsidies. Over the previous thirty years, total industrial and agricultural output value increased fourfold, while state subsidies increased by 65 times. An increase of one yuan in output value required an increase of 1.21 yuan in state subsidies—that is, Tibet had a *negative* multiplier effect on investment. The average annual increase in output value was 5.45 percent, while the average annual increase in state subsidies was nearly 15 percent. For the TAR to double its total industrial and agricultural output value in fourteen years, using the output value of 1981 as a base, the central government would have to provide subsidies of 4.5 billion yuan. Quadrupling the region's output value in twenty-seven years would necessitate state subsidies of 27.5 billion yuan.[25] This was an unthinkably large sum; the PRC's defense budget in 1985 was, by comparison, only 18.67 billion yuan.[26]

As will be seen, the unnamed author's views were echoed more than a decade later by a group of economic scholars and officials in Tibet. One important reason for the failure of state subsidies to generate economic growth has been that the subsidies are used to support an overly large administrative superstructure. In essence, organizational forms designed for highly populated provinces in Han China were exported to sparsely populated Tibet. A second reason is the large PLA force stationed in Tibet to guard against infiltration from abroad and dissidence within. A third is the cost of subsidies for Han workers in Tibet. A fourth is that much of the state's subsidies are used to buy the state's goods from other parts of the country, rather than in order to develop local commodity production. A vicious cycle had developed in which Tibet was becoming more, not less, dependent on central government outlays, rather than using them to develop internal productive forces. To the extent that these existed, they were state-owned enterprises which, as elsewhere in the PRC, were inefficient money-losers.[27]

More friction was produced by a policy begun in 1985 of sending young people to be educated in Han China. Since, the government declared, Tibetans' lack of skills and the region's poor educational system were impeding economic progress, the youngsters would attend superior Chinese schools where they could acquire knowledge of use to their home areas. Four thousand middle school students were dispersed among seventeen provinces and municipalities where, needless to say, the language of instruction was Chinese rather than Tibetan. Although official propaganda emphasized how proud their parents were of them and the great hopes that everyone held for what they could do for Tibet in the future,[28] there were also lurking suspicions that the real motivation of the program was assimilation rather than economic development.

Tourism caused other problems. It definitely contributed to the region's gross domestic product and helped some Tibetans, who sold traditional handicrafts such as ceremonial scarves, weavings, and the area's distinctive turquoise, coral, and silver jewelry. Others felt that they were being exploited. One of these stated forcefully to a Western reporter that "First the Chinese cut our trees, mined our gold, and took our grain. Now there's nothing left, and they're selling our country to the foreigners."[29] There was a widespread perception that most of the benefits of tourism went not to natives but to Han immigrants. Tibetans became a minority in Lhasa, with most small businesses run by Han. This does not seem to have been the result of a conscious central government policy of ethnic swamping. Beijing had exempted Tibet from the general rule that one must be a permanent resident of an area in order to open a business there. In addition, taxes were low. A "floating population" of mostly impoverished young people from provinces like Sichuan, Gansu, and Yunnan had arrived and seemed to thrive even though, unlike the workers brought in under party/government sponsorship, they did not receive salary supplements. Tibetans were either unaware that the central government had not planned the influx or they were indifferent to the issue of whether it was culpable or not. More important to them were the realities that Han were present, and that they were taking jobs away from Tibetans. The locals were angry. Although Beijing argued that non-Tibetans stayed in urban areas, and that nearly 88 percent of Tibetans lived in rural areas, natives complained that the estimated 200,000–250,000 Han in the TAR represented a solid 15 percent of the area's population.

Phase V: Economic Development Under Strict Political Control, 1987–Present

This anger was a major factor in demonstrations in 1987. Tourists tended to sympathize with Tibetans rather than the government, particularly when they saw police beating unarmed protestors. Some tourists had not come simply to see the sights, but represented human rights groups on fact-finding missions. After learning this, party and government concluded that outside instigation had been behind the demonstrations, and took measures to restrict it. For a time, individual tourists were forbidden to enter Tibet, the assumption being that the activities of those who traveled in groups could more easily be monitored.[30] The restriction appeared to have a relatively minor affect on tourism and, concomitantly, on the amount of economic return realized from it. But even larger demonstrations in 1989 and the declaration of martial law that accompanied them would reduce tourism to a bare trickle for several years (see Appendix 6D).

In 1990, infrastructure development became a major concern. The State Planning Commission approved a program to develop the valleys of the three major waterways in central Tibet—the Yarlung Zangbo, Nyang Qu, and Lhasa rivers. Noting that the three comprised the political, economic, and cultural heart of the TAR and contained 35 percent of its population, the Commission pointed out that, collectively, they possessed significant potential for raising the grain output of existing farmland as well as afforestation projects. It was hoped that Tibet could become self-sufficient in grain by 2000, since about 150 million kilograms of grain had to be sent to the TAR from other parts of China every year, costing the government nearly 300 million yuan (US$64 million) in transportation fees.[31] Modern industry, said to have been non-existent at the time of liberation, now had three pillars: electricity, textile/handicrafts, and mining.[32] A fourth pillar, tourism, would later be added; 1990 would have been an inappropriate time to do so, since a declaration of martial law in Lhasa in 1989 had drastically reduced the number of tourists.

Echoing a theme applied to other minority areas of China, although of dubious validity—that economic development would erase ethnic tensions—a State Council inspection group opined that development of the three valleys was important to "stabilizing the situation in Tibet."[33] Work on these projects would dominate economic news from the TAR for the next several years. Four counties were designated "agro-tech demonstration counties" in 1990; another six were added in 1991. These ten received training in crop enhancement from outside experts plus funds for water conservation, land improvement, and farm machinery.[34]

In 1991 also, it was decided to divide Tibet into four economic zones for developmental purposes, based on the differing resource bases of the regions. A central zone, encompassing the eighteen counties through which the three above-mentioned rivers pass, would become the TAR's production base for commodity grain, nonstaple foods, light industry, textiles, and handicrafts, as well as be the focus of scientific and technological inputs. The geographically central zone was to become the center of the area's economic growth as well. The western zone, comprising Xigaze (Shigatse) and part of Ngari, was to take advantage of its frontier location by adopting special and flexible policies to promote border trade. The eastern zone, Nyingchi and Qamdo prefectures, with their milder climate and plentiful resources, was to boost infrastructure construction, including transportation and communications systems, and enlist human, material, and financial resources both within the zone and from elsewhere to build processing industries for minerals, forest products and by-products, Chinese medicinal materials, and wool. A northern zone, including Nagqu and the remainder of Ngari, would concentrate on developing animal products. Traditionally a pastureland, the northern zone would "build up animal husbandry, exploit energy resources, promote an animal commodity economy, and develop processing industries for animal products." It was also to develop its mineral and medicine material resources.[35]

Nineteen ninety-four proved a watershed year for development. Beijing and the

Dalai Lama's government were in the process of reaching different conclusions on the reincarnation of the Panchen Lama, engendering considerable tension, particularly after the child chosen by the Dalai Lama disappeared. Hu Jintao had gone on to higher office and was replaced by Chen Kuiyuan. Hu's lack of achievement in Tibet's economic development was clearly not held against him; one expert commented laconically, "when Hu arrived, there were riots. When he left, there weren't."[36] A third forum on work in Tibet was held in July. The annual growth rate was set at 10 percent for the rest of the decade—a highly ambitious goal—with the intent of doubling the TAR's gross domestic product by 2000, when compared with 1993. To further this goal, "relevant central departments and provinces" were to render long-term aid to Tibet in addition to ongoing state subsidies and preferential policies. These relevant central departments and provinces would take charge of the construction of 62 projects and provide an estimated investment of 2.38 billion yuan (US$270 million), almost exactly one-fourth of the projected total cost of the projects. When completed, the projects were expected to have "played a great role in the all-around development of Tibet."[37]

Almost immediately, concerns about how these projects would impact an environmental situation already perceived as deteriorating were voiced. They were emphatically dismissed by official sources. Other concerns were raised as well. A Western diplomat in Beijing opined that "If Tibetans want to cash in on the economic boom [created by the development projects], they will in effect have to become honorary Chinese," and the Hong Kong press construed party General Secretary Jiang Zemin's comment to the forum that social stability was an essential factor in Tibet's development as portending more repressive policies toward Tibetans.[38] New party secretary Chen Kuiyuan did indeed introduce harsh policies aimed at dealing with resistance. Tibetans were told, point-blank, that if religion interfered with socialism and economic development, it was religion that would have to give way. Among other measures, Chen curtailed the teaching of Tibetan in schools, closed monastic schools, and restricted the number of monks and nuns to 46,000, as well as forcing the remaining clergy to undergo patriotic re-education. Tibetan bureaucrats who could not write in Chinese were fired, as were people who had been educated in India, including tour guides. An additional 13,000 Tibetans were sent to be educated in the interior of China where, it was said, they could better obtain the necessary skills the TAR needed to develop economically and culturally.

Whole neighborhoods in Lhasa were razed, ostensibly to provide better modern housing and a smoother traffic flow. Family planning measures, which had been much less strictly applied than in most other areas of China, were tightened, again in the name of economic development and prosperity.[39] Since Han were coming into the TAR in sizable numbers to assist in economic development at the same time as Tibetans were being urged to limit the size of their families to help with economic development, some Tibetans concluded that the real motive behind family planning was genocide.

Official sources repeatedly denied that Han were flooding into Tibet. Ignoring a PLA presence variously estimated at between 100,000 and 300,000 and the un-registered floating population, with neither group being counted in census statis-tics, they pointed out that the population of the TAR was well over 90 percent Tibetan. The large numbers of Han who had come to help with economic develop-ment were not expected to stay longer than the terms of their contracts, which could be as long as ten years, and they would not in any case receive registration certificates. An article in *Tibet Daily* explained that having more Han than other nationalities was not a bad thing and was absolutely crucial to economic develop-ment. It warned that "unless people change their way of thinking, it will be very difficult for Tibet to enjoy development."[40] Han became the majority of the popu-lation in Lhasa and in the TAR's second city, Xigaze.

In mid-1996, a group of scholars and officials gathered to address the gap in living standards between Tibet and the interior, a discussion broadcast on Lhasa Television's weekly report. The economic growth rate in 1995 had been 10.6 per-cent, exceeding the average for the entire country. However, the interviewees stressed that the gains had been quantitative rather than qualitative. Development was extensive, resulting from higher subsidies, rather than intensive: economic rates of return were low, and dropping. Whereas the TAR's total factor productiv-ity was a meager 0.3 during the Seventh Five-Year Plan, 1.4 percent lower than the national level, it had dropped to −0.1 percent during the Eighth Five-Year Plan, 4.2 percent below the national level. Even though Tibet's gap with the interior of China had narrowed, it had widened in quality terms.[41] Exactly as predicted a decade before, the TAR had become still more dependent on subsidies.

There were also indications from exile groups that the government's statistics on development were being inflated. According to the *Tibetan Review,* premier publication of the exile community, the hydropower station at Yamzhong Yumco was symbolic of the central government's failures. Beijing's biggest project in the TAR thus far, the station had been built near a lake of the same name at an eleva-tion of 3,900 meters above sea level. The Yamzhong Yumco station cost an esti-mated US$120 million to build, but had never worked properly. Other large-scale construction activities had caused flooding along the Yangtze and left 4,000 square kilometers of desert elsewhere. And, citing a United Nations Development Pro-gram Report, *Tibetan Review* reported that life expectancy at birth in the TAR had fallen from 63.9 years in 1982 to 59.8 years in 1990.[42] The *Los Angeles Times* described a situation in which young Tibetan women seeking employment had a choice between heavy construction work or prostitution.[43]

Fueled by huge influxes of money from outside, the TAR's officially reported economic growth rate averaged an impressive 12.8 percent between 1993 and 1999, substantially in excess of the 1994 forum's already ambitious plans. Spurred by an expansion in service industries and state investments, a 9.3 percent rate was ex-pected for 2000.[44] The rate eventually reported was still higher—10.2 percent,[45] with increases of over 12 percent projected for the coming years. These are in fact being reported to date for the Tenth Five-Year Plan that was to run from 2001 to 2005: GDP for the latest year available, 2002, was 18 percent higher than 2001, adjusted for inflation to 12.4 percent.[46] Heightened attention to development in Tibet was consonant with the PRC's ambitious plans to develop the west. In the case of the TAR, these plans included construction of a very expensive railroad from Golmud, in Qinghai, to Lhasa. The cost of the railroad was a major factor in the expectation that growth rates would exceed 12 percent over the coming five years. Not surprisingly, this latest effort to develop Tibet entailed a large increase in the subsidies that, the central government has frequently reminded Tibetans, are already generous. During the Tenth Five-Year Plan, central government subsidies to the TAR were scheduled to reach 37.9 billion yuan, which is said to be twice those of the Ninth Five-Year Plan.[47] An additional 32.2 billion yuan is to be provided by the central government in cooperation with other areas of the country for 187 designated projects; other preferential policies were promised as well.[48]

The railroad project is highly controversial, both from an engineering/ecological perspective and for what its goals are perceived to be. With regard to the first obstacle, official sources insist that the technological problems of building a rail line through permafrost can be solved, and that Tibet's fragile environment will not be harmed. As for the motive behind building the road, two simultaneously published magazines reflect diametrically opposing views. *Beijing Review* concentrates on the economic benefits that the line will bring to ethnic minorities who live along it and the enhancement of ethnic unity.[49] By contrast, *Tibetan Review*, published in India, contains a cartoon depicting the railroad as the body of a sinuous dragon, symbolic of China, boring through the mountain under the Potala Palace, the symbol of Tibet, and dislodging it from its foundations. Out of the dragon's open mouth emerge thousands of tiny termite-like Han, each wearing an army cap.[50]

As if to underscore central government concerns about Tibet, a fourth Tibet work forum was held in Beijing at the end of June 2001. The forum report averred that economic development could not take place without stability, and named "the Dalai Lama clique" as the main source of Tibet's instability. To thwart the clique's nefarious designs, more than 10,000 cadres had been formed into work groups and rushed to agricultural and pastoral areas "to rectify and improve grass-roots party organizations." If they did not succeed, the report stated, the gap between the living standards of Tibet and other parts of China would continue to widen. Development was the key to stability.[51] It is not clear that forum participants comprehended the circularity of the chicken–egg dilemma their report outlined, that is, that instability causes failure to develop and failure to develop causes instability.

If the anticipated high growth rates can be sustained for five additional years, officials predict that the TAR can expect to "attain the mid-level of the country in ten years."[52] However, such statements contain the tacit assumptions that, first, large external subsidies will continue, and second, other provinces will continue to grow at the same rates they have been. Neither of these can be taken for granted. Other provinces are likely to experience changes in their growth rates, perhaps upward, which will make it more difficult for Tibet to attain the middle range, or perhaps downward in response to changes in the world economy or to unforeseeable natural disasters. The latter could inhibit their ability to contribute to the TAR's development. More important than this, perhaps, is that provinces are already reportedly reluctant to funnel to the TAR funds that could be used to better advantage in their own areas. There is increasing willingness to state this openly, as did Sichuan First Party Secretary Zhou Yongkang in March 2000, when he accused Tibetans of wasting money by donating to monasteries ("What's the point of talking about the future when you ignore the present?") and the government of wasting money by insisting that Tibetan be taught in schools ("The whole world is learning English. Why bother?").[53] In essence, this attitude holds Tibetans responsible for their own poverty, and argues that money should be spent where it yields a better return. While the attitude itself is not new, there are fewer inhibitions to stating it publicly.

At the same time, some Han feel more free to express opinions about the TAR's economic development that are critical of party and government efforts for other reasons. Wang Lixiong, a scholar-author who spent fifteen years collecting data in various areas of Tibet, argues that modernization has not succeeded there because it was forced in from the outside rather than at the behest of the people and with no regard for their culture. Since the sole driving force of development is massive financial support from Beijing, it cannot become self-sustaining. Wang argues, for example, that the main goal of road building was not, as the party claimed, economic development, but rather the creation of a stabilizing group (*wending jituan*) of Han—administrators and soldiers. The highways mainly carry goods to benefit them and the small number of Tibetans who have joined the stabilizing class. Hence the roads have little relevance to the lives of the great majority of Tibetans, who live in small, dispersed communities in the high plateaus. Development is, moreover, concentrated on showcase projects in major cities, mainly Lhasa. The result is a polarization of Tibetan society. Tibetan members of the stabilizing class play a dual role: on the one hand, they have common cause with party and government; they do not want the Dalai Lama to return from exile, fearing their privileged status will be adversely affected. On the other hand, wishing to enhance their value to the central government as stabilizers, they encourage small incidents of instability that they can soothe. Ordinary Tibetans are not inherently lazy in Wang's view; they have simply lost their work incentive due to the unnatural way in which development has come to the TAR.[55]

Another taboo that began to be addressed concerned the number of TAR residents who live below the poverty line. Official figures place the number at only 70,000 out of a total population of 2.6 million, and falling steadily. Representatives of the Hong Kong press who felt this figure was suspiciously low were able to ascertain that the standard for poverty had been set in 1990, at 600 yuan a year for farmers and 700 yuan a year for herders, both well below World Bank figures and not adjusted for inflation.[54]

Another scholar has hypothesized that economic development in Tibet is a dichotomy that is urban versus rural rather than Han versus Tibetan.[56] This falls athwart two problems. The first is one of data: Beijing releases income figures that are broken down only by rural versus urban, not urban Han and urban Tibetans on the one had and rural Han and rural Tibetans on the other, so the validity of this hypothesis cannot be tested. The second difficulty is one of perception: since an estimated 88 percent of the TAR's rural dwellers are Tibetans, the gap will be *perceived* as an ethnic one by the majority of those who feel themselves disadvantaged. Should the proportion of Han in Tibet be reduced while the Tibetan members of the stabilizing class increase, this urban/rural cleavage in development could become a reality, with a sinicized, relatively prosperous urban Tibetan ruling class governing a group of more impoverished, more traditional rural dwellers.

Conclusions

Even assuming that current high growth rates continue, there are questions about what they mean. Roads have brought not only Han Chinese soldiers and administrators, but access to better markets—for example, cashmere for the herders of the northern plateau[57] and, for Yunnan Tibetans, gourmet matsutake mushrooms for the tables of Japan.[58] A sadder example of what markets can do concerns the near extinction of the Tibetan antelope, hunted so that its exceptionally soft hair can be woven into *shatoosh* scarves. These have been sold in South Asia and the West for prices exceeding a thousand dollars.[59]

The average person has more food, and more varied food. Clothing and small consumer goods are more readily available, as even publications from the exile Tibetan community acknowledge.[60] Although official statistics are notoriously inaccurate, the data presented in the appendices at the end of this chapter provide at least a rough outline of increasing food supplies. Exiles are also aware that, particularly for those who settled in India, living abroad has not necessarily meant prosperity, either. On the other hand, to the extent that development has produced better lives, its chief beneficiaries have been urban dwellers, most of whom are Han. The gap between rich and poor has widened; an exile website states that rural household incomes in 2003 remained below 1992 levels.[61] And, despite Beijing's offering foreign investors in the TAR better incentives, involving privileged rates on taxation, borrowing, and land transactions, there is not a single example of foreign direct investment (FDI) in Tibet to date. Ninety-five percent of Tibet's trade is with Nepal,[62] itself a desperately impoverished country, and the trade is characterized by various irregularities, including rampant smuggling.[63] Trade with India has been severely restricted for political reasons, though the warming trend in Sino-Indian relations that began in the latter half of 2003 may result in facilitating commercial transactions between the latter and Tibet.[64]

This raises an interesting issue pointed out to the author by a prominent human rights activist: the tacit Chinese assumption that the only way to develop the Tibetan economy is by integrating it with the Chinese economy.[65] A few qualifications are in order, however. Beijing would not be encouraging trade with Nepal had it not approved of trade with the outside world. External links would doubtless be more welcome if Sino-Indian relations were warmer and relations between Beijing and the Tibetan exile community less tense. Given several decades of infiltration and exfiltration of Tibetan dissidents through India, Beijing's fears about restricting trade with that nation seem justified.

Efforts to produce more food and different foodstuffs as well as develop other areas of the economy have, however, caused significant environmental degradation. Deserts increase in area as do the sandstorms they produce. These impact both animal husbandry and agricultural production. Concern that the central government's plans for intensive development may cause irreversible ecological damage in Tibet is the central theme of a study published by the U.S. Embassy in Beijing in 2002. It notes that, although there are several different ecosystems in Tibet, their common attribute is that they are easily upset by overexploitation to support human activity.[66]

There has also been a degradation of Tibetan culture, which has been modified and "developed" by party and government rather than by Tibetans themselves. Han prejudice against Tibetans definitely exists, and has an adverse effect on economic development. For example, technology supplied by a Western philanthropical organization enabled Tibetans to turn yak milk into a tasty, Brie-like, cheese. However, when the cheese cooperative's representatives tried to market their product to Chinese hotel managers in Beijing they were refused on the grounds that if it came from Tibet, it must be filthy.[67] In another example, a Han bus driver refused to stop for a group of Tibetans, remarking loudly over her shoulder to the rest of the passengers, "we don't want that smell in here."[68] And, the government's claims to have Tibetanized the governing structure notwithstanding, the TAR has never had a first party secretary who is a Tibetan. In the end, the benefits, or lack thereof, of economic development are in the eye of the beholder.

Appendices

6A. Livestock Production

According to the official Xinhua news agency, the TAR had 11.14 million head of livestock in 1958 and 9.58 million in 1959, presumably because the rebellion affected production.[69] In 1961 and 1962, said to be years of natural disaster in the TAR, there were 11.5 million.[70] The year 1963 saw a sizable increase, to 13.7 million; in 1964, there were 16 million.[71] The total in 1965, calculated as an increase of 36 percent over 1958, comes to 15.544 million, possibly reflecting losses from poor weather. By 1968, the figure had risen to 17.36 million, and in 1970, to 17.86 million. In 1971, under the influence of radical policies prevalent in Beijing as a result of the Great Proletarian Cultural Revolution, communes were founded in the TAR. As if on cue, livestock production again leaped forward, to 18.5 million in 1973, 19.2 million "despite a major wind disaster" in 1974,[72] and 19.3 million in 1975—"up two percent over 1974."

No figures were reported for 1976, but 1977's was 22 million, "32 percent higher than 1965,"[73] and consistent with "17 percent higher than 1970, despite natural disasters." In 1978, the number of animals was reported to be 1.5 times that of 1958, or 17.25 million; in 1979, livestock production was expected to increase by 2 percent over 1978, or to 17.6 million. In 1980, the year that communes were disbanded, one source announced that livestock production had "increased somewhat," another that the number of privately owned stock had increased from 1.21 million to 3.48 million head, or 15 percent of the TAR's total livestock. This would yield a figure of 23.2 million livestock, a 31.8 percent increase, or far more than the modest increase claimed by the first source. This is consistent with the 23 million figure announced for 1982.[74]

No figures were released for 1983 during and shortly after that year. Nineteen eighty-four saw a drop to 21.68 million, claimed to be an *increase* of 1.4 percent over the previous year, which would have meant the number of livestock in 1983 was 21.38 million. The next figures to be released put the number of livestock at 23 million, said to be 1.4 times the number in 1959.[75] This is inconsistent with previous figures of 9.58 million in 1959.[76] It is, however, consistent with the 23 million figure given for 1990[77] and 22.8 million for 1991, "roughly the same as last year," with a slaughter rate up 1 percent from 1990.[78] In 1996, the figure was 22.5 million, with outputs of meat and sheep's wool "basically the same as last year."[79] For several years thereafter, numbers of livestock went unmentioned, though the 2001 Tibet White Paper put the figure for 2000 at 22.6 million. The apparent stabilization of numbers of livestock, which can reasonably be attributed to the numbers that the ecosystem can sustain, began to change in 2001, when the numbers reached 23.6 million, and again in 2002, with 24.39 million reported.[80]

It is somewhat puzzling that the number of livestock in the TAR should have had its greatest increase during the period of communes, which were a failure elsewhere in China. In Xinjiang and Inner Mongolia, the institution of communes resulted in some herders slaughtering all their animals rather than turning them over to the communes, leading to severe shortages of meat in the ensuing years.

Also puzzling is the government's attempt to take credit for avoiding the problem of overgrazing after communes were disbanded by persuading herders to limit the numbers of their livestock. While independent entrepreneurs would certainly have an incentive to increase the size of their herds, until two years ago the government's own statistics did not show an appreciable rise in the period since the demise of communes. Goldstein and Beall, who lived among the nomads of the TAR's northern plateau in 1986–87, discovered a well-developed traditional system for avoiding overgrazing and an understanding of the carrying capacity of the environment.[81]

6B. Agriculture

Official agricultural statistics suffer from the same problems as those of livestock, with the additional complication that for several decades they were sometimes reported as catties or *jin* (catty), without specifying whether these are *gong jin* (one kilogram) or *shi jin* (1.1023 English pounds, or exactly one-half kilogram). While it should be simple to infer which is meant, some figures are not consonant with either measure unless one assumes improbably large deviations in the harvest. In other years, grain totals are reported as kilograms or tons. Since the amounts reported are rounded, translating rounded catties into tons, for example, introduces further bias. By excluding clear outliers, one can, however, come up with a rough time series.

The 1952 harvest, calculating back from 1982 figures ("more than three times the 1952 harvest") was less than 158,333 tons.[82] In 1971, the harvest reached 315,000 tons.[83] In 1974, for the first and only time since liberation, the TAR was reported to be self-sufficient in grain.[84] The figure for 1979 was 423,000 tons— "dropping by a large amount, which will cause difficulties in the people's livelihood, due to natural disasters and some work problems; we must not neglect animal husbandry to raise grain."[85] In 1981, 483,500 tons was reported, an improbably large increase that may reflect grain shipped in from outside to alleviate food shortages.[86] In 1982, grain production was reportedly down to 475,000 tons.[87] In 1986, the harvest was down again, to 450,000 tons, reportedly due to "various serious disasters";[88] in 1988, 520,000 tons;[89] in 1989, 549,500 tons according to one source,[90] 532,000 according to a second,[91] and 530,000 according to a third.[92] Statistics for 1990 put the grain harvest at 560,000 tons;[93] 1991, 580,000 tons;[94] 1995 was a peculiar year in that five-year statistics only were presented, possibly because of poor results; grain was projected to reach 625,000 tons;[95] 1996, 777,000; 1997, 820,000; 2000, 922,000.[96] In 2000, the figure reached 962,234 tons as well as the assertion that self-sufficiency in grain and oils had been "basically realized."[97] The 2001 figure was 982,508 tons, up 2.1 percent over 2000, and for 2002, 983,970 tons, up one-tenth of a percent over 2001.[98]

6C. Roads

According to a 1981 source, Tibet had only a five-kilometer highway at the time of liberation;[99] by 1979, official sources reported 22,200 km of motor roads.[100] In 1981, the figure was lowered to 21,100,[101] and in 1982 it was listed simply as "over 20,000."[102] Figures hovering slightly over 21,000 continued throughout the 1980s and 1990s;[103] in 1987, a delegate to the Thirteenth Party Congress from the TAR's Medog County was described as having to walk three days to get to a road, followed by a three-day automobile trip to reach Lhasa. In 2000, it was announced that 1.1 billion yuan would be spent to bring the TAR's total highway length to 25,300 km, with a goal of 27,000 km by the end of 2005, though most of the additions would be in the form of basic roads to open access to hitherto isolated rural communities. The figure reported for 2000 was 22,500 km, said to reach all of the TAR's counties and 80 percent of its townships.[104] The goal for 2005 was surpassed the year after it was announced by an apparently chance discovery: a highway census conducted in 2001 discovered 13,000 km more roads than previously reported. Tibet scholar Barry Sautman hypothesizes they had been built by localities whose officials did not trouble themselves to report the roads to higher authorities. No information was supplied on the condition of the newly discovered routes. In 2001, 35,537 km of roads were reported, and in 2002, 35,538 km.[105]

Ninety-four percent of the TAR's cargo and 85 percent of its human travelers move over these roads. Only 2,000 km of them are asphalted. The others are described as rugged and vulnerable to harsh weather and other natural disasters.[106] According to official sources, the Qinghai–Tibet highway is the only one of the region's four major routes—the other three being the Sichuan–Tibet, Yunnan–Tibet, and Xinjiang–Tibet highways—to function on a year-round basis. The Qinghai–Tibet route carries fully 80 percent of the TAR's cargo and passenger transport.[107] Ambitious plans to extend a railroad from Golmud to Lhasa face formidable problems of engineering, given the difficult terrain and harsh climate.

6D. Tourists

The TAR was opened to tourism in 1980, and despite considerable added costs, the difficulty of getting there, and problems associated with adjusting to Tibet's thin air, proved an immensely popular destination. By 1986, Tibet was hosting approximately 30,000 tourists a year; in 1987, 40,000. In 1989, the imposition of martial law dropped the number to 3,700;[108] by 1990, the total improved to 11,000.[109] In 1991, it was 16,755;[110] in 1993, 24,900;[111] and in 1994, 28,000.[112] Interestingly, despite tremendous foreign interest in Tibet, the figures had not recouped to pre-1989 levels, although they rose quickly thereafter. In 2000, the TAR received 598,300 tourists, of whom 148,900 were from overseas and 449,400 from elsewhere in China. The direct income realized from tourism was 780 million yuan, or 6.6 percent of the autonomous region's budget. Indirect income was 2.98 billion yuan, or 25.38 percent of GDP.[113]

Numbers continued to increase: in 2001, there were 686,116 tourists, of whom 558,968 were domestic and 127,148 international; in 2002, the figure reached 867,320, with 725,041 domestic and 142,279 international.[114] Clearly tourism had, as hoped, become one of the region's pillar industries and an impetus to the development of other industries such as handicrafts.

6E. Per Capita Income

Statistics here are sometimes reported as regional averages; at others, for peasants and herders on the one hand and urban dwellers on the other. They are not reported for Han versus Tibetans, though since nearly all Han live in cities and the large majority of Tibetans live in the countryside, it can be assumed that a significant proportion of the higher urban incomes go to Han. The most consistent series of data are for peasants and herders only. In 1996, the per capita income figure was 975 yuan.[115] Data from earlier periods include 218 yuan in 1979 reported in 1987, and 343 yuan for 1986, reported at the same time.[116] Income figures throughout the 1980s hover in the 300–plus yuan range until 1990, when the figure rises to 430 yuan.[117] In 1992, it was 490 yuan,[118] and in 1993, 521 yuan.[119] In 1995, per capita average net income of peasants and herders was 878 yuan, while that of staff and workers was 7,382 yuan, showing a worrisomely large gap.[120] Per capita income of the TAR's farmers and herders in 1999 was 1,258 yuan (US$151.56), or 53.3 percent of the national average, and the country's lowest.[121] In 2000, figures were reported as percentage increases, up an astounding 62.9 percent for farmers and herders, which can be calculated to be 2,049 yuan, and 93.6 percent for urban residents.[122] There is likely to have been a misplaced decimal, with the actual rise of 6.29 percent to 1,337 yuan, since per capita income in 2001 was 1,404 yuan for rural dwellers and 7,119 for urbanites; in 2002, the amounts rose to 1,521 and 7,762 yuan, respectively.[123] These figures do not appear to be adjusted for inflation, which, given the huge infusions of capital from the central government, is substantial. Note that the difference between urban and rural incomes is more than five to one.

6F. Gross Domestic Product

In 1987, gross domestic product (GDP) was 1.77 billion yuan[124]; in 1993, 3.72 billion.[125] Tibet's reported GDP in 1994 was 4.23 billion yuan,[126] in 1995, 6.45 billion yuan,[127] and in 1998, 9.1 billion yuan.[128] In 1999, it reached 10.661 billion yuan,[129] and in 2000, 11.746 billion yuan.[130] The figure for 2001 was 13.873 billion yuan and in 2002, 16.420 billion yuan, each up 18 percent over the previous year but reported as 12.4 percent, presumably adjusted for inflation.[131] As pointed out by numerous sources, much of the GDP growth reflects massive state subsidies.

Notes

An earlier version of this chapter appeared in the *Journal of Contemporary China* 12, no. 36 (2003): 411–430; the current version appears here with the permission of the editors thereof.

1. "Tibetan Farmers, Herdsmen See Lifestyle Changes," Xinhua (Beijing, in English), March 12, 2002.

2. Xinhua, May 27, 1951, in *Tibet, 1950–1967* (Hong Kong: Union Research Institute, 1967), 20.

3. Ngapo Ngawang Jigme, quoted in *Guangming Ribao* (Beijing), May 28, 1983, 3.

4. *Peking Review* (subsequently known as, and hereafter cited as, *Beijing Review*), February 16, 1962, 4.

5. *Beijing Review*, November 8, 1974, 5.

6. *Renmin Ribao*, January 16, 1969, 2.

7. *Beijing Review*, July 31, 1970, 30.

8. Lhasa Radio, August 9, 1973.

9. Xinhua, September 27, 1974.

10. Xinhua, December 25, 1975.

11. *Beijing Review*, July 18, 1975, 24.

12. Lhasa Radio, February 18, 1975.

13. Charles Bell, *Tibet Past and Present* (Oxford: Clarendon Press, 1924), 31.

14. Lhasa Radio, December 17, 1980, in Foreign Broadcast Information Service/China (hereafter FBIS), December 18, 1980, Q4.

15. Lhasa Radio, November 6, 1980, in U.S. Department of Commerce, *Joint Publications Research Service: China*, No. 77089 (December 31, 1980), 81.

16. George B. Schaller, "Tibetan Passage," *Animal Kingdom*, December 1980–January 1981, 14–19; S. Dillon Ripley, "Tibet: The High and Fragile Land Behind the Ranges," *Smithsonian*, January 1981, 96–105.

17. Beijing, Xinhua, November 20, 1979, in FBIS, November 23, 1979, Q2.

18. Lhasa Radio, January 6, 1981, in FBIS, January 7, 1981, Q1.

19. See, for example (no author), "New Principles for Building Up Tibet," *Beijing Review*, June 16, 1980, 3–5; Wang Yao, "Hu Yaobang's Visit to Tibet, May 22–31, 1980," in *Resistance and Reform in Tibet*, ed. Robert Barnett and Shirin Akiner, 285–289 (London: Hurst and Company, 1994); Ngapoi Ngawang Jigme, "Build a United, Prosperous, and Highly Civilized New Xizang," Beijing Radio, May 2, 1981, in FBIS, May 27, 1981, Q12.

20. Wang Yao, "Hu Yaobang's Visit."

21. Christopher Wren, "Chinese Trying To Undo Damage in Tibet," *New York Times*, May 3, 1983, 1, 5.

22. Xinhua (Beijing), June 10, 1996.

23. Lhasa Radio, January 3, 1986, in FBIS, January 7, 1986, Q2–Q3.

24. Lhasa Radio, August 12, 1986, in FBIS, August 19, 1986, Q3.

25. "An Exploration of a New Method for Reinvigorating Xizang's Economy," *Shijie Jingji Daobao* (World Economic Herald, Shanghai), January 21, 1985, 5.

26. International Institute of Strategic Studies (IISS), *The Military Balance, 1986–1987* (London: IISS, 1986), 142.

27. See Tseten Wangchuk Sharlho, "China's Reforms in Tibet: Issues and Dilemmas," *Journal of Contemporary China* 1, no. 1 (Fall 1992): 45–46.

28. See, for example, Lu Yun, "Training Qualified Personnel for Tibet," *Beijing Review*, May 30–June 5, 1988, 21–22.

29. *Asian Wall Street Journal Weekly*, June 29, 1987, 48.

30. Han Guojian, "Tibet Reopened to Individual Tourists," *Beijing Review*, March 28–April 3, 1988, 31.

31. "Commission Approves Tibet Development Program," Xinhua (Beijing), July 18, 1990.

32. Liu Wei, "Three Industrial Pillars Formed in Tibet," *Renmin Ribao*, July 4, 1990, 1, in FBIS, July 17, 1990, 41.

33. "State Council Inspection Group Visits Tibet," Tibet Television Network (Mandarin), July 6, 1990, in FBIS, July 18, 1990, 46.

34. "Gyaincain Norbu Views Economic Development," Xinhua (Beijing), December 21, 1991 (no author).

35. Wu Huijing, "Tibet to Develop Four Economic Zones," Xinhua (Beijing), February 27, 1991.

36. Professor Barry Sautman, personal comment to the author, March 24, 2001.

37. Commentator, "Policy on Tibet," *China Daily* (Beijing), July 28, 1994, 4.

38. Geoffrey Crothall and Willy Wo-Lap Lam, "Economic Growth Causing Tibetan Cultural 'Erosion,'" *South China Morning Post* (Hong Kong), July 28, 1994, 10.

39. The exception being among the Turkic Muslims of Xinjiang, where efforts to get the population to reduce fertility rates frequently resulted in violent countermeasures.

40. Cited in "Han Influx Deemed Good for Tibet's Economic Development," *Far Eastern Economic Review*, February 19, 1998, 29 (no author).

41. Ni Song, "May I Ask About the Direction?—The Gap Between Tibet and the Hinterland," Tibet Television Network (Mandarin), June 23, 1996, in FBIS, July 16, 1996, 57.

42. *Tibetan Review* (Delhi), November 1998.

43. Ni Ching-Ching, "Tibet's Women of Misery," *Los Angeles Times*, October 7, 2003, www.latimes.com.

44. Liu Wei and Wu Yilong, "We Should Grasp Stability and Development Simultaneously," Xinhua (Beijing), November 2, 2000.

45. Calculated from a GDP of 11.746 billion yuan for 2000 vis-à-vis the 1999 figure of 10.561 billon yuan as reported by the Tibet White Paper entitled "Tibet's March Toward Modernization," hereafter cited as Tibet White Paper 2001, issued by Xinhua on November 9, 2001.

46. Wang Jianxin and Yue Furong, "Milestone in Tibet's Reforms, Development, and Stability," *Renmin Ribao* (Beijing), in FBIS CPP22010719000028, July 19, 2001, 2.

47. Ibid.

48. Ibid.; see also Tibet White Paper 2001.

49. Wang Wen, "Train Will Run on the Roof of the World," *Beijing Review*, April 12, 2001, 16–17.

50. Loten Namling, "Khari Khathug," *Tibetan Review*, May 2001, 20.

51. Wang Jianxin and Yue Furong, "Milestone in Tibet's Reforms."

52. "Tibet Expects 9.3 Percent Growth," Agence France-Presse (Hong Kong), December 26, 2000.

53. Josephine Ma, "Tibetans 'Wasting Money' on Donations to Monasteries," *South China Morning Post* (Hong Kong), March 14, 2000, www.scmp.com.

54. Daniel Kwan, "Figures Hide Scale of Poverty in Tibet," *South China Morning Post*, August 16, 2001.

55. Wang Lixiong, *Tianzang: Xizang de Mingyun* (Sky Burial: The Fate of Tibet) (Hong Kong: Mirror Books, 1988), passim.

56. Anonymous paper entitled "Tibet: Development for Whom?," Summer 2001.

57. Melvyn C. Goldstein and Cynthia M. Beall, *Nomads of Western Tibet* (Berkeley: University of California Press, 1990), 83, 105.

58. Emily T. Yeh, "Forest Claims, Conflicts, and Commodification: The Political Ecology of Tibetan Mushroom-Harvesting Villages in Yunnan Province, China," *China Quarterly* (London), January 2000, 264–278.

59. "Profits Keep Shahtoosh Trade Alive and Antelope Dying Out," Reuters, July 10, 2001; Daniel Kwan, "Antelope Still Victims of Fashion Foibles," *South China Morning Post*, August 17, 2001.

60. Tsering Topgyal, "The *shou* and *fang* of China's Tibet Policies," *Tibetan Review*, April 2001, 21.

61. "Despite Economic Boom, Rural Standards of Living in the Tibet Autonomous Region Still Below 1992 Levels," Tibet Information Network (London), February 6, 2003, www.tibetinfo.net/news-updates/2003/0602.htm.

62. Xinhua, Lhasa, October 15, 2001.

63. Bijaya Ghimire and Gopal Devkota, "Nepalese Army to Crack Down on Sino-Tibetan Border Smuggling," *Kathmandu Post*, March 2, 2001, www.nepalnews.com.np/ktmpost.htm.

64. C. Raja Mohan, "Cracking India's Two-Front Problem," *The Hindu* (Chennai), January 15, 2004, provides a pithy summary of recent démarches between the two countries; see www.hindu.com/2004/01/15htm.

65. Robbie Barnett, personal communication, March 4, 2001.

66. "Environmental Conditions in Tibet," www.usembassy-china.org.cn/sandt/ptr/TibetEnvironment-prt.

67. Calum MacLeod, "Tibetan Nomads Say Cheese," *South China Morning Post*, November 15, 2000, www.scmp.com.

68. Told to the author by a Western passenger aboard the bus, April 2000.

69. Calculated from statement in *Qiushi*, February 1, 1989, 3, that the 1988 figure was 23 million, up 1.4 times over 1959.

70. *Minzu Tuanjie* (Beijing), July 1964, 4–6.

71. *Beijing Review*, December 18, 1964, 4.

72. Lhasa Radio, November 8, 1974, in FBIS 74–246, J2.

73. Lhasa Radio, December 7, 1977, in FBIS 77–238, J4.

74. Ngapo Ngawang Jigme, quoted by *Guangming Ribao*, May 28, 1983, in FBIS, June 10, 1983, Q2.

75. Li Weihan, "The Road of Liberation of the Tibetan Nationality," Beijing Radio, May 25, 1981, in FBIS, May 27, 1981, Q13.

76. *Qiushi*, February 1, 1989, 2–8, in FBIS, February 22, 1989, 45.

77. Xinhua (Beijing), August 25, 1990.

78. Lhasa Radio, May 6, 1992.

79. Lhasa Radio, July 1, 1997.

80. 2001 and 2002 data from *Xizang Tongji Nianjian* (Beijing: Zhongguo Tongji Chubanshe, 2003), 170.

81. Goldstein and Beall, *Nomads of Western Tibet*, 69–71, 177–181.

82. Ngapo Ngawang Jigme, quoted by *Guangming Ribao*, May 28, 1983, in FBIS, June 10, 1983, Q2.

83. Lhasa Radio, August 6, 1973, in FBIS, 73–153, E1.

84. Lhasa Radio, November 8, 1974, in FBIS 74–220, Q3.

85. Lhasa Radio, November 29, 1979, in FBIS 79–234, Q4.

86. Xinhua (Beijing), August 12, 1982, in FBIS, August 16 1982, Q3.

87. Ngapo Ngawang Jigme, "Xizang Marches Along a Bright Road," *Guangming Ribao*, May 28, 1983, 3, in FBIS, June 10, 1983, Q2.

88. Lhasa Radio, March 10, 1987, in FBIS, March 13, 1987, Q2.

89. Xinhua (Beijing), December 14, 1988, in FBIS, December 16, 1988, 63.

90. *Renmin Ribao*, January 14, 1990, 1, in FBIS, February 16, 1990, 82.

91. Xinhua (Beijing), February 28, 1990, in FBIS, March 9, 1990, 47.

92. Xinhua (Beijing), April 29, 1990, in FBIS, May 2, 1990, 84.

93. Xinhua (Beijing), October 21, 1990, in FBIS, October 22, 1990, 49.

94. Lhasa Radio, May 6, 1992, in FBIS, May 11, 1992, 47.

95. Lhasa Radio, June 23, 1996, in FBIS, July 16, 1996, 57.

96. Yang Yung-nian, "Legqog, 'Seize Opportunity, Speed Up Construction,'" *Wen Wei Po* (Hong Kong), October 16, 2000, D1, in FBIS CPP20001016000063, at www.fbis.gov.

97. 2001 Tibet White Paper.

98. *Xizang Tongji Nianjian* (Beijing: Zhongguo Tongji Chubanshe, 2003), 164.

99. Xinhua (Beijing), June 17, 1981, in FBIS, June 19, 1981, Q5.

100. Xinhua (Beijing), October 12, 1979, in FBIS, October 12, 1979, Q2.

101. Xinhua (Beijing), June 17, 1981, in FBIS, June 19, 1981, Q5.

102. Beijing Radio to Taiwan, June 27, 1982, in FBIS 82–129 (July 2, 1982), K16.

103. Xinhua (Beijing), February 21, 1990, in FBIS, March 9, 1990, 47.

104. 2001 Tibet White Paper.

105. *Xizang Tongji Nianjian* (Beijing: Zhongguo Tongji Chubanshe, 2003), 225.

106. Raymond Li, "Tibet to Benefit from 20 Billion Yuan Highway Plan," *South China Morning Post*, August 2, 2000, at www.scmp.com.

107. Wang Wen, "Train Will Run on the Roof of the World," *Beijing Review*, April 12, 2001, 16–17.

108. Xinhua (Beijing), March 5, 1990, in FBIS, March 9, 1990, 45.

109. Calculated from the 1991 figure of 16,755, "an increase of 51.75 percent over 1990." Lhasa Radio, May 6, 1992, in FBIS, May 11, 1992, 46.

110. Lhasa Radio, May 6, 1992, in FBIS, May 11, 1992, 46.

111. Calculated from the 1994 figure of 28,000 "an increase of 12.5 percent over 1993." Xinhua (Beijing), May 16, 1995, in FBIS, May 16, 1995, 60.

112. Xinhua (Beijing), May 16, 1995, in FBIS, May 16, 1995, 60.

113. 2001 Tibet White Paper.

114. *Xizang Tongji Nianjian* (Beijing: Zhongguo Tongji Chubanshe, 2003), 248.

115. Xinhua (Beijing), February 26, 1998, in FBIS, February 28, 1998.

116. *China Daily* (Beijing), July 6, 1987, 4.

117. *Liaowang* (overseas edition), no. 22, June 3, 1991, 13.

118. *Renmin Ribao* (overseas edition), June 12, 1993, 3.

119. *Renmin Ribao* (Beijing), August 9, 1994, 10, in FBIS, August 15, 1994, 53.

120. Tibet Television (Mandarin), June 23, 1996, in FBIS, July 16, 1996, 57.

121. Xinhua (Chengdu), November 13, 2000.

122. 2001 Tibet White Paper.

123. *Xizang Tongji Nianjian* (Beijing: Zhongguo Tongji Chubanshe, 2003), 118.

124. Lhasa Radio, July 25, 1988, in FBIS, July 26, 1988, 53.

125. *Renmin Ribao* (Beijing), August 9, 1994, 10, in FBIS, August 15, 1994, 53.

126. *Xizang Ribao* (Lhasa), June 8, 1995, 1–3, in FBIS, July 21, 1995, 63.

127. *Xizang Ribao*, June 5, 1996, 1–3, in FBIS, July 9, 1996, 56.

128. Mary Kwang, "Beijing Lifeline," *Straits Times* (Singapore), November 6, 1999, at www.straitstimes.asia1.sg.

129. Xinhua (Lhasa), January 20, 2000, in FBIS FTS20000120000190, at www.fbis.gov.

130. 2001 Tibet White Paper.

131. *Xizang Tongji Nianjian* (Beijing: Zhongguo Tongji Chubanshe, 2003), 21.

7

Economic Policy and
Practice in Contemporary Tibet

Dawa Norbu

Most experienced Tibetologists would agree that their field has been hell for statisticians but heaven for anthropologists. Indeed, Tibetology is characterized by a poverty of statistical data. One can recall only one census from pre-1950 Tibetan history, namely that of 1268, conducted by the Mongols.[1] In other words, Tibetan culture is highly literate but numerically weak. It was against the backdrop of this statistical poverty, or in the absence of any statistical tradition, that Chinese Marxists introduced and popularized the concept and practice of statistics. Not, unfortunately, as a value-neutral academic tool but essentially as a propaganda-driven means of measuring "progress" under the Communist regime. Hence, most of the statistics on contemporary Tibet are suspect for a number of reasons. The base year is not stated; there is also built-in ideological pressure at the village level, as well as a political tendency to inflate figures at the state level. This is particularly true of production and central assistance figures.

Therefore, to study economic development in Tibet is not the same as studying the economics of Hong Kong. In the former case, figures are used to substantiate ideological and historical claims. In the latter case, it is pure, essential, and simple economics, and figures are to be trusted. Not so in the case of contemporary Tibet.[2] That being the case, one of the least controversial things one can do at the present is to carry out a qualitative analysis of economic policy and practice in contemporary Tibet. In order to do so from a comparative perspective, I begin with a tentative outline structure of the pre-Communist Tibetan economy.

The pre-Communist economy of Tibet was purely traditional in the sense of being pre-industrial in all sectors of economic life for the country as a whole, except for the area around Lhasa, which was partially urbanized and superficially touched by modernity during the Thirteenth Dalai Lama's rule. In its traditional form, the Tibetan economy consisted of three vital sectors: subsistence agriculture, harsh pastoralism, and lucrative trade, which included barter and inter-regional trade as well as long-distance trade with India and China. Of the three sectors, agriculture was dominant. But land ownership, in theory, was not based on private property. It was heavily embedded in the practice of feudalism, which formed the economic base of the government (*bde-wa gzhung*), its officially recognized landed aristocracy, and the large monastic establishment(s). So there was plenty of room for exploitation. However, the common populace derived a great deal of psychic satisfaction from the feudal relations, especially with the monastic establishments and the government headed by the Dalai Lama. In fact, the economic surplus from agro-nomadic production and long-distance trade, to a large extent, was willingly and voluntarily on the part of private individuals spent on the monastic establishments as the principal means of earning merit (*dge-wa/bsod-nams*).

Tibetan feudalism, especially in its conceptual foundation, sounds so oppressive and exploitative to the Marxist. The real irony is that in all probability, supported by personal experience,[3] traditional commoners in pre-1950 Tibet enjoyed more freedom than their contemporary counterparts. The reason is simple. Because of the difficult terrain and huge geographical space, even the most rapacious feudal lords were ineffective in exercising the total control that feudalism in theory dictated. As a result, "serfs" enjoyed considerable relative freedom that was not legislated by *zhung* (government) but facilitated by geography and reinforced by Buddhism since the tenth century A.D.

Finally, because the land to population ratio on the Tibetan plateau was no problem, and because Tibetans in general tended to be hard working, there is no recorded famine in pre-1950 Tibetan history. This is confirmed by British colonial officers' observations based on their visits to Tibet before the Communist takeover. They concur that the Tibetan economy was not developed in the sense they were accustomed to, but observe that the economic conditions of the average Tibetan was better than the living standard of average Asians in several of the premodern larger Asian economies known to the British. There was no striking gap between rich and poor in traditional Tibet. Yet, on historical balance, the Chinese Communist destruction in 1959 of Tibetan feudalism, the feudal class, and above all, the enduring feudal economic base of the Buddhist church, may be considered a positive outcome of the Communist-exported revolution in Tibet. A critical and theoretical question still remains. Can the Tibetans, freed from feudalism, imagine and build a new community based on the essence of freedom and democracy, yet in harmony with their cultural heritage and their peculiar environment? Can they still fight for a relatively modern economic system in which they might stand a chance to survive and benefit economically rather than face an unfair and unequal competition in a bulldozing economic system in the name of development, an unfair game for which most Tibetans are educationally and culturally ill-equipped?[4]

In what follows, I shall enumerate the major turning points in Chinese Communist economic policy and practice in contemporary Tibet, starting from the take-over in the 1950s. Whether the takeover was motivated by strategic necessity or a liberation project will be debated by future historians. What is clear from scattered available evidence is that a major portion of the expenditure in the 1950s, supposedly earmarked for development, went into road building on the Tibetan plateau.

Development in the Early Years of the Communist Occupation

The Chinese Communists poured in silver dollars, called in Chinese *da yuan*, for road-building and political projects in Tibet in the 1950s. While it is difficult to know exactly how much the Communists spent on these projects, we can get a rough idea if we piece together the shreds of available and fairly reliable published statistics. For example, during the First Five-Year Plan (1953–1957), China spent $4.232 billion on transport and communication for the whole of the People's Republic of China, which constituted 11.7 percent of total development expenditure.[5] And there is evidence to suggest that a large portion of that total amount was actually spent on road-building projects in Tibet or the Tibetan plateau. To pay for all these urgent projects, Communists introduced not paper currency, which was not then acceptable to the Tibetans, but cash payments in *da yuan*. Thus in the 1950s the Tibetan economy and the market were flooded with *da yuan*, paid handsomely to the common laborers on road construction whose hard labor made the "liberation" a reality, as well as most generously to the traditional ruling class whose cooperation and cooptation were so essential for the takeover. In his party-approved book on minority nationalities in the PRC, Zhang Zhiyi, who was then a deputy director of the United Front Work Department of the party, the key outfit entrusted with formulation and implementation of Communist policy toward minorities, especially Tibetans, notes:

> With respect to communications and transportation, the greater part of the new highway construction throughout the country since Liberation has been located in the frontier regions of the motherland and in areas inhabited by national minorities. . . . The highway routes involving major engineering were, among others, the following: Kangting–Tibet, Tsinghai–Tibet, Tsinghai–Sinkiang, Chengtu–Apa, Lanchow–Langmuszu, Kunming–Talo, Lhasa–Shigatse, Shigatse–Gyangtse, and Phari–Yatung.[6]

It should be noted that most of the highways listed above are in Tibet proper and the rest in the Tibetan cultural areas neighboring the southwestern Chinese provinces. With hindsight we can say that they are all strategically important. In the 1950s' context we can say that they were for transport and communications purposes, equally valuable for the takeover and the long-term liberation project. But since 1959 and especially after 1962, Communist China saw a new dimension and a new urgency in the development of Tibet that would henceforth define its basic nature in Central Asia: the progressively *strategic* dimension, in the military sense of the term. Communists increasingly realized the strategic location of Tibet and its vulnerability. Henceforth they would subordinate Tibetan economic development to the Chinese strategic imperative, but give it an ideological twist. They might initiate new economic reforms such as the current campaign to "develop the western region" and invite partners in the Tibetan development who submit to the Chinese strategic imperative in Tibet, or at least do not question Chinese strategic supremacy in Inner Asia.

Development in the Period Post-Revolt

Once the party-state made the decision to subordinate the proclaimed Marxist mission in Tibet (i.e., economic development) to strategic considerations, statistics became increasingly suspect. To conceal this non-Marxist nature of development, namely, the heavily defense-related development that overshadowed the Chinese exported revolution in Tibet, Communists gave the whole process an ideological twist and coloring. This was manifested in the frequent use and almost exclusive reliance on statistics as the "objective" measurement of "progress" in Tibet. Inflation of figures and statistics was inevitable. Since the party-state held a virtual monopoly over statistics during the 1960s and early 1970s, there were few alternative sources of information on Tibet, let alone reliable statistics. Moreover, after the Dalai Lama's escape in 1959, and the political dynamics which engulfed the Tibetan Question increasingly in the ocean of the Cold War, the Communist closure of the Tibetan economy to the outside world was complete. Against this background, Beijing did feel the political necessity to invite some Western but regime-friendly journalists to examine the Tibetan economy and social change. But unfortunately their statistics were neither independent nor neutral; they seemed only to echo and substantiate the official Communist claims. So I would not rely on statistics of any kind for the 1960s and much of the 1970s concerning the Tibetan economy.

The 1960s began on a positive note: historically significant land reform, wasteland reclamation, small-scale but useful mini-irrigation projects. If these down-to-earth and much-needed reforms had continued, Tibetan peasants and nomads would have benefited much more than ever before. But soon the Tibetan economy and peasants were subjected to a series of Mao Zedong's radical ideological projects such as communes, which deprived Tibetans of operational private property, especially land and geography-granted freedom; and the Great "Proletarian Cultural Revolution," which destroyed Tibetan traditions and brought much human suffering to the Tibetan commoners.

In the early 1960s China suffered from famine,[7] which naturally affected the Tibetan region as well. As a result, Tibetan peasants and nomads experienced famine for the first time in their recorded history.[8] However, the Tibetan economy, though entirely pre-industrial in its basic structure, was able to overcome the food shortages. In fact, thanks to land reform, wasteland reclamation, and mini-irrigation works, agro-nomadic production as a whole steadily increased. This leads to one of the fundamental anomalies in the Chinese Communist economic policy of the 1960s and 1970s in Tibet, which might have implications even today: Where did the Tibetan economic surplus go? Even under the *ancien régime* there used to be some surplus that was willingly and voluntarily given to religious institutions. The Tibetan surplus was even larger under the irreligious communist system because of land reform and improvements in agricultural techniques, which boosted agro-nomadic production. Simply put, the surplus was squeezed out of the peasants and nomads by the Communists much more effectively than the Tibetan feudal lords ever could manage, in order to meet the growing military and political needs of the expanding Chinese state in Tibet.[9] To meet such requirements, the state tried to alter even the Tibetan crop patterns. Wheat cultivation was one such official attempt. There was no visible improvement in the living standard of the average Tibetan during this period.

Radicalism Dismantled: Decollectivization, the Open Door, and Population Transfer

With Deng Xiaoping's return to power in 1979, the Chinese economy and society began to open up to the outside world, particularly to the West. This open-door policy benefited Tibet as well, and the Tibetan economy and society gradually opened up, though to a lesser extent. In fact, in the 1980s there emerged the possibility of alternative sources of information on contemporary Tibet and the official statistics became realistic for the first time since the Communist takeover.

The decade of the 1980s began with the official dismantling of the radical (Maoist) economics and politics that had affected the Tibetan region for decades. Decollectivization was the most dramatic measure in Tibet, restoring Tibetan property and social freedom. Between May 22 and June 1, 1980, Hu Yaobang, then the party secretary, led China's fact-finding delegation to central Tibet and issued a six-point directive. First on the directive, autonomy (*rang-skyong ljong*) was defined as "having the right to decide for oneself," but this definition did not pertain to the political plane; it referred mainly to economic decentralization. Second, as a corollary, the policy directive instructed that the Tibetans should be exempted from taxes and work without pay. They would also be free from meeting compulsory state purchases and their products could be purchased at negotiated prices (market values). Third, the new policy suggested a flexible economic policy suited to the specific and actual conditions in the TAR, which would be carried out with a view to applying to the whole of the Tibetan economy. Fourth, the central government (Beijing) would increase funding to the autonomous region in order to develop the local economy and improve living standards. Fifth, within the "socialist" framework, Hu admitted it would be necessary to make "vigorous efforts to revive and develop Tibetan culture, education and science." Sixth and last, the directive strongly recommended that Tibetan participation in the local administration should be enlarged: full-time Tibetan cadres should account for more than two-thirds of all government functionaries in the TAR within two to three years.[10]

The effect of this new economic policy was immediately felt in Tibet in the early 1980s. Not only did average Tibetans, especially peasants and nomads, breathe a great sigh of relief after the two decades of Maoist radicalism, but the Tibetan economy showed signs of recovery. Agro-nomadic production increased and returns for the first time actually went into poor Tibetan hands and mouths. Along with this marked improvement in the Tibetan living standard and general economic conditions was the quality of social freedom visible all over the Tibetan plateau. If such positive trends in the Tibetan economy, which directly flowed from Hu Yaobang's sane and moderate new economic policy for the TAR, had continued, Tibetan peasants and nomads would have benefited more than during the "liberation" of 1950 or "democratic reform" of 1959. But by September 1983, the party-state put into effect its long-term population transfer policy, with unprecedented impact on the Tibetan economy and calling into question the survival of Tibetan identity on the plateau. Almost immediately, in 1983, 50,000 Han Chinese workers migrated to Tibet; in 1984, about 10,000 Chinese households from neighboring Sichuan and Gansu provinces settled in the TAR's few urban locations. In May 1984 about 60,000 Chinese "peddlers and craftsmen" from twenty Chinese provinces and cities arrived at Tibetan urban centers to work on the new major projects.[11] These figures are not entirely dependable, but they can be considered credible indicators of a significant and even crucial component of a new economic policy and practice operational since 1983: population transfer policy, not only as a long-term hidden intention, but as a public policy now implemented and announced by the party-state to its media.

The timing of the Chinese Communist official policy of population transfer in 1983, at a time when the Tibetan economy was showing signs of recovery and normalcy, calls into question Chinese Communist intentions toward the Tibetan population. Was their timing dictated by the Marxist mission in a pre-industrial Tibet (i.e., economic development), or by the Han Man's burden, which envisages the final solution to Tibet as the total and eventual Tibetan assimilation into a greater China? There is some evidence to suggest that the state's first and foremost objective in Tibet is not economic development; instead, control of the area seems to be an increasingly important means to achieve China's politico-military or strategic objective in Inner Asia. We might recall that Hu Yaobang's tax exemption limits and his agreement to increase Tibetan participation in the local administration by two-thirds were limited to three to five years. And the three-year limit was over by 1983. This is what I call the cunning of history in Chinese economic policy and practice in Tibet, which occurs frequently in each phase of Sino-Tibetan development since 1950.

According to informed sources,[12] prior to 1983, any Han Chinese who desired to visit and settle in the TAR, apart from soldiers and those working in the Chinese administration, was required to obtain a special permit from the TAR government.

From 1983 onward this requirement was lifted and henceforth any Han Chinese desiring to do business or settle in the TAR was welcomed. Therefore, the year 1983 marked the formalization and operationalization of population transfer and henceforth the TAR was open to Chinese immigration. Much earlier, other urban centers and fertile flatlands in neighboring Amdo and Kham were subjected to surreptitious and gradual Han immigration as Chinese authorities pretended to ignore such Han settlements. But the TAR was a special case as agreed in the Seventeen-Point Agreement of 1951, and no such surreptitious Han immigration could be openly and formally tolerated.

Since Tibet's geography and climate on the whole are unsuited to a wholesale Han Chinese migration, Chinese authorities decided that population transfer had to be selective and strategic. It could not be like Manchuria whose rich resources and bearable climate attracted so many Han colonists that they now completely outnumber the original inhabitants. However, there are fertile flatlands and warm rich valleys on the plateau that are suitable for Han settlements. Apart from such oases, the semi-official rationale for the post-1983 population transfer seems to be to let in Han Chinese migrants and immigrants who would occupy strategic positions in all the modern sectors of the emerging Tibetan economy. Toward such demographic ends, we see the Han concentrated in politically and economically strategic urban centers such as Lhasa and Chamdo, where the local economy is dominated, if not already monopolized, by the Hans. In particular, the TAR is prone to massive Han migration from Sichuan, one of the most densely populated provinces in China. The Chinese population transfer has been selective and compared to the total Chinese population of 1.3 billion, small. But when the whole Tibetan plateau is declared open for Chinese business, immigration, or tourism, among the over one billion Chinese, there might be some enterprising, energetic men and women who long for new frontiers outside of a crowded China. Hence there is a danger that the Chinese "small scale" might become the new majority in a sparsely populated Tibet, and what is more pertinent to our discussion, the new dominant majority in the new economy.

Recent Efforts at Economic Development

The Chinese Communist practice of selective population transfer, the recently announced Golmo–Lhasa railway construction, as well as the state's deliberate neglect of Tibetan education are part and parcel of a gigantic Han-centric economic vision in the current campaign to "develop the western region."[13] This campaign seeks the ultimate political solution to the Tibetan Question under the guise of economic strategy in the age of globalization. This is clear from the current Communist sources. Chen Dongsheng, one of the key master planners for the development of the western region, stated that one purpose of the scheme is to "guarantee the inviolability" of the PRC's borders in the western region. Chen confessed that the other purpose of his scheme is to "smash our enemies who want to use the poverty and the contradictions between races to create a Kosovo-style crisis in Asia."[14] Nor is the construction of a railway in Tibet for economic purposes, even primarily. Communist authorities admit that railway construction is absolutely necessary in order to "consolidate national defense and unity of nationalities" in view of Tibet's geostrategic location. It is quite clear that it is a political decision made by the party-state for security and strategic reasons.[15]

Thus, strategically motivated and conceived, China's economic vision of "develop the western region" is Han-centric in its essence and effect, and envisages a classical colonial pattern of development. The western region and particularly the Tibetan plateau will, according to this Communist manifesto, provide raw materials for a Middle Kingdom manufacturing metropolis. In this scenario, the PRC hopes it can ensure and sustain the high growth rate of the Han areas in a twenty-first-century world of fast-dwindling resources. This is stated in a Chinese history textbook entitled *Tonghua-lu:* "On the one hand, the expansive western areas have rich deposits of natural gas, petroleum, hydro-electric power, and other important resources, [yet a] huge volume of hydro-electric power is wasted there; on the other hand, the rapidly developing eastern region needs the import and supplement of various resources and energy."[16]

China's Tenth Five-Year Plan (2001–2005) selected four key projects to accelerate "develop the western region." These priority projects include "west-to-east gas transfer, west-to-east power transmission, south-to-north water diversion, and Qinghai–Tibet railway projects."[17]

Of particular urgency to China's current and future economic needs are oil and natural gas to be transferred from the resource-rich western region to the power-hungry industries in the Han hinterland and the eastern region. China imported 40 million tons of oil in 1999 and 60 million in 2000. Experts believe that China's energy needs will further escalate in the years to come. Therefore, the PRC places a high priority on the development of oil fields in the Tarim Basin in southern Xinjiang, the Tsaidam Basin in northeastern Tibet, and the Ordos Basin in Inner Mongolia.

No less important is the South-to-North Water Diversion Project. Northern China, being densely populated, has been experiencing chronic water shortages. Centuries of intensive agriculture, rapidly expanding population, and recent industrialization have drained almost all the available water resources in the north. All this has resulted in sinking water sources, increased salinity, and dry rivers and lakes in the region. Of China's 668 cities, 400 face water shortages, and peasants riot over precious water supplies. Water is directly related to China's decline in agricultural output. In the future, China will have to import much more grain than now; by 2025 this figure will reach nearly 175 million tons.[18] In order to resolve this serious water crisis, Beijing decided in 2000 to revive the long-abandoned South-to-North Water Diversion Project with three possible routes from the Drichu (Yangtze) River to northern China. According to China's Ministry of Water, 48 billion cubic meters of water will be drained annually from this Tibetan river.

The authorities have observed that a huge volume of hydro-electric power is wasted in the region, probably referring to the Tibetan plateau. The Tenth Five-Year Plan is undertaking power projects with a combined installed capacity of 29.2 million kilowatts in the western region, accounting for one-third of China's power projects. They would have an installed capacity of 14.84 million kilowatts, 59.7 percent of which would be built in the western region. Currently, of the potential hydro-power resources of 378 million kilowatts installed capacity, only 9 percent of the resources have been developed. Seventy percent of PRC's hydro-power resources and 64 percent of its coal resources are located and found in the western region.

These gigantic industrial projects conceived by the Chinese Communists derive their inspiration and structure from Stalinism. Stalin, as we know, without any compunction, indulged in industrial gigantism in his ruthless rush for "progress" in the former Soviet Union of the 1930s. Today the Chinese Communists are executing such gigantic and ruthless projects that have absolutely no room for indigenous people and their identity, nor for the trans-Himalayan environment and the fragile ecology of the region.[19] Being so gigantic as well as so Sinocentric, these projects, if allowed to proceed and succeed, will push the Tibetan people and their identity to the peripheries of the economy and will ultimately lead to the disappearance and extinction of the Tibetans as such from the Tibetan plateau. The scope of these projects is so sweeping that it is like the strategic scope of the 1950 "liberation," which altered the very balance of power in Asia. These mammoth projects are designed to create a futuristic Han-centered economy that will not only exploit the Tibetan resources to benefit the party-state, but will make Tibetan labor (or participation) *redundant,* and declare Tibetan education and culture *functionless.* Economics and economic mechanisms in the process are given the negative task of effecting the final disappearance of Tibetans if they do not willingly subject themselves to the economic process of Sinicization.

Some Western leftist Sinologists have been quite successful in painting the Chinese Communists as quite different from the Soviet Communists. They may be correct in relation to Communist behavior and deeds in China proper. But in relation to Tibet or Tibetans in general, Chinese Communists are as sophisticated as Stalinists—thanks to their Confucian cultural background. Take, for example, their propaganda approach to projecting the gigantic Stalinist industrial projects in the western region. They seem to know that their "projects" will face hostile international reaction and criticism. In order to blunt such reaction and criticism, they have sought American "involvement,"[20] however symbolically. There was a Sino-U.S. seminar in May 2001 held in Beijing on the Qinghai–Tibet Railway Project, organized by the Construction Industry Manufacturers Association (CIMA) from Milwaukee, Wisconsin, and the PRC Ministry of Railways.

The economic and demographic future of the Tibetans on the plateau in this Communist vision of a gigantic Sinocentric, Han-centered economy in the western region is reflected and manifested in the current situations in Lhasa and Golmo, the starting point of the Qinghai–Lhasa railway now under construction. The proposed railway, when completed, is scheduled to run eight trains daily in each direction. Apart from increasing strategic mobility and enhancing Communist logistics on the Tibetan plateau, the railway will definitely increase the influx of Chinese immigrants, especially from Sichuan. For instance, Qinghai's population increased from 1.3 million in 1949 to nearly 5 million today due mainly to the railway connection. Golmo was once a vast pastoral land inhabited by a few hundred Tibetan nomads. Today it is the second largest town in Amdo (Qinghai). In 1994, Golmo had a population of 88,500, of which only 3,600 were Tibetans (4.4 percent). The Tenth Five-Year Plan envisages further expansion and "urbanization" of Golmo.

Besides the Stalinist industrial gigantism I have described in this section, Chinese Communists have, in recent years, engaged in more specific but massive projects to facilitate the migration of Han settlers into Tibet. The so-called western poverty reduction project is a clear example. An initial component of this project was to develop agriculture in the Dulan area of Amdo, and to transfer 58,000 Han settlers there. In 2000, the World Bank withdrew its US$40 million loan to this project in the face of stiff protests from Tibetan exiles and their international supporters.

The Chinese population transfer to Tibet has had devastating economic effects on the indigenous population. The Han settlers and their children take away better houses, jobs, schools, businesses, and hospitals from the indigenous people, who are automatically pushed to the peripheries of this new economy as tourist curios. In 1992, a curious western tourist conducted a covert survey in the TAR. He observed that there were 12,227 shops and restaurants in Lhasa (excluding the Barkhor) of which only 300 were owned by Tibetans.[21] In Tsawa Pasho, southern Kham, the Chinese owned 133 business enterprises whereas the Tibetans owned only 15. The ownership ratio is similar in other Tibetan towns: 748 to 92 in Chamdo, 229 to 3 in Powo Tramo.

I have been quite critical of the Communist attempt at Stalinist industrial gigantism in the name of internal globalization and development because I see an alternative to Stalinism for the Tibetan culture areas within China.[22] In this post-Communist era, tradition need not be negated, rejected, and consigned to the dustbin of history, as Stalin did and as the Chinese Stalinists are doing today. In fact, tradition and culture, if judiciously used, could and can be the maidservant of an industrial revolution and an effective lubricator of development, as modern Asian history indicates. This means we must consider not only state intervention in the economy, but also social sources of productivity that owe their origins to a great living tradition, namely Buddho-Confucian culture.

More specifically, I believe it would be unfair and incorrect to dismiss the Tibetans as unfit for, or incapable of, modernization as the Chinese Stalinists and Han nationalists are currently doing. I feel this is done out of sinister motives and a diabolical design to ultimately obliterate the Tibetan race and identity from the Tibetan plateau by justifying the Han Man's burden in pre-industrial Tibet and Chinese population transfer to the Tibetan plateau.

Tibetan refugee experiences in India, Nepal, and Canada indicate that given favorable conditions of freedom and fair opportunity, Tibetans can modernize in their own ways, which are by no means unique or eccentric. They conform to the Asian general pattern: modernization mediated by culture, not subjected to systematic Stalinist industrial gigantism. In Nepal former subjugated peasants and nomads of *bstod* (western Tibet) and warriors of Kham (eastern Tibet) have demonstrated considerable entrepreneurial skills in setting up and managing their carpet factories and competing in the world market, which I saw in the summer of 1997. In the early 1970s a number of Tibetan refugees were invited to immigrate to Canada. The first generation worked in factories, but their sons and daughters have become doctors, engineers, and lawyers, many of whom I have met in the West. And the most amazing thing about Tibetan refugees' experience in India is the ingenious ways in which Tibetan commoners, most of whom are illiterate, have demonstrated their elementary or almost instinctive sense of business enterprise: sweater-selling in the winter throughout India. I have witnessed firsthand their sense of enterprise, business leadership, and voluntary organization at the grass-roots level, all of which have made them economically better off than their host society, rural India.

But do we as academics see a successful alternative to the Chinese industrial gigantism for the Tibetan plateau and the Tibetan culture areas? We do. Bhutan is an independent nation and a member of the United Nations. Its culture and tradition are a distinct and distinctive variation on the Tibetan civilizational pattern, and most Bhutanese are of the Tibetan racial stock. They have four decades of successful engagement with modernity and industrial development during which they have negotiated well with tradition and have utilized successfully their cultural resources to modernize yet maintain their identity. Their model of development is exemplary: people-oriented, ecology-friendly, and congruent with their cultural patterns. By the end of the twentieth century the Bhutanese model of development was quite successful, recording a 13.5 percent growth rate in certain industrial sectors of the economy,[23] thanks to Indian assistance and support.

Bhutan's positive engagement with modernity, and the consequent recorded success of the Bhutanese model of development, presupposes modern education. So does the relative success with which post-1959 Tibetan diaspora communities have integrated into modern, competitive industrial economies. Modern education is the gateway to modernity and development. But unfortunately the Chinese Communist authorities in Tibet, since their takeover and especially since 1959, have shown no interest in Tibetan education. They have, in retrospect, deliberately neglected the field of Tibetan education in order to leave the field open to Chinese education as the only alternative to modernity in the Sino-centric Stalinist industrial gigantism. In such a perspective and process, education automatically becomes the indirect but effective instrument of Sinicization. Tibetans oppose Sinicization not because they dislike Confucian culture, but because they, like other ethnic groups, prefer their own language and culture.

Tibetan public figures in the PRC, such as the former Panchen Lama and Ngabo Ngawang Jigme, strongly advocated Tibetan education in the TAR as one of their constitutional rights. A number of eminent Tibetan scholars in China, such as Dungkar Lobsang Trinley, Dherong Tsering Thondup, and Khenpo Jigme Phuntsog,[24] deplored the party neglect of Tibetan education and strongly recommended Tibetan language as the medium of instruction in the TAR. These scholars were not and are not interested in Tibetan language as the vehicle of traditional Buddhist scholarship. Their interests in the Tibetan language are technical and scientific, and they hoped that a Tibetan medium of education would meet the scientific and technical requirements of the new economy and society. Their academic recommendation of a Tibetan-medium education system as most suitable in the TAR was supported by a scientific educational experiment. In 1995 a Tibetan school pilot project in the TAR showed that Tibetan students studying in a Tibetan-medium school passed school graduation examinations with an average of 80 percent, and Tibetan students studying in a Chinese-medium secondary school scored an average of 39 percent.[25] Despite such encouraging results and strong evidence for Tibetan-medium education in Tibet, the party-state not only ignored Tibetan education but opted for their not so hidden agenda, Chinese. In 1997 TAR Deputy Party Secretary Tenzin disclosed a party decision to make Chinese mandatory and compulsory for Tibetan students from primary school onward.[26] The party sees the Chinese medium as the most efficacious instrument of Sinicization of the Tibetan race in order to wipe out their identity from the Tibetan plateau. It means that hardliners in the state, party, and army who are Han nationalists to the core have come forward to dominate economic policy and practice in Tibet, especially since 1983. Han nationalists are always conscious of the fact that imperial China in the past had coveted Tibet, but it took the PRC to realize that dream. Consequently, it would seem to such hardliners that it is the sacred duty of the Communists to kill the very idea of Tibetan identity "once and for all"[27] through Sinicization and Stalinist industrial gigantism. Economics in the age of globalization would do its trick and realize the cherished Communist dream without the PLA firing a single shot.

Conclusion

The current campaign to develop the western region reveals the Chinese Communists' latest strategy and tactics in their information war on Tibet. The strategy is to put the Tibet Question in a global economic context and thereby make Tibet policy appear congruent with the basic tenets of the international discourse on globalization. The tactical assumption is that by putting the question in a global context it will sharply blunt any Tibetan aspirations and possible articulation of even a limited quest for Tibetan autonomy, and will make identity irrelevant and in the long run redundant. In this way, the Leninist subjectivity (i.e., the Communist agenda and Mao's interventionist political and economic blueprint for the Tibetan plateau) might be "efficiently" achieved by economic objectivity and globalization processes, processes in which the lone superpower and other economic powers are economically glued together. It is sophisticated information warfare whose consequences will have the negative effect on Tibet intended by the Communists. The cost will be Tibet's autonomy and identity vis-à-vis China and the rest of the world.

Notes

Economics has not been my academic training nor one of my areas of specialization. Yet I realize the importance of economics in our age, and particularly for the Tibetans inside and outside Tibet. In this academic endeavor, I am grateful also to William Alford, S.K. Jha, Lobsang Sangay, Thubten Samphel, Tanka Bahadur Subba, H.K. Taneja, Kunchok Tsundue, and Kesang Yangdon for their inspiration and information. I am grateful also to professors William Kirby and Deirdre Chetham for inviting me to the Harvard University Asia Center in 2002.

1. Luciano Petech, "The Mongol Census in Tibet," in *Tibetan Studies in Honour of Hugh Richardson*, ed. Michael Aris and Aung San Suu Kyi (Warminister: Aris and Phillips, 1980), 234.

2. For a Marxist analysis of the political economy of Chinese Communist rule in Tibet, see Hansvir Singh, "Political Economy of Chinese Rule in Tibet," unpublished Ph.D. dissertation, Jawaharlal Nehru University, 2000, 39–211.

3. Dawa Norbu, *Red Star over Tibet* (London: William Collins, 1974).

4. I use the terms *fair* or *fairness* in the sense advanced by John Rawls in his book *A Theory of Justice* (Oxford: Clarendon Press, 1972). See especially the first chapter of this profound book, "Justice as Fairness," 3–53.

5. Feng-hwa Mah, "The First Five Year Plan and Its international Aspects," in *Three Essays on International Economics of Communist China*, ed. C.F. Remer (Ann Arbor: University of Michigan Press, 1954), 49.

6. Translated by George Moseley under the title *The Party and the National Question in China* (Cambridge, MA: MIT Press, 1966), 107.

7. Jasper Becker, *Hungry Ghosts: China's Secret Famine* (London: John Murray, 1996), 171.

8. Panchen Lama, *A Poisoned Arrow: The Secret Report of the 10th Panchen Lama* (London: Tibet Information Network, 1997), 103.

9. According to some Amdo lamas resident in the PRC, the Tibetan economic surplus is, as they could observe in Qinghai, squeezed out of Tibetan peasants and nomads, and goes to the party-state in the form of taxes of which, they write, the Communists collect nine. See Nammkha, *Bya-khog gi deb-ther norbu' mgyl-rgyan* (China, 2000), 19.

10. For a translation of Hu Yaobang's six-point policy directive, see Foreign Broadcast Information Service (FBIS)—PRC, no. 108 (1980): Q3–6.

11. *Tibet Information Network News Update* (London). TIN is what I call one of the alternative sources of information on Tibet, quite reliable and credible. See also Radio Beijing, 1700 hrs, May 14, 1984.

12. Dr. Kunchok Tsundue, who did his Ph.D. fieldwork in the TAR, Sichuan, and Yunnan during 1993–94 for a German university (Ruhr).

13. We come across the term "western region" in the history of Qing–Dalai Lama relations in which some of the Qing (Manchu) emperors referred to Tibet as the western region. As used by the Communists, especially in the wake of their current campaign to "develop the western region," it refers to western China, which encompasses 5.6 million square km and 300 million people in five Chinese provinces neighboring Tibet, namely Gansu, Qinghai,

Shanxi, Sichuan and Yunnan, three autonomous regions (Ningxia, Tibet, and Xinjiang), and one city (Chongqing). Communists have incorporated Tibetan cultural areas in eastern Tibet into the neighboring Chinese provinces such as Qinghai, Sichuan, Gansu, and Yunnan, constituting 2.5 million square km of the total 5.4 million that the western region constitutes today.

14. *South China Morning Post* (Hong Kong), February 17, 2000.

15. See President Jiang Zemin's interview with the *New York Times*, August 10, 2001.

16. Cited in Consulate General of the People's Republic of China in Houston, Texas, "Four Major Projects Will Redraw China's Economic Division Map," March 18, 2001, at www.chinahouston.org/news/200131720.5006html.

17. See an unusually interesting and useful publication from the Dalai Lama's exile government *Tibet under Communist China: 50 Years* (Dharamsala, India: Department of Information and International Relations, 2001), 73–79.

18. International Centre for Integrated Mountain Development (Kathmandu Newsroom), "China: Drought Leaves Water Shortages, Larger Deserts," August 14, 2000.

19. Chinese environmentalists Song Xinyu and Yao Jianhua report the destructive consequences of these gigantic Stalinist projects on the environment in *Raiding the Treasure House: Oil and Mineral Extraction in China's Colonization of Tibet* (New York: Milarepa Fund, 2000), 13.

20. *Tibet under Communist China*, p. 75.

21. Cited in Habitat International Coalition Israel in Occupied Territories and China in Occupied Tibet, Representative, Statement, Agenda No. 9, Right of Peoples to Self-determination and its Application to Peoples under Colonial or Alien Domination or Foreign Occupation, 49th session of United Nations Commissioner of Human Rights in Geneva, February 8, 1993.

22. Dawa Norbu, "Is Tibetan Culture Congruent with Modernity? Some Clues from the Asian Experience," *Tibetan Review* 34, no. 2 (February 1999): 8–14.

23. Bhabani Sengupta, *Bhutan: Towards a Grass-root Participatory Polity* (Delhi: Knoark Publishers, 1999), 86.

24. *Tibet under Communist China*, 40–41.

25. Catriona Bass, *Education in Tibet: Policy and Practice Since 1950* (London and New York: Zed Books, 1998), 237.

26. Xinhua (Beijing), March 9, 1999.

27. Dawa Norbu, "China's Dialogue with the Dalai Lama 1978–90: Prenegotiation Stage or Dead End?" *Pacific Affairs* 64, no. 3 (Fall 1991): 367.

8

Market Formation and Transformation

Private Business in Lhasa

Hu Xiaojiang and Miguel A. Salazar

Introduction and Research Questions

The purpose of this chapter is to analyze the development of the private business sector in Lhasa, capital city of the Tibet Autonomous Region (TAR) of the People's Republic of China, and its relation to migration from other provinces. The issue of rural labor flows into the TAR has long been debated, almost exclusively in the context of the ongoing political struggle over the status of the region and as part of the macro political strategy, with very little reference to matters of economic development or established migration theory.

Besides the inevitable politicization of almost any topic related to Tibet, this scholarly neglect is the result of three main reasons. First, compared to other parts of China, migration from and to Tibet is both more recent and on a much smaller scale,[1] which has caused most studies of internal migration in the PRC to ignore the TAR. Second, scholars who study migration in general, or China's migration in particular, rarely interact with Tibetan studies scholars, who are mostly historians and researchers on religion, language, literature, and the arts. Third, accurate data on migrants in the TAR in general and Lhasa in particular are intrinsically difficult to obtain. This is not so much the result of official obfuscation and data-massaging as it is the simple result of a lack of accurate knowledge, even on the part of officials in Tibet and the rest of the PRC. Estimates from different sources are usually based on very different definitions of migration and inevitably vary greatly.[2]

Moreover, because of the politicization of the debate over this issue, public arguments often deploy claims about the effects of migration that have long been discredited in the economic, sociological, and demographic study of migration, without any reference to already available theoretical models and empirical evidence from comparable settings. One of the most oft-cited claims is that economic migrants have caused unemployment among local Tibetans and therefore Tibetans are grievously losing out from in-migration.[3] This argument works only under a problematic and highly outdated zero-sum assumption regarding the economic impact of labor migration.

Even this seemingly straightforward claim of "job-stealing newcomers" actually needs to be dissected further. First, are non-Tibetan migrants to Lhasa causing local urban Tibetans to lose their original jobs, either in the public sector or private sector? Second, are non-Tibetan migrants causing Tibetan rural migrants to lose out in absolute terms, meaning that a fixed number of employment opportunities existed before, and independent of, the influx of non-Tibetan migrants, so that non-Tibetans migrants have taken over jobs that otherwise would be filled by Tibetan migrants? Third, are non-Tibetan migrants causing Tibetan migrants to lose out in relative terms, meaning that despite a clear increase in employment opportunities as a whole, the proportion of new opportunities held by Tibetans is smaller than the proportion held by non-Tibetans and the Tibetan proportion is still decreasing?

Economists are in general agreement that China's gradual approach to economic reforms is, overall, Pareto-improving, thanks to its dual-track strategy,[4] though there are concerns about how long such a policy can be sustained.[5] A Pareto-improving economic reform ensures that all segments of the society benefit economically, or that at least none is worse off in absolute terms. Studies of rural migration in many Chinese cities also find that migration is generally Pareto-improving. Despite almost universal local resentment and widespread negative stereotypes that are usually attached to rural migrants,[6] urban dwellers in Chinese cities not only do not lose, but actually gain considerably from the rural labor influx.[7] Studies of immigration around the world have generally supported the idea that migrant-receiving countries tend to experience positive effects on their economies.[8]

This overall beneficial effect, however, comes with fairly significant changes to the relative positions of the various economic actors. The fundamental transition from a planned economy to a market economy in China and East European countries has changed significantly the relative importance of the assets possessed by various social groups. It is therefore inevitable that some groups gain more from economic reforms than others.[9] Though this conclusion is based on cross-sectoral comparisons, the same idea applies to people within the same economic sector. Migrant laborers are very heterogeneous to begin with. This is especially the case if migrants from multiethnic and cross-regional backgrounds interact in the business context of an urban setting. The different aspects of these migrant assets, be they personal, social, cultural, or economic, can therefore act to their advantage or disadvantage depending on the specific context.

How does this process of "asset revalorization" apply in the context of Lhasa? Lhasa is not an industrial city; the only economic opportunities for rural migrants are found in the city's commercial and service sector. In other cities (mostly in coastal regions), however, it is industry, especially the labor-intensive manufacturing sector, that absorbs the largest proportion of rural migrants. Moreover, Lhasa is not a rich city in a rich region. The TAR's GDP is among the lowest of all PRC provinces and it would be a common-sense assumption that migrants should follow the gradients of prosperity. Furthermore, the TAR was the last region to become open to migrant economic activities. Only by understanding the mechanisms by which migrants enter Tibet's economy can we start to reasonably assess the economic and social consequences of labor migration to Tibet, with respect to both its intended and unintended consequences.

This chapter will focus on the development and transformation of Lhasa's current, largely migrant-dominated, private business market and answer the question of what factors bring a specific group into a specific business field.

Data Sources

To address the evolution of Lhasa's private market, this chapter analyzes data from two sources, presenting a fairly complete, dynamic, and detailed picture of market formation and transformation.

The first source is general statistics on the overall pictures of the TAR and Lhasa private economies, collected from an assortment of media and government sources, or from the work of other researchers. These general statistics provide a picture of the scale of market development in Lhasa. The government of the TAR has often used these statistics to demonstrate the overall achievement of the opening and reform program, and the growth of the private sector.[10] At the same time, some scholars have made use of these aggregate statistics to draw conclusions regarding the overall migrant-heavy nature of the market, spelling out negative social consequences.[11]

However, the market economy, by its very nature, is resistant to planning. Economic fields grow and change independently of each other and are interdependent with each other. Therefore, this chapter will use only macro statistics to set up a general background that will facilitate the analysis of more nuanced data obtained from middle-level data sets.

The second source of data are the business registration data (hereafter BRD) of individual businesses in Lhasa City, 1990–2000. BRD are the complete original records maintained by the Lhasa Industrial and Commercial Bureau (ICB). They contain all the private businesses registered in Lhasa City (not including the seven counties subject to Lhasa Municipality), from 1990 to June 30, 2000—a total of 34,000 business records. Every person who registers a business needs to fill in a form at the ICB and pay fees. On the registration form, the owner is asked to enter his personal information: name, age, gender, ethnicity, education, province of origin, and so forth, plus basic business information: business name, address, business area, specialty, number of employees, size of initial investment, source of products, and so on. In the BRD, there is no information about how long the business had existed, and if and when it was closed, though this information does appear in the aggregated statistics of the ICB report.

There was a two-tier classification system for business licenses. People who have permanent resident registration in the TAR got a "Regular Business License" valid for a year. People without permanent residence were only allowed a "Temporary Business License," valid for three months, which was supposed to be renewed every three months in case of longer stays. The rationale for giving such short-term licenses was the informal, and not ungrounded, belief that migrants without *hukou* (residence registration) would not stay long regardless.[12] Many migrant small-businesspeople close their shops when winter comes and head home. Some suspend their licenses; most just leave without informing the ICB. There is a large level of circulation of people every year in Lhasa's private business sector.

From the second half of 1998, as a modernizing measure, the ICB conducted a complete re-registration of all existing businesses at the time, in addition to the registration of new ones. The re-registration, using new forms and giving for the first time unique numbers to each application, was a major modernization of the public regulation of business management, at least from the perspective of officialdom.[13]

During the time of re-registration, the registration fee was lowered. With increased personnel at the ICB, better planning, and an increased determination to catch all previously unregistered businesses, the re-registration results showed a large growth in registrations between 1998 and 2000 (the end date of this study). The ICB estimates a 90 percent registration rate for fixed-location businesses (as opposed to the more elusive sidewalk peddlers). Observations in the field largely confirm this estimate. The rate of registration was very high among all small businesses interviewed, as there is relatively little incentive to avoid it.

Therefore, without the necessary detailed statistics on the business development of each business, some patterns can be determined when we compare the two data sets of registration and re-registration. Apart from the information of each year's new businesses, we can also see from the re-registration how many of the previously registered businesses stayed in business long enough to be re-registered, which gives us a rough sense of the average duration of each type of business.

It is important to note that all the data used in this chapter were obtained in raw, untabulated paper form. Because of a lack of computing facilities, all public statistics from the ICB had to be tabulated by hand; published statistics were therefore simple, with little detailed cross-tabulation. There was no breakdown and cross-tabulation of registration data in terms of ethnic group, province of origin, or other variables.

The fact that the data were found largely in the form of undigested slips of paper has the effect of increasing its credibility. It is unlikely that officials would massage data at such a raw level without losing the incentive to collect the data in the first place.

A final data source was gathered by conducting direct interviews with private business owners and government officials in Lhasa. These interviews were conducted in 1999–2000, and we shall use them to provide descriptive depth to specific business fields and specific outfits.

The Formation of Lhasa's Private Economy Sector

In this section we sketch a general picture of Lhasa's private economy. Specifically shown are the scale of the businesses in general, the annual influx of migrants, profiles of newcomers, the estimated turnover rate, and business specialization by region of origin or ethnicity.

Lhasa Municipality contains seven rural counties and one urban district. The urban district, Chengguanqu, is commonly referred to as Lhasa or Lhasa City. This chapter talks only about Lhasa City, a relatively small city with an area of 53 km^2 (20.5 square miles). It is located in the Lhasa River valley at an altitude of 3,600 meters (12,000 ft.) above sea level, with a permanent urban population of 140,000.

Overall Development of the Private Sector in the TAR and Lhasa, 1980–2000

The technical term for "business" used by the ICB is "individual industrial and commercial household" (*geti gongshang hu*). It refers to privately owned commercial or industrial establishments with eight or fewer employees. The term therefore refers mostly to small businesses. Table 8.1 shows data on the development of small businesses from 1980 to 2000.

As mentioned above, the question of who lost out can be divided into absolute and relative losses. The question of absolute loss is fairly straightforward to address. Given that most outsiders in Tibet before the opening reforms were state employees, and cross-regional private economic activities were strictly forbidden and harshly punished, it is reasonable to assume that in 1980 nearly 100 percent of all private business registered in the TAR were owned by local Tibetans. We can, therefore, easily estimate that in absolute terms, the number of Tibetan-owned businesses in the private sector increased from 489 of 1980 to about 30,000[14] in 2001, at least a 55–fold increase. The number of Tibetans employed in these businesses also increased at a comparable rate because Tibetan-owned businesses usually recruit relatives or other ethnic Tibetans as shop assistants and employees.

The question of relative losers is much more complicated. The ratio of regular licensed business (i.e., permanent residents) to temporary licensed business (i.e., migrant businesses) in Lhasa City is about 3:7. However, for the TAR as a whole, this ratio is inverted to 7:3.

These ratios reflect several phenomena. First, there is the urban, Lhasa-centered nature of the migration economy.[15] Second, the urban 3:7 local-to-migrant ratio found in Lhasa is in fact fairly common in the context of the post-reform PRC. The influx of migrant petty entrepreneurs, although both a dramatic change from the

Table 8.1

The Development of Private Small Businesses, 1980–2000

	Tibet Autonomous Region (TAR)				Lhasa City (Lhasa Chengguanqu) (not including the surrounding seven rural counties)					
Year	Number of businesses	Number of people employed	Registered capital (RMB)	Sales (RMB)	Permanent population	Number of private businesses	Number of people employed	Registered capital (RMB)	Sales (RMB)	Tourists
1980	489[1]	501[2]	0.513m[3]							
1986										(1,400 int'l)
...	...	...	...							
1992	41,830[4]	37,711[5]	101.64m[6]	740m[7]		+3400[8]				22,600[9]
1993	41,830[10]	65,579[11]	174.46m[12]	900m[13]	129,805[14]	+5300[15]				26,000[16] (23,000 int'l)[17]
1994	33,800[18] (12,110 temporary licenses)[19]		154m[20]			Reached 10,000[21]			560m[22]	(28,000 int'l)[23]
1995					136,022[25]					(30,000 int'l)[24]
1996					138,106[26]					
1997	39,000[28]	54,000[29]			140,469[30]					350,000[27]
1998										448,000 (108,000 int'l)[31]
1999	41,125[32]					11,197[33]	16,366[34]		752.99m[35]	445,800[36]
2000	43,000[37]	69,000[38]			140,000[39]	11,389[40]	17,056[41]	45.10m[42]	927.00m[43]	598,300 (148,900 int'l)[44]

(continued)

Table 8.1 (continued)

	Tibet Autonomous Region (TAR)				Lhasa City (Lhasa Chengguanqu) (not including the surrounding seven rural counties)					
Year	Number of businesses	Number of people employed	Registered capital (RMB)	Sales (RMB)	Permanent population	Number of private businesses	Number of people employed	Registered capital (RMB)	Sales (RMB)	Tourists
2001	42,348[45]	63,198[46]	422.21m[47]							
2005										Projection: 1,400,000 (240,000 int'l)[48]

Sources:

1. *Xizang ribao* (Tibet Daily), February 4, 1994.

2. Ibid.

3. *Introduction of TAR Industrial and Commercial Bureau*, 2001. www.tibet-50.gov.cn/cjzs/jingji/32gongshang/2.htm.

4. Data of 1992 are calculated from the information, "although the total number of individual businesses [of 1993, 41,830] was about the same as that of 1992." *Xizang ribao* (Tibet Daily), February 4, 1994. Note from the authors: the numbers of 1992 and 1993 seem to be inconsistent with those of 1994 and later years. It is likely that the statistical criteria have changed during this period of time. The 1994 and later data are more accurate and relevant to this study.

5. Data of 1992 are calculated from the information, "the number of workers they employed [in 1993, 65,579] is 73.9% over 1992." *Xizang ribao* (Tibet Daily), January, 31, 1994.

6. Data of 1992 are calculated from the information, "[1993 figure 174.46m] is up 71.64% over 1992." *Xizang Ribao* (Tibet Daily), January 31, 1994.

7. Data of 1992 are calculated from the information, "the total volume of trading [of 1993] went up by 21.6%." *Xizang Ribao* (Tibet Daily), February 4, 1994.

8. Total number of 1992 is unknown. The increase over 1991 is calculated as 3400 from the information: "5300 were added last year, an increase [of the same index] over 1992 [over 1991]." *Xizang Ribao* (Tibet Daily), February 4, 1994.

(continued)

9. Data of 1992 are calculated from the information, "tourism numbers [of 1993, 26,000] were up 15 percent over the year-earlier [1992] figure." China News Agency, January 19, 1994.

10. *Xizang ribao* (Tibet Daily), February 4, 1994.

11. Ibid.

12. *Xizang ribao* (Tibet Daily), January 31, 1994.

13. *Xizang ribao* (Tibet Daily), February 4, 1994.

14. TAR Press Office, Response to Foreign Journalists' Questions, July 27, 1995. Also "for the entire municipality [including seven rural counties], Tibetan residents took up 87.20%, Han nationality took up 11.95%, and other nationalities took up 0.85%."

15. Total number of 1993 is unknown. But "5,300 were added last year [1993]." Xizang ribao (Tibet Daily), February 4, 1994. Also, "500 came in June and July 1993 alone" according to Kransky, "Central Lhasa and Migration," *Provincial China*, no. 2 (October 1996), p. 21.

16. China News Agency, January 19, 1994.

17. Xinhua Overseas News Service, Feburary 6, 1994.

18. Xinhua News Agency, February 17, 1995.

19. TAR Press Office, Response to Foreign Journalists' Questions, July 27, 1995. It also specifies that "60% of them invest in food services."

20. Xinhua News Agency, February 17, 1995.

21. Lhasa Municipality Economic and Commercial Administration Office, *Investment Guide for Lhasa Municipality*, TAR, China, July 1994.

22. Ibid.

23. *People's Daily*, January 3, 1995. Number of overseas tourists only. The total number is unknown.

24. Xinhua News Agency, January 12, 1996. Number of overseas tourists only. The total number is unknown.

25. Lhasa HIV/AIDS Situation Analysis, August 2000, 4. Said obtained from the TAR government.

26. Ibid.

27. Xinhua News Agency, Febuary 1, 1998.

28. Data by the end of 1998. *China Statistics Year Book* of 1999, found at www.stats.gov.cn/yearbook/1999/e16c.htm.

29. Ibid.

30. Lhasa HIV/AIDS Situation Analysis, August 2000, 4. Said obtained from the TAR government. The number given is 105,023. Seems to be an error. The current number is the result of subtraction of the rural population from the total. It seems more reasonable, especially when compared with the data of 1996, 1997, and 2000.

31. Lhasa HIV/AIDS Situation Analysis, August 2000, 6. Said obtained from the TAR government.

32. Speech given to the TAR Individual and Private Business Association, 2nd Board Member Meeting, by Jiangbian Enzhu, associate director of TAR ICB, January 10, 2000.

33. Lhasa ICB, end of 1999.

34. Ibid.

35. Ibid.

36. Data from 1999 are calculated from the information, "Tourists number of 2000 was 608,300, an increase of 36.45% over 1999." *Zhongguo Xibu: Xizang* [China's West: Tibet] (Beijing: China Continental Press, 2001), 21.

37. *People's Daily*, April 7, 2001, http://english.peopledaily.com.cn/200104/07/eng20010407_67131.html.

38. Ibid.

39. Lhasa (Beijing: China Continental Press, 2000).

40. Lhasa ICB, July 2000.

41. Ibid.

42. Ibid.

43. The whole-year sales are estimated based on the half-year sales (463.55 million). Lhasa ICB, July 2000.

44. *White Paper on Tibet's Modernization*, 2001. Information Office of the State Council of the PRC.

45. Data at the end of March 2001. Introduction of TAR ICB, 2001, www.tibet-50.gov.cn/cjzs/jingji/32gongshang/index.htm.

46. Ibid.

47. Ibid.

48. Projected figure. *People's Daily*, March 23, 2001.

1980 state of affairs and obviously contrary to the romantic image of an unchang-
ing Tibet unsullied by external influences, cannot simply be dismissed a priori as
a negative invasion by outsiders. Many cities in the PRC (and a few abroad, like
Phnom Penh) have seen their small business sector numerically dominated by outsiders. The proportion of Tibetan-owned businesses has undoubtedly decreased
from the 100 percent (of a tiny base) of the pre-reform years. Whether the pre-
reform state of affairs of a purely Tibetan but minuscule private sector was to the
benefit of the local population is highly debatable.

Nevertheless, the question remains as to whether the development of a private
market has damaged or marginalized local Tibetans in ways that cancel out the
benefits of increased absolute levels of economic growth.

In the existing business climate in Lhasa, the direction in which the current 3:7
local-to-migrant ratio might go is not easy to predict. As a component of an increasingly marketized economy, it seems the macroeconomic development of the
PRC in general and the TAR in particular, the capacities of businesspeople, migration patterns, the capacity of local consumers, competition in the local market, and
so on are all going to affect such ratios.

Table 8.1 above shows the rapid increase in the number of small businesses in
the TAR and in Lhasa. From 489 households in 1980 to 43,000 in 2000 represents
an increase of almost 100 times. Two trends are shown in this macro picture. First,
from 1994 Lhasa witnessed an astonishing development of the private sector. The
number of small businesses jumped over 50 percent from 1992 to 1993 and almost
doubled from 1993 to 1994. Second, after 1994, the growth rate of Lhasa's private
sector slowed considerably: while it reached 10,000 in 1994, by 2000 the number
had only increased 10 percent to 11,389.

Profile of Migrant Small Business

While the total number of migrant businesses is large, the size of each business is
very small. ICB 1999 statistics show an average size of 1.4 to 1.5 persons per outfit
among all of Lhasa's private businesses. This average reveals the predominance of
mom-and-pop street shops, plus a very large number of single-person businesses,
mostly stall tenders inside market places. Moreover, the average educational level
of these small business owners is very low. BRD data show that 25 percent of
businesspeople in Lhasa are illiterate, 25 percent have primary school education,
42 percent have junior high school education, 7.5 percent have senior high education, and only 0.5 percent have some kind of tertiary education. The mean educational level is some years of junior high schooling (six to nine years of schooling),
but below junior high graduation level.[16] These statistics, if anything, inflate the
actual levels, as it is likely that in an establishment with more than one person, the
most educated person will be entrusted with registration, not to mention the well-
known tendency to add a couple of years to one's actual education in order to
"look good."[17]

The turnover rate of Lhasa's migrant businesses is strikingly fast. There are no detailed data on how long an average business stays in Lhasa. However, studies of migrant labor in the PRC generally agree on a pattern of short-term work-and-move, similar to the fast-moving *dekasegi* itinerant workers of pre-war Japan. To account for this phenomenon, the terms "temporary migration" and "circular migration" have been coined.[18] The only study on this issue in the TAR is a survey that asked migrants in Lhasa about their intended length of stay.[19] Needless to say, the problem of a major censoring of data is hard to circumvent: those most likely to stay for short terms are obviously most likely to have gone already at the time of a survey. Even considering this inevitable sampling weakness, a genuine statement of intention by a temporary migrant is still often not a reliable indicator of the actual length of stay.

Most migrants adjust their business plans with the utmost flexibility, reacting to changes in economic opportunities and the business climate. Fixed long-term plans never survive contact with changing profit rates. Many ethnographic studies on PRC migrants seem to confirm the wide predominance of that short-termism.[20]

In the case of Lhasa, the availability of the two complementary data sets mentioned above offers a rare opportunity to analyze longitudinally the operation of migrant business. Comparing the two data sets, those who stayed long enough to be registered again in 1998 should have at least two records. Based on the longitudinal model, we are able to track these people and find their mobility pattern. Table 8.2 shows the number and percentage of people who registered each year from 1990 to 1998, and who are also then found in the post-1998 re-registration.

Two things need to be addressed in reading this result. First, how to access the average length of stay of those who didn't register? If obtaining an official registration is a reasonable indication of a level of commitment, it can be assumed that unregistered businesses are more likely to leave a place than registered ones. So if there is a bias caused by the missing registrations, the turnover rate should be higher than registered business data reveal. Second, in this study, only the names of the business owners, not the names of the businesses, have been tracked. That is to say, if one person registered different businesses at different times, he would be counted more than once. But if a business under one name is owned by different owners at different times, it is counted as different businesses. In reality, a business is often sold or transferred to a newly arrived relative rather than to a total stranger. Therefore, continuity and stability inside migrant networks is not captured by the high turnover rate of individuals. However, that issue will not be analyzed in this chapter.

We can tell several things from Table 8.2. First, data confirm the observation of a very high mobility rate among Lhasa businesspeople. Second, the first-year mobility rate is the highest. Among the 2,465 businesses opened in the first half of 1998, less than 30 percent re-registered in the 1998–2000 process. It is reasonable to estimate a 60–70 percent departure rate for newcomers in the first or second year after arrival. Third, the departure rate slows down after the second year of

Table 8.2

The Retention of Migrant Business of Each Year in Lhasa

Year of initial registration	Number of registrations in that year	Number of businesses that also appear in the post-1998 re-registration	Percentage of "lingering" outfits
1990	58	5	8.62
1991	195	16	8.21
1992	859	128	14.90
1993	436	54	12.39
1994	4,998	564	11.28
1995	4,011	430	10.72
1996	4,457	569	12.77
1997	2,823	421	14.91
1998	2,465	697	28.28

residence and stabilizes after five years. This observation fits the predictions of cumulative causation theory:[21] the longer one stays, the more likely one is going to stay. Among each year's migrant cohort, about 10–15 percent stayed in Lhasa over a relatively long period of time. These semi-stable settlers comprise a very small portion of Lhasa's small businesses, at least in comparison to the high yearly influx of newcomers.

Business Concentration

It is evident to any observer that there is a large degree of specialization of trades and businesses by ethnicity or region of origin. Every resident in Lhasa knows whom to go to for what kind of service or products. Corner grocery stores are owned and patronized by a very wide variety of people, but when it is time to have a new dress made, either Western or Tibetan style, the average buyer will go to a tailor from Zhejiang. Tourists who want to buy a ready-made Tibetan dress will go to a Tibetan-owned clothing store. Grain will likely be bought from an ethnic Tu vendor from Qinghai, while measured window glass and aluminum frames will be ordered in a shop run by migrants from Hubei. For gold jewelry, shoppers would go to a Fujian goldsmith, but for silver decorations and accessories, they would undoubtedly resort to a Bai silversmith from Yunnan. To buy jewelry, perfume, antiques, sutras, prayer flags, and so on, they will go to fellow Tibetan traders.

The published aggregate statistics from the ICB show a clear advantage of migrants in absolute numbers, even in prima-facie traditional fields such as "crafts." This aggregate predominance of migrants has led some observers to the conclusion that local Tibetans are at a clear, across-the-board disadvantage vis-à-vis migrants.[22] However, a further breakdown of categories in each field shows a much more complex story.

In the self-completed registration forms, businesspeople often list in great detail the products and services they provide. In fact, the information on the forms is so detailed that it is often difficult to classify. A rough illustration of field specialization by region of origin and ethnicity is shown in Table 8.3.

It is important to clarify further the classification of small businesses into fields. First, the categories of business activities used here are not taken from the administrative sources that collected the original data, but directly from what the business operators and customers in Lhasa classify and perceive their own activities to be. These self-perceptions may be different from the administrators' point of view, or from the point of view of external observers. For example, silverware processing, gold and silver processing, and jewelry are considered three mutually unrelated fields by the entrepreneurs themselves. Cotton quilt reprocessing is an activity distinct from bedding. A tea garden (*cha yuan*) serving green tea is considered a totally different concern from that of a tea house (*cha guan*), which serves traditional Tibetan sweetened tea.

From this table, we see that traditional products (Tibetan food, sweetened tea, brick tea, etc.) are still firmly in the hands of Tibetans. Migrants have come to dominate the fast-growing nontraditional fields instead. Traditional fields, generally speaking, consist of a market of fixed size, primarily determined by the size of the ethnic Tibetan population in and around the city. This is a market with limited growth potential for entrepreneurs, unless it is possible to convince non-Tibetans to adopt a more Tibetan lifestyle.

On the other hand, initial success in nontraditional fields seems to depend on having connections and links with producing regions or else having access to the complex and mostly informal distribution channels that characterize present-day China. Most forms of consumer goods trade require a level of personal relationships with intermediaries and distributors. Lacking an industrial base, Tibet imports the vast majority of the manufactured goods it consumes. Ethnic Tibetans without those links find themselves at an initial and persistent disadvantage to outsiders. Some exceptions are the trade of handicrafts from Nepal that feeds the tourist trade, and the perfume trade. This Tibetan connection with Nepal and India is so far underutilized due to relatively poor communications and other limitations on trade. Smuggling is the most common form of border trade.

In Lhasa's market, we can find various types of ethnic concentrations in specific businesses. First, we find traditional skill-based businesses. These involve skills that are normally passed on only to family/kin members within a strict master–appentice system. Therefore, this kind of artisanship-based business tends to be heavily concentrated in one ethnicity or is geographically based. Examples are the Bai silversmiths of Deqing County, Yunnan Province, and the goldsmiths of Putian County, Fujian Province.

A second type of ethnic specialization is, on the contrary, based on modern knowledge and skills. Specialization in these areas seems to depend largely on the exploitation of first-mover advantage. Skill acquisition forms a temporary barrier to entry, but allows much wider profit margins.

Table 8.3

Business Specialization by Region of Origin and Ethnicity

Specialty	Place of origin	Ethnicity
Knives and boneware	Aba Prefecture, Sichuan	Tibetan
Jewelry	Aba Prefecture, Sichuan; TAR	Tibetan
Antiques	TAR	Tibetan
Brick tea	TAR	Tibetan
Chang[1]	TAR	Tibetan
Hair strings	TAR	Tibetan
Hats	TAR	Tibetan
Dairy crumb	TAR	Tibetan
Pedicabs[2]	TAR	Tibetan
Perfume (from India)	TAR	Tibetan
Pulu[3]	TAR	Tibetan
Sutras, candles	TAR	Tibetan
Thangka[4]	TAR	Tibetan
Tibetan furniture	TAR	Tibetan
Tibetan restaurants	TAR	Tibetan
Tibetan-style clothes (retail)	TAR	Tibetan
Tibetan sweetened tea	TAR	Tibetan
Tsampa[5]	TAR	Tibetan
Vegetable oil	TAR	Tibetan
(Pirated) music cassettes	TAR; Gansu	Tibetan and Hui
Grain	Minhe County, Qinghai	Tu
Beef	Gansu	Hui
Green stone	Gansu	Hui
Woolen tread	Gansu	Hui
Handbags	Guanghe County, Gansu	Hui
Welding	Kangle County, Gansu	Hui
Cooking oil	Linxia County, Gansu	Hui
Handbags	Linxia County, Gansu	Dongxiang and Hui
Auto parts	Henan; Sichuan	Han
Banners	Shaanxi; Sichuan	Han
Bikes, parts and repair	Sichuan	Han
Blacksmiths (white iron)	Qingtian County, Zhejiang	Han
Cotton quilt reupholstering	Yongjia County, Zhejiang	Han
Dongfeng truck parts[6]	Pengxi County, Sichuan	Han
Eyeglasses	Jiangsu; Zhejiang; Hunan	Han
False teeth	Yongkang County, Zhejiang	Han
Fresh flowers	Sichuan	Han
Gas stoves	Jiangsu; Hubei; Sichuan	Han
Glass and aluminum alloys	Jianli County, Hubei	Han
Goldsmiths	Putian County, Fujian	Han
Hair and beauty salons	Sichuan	Han
Karaoke bars	Sichuan	Han
Motor repair	Sichuan	Han
Shop signs	Zhejiang	Han
Solar stoves	Nantong County, Jiangsu	Han
Steamed bread and noodles	Henan; Shaanxi	Han

(continued)

Table 8.3 *(continued)*

Specialty	Place of origin	Ethnicity
Tailors	Yueqing County, Zhejiang	Han
Tea leaves	Sichuan	Han
Telephones and cell phones	Anhui; Sichuan	Han
Vegetables	Sichuan	Han
Hardware	Mixed	Han
Window curtains	Mixed	Han
Silverware and copperware	Heqing County, Yunnan	Bai
Books	Mixed	Ethnically mixed[7]
Cold and hot drinks	Mixed	Ethnically mixed
Carpets	Mixed	Ethnically mixed
Cosmetics	Mixed	Ethnically mixed
Fabric	Mixed	Ethnically mixed
General clothing	Mixed	Ethnically mixed
Groceries	Mixed	Ethnically mixed
Kadian[8]	Mixed	Ethnically mixed
Photo taking	Mixed	Ethnically mixed
Shower houses	Mixed	Ethnically mixed
Snacks	Mixed	Ethnically mixed
Solar energy equipment	Mixed	Ethnically mixed
VCR rental and playing	Mixed	Ethnically mixed

Notes:

1. *Chang* is Tibetan barley beer.

2. Pedicabs are allocated to some Lhasa ethnic Tibetan residents as a welfare measure, so the ownership of pedicabs is 100 percent Tibetan. The owner can then rent them out to peddlers, who are about half Tibetan, half Han, and some Hui.

3. *Pulu* is a kind of Tibetan woolen fabric. It is used to make the usually heavy traditional-style clothing.

4. A *thangka* is a traditional Tibetan Buddhist painted scroll.

5. *Tsampa* is roasted barley flour, the staple of a traditional Tibetan meal.

6. Dongfeng is a brand of truck made in Hubei Province and widely used in Tibet.

7. "Ethnically mixed" here means there are substantial numbers of people of at least three ethnic groups in the businesses.

8. *Kadian*, a cushion made of wool and tapestry, like a small carpet, is used to cover a bed.

A third type is capital-intensive businesses. Here what is critical is the financial advantage of extensive social networks from which financial resources can be tapped at much lower costs than the underdeveloped formal financial markets. A fourth type is niches based on the aforementioned access to production and/or distribution of products. A fifth type is more dependent on local advantage. This includes knowledge of language, customs, and location, which heavily favors local people. In the case of Lhasa, this involves the market for sutras, prayer wheels, and flags, *chang*, sweetened tea, and so forth.

Some authors have suggested that due to the lack of "capitalization, education, and connections," local businesspeople cannot compete with migrants inured and prepared for the "modern sector."[23] However, there is no intrinsic reason why the "traditionalness" or "modernness" of a sector per se should be the crucial determiner of who successfully enters and establishes businesses in what sector. Many tourists have noticed that Hada (Katak), the distinctive, traditional Tibetan greeting scarves, are almost solely sold by Han. On the other hand, Internet cafés in Lhasa are mostly owned by local Tibetans, both rather counterintuitive examples of niche formation.

Below we shall discuss the examples of two fields that are currently migrant-dominated. We want to show that the different patterns of market formation for each field and the different market transformation of such fields are the result of factors and processes much more complex than simple invasion and usurpation by "modernized" outsiders.

Case Studies: Grain/Cooking Oil and Dry Cleaning

In this chapter, two migrant-dominated fields are analyzed to illustrate patterns of market formation and transformation in Lhasa. The first field, grain and cooking oil, is a trade-oriented business in which access to production and/or distribution channels is the key to competition. The business is low-capital intensive, with no requirement of operator formal education or special skill. The consumer in this market is the entire population in the city. The second field, dry cleaning, is chosen for its almost opposite nature. It is a capital-intensive, service-oriented business. Modern knowledge and some skills are required. It is a stranger to the traditional local economy and lifestyle and only caters to "high-brow" consumers.

The Case of Grain and Oil

What is usually referred to as the "grain and oil" sector is large, supplying the most basic staple to the widest possible market.[24] This is a business that requires relatively low initial capital layouts and no special education or skills. As with grocery stores, the most important factor is probably a convenient location. These factors would seem to give Lhasa residents, who control most of the real estate, natural advantages to get a fair share of the grain business. However, by 2000, only 19 (11 percent) of Lhasa's 172 grain stores were owned by permanent TAR residents, and just over half of these 19 owners were ethnic Tibetan. The rest were Han and Hui with broader connections to other provinces.

On the other hand, almost two-thirds of the 172 Lhasa grain stores are owned by ethnic Tu. More specifically and notably, around 90 percent of the Tu in Lhasa are from the same town in the same county of the same province: Guanting Town, Minhe Hui and Tu Autonomous County, Qinghai Province. To a fair degree, the grain business in Lhasa is an ethnic enclave dominated by Tu.

There are no apparent reasons why Tu, and Tu from Minhe County alone, should specialize in, and dominate, the grain and cooking oil trade in Lhasa. The Tu are a tiny group with a total population of only 192,568 (1990)[25] in all of China. Most of them live in four counties at the eastern corner of Qinghai Province. Moreover, Qinghai Province is not a grain-producing province and Minhe County is even less so. Minhe is a mountainous rural backwater, only opened to foreigners in 1997.[26] Farmland is scarce, and drought, floods,[27] and desertification make farming even harder. Traditionally, the Tu were shepherds, not farmers.

Minhe's modern industry is based solely on natural mineral resources and there is a large magnesium smelter and foundry. While relatively large employers, these concerns provide a livelihood for only a fraction of the population. Minhe and its surrounding areas suffer from a very low ratio between arable land and population. This, and the harshness of the weather, has made the whole area into one of the poorest regions in China, constantly dependent on state aid to survive. The World Bank once chose it as a target area for the Western China Poverty Reduction Project.

Minhe County's sole advantage is its geographic location at the juncture of Gansu and Qinghai provinces. It is 120 km west of Lanzhou, the capital city of Gansu Province, and 110 km east of Xining, the capital city of Qinghai Province. The main railroad and highway between Gansu and Qinghai provinces pass through this area. At the western end of the railway is the city of Golmud, the starting point of the 1,937–km-long Qinghai–Tibet plateau highway, and thus the effective railhead for Lhasa. Eighty-five percent of all goods shipped to and from Tibet[28] pass along this route, making Golmud the trade entrepôt for Tibet.

However, the relatively convenient location and the bleak economy of Minhe County alone cannot explain why Tu from Minhe should have such a strong presence in Lhasa's grain market. Tu people of other counties in the same area do not go to Lhasa, nor do Hui from Minhe; other peoples from the vicinity of Golmud do not enter the market either. Is there any specific trait unique to Minhe Tu that has allowed them to corner such a large part of the grain market?

Digging into the history of ethnic Tu business in Lhasa, it seems that the entry of the Minhe Tu into the grain market was accidental. The first business registered by an ethnic Tu in Lhasa appeared in 1992. This Tu was from Gansu Province and set up a mini-grocery. It was only in 1993 that there appeared the first ethnic Tu grain and oil store.[29] In 1994, two Tu brothers came from Huangzhong County, Qinghai Province, and each opened a snack stall. In 1995, however, an avalanche of Minhe Tu into the grain market began. That year, 23 Tu businesses were registered. Of these, 22 were from Minhe County and all were in the grain business. In 1996, 33 Tu businesses opened, all from Minhe, and 32 in the grain business. The trend continued. In the first half of 2000, 99 of the 109 newly registered Tu businesses were in grain. The Tu now own nearly 70 percent of the 144 grain stores registered in 2000.

Most of the Tu grain stores are husband-wife outfits that look very much alike. Shop signs contain exactly the same characters: Grain and Oil Store. The products, services, and prices are almost identical. At the beginning, all the grain was purchased wholesale in Golmud and trucked to Lhasa by relatives, to be distributed to individual stores. Even most of the Tu business registration forms are filled in exactly the same way, apparently following the same template.

The fast growth of the private grain retailing sector coincides with the rapid retreat of the decades-long state-owned grain supply system and the turning over of the distribution of grain to private markets. Private retailers bring in grains that are fresher, better quality, and more varied compared to the old state grain system.

With the growth of a grain retailing sector, the market diversified. People from several other provinces are filling the half of the grain market not filled by Minhe Tu. In 2000, though Tu businesses held a half share of the grain market, people from eight other provinces were also operating. People from Gansu (Hui), Sichuan, Henan, Hubei, Jiangsu, and Shaanxi have all registered grain shops of various kinds. The grain available to Lhasa residents is not only from Golmud, but also Hubei and Jiangsu, both famous high-quality rice producers, and from Henan, which has high-quality flour. Thus, stores started to add specifications in their signs, such as "Qinghai Rice," "Jiangsu Rice," or "Henan Flour."

Regular license holders, that is people with TAR residence registrations, have never been a big presence in this market. Available data show that in 1999 only 7.4 percent of grain stores were owned by permanent TAR residents, that is, 9 of 122. In 2000, this proportion increased to 11 percent, 19 out of 172. Of the TAR permanent residents in the grain market, only half are ethnic Tibetans; the others are Hui and Han. It seems that this distributive business is hard to enter without friends or relatives somewhere in the chain.

Dry Cleaning

Dry cleaning is chosen here as an example because it is clearly one of the least traditional business fields in Lhasa. It requires intensive and ongoing investment that is hundreds of times higher than that needed for a stall or a street-corner grocery shop. The operators need to have knowledge in handling modern machinery, chemicals, and expensive fabrics. Dry cleaning is also regarded as a luxury service, and presumably only caters to a small, high-end customer base. It is completely alien to both traditional Tibetan and Han lifestyles. All the characteristics of this business run counter to the likelihood of local participation in Lhasa, in particular if the modern invasion theory holds. Table 8.4 illustrates the development of the Lhasa dry cleaning market over time.

The table reveals several patterns of how this market was formed, transformed, and saturated in a very short period of time. First: the overall pattern of the dry cleaning business is very similar to the macro pattern of private businesses shown in Table 8.1. The number of newly registered dry cleaners has grown rapidly since 1994, especially in 1996 and 1997, but the trend slowed down after several years. Two: the sector gradually shows a dispersion of the owners' provinces of origin. Though Jiangsu people, mainly from Qidong County, still hold a large share of the market, people from more and more provinces also participate. In 1999, apart from 8 businesses belonging to TAR people, 53 new businesses belonged to people from 13 provinces. Third: TAR people's entry into this totally new and alien field was not

Table 8.4

Registration of Dry Cleaning Business in Lhasa, by Year

Year	New businesses registered each year							Re-registration		
	1992	1993	1994	1995	1996	1997	1998 (half year)	1998	1999	2000 (half year)
Total registered	2	2	11	9	20	23	15	56	61	11
By TAR people			1	1	7	13	3	9	8	0
By others	2	2	10	8	13	12	12	47	53	11
(From number of provinces)	(2)	(1)	(4)	(3)	(5)	(7)	(6)	(7)	(13)	(3)
Total survived	–	–	–	–	–	–	–	–	82	85

late. The first TAR-owned dry cleaners appeared in 1994, only two years after the service first appeared in Lhasa, and they became the third largest market holders after people from Jiangsu and Sichuan.

During the 1998–99 re-registration, 17 dry cleaning shops (9 in 1998, 8 in 1999) were registered by TAR *hukou* carriers (mostly ethnic Tibetans), and 100 (47 in 1998, 53 in 1999) were registered by migrants. Aggregate statistics from the ICB show that at the end of 1999, 82 dry cleaning stores were still in business, 12 owned by TAR people and 70 by migrants. TAR people thus took a 15 percent of market share. Twelve of the 17 TAR shop owners were still in business at the end of 1999, and 70 out of 100 belonging to migrants were in business at the same time. Each group had the same survival rate of 70 percent.

ICB statistics show that in the first half of 2000 there were 85 dry cleaning shops in service, 12 owned by TAR people and 73 by migrants. The net increase in the number of businesses was only 3. In this period, no TAR people registered a new dry cleaning business, as all 11 new registrations belonged to migrants. These statistics mean that the 12 TAR-owned dry cleaners founded in 1999 were still in business in 2000. And among the 73 migrant businesses founded in 1999, 8 had been closed or transferred.

The stabilization of the dry cleaning market is an example of the whole market in Lhasa. Despite the long-argued advantage of migrants in capitalization and know-how, the above pattern indicates a common reaction to market pressures, rather than a result of endogenous advantage for either group. The market pressure in play seems to be simple saturation.

There were 85 dry cleaning shops in Lhasa in 2000. The city of Lhasa has an urban population of 140,000, with an average income of 7,090 yuan (2001).[30] Even adding another 100 percent floating population at peak season, as per the highest estimates (though tourists and rural migrant laborers are unlikely to frequent dry cleaning services) gives us one dry cleaning shop per 3,300 people.

Compare that with Guangzhou, the capital city of Guangdong Province. Guangzhou has an urban population of 9.94 million (7.03 million permanent residents and 2.91 million migrants),[31] with an average income of 14,416 yuan (2001), claimed to be the highest among Chinese big cities and even higher than Beijing and Shanghai.[32] It is one of the first cities in China to have entered the reform era, and is far more modern than Lhasa. In Guangzhou, there are 2,000–plus dry cleaning services[33] for an average of one shop per every 5,000 people. It is easy to see that Lhasa's dry cleaning industry has in all likelihood reached saturation. Nevertheless, in this crowded market we can still find new entrants and, noticeably, an increasing number of local Tibetans.

This rush-to-saturation development pattern of the dry cleaning business is rather representative of Lhasa's service sector. It fits well with the following observations from an ICB official: "Lhasa is after all a small place; you can't compare it with Beijing and Shanghai. How many consumers does Beijing have?[34] How many do we have? There is only so much demand. If you think that Lhasa doesn't have something, then you sell it, and then he also sells it, then ten shops open up, then, Boom!, suddenly the market is full. Unless you bring out newer, fancier products, you can't make money. The price is falling now. It is good for consumers but not good for businesses. Unlike before."[35]

As the market has saturated, competition within the dry cleaning business has become fierce. Profit margins had already become quite thin by the year 2000. Operations costs were becoming more and more of a concern. Thus, cleaners began to hire rural ethnic Tibetans due to the significantly lower wages necessary to hire them.

The competition for new customers is also very fierce. To attract foreign tourists, dry cleaning owners copy each other's often misspelled English signs to add foreigner appeal. Ethnic Tibetans from Sichuan Province have also become a coveted group of new customers. This group, especially males, is believed to spend lavishly and to be able to afford luxuries because most of them are in the antique and precious stone trade. The preference for leather jackets among Lhasa residents is also believed to be an untapped source of customers for dry cleaning.

Cutting corners is fairly universal. Water washing, followed by careful ironing, is often carried out instead of genuine dry cleaning. But unlike in other cities where complaints on the quality of dry cleaning have already made it into both the news and official notice, in Lhasa there simply is not yet enough local knowledge (or concern) about such a recent luxury. Even an official from the Quality Control Bureau admits: "I have never had anything dry cleaned; I don't know how you can wash clothes dryly."[36]

It is significant that ethnic Tibetans are joining this unlikely and very competitive business at a steady rate, competing successfully, and having a substantial share of this market. The factors facilitating and inhibiting participation of ethnic Tibetans in the private market are more complex than a simple modern-versus-traditional dichotomy. Tibetans are exploiting a better understanding of the local market (the local preference for leather is one) and their better position vis-à-vis local authorities to establish their relatively late-coming business.

Comparison of the Two Cases

Comparing these two migrant-dominated cases, we can venture the following hypotheses. First, in the commercial sector, that is, those enterprises related to the trade and distribution of (mostly) consumer goods produced elsewhere, it is likely that the dominance of migrant entrepreneurs will remain for as long as intermediary markets and distribution channels are dependent on personal connections and informal contacts based on kinship and in-group trust. Ethnic Tibetans may improve their relative position in the consumer goods trade if they are able to exploit their existing connections with South Asia. For example, the perfume trade is now controlled almost solely by ethnic Tibetans because of their access to the source of smuggled perfumes in India and Nepal.

Nevertheless, as the market matures and new forms of consumer demand emerge, we can expect new opportunities to open, opportunities that can best be exploited by groups other than the current incumbents. We should thus expect that consumer goods markets will tend to diversify somewhat, to be exploited by new groups and social networks that may well, like the Tu, seem unlikely candidates at first sight. We should expect greater levels of ethnic diversification both within (members of a regional or ethnic group dispersing in a wider field of activities) and without (more groups entering a given activity field).

The second main hypothesis is that the main barrier to entry in which ethnic or regional origin is critical is access to the informal social networks on which trade depends in the PRC at present. Thus, in those fields in which that access is not so critical we will find a much faster increase of ethnic and regional diversification. While factors such as initial capital, skills, and knowledge may give a significant first-mover advantage, facilitating the formation of an ethnic niche, these factors have limited force as barriers to entry for second-wave entrepreneurs, including locals. We can thus expect both higher ethnic and regional diversity in those sectors and an increasing local resident share. While novel products and services, by definition, are initially brought into a place by outsiders, locals will find the way easier as second movers, able to exploit their relative advantage of better knowledge of local conditions and their superior local social capital networks.

Conclusion

Among the large body of literature on the study of immigration,[37] it is accepted wisdom that permanent labor demand is inherent in the very nature of modern industrial societies. As an inherent element of urbanization and industrialization, and through the swift penetration of the market to formerly untouched parts of the economy, modern cities will absorb labor from other, less modernized parts of the economy. This pattern of labor absorption can be observed in most parts of the PRC in the past twenty years. The cities of the TAR, although relative latecomers to economic reform, do not have any special characteristics that shield them from these effects.

It is important to shift attention for a moment from the effects of migration on Tibetans to the ways in which migrants succeed in surviving and thriving in a fairly hostile host social setting in which they have to deal with both an unwelcoming officialdom that, in essence, gives them the status of illegal migrants, and an unpromising economic environment. Students of migration have often wondered about the puzzling success of migrant entrepreneurship. Once-popular theories that depended on the idea of a migrant entrepreneurial personality (or culture) have long been discredited. Attention has shifted to other characteristics that come with the status of migrant, namely the powerful effect that comes from the distinct social networks that migrants form and belong to.

One of the consequences of the importance of social capital in the establishment of migrant enterprises is a marked path-dependency effect in the formation of ethnic niches and enclaves. The relatively accidental initial settling of a small number of pioneers is likely to generate a chain effect that will result in dominance in a given niche.

The serendipity of Minhe Tu concentration on grain is a good example of this path dependency. Ethnic networks greatly influence the recruitment of personnel and the induction of new entrepreneurs, funneling more members of the same group into the field and sometimes resulting in an "ethnic colonization" of the niche. This, rather than an overall modernity advantage, an ethnic conquest of unprepared natives, or official support, seems to be the driving force of the ethnic and regional pattern of specialization we find in Lhasa.

On the receiving end, we also find the patterning effect of the specific structural opportunities provided by the receiving cities. In the case of Lhasa, no jobs in the most coveted public sector occupations are open to rural migrants (of any ethnic group), and there is a marked lack of the industrial assembly line jobs that characterize rural migration into the coastal regions. Instead, the opportunities that exist are in the commercial and service sectors. Both sectors were woefully unprovided for in the days of the planned economy. They are now fueled by increased demand for consumer goods and creature comforts on the part of the heavily subsidized permanent residents of Lhasa. The city, lavished with government largesse due to its delicate political status and having also a tourist industry, is always hungry for services and goods.

The nature of a specific business field—labor-oriented, skill-oriented, trade-oriented, service-oriented, or some combination thereof—intersects with local conditions and characteristics of various entering groups, in particular the nature of their social capital networks and random contingencies of their historical paths to enterprise. The opening up has created an entire virgin field of economic opportunity, a veritable wild highlands of virtually unoccupied economic sectors into which migrants rush.

The most basic of these intersections has been the emergence of middleman outsider groups in charge of supplying the new demand for out-of-region consumer goods. The traditional sectors, because of their cultural and/or skill exclusivity, remain locally controlled. These sectors are also expanding, but at a much slower rate.

In between these two fields lie many potential niches that are not constrained by such barriers to entry. The ethnic and regional participation in these areas is much more mixed, even where a "pioneer" group established an early lead, as in the case of dry cleaning.

This chapter does not address a very important dimension of market formation, the public sector in Lhasa and the TAR, which still employs the best and the brightest of Tibet's working population, and is still considered the most desirable occupation for those entering the job market. The lingering attraction of this latter-day "iron rice bowl" has effects in the private sector that we intend to explore in future papers.

In conclusion, only when we see migration in Lhasa as a phenomenon of *migration,* as opposed to being just another development in a political conflict, can we effectively assess its social consequences. Many questions need to be researched further. Most existing research focuses on the migration pattern to China's booming industrial coastal regions, neglecting the flows into western economies that, like Tibet's, operate in a very different mode. First, in what ways do different economic compositions in Tibet and the industrial coastal regions affect the pattern of migration? Second, most of China's internal migration happens within the Han sphere. Even though regional differences are marked and significant tension can be detected, the issue of ethnic conflict is maximized in minority regions such as Tibet. How does the fact that Tibet is an ethnic region affect migrants' decision making, duration of stay, and expectations? Third, overwhelming evidence has pointed to the pattern of urban/rural dichotomy in China, where social class is largely defined by one's *hukou* status. How does the dynamic of social class interact with ethnic classification in determining the relation between locals and migrants? Last, most research on migration is based on scenarios in which an ethnic minority migrates to a majority region. What factors come into play when the migrants are from the country's ethnic majority and enter a minority region in which as migrants they find themselves the numerical minority?

All these questions, like any academic endeavor, need to be answered with solid empirical evidence from the specific field, with reference to the framework of similar phenomena in the world. We hope this chapter can point out some directions for future research and provide some academic base for future debates on these issues.

Notes

1. The biggest wave of rural migration in China appeared in the mid-1980s, while the peak in Lhasa appeared in the mid-1990s. It is generally estimated that China's rural migration numbers total 100 million. Big cities like Beijing and Shanghai attract more than 3

million migrants each, per year, while the high estimate of migrants to Lhasa in the peak summer season is 200,000.

2. For a detailed discussion of this issue, see Barry Sautman, "Is Tibet China's Colony?: The Claim of Demographic Catastrophe," *Columbia Journal of Asian Law* 15, no. 1 (Fall 2001): 82–131.

3. Tibet Information Network, *China's Great Leap West* (London: Tibet Information Network, 2000), and other pro-Tibet publications and media reports.

4. See, for example, Lawrence Lau, Yingyi Qian, Gerard Roland, "Reform Without Losers: An Interpretation of China's Dual-Track Approach to Transition," *Journal of Political Economy* (February 2000): 120–143; Barry Naughton, *Growing Out of the Plan: Chinese Economic Reform, 1978–1993* (Cambridge: Cambridge University Press, 1996); Terry Sicular, "Plan and Market in China's Agricultural Commerce," *Journal of Political Economy* 96 (April 1988): 283–307.

5. Leong Liew, "Chinese Economic Reform Experience: Limits of a Pareto-Improving Policy," paper presented at the conference "China, India and Russia: Progress and Challenges of Economic Transition" (Kellogg Center, Michigan State University, October 23–25, 1998).

6. Dorothy J. Solinger, *Contesting Citizenship in Urban China: Peasant Migrants, the State, and the Logic of the Market* (Berkeley: University of California Press, 1999).

7. Delia Davin, *Internal Migration in Contemporary China* (London: Macmillan, 1999), 120.

8. Jeffrey Passel, *Immigrants and Taxes: A Reappraisal of Huddle's "The Cost of Immigrants"* (Washington, DC: Urban Institute, 1994); and National Academy of Sciences/National Research Council Report, *The New Americans*, May 1997.

9. Victor Nee, "The Emergence of a Market Society: Changing Mechanisms of Stratification in China," *American Journal of Sociology* 101 (1996): 908–949.

10. See *White Paper on Tibet's Modernization*, 2001, by Information Office of the State Council of the PRC and other TAR official publications on economic development.

11. See John Kransky, "Central Lhasa and Migration: Economic Development and Social Consequences," *Provincial China*, no. 2 (October 1996): 16–44, as well as many publications by the Tibet government in exile on economic issues.

12. Interviews with ICB officials, 2000. However, interviews with businesspeople show that they believe that such a practice was designed by the ICB as a "local protection measure" to collect more renewal fees from migrants, which "regular license" holders can skip.

13. A more recent upgrading measure has taken place from July 1, 2000, when the ICB started to use the national standard five-year business license for all businesses regardless of the applicant's *hukou* status, as a measure to keep up the pace of national development after the PRC entered the WTO. The TAR is the last provincial-level region to adopt this national standard, which has been used for years elsewhere. The reason for this delay was said to be that in the TAR all licenses have to be bilingual, placing added demands on the ICB's facilities and manpower, and making it take longer for the ICB to adapt. Interviews with ICB officials, 2000.

14. There are no exact statistics at the TAR level on the proportion of migrant- versus TAR-owned business. This number is calculated by the rather stable total number of private businesses from 1994 to 2001 in proportion to the number of migrant-owned businesses at the TAR level in 1994, assuming the proportion stays constant.

15. For the urban-centered nature of migrant business in Lhasa, see Sautman, "Is Tibet China's Colony?" 82–131; Wang Lixiong, *Tianzang: Xizang de Mingyun* [Sky Burial: The Fate of Tibet] (Hong Kong: Mirror Press, 1998).

16. Educational level is calculated from the data set.

17. Interviews with businesspeople in Lhasa, 1999–2000.

18. Davin, *Internal Migration in Contemporary China*, 120.

19. Kransky, "Central Lhasa and Migration," 16–44.

20. Xiang Biao, *Kuayue Bianjing de Shequ: Beijing Zhejiangcun de Shenghuoshi* [Community Beyond Borders: Life History of Zhejiang Village in Beijing] (Beijing: Sanlian Press, 2000).

21. Howard Becker, *Outsiders: Studies in the Sociology of Deviance* (New York: The Free Press, 1963).

22. Arthur Holcombe, "Impacts of Economic Reform and Opening Up Policies on Local Ethnic Population Living Standards in China: The Case in Tibet," paper presented at Conference on Financial Sector Reform in China, Kennedy School of Government, Harvard University, September 2001; Kransky, "Central Lhasa and Migration," 16–44.

23. Holcombe, "Impacts of Economic Reform."

24. Despite the stereotypical impression that Tibetans live on *tsampa* (barley), Lhasa's Tibetan residents have long preferred rice and wheat flour when available. *Tsampa* has become a flavored snack rather than a staple for urban residents.

25. Fourth National Census.

26. See www.chinainformat.com/Archive/x9709/970930.html.

27. From August 4–7, 1999, torrential rains flooded the upper reaches of the Yellow River and its Huangshui tributary. Minhe and 14 other counties and 100 townships in Qinghai were flooded. The flood displaced 24,000 people, caused 20.5 million U.S. dollars in economic losses, and damaged 66,700 hectares of farmland. See www.dartmouth.edu/artsci/geog/floods/1999sum.html.

28. *Renmin ribao* (People's Daily), July 5, 2000.

29. Unfortunately, this person didn't write down which province he came from on the registration form, although it is likely that he was the first Tu from Minhe County to do grain trading.

30. Data from 2001. Xinhuanet: Tibet channel, January 8, 2002. Obtained 6/25/02 from www.tibetinfor.com/tibet50.jjxz/new/c01956.html.

31. Guangdong Statistics Bureau. Data from 2000 Fifth National Census. Obtained from www.cpirc.org.cn/5cendata22.htm.

32. *Renmin ribao*, local news, January 30, 2002. Obtained on 6/16/02 from www.unn.com.cn/GB/channel2200/2203/200202/30/155367.html.

33. *Xinkuaibao* (New Quick Paper), June 17, 2002. Obtained 6/17/02 from http://news.sina.com.cn/s/2002–06–17/0925607242.html. "According to Dry-Cleaning Professional Association in Guangzhou."

34. Beijing has a population of 10 million; Shanghai has 13 million.

35. Interview with Tibetan official from the ICB, February 2000.

36. Interview, Lhasa Quality Control Bureau, March 2000.

37. For important works on the study of immigration, see Michael J. Piore, *Birds of Passage: Migrant Labor in Industrial Societies* (New York: Cambridge University Press, 1979); Douglas Massey, et al., *Worlds in Motion: Understanding International Migration at the End of the Millennium* (Oxford: Clarendon Press, 1998); Edna Bonacich and John Modell, *The Economic Basis of Ethnic Solidarity: Small Business in the Japanese American Community* (Berkeley: University of California Press, 1980); Alejandro Portes, ed., *The Economic Sociology of Immigration: Essays on Networks, Ethnicity, and Entrepreneurship* (New York: Russell Sage Foundation, 1990); Oded Stark and Yong Wong, *Migration Dynamics* (Vienna: Institut fur Hohere Studien, 2002).

PART III

Society and Identity

9

Development and Change in Rural Tibet

Problems and Adaptations

Melvyn C. Goldstein, Ben Jiao, Cynthia M. Beall, and Phuntsog Tsering

The manner in which China's economic reforms have impacted on Tibet's[1] rural farmers is one of the least-understood aspects of the controversy over China's management of Tibet. Many in the West have criticized China, arguing that Beijing's overall development policy in Tibet benefits Han (Chinese) rather than Tibetans. Pierre-Antoine Donnet, for example, states, "From the point of view of economic performance, after forty years of Chinese Marxism, Tibet's situation looks disastrous from any angle."[2] Gabriel Lafitte similarly argues that despite large inputs of development funds from Beijing, Tibet would rank at the very bottom of the United Nations' list of nations (if it were a nation), along with countries like Rwanda, Somalia, Sudan, Afghanistan, and Mozambique.[3]

The Chinese government, not surprisingly, argues otherwise. Although it recognizes that Tibet is one of the poorest areas in China, Beijing consistently cites official government statistics to demonstrate the success of its policies in improving economic conditions there.[4] In a similar vein, an academic study of macro development in Tibet concludes that "Tibet has moved from quasi-stagnation before 1959 to a plateau of rapid dependent growth today," the term "dependent" here meaning that the growth derives from central government funding.[5]

In one sense, such a divergence in views is not surprising, given the dearth of independent research data. Virtually all publications on development in Tibet are based on picking and choosing from often-dubious official Chinese government statistics. Despite the fact that roughly 81 percent of Tibet's population reside in

This chapter is copyright 2003 by The Regents of the University of California. Reprinted from *Asian Survey*, vol. 43, no. 5, pp. 758–79, by permission of The Regents.

rural villages, virtually no data deriving from firsthand fieldwork in farming communities exist.

This article addresses that gap by examining current conditions in village Tibet and the manner in which the economic changes engulfing the rest of China have played out there. In particular, the paper examines the interaction of three critical areas of change—decollectivization and land division, population and family planning, and economic development and labor migration—and the manner in which Tibetan farmers are adapting to it.

The data presented in this paper are based on a study of life in rural Tibet that was conducted from 1997 to 2000 by Case Western Reserve University's Center for Research on Tibet and the Tibet Academy of Social Sciences in Lhasa, with support from the Henry Luce Foundation. Thirteen farming villages from four rural townships (Chinese: *xiang*) in the two main cultural divisions in central Tibet (Tibetan: *dbus* and *gtsang*) were selected based on the authors' knowledge of rural Tibet and discussions with other Tibetan researchers. The aim of this research design was to include a mix of subsistence situations. Two of these four *xiang* were located close to county seats and better off economically (Panam County's Norgyong *xiang* and Lhundrup County's Khartse *xiang*). The other two *xiang* were located farther from county seats and were less well off (Medrogongkar's Tsashol *xiang* and Panam's Mag *xiang*) (see Table 9.1).

Official statistical data for Tibet's counties give a sense of these economic differences: Panam County placed seventeenth in Tibet's seventy-three counties, Lhundrup forty-seventh, and Medrogongkar ranked near the bottom at sixty-sixth.[6] There are no comparable published statistical data for *xiang* in Tibet.

The study collected a wide range of information including data on social, economic, reproductive, and cultural issues. Traditional anthropological interview methods were used, along with focus groups, participant observation, and informal discussions. In addition, two surveys were conducted: a detailed socioeconomic survey of each household and a separate reproductive survey with all women 18 years and older.

There was no interference from the government in the design or analysis of queries, and no government officials accompanied us to interviews with villagers. Nor did we have to make appointments through officials to see villagers. We were free to visit households whenever we wished, day or night.

Characteristics of the Study Population

The 13 study villages contained 780 households, all of which were included in the study; 49.8 percent of the population were males and 50.2 percent were females. The median age of the sample was 22; 63.7 percent of the respondents 18 years and older were married, 4.9 percent were widowed, and less than 1 percent were divorced. Household size was large, the average containing 7.1 persons, with a range from one to 15 people.

A breakdown of the composition of the population by age and sex reveals an expansive triangular shape, with 34 percent of the population under the age of 15.

Table 9.1

Location and Size of the Study Population

	# of households	% of households
Ü		
Lhasa Municipality		
Lhundrup county	199	25.5
Khartse *xiang*	199	25.5
Chokartse Village˙	31	4
Nemna	21	2.7
Khartse	49	6.3
Bhondrong	33	4.2
Thongman	65	8.3
Medrogongkar county	199	25.5
Tsashol *xiang*	199	25.5
Tsashol Village	93	11.9
Thagya	105	13.5
TSANG		
Shigatse Prefecture		
Panam1	382	49.1
Norgyong *xiang*	198	25.4
Norgyong Village	108	14
Shobo	69	8.7
Panam2		
Mag *xiang*	185	23.7
Monkhang Village	60	7.7
Thondrog	35	4.5
Dechen	90	11.5
Total	780	100

*All village names are pseudonyms.

This is intermediate between adjacent Third World countries such as Nepal and Bhutan, which have 43 percent of their population under 15, and China as a whole, with 26 percent. The age-dependency ratio—the proportion of the population in the dependent ages (under 15 and over 65) relative to those in the productive ages (15–64)—was 63.6. This also was intermediate between Nepal/Bhutan (respectively, at 88.7/85.2) and China as a whole (47.1 percent).[7]

All 5,590 individuals in the 13 villages were ethnic Tibetans. There were no Han or Hui (Muslim) Chinese living there, either as residents or as temporary workers. Nor were any Chinese working in the four study rural *xiang* centers as officials or shopkeepers. The villages were entirely Tibetan in language and culture.

The study villages were farming communities, although all also kept some animals for milk and meat. In a few areas where sizable adjacent pastures existed, larger numbers of sheep and goats were raised. The diet was traditional Tibetan,

Table 9.2

Religious Activities That Households Engaged in During 1997

Item	Yes %	(n)	No %	(n)
Invite monks to one's house to do prayers	50.9	(396)	49.1	(382)
Purchase religious items such as incense	43.8	(341)	56.2	(437)
Give alms to monks or monasteries	38.7	(301)	61.3	(477)
Do religious rituals like Lhapsö	33.2	(258)	66.8	(520)
Consult astrologer, shaman	3.3	(50)	96.7	(1,504)
Arrange for monastery to do prayers for one's household	3.3	(26)	96.7	(754)

with parched barley flour *(rtsam ba)* being the staple food in all areas. Villagers, however, now eat a range of non-traditional foods like rice, sweets, and, in some villages, chicken, eggs, and pork.

Constraints on religion in contemporary Tibet exist, but religion is an important part of rural society. In terms of formal practitioners, 3.6 percent of all males were monks, and 2.6 percent of all females were nuns; 16.3 percent of households had one member living as either a monk or nun. These numbers would certainly have been considerably higher if there were no government limits on the number of monks and nuns.

Households were queried about their engagement in a range of traditional Tibetan religious activities during the previous year (1997). Table 9.2 reveals that 50.9 percent of households invited monks to do prayers/rites in their home; 43.8 percent spent money on religious items (prayer flags, incense, etc.); and 38.7 percent gave alms to monks/monasteries. The average household expenses for all religious activities in 1997 was estimated by respondents at 128 yuan ($15.50), but there was a substantial range, depending on the economic status of the households. For example, whereas rich and middle households spent on average 209 yuan ($25.30) and 206 yuan ($25), respectively, poor households spent on average only 15 yuan ($1.80). Other communal religious practices like the pre-harvest village religious procession through the fields *('ong skor)* were also performed.

During a 2002 follow-up stint of fieldwork in Mag, one of the study *xiang,* all 26 elderly (age 60+) were interviewed about the status of the elderly, including their religious activities. The fieldwork revealed that all the elderly engaged in daily religious prayers, but in differing amounts: 35 percent said they spent over one hour a day doing prayers (using rosaries, prayer wheels, or doing circumambulation); 27 percent spent one-half to one hour; 23 percent spent five to 30 minutes; and 11 percent spent very little time. The least-religious interview subject said he spent "very little" time but went on to elaborate that he was atypical, saying, "My children say our father is a strange man who doesn't do prayers or circumambulation. It's true. I do not have a strong religious feeling." But then he added, "We have an altar in our house and our [family member who is a] nun offers butter lamps and the water offering [on our altar]." Consequently, it is clear that villagers in this study engaged actively in a variety of overt religious activities.

Notwithstanding this pattern, government policy considers Tibetan Buddhism in a negative light and constrains/controls it in various ways. For example, limits on the size of existing monasteries or nunneries are enforced, and there are prohibitions against the creation of new religious institutions. Moreover, in the 1990s, many monasteries and nunneries that had unilaterally exceeded their limits were forced to send the "excess" monks and nuns back to their families. At the same time, the government also began to enforce more strictly a rule that prohibits males under 18 years of age from becoming monks, despite the Tibetan tradition of boys becoming monks before they reach their teens.[8] Similarly, the government strictly prohibits the exhibition of the Dalai Lama's photo. There is also an official culture that criticizes traditional religious practices like divination, disparages expenditures on religious rites, and invokes tight regulations on other folk practitioners like shamanic mediums. Informal discussions with Tibetans revealed widespread resentment of this. A few villagers explicitly voiced the view that these policies are incompatible with the state's claim of religious freedom.

Educationally, Khartse, Tsashol, and Mag *xiang* all had primary schools. The first two *xiang*'s schools included first to sixth grade, and the latter only grades 3–6, as students in that *xiang* go to village schools for grades one and two. Norgyong *xiang* did not need a primary school since it is contiguous with Panam's county seat and its students attend the county's primary school after completing grade three in their village level school. On average, 48.4 percent of all individuals in the study had been to school for some period. However, among children 7–15 years of age, it was reported that 80.6 percent had attended school at some time, and 75.4 percent were currently attending school.[9] Of those currently in school, 54.1 percent were male.

We did not try to assess the quality of teaching or levels of knowledge, but 53.5 percent of males and females aged 15–45 reported that they can read Tibetan. Official statistics for 1995 reported 38.5 percent literacy, but this was for *all* persons 15 years and older.[10] In our sample, this percentage increased to 73 percent when only males of that age range were examined. By contrast, only 9.5 percent of individuals aged 15–45 reported that they can speak some Chinese (including the local village officials). Most of those reporting an ability to speak some Chinese resided in Norgyong, the *xiang* located just beside the county seat.

With this general introduction, let us now turn to the major changes in post-Mao Tibet, beginning with decollectivization.

Decollectivization and the Post-Mao Agricultural Economic Structure

As in the rest of China, decollectivization in the TAR from 1981 saw the division of virtually all commune land among member households. In Tibet, this was normally done on a per capita basis.[11] Once land division was implemented, the basic

Table 9.3

Responses to the Query: "Do You Have a Better Life Now Than Your Parents Did?" (percent)

Current age	Better	Worse	Same
60–69 (N = 111)	87.4	6.3	6.3
70–79 (N = 39)	92.3	5.1	2.6

productive resource—arable land—typically was fixed in the household. Children born after land division did not (and still do not) receive land, and households, with a few exceptions, have no way to increase their holdings, because land cannot be bought and sold.[12] Households, therefore, essentially hold their land indefinitely, albeit on an unspecified long-term lease arrangement.

Despite this limitation, land reforms have had a profound effect. Households were once again the basic unit of production that they had been in the pre-communal era. They controlled their labor and capital and, by and large, could manage their farms as they saw fit.[13]

The impact of these reforms on farmers' standard of living is almost universally perceived by villagers to be positive; 94 percent of all 780 households felt their livelihood had improved since decollectivization, and in even the poorest *xiang*, Medrogongkar, 93.4 percent of respondents responded positively, saying their livelihood had improved. When responses were analyzed by socioeconomic status, it was found that 99.1 percent of rich and 81 percent of poor households reported that they had better livelihoods. The almost universal reason villagers offered for this was not new technology but rather their newly acquired freedom to work hard on their own resources for personal profit.

Similarly, when respondents were asked whether they think they now have a better life than their parents, 85.5 percent responded positively. Only 8.6 percent said they were worse off. As Table 9.3 illustrates, even older villagers in the age category 60–79 years held this view—and their parents would have been adults at the end of the traditional society, i.e., they would have been between 40 and 60 years of age when the socialist period began in 1959.

There was also optimism about the future. When asked whether they think their children will be able to have a better livelihood than they now have, 92 percent said yes. In sum, villagers overwhelmingly reported that their material lives had improved since the end of the communal system. A number of specifics about village life were examined in order to compare these reports with actual conditions.

At the time of decollectivization, each household received a share of the commune/state farm's livestock, on a per capita basis, in addition to arable land. These animals (sheep, cow, ox, *dzo* [yak-cow hybrid], yak, mule, donkey, and horse) became private property that households were free to sell or buy as they wished. Table 9.4 reveals that the number of livestock per household has increased 82

Table 9.4

Number of Animal Holdings Per Household

	# of animals/household at decollectivization	# of animals/household in 1996	Amount of change	% Change	# of animals/household in 1996 minus chickens and pigs	Amount of change	% Change
Lhundrup	9.2	18.5	+9.3	+172	15.8	+6.6	+72
Medro-gongkar	7.1	24.9	+17.9	+252	23.7	+16.6	+234
Panam1	20.1	35.1	+15.1	+75	28.0	+7.9	+39
Panam2	22.2	43.0	+21.1	+95	38.5	+16.3	+73
Total	14.5	30.1	+15.8	+109	26.2	+11.9	+82

Source: Local *xiang* and village records.

Table 9.5

Changes in the Number of Milch Animals Per Household from Decollectivization Until 1997

	# of milch animals at decollectivization		# of milch animals in 1997		Amount of change	Percent of change
	Cases	#	Cases	#	#	
Lhundrup	181	0.2	198	3.7	+3.5	1519.3
Medrogongkar	183	1.1	198	4.7	+3.6	327.8
Panam1	179	0.2	197	3.5	+3.3	1415.1
Panam2	168	0.4	185	3.5	+3.0	694.4
Total	711	0.5	778	3.9	+3.4	668.4

Source: Local *xiang* and village records.

Table 9.6

Change in Number of Plow/Transport Animals Per Household from Decollectivization Until 1996

	# of plow animals at decollectivization	# of plow animals now	Amount of change	Change rate (%)
Lhundrup	0.376	1.121	0.745	+198.3
Medrogongkar	1.799	6.696	4.525	+208.4
Panam1	1.119	1.964	0.845	+75.6
Panam2	1.880	2.589	0.709	+37.7
Total	1.382	3.093	1.712	123.9

Source: Local *xiang* and village records.

percent since land division, and more so (109 percent) if nontraditional animals like pigs and chickens are included.

For villagers, milch animals (cows, female yak, and *dzo)* are one of the most important types of livestock because they provide the milk that Tibetans process into butter and consume in Tibetan tea, which is considered essential to a high-quality diet. Table 9.5 reveals a striking 668 percent increase in such milch animals. Not surprisingly, this increase has made butter tea (versus black tea) a staple for most households, 91 percent of which reported they drank butter tea every day. Ninety-five percent of the households also reported that they use more butter now than during the commune era.

Animals are also used for plowing. With the exception of study villages in Lhundrup County that have used tractors to plow their fields since the early days of the state farm in the 1960s, the other village sites all used animal power (pairs of *dzo,* yaks, horses, or oxen) to plow. As Table 9.6 shows, there was an average increase of 124 percent in the types of animals that can be used for plowing.

Agriculture was the core of the local subsistence economy in all of the study

Table 9.7

Perceptions of Changes in Crop Yields After Decollectivization

	Barley		Spring wheat		Mustard seed		Lentils		Potatoes	
	N	%	N	%	N	%	N	%	N	%
Same	98	13	88	13	97	13	44	8	105	14
Less	48	6	51	7	35	5	8	1	28	4
A little more	428	55	360	52	420	56	338	60	413	55
Much more	149	19	139	20	146	19	119	21	146	20
Don't know	55	7	56	8	55	7	58	10	57	8
Total	778	100	694	100	753	100	567	100	749	100

villages, and five main crops were planted: barley (57 percent of fields), wheat (20 percent), mustard seed (12.7 percent), lentils (10.8 percent), and potatoes (3.6 percent). Between 72 percent and 81 percent of respondents reported that the yields of these crops had increased since decollectivization (see Table 9.7). However, it should be noted that only 19 percent of households reported that their yields are now much larger than during the commune era.[14] These reports of moderate increases in yields were supported by our in-depth and focus group interviews.

The critical question for rural households is whether they are able to produce enough grain to meet their family's food needs. Focus group discussions were held to discuss in detail the grain situation of all households in each village. These discussions revealed that 77 percent of households produced either enough grain or a surplus of grain. Direct survey questioning of each household revealed a similar result—67 percent said they had one or more year's grain stored away, and another 21 percent said they had six months' to a year's grain in storage.

Key Indicators

Barley is not only used for parched barley flour, the Tibetan staple food, but also fermented to produce beer. This is consumed in large quantities and is another key "high-quality" traditional food; 95.4 percent of households said they consumed more beer than during the commune era, and 76 percent of households said they now make beer regularly. On average, households reported using approximately 416 kilograms of barley per year for making beer. That amount of grain is roughly equivalent to the output of 3 *mu* (2 hectares) of land which, in turn, is roughly equivalent to the share of land one person received at the time of decollectivization. Thus, conditions are such that most households are able to divert substantial amounts of the main staple crop to the production of a high-quality, non-staple food.

Another important measure of Tibetans' diet and living standard is the consumption of meat. Table 9.8 reveals that the majority of families in Lhundrup and Medrogongkar reported that they ate meat/fat frequently, either daily or several times a week. For example, in Medrogongkar's Tsashol *xiang,* the poorest one in

Table 9.8

Consumption of Meat/Fat in Two Counties

Site	(n) daily	(n) 1–3 times a week	(n) once or twice a month	(n) holidays and the busy work season	(n) rarely or never	Total
Lhundrup	26.1 (52)	45.2 (90)	14.6 (29)	12.6 (24)	1 (2)	100 (198)
Medrogongkar	18.7 (37)	37.9 (75)	12.1 (24)	25.8 (51)	4.5 (9)	100 (196)
Total	22.6 (89)	41.9 (165)				

the study, the proportion was 56.6 percent of households, and in Lhundrup's Khartse, the second richest *xiang,* it was 71.3 percent.[15]

Another empirical indicator of improved livelihood and quality of life is housing. Fifty-five percent (N = 430) of households reported that they had either built a new house or expanded their old house since decollectivization. The average reported cost of these improvements was 5,078 yuan ($614) (median = 3,000 yuan [$363]). Even in Medrogongkar, 42.4 percent of households reported they had either built a new house or expanded their old house.

Thus, despite many reports of extreme poverty in rural Tibet, our data reveal that the majority of inhabitants in the areas studied have made marked progress since decollectivization and secured basic subsistence, in the sense of good food and housing, according to traditional Tibetan standards. However, despite these improvements, because conditions during the communal period in Tibet were poor, the current level of development and the standard of living in rural Tibet are still limited. Compared to rural eastern China, Tibetans clearly have a long way to go, even in the better-off areas. For example, none of the 13 villages we studied had running water in houses, and only the village immediately adjacent to a county seat had a running water tap for the village. Similarly, only that village had electricity. None of the areas had improved dirt roads, let alone paved roads.

Moreover, roughly 14 percent of sample households were poor by our criteria,[16] and another 28.5 percent fell into the category of lower-middle households (which we defined to mean that they had a difficult time meeting their basic subsistence needs). Table 9.9 further reveals that in the two poorest *xiang*—Medrogongkar and Panam2—roughly one-third of the households were poor (37 percent and 31 percent, respectively). And, in Medrogongkar, 47.2 percent of the households reported they were not producing enough grain for their own subsistence from their land. By contrast, government statistics for China as a whole report that less than 5 percent of the rural population was below the poverty line.[17]

Another indication of deficiencies in the rural standard of living derives from

Table 9.9

Percentage of Households in Different Economic Strata by Site

	Lhundrup	Panam1	Panam2	Medrogongkar
Rich	28	40	19	14
Middle	24	30	23	23
Lower Middle	27	19	24	30
Poor	24	8	31	37

the project interviewers' subjective assessments of the physical condition of each family's house. They reported that two and a half times as many houses were considered to be in poor condition than were considered to be in good condition (12.5 percent good, 55.1 percent average/adequate, and 32.5 percent poor).

Still another area where rural Tibetans lag behind is education. Although improvement is clearly being made, and the majority of children now go to school for some period of time, 19.4 percent of children aged 7 to 15 had never been to school (69.4 percent of these were females); only 17.3 percent of individuals who had ever gone to school had completed primary school (six years). Furthermore, only 7.1 percent had gone beyond primary school. Given the rapid modernization of Tibet's economy, it could be argued that rural Tibetans were not getting adequate education for competing effectively in the new market economy.

The material situation of village households is another empirical way to assess standard of living. We addressed this by asking households about their ownership of a range of durable consumer goods that went beyond the "basics" of pots, pans, beds, and bedding. As Table 9.10 reveals, the results were mixed. For example, while 71 percent of households owned a pressure cooker and 60 percent had a Tibetan carpet set, just slightly more than half had a metal stove (57 percent) or a bicycle (53 percent). Moreover, less than half had a tape recorder (43 percent), and only 30 percent had a sewing machine.

Thus, although virtually all villagers felt that village material life had improved considerably as compared with the commune era, there is an obvious need for improvement in rural conditions. However, whether the gains made since decollectivization are a trend that will continue is linked to two other trends: population increase and non-farm income.

Population Dynamics

While China's new semi-market economic system was unfolding in rural Tibet, decisions were made in Beijing and Lhasa with regard to family planning that had an important impact on rural society.[18] In contrast to inland China, from the mid-1970s to the late 1980s, the government opted not to emphasize birth limits and family planning in Tibet. No official birth limits for rural Tibetans were set until the early to mid-1990s, and even today, such limits are not only higher than in

Table 9.10

Material Possessions Owned by Households

Item	Percent of households owning at least one
pressure cooker	71.4
one set of knotted carpets	60
metal stove	57
bicycle	53
coleman lantern	49
tape recorder	43
altar	36
sewing machine	30
wristwatch	26
radio	25
small tractor	18
clock	7
solar stove	8
television (only one village had electricity)*	5.8
truck	2.8
solar generator	1.5
large tractor	0.9
motorcycle	0.4

*In the one village that had electricity, 18.7% of households had television sets.

inland China but are not strictly enforced. Not surprisingly, rural Tibet has been, and still is, characterized by relatively high fertility.

As Table 9.11 illustrates, the 141 currently married women aged 50–54 and 55–59 (i.e., women who have completed their reproduction) had, on the average, 6.9 and 7.1 live births, respectively. Similarly, women under the age of 44 (i.e., women who started their reproduction after decollectivization) also had high fertility. For example, currently married women aged 35–39 had, on the average, 4.1 live births, and those 40–44 had 5.7.

The proportion of births that were third, fourth, or a higher birth order also indicates high fertility and is evidence of the absence of any program of systematic forced birth limits in Tibet's rural areas. Of the 131 births that occurred in 1997 to the women in our study, 45.4 percent were third or higher birth order, 31.5 percent were fourth birth order or higher, and 20.8 percent were fifth or higher. Similarly, 70.1 percent of the 1,110 women who have ever given birth (i.e., who are everparous) had three or more live births, 55.9 percent had four or more, and 41.4 percent had five or more. The absence of a policy of birth control in Tibet's rural sector is also reflected in the fact that even local officials had large families. The average number of surviving children for the 20 local village heads for whom we had information was 5.1.

This high fertility, moreover, was coupled with moderate/low mortality. For example, only 12.9 percent of children born to the oviparous women in our sample

Table 9.11

Mean Number of Live Births and Surviving Children to Currently Married Women Ages 20–59 (by 5-year age-categories)

Age Category	# of women	Mean (median) # live births	S.D.	Range	Mean # live births surviving	S.D.	% of live births deceased
20–24	73	1.1 (1)	0.8	0–3	1.0	0.8	9.1
25–29	144	2.3 (2)	1.2	0–6	2.1	1.1	13
30–34	142	3.4 (3)	1.4	0–7	3.0	1.3	11.8
35–39	137	4.1 (4)	1.7	0–8	3.8	1.6	7.3
40–44	93	5.7 (6)	2.4	0–14	5.0	2.0	12.3
45–49	85	6.5 (6)	2.7	0–15	5.6	2.3	13.9
50–54	78	6.9 (8)	2.7	0–13	6.1	2.6	11.6
55–59	63	7.1 (7)	2.8	0–12	6.0	2.6	15.6
Total	815	4.3 (4)	2.8	0–15	3.8	2.4	11.6

had died.[19] Of these women, 65.2 percent had no children die, 21.2 percent had one child die, and only 13.6 percent had two or more children die. In other words, on average, 87.1 percent of all children born to women in the study survived. This mortality rate is moderate to low in comparison with indigenous Tibetan populations in northwest Nepal that had no modern health care when they were studied in 1976. For example, in Limi, 43 percent of the children born to living women had died,[20] and during the same time period in nearby Nyinba, 54.3 percent of children born to living women had died.[21] However, it should also be noted that relative to other groups in China, the offspring mortality experienced by women in the present sample is still high. For example, Chinese statistics indicate that the Han Chinese, Koreans, Mongols, and Hui had lower proportions of children dying: 2.6 percent, 5.5 percent, 6.8 percent, and 8.6 percent, respectively.[22]

The laissez-faire population policy that characterized rural Tibet in the 1980s changed in the 1990s, and birth controls are currently being emphasized in rural areas, where the official limit is normally considered to be three births per couple. However, it is clear that for most of the period since decollectivization, Tibetan villagers had no birth limits, and even today, the official three-child birth limit is not strictly enforced. The result of this has been population growth. For example, in the TAR as a whole, the number of ethnic Tibetans increased 35.3 percent in the 17 years from 1982 to 1999 (1,764,000 to 2,388,009).[23] Data from the localities in our study sites revealed similar increases.

Land Holdings Per Capita

The absence of an active family-planning policy has fostered population growth which, given the matrix of fixed land resources, has impacted negatively on rural Tibetans by fostering a decrease of 19.9 percent in per capita land holdings since

Table 9.12

Change in Number of *Mu* per Capita from Decollectivization to 1996

	# of *mu* per capita at decollectivization		# of *mu* per capita now		Amount of change in *mu*	Percent of change
	Cases	#	Cases	#	#	
Lhundrup	180	5.1	199	4.3	−0.7	−14.5
Medro-gongkar	176	2.6	198	2.1	−0.5	−21.1
Panam1	181	3.3	198	2.4	−0.9	−28.6
Panam2	163	2.3	185	1.9	−0.5	−20.7
Total	700	3.3	780	2.7	−0.7	−19.9

Source: Local *xiang* and village records.

decollectivization (see Table 9.12). This decrease would be slightly higher if the farm land that was taken out of production for new house sites or lost to flooding were included in government statistics. Not surprisingly, 33 percent of all study households said that in 1997 their fields in general did not produce enough grain for household needs, and 26 percent reported that they did not produce enough during the previous year.

At the same time, Tibet, as in the rest of China, experienced inflation in the price of manufactured goods and other essential products such as fertilizers. For example, in the TAR, the cost of deep dressing fertilizer increased 107 percent between 1988 and 2000, and sugar, tea, cooking oil, and rice increased by 133 percent, 188 percent, 336 percent, and 400 percent respectively, between 1984 and 2000.[24] By contrast, the price of barley, over the period 1985–98, increased only 56 percent.[25] There have also been increases in taxation and fees for services previously provided free by the government, e.g., salaries of local leaders and health care. All individuals 18 to 60 years of age are required to provide 20 days of free labor annually. This inflation has leveled off over the past two years, but the overall effect has been to exacerbate the income shortfall of many families.

One obvious solution to these problems would be to open up new land for farming. However, in our study areas, there is virtually no land available for this. Nor is arable land available for leasing from others, because there has been very little permanent outmigration. Increasing yields on existing land is also not a viable option without large outlays of new funds for irrigation works. Similarly, the value of Tibetans crops is unlikely to increase in the future, as Tibetan barley and wheat have no marketability in the rest of China. They are only consumed by ethnic Tibetans, and urban (and many rural) Tibetans actually prefer flour from Nepal or China to that made from Tibetan wheat.

Villagers are trying to cope in a number of traditional and non-traditional ways. One traditional option—making sons monks and daughters nuns—could relieve some of this pressure, because monks and nuns relinquish their shares of land to their household when they join the monastery. However, its utility is limited because, as mentioned earlier, there are membership limits on monasteries and nunneries. In the 1990s, not only were these limits enforced in the areas we studied, but monasteries and nunneries with residents in excess of government-set limits were forced to return the "excess" monks and nuns to their home villages. This, of course, exacerbated the decreasing land-person ratio. Goldstein witnessed in 1997 an interesting interchange about this between the mother of an expelled nun and the local party secretary at the former's house. The party secretary was a local man and knew the family well. The mother served him a cup of local Tibetan beer, and after some small talk, she launched into a diatribe about the recent expulsion of her daughter from the nunnery. She was very verbal and basically said that this policy was destroying the lives of monks and nuns like her daughter who, after returning to the village, were neither real nuns nor real villagers. The party secretary didn't try to enlighten her with any of the official rhetorical justifications. He just shook his head and, with a forlorn look on his face, said, in effect: "There is nothing I can do. There is nothing anyone can do. You will have to try to make the best of it."

Villagers are trying to cope in a number of other traditional and nontraditional ways. One strategy employed in many areas was the revival of traditional marriage patterns such as fraternal polyandry (two or more brothers jointly marrying a wife), since this helps to conserve land intact across generations and concentrates adult male labor in households.[26] Another was the revival of traditional inheritance norms that favor the main household against segments that fission off. From the standpoint of the main household, this helps to ensure that it will remain economically strong, although the practice creates weak new households. A third, and unexpected, strategy was the use of modern contraception to bear fewer children.[27] There was widespread feeling that the cost of having many children is high, especially for poorer households. Our reproductive survey revealed that of the 515 currently married women aged 25–44, 52.6 percent were using modern family planning, and of the 372 currently married women aged 30–44, 58.1 percent were using contraception. However, most of these users have been utilizing contraception only since the mid-1990s, and over half (52 percent) of these women began using contraception only after they had had four or more children. Thus, this high usage is recent, and appears primarily aimed at preventing fifth and subsequent pregnancies and, to a lesser extent, birth spacing. Contraception has not, therefore, yet had a large impact on overall fertility and population growth. Moreover, even if contraceptive use increases in the coming years, as we think it will, population growth is likely to continue for the indefinite future because of the young age structure of the population, albeit probably at slower rates.

This leads to the fourth major adaptive strategy—participation in off-farm work.

Table 9.13

Percent of Households Having One or More Non-Farm Laborer

Lhundrup	53.8
Panam1	55.6
Panam2	62.7
Medrogongkar	24.2
Total	48.8

Note: Focus group interviews reported 70.7 of households usually send at least one member for non-farm income.

Development Policy and Off-Farm Work

Although the rural Tibetans in our study are generally unable to participate in the migrant labor market in inland China because they do not know the Chinese language and, even if they did, there is already a scarcity of jobs for ethnic Chinese there, they do pursue non-farm work opportunities in the TAR. In fact, they see this as critical for their economic well-being.

The study found that 48.8 percent of the 780 households surveyed had one or more members engaged in non-farm labor for part of 1997–98. Table 9.13 shows that in three of the four study areas, the percent of households sending one or more non-farm laborers averaged 57 percent, while in the fourth and poorest area, Medrogongkar, only 24.2 percent of households did so. A total of 19.4 percent of all individuals between the ages of 15 and 49 engaged in some form of non-farm work that year, and 27.2 percent of individuals between ages 20 and 34 did so. Forty-four percent of males between the ages of 20 and 34 engaged in non-farm work.

Villagers engaged in five basic types of non-farm work: (1) migrant manual and low-skill labor (usually construction); (2) skilled and craft labor (usually carpentry, masonry, or painting); (3) private business (running a shop, trading, transportation); (4) ritual work (such as mantra specialist); and (5) government employment (such as official, teacher, health aide). Migrant laborers typically left the village for a four-month period beginning with the end of planting and ending at the start of harvesting.

Villagers consider off-farm income essential for achieving a high standard of living, and Table 9.14 provides data in support of this. It shows, for example, that whereas 61.6 percent of rich families had one or more members engaged in non-farm, income-producing activities, only 30.8 percent of the poorest families did. And while 21.5 percent of rich households had two or more non-farm income earners, only 3.7 percent of poor households did.

Households in the study earned a wide range of income. Because a few households had incomes over 10,000 yuan ($1,209) per year—these operated trucking

Table 9.14

Percent of Households Having One or More Non-Farm Laborer, by Economic Status

Economic status	having one or more wage laborer	of households having 2 or more wage laborers
Rich	61.6	21.5
Middle	54.6	15.4
Lower middle	42.3	2.8
Poor	30.8	3.7

Table 9.15

Median Income in Yuan for Households from Non-Farm Work by Economic Status

	Median income
Rich	3,900
Middle	1,500
Lower middle	1,000
Poor	700

and construction businesses—median-income figures are used in the following analysis in order that these few households do not skew the results. For households that had a member engaged in non-farm work, the median income earned was 1,280 yuan ($155). That was equivalent to approximately 29 percent of the cash value of their total agricultural production.[28] In Table 9.15, the importance of non-farm income for standard of living is illustrated by the fact that rich households had 5.6 times as much non-farm income as poor households, and middle-income households had 2.1 times as much. It is not surprising, therefore, that villagers explicitly consider securing income from non-farm work essential for a high standard of living in today's world.

However, despite this involvement in non-farm work, villagers and their leaders almost universally complain that there are not enough jobs for them, and because their skill levels are low, most of those who find jobs get only the lower-paying jobs. Thus, the income they earn is low. For example, roughly 52 percent of those who worked at off-farm labor engaged in manual labor, whereas only 26 percent engaged in skilled work, 18 percent in business, and 4 percent in government jobs. The different earning capacities of these types of jobs is substantial. In 1997–98, the reported median income earned per worker in manual labor was only 1,000 yuan ($121), while that of those in skilled labor was 65 percent higher at 1,650 yuan ($196), and in business it was 100 percent higher at 2,000 yuan ($242). Working for the government provided the highest income at 2,160 yuan ($261).

Villagers and many of their leaders are frustrated by the dearth of job opportunities in construction projects, blaming this not on the lack of economic investment in Tibet but rather on the unrestricted influx of non-Tibetan migrant laborers. Thus, the third area of policy change that has had a critical impact on rural Tibet in the post-Maoist era is the type of development policy that has been implemented in Tibet and its impact on non-farm wage labor opportunities.

Throughout China, the post-Mao reforms have freed villagers to move from their official village residence and allowed them to seek work elsewhere. However, minority areas pose a special problem to economic development policy, since minority autonomous regions were explicitly created to preserve minority cultures and benefit minorities. The autonomy law of 1984 gave autonomous regions the right to override national laws when they were deemed not suitable for the needs of the minority population, including economic and development issues.[29] A question for the government, therefore, was how to implement the market-development and migrant-labor policies in Tibet where, for many reasons, Tibetans were clearly disadvantaged vis-à-vis non-Tibetans (Han and Hui). Two models were discussed in the 1980s. In one, rapid development in Tibet would be stressed, with the door to Tibet being open to all Chinese without restraints. The government would provide huge amounts of infrastructural development money, and whoever came to compete for jobs was fine. The overt rationale for this was the need to accelerate the pace of development in Tibet.

In the other model of economic development, Tibetans would be given preferential treatment for jobs, contracts, and so forth. The aim was still rapid development, but this would be tempered somewhat so that the citizens of the minority autonomous region would be the primary beneficiaries of economic growth. This approach is somewhat analogous to the model being used in China's dealings with more advanced Western companies, where combinations of preferences and constraints are used so that the less skilled group—the Chinese—has time to catch up and compete.

The debate over these alternatives was settled in the mid-1980s, when China opted for the former model. The result has been an influx of huge numbers of non-Tibetan migrant laborers and businesspeople (mainly Han). The majority of the residents in Tibet's capital, Lhasa, now are Han Chinese, and the secondary towns are moving in that direction. Thus, as rural Tibetans found it increasingly necessary to compensate for decreasing per capita land holdings and turned to off-farm labor, they found (and find) themselves in difficult competition with large numbers of better-skilled, experienced Han workers and businesses. Given the current policy, this competition from non-Tibetans will certainly increase as the new western region development policy pumps more funds into infrastructural projects in Tibet. Tibet's economy is likely to shift further and further into the hands of Chinese firms and laborers. The development of a rail link between Tibet and inner China will further exacerbate this trend.

Conclusion

Decollectivization in Tibet has clearly brought improvement to the livelihood and standard of living of rural Tibetans, although it has also created economic stratification and a stratum of very poor households. However, the state's policies on land tenure, family planning, and development/migrant labor have interacted to create serious structural problems for rural Tibetans. Tibetan villagers now cope with increasing population, decreasing land per capita, and increasing prices and taxes, by utilizing a variety of traditional strategies such as fraternal polyandry and adopting new coping strategies such as family planning and non-farm wage labor. However, although the government is trying to improve this situation by making a more concerted effort to reduce fertility and population growth in Tibet by increasing the use of contraceptives, with regard to the key problem area—access to income from off-farm labor—there is no sign that the government is considering reforming the current "open door" policy to provide, for example, job preferences or set-asides to citizens of the autonomous region in the government-funded construction sector, or to establish tax-rebate programs for construction projects that hire Tibetans. Thus, unless major changes in development policy such as these are instituted, the progress rural Tibetans have made since decollectivization may not continue, let alone increase, in the coming decade.

Notes

1. Tibet here refers to the Tibet Autonomous Region (TAR) of the People's Republic of China, not to the ethnic Tibetan areas in Sichuan, Gansu, Qinghai, and Yunnan provinces. See Melvyn Goldstein and Cynthia Beall, "China's Birth Control Policy in the Tibet Autonomous Region," *Asian Survey* 31:3 (March 1991), pp. 289–91, for a discussion of the reasons for this distinction.

2. Pierre-Antoine Donnet, *Tibet: Survival in Question* (London: Zed Books, 1994), p. 139. See also Ronald Schwartz, "The Reforms Revisited: The Implications of Chinese Economic Policy and the Future of Rural Producers in Tibet," in *Development, Society, and Environment in Tibet*, ed. Graham Clarke (Graz, Austria: Austrian Academy of Sciences Press, 1995).

3. Gabriel Lafitte, "Tibet as a Developing Society," paper presented to the Future of Tibet Colloquium, Canberra, Australia, September 2, 1995, p. 4.

4. Information Office of the State Council of China, "Tibet—Its Ownership and Human Rights Situation," *Beijing Review*, September 28–October 4, 1992, pp. 9–42, www.tibetinfor.com.cn/tibetzt-en/whitebook/.

5. Barry Sautman and Irene Eng, "Tibet: Development for Whom?" *China Information* 15:2 (2001), pp. 20–74.

6. Tibet Statistical Bureau, *Xizang tongji nianjian: 1995* [Tibet statistical yearbook: 1995] (Beijing: China Statistical Press, 1995), p. 178.

7. Population Reference Bureau, *World Population Data Sheet* (Washington, DC: Population Reference Bureau, 1999).

8. Tibetans believe that to create excellent monks it is essential for them to join the monastery at a young age.

9. This is similar to the primary school statistics for the TAR, which for 1997 reported

that 78.2 percent of all children aged 7 to 13 were enrolled in primary schools *(Xizang tongji nianjian: 1998)* [Tibetan statistical yearbook: 1998] (Beijing: China Statistical Publishing House, 1998).

10. *1995 nian quanguo 1% renkou chouyang diaocha ziliao: Xizang fence* [1995 national 1 percent population sample results: Tibet section] (Beijing: China Statistical Publishing House, 1996).

11. In the areas in the study that had been part of communes, all individuals, regardless of age or gender, received equal shares on the day of decollectivization. In Lhundrup, an area that had been part of a state farm, non-working members were allocated only 70 percent of the share of working members.

12. The main exception to this involves marriage. Generally, children who marry into other villages do not keep the share of land they acquired at the time of land division. However, when a marriage takes place in the same village, land does shift to the household receiving the bride or groom. It should be noted that there appear to be a few village areas in the TAR where land reverts back to the government at death, and is reallocated to children born after decollectivization. This is not usual and was not the case in any of our study sites.

13. There are some exceptions to this. For example, farmers were required to buy set amounts of fertilizer for their fields, and in some areas, households were made to sow specific crops in delimited areas so that whole sections of farmland could be planted with the same crop.

14. At all sites, the official *xiang* statistics were found to be overstatements, and thus are not used in this article. The issue of farm yields will be dealt with in a separate paper.

15. Data from Panam1 and Panam2 had to be discounted because of a linguistic error in our survey question about consumption of meat (Tib. *sha*). Unbeknownst to us, the referent of the term *sha* in Panam does not include meat fat, as it normally does in other areas like Lhundrup and Medrogongkar, so the Panam responses did not answer the question we asked.

16. After extensive discussion with local officials, individual villagers, and focus groups, we operationalized a household as poor if it did not have sufficient grain either from its own fields or from income earned in work, and had to borrow or get welfare to meet its needs. In borderline cases, other factors such as the quality of the house, the number of possessions in the house, and the number of animals were also considered.

17. World Bank, *China: Overcoming Rural Poverty* (Washington, DC: World Bank, 2000), p. vi.

18. This section derives from Melvyn C. Goldstein, Ben Jiao (Benjor), Cynthia M. Beall, Phuntsog Tsering, "Fertility and Family Planning in Rural Tibet," *China Journal* 47 (January 2002).

19. Another recent survey reported 13.2 percent. See Nancy Harris et al., "Nutritional and Health Status of Tibetan Children Living at High Altitudes," *New England Journal of Medicine* 344:5 (February 2001), p. 345.

20. Cynthia M. Beall and Melvyn C. Goldstein, "Fraternal Polyandry in N.W. Nepal: A Test of Sociobiological Theory," *American Anthropologist* 83:1 (March 1981), p. 8.

21. Nancy Levine, *The Nyinba: Population and Social Structure in a Polyandrous Society*, Ph.D. dissertation, University of Rochester, 1977, p. 304.

22. Tianlu Zhang and Mei Zhang, "The Present Population of the Tibetan Nationality in China" (in English), *Social Sciences in China* 15 (Spring 1994), p. 57. This paper also reports a higher 1990 mortality rate for the TAR (17.4 percent) than we found. Data also came from Jianhua Shi and Shuzhang Yang, "Xizang zizhiqu renkou shengyu zhuangkuang" [Fertility status in the Tibet Autonomous Region], in *Dangdai Zhongguo Xizang renkou* [Tibetan population in China today], ed. National Population Census Office under the State

Council and the Population Census Office of the Tibet Autonomous Region (Beijing, 1992), pp. 266–82.

23. Rong Ma, *Xizang de renkou yu shehui* [Population and society in Tibet] (Beijing: Tongxin chubanshe, 1996), p. 37; Tibet Population Sampling Bureau, *Xizang tongji nianjian: 2000* [Tibet statistical yearbook: 2000] (Beijing: China Statistical Press, 2000), p. 325.

24. Local records and *Xizang wu jiazhi* [Tibet merchandise price history], ed. Economic Planning Bureau (Lhasa, 2000), manuscript.

25. Local records. According to *Xizang wu jiazhi*, between 1984 and 2000, there was an 89 percent increase.

26. Ben Jiao, *Socio-economic and Cultural Factors Underlying the Contemporary Revival of Fraternal Polyandry in Tibet*, Ph.D. dissertation, Case Western Reserve University, 2001.

27. This topic is examined more fully in Goldstein et al., "Fertility and Family Planning in Rural Tibet."

28. To obtain this estimated cash value of crops, we multiplied the average number of *mu* [1 *mu* = 0.067 hectares] per household (17.4) by the average seed sown for barley (30 *jin*) [1 *jin* = 0.5 kilograms] by an average yield of 11 times the seed sown to get the total yield in barley. The price for a *jin* of barley in 1998 was 0.78 yuan, so this was multiplied to get the cash value. This is a rough estimate, since a portion of the crop is wheat and oil seed, but it suffices to give a general idea of the importance of this income.

29. The law is cited at www.novexcn.com/regional_nation_autonomy.html.

10

Riding High on the Manchurian Dream

Three Paradigms in the Construction of the Tibetan Question

P. Christiaan Klieger

It has been argued that the concept of the existence, or former existence, of the Tibetan state is a construct of the Tibetan government in exile under the Dalai Lama in Dharamsala, India. Similarly, pan-Tibetan identity is considered by some to be an "invented" tradition of the post-1959 diaspora of refugees living abroad. But the reality of the "Tibetan Question" defies simplistic, reductionistic conclusions. What is perhaps more useful is to develop an understanding that several parallel, competing, and perhaps mutually exclusive paradigms have existed that work to define the notion of the Tibetan state in history. Although distinct, the three primary historical ideologies share a common trait: all are positioned to include the personal and experiential, the dreams and personalities of the political actors, and the power of religious affect in the various constructions of Tibet.

The continuing use of the Tibetan Question (see Goldstein 1995) in area studies, political science, and international relations indicates not a difficulty in assessing historical data but an affirmation that Tibet as political entity is defined differently from source to source, audience to audience. Perhaps no other place or civilization on earth has been more written about in so many, often contradictory, styles. Histories of Tibet have also differed regionally, both between the great monasteries, and externally, from British to Russian colonials, to Qing, Guomindang, and Communist sources. The state that was once Tibet has itself articulated contradictory messages, both in regard to external powers and internally, within its own leadership structures.

In addition to the largely official, state-sponsored histories from China and Tibet, there is also a powerfully constraining, bifurcated orientalist paradigm in the West that views the Tibetan region either as the pinnacle of an exotic Shangri-La, a realm of lost wisdom of an ancient civilization, or a degraded society addicted to demon worship. This plethora of Tibets has not only kept the Tibetan Question alive, it has had the effect of keeping the region in a state of perpetual dissatisfaction, "prisoners" of Shangri-La (Lopez 1998). The unending global debate on the Tibetan Question has not only tended to stifle indigenous nationalism, it has also prevented Tibet's assimilation into the Chinese polity.

This chapter examines the three most prominent paradigms that have constructed modern Tibetan history. Each is born of different historical circumstances, and each is maintained for unique sociocultural purposes: (1) The Tibet that developed under modern PRC ideology borrows heavily from dynastic centrist Confucian imagery and is tempered by Marxist and Stalinist views of secular national self-determination. Chinese official history, both imperial and republican, paints Tibet as a realm fertile for China's civilizing mission. Seen as an integral part of Chinese territory since the Yuan dynasty, present Han activity in Tibet is merely a fulfillment of this centuries-old directive. The second component of this paradigm illustrates the position of the emperor, especially the innovations of the Qing emperors, in regard to Tibetan Buddhist practice and sponsorship. (2) Conditioned by Buddhist ideology from India, native Tibetan historians have chronicled interactions with their neighbors for over 1,500 years. In indigenous history, Chinese and Mongol emperors are generally subsumed into the role of secular patrons supporting a superior Tibetan theocracy, or accorded divine status compatible with the development of rule by reincarnating lamas. The language of these representations tends to be intimate and flowery. (3) The popular image of Tibet as a Shangri-La is deeply ingrained and important for a complete view of the Tibetan Question. Tracing back through several centuries of Western literature, Tibet as a utopian land full of mythical beasts and magical lamas has persisted to the present day. Although it continues to work to popularize the region, this classical orientalist paradigm arguably has limited the acceptance of the Tibetan state as a realistic candidate for sovereignty by the international community.

The "Chinese" Historiographic Paradigm

Conventional wisdom suggests that the 500–year-old institution of the Dalai Lama and dominance of the Gelugpa hierarchy in Tibetan affairs is but a relic of Qing administration: that the Dalai Lama and other high lamas represent an aspect of state ritual that is no longer practiced in the secular People's Republic of China. Even in the past, Qing emperors are widely believed to have simply used Tibetan Buddhist monasticism as an agency of state administration throughout Inner Asia. Yet one wonders, given the current romanticization of the Manchus as seen in the works of Crossley (1987, 1999), Rawski (1998), Warner (1972), and especially in the imagery of Bertolucci's *Last Emperor*, that the Manchus were not quite the robots of sinification they were once thought to be. In fact, neither the Mongol khan Chinggis nor the Manchu headman Nurgaci 400 years later probably gave too much thought to "uniting the Chinese Motherland." They ruled by political domination of the Han and other peoples. Through both the Yuan and Qing dynasties, the participation of the Tibetan Buddhist hierarchs in legitimizing the ruling class was essential.

A pattern distinctly different from the centralist, Confucian view of the imperial role of ruler and subject is clearly seen in the creation of the Manchu tribe and the foundation of the Great Pure Dynasty. In fact, it was the Aisin-Gioro clan leader, Nurgaci, who began to weld the Jianzhou and other tribes in the Northeast into a formidable fighting force. His heir, Hongtaiji, declared that all under his rule were to be known as Manchu (Rigger 1995, 187). He invented an identity construct for his warriors, one not based on normative and essentialist criteria of ethnicity, but based on participation in the overthrow of the Ming dynasty. Mongols and even Han were brought into this force, and were supported by the rising Gelugpa Church of Tibetan Buddhism under the Dalai Lamas. As the dynasty matured, Manchu identity was tempered by Qing elites attempting to codify Manchu-ness through sumptuary laws, residence patterns, endogamy, and occupational restrictions. The Manchus were the descendents of the original invasion force, except for the reserve of bannermen and tribal groups in the homeland. The Manchus remained a political cadre, rather than a culture-and-language-based ethnic group, until the end of the dynasty. One could become a Manchu by being a loyal subject of the Aisin-Gioro clan, fighting its battles, and living in its banner organizational structure. One could also become a Manchu by practicing the clan's shamanistic rituals, doing archery, engaging in horsemanship, wearing its distinctive riding habit clothing, and by taking a Manchu name. But the definitive symbolic criterion of Manchu identity was loyalty (Rigger 1995, 191). Who would have imagined that 300 years later the chief of the Aisin-Gioro clan would again call on the people of the northeast to rally around the creation of Manchukuo? From Nurgaci to Puyi, the circumstantial ethnicity of the Manchus depended on the group's fortune as a conquering army and its ability to receive legitimacy from broadly revered religious figures—mainly the hierarchs of Tibetan Buddhism.

Buddhism was a keystone to the success of the Manchu dynasty and an integral part of its ruling philosophy. Certainly Qing policies from the start of the consolidation of the tribes and banners rallied under Nurgaci had the effect of facilitating the spread of Buddhism among the Mongols (Rawski 1998, 254). As in Tibet, monasteries were built in Mongolia by the Qing emperors on previously established sites sacred to shamanistic practice. The incorporation of the Mongols into the Manchu politico-military ruling class was a key component of the success of the Manchu invasion and its successful establishment of the Qing dynasty in Beijing. Were the Manchus and the court also converted in the process? The Tibetan *gompa* became the primary centralized state institution of a decentralized nomadic society throughout the steppes and pastoral regions of Inner Asia and the Northeast (see Rawski 1998).

Were not the Tibetans themselves active agents in the conversion of the Mongols and the Manchus to Tibetan Buddhism? It is speculated that a considerable amount of friction in trying to resolve the Tibetan Question deals with the absolute discordance between ruler–subject directives and more egalitarian priest–patron ideologies in the relations between the empire and Tibet. These persist to the present day.

An example of a ruler–subject interpretation of the Sino-Tibetan relationship is seen in a modern PRC publication for foreign consumption, which states, "The building of the Potala Palace [in Lhasa, Tibet] . . . is a story of national co-operation and international cultural exchange in the history of Chinese architecture" (Cultural Relics Administration Committee 1982). The Tibet contribution is here considered national. The rather unvarying claim of official China, from imperial through modern times, is that the acceptance of the Tibetan lama, Sakya Pandita, to become Buddhist guru to the Mongols under Chinggis's grandson, Godan Khan, in 1247 (Shakabpa 1984, 61–62), led to the submission of Tibet under Chinese rule. A vice royalty of Central Tibet was indeed established under Mongol patronage, and the arrangement was reaffirmed with respective successors Phagpa Lodro Gyaltsen and Khubilai Khan, the first Yuan emperor of China. These acts established the priest–patron relationship for Tibetans (*mchod-yon*) and their Mongol converts, a mutual role of religious prelate and secular patron that generated goodwill and Buddhist merit for the participants. For the Chinese, it became the prime assertion for subsequent claims and eventual occupation of Tibet. Although agreements were made between Tibetan leaders and Mongol khans, Ming and Qing emperors, it was the Republic of China and its Communist successors that assumed the former imperial tributaries and subject states as integral parts of the Chinese nation-state.

Similarly, the much publicized contemporary outrage over the battle for recognition of rival Panchen Lamas, one claimed by the Fourteenth Dalai Lama and one chosen by the Chinese, is not a recent disjuncture. Manchu rulers had been asserting their rights to recognize Tibetan Buddhist *tulku* (reincarnate lamas) since the seventeenth century (Rawski 1998, 255). This policy had been especially successful in Mongolia. The selection of incarnate Gelugpa lamas was formalized in the drawing of lots from a golden urn, beginning in 1792. But in actuality, the three principal Gelugpa hierarchs of the Manchu empire, the Dalai Lama in Lhasa, Panchen Lama in Shigatse, and the Mongol Jetsun Dampa Khutukhtu in Urga, acted with a strong degree of independence, and usually contrary to the wishes of Qing administrators. The court attempted to control by inflating the number of *tulku* lines, then raised others to the ranks of the three principal hierarchs.

The concept of the state preceptor (*guoshi* or *tishi*), another major factor in the relationship between Tibet and the empire, first appeared at the court of Mongke Khan at Karakorum in the twelfth century. It was used by the Ming beginning in the 1390s between Emperor Yongle and the Karmapa hierarch of the Kargyupa lineage of Tibetan Buddhism (Sperling 1983). Ming policy of support for high lamas was designed to help stabilize border regions and protect trade routes. The

Ming position continued until the activities of Altan Khan in 1522–66 reduced Ming influence in the west.

According to Rawski (1998) and Klieger (1992), the priest–patron relationship between the empire and Tibet included two principal elements: First, the concept of the *dharmarāja* (or Tibetan, *chos-rgyal*) began to be applied to the secular ruler of Buddhist states in the region. This was an ancient Indian concept, largely adopted in Buddhist countries throughout history. It was ascribed to the ancient Yarlung Valley kings of Tibet, who were said to rule as *chos-rgyal,* and was assumed by Qing emperor Qianlong (Rawski 1998, 247). The second was the *cakravartin,* the world conqueror, whose prototype is seen in the Indian Maurian emperor Ashoka. The concept of *tulku,* or reincarnation lineages of ruling hierarchs, is perhaps uniquely Tibetan. Each ruler of this order has the power to select his (or her) rebirth and foretell the circumstances of his rebirth. The Dalai Lama institution, in particular, collapsed the notion of *dharmarāja* of Tibet with his manifestation as the God of Compassion, Avalokiteśvara. With this, he became not only the divine protector of Tibet and the reincarnation of all previous Dalai Lamas, but also a reincarnation of the founding Buddhist king Songsen Gampo of seventh-century Tibet. He was even seen as an avatar of the monkey god, who was the father of the Tibetan people (Klieger 1992). Rawski's succinct summation is that the expanded concept of reincarnating lineages stimulated Inner Asian rulers to attempt to combine religious and secular authority in a new concept during the foundation of rulership (1998, 249). Klieger (1992) has described this in post-structuralist terms.

The Fifth Dalai Lama, who was instrumental in the founding of the Qing dynasty in Beijing, had successfully combined many of these roles (Klieger 1992). He visited the Manchu capital of Mukden (Shenyang) in 1642–43, just prior to the successful Manchu invasion of China. At this time Emperor Hongtaiji adopted the Mahākāla cult, which transferred symbolic *yi-dam* powers of this protective deity of Tibetan Buddhism to Hongtaiji (Grupper 1984). Thus, through tantric initiation, the Manchu leadership surpassed the hereditary principle, becoming an incarnation of the Mongol emperor as well. The Manchu emperor could lay claim to being an incarnation of Khubilai Khan, the bodhisattva Mañjuśri, and the protector deity Mahākāla in the Tibetan pantheon. All served to create an imperial mythology upon which the emperor's legitimacy could be built. This notion went against the Confucian Chinese ideology of imperial rule. Early imperial Manchu politics were characterized by multiculturalism, power-sharing, and joint decision-making. This attitude was articulated with the founding of the Ganden Phodrang administration of the Gelugpa hierarchs in Tibet, which by no mere coincidence occurred at roughly the same time as the establishment of the Qing empire in the middle of the seventeenth century.

The Qing patronage of the Gelugpa sect was extensive. Thirty-two Tibetan Buddhist temples were built in Beijing, 11 temples in Chengde, and 32 temples at Wutaishan, all through imperial donations (Rawski 1998), not to mention support for projects in Tibet and Mongolia.

Some of the most eminent evidence of the revived priest–patron relationship during Qing times consists of the six extant *thangka,* or scroll paintings, of the emperor as the bodhisattva Mañjuśri. All the *thangka* depict the lineage of the great eighteenth-century imperial preceptor, Rol pa'i rdo rje, in association with the central figure of the emperor. Mañjuśri is the Tibetan Buddhist God of Wisdom, also associated with the great Chinese pilgrimage center, Wutaishan; the emperor may also appear as Mahākāla, Mañjuśri in a wrathful form. In this case, the emperor assumes the roles of a Buddhist deity, an incarnation of Chinggis, and other predecessors all in one. In noting the developing cult of personality of the emperor as bodhisattva, Rawski finds that the elements of relations between the Qing and Tibet were managed by the Sutra Recitation Office in the palace, rather than by offices directed to regulate provincial and tributary affairs. This blurred "the boundary between the emperors' personal affairs and affairs of state" (Rawski 1998, 180).

Ruegg (1991) notes that by the time of the matriculation of the Manchus in Beijing, the relationship between the Dalai Lama and the emperor was developing beyond the priest–patron model into a diarchy of rule. He sees an inherent ambiguity in the relationship that clouded Tibet–imperial relations during the last half of the Qing dynasty. The emperor and the Tibetan hierarch, both bodhisattvas and both secular rulers, could be seen as technically equivalent. The evolution of this idea is a major point in the claim of Tibetan independence in indigenous Tibetan histories and contemporary refugee commentaries. Rawski states that it is no surprise, therefore, that Tibetan-language accounts of the Qing–Tibetan relationship vary widely from those of the Han Chinese (1998, 261).

The growing ambiguity between the reciprocal roles of the empire and Tibet is seen at many levels—in agreements, treaties, relationships with outside powers, and in iconography even within the Potala Phodrang in Lhasa. Here, in the palace of the Dalai Lamas, the layout of four murals illustrates four different proximal relationships between the emperor and the Tibetan hierarch. One depicts the Karmapa and Ming emperor Yongle, with the Karmapa hierarch in the center of the picture. Another depicts the Fifth Dalai Lama, Ngawang Lopsang Gyatso, with the Shunzhi emperor. Here the Manchu ruler is in the center, flanked by a gigantic Dalai Lama. The third mural in the Potala illustrates the Thirteenth Dalai Lama, Thupden Gyatso, at audience with Empress Dowager Cixi. The Dalai Lama is kneeling before the emperor's symbolic mother, and is presenting a statue of Amitāyus. The fourth painting depicts the Thirteenth Dalai Lama seated to the side of and slightly below Cixi.

Heissig (1970) claims that the Kangxi emperor (r. 1662–1722), whose mother was a Khorchin Mongol, was the last Manchu emperor with a personal interest in lamaism. However, the Gelugpa state preceptor of the eighteenth century, lCang skya II, Rol pa'i rdo rje, states that Emperor Qianlong was a genuine student of Tibetan Buddhism (Rawski 1998, 257). His most private temples were largely Tibetan Buddhist. In addition to Qianlong's interest, the writings of Warner (1972), courtesan Princess Der Ling, and the autobiography of Puyi himself suggest that the last emperors may have been true Tibetan Buddhists. The appearance at court of the Thirteenth Dalai Lama in 1908 was not a simple tribute visit—it was perhaps more of a desperate attempt to extract legitimacy from the leader of Tibetan Buddhism and maintain the Mandate of Heaven. The Dalai Lama officiated during the funerals of the Empress Dowager Cixi (1835–1908) and the Guangxu emperor (r. 1875–1908). He stayed on for the installation of Xuantong (Puyi) as last emperor (r. 1908–1911). Dalai Lama Thupden Gyatso finally returned to Lhasa, whereupon at the fall of the dynasty he proclaimed that the *mchod-yon* was at an end. Despite the fact that the Dalai Lama and the Mongol Khutukhtu essentially declared independence for their respective countries, the former Qing court may have remained loyal to their principal faith:

> From the age of about eleven I became an addict of books and stories of the supernatural (which eunuchs brought for me) and these, combined with the incessant sacrifices to gods and Buddhist worship, the spirit dances of the *shaman* wizards and so on, made me even more afraid of ghosts and spirits, of the dark, of thunder and lightning, and of being alone in a room. (Aisin-Gioro Puyi 1964)

The autobiography of Aisin-Gioro Puyi reveals a personal side to the end of the Qing dynasty and the priest–patron relationship with Tibet that perhaps no other source could approach in authority. Many scholars are prone to dismiss Puyi's statements as products of the forced confession of a political puppet, communist propaganda, or anything other than candid expressions of free will. But these statements recall the writings of other Qing sovereigns who have previously discussed their own Tibetan Buddhist practice. Are these exercises pure statecraft or simply marginalia? What a difference the understanding of the court's relationship to Tibet would make if the practice of Tibetan Buddhism was genuine. Within these personalized narratives and valedictoria lie clues to the much-occulted relationship between the Chinese empire and its successors and the Tibetan state. Tibetan archives also discuss the personal nature of the priest–patron relationship as it existed at the imperial level. It is to these accounts that we now turn.

Indigenous Tibetan Historical Accounts

The Ganden Phodrang, the government of Tibet under the system of reincarnating Dalai Lamas, defined the ideology of rule and its relationship to the Qing emperor as a personal and spiritual relationship between the two leaders. The Tibetan term *mchod-yon* refers to the dyadic interaction between religious prelate and secular patron. It is the state-level expression of a more general client–patron relationship that is widespread in Tibetan culture (*sbyin-bdag*). The secular patron receives merit and legitimacy for his or her gifts while the priest receives material support, military protection, and so on. The Ganden Phodrang relationship to the Qing court is the inverse of the standard tribute giver–tribute receiver relationship that defined the position of other vassal states to the imperial order, especially the Confucian order. In the ideal relationship between the Manchu emperor and the Dalai Lama and other high Tibetan Buddhist hierarchs, it was the emperor who received merit in exchange for supporting the worldly needs of the lama. With all other genuine tributaries, the wealth of the outlying states flowed from the periphery to the center. While the later system was a political device to help reify the hierarchical relationship of the Qing court to local rulers in the empire, the relationship between the emperor and the Dalai Lama in the priest–patron relationship is best not expressed in vertical or hegemonic terms. It was a personal relationship between a religious teacher and a secular student; it was full of duties, obligations, and emotional affect—all of which were lost at the fall of the empire in 1911.

The patron–client relationship adopted by the Tibetan theocracy is an ancient idea from early Buddhism in India. Here, the renunciate (Sanskrit *śramana*), is considered a holy vessel upon which worldly offerings may be made by the gift-givers, *dānapati*. Inherent in the relationship is the transformative exchange, where worldly goods passing from the gift-giver to the receiver are converted to intangible merit (Klieger 1992). This interaction underpins the ideal relationship between religious teacher and student in Indo-Buddhist philosophy, where it is manifest as *guru-bhakti* or guru devotion. By his or her sacred status, the mendicant was considered ultimately superior to the patron. But the language of the interaction is often couched in sentiments of kindly love, respect, and humility. Guru devotion was an integral component of Buddhist tantric practice imported into Tibet starting in the seventh century A.D. and has conditioned the affective relationship between religious hierarchs and outside patrons ever since.

According to one official Tibetan history, Mongol armies under Chinggis Khan invaded the Tangut empire (parts of modern Gansu and Inner Mongolia) in 1207. Tibetan rulers, fearing imminent invasion, sent a delegation to the khan and secured a peace treaty with the Mongols. After the death of Chinggis in 1227, the Tibetans discontinued tribute payments. Godan Khan, a grandson of Chinggis, invaded Tibet in 1240 and sent an ultimatum to the high lama Sakya Pandita Kunga Gyaltsen residing in southern Tibet:

> I, the most powerful and prosperous Prince Godan, wish to inform the Sakya Pandita, Kunga Gyaltsen, that we need a lama to advise my ignorant people on how to conduct themselves morally and spiritually. (Shakabpa 1984, 246)

The Sakya Lama and his nephew Phagpa Lodro Gyaltsen answered this call in 1247. The Sakya Lama instructed the khan in Buddhism, while Godan invested him with temporal authority over Central Tibet, thus assuring the ascendancy of the Sakya sect over others. Both figures were succeeded by Phagpa Lodro Gyaltsen and Khubilai Khan, the latter establishing the Yuan dynasty in China. The new emperor awarded Phagpa the Chinese title of imperial preceptor, invested with temporal and spiritual authority over the three provinces of Tibet—Ü-tsang, Kham, and Amdo. In meetings between the two, the khan would assume a lower throne than the lama when taking religious initiation (*bdang*).

This general stance was taken in subsequent Tibetan official histories, especially those produced during the reestablishment of the priest–patron relationship between the Gelugpa hierarchs and the new Manchu emperors:

> From the Tibet legal codes of the mid-seventeenth century, these are the laws founded by the *mchod-yon*, sun and moon:
>
> Like in the Tara Age, the dawning of an auspicious epoch, the *mchod-yon*, sun and moon, became the Universal Monarch [*cakravartin*] through the power of the law they founded.
>
> Because of the achievements of the 5th Dalai Lama and the good laws of the two, priest and patron, the people enjoy peace and prosperity.
>
> Related here is just a drop from the ocean of good deeds of the *mchod-yon*.
>
> In the past in India with the coming of each Buddha, there was a universal monarch. In the same way at the time of Sonam Gyatso, the third Dalai Lama, there came the very powerful religious king [*chos-rgyal*] Altan Khan. It was prophesied in a sutra, "May this religion spread northward from the North." And as a result, Sonam Gyatso and Chos-rgyal Altan became *mchod-yon*.
>
> At the time of His Holiness Yonten Gyatso, the 4th Dalai Lama, who was of the Tho-me lineage [Altan's family], there was a very powerful king, Khor-lo Che. Under these two, *mchod-yon*, Buddhism in general and the secret mantra path or Vajrayana in particular spread.
>
> The regent, Sonam Chosphel, who was also born of this lineage, performed superbly in his spiritual and temporal capacities. On account of this, he was respected by all people, high and low. Due to their aspirations and karmic connections, the Dalai Lama and Regent arrived at the same time and drew the Dharma chariot up the slope. The Regent also helped Gushri Khan and they became friendly like the sun and the moon and the names of the *mchod-yon* spread throughout the land. Sonam Chosphel caused Buddhism to dawn. He also became *mchod-yon* with the Chinese Emperor and traveled to China, arriving in one and a half years. Sonam Chosphel was able to accomplish even more than Drogon Chosgyal Phagpa who previously went to China and became *mchod-yon* with the Emperor.
>
> . . . From among all the *mchod-yon*, the achievements of these three were unparalleled. The spiritual and temporal laws of the priest–patron relationship were proclaimed in the Red and Black edicts and spread from the upper region of Dzata'i gyupe lung-pa to the lower region of Mo-dar thag-pa in China.
>
> The three *mchod-yon*, the 5th Dalai Lama, Sonam Chosphel, and Gushri Khan, spread Buddhism through temporal and spiritual methods. (Anonymous 1653–1658)

The imagery of the universal monarch is evident in the foregoing. The Dalai Lama, as vicar of Buddha during this *yuga*, should be supported by a powerful *cakravarin* patron. The discourse suggests that the present Gelugpa relationship is more auspicious and efficacious than the priest–patron system established under the Yuan-Sakya rule.

This mode of representation continued throughout the Qing. The image of two equal-status partners again emerges from a document of the late eighteenth century, at a time that many considered to be the period of the greatest Qing influence. The meeting of the Third Panchen Lama, the effective ruler of the time due to the minority of the Dalai Lama, and the Qianlong emperor was chronicled by contemporary historian Dkon-chog' Jigs-med dBang-po ('Jam-dbyang bZhad-pa of bLa-brang bKra-shis 'Khyil) (1728–1791):

> [The Panchen Lama] saw the Emperor surrounded by thousands of his subjects. Here the two, *mchod-yon* met each other for the first time. The Panchen Lama offered a scarf, a statue made of precious metals, and a pearl rosary to the Mañjuśri emperor. The Emperor was extremely pleased, and *with all due respects*, offered a very long scarf and asked about the Panchen Lama's journey. . . .
> The Emperor took Lord Lama's hand and led him unto his inner apartments. They sat together on an exceptionally large throne, and talked for a long time while facing each other. LCang-skya Rinpoche offered a scarf to the two, *mchod-yon* . . . they drank tea at the same time. (315–324, emphasis added)

Equal status between the *mchod* and the *yon* is enhanced by the ascription of *bodhisattva* status for both—Mañjuśri for the emperor and Amitāba (God of the Western Paradise) for the Panchen.

Toward the end of the Qing dynasty, a reference to the seventeenth century meeting of the Fifth Dalai Lama and Shunzhi is noted in a manual for Tibetan officials of the Ganden Phodrang administration of the Dalai Lama, written by Dbang-'dus Tshe-ring Nor-nang in 1886–1888:

> The first emperor of the Manchu dynasty, Shunzhi, the fifth of his lineage, invited the 5th Dalai Lama to his palace in the year of the Earth Ox [1649]. The subjects carried out the preparations for the reception according to the orders given by the emperor. The Dalai Lama was then 36 years old.
> On the 27th day of the 3rd month of the Water Dragon Year [1652], the Dalai Lama went from Drepung to Beijing and met the emperor. The emperor received the Dalai Lama with *homage* and from then on the *mchod-yon* were united. (emphasis added)

Again, while much of the official language from the court to the leaders of Tibet was couched in centrist, ruler–subject language, the Tibetan histories generally are couched in the theme of mutual respect between priest and patron, actions that are considered generators of considerable merit for all sentient beings.

Utilizing Manchu-language texts, some scholars indicate that the private–public aspect of the Qing attitude toward Tibet's religious leaders is itself somewhat artificial (see Rawski 1998). The Manchu empire was founded on the basis of an

alliance between various Tungusic and Mongol tribes, with the religious sanction of Tibetan Buddhist hierarchs. The so-called private aspect of the emperor's
relationship with the Tibetan leader in any case was largely ignored with the
establishment of the Republic in 1911–12, and was further distanced with the
Communist victory in 1949. Thus shorn of religious and emotive affect, the actions of piety, flattery, and respect by the ruling elite toward Tibetan hierarchs
are seen as merely pragmatic attempts to manipulate Tibetan hierarchs into submission to the imperial will.

We may never know for certain the extent of religious sympathies, beliefs, and
practices of the Qing court, especially that of the emperors. Official biographies
and reign histories tend to follow Confucian styles that view the emperor as residing at the center of the universe, on the *axis mundi* between Heaven and Earth.
This philosophy permeates Chinese imperial architecture at the Forbidden City in
Beijing, at the former Manchu capital palace at Mukden, and throughout Chinese
arts and letters. The concept of the emperor as a unique node in the transmission of
divine blessing to the world, the Mandate of Heaven, prevented many memorial-
ists and scholars to record a more personal relationship between the emperor and
any mortal human. The centrist relationship between emperor and other was mirrored in the ideal, hierarchical relationship between state and subject, and between
the empire and all other countries. Thus the relationship between the emperor and
the ruler of Tibet could not be viewed officially as anything other than a hierarchical relationship between ruler and subject. To the Tibetans, it was one of student to
teacher, perhaps more closely conforming to the ideals of the Manchus at the founding of their state.

The Chinese Republican revolution of 1911 and Communist victory in 1949
changed nothing of the centrist, Confucian view on the Tibetan region. The former
empire strived for an integrated nation-state based on Han language and culture.
The *minzu* (national) minorities of Manchu, Tibetan, Mongol, and Hui were recognized, but largely within a subordinate younger brother relationship with the
Han majority.

Tibet as Shangri-La

The third major paradigm in the construction of Tibetan history is the least scholarly and least official, but the most influential. The myth of Shangri-La has been
the most popular way of looking at the Himalayan peoples for many outside the
Sino-Tibetan region. Tibet and the Tibetans have manifested themselves in a thousand different fantasies, from the headless Blemmyae of the Middle Ages to the
cartoon visions of Walt Disney. The basic difficulty with considering Tibet as a
utopian, magical land is that such distancing from reality also relegates any genuine consideration toward national sponsorship to the political fringe. While the
Tibetan cause may be currently fashionable in Hollywood and on the bumpers of
college students' automobiles, the topic of Tibetan nationalism is usually side-

stepped in the world's political power centers. Tibet is not a viable country because Tibet was not real.

The Shangri-La model in the West is ancient. It can be traced back to the Greek historians Herodotus and Megasthenes, who wrote of giant gold-digging ants living in the distant Himalayas (Klieger 1997). For most of the last millennium, the Tibetans and their religious pursuits were bound together with the activities of the expansionistic Mongols, most of whom were labeled with the gloss "Tartar" and darkly identified with the inhabitants of the Greek realm below Hades, Tartarus. Far from being the source of all light and blessings, the Tartars were the scourge of Europe from the twelfth to fourteenth century and beyond. One Catholic monk writing in 1245–47 noted:

> Towards other people, the Tartars are most insolent, and they scorn other persons, noble and ignoble. Moreover they are angry and of a distasteful nature unto other people, and beyond all measure deceitful, and treacherous towards them. Whatsoever mischief they intend to practice against a man, they keep it wonderfully secret, so that he may by no means provide for himself, nor find a remedy against their conspiracies. (Friar John 1928, 7)

In the fourteenth century another Catholic cleric described Tibet proper, the white land of snows:

> Going on further, I came to a certain kingdom called Tibet, which is in subjection to the great Khan also. . . . Many other vile and abominable things does this nation commit, which I mean not to write, because men neither can nor will believe, except they should have sight of them. (Friar Odoric 1928, 244–245)

The Western paranoia toward Asia was based on a slowly fading memory of the Mongol invading hordes, persisting in fits and starts along the old Tartar marches of Europe right up to the twentieth century (Klieger 1997, 64). Western missionaries and explorers continued to cautiously approach the high heathen lands at the beginning of the great era of exploration. They saw not the pure, ascetic Buddhism of India, Sri Lanka, and China, but the dramatic Vajrayana form, complete with wrathful deities, shaman-oracles, tantric deities in union, and living god-kings. Many felt that this was a highly debased practice compared with more orthodox, or exoteric forms of Buddhism (see Guibaut 1949; Humphreys 1962, 189).

Another line arose in the wake of great nineteenth-century colonial scholarship from orientalists who painted an opposite view of Tibet. The Russian mystic Helena Blavatsky and the theosophists embraced Tibet's occultism as mankind's salvation. The works of explorer Alexandra David-Neel, the German Lama Govinda, and others were strongly influenced by these violet-scented treatises. Perhaps the most extreme in this genre were the highly popular but distorted writings of the son of an English plumber, Cyril Henry Hoskin, who took on the name of a fictitious lama, T. Lobsang Rampa (see Rampa 1964 [1956]).

The two extremes of the Shangri-La image of Tibet coexist, serving to generate countless popular tales of life in one of the world's most exotic lands. But just like in the Chinese paradigm of public and private imperial attitudes toward Tibet, two extremes in Shangri-La work together. Lopez suggests in his analysis of Rampa: "The representation of Tibetan Buddhism historically has been and continues to be situated in a domain where the scholarly and the popular commingle, a domain that is neither exclusively one or the other" (Lopez 1998, 110)

The saccharine variety of Shangri-La, while continuing to serve as a mnemonic for the passing of the Tibetan state, is the chief paradigm chosen by the government-in-exile of the Dalai Lama to present to the West. It reflects upon the past and creates a future for a free Tibet. In this format, Tibet, its people, and its institutions are special and unique: they are the holders of occult knowledge that is of great potential benefit for the world in the form of the complete set of Tibetan Buddhist teachings. Tibet, as a "Zone of Peace," can set an example for other nations. Tibetans, being a peaceful, Buddhist people, practiced deeply seated environmental conservation, never killing animals and never exploiting the forests, according to this construct (see Huber 1991, 1997). Tibetans, being conscious of the strength and blessings of women, have never practiced gender discrimination (see Michael 1982, 127). And they are democratic, having created several constitutions in exile that are roughly based on that of the United States (Bureau of His Holiness the Dalai Lama 1963).

Unfortunately, the Tibet that is presented in this manner never existed. The refugee paradigm of an ideal, antebellum Tibet homeland is the ossified, premodern Western model of Tibet as Shangri-La. It was born in the West, adopted by Dharamsala as the construct most likely to be acceptable to the West, and represented to the West as a reality. It follows closely the Kiplingesque colonial memoirs of men such as Charles Bell, Lowell Thomas, Heinrich Harrer, and dozens more who were active in Tibet from 1904 to 1950.

The romance between Tibetan exiles and Western supporters has only led to the reproduction of the ideal Shangri-La model—it has not substantially furthered the cause of Tibetan autonomy in China, much less independence. Many Tibetan refugees, caught in the web of popular Western misconceptions about Tibet, have indeed become prisoners of Shangri-La.

The perpetual reproduction of Shangri-La has created a type of hyper-reality—a vehicle that derails time. The hyper-real state perpetually inhabits a never-never land where nothing changes (Klieger 1997, 66). The outreach messages from Dharamsala and other refugee communities under the exiled Dalai Lama are reproduced and articulated through Western friends and religious and cultural institutions throughout the world. Popular motion pictures such as *Kundun* and *Seven Years in Tibet,* the latter adapted from Harrer's story, are good examples of the incorporation of Shangri-La into the modern diaspora Tibetan political cause. These vehicles generally include the messages that (1) Tibet has enjoyed a historically different past, independent of China and other powers, (2) Tibet possesses a unique culture, (3) Tibet is a sacred land, a repository of the full Buddhist teachings that have degenerated elsewhere, and (4) Tibet as a place and Tibetans as a people are real, and thus have a right to self-determination. The messages create national solidarity by representing a culture of difference—difference from their Indian and Nepalese neighbors, difference from China, and difference from the matter-bound consumerism of the West. It is the Tibetan diaspora strategy to remain the exotic Other, inhabiting the Western-created golden Shangri-La until some unknowable time when the present national misfortunes are reversed.

Conclusion

The foregoing presentation briefly examines three ways of looking at the Tibetan Question. Undoubtedly there are others. As in Confucian ideology, the Chinese paradigm of the history of Sino-Tibetan relations can be represented in centrist ruler–subject rhetoric. But recent scholarship, much of it utilizing Manchu-language texts, illustrates a more cooperative, alliance-based relationship between Tibet and the empire. Furthermore, there is considerable evidence that many members of the Manchu elite, including the emperors themselves, followed Tibetan Buddhist practices as a matter of affect rather than statecraft. Like the foundation of the Mongol empire before it, the Manchu *imperium* was based on a dream, a dream that was shared by the voluntary participation and inclusion of tribes throughout Inner Asia who had many elements of culture, including nomadic pastoralism, horsemanship, shamanism, and Buddhism, in common.

The private, personal relationship between Buddhist teacher and emperor, priest–patron, is the dominant paradigm in indigenous Tibetan history. In exchange for helping to legitimate the emperor's mandate and instruct him in Buddhist practice, Tibetan hierarchs received military and material support when requested. It was an alliance based on mutual respect and clearly defined, nonhierarchical roles.

The Shangri-La model of Tibet was born in the West and generated in the interplay of two polar views of Tibet as heaven or hell on earth. Hoping to build sympathy for the current Tibetan national cause, the government-in-exile of the Dalai Lama has chosen this poetic Western construct to represent both the past and the ideal future for a Tibetan state.

But Tibet is not just a construct of Dharamsala, nor a utopian repository for Western cravings and fears. Tibet is not just a segment of Nurgaci's dream of a united, multicultural Asian empire led by his Manchus. Yet in a sense, the real Tibet is present in all of these paradigms. Tibet, although geographically remote and politically difficult to enter at times, has never been isolated. It has interacted with the outside world for 1,500 years, assimilating ideas from others and creating models of itself for external and internal use. It cannot be reduced to a binomial equation of right and wrong. The Tibetan Question is a complex and often contradictory issue that requires, above all, broad knowledge and an open mind.

References

Aisin-Gioro Puyi (Hsuang T'ung). 1964. *From Emperor to Citizen*. Vol. 1. Peking: Foreign Languages Press.

Anonymous. 1653–1658. *Rdzong gsang sngags bde chen* (Tibetan Legal Codes). Manuscript in Library of Tibetan Works and Archives, Dharamsala.

Bureau of His Holiness the Dalai Lama. 1963. *Bod kye rtsha khrems* (Constitution of Tibet). New Delhi.

Crossley, Patricia. 1987. "*Manzhou Yuanliu Kao* and the Formalization of the Manchu Heritage." *Journal of Asian Studies* 46, no. 4: 761–790.

———. 1999. *A Translucent Mirror: History and Identity in Qing Imperial Ideology*. Berkeley: University of California Press.

Cultural Relics Administration Committee (TAR). 1982. *The Potala Palace of Tibet*. English edition. Beijing: Chinese Academy of Social Sciences.

Dbang-'dus Tshe-ring Nor-nang. 1886–1888. *Gzhung zhabs rnam la nye bar mkho ba bla dpon rim byon gyi lo rgyus tham deb long ba'i dmigs bu*. (A Manual for Officials of Gaden Phodrang). New Delhi: Gedan sun grab nuiyam gyuk phel Series, 139.

Dkon mchod 'igs me dbang po, the second 'Jam dbyangs bzhad pa of La bran bkra ski 'khyil. 1971. Biography of the 3rd Panchen Lama, Blo Bzang dpal ldan ye she (1738–1780), *Collected Works*. (late eighteenth century). New Delhi: Ngawang Gelek Demo.

Goldstein, Melvyn. 1995. *Tibet, China, and the United States: Reflections on the Tibet Question*. Washington, DC: The Atlantic Council.

Grupper, Samuel. 1984. "Manchu Patronage and Tibetan Buddhism During the First Half of the Qing Dynasty: A Review Article." *Journal of the Tibet Society*, no. 4 : 47–75.

Guibaut, André. 1949. *Tibetan Venture*. London: John Murray.

Heissig, Walther. 1970. *The Religions of Mongolia*, trans. Geoffrey Samuel. Berkeley: University of California Press.

Huber, Toni. 1991. "Traditional Environmental Protection in Tibet Reconsidered." *Tibet Journal* 16, no. 2: 63–77.

———. 1997. "Green Tibetans: A Brief Social History." In *Tibetan Culture in the Diaspora*, ed. Frank J. Korom, 103–119. Vienna: Österreichsche Akademie Der Wissessenschaften. Vol. 4, *Proceedings of the 7th Seminar of the International Association for Tibetan Studies*, Ernst Steinkellner, general editor.

Humphreys, Christmas. 1962. *Buddhism*. New York: Barnes and Noble.

John, Friar. 1928 [1245–1247]. "The Journey of Friar John of Pian de Carpinin to the Court of Kuyuk Khan." In *Contemporaries of Marco Polo*, ed. Manuel Komroff. New York: Liveright Publishing.

Klieger, P. Christiaan. 1992. *Tibetan Nationalism*. Meerut, India: Archana Press.

———. 1997. "Shangri-La and Hyperreality: A Collision in Tibetan Refugee Expression." In *Tibetan Culture in the Diaspora*, ed. Frank J. Korom, 59–68. Vienna: Österreichsche Akademie Der Wissessenschaften. Vol. 4, *Proceedings of the 7th Seminar of the International Association for Tibetan Studies*. Ernst Steinkellner, general editor.

Lopez, Donald S., Jr. 1998. *Prisoners of Shangri-La*. Chicago: University of Chicago Press.

Michael, Franz. 1982. *Rule by Incarnation: Tibetan Buddhism and its Role in Society and State*. Boulder, CO: Westview Press.

Odoric, Friar. 1318–1330. "The Journal of Friar Odoric." In *Contemporaries of Marco Polo*, ed. Manuel Komroff. New York: Liveright Publishing.

Rampa, T. Lobsang. 1964 [1956]. *The Third Eye*. New York: Ballantine Books.

Rawski, Evelyn S. 1998. *The Last Emperors*. Berkeley: University of California Press.

Rigger, Shelley. 1995. "Voices of Manchu Identity, 1635–1935." In *Cultural Encounters on China's Ethnic Frontiers*, ed. Stevan Harrell. Seattle: University of Washington Press.

Ruegg, D. Seyfort. 1991. *"Mchod yon, yon mchod* and *mchod gnas/yon gnas:* On the Historiography and Semantics of a Tibetan Religio-Social and Religio-Political Concept." In *Tibetan History and Language: Studies Dedicated to Uray Geza on His Seventieth Birthday,* ed. Ernst Steinkellner, 441–453. Vienna: Arbetskreis für Tibetische und Buddhistische Studien, Universität Wien.

Shakebpa, Tsepon W.D. 1984. *Tibet: A Political History.* New York: Potala Publications.

Sperling, Elliot. 1983. "Early Ming Policy Toward Tibet: An Examination of the Proposition that the Early Ming Emperors Adopted a 'Divide and Rule' Policy Toward Tibet." Ph.D. dissertation, Indiana University.

Warner, Marina. 1972. *The Dragon Empress.* New York: Macmillan.

11

"Demographic Annihilation" and Tibet

Barry Sautman

There were two 'Reigns of Terror,' if we would but remember it and consider it; the one wrought murder in hot passion, the other in heartless cold blood; the one lasted mere months, the other had lasted a thousand years; the one inflicted death upon ten thousand persons, the other upon a hundred millions; but our shudders are all for the 'horrors' of the minor Terror, the momentary Terror, so to speak; whereas, what is the horror of swift death by the axe, compared with lifelong death from hunger, cold, insult, cruelty, and heart-break?

—Mark Twain

At the time when American novelist Mark Twain wrote of two "Reigns of Terror," the French Revolution had been the only modern social revolution. In Twain's time, it was recognized by even the elite members of the U.S. Supreme Court (1872, 1883) that the French Revolution's abolition of the badges and incidents of feudalism set the standard for a thoroughgoing extirpation of the legacy of slavery in the United States. France's revolutionary Terror, however, was seen by ruling elites as the ultimate horror. Twain in contrast measured the wrongs of the short-lived Terror against the millennial injustices suffered by the overwhelming majority of French people under the feudal system the Revolution had overthrown.

The Dalai Lama (1962; Thurman 1992, 1997) and some of his supporters (Sangay 2003) acknowledge that Tibet was a feudal society. Unlike Twain, however, they contend that the wrongs committed in the course of the abolition of feudalism in Tibet were incomparably greater than any oppression formerly experienced by those who lived under it. Exceptionally in the world, they refuse to recognize the oppressiveness of feudalism; if the Tibetan émigré leaders in India criticize feudalism, it is only as an obstacle to development and diplomacy. Indeed, they have long made use of the Western-invented Shangri-La image to represent "old Tibet" as a contented society whose halcyon days were ended by China's reduction of a free and prosperous society to a degraded colony (ICJ 1960; DIIR 1993; Dalai Lama 1998; Kyabje Gelek 1999).

Although the world's states universally recognize that Tibet is part of China, the émigré leaders and their supporters position the international discourse of Tibet as anti-colonial ("Tibetans at Earth Summit" 2002; ICT 1994; Tsering 1998; Tsarong 1997). Tibet Government in Exile (TGIE) *kalon tripa* (premier) Samdhong Rinpoche has stated, "China is now attempting to exterminate Tibet's unique way of life through renewed colonization" ("China Seeking" 2001). Émigré parliament vice-chair Dolma Gyari speaks of "Chinese colonial masters of occupied Tibet" ("Tibetans Challenge India" 2002), while President of the Tibet Justice Center Dennis Cusack refers to "classic colonial exploitation" ("California" 2002). Based on the Dalai Lama's authority, antagonism to the Chinese Communist Party (CCP), and other factors, support for the Tibet-as-colony position comes from many politicians (Kranti 2000; Cleven and Koren 1995; "EU MP" 2000) and journalists (Bruno 1999; McGrory 1999; Safire 2000), and some scholars (Pommaret 2003, 120; Bishop 2000, 655; Johnson 2000, 165; Leccardi 1993; Goodman 1983, 111; Horvath 1972, 45).

The representation of Tibet as a colony is not the metaphorical use of colonialism that many scholars deplore as a turning away from the specific historical realities of colonialism (Landow 2001; Suleri 1992; Mohanty 1991). Rather, proponents of the concept aim to establish that Tibet is as much a colony as were the lands held by European powers, the United States, and Japan from the sixteenth to seventeenth centuries. Robert Thurman (1999), for example, speaks of "total, rapid, mass Chinese colonization" and "blatantly genocidal activity" in Tibet. By virtue of its colonization, it is argued, Tibet gains the right to self-determination, including independence (Dulaney 1993; Smith 1999; McCorquodale and Orosz 1994, ch. 8). Proposals for association, federation, or "genuine autonomy" for Tibet, advanced by the émigrés since 1987, incorporate that right (Sautman 2001). If, however, Tibet is not a colony, nor under alien occupation (also know as alien subjugation or alien domination), nor a place where minorities are denied access to government, no self-determination is required (Can. S.C. 1998, 132–135; UNGA 1995). A compromise then must be forged that would likely retain Tibet's status as part of China and much of its governance system, but with power shared by the CCP and the Dalai Lama. Such a solution is now within the contemplation of some PRC Tibet specialists (Wang 2000).

An assessment of whether Tibet is a colony would involve a delineation of the contours of classic, modern, external colonialism and an explication of the theory of internal colonialism (Hechter 1998 [1975])—matters to be treated in a future, more comprehensive work (Sautman, in progress). In the present essay, we consider only one phenomenon associated with classic modern colonialism—depopulation—and examine the claim that it has occurred in both political and ethnographic (cultural) Tibet (Goldstein 1997, 16). We find no evidence for the demographic catastrophe claimed by Tibetan émigré leaders, but instead an overall increase in the number of Tibetans after 1949 that markedly contrasts with the population disasters that befell colonized peoples over decades and even centuries. This result does not itself negate the possibility that Tibet is a colony, but it does indicate that Tibet's experience has diverged in at least one significant way from that of most classic colonies.

This essay deals only with the issue of whether a colonial-style "demographic annihilation" was practiced against Tibetans in the first decades of China's reassertion of its authority in Tibet. A longer companion essay, to appear elsewhere (Sautman forthcoming), treats the question of whether China now practices "demographic aggression" against Tibet through population transfer and family planning measures. It concludes that there is no population transfer to Tibet in the sense that the term is understood in international law. There was, moreover, a net *out-migration* of Han Chinese residents from the Tibetan areas over the course of the 1990s, the latest period for which we have census data. State-coerced family planning exists for some Tibetans, but the degree of coercion is markedly lower than for Han. The Tibetan population is fast-growing, more than doubling in a half-century, with the percentage of Tibetans in the populations of the Tibet Autonomous Region (the TAR or central-western, "political" Tibet) and almost all the Tibetan autonomous prefectures and counties on the eastern Tibet Plateau (ethnographic Tibet) increasing in the 1990s. Growing trade and tourism do make Han more visible than before in Tibetan areas. The idea of demographic aggression against Tibet, like the notion of the demographic annihilation of Tibetans, is, however, a nationalist-crafted illusion designed to foster support for the émigré leaders' political goal of restored power in Tibet.

Demographic Catastrophes in the Classic Colonies

In a well-known lyrical passage of *Das Kapital*, Karl Marx (1954 [1867], 751) observed that Europe's "primitive accumulation" was based on "the discovery of gold and silver in America, the extirpation and entombment in mines of the aboriginal population, the beginning of the conquest and looting of the East Indies [and] the turning of Africa into a warren for the commercial hunting of black skins." The most elemental effect of these depredations was the extinction of a significant part of the native population in the colonies of the Americas, Africa, and other regions.

Most colonies were created by invasion, without a prior history of contact that could give rise to a colorable claim of sovereignty. Wars of subjugation were perpetually waged in the colonial empires; indeed, the British army was engaged in a colonial war during every year of Queen Victoria's sixty-four-year reign (Farwell 1972). Britain's nineteenth-century architect of colonialism, Prime Minister Joseph Chamberlain, alluding to a Roman practice of keeping a certain place of worship open round-the-clock for prayers in wartime, stated "In the wide dominions of the Queen, the doors of the temple of Janus are never closed" (Wesseling 1997, 9).

Gutto (1993, 58–59) has summed up the effects of continuous wars of subjugation waged by the European colonialists against Africans:

[N]umerous cases of massacre and genocide of African people could be established against Britain, Holland, France, Germany, Belgium, Italy, Spain and Portugal. Colonialists routinely practiced torture, cruel and inhuman treatment on the African people. They committed crimes against humanity such as sexual assault on African women. They plundered wealth, expropriated and privatized African land and domestic animals; they decimated African wildlife and plants; and they destroyed and looted Africa's cultural property. A large proportion of African cultural heritage is to be found in private and public collections in Europe and North America.

Wars, diseases, enslavement, and economic ruin brought by the colonialists had a devastating demographic effect. The populations of the post-colonial Americas and late-colonial Africa and Asia did eventually stabilize and then rapidly increased, not surprisingly as it was in the interests of colonialists to have an adequate labor force for their exploitation of land, minerals, and other resources. Indeed, the population increase in late colonialism may have played a role in ending colonialism, as it boosted the potential return to the "subversive activity" of extralegal appropriation of the profits of colonial companies (Grossman and Iyigun 1997). In the early and middle stages of colonialism, however, demographic catastrophe affected many colonies.

The New World indigenous population of 75–145 million declined by three-fourths in the sixteenth century and by 95 percent if a longer time frame is used. This occurred not only because of Old World diseases, but also through repression and forced labor for the colonialists (Blaut 1992, 184, 194; Diamond 1998, 78; Stannard 1992, 268; Cook and Borah 1971). Jackson (1994) and Jackson and Castillo (1995), for example, analyzed the demographic collapse of indigenous populations in the Spanish colonial missions of northwest New Spain and found that it resulted mainly from epidemics in some areas and mainly from working and living conditions in others. Livi-Bacci (2003) found that the indigenous population of the large Caribbean island of Hispaniola was already on the road to extinction through colonialist-enforced labor, repression, and social dislocation before there were any widespread epidemics. The number of indigenous dead due to colonialism in the Americas about equaled the total population of China in 1500 or Europe (excluding Russia) in 1750 (Durand 1977, 259).

There were population losses in Australia and Oceania as well. The 300,000 indigenous people in Australia in the 1700s declined to 60,000 by 1900. Native Hawaiians who numbered 300,000–800,000 in 1778 were 48,000–70,000 in 1900, despite Hawaii's nominal independence until 1898. The Chamorro people of Guam and other islands were 80,000 in 1668, but only 1,500 by 1783 (CS 1993, 74). By no means can these losses be mainly attributed to disease; wars of extermination were waged against the peoples of these regions (Latham 1975; Elder 1996).

Some 18 million African slaves were traded from 1600 to 1800. More than 9 million were exported, 3.5 million in British ships and 5.8 million by non-British slavers. An additional 5.6 million slaves were exported in the nineteenth century (Marshall 1998, 443; O'Brien 1990, 165; Lovejoy 2000, 65–66, 142). Millions of

Africans died in the slave trade—there was a 15 percent mortality rate in the Atlantic crossing alone—and Africa's share of the world's people fell from 18–20 percent in 1500 to 12 percent in 1800 (Hyam 2002, 78; Blaut 2000, 112). Demographic decline also accompanied the last wave of colonization, which took place in Africa in the late nineteenth and early twentieth centuries. Africa's population was then no more than 120 million, with 80–90 million in the sub-Sahara (Durand 1977, 259; Caldwell 1985, 486). The population of the Belgian Congo, under King Leopold's regime of slave labor–like rubber production, declined by half over several decades, with a net loss of 10 million people, partly through disease, but mainly by murder, starvation, and an attendant plummeting birth rate (Hochschild 1998, 233). The roots of the poverty in central and southern Africa that persists today can be traced to colonial population and economic disasters (Parsons and Palmer 1977, 1–32).

In what is now Namibia, German troops exterminated 80 percent of the indigenous Hereros and half the Namas in 1904–1907. The entire tribal property, including the land and stock of the scattered survivors, was confiscated and Africans could thereafter acquire neither without permission of the colonial governor. The military commander von Trotha stated that "the [Herero] nation must be annihilated as such." Speaking of the survivors, Germany's Commissioner for Settlement averred that "Our job is to strip the Herero of his heritage and national characteristics and gradually to submerge him, along with other natives, into a single colored working class" (Wirz 1982, 397, 412; Dedering 1999, 211; Dreschler 1980, 213–214). In what is now Tanzania, up to half a million Africans died as a result of Germany's scorched-earth policy in suppressing the 1905–1906 Maji Rebellion (Martin 1961).

Three-fourths of British imperial subjects resided in India, where colonialism also produced huge population losses, in the first instance through repression. The eighteenth-century Scottish writer James Callender (1792, quoted in Davidson 2000, 110) stated:

> In Bengal only, we destroyed or expelled within the short period of six years, no less than five millions of industrious and harmless people; and as we have been sovereigns in that country for about thirty-five years, it may be reasonably computed that we have strewn the plains of Indostan with fifteen or twenty millions of carcasses.... The persons positively destroyed must, in whole, have exceeded twenty millions. These victims have been sacrificed to the balance of power, and the balance of trade, the honour of the British flag.

Economic decline wrought by British colonialism, especially after the Raj was established in 1813, contributed to population loss. The destruction of indigenous industry, especially textile production, through colonial laws designed to create a monopoly for British goods and a neglect of infrastructure never witnessed in precolonial India increased dependence on agriculture while reducing the size of peasant holdings. From 1700 to 1890, India's share of world GDP was halved, from 22.6 percent to 11 percent, and fell to 3.8 percent by 1952 (Maddison 1998, 40). In manufacturing output, India's share fell from 24.5 percent in 1750 to 2.8 percent in 1880 and 1.7 percent in 1900 (Davis 2001, 294). Colonialism was largely the proximate cause of poverty in India. Laborers in eighteenth century South India had higher earnings and greater financial security than their British counterparts (Parthasarathi 1998) and the mean standard of food consumption was higher in pre-Raj India than in India of the 1960s (Desai 1972, 40–52).

Economic decline in India fostered famines, during which colonialist Malthusian policies led to the death of millions. Estimates of mortality from famines in 1876–1879 and 1896–1902 alone range from 12.2 to 29.3 million. Population growth was negative for several decades before the 1920s (Davis 2001, 7). Life expectancy for ordinary Indians during the height of the Raj, from 1872 to 1921, fell by 20 percent (Davis 1951, 8). Famines were not endemic to India. Walford (1878) showed that there were 31 serious famines in 120 years of British rule, but only 17 recorded famines in the previous two millenia. G.V. Josh estimated in 1890 that half of the net savings of India was confiscated as revenue by the colonial government (Chandra 1991, 102). Military and police expenditures were one-third of colonial India's budget (Hobson 1993); public works expenditures were only 4 percent (Stein 1998, 263). The tax burden for colonial administration caused a shift from subsistence to commercial crops, exported to feed Britain's industrial revolution, and to an increase in the frequency and severity of famines, which grew dramatically worse after the Suez Canal opening in 1869 cut sailing time from India to Britain by half. Nothing was done by the Raj to curtail exports during famines, and commercial interests were encouraged to profit from famine prices (Bhatia 1967; Harris and Ross 1987, 138–143; McAlpin 1983).

Ireland, Britain's closest colony, also experienced colonialism-induced demographic catastrophe. Potatoes became an Irish staple in the seventeenth century when landlords found that they yielded more calories per acre than wheat and could thus reduce the land needed for tenant sustenance. In 1740, when Ireland's population was some 3 million, there was a devastating famine after the potato crop failed, but over the next century the losses were more than recouped as demand for labor to produce grain for the British market swelled. The Irish population reached 8.2 million in 1841. At the same time, Ireland's economy came more completely under British domination. About a thousand people, all British or Anglo-Irish, owned half the land, Irish Catholics having long been forbidden its purchase. Absentee landlords resident in Britain controlled one-fourth of Ireland's territory. By 1840, the landlords had turned half of Ireland's land to cattle and pig breeding for the British upscale and military markets; about 10 percent was used to produce potatoes for animal fodder and 20 percent was planted in potatoes for human consumption. Remaining land was devoted to flax and wheat for export to Britain. To force this shift from a subsistence to a colonial commercial economy, the landlords, backed by the state, drastically decreased the size of tenant plots and increased rents.

A potato blight hit Ireland in 1845. Over the ensuing decade, landlords, including Prime Minister Russell and Foreign Minister Palmerston, forced almost 2 million people to emigrate, with vast numbers dying at sea or in quarantine abroad, while about 1.5 million in Ireland died of starvation or famine-related diseases. Meanwhile, the British government passed legislation expediting the process of land concentration and eviction. Exports of food to Britain actually increased during the Great Famine because the price of Irish grain fell when Britain repealed the protectionist Corn Laws in 1846, forcing tenants to sell more foodstuffs to make their rents. After the famine, the threat of starvation did not abate; in the western province of Connacht, which lost 29 percent of its population in 1841–1851 and had a declining population over the next three decades, a famine hit in 1879–1880. Between 1855 and 1914, another 3.5 million emigrants left Ireland (Silvester-Carr 1996; Ross 1986; Steele 1974, 3; Lee 1973, 6).

Demographic disaster for native peoples was thus a signal characteristic of colonialism. Population calamity attendant to conquest occurred in the pre-colonial world as well, for example in the depredations of the great medieval Central Asian leaders Timur and Chinggis Khan. The scale of demographic catastrophe caused by colonialism was, however, historically unique, and came to be matched only by the genocidal ethnic slaughters of the twentieth century.

"Demographic Annihilation"

Tibetan émigré leaders and supporters assert that the classic colonial concomitant of population disaster has occurred in Tibet through the "demographic annihilation" of Tibetans and "demographic aggression" against them. These claims are the elements of émigré ideology most widely and unquestioningly repeated in the West. Chalmers Johnson (2000, 166), for example, has stated that demographic catastrophe comparable to what befell indigenous Americans with the arrival of the Europeans has affected Tibetans. Evidence of a population cataclysm is lacking however, calling into question a significant aspect of representations of Tibet as a colony.

A fall in the indigenous population of many colonies and an influx of settlers in some of them were key demographic consequences of colonialism. Émigré leaders speak of a "demographic annihilation" of Tibetans and a policy that "aims at the extermination of the Tibetan race" (Thinley 2000; TYC 1994, 4). The Dalai Lama has invoked visions of the Holocaust by talk of the "extermination of the Tibetan race" and a "final solution" plotted by China (Saklani 1984, 265; Dalai Lama 1987, 1996). Such statements are ironic: the Dalai Lama has said that the Nazis had a "seed of human compassion" ("Israeli Minister" 1994), and émigré leaders have defended Heinrich Harrer, an "unrepentant Nazi" (Schell 2000), whose tale of seven years in Tibet became Hollywood's contribution to the "Free Tibet" campaign. A spokesman for the Dalai Lama has called Harrer a "good friend" (Brown 1997; Hellen 1996), and more than five years after the 1997 exposure of Harrer's long-denied past as a Nazi storm trooper and SS-man, the International Campaign for Tibet gave him its "Light of Truth" award, while a picture of Nazi

Table 11.1

Deaths Attributed by Tibetan Émigrés to PRC Actions in Tibet, 1949–1979, by Former Ethnic Tibetan Region

Cause	U-Tsang	Kham	Amdo	Total
Prisons and Camps	93,477	64,977	14,784	174,138
Execution	28,267	32,266	96,225	156,758
Battle	143,255	240,410	49,042	432,067
Starvation	131,253	89,916	121,982	413,151
Torture	27,951	48,840	15,940	92,931
Suicide	3,375	3,952	1,675	9,002
Total	427,478	480,261	299,648	1,207,387

Sources: Samdup (1993, 3); "Exiled Tibetans Say 1.2 Million Killed During Chinese Rule," United Press International, September 17, 1984.

war criminal Bruno Beger with Harrer and the Dalai Lama continued to appear on the latter's official website (ICT 2002; Douglas 1997; French 2003). SS chief Heinrich Himmler had deemed Tibetans "racially pure" relatives of the "Aryans" because isolation had kept them from the pollution of intermarriage (Hale 2003; Cash 1997). In 2003, Samdhong Rinpoche denounced intermarriage between Tibetans and others and stated that "to protect a pure Tibetan race is also one of the challenges which the nation is facing" (McDonald 2003).

The émigré leaders' claims of demographic annihilation are echoed by foreign supporters who assert that "What we are seeing is genocide" (McElroy 2000), that 1.2 million Tibetans were "killed by the Chinese" before 1979, and "since then, the death toll is believed to have reached 1.5 million" (Billington 1997). The claim of 1.2 million unnaturally dead Tibetans is a constant theme of émigré leaders. For example, TGIE former *kalon tripa* Tenzin N. Tethong stated in 2003 that "Of the six million Tibetans who lived there at the time of the [Chinese] invasion, over 1.2 [million] have been killed" (Benson 2002). Western media assiduously repeat the figure (Watanabe 2000; Crace 1999) and link it to colonialism (Butterfield 1989). The U.S. Congress essentially endorsed the claim in the 1988–1989 Foreign Relations Authorization Act Sec. 1243 by stating that "over 1,000,000 Tibetans perished from 1959 to 1979 as a direct result of the political instability, executions, imprisonment, and wide scale famine engendered by the policies of the People's Republic of China in Tibet."

The claim that 1.2 million Tibetans "died of unnatural causes during the years of Chinese occupation" was first made by the TGIE in 1984, based on a precise breakdown of deaths arising from six causes in three areas of the Tibet Plateau, U-Tsang (central-west), Kham (east), and Amdo (northeast) (see Table 11.1).

Figures at this level of specificity are meant to impress, but the émigré approach to numbers is quite elastic. In a 1990 book widely circulated by the TGIE, the number of famine victims is given as 343,000, not 413,000 (Ingram 1990,

297). In 1991, the Dalai Lama stated that 200,000 Tibetans had died from starvation ("McLaughlin's One on One" 1991), less than half of what had originally been claimed. These discrepancies are not surprising: some of the statistics are based on citation of documents that do not contain the figure at all (Yan 2000, 20) or have not been made public by the émigrés.

Other figures in claims of demographic annihilation derive from interviews with Tibetan refugees in India (Samdup 1993, 3). Émigré informants often have political agendas that make them unreliable sources. For example, the leading Iraqi émigré Ahmad Chalabi was the main source of disinformation on Saddam Hussein's alleged chemical and biological weapons and ties to al-Qaeda, supplied to the second Bush administration before the war in Iraq (Rich 2003). Lois Lang-Sims (1963, 132–133), a leader of the pro-TGIE Tibet Society of the UK, wrote that statements of refugees examined in the years after the Dalai Lama arrived in India have "an extreme and inevitable unreliability," which she contrasts with the "ring of authenticity" she encountered in Jewish refugee accounts of Nazi atrocities. The U.S. anthropologists Melvyn Goldstein and Cynthia Beall (1991, 301), who have done years of fieldwork in Tibetan areas, also found refugee reports to often be exaggerations designed to show support for the émigré cause. Another U.S. anthropologist reports that her informants in the Tibetan community in India imparted "information" that reflected their goal of promoting the émigré political cause (Mountcastle 1997, 121), and yet another U.S. anthropologist was told by a refugee recently arrived from Tibet that "Tibetans living in India have a set story that they want to hear about Chinese oppression and persecution as it confirms the reasons behind their continued exile" (Hess 2003, 212). Hyperbole pervades responses of Tibetans interviewed in the early 1970s by an Indian scholar sympathetic to the émigré cause (Saklani 1984, 265):

> The Tibetan respondents reported that soon after the Chinese occupation, they had been deprived of all basic freedom and rights, in their own country, such as freedom of profession, marriage, religion, property, thought and action. It was expressed that China took away their land, property, religion and teacher.

The proportion of unnaturally dead Tibetans to the total Tibetan population was initially said to be one-seventh, but was later raised to one-fifth (Avedon 1984; "McLaughlin's" 1991). In 1994, the same émigré official who used 1.207 million in the 1993 TGIE official report cited above spoke of 1.5 million Tibetan deaths and of that amounting to a fifth of the Tibetan population ("Communism" 1994). No explanation was given for the additional 293,000 deaths, or for how 1.5 million can be one-fifth of a Tibetan population that the émigrés always peg at 6 million. In any case, the 1.5 million figure was picked up by politicians; 200 members of the French parliament used it in demanding that China withdraw from Tibet ("The China Trap" 1996) and the ultra-nationalist governor of Tokyo Ishihara Shintaro has employed it in his frequent fulminations on the "China threat" ("Tokyo Governor" 1999).

The writer Patrick French (2003, 288–292), former head of the Free Tibet Campaign in Britain, has plumbed the claim of 1.2 million unnatural Tibetan deaths. Noting that as there were only about 2.5 million Tibetans in 1951, the 1.2 million figure would mean that nearly half of all Tibetans had died, French learned that the TGIE had compiled the total based on refugee interviews, but subsequently "stopped outside researchers from having access to the documentation on which it is based." French gained access and found no list of names, but "the insertion of seemingly random figures into each section, and constant, unchecked duplication," while "the death tolls in some sparsely populated parts of northern and eastern Tibet were unfeasibly high." He lists examples of improbabilities and duplications in the data, each involving tens of thousands of claimed victims. French also found that of nearly 1.1 million deaths listed, only 23,364 were female, meaning that 1.07 million of the approximately 1.25 million Tibetan men would have died. French concluded that the survey was a "statistically useless attempt to satisfy Western demands for data and tabulation."

Famine Deaths

Émigrés and Western journalists claim that there were hundreds of thousands of Tibetan famine deaths. Some assert that 500,000 Tibetans starved to death in the early 1960s because their crops were seized and transported to China proper to alleviate the famine there (Adams 1993). This scenario is improbable given the few roads in Tibet and the petrol shortage of those years. Others claim that Tibet was the region worst hit by China's famine of 1959–1962 ("Secret Panchen Lama Report" 1996), based not on statistics gathered in Tibetan areas, but on anonymous refugee reports lacking in numerical specificity.

The British journalist Jasper Becker (1996a) devotes a chapter to Tibetan famine deaths in his work on the PRC famine of 1959–1962. Becker provides only one local statistic about Tibetan famine deaths, based on an interview with an official in the Dalai Lama's birthplace, Ping'an County, Haidong Prefecture, Qinghai, an ethnically mixed area on the edge of the Tibet Plateau where Han greatly outnumber Tibetans ("Dalai Lama" 1999). He asserts that there, "at least 50 percent of the population starved to death" and "as many Chinese as Tibetans died of hunger" (166–167). Ping'an had 110,000 residents in 1999 (*QHTJNJ* 2000, 37) and, given Qinghai's overall growth rate, likely had half as many four decades earlier. Even if famine in Ping'an were as devastating as Becker claims, some 15,000 famine-dead Ping'an Tibetans would account for only 3 percent of the Tibetans that he asserts perished from starvation in the PRC. Becker (1996a, 181) writes that the Tibetan "population may have declined by 500,000 and that one in six may have perished" through starvation, based on a very rough estimate of 3 million Tibetans in China made in 1962 by the Panchen Lama (1997 [1962]). The Panchen Lama, however, made no estimate of the number of Tibetans *before* the famine, and a decline of 500,000 in the PRC Tibetan population does not mean that most of the loss was from famine deaths. More to the point, however, Becker provides no data about the other 97 percent of the supposed 500,000 dead.

There are in fact no reliable direct estimates of the number of Tibetans who died in the famine because there was no accurate tally of Tibetans before the PRC's 1990 census. The Chinese government averred in 1907 that there were 6.43 million Tibetans; fifteen years later it said there were 1.5 million (Mehra 1968, 22). Hugh Richardson (1962, 6), a British diplomat posted to Tibet from 1946–1950, could be no more exact about the Tibetan population than to say that it was 2–3 million. There were many other speculative figures about the number of Tibetans before and at mid-century.

The PRC 1953 and 1964 censuses, which are the national population estimates closest in time to the famine years, were not direct surveys: that is, they were not an enumeration of individuals. In Tibet as elsewhere in China, they were "a product of an 'administrative estimate'" (Orleans 1966, 120), a rough attempt made rougher in infrastructure-poor areas like the Tibetan Plateau. Graham Clarke (1991) observed that pre-1982 censuses in China cannot be taken at face value, especially where remote areas in times of conflict are concerned. Geoff Childs (2001, 20) has stated that "all those who have reviewed population figures for Tibet prior to the 1960s (Chinese and Western scholars alike) have pronounced the figures to be unfounded estimates, dubious speculations, and highly unreliable at best." Early censuses had something of the character of the surveys described by Chen and Murray (1976, 241): "A rural Third World survey is the careful collection, tabulation and analysis of wild guesses, half truths and outright lies meticulously recorded by gullible outsiders during interviews with suspicious, intimidated but outwardly compliant villagers." Even the same government agency may make different retrospective estimates of the number of Tibetans in an area in the 1950s. The 1993 Qinghai Province statistical yearbook, for example, states that in 1957 there were 513,415 Qinghai Tibetans, while the 1996 Qinghai yearbook puts the number in 1957 at 486, 269 (*QHTJNJ* 1993, 75; 1996, 48).

The estimate of PRC Tibetans given in 1953 was 2.753 million; in 1964 it was 2.501 million, a decline of 250,000 or 9.2 percent (*ZGMZTJNJ 1949–1994* 1995, 155). The 1953 estimate of Tibetans in the future Tibet Autonomous Region (TAR), 1.274 million, is said however to be only an approximation "not meant for close scrutiny" (Orleans 1966, 121). It was later revised to 1.05 million ("State Council White Paper" 1991), a revision accepted by China's leading demographer of the minorities areas (Zhang 2001, 6). Assuming that revised estimate, the 1953 estimate for all PRC Tibetans is 2.529 million and the decline by 1964 is 28,000 or 1.1 percent. There is, moreover, no reason to believe that estimates of the number of Tibetans elsewhere in China were other than rough approximations. Attempts to make use of the resulting figures to claim that hundreds of thousands of Tibetans must have died or otherwise failed to reproduce (Smith 1996, 600, 607) are thus unavailing.

The immediate famine-era decline (1959–1962) in the number of PRC Tibetans would have been greater than the Tibetan population loss between the 1953 and 1964 estimates, as the Tibetan population grew both before and after the famine. Whatever decline did occur had several causes, however, and we cannot know with any precision the degree of decline or even the share of the decline caused by famine. Starvation was nevertheless likely to have been less common among Tibetans than non-Tibetans. The population of Qinghai, the area on which most discussion of famine deaths among Tibetans centers, was one-quarter Tibetan in 1957, and Qinghai had the third highest increase in mortality among PRC provinces in 1959–1962 (*QHSSHJJTJNJ* 1989, 129; *QHTJNJ* 1993, 75; Yang 1996, 57). Its population dropped an estimated 352,000, from 2.425 million in 1959 to 2.073 million in 1963 or by 19.2 percent (*QHTJNJ* 1993, 74). The death rate rose from 1.3 percent in 1958 to 4.0 in 1960 and dropped to 1.2 in 1961; the concomitant decline in the birth rate (delayed by a year) was from 2.8 percent in 1958 to 1.14 in 1961, rising to 3.57 in 1962. The numbers of deaths and births per year indicate about 100,000 more deaths in Qinghai than would have been expected had there been no famine, and roughly 60,000 fewer births (*QHSSHJJTJNJ* 1989, 129). The remaining half of the population decline had other causes; some were related to the famine, but were not famine deaths, such as migration from the hard-hit provinces.

As for Qinghai Tibetans, their numbers declined from an estimated 477,994 in 1959 to 408,132 in 1963 (*QHTJNJ* 1993, 75). The decline of almost 70,000 or 14.6 percent was due not only to famine and reduced births, but also to nonfamine factors found especially among Tibetans. Battle and imprisonment played roles, but transnational migration by Tibetans was likely the most important Tibetan-specific factor, and not only in the case of Qinghai. Some 30,000 Amdowas and Khampas, from the northeast and eastern Tibet Plateau, were among 70,000 Tibetans who left China during or soon after the Dalai Lama's departure in 1959; 30,000 more left in the next few years. Amdowas (from Qinghai and south Gansu) accounted for about 20,000 of the émigrés, and eastern Tibetans continued to migrate to what became the TAR even after the suppression of the Lhasa revolt (Smith 1996, 600, fn. 8; Sun and Li 1995, 36; Saklani 1984, 46). Even if famine deaths had the same influence in a population decline among Qinghai Tibetans that they did in the decline in the number of all Qinghai people (less than three-tenths), that would mean that some 20,000 Qinghai Tibetans died of famine, or one-fifth the number the émigrés claim for Amdo.

There is reason however to surmise that the death rate from famine among Qinghai Tibetans was lower than for Qinghai as a whole. The increased morbidity in the part of Qinghai with the lowest percentage of Tibetans, Xining, was even higher than the increase in the province as a whole. Xining is the only large urban area in Qinghai and has a city and six rural counties. Its 1958 population was 25 percent of Qinghai's total (*QHSSHJJTJNJ* 1989, 129; *RMXN50N* 1999, 277–278). Because Xining's death rate was so high, and because urbanites fared better than peasants during the famine, it is not surprising that it was Xining's rural counties (including the present Haidong Prefecture), where few Tibetans lived, that were the areas of Qinghai most deeply affected by the famine (Tibet Information Network 1999, 5). The hyperdevelopment schemes that caused the famine could more easily be applied in these densely populated, largely non-Tibetan areas than in the scattered Tibetan settlements high on the plateau.

In this respect it is worth noting that the Panchen Lama, upon whose writings the charges of a massive famine among Tibetans mainly rest, is said to have only visited three counties in "Tibet" prior to writing his report in 1962. These were Ping'an, Hualong, and Xunhua, and his comments on the famine pertain to his home county, Xunhua (Becker 1996b; Panchen Lama 1962, 112–113). All three counties are in Haidong Prefecture, an area whose population is 90 percent non-Tibetan and not in "cultural" Tibet. A former TAR leader, moreover, disputes that the Panchen Lama visited any Tibetan areas during the famine (Becker 1998).

While there is no direct method to estimate total famine deaths of Tibetans, the Australian-Chinese demographer Yan Hao (2000, 22–26) has used indirect methods. Preliminarily, he notes that émigré claims would, if accurate, mean that Tibetans died in the famine at a rate four times the national rate. This is counterintuitive, as Tibetans in U-Tsang (the central-western Tibetan area) were not exposed to the policies that induced the famine, but were recent beneficiaries of a land-to-the-tiller program and tax exemptions that increased their production. For example, a study of Yid-Chab Village, Amdo County, TAR, about 500 kilometers north of Lhasa, found that before the 1959 reform, there were 56 animals per capita, while after 1959 there were 93. Average household size, 5.2 people before the 1959 reform, grew first to 5.6 in the years after the reform and reached a peak of 6.1 during the commune period of the Cultural Revolution. In contrast, during the famine in China as a whole, total fertility dropped by 45 percent (Hai 1998, 23, 33, 46). There is thus no indication of a famine in this period (Barnett 1997, xvi). The population of "Tibet" (U-Tsang) in the Great Leap Forward (GLF) period (1959–1962), a time in which there was widespread famine in many parts of China, is said to have gone from 1,228,000 in 1959 to 1,301,700 in 1962 (Sun 1994, 20); figures for 1958 and 1969, accepted by the UN Economic and Social Commission for Asia and the Pacific (UNESCAP), are 1,206,200 and 1,480,500. The high growth rates during these periods (over 2 percent per annum), despite the emigration from U-Tsang of tens of thousands, are hardly compatible with famine. The same can be said of the subsequent TAR crude birth rate of 25 per 1,000 in 1970–1985 (UNESCAP 2003). Moreover, many Tibetans outside U-Tsang were in situations similar to those within it: they were peasants or pastoralists in very remote areas, where Great Leap Forward policies could scarcely be applied.

Yan examined the Tibetan age–sex cohorts in the 1990 census and determined that there is an extraordinarily low male-to-female sex ratio among Tibetans who were 20–34 years of age in 1960. The ratio indicates a sharper decline during the famine years among young males than among other Tibetans, which is more compatible with emigration or death in prison or battle than with famine, as famine tends to equally impact men and women and especially harms the very young and old. Yan also shows that the birth decline among Tibetans in the famine period was 11.5 percent, while among Han it was 40 percent. The decline in Han births was solely because of the famine, while there were additional reasons that account for the much smaller decline among Tibetans, including the political turmoil in the Tibetan areas. Yan estimates the national excess death rate during the famine period as 1.2 percent of the PRC population per year. Even if it is assumed that famine had the same degree of causality in the decline in Tibetan births, because the Tibet birth decline was proportionately one-quarter of the decline in Han births, the Tibetan excess death rate would have been 0.3 percent. If there were 3 million PRC Tibetans at the outset of the famine—and there were likely fewer—then fewer than 30,000 Tibetans would have died of starvation in the famine years, a number one-fourteenth that claimed by the émigrés.

The most serious history of modern Tibet by an émigré scholar advances a much smaller estimate of famine deaths than the TGIE. Shakya (1999, 504 fn. 91) states that in Qinghai, Sichuan, and Gansu, "thousands of Tibetans . . . were either killed in the suppression of the revolt or died as the result of economic disaster." The pro-independence Tibetan Youth Congress, in a work on development in Tibet, fails to mention a famine associated with the Great Leap Forward. It does claim that during the late Cultural Revolution period in U-Tsang, "tens of thousands of Tibetans" died as a result of overcultivation of land sown with wheat (TYC 1995, 18–19). Shakya (1999, 356), however, states only that "economic setbacks" resulted from the failed wheat cultivation, while Zhang (1989), in a study of wheat cultivation during this period in the TAR's Nyemo County, states that the population increased. In short, a number of scholarly sources diverge from the TGIE's inflated famine death claims.

Finally, it should be pointed out that even had famine deaths been on the scale claimed by the TGIE, this would not amount to an association with colonialism. The demographic catastrophes in classic colonies had no counterpart in Europe. Tens of millions of colonized peoples died from starvation and epidemics; Western colonizers did not. Harris and Ross (1987, 105–109) speak of "demographic rewards of colonialism" for Britain: wealth flowing in from colonies sped the reduction of mortality, and the sharp rise in the English population from the late eighteenth century was based on growing demand for child labor occasioned by the expansion of exports to the colonies. In the Chinese case, however, Han were the main famine victims, likely to a much greater extent than Tibetans. The worst-hit province by far was Anhui, with a 99 percent Han population.

Far from being subject to massive population depletions from diseases, moreover, the life expectancies of Tibetans were rapidly raised through the development of a system of medical care that wiped out the worst communicable diseases and sharply lowered infant mortality, beginning as early as the 1950s. The average TAR Tibetan life expectancy, which was about thirty-five years in 1950, has, according to PRC statements, increased to sixty-eight, three years lower than the PRC national average (ZGMZTJNJ 1998, 335). Given the health disadvantages of life on a high plateau (see Zhang 1997, ii–iii), this means that, ceteris paribus, TAR Tibetans have the same longevity opportunities as Han, despite Tibet's relative poverty. If this is so, it is most likely because health care is provided at low cost to rural TAR Tibetans (85 percent of TAR Tibetans) ("Overview" 2003; Soinam 2003) while the population of China proper must pay dearly for it. Moreover, the ratio of health care providers to population in the TAR exceeds the national average (Sautman and Eng 2000). While official estimates of present-day life expectancies have yet to be independently confirmed, even if expectancies were somewhat lower, they would still stand in marked contrast to the predicament of indigenous peoples elsewhere. The average life expectancy of Australian aborigines has been reduced since the mid-1990s, and at 55.8 years for men and 63 years for women, it is 20 years less than the average for Australian men overall and 19 years less than for Australian women (Neill 2001; Ryan 2001).

Other "Excess Deaths"

Accurate direct estimates of Tibetan deaths from causes other than famine are not available, as data on such matters are a state secret in the PRC and émigré witnesses possess only localized, problematic knowledge. Testimony on executions, for example, has been found to be contradictory and incredible (Shalom 1984, 74–75). French (2003, 291) observes, for example, that "a figure of 69,517 executions in Amdo had no clear origin, and seemed to have been taken from a contentious report issued by the [CIA-financed] International Commission of Jurists [ICJ]," while "one informant asserted with no evidence that nineteen thousand people had been executed near Kongbo." Many estimates were made of battle deaths after 1959, but not of prison deaths, which should include most executions, torture deaths, and suicides. The few estimates of prison deaths are highly unreliable: French found in the TGIE documents that "a single interviewee claimed that twenty thousand people died in prisons near Karon," and "a table of those tortured to death in Kham included ten thousand who had already been listed under the heading of executions."

China has asserted that 5,600 Tibetans were killed, wounded, or captured in the Lhasa revolt of March 1959 (Strong 1976 [1959], 75–76). The Dalai Lama and Trikamdas, the head of the ICJ, both claimed in June 1959 that there had been 65,000 Tibetan battle deaths. The number was not repeated in subsequent ICJ reports on Tibet, however, and the figures on Tibetan deaths in the Lhasa revolt provided by the émigrés and their supporters range from hundreds to 15,000 (Shalom 1984, 160, fn. 149–150). The other source of battle deaths was fighting on the eastern Plateau in 1956–1959. Émigré leaders maintain that most of the "anti-China" struggle took place in Amdo and Kham ("Tokyo Governor" 1999) and it was migrant Amdowas and Khampas who led the Lhasa revolt (Wolff 1997). Andrugtsang, the Khampa guerrilla leader whose memoirs (1973, 89) are credited by the émigré scholar Dawa Norbu (1979, 93), states that his units suffered 118 casualties from August 1958 to March 1959, the peak of the struggle in Amdo. There thus seems to be no basis for a claim of 65,000 battle deaths.

From the mid-1960s, however, the Dalai Lama upped his claim of the number of battle deaths. He is quoted by Bradsher (1969, 763) as stating that based on "secret documents," 87,000 died in the Lhasa Revolt; Bradsher himself states that 3,000 or more died (1969, 755). The Dalai Lama's source is a 1960 PLA document, *Xizang xingshi he renwu jiaoyu de jiben* (Basic teaching materials on education about Tibet's situation and tasks), said by the TGIE to have been captured by Tibetan guerrillas in 1966. It states that "87,000 enemies were eliminated" in central Tibet from March 1959 to October 1960 (Ingram 1990, 356–357; DIIR 1993). The Chinese term said to be used in the document, *xiaomie*, however, is as ambiguous as its English equivalent, "eliminated." Elsewhere, moreover, the TGIE and its supporters do not cite the PLA document, but state that the figure of 87,000 dead was heard on an unverifiable Radio Lhasa broadcast of October 1, 1960 (Samdup 1993). The TGIE has also stated that 5,000–10,000 people died in the Lhasa revolt (CTS 1976), itself a questionable figure, given that Lhasa then only had about 40,000 inhabitants and Tibetans who were there at the time do not attest to the loss of a large part of the city's population (Erickson 1997, 197). In any event, the émigré leaders continue to publicize the figure of 87,000 dead (Gyari 1997; Gombu 1997), a "fact" frequently repeated by Western media (Schvindlerman 2001; "Tibetans, Americans" 1999; "Tibetans Confident" 1998).

The TGIE claim of 432,000 battle deaths comes out of nowhere. If accurate it would mean Tibetan battle deaths were 17 percent of the population—proportionately more than five times higher than those of Britain in World War I (9 percent of under-45 males, or about 3 percent of the population) (Hyam 2002, 335), a war with such colossal slaughters as the Somme and Verdun; it would also be more than four times the proportional battle deaths of Nazi Germany (3.25 million military dead among 80 million Germans) (Ambrose 1995), a country that waged a total war on long fronts against the most formidable armies ever assembled.

We cannot surmise how many Tibetans died in prison settings, but we can discount unreasonably high figures. The claims of 175,000 Tibetans prison/labor camp deaths and 866,000 deaths from all nonfamine causes, most of which would have happened in confinement, are untenable. Shalom (1984) examines the welter of assertions made about the number of such deaths in China generally. He concludes that even making "assumptions that are likely to err in the direction of overestimating the number of deaths," perhaps one million died in China's prisons and labor camps from 1950 to 1970 (1984, 109–110). If this estimate and émigré figures are both accepted, then Tibetans would account for a very high proportion—anywhere from 17 percent to 85 percent—of PRC prison deaths. Yet Tibetans are less than one-half of 1 percent of the PRC population, and no studies show that Tibetans were disproportionately imprisoned or subjected to a harsher prison regime than non-Tibetans.

The vituperatively anti-Communist writers Domenach (1992, 242) and Courtois et al. (1999, 498) have made the highest claims of mortality among Mao-era prisoners: 5 percent of 10 million detainees each year, for a total of 20 million, including 4 million from the famine in 1959–1962. Even applying an analogous estimate, the TGIE figures on Tibetan deaths are implausible. To achieve the same death rate as for all PRC prisoners, based on the claimed 174,000 Tibetan prison deaths, no less than 116,000 Tibetans would have to have been imprisoned during every year from 1950 to 1979, that is, about 3–4 percent of the Tibetan population. If one assumes that more than 50 percent of all executions, deaths through torture, and suicides of Tibetans from 1950 to 1979 also took place in prison settings, then about 450,000 people, or some 10 percent of all Tibetans, would have had to have been imprisoned during every one of those years.

Domenach and Curtois et al. claim, however, that 1–2 percent of Chinese were in some form of imprisonment at any given time in the Mao era. Although armed rebellion in Tibetan areas surely resulted in thousands of Tibetans being imprisoned, major PRC political campaigns that led to imprisonments and deaths generally touched Tibetan areas more lightly than China proper. Tibet is remote and most campaigns disproportionately affected urban areas, while nine-tenths of Tibetans lived in the countryside. China's violent land reform and the Great Leap Forward were rural phenomena, but Shakya (1999) and other scholars report no executions or imprisonment of Tibetan landlords for past oppression of peasants, in contrast to the policy in China proper, while the Great Leap produced famine, not executions and imprisonments. The campaigns attended by large-scale imprisonments, such as the Anti-Rightist Movement of the late 1950s or mass executions, such as the Purifying of Class Ranks and Anti–May 16th Movement campaigns of 1968–1970, are not reported to have impacted Tibetan areas.

If Tibetans died in imprisonment at the same rate as prisoners in China proper, then based on Domenach and Curtois et al.'s claimed rate of PRC prison death rates—5 percent each year of 1–2 percent of the total population—Tibetan prison deaths would have been 75,000–100,000. It is unlikely, however, that the highest estimates are an accurate gauge of prison deaths in China, or that Tibetans were imprisoned at the same rate as Chinese generally, or that émigré claims of Tibetan prison deaths do not involve double-counting deaths from execution, torture, and suicide (Shalom 1984, 108; French 2003, 291). "Excess" deaths, moreover, are those above normal mortality in the general population, so that a portion of prison deaths are necessarily not excess.

Conclusion

There is no evidence of a special repression of Tibetans, let alone demographic annihilation. The lack of credible evidence contrasts sharply with what was known about documented demographic catastrophes in such places as Cambodia and East Timor, long before their mass murderous regimes were overthrown (Kiernan 2003). There is a harsh state response to any political challenge to CCP rule in any part of

Table 11.2

Number of Tibetans in the PRC by Census Date

1953	1964	1982	1990	2000
2,753,081	2,501,174	3,847,875	4,593,072	5,416,021

Source: ZGMZGZNJ (2002, 698).

China. State organs involved in suppressing separatism have often violated the rights of those seeking independence through beatings and torture, but the suppression of separatism is not per se illegitimate under international law. The consensus of international organizations, states, and scholars is that states are allowed to use military and police measures to prevent secessionist activities, except in the special circumstance where to do so would endanger international peace and security (Charney and Prescott 2000; Hsiao 1998; Duursma 1996, 427–428; Weller 1992, 572). The suppression of Tibetan separatism has been no more brutal than the repression that accompanied many political campaigns waged during the PRC's first four decades and no more egregiously violent than more recent actions against dissident Han organizations. The lack of a sharp dichotomy in the degree of repression against majority and minority people distinctly contrasts with the practices of the colonial era.

In contrast to the fate of many colonized peoples, Tibetans have proliferated, not diminished, in number, during the more than a half-century of Communist rule (see Table 11.2). The Tibetan population increased by about 150 percent over almost seven centuries, from some 1 million in 1268 to about 2.5 million in 1950, and Tibetans have more than doubled in number since then. Despite a large and growing economic gap between Tibetans and Han, reflecting their different rates of urbanity, education, and other factors, the proliferation of the Tibetan *ethnie* evidences a key distinction from the main contour of colonialism.

The finding that there is no evidence of demographic annihilation of Tibetans calls into question a claim central to the émigré leaders' ideological construct of a colonial occupation and shifts the burden to them to recast their argument, which is currently tangled in all manner of unsupported claims about a special oppression of Tibetans. Supporters of the émigré cause claim, for example, that one in every 100 Tibetans is in prison (Barlow 1999). The implication is that this high incarceration rate reflects state ethnic discrimination. The PRC has put the all-China incarceration rate at just under 1 per 1,000 ("State Council White Paper" 1991). Western specialists say that it may actually be 1.66, higher than the world average of 1.05 per 1,000, but not hugely so (Seymour 1998). In 2000, the United States had the world's highest rate: 7.12 inmates per 1,000 population ("U.S. System" 2000; "Nation's Prison Population" 2000), almost seven times the world average and higher than the next contender, Russia, with 6.50 (Working 2001;

Dillin 2001). Despite the very high U.S. rate of imprisonment, it was nevertheless lower than the incredible rate of 10 per 1,000 claimed for Tibetans by the émigrés and their supporters.

The incarceration rate for TAR Tibetans, according to the PRC, is about 0.7 per 1,000 (Xinhua 17 April 2000), seven-tenths of the official all-China rate. In the United States, black males are incarcerated at 8 times the rate for white males ("A Land of Bondage" 1999), that is, 80 times the TAR Tibetan rate. Not only were one in 143 persons in the United States in prison as of the end of 2001, but one in 37 U.S. adults was either in prison or had once been there. The official estimate is that 6.6 percent of U.S. residents born in 2001 will go to prison at some point, with black males having a 1–in-3 chance, Hispanic males a 1–in-6 chance, and white males a 1–in-17 chance (Liptak 2003; "Unfree" 2003). In contrast, Qinghai, with 1.2 million Tibetans, has 1,200–1,500 Tibetan prisoners under any form of detention, mostly in local jails (Seymour and Anderson 1998, 168). Qinghai Tibetans are thus incarcerated at 0.12–0.15 per 1,000, or one-seventh to one-eighth of the all-China rate and one four-hundredth the rate for black Americans. Tibetans are mainly rural people, while African Americans are mainly urban, so a significant difference in incarceration rates is to be expected. The gap between the rates is so enormous, however, that it indicates that racial discrimination is much more likely to be a factor accounting for the racial differential in the United States than it is in the Tibetan areas of China.

Some émigré claims reach fantastic proportions. A Japanese magazine, responding to Chinese criticisms that the Japanese government is not forthright about World War II atrocities, published an article by Tibetan émigré researcher Pema Gyalpo in which he claimed that there are 2 million political prisoners in Qinghai (Hoffman 1999). "Tibet activists" have asserted that there are more than 100,000 Tibetan political prisoners (Avedon 1984). Human rights groups quote much lower numbers. Asia Watch (1994) has stated that there were 1,710 people of all PRC ethnic groups known to be in prison due to political, ethnic, or religious activities. Amnesty International (1996) pegged the number at 2,000, as have more recent Western estimates ("Please Shout Quietly" 1999). Others claim that the number may be as high as 10,000 ("China's Communist Regime" 1999). Emigrés claim that Tibetans are disproportionately represented among PRC political prisoners—there were estimates of "over one hundred" and "about 150" in 2003 ("Amnesty" 2003; "Change in Pattern" 2003). This is because there is an émigré-supported separatist movement; there is no evidence that Tibetans who commit what the PRC government considers "subversion" are selectively prosecuted, or any firm reason to conclude that they are imprisoned for longer periods than others convicted of the same crime. The average sentence imposed on all Tibetan political prisoners convicted in 1987–2000 was four years, nine months (U.S. State Department 2002). Although there has yet to be a systematic study, among (overwhelmingly Han) labor activists convicted of "endangering state security," sentences seem to be longer, with sentences of ten to twenty years for organizing an independent trade union not at all unusual (UAW 2003; LRN 2003).

Winston Churchill (1906, vii) once described the claims of ex–Colonial Secretary Joseph Chamberlain for intra-empire protectionism as full of "morose, sordid and often absurd extravagancies," words that fit assertions of demographic aggression in Tibet. These claims are not unique in being taken as "facts" by Western media; there are other examples of assertions of demographic catastrophe that were first accepted and then disproved. For example, Canadian novelist James Bacque (1989) wrote a much publicized work asserting that the United States and France likely killed a million Germans in post–World War II prisoner-of-war camps. The German government found that about 56,000 of the 5 million Germans held in custody died, while Bischof and Ambrose (1992) and others demolished Bacque's sensational assertions. He nevertheless was able to bring out another book with a reputable U.S. publisher (Bacque 1997) in which he asserted that the Allies were responsible for between 9.3 and 13.7 million German deaths *after* the war, including 2.1–6 million civilians who died being expelled from countries east of Germany.

It is quite possible that dissident émigrés will take a page from the book of U.S. secretary of defense Donald Rumsfeld, who stated with regard to U.S. claims that Saddam Hussein possessed weapons of mass destruction in the run-up to the 2003 war against Iraq that "the absence of evidence is not evidence of absence. . . . Simply because you do not have evidence that something exists does not mean that you have evidence that it doesn't exist" (quoted in O'Toole 2002). In the Tibet case, that in effect would have the émigré leaders saying that since the PRC government cannot directly prove that it did not annihilate a significant number of Tibetans (i.e., prove a negative), the TGIE will continue to revile it for having committed "genocide." The continued leveling of such charges without evidence is no more logical than the Rumsfeld argument that war can be waged even without any evidence to support its principal justification. Imputations of demographic annihilation have mislead ordinary Tibetan exiles and those who sympathize with them. More importantly, they are an obstacle to solving the Tibet Question, affecting as they do the credibility of the Tibetan émigré leaders and thus diminishing the confidence of PRC leaders that TGIE assertions of a desire for a solution short of independence can be trusted.

References

Adams, Robert. 1993. "Tibet: Brutal Chinese Policies Crush Local Buddhist Culture." InterPress Service, May 12.

Ambrose, Stephen. 1995. "Recalling a Land's Bloody History." *Times-Picayune*, December 24, B7.

"Amnesty Highlights Chinese Repression of Tibetans Before EU-China Summit." 2003. World Tibet Network, October 28.

Amnesty International. 1996. *China: No One Is Safe—Political Repression and the Abuse of Power in the 1990s.* London: AI.

Asia Watch. 1994. *Detained in China and Tibet: A Directory of Political and Religious Prisoners.* New York: Asia Watch.

Avedon, John. 1984. "China's Tibet Problem." *New York Times*, June 23.

Bacque, James. 1989. *Other Losses: The Shocking Truth Behind the Mass Deaths of Disarmed German Soldiers and Civilians Under General Eisenhower's Command.* Toronto: Stoddard.

———. 1997. *Crimes and Mercies: The Fate of German Civilians Under Allied Occupation.* New York: Little, Brown.

Barlow, Jude. 1999. "Strangers in Their Land," *Christchurch Press* (New Zealand), September 27, 11.

Barnett, Robbie. 1997. "Preface." In *Panchen Lama* (1997 [1962]): xi–xxiii.

Becker, Jasper. 1996a. *Hungry Ghosts: Mao's Secret Famine.* New York: Free Press.

———. 1996b. "China's Northern Nomads Face a Bleak Future." *South China Morning Post* (*SCMP*) (Hong Kong), September 28, 18.

———. 1998. "Tibet Elder Scorns 'Fantasy' Film." *South China Morning Post*, March 30, 1.

Benson, Adam. 2002. "Tibet Shares Personal Exile Experience." *Daily Utah Chronicle*, March 15, in World Tibet Network, March 18.

Bhatia, B.M. 1967. *Famines in India: A Study of Some Aspects of the Economic History of India.* London: Asia Publishing House.

Billington, John. 1997. "Power Before Prayer." *Independent*, October 12, 5.

Bischof, Gunter, and Stephen E. Ambrose. 1992. *Eisenhower and the German POWs: Facts Against Falsehood.* Baton Rouge: Louisiana State University Press.

Bishop, Peter. 2000. "Caught in the Cross-fire: Tibet, Media, and Promotional Culture." *Media, Culture & Society* 22: 645–664.

Blaut, J.M. 1992. *The Colonizer's Model of the World: Geographical Diffusionism and Eurocentric History.* New York: Guilford Press.

———. 2000. *Eight Eurocentric Historians*, vol. 2: *The Colonizer's Model of the World.* New York: Guildford Press.

Bradsher, Henry. 1969. "Tibet Struggles to Survive." *Foreign Affairs* 47, no. 4: 755–763.

Brown, M. 1997. "His Holiness—My Brother." *Daily Telegraph*, November 7, 23.

Bruno, Philip. 1999. "Ombres chinoises au pays des neiges" (Chinese shadows in the land of snows). *Le Monde*, March 1.

Butterfield, Fox. 1989. "Tibet's Days of Despair and China's Harsh Response." *New York Times*, March 12, 3.

Caldwell, J.C. 1985. "The Social Repercussions of Colonial Rule: Demographic Aspects." In *General History of Africa*, vol. 7: *Africa Under Colonial Domination 1880–1935*, ed. Abu Boahen, 458–486. Berkeley: University of California Press.

"California Assembly to Meet with Tibetan Puppet Government—Tibet Groups Issue Warning." 2002. World Tibet Network, May 29.

Callender, James. 1792. *The Political Progress of Britain or an Impartial Account of the Principal Abuses in the Government of This Country from the Revolution in 1688.* Edinburgh (privately published pamphlet).

Can. S.C. [Canadian Supreme Court]. 1998. *Reference re Secession of Quebec*, 2 Can. S.C.R. 217.

Cash, William. 1997. "Heil Hell in Brad's Glorified War Epic." *Sunday Star-Times* (Auckland), November 30, 3.

Chandra, Bipan. 1991. "Colonial India: British Versus Indian Views of Development." *Review* 14, no. 1: 81–167.

"Change in Pattern of Political Detention." 2003. Tibet Information Network, March 10. Available at www/tibetinfor.net.news-updates/2003/1003.htm.

Charney, Jonathan, and J.R.V. Prescott. 2000. "Resolving Cross-Straits Relations Between China and Taiwan." *American Journal of International Law* 94: 453–475.

Chen, K.H., and G.F. Murray. 1976. "Truths and Untruths in Village Haiti: An Experiment in Third World Survey Research." In *Culture, Natality and Family Planning*, ed. John Marshall and S. Polgar. Chapel Hill, NC: Carolina Population Center.

Childs, Geoff. 2001. "When Conjecture Becomes Fact: Tibet's Vanishing Population Before 'Liberation.'" *Tibetan Review* 36, no. 8: 20–22.

"China Seeking to Colonise Not Modernize Tibet: Exiled Premier." 2001. Agence France-Presse, December 10.

"The China Trap." 1996. *The Times* (London), June 26.

"China's Communist Regime Crushes Dissent with Iron Fist 50 Years On." 1999. Agence France-Presse, September 26.

Churchill, Winston. 1906. *For Free Trade: A Collection of Speeches Delivered at Manchester or in the House of Commons During the Fiscal Controversy Preceding the Late General Election.* London: Arthur L. Humphreys.

Clarke, Graham. 1991. "Research Design in the Use of China's Census and Survey Data for Rural Areas and Households." In *From Peasant to Entrepreneur: Growth and Change in Rural China*, ed. Edward Vermeer, 217–240. Hague: PUDOC/Centre for Agricultural Publishing and Documentation.

Cleven, Eric, and Chungdak Koren. 1995. "The Correct Route to Independence." *Tibetan Review* 30, no. 6: 17–18.

"Communism in the Land of the Gods." 1994. Cable News Network (hereafter CNN), December 26.

Cook, Sherburne, and Woodrow Borah. 1971. *Essays in Population History: Mexico and the Caribbean.* 3 vols. Berkeley: University of California Press.

Courtois, Stephane, Nicholas Werth, Jean-Louis Panne, Andrej Paczkowki, Karel Bartosek, and Jean-Louis Margolis.1999. *The Black Book of Communism: Crimes, Terror, Repression.* Cambridge: Harvard University Press.

Crace, John. 1999. "Forbidden Territory: The Dalai Lama Has Been in Exile for Forty Years." *Guardian*, March 9, 10.

CS [Cultural Survival]. 1993. *State of the Peoples: A Global Human Rights Report on Societies in Danger.* Boston: Beacon Press.

CTS [Central Tibetan Secretariat]. 1976. *Tibet Under Chinese Communist Rule: A Compilation of Refugee Statements, 1958–1975.* Dharamsala: Information and Publicity Office of His Holiness the Dalai Lama.

Dalai Lama. 1962. *My Lands and My People: The Original Autobiography of the Dalai Lama of Tibet.* New York: Warner Books.

———. 1987. "Five Point Peace Plan for Tibet." At www.tibet.com/Proposal/5point.html.

———. 1996. "Statement by His Holiness the Dalai Lama to the Foreign Affairs Committee of the Folkletingets Udenrisudalg, Denmark." In "Prepared Testimony of Lodi G. Gyari" Before the U.S. Senate Finance Committee, June 6.

———. 1998. Remarks (on cover) in Steve Lehman, *The Tibetans: A Struggle to Survive.* New York: Umbrage Press.

"Dalai Lama Remains Taboo Subject in Home Region." 1999. Agence France-Presse, August 10.

Davidson, Neil. 2000. *The Origins of Scottish Nationhood.* London: Pluto Press.

Davis, Kingsley. 1951. *Population of India and Pakistan.* Princeton: Princeton University Press.

Davis, Mike. 2001. *Late Victorian Holocausts: El Niño Famines and the Making of the Third World.* London: Verso.

Dedering, Tilman. 1999. "'A Certain Rigorous Treatment of All Parts of the Nation': The Annihilation of the Herero in German South West Africa, 1904." In *The Massacre in History*, ed. Mark Levene and Penny Roberts, 205–222. New York: Berghahn Books.

Desai, Ashok. 1972. "Population and Standards of Living in Akbar's Time." *International Economic and Social History Review* 9, no. 1: 40–52.

Diamond, Jared. 1998. *Guns, Germs and Steel: A Short History of Everybody for the Last 13,000 Years.* London: Vintage.

DIIR [Department of Information and International Relations, Tibet Government-in-Exile]. 1993. *Tibet: Proving Truth from Facts.* Dharamsala: DIIR.

Dillin, John. 2001. "The Incredible Shrinking Russia." *Christian Science Monitor*, February 22, 15.

Domenach, Jean-Luc. 1992. *Chine: l'archipel oublie.* Paris: Fayard.

Douglas, Ed. 1997. "Dalai Lama's Nazi Friends." *Observer*, November 2, 15.

Dreschler, Horst. 1980. *'Let Us Die Fighting': The Struggle of the Herero and Nama Against German Imperialism (1884–1915).* London: Zed.

Dulaney, Andrew. 1993. *Resolving Claims of Self-Determination: A Proposal for Integrating Principles of International Law with Specific Application to the Tibetan People.* Berkeley: International Committee of Lawyers for Tibet.

Durand, John. 1977. "Historical Estimates of World Population: An Evaluation." *Population & Development Review* 3, no. 3: 253–296.

Duursma, Jerri. 1996. *Fragmentation and the International Relations of Micro-States.* Cambridge: Cambridge University Press.

Elder, Bruce. 1996. *Blood on the Whattle: Massacres and Maltreatment of Australian Aborigines Since 1788.* French's Forest, NSW: National Book Distributors.

Erickson, Barbara. 1997. *Tibet: Abode of the Gods, Pearl of the Motherland.* Berkeley: Pacific View Press.

"EU MP Olivier Supuis's Letter to the President of the EU Re: Remarks on Tibet." 2000. World Tibet Network, December 1.

"Exiled Tibetans Say 1.2 Million Killed During Chinese Rule." 1984. United Press International, September 17.

Farwell, Byron. 1972. *Queen Victoria's Little Wars.* New York: Harper & Row.

French, Patrick. 2003. "The Master Race in the Mountains." *Daily Telegraph*, September 1.

Goldstein, Melvyn. 1997. *The Snow Lion and the Dragon: China, Tibet and the Dalai Lama.* Berkeley: University of California Press.

Goldstein, Melvyn, and Cynthia Beall. 1991. "China's Birth Control Policy in the Tibet Autonomous Region: Myths and Realities." *Asian Survey* 31, no. 3: 285–300.

Goodman, David. 1983. "Guizhou and the People's Republic of China: The Development of an Internal Colony." In *Internal Colonialism: Essays Around a Theme,* ed. David Drakakis-Smith and Stephen Williams, 107–123. Edinburgh: University of Edinburgh.

Gombu, Phinjo. 1997. "A 966–km March to Save Tibet." *Toronto Star*, March 11, A3.

Grossman, Hershel, and Murat Iyigun. 1997. "Population Increase and the End of Colonialism." *Economica* 64: 483–493.

Gutto, Shadrack. 1993. *Human and Peoples' Rights for the Oppressed: Critical Essays on Theory and Practice from Sociology of Law Perspectives.* Lund: Lund University.

Gyari, Lodi. 1997. Prepared Testimony . . . Before the U.S. Senate Foreign Relations Committee. Federal News Service, May 13.

Hai Miao. 1998. "Changing Patterns in Family Size and Structure in the Tibet Autonomous Region: Adaptions to Reform of Pastoral Management." Unpublished MA thesis, UCLA.

Hale, Christopher. 2003. *Himmler's Crusade: The True Story of the 1938 Nazi Expedition into Tibet.* New York: Wiley.

Harris, Marvin, and Eric Ross. 1987. *Death, Sex and Fertility: Population Regulation in Preindustrial and Developing Societies.* New York: Columbia University Press.

Hechter, Michael. 1998 [1975]. *Internal Colonialism: The Celtic Fringe in British National Development.* New Brunswick, NJ: Transaction Books.

Hellen, Nicholas. 1996. "The God-king and the Darling of the Nazis." *Sunday Times*, July 14.

Hess, Julia Meredith. 2003. "Stateless Citizens: Culture, Nation and Identity in the

Expanding Tibetan Diaspora." Unpublished Ph.D. dissertation, University of New Mexico.

Hobson, John. 1993. "The Military Extraction Gap and the Wary Titan: The Fiscal Sociology of British Defense Policy, 1870–1913." *Journal of European Economic History* 22, no. 3: 461–506.

Hochschild, Adam. 1998. *King Leopold's Ghost: A Story of Greed, Terror and Heroism in Colonial Africa.* Boston: Houghton Mifflin.

Hoffman, Michael. 1999. "Chinese Bluster Hides History of Butchery." *Mainichi Daily News*, November 25, 9.

Horvath, Ronald. 1972. "A Definition of Colonialism." *Current Anthropology* 13, no. 1: 45–51.

Hsiao, Anne Hsiu-an. 1998. "Is China's Policy to Use Force Against Taiwan a Violation of the Principle of Non-Use of Force Under International Law?" *New England Law Review* 32: 715–742.

Hyam, Ronald. 2002. *Britain's Imperial Century, 1815–1914: A Study of Empire and Expansion.* 3rd ed. London: Palgrave.

ICJ [International Commission of Jurists]. 1960. "Manifesto by Tibetan Leaders." In *The Question of Tibet and the Rule of Law.* Geneva: ICJ.

ICT [International Campaign for Tibet]. 1994. *Tibet 'Transformed': A Pictorial Essay Documenting China's Colonization of Tibet.* Washington: ICT.

———. 2002. "Heinrich Harrer and Petra Kelly to Be Honored for Contributions to Tibet with Award Presented by the Dalai Lama." World Tibet Network, September 27.

Ingram, Paul. 1990. *Tibet: The Facts.* 2d rev. ed. Dharamsala: Tibetan Young Buddhist Association.

"Israeli Minister Upbraids Dalai Lama for Finding Humanity in Nazis." 1994. Associated Press, March 21.

Jackson, Robert. 1994. *Indian Population Decline: The Missions of Northwestern New Spain, 1687–1840.* Albuquerque: University of New Mexico Press.

Jackson, Robert, and Edward Castillo. 1995. *Indians, Franciscans and Spanish Colonization: The Impact of the Mission System on California Indians.* Albuquerque: University of New Mexico Press.

Johnson, Chalmers. 2000. *Blowback: The Costs and Consequences of American Empire.* New York: Metropolitan Books.

Kiernan, Ben. 2003. "The Demography of Genocide in Southeast Asia: The Death Tolls in Cambodia, 1975–79, and East Timor, 1975–80." *Critical Asian Studies* 35, no. 4: 585–597.

Kranti, Vijay. 2000. "Pilgrim's Progress." *Pioneer Daily*, December 21; World Tibet Network, January 17, 2001.

Kyabje Gelek Rinpoche. 1999. "A Clear-Eyed Reminiscence." World Tibet Network, December 27.

"A Land of Bondage." 1999. *Economist*, February 13, 33.

Landow, George. 2001. "The Metaphorical Use of Colonialism and Related Terms." At www.thecore.nus.edu.sg/landow/post/poldiscourse/colony2.html.

Lang-Sims, Lois. 1963. *The Presence of Tibet.* London: Cresset Press.

Latham, Linda. 1975. "Revolt Re-examined: The 1878 Insurrection in New Caledonia." *Journal of Pacific History* 10, no. 3: 49–62.

Leccardi, Carmen. 1993. "Ethnic Conflict and Prejudice in a Colonial Context: The Case of Tibet." *International Journal of Group Tensions* 23, no. 3: 193–224.

Lee, Joseph. 1973. *The Modernisation of Irish Society, 1848–1918.* Dublin: Gill & Macmillan.

Liptak, Adam. 2003. "Crime and Punishment." *New York Times*, August 24, 3.

Livi-Bacci, Massimo. 2003. "Return to Hispaniola: Reassessing a Demographic Catastrophe." *Hispanic American Historical Review* 83, no. 1: 3–51.

Lovejoy, Paul. 2000. *Transformations in Slavery: A History of Slavery in Africa.* 2d ed. Cambridge: Cambridge University Press.

LRN [Labor Rights Now]. 2003. "China Action." Available at www.laborrightsnow.org/China.htm.

McAlpin, Michelle. 1983. "Famines, Epidemics and Population Growth: The Case of India." *Journal of Interdisciplinary History* 14, no. 2: 351–366.

McCorquodale, Robert, and Nicholas Orosz. 1994. *Tibet: The Position in International Law.* London: Serindia.

McDonald, Angus. 2003. "Love Across the Divide." *South China Morning Post*, August 30, A5.

McElroy, Damien. 2000. "Tibet's Cultures and Vultures Clash," *Sunday Telegraph*, November 19, 37.

McGrory, Mary. 1999. "Not What the Founders Had in Mind," *Washington Post*, July 4, B1.

"McLaughlin's One on One: Interview with the Dalai Lama." 1991. Federal News Service, April 19.

Maddison, Angus. 1998. *Chinese Economic Performance in the Long Run.* Paris: OECD.

Marshall, P.J. 1998. *The Eighteenth Century*, vol. 2: *Oxford History of the British Empire.* Oxford: Oxford University Press.

Martin, C.J. 1961. "Population Census Estimates and Methods in British East Africa." In *Essays on African Population*, ed. Kenneth Barbour and R. Mansell Prothero, 49–62. London: Routledge & Kegan Paul.

Marx, Karl. 1954 [1867]. *Capital.* Vol. 1. Moscow: Progress Publishers.

Mehra, Parshotam. 1968. *The Younghusband Expedition.* New York: Asia Publishing House.

Mohanty, Chandra. 1991. "Under Western Eyes: Feminist Scholarship and Colonial Discourse." In *Third World Women and the Politics of Feminism*, ed. Chandra Mohanty, Ann Russo, and Lourdes Torres, 51–80. Bloomington: Indiana University Press.

Mountcastle, Amy. 1997. "Tibetans in Exile: The Construction of Global Identities." Unpublished Ph.D. dissertaion, Rutgers University.

"Nation's Prison Population Climbs to Over 2 Million." 2000. *Washington Post*, August 10, A04.

Neill, Rosemary. 2001. "Where Reconciliation Becomes a Cruel Joke," *Australian*, February 23, 15

Norbu, Dawa. 1979. "The Tibetan Rebellion: An Interpretation." *China Quarterly*, no. 77: 74–93.

O'Brien, Patrick. 1990. "European Industrialization: From the Voyages of Discovery to the Industrial Revolution." In *The European Discovery of the World and Its Economic Effects on Pre-Industrial Society, 1500–1800*, ed. Hans Pohl, 154–177. Stuttgart: Franz Steiner.

Orleans, Leo. 1966. "A Note on Tibet's Population." *China Quarterly*, no. 27: 120–122.

O'Toole, Fintan. 2002. "Bizarre Logic Behind Bush's War on Terror." *Irish Times*, July 30, 14.

"Overview of the Tibetan Population in the PRC from the 2000 Census." 2003. *Tibet Information Network News Update*, September 30. Available at www.tibetinfo.net.

Panchen Lama. 1997 [1962]. *A Poisoned Arrow: The Secret Report of the 10th Panchen Lama.* London: Tibet International Network.

Parsons, Neil, and Robin Palmer. 1977. "Introduction: Historical Background." In *The Roots of Rural Poverty in Central and Southern Africa*, ed. Robin Palmer and Neil Parsons, 1–32. Berkeley: University of California Press.

Parthasarathi, Prasannan. 1998. "Rethinking Wages and Competitiveness in Eighteenth Century Britain and South India." *Past and Present*, no. 158: 82–87, 105–106.

"Please Shout Quietly." 1999. *Guardian* [London], October 19, 19.

Pommaret, Francoise. 2003. *Tibet: An Enduring Civilization.* New York: Harry Abrams.

QHSSHJJTJNJ [*Qinghai sheng shehui jingji tongji nianjian*] (Qinghai social and economic statistical yearbook). 1989. Beijing: Zhongguo tongji chubanshe.

QHTJNJ [*Qinghai tongji nianjian*] (Qinghai statistical yearbook). 1991, 1993, 1996, 2000, 2001. Beijing: Zhongguo tongji chubanshe.

Rich, Frank. 2003. "Reality Makes Way for the Bush Script." *International Herald Tribune*, October 25, 10.

Richardson, Hugh. 1962. *A Short History of Tibet*. New York: Dutton.

RMXN50N [*Renmin Xining 50 nian*] (50 years of People's Xining). 1999. Beijing: Zhongguo tongji chubanshe.

Ross, Eric. 1986. "Potatoes, Population and the Irish Famine: The Political Economy of Demographic Change." In *Culture and Reproduction: An Anthropological Critique of Demographic Transition Theory*, ed. W. Penn Handwerker, 196–220. Boulder, CO: Westview.

Ryan, Siobhain. 2001. "Statistics Highlight Aboriginal Tragedy." *Courier Mail* (Australia), August 31, 2.

Safire, William. 2000. "The Biggest Vote." *New York Times*, May 18, A14.

Saklani, Girija. 1984. *The Uprooted Tibetans in India: A Sociological Study of Continuity and Change*. New Delhi: Cosmo Publications.

Samdup, Tseten. 1993. "Chinese Population—Threat to Tibetan Identity." Website of the Tibetan Government in Exile, www.tibet.com/Human rights/poptrans.html.

Sangay, Lobsang. 2003. "Tibet: Exiles' Journey." *Journal of Democracy* 14: 119–130.

Sautman, Barry. 2001. "Association, Federation and 'Genuine Autonomy': The Dalai Lama's Proposals and Tibet Independence." *China Information* 14, no. 1: 31–91.

———. 2003. "'Demographic Aggression' and Tibet." Paper under submission to a journal.

———. *The Tibetan Émigré Ideology: Manichean Politics and the "Colonial" Thesis*. Monograph. (In progress).

Sautman, Barry, and Irene Eng. 2000. "Tibet: Development for Whom?" *China Information* 15, no. 2: 20–75.

Schell, Orville. 2000. *Virtual Tibet: Searching for Shangri-la from the Himalayas to Hollywood*. New York: Metropolitan Books.

Schvindlerman, Julian. 2001. "The Coddling of Arafat." *Jerusalem Post*, January 1, 55.

"Secret Panchen Lama Report Confirms Chinese Atrocities?" 1996. Agence France-Presse, October 5.

Seymour, James. 1998. "Inflating Prisoner Statistics Counter-Productive." *South China Morning Post*, March 30, 18.

Seymour, James, and Richard Anderson. 1998. *New Ghosts, Old Ghosts: Prisons and Labor Reform Camps in China*. Armonk, NY: M.E. Sharpe.

Shakya, Tsering. 1999. *Dragon in the Land of Snows: A History of Modern Tibet Since 1947*. London: Pimlico.

Shalom, Stephen. 1984. *Deaths in China Due to Communism: Propaganda Versus Reality*. Tempe: Center for Asian Studies, Arizona State University.

Silvester-Carr, Denise. 1996. "Ireland's Famine Museum." *History Today* (December): 20–32.

Smith, Warren. 1999. "History Is Not Complete Answer to Tibet's Future: A Reply to Michael van Walt." *Tibetan Review* 34, no. 2: 19–20.

Smith, Warren W. Jr. 1996. *Tibetan Nation: A History of Tibetan Nationalism and Sino-Tibetan Relations*. Boulder, CO: Westview.

Soinam, Dagyi. 2003. "Cooperative Medicare System: A Boon for Farmers and Herders." *China's Tibet* 5: 8–9.

Stannard, David. 1992. *American Holocaust: Columbus and the Conquest of the New World*. New York: Oxford University Press.

"State Council White Paper on Human Rights." 1991. Xinhua, November 2.

Steele, E.D. 1974. *Irish Land and British Politics: Tenant Rights and Nationality, 1865–1870*. Cambridge: Cambridge University Press.

Stein, Burton. 1998. *A History of India*. London: Blackwell.

Strong, Anna Louise. 1976 [1959]. *When Serfs Stood Up*. San Francisco, CA: Red Sun.

Suleri, Sara. 1992. "Woman Skin Deep: Feminism and the Post-Colonial Condition." *Critical Inquiry* 18, no. 4: 756–769.

Sun Huayang, and Li Xiru. 1995. "Zhongguo Zangzu renkou de yanbian he xianzhuang" (Evolution and situation of China's Tibetan population). *Zhongguo renkou kexue* 51: 35–39.

Sun Jingxin. 1994. *Zhongguo Zangzu renkou* (China's Tibetan population). Beijing: Zhongguo tongji chubanshe.

Thinley, Pema. 2000. "Editorial: Who Says Colonialism Has Ended?" *Tibetan Review* 35, no. 1: 3.

Thurman, Robert. 1992. "The Potomac Conference: Sino-Tibetan Relations: Prospects for the Future." At www.columbia.edu/cu/web/data/indiv/area/Tibet.potomac/historical/recent/histdsc2.html.

———. 1997. "The Realpolitik of Spirituality: An Interview with His Holiness the Fourteenth Dalai Lama." Shambala Online, available at www.shambalasun.com/Archives/Features/1996/November 1996/Dalai Lama.

———. 1999. "Introduction." In *The Tibetans: Photographs*, ed. Art Perry. New York: Viking Studio.

Tibet Information Network (TIN). 1999. *The Politics of Population Transfer: An Ethnographic and Historical Survey of Haidong and Haixi*. London: Tibet Information Network. Available at www.tibetinfo.net/news-updates/nu281099.html.

"Tibetans, Americans Mark 40th Anniversary Since Tibetan Uprising." 1999. Agence France-Presse, March 10.

"Tibetans at Earth Summit Protest Against Chinese Rule." 2002. Agence France-Presse, August 27.

"Tibetans Challenge India, China's Rights to Hold Border Talks." 2002. Press Trust of India, January 12.

"Tibetans Confident of Change—at Last." 1998. InterPress Service, March 10.

"Tokyo Governor Meets Tibetan Foreign Minister-in-Exile." 1999. *Kyodo*, October 15.

Tsarong, Paljor. 1997. "Understanding Decolonization and Its Implications for the Tibetan Movement." *Tibetan Review* 32, no. 11: 14–19.

Tsering, Dawa. 1998. "Dui Xizang de Zhimin yu Zangren de shengcun weiji" (The colonization of Tibet and the Tibetan survival crisis). *China Spring*, no. 173: 63–88.

Twain, Mark. 1997 [1887]. *A Connecticut Yankee in King Arthur's Court*. Oxford: Oxford University Press.

TYC [Tibetan Youth Congress]. 1994. *Strangers in Their Own Country: Chinese Population Transfer in Tibet and Its Impact*. Dharamsala: TYC.

———. 1995. *Development for Whom? A Report on the Chinese Development Strategies in Tibet and Their Impacts*. Dharamsala: TYC.

UAW [United Auto Workers]. 2003. "China Has Jailed Many Labor Activists." Available at www.uaw.org/action/china/free03.html.

UNESCAP [United Nations Economic and Social Commission for Asia and the Pacific]. 2003. "Tibet: Population Situation." Available at www.unescap.org/pop/database/chinadata/tibet.htm.

"Unfree in America." 2003. *Boston Globe*, August 31, D10.

UNGA [United Nations General Assembly]. 1995. "Declaration on the Occasion of the Fiftieth Anniversary of the United Nations." GA Res. 60/6, November 9.

U.S. Congress, "United States Foreign Relations Act, Fiscal Year 1988–1989," on Tibet Government-in-Exile Website, www.tibet.com/Resolution/us8889.html.

U.S. State Department. 2002. *China Country Report on Human Rights Practices for the Year 2001*. Washington, DC: U.S. State Department. Available at www.state.gov/drl/rls/hrrpt/2001/eap/P289.htm.

U.S. Supreme Court. 1872. *Slaughter House Cases*, 83 U.S. 36.
———. 1883. *Civil Rights Cases*, 109 U.S. 3.
"U.S. System Is Not a Perfect Model for Canada." 2000. *Gazette* (Montreal), April 24, B2.
Walford, C. 1878. "The Famines of the World: Past and Present." *Journal of the Statistical Society* 41, no. 3: 434–442.
Wang Lixiong. 2000. "Zhu ceng di xuan zhi yu minzhu zhi: jiejue Xizang wenti de fangfa bijiao" (Level-by-level successive choice or democratic system: A comparison of methods to resolve the Tibet Question). *Zhongguo shehui kexue jikan* 9, no. 1, reprinted at www.usembassy-china.org.cn/sandt/tibetres-demosystem.html.
Watanabe, Teresa. 2000. "Dalai Lama Urges Local Unity Against China." *Los Angeles Times*, June 26, 1.
Weller, Marc. 1992. "The International Response to the Dissolution of the Socialist Federal Republic of Yugoslavia." *American Journal of International Law* 86: 568–607.
Wesseling, H.L. 1997. *Imperialism and Colonialism: Essays on the History of European Expansion*. Westport, CT: Greenwood Press.
Wirz, Albert. 1982. "The German Colonies in Africa." In *European Colonial Rule, 1880–1940*, ed. Rudolf von Albertini, 388–417. New York: Greenwood.
Wolff, Diane. 1997. "The Pitiless Measurement of History: China and Tibet, Past, Present and Future." Available at www.geocities.com/Capitol Hill/1730/pmh_5.html.
Working, Russell. 2001. "Desperate for a Life Behind Bars." *South China Morning Post*, February 14, 14.
Yan Hao. 2000. "Tibetan Population in China: Myths and Facts Re-examined." *Asian Ethnicity* 1, no. 1: 11–36.
Yang Dali. 1996. *Calamity and Reform in China: State, Rural Society, and Institutional Change Since the Great Leap Forward*. Stanford: Stanford University Press.
ZGMZGZNJ [*Zhongguo minzu gongzuo nianjian*] (China ethnic work yearbook). 2002. Beijing: Zhongguo minzu gongzuo nianjian bianji weiyuanhui.
ZGMZTJNJ, 1949–1994 [*Zhongguo minzu tongji nianjian, 1949–1994*] (China ethnic statistics yearbook, 1949–1994). 1995. Beijing: Minzu chubanshe.
ZGMZTJNJ 1998, 2000 [*Zhongguo minzu tongji nianjian 1998, 2000*] (China ethnic statistical yearbook, 1998, 2000). Beijing: Minzu chubanshe.
Zhang Rongzu [Chang Jung-tsu]. 1989. *Case Study on Mountain Environmental Management: Nyemo County*. Kathmandu: Center for Integrated Mountain Development.
Zhang Tianlu. 1997. *Population Development in Tibet and Related Issues*. Beijing: Foreign Languages Press.
———. 2001. "Peaceful Liberation and Population Growth." *China's Tibet*, no. 4: 6–7.

12

Life in Lara Village, Tibet

Yu Changjiang

This fieldwork report reflects on the old stereotypes of Tibet and aims at a renewed understanding of Tibet by mainstream Chinese society. A decisive factor in ethnic relations within China is the stereotype that Han Chinese have of ethnic minorities.[1] Up to the 1980s, mainstream Han viewed Tibetans from a perspective that was mainly conditioned by four basic premises:

1. the assumption of social evolution and "progress" introduced into China from the West at the end of the nineteenth century (Yuan 1999, 17–34);
2. the traditional Confucian "Hua-Yi" ("civilized-barbarian") framework based on *jiaohua*, or educational determinism (Fei 1999, 332–347);
3. the confusing concept of *minzu* (nation, nationality, ethnic groups) introduced into China around the end of the nineteenth century (Ma 2001, 111–119; 141–159);
4. the Marxist ethnic theory of the Soviet Union, based on Marx's five stages of social development[2] (Ma 2000, 105–111).

Social evolution and, accordingly, a rough "progressivism" were introduced in China by intellectuals at the end of the nineteenth century. These concepts were viewed as an enlightening gospel to save the nation and revitalize China at a time when the country was in the midst of a serious social crisis brought on by a succession of attacks from the West. As a result, many Han Chinese intellectuals changed dramatically from traditionalists into anti-traditionalists. In addition, at a somewhat later date, the social elite began to advocate Marxism, especially Marx's five-stage theory of evolution from primitive communism through post–industrial revolution communism. The progression from backward to advanced thus became the basic frame of reference for social analysis. "Tradition" was juxtaposed with "modern" or "progressive" in a zero-sum way, becoming synonymous with "back-ward" or even "reactionary." Many people were infatuated with the principle "there can be no construction without destruction." Such "progressivism" finally led to nationwide spasms of anti-traditionalism that elicited both large-scale orchestrated criticism and the destruction of much of traditional Han culture. The best known of these are the New Culture Movement of 1915, the Cultural Revolution of the 1960s, and the Culture Discussions of the 1980s.

The hatred that some of the Han elite feel for their own tradition is another form of worship of "the West." They imagine they are catching up with the West when in fact they may simply be ruining their own tradition. The new things they hope to build on the ruin of the old are, in their imagination, associated with the West, though in fact they are often strange to Westerners. It is difficult for most Han to understand why Western people often criticize them for damaging their culture when they feel they are just struggling to follow and learn from the West.

The backward/advanced progression and anti-tradition sentiment also consti-tute the foundation of the Han elite's psychology and attitude toward ethnicity. Internationally, most Han believe that they are backward compared with people in more technologically advanced Western nations. Domestically, however, Han tend to believe they are more advanced than Chinese minorities, not only historically, since they were already in what they called a mature feudal stage, but also cur-rently, since they first accepted capitalism and communism from the West. The "advanced" Han genuinely feel a calling to help the "backward" minorities, in-cluding Tibetans, to develop and leap into an advanced stage.

Culturally, radical Han and some members of the educated minority elite tended to disdain all "backward" ethnic traditions. In the case of tradition-oriented Tibetan society, a lot of "backwardness" was found and juxtaposed with "social develop-ment." From the 1950s to the 1980s, this backward-versus-advanced perspective dominated nearly all the surveys, reports, and descriptions of mainstream writers.

The most extreme expression of the backward/advanced dichotomy was the destruction of traditional relics during the Cultural Revolution in the name of anti-feudalism and anti-superstition. This was also the period during which the most serious destruction of Tibetan historic sites occurred. Although most of the perpe-trators were not really ethnic Han, the concept of extreme anti-traditionalism was definitely introduced from Han society. One of the chief motivators of this re-search is the desire to change the negative view of tradition.

Following the extreme animosity toward tradition in the 1960s and 1970s, a new tendency appeared in the 1980s: that of the overmystification of Tibet. "Mys-terious" became almost the only label of Tibet, and produced a new vision or myth of Tibet that is often at odds with local feelings and concerns. Both the denigration of tradition and the mystification of the new Tibet contribute to misunderstanding and prejudice, distorting the public's knowledge of Tibet and of the Tibetan people. Only when the mainstream Han society is able to communicate with Tibetans as with any other people can there be a truly "normal" ethnic relationship.

This research aims to dispense with both the backward stereotypes and the pseudo mystique of Tibet, and to understand Tibetans as they see themselves. Through this work, I hope to help mainstream Han society see Tibetans and their land as ordinary and normal.

The Project

At the end of the 1980s, China made a new round of efforts to promote economic development in Tibet. A large amount of investment was poured into the region. This research was designed as part of a national social and economic development project jointly supported by Beijing University's Institute of Sociology and Anthropology and the Tibetology Research Center of China. My Tibetan colleagues and I believed that a new and effective way of thinking on Tibet could not be found unless mainstream society could consider Tibet from a new perspective. This new perspective should be built on the principles of sociology and anthropology, rather than evolutionism or stage-theory. Hence, I turned to basic anthropological fieldwork and participant observation. Functionalism and cultural relativism were reviewed as theoretical references. Although already commonplace in the West, this was considered quite radical in the China of the late 1980s. I strove to present neutral observations and an objective record, trying to avoid judgment of right and wrong, this being quite different from the mainstream formulation at that time.

In order to improve my descriptions, other methodologies, including phenomenology and ethnomethodology, were utilized as well. The narratives and descriptions of local people and their activities were recorded and described as facts, regardless of mis-remembrances and mistakes. Superficial substantialism or reductionism was also avoided. For instance, cultural or spiritual phenomena were not simply explained by economic, political, or social reasons.

This study did not aim to test a theory or discover new facts, but rather to explore a new viewpoint and framework to understand a familiar society, and lay a foundation for further study. Most of what is recorded in this report has been known to other observers.[3] But this study contains new observations and descriptions, reflecting Tibetan life inside today's China as recorded by a Han scholar who had been educated and trained completely with a Han background. The participant-observation framework conducted in a Tibetan community by a Han scholar is itself an attempt to prove the possibility of a cross-ethnic understanding between Han and Tibetans.

Fieldwork and Report

I made my first visit to a Tibetan area in 1988. Since then, Tibetan colleagues and friends helped me to become more and more involved with the area and its people. This research was conducted from July to November of 1990 in a small village called Lara around 70 kilometers from the capital city of Lhasa. In 1991 and 1993,

I went there again for a brief stay.[4] This site was selected because it is located in the center of the Tibetan region, influenced by the city, but still a typical agricultural community. The relative density and concentration of the agricultural lifestyle provide good conditions for the participant-observer to be efficiently and easily involved in daily life.

Because anthropologists find it difficult to accept that any community is typical or representative of the larger society, I cannot presume to make such a claim on behalf of Lara. The diversity of the locality and the subcultures among Tibetans means that this case can be seen as only one among many local cultures, though some of the basic cultural elements described do in fact exist generally.

As part of the participant-observation methodology of this study, I stayed with one Lara family, took part in daily village life, work, and religious activities, and learned their language and customs. The villagers knew my identity, background, and purpose. This was not a commercial venture; villagers helped me voluntarily. All of my food and accommodations were free, although when I went to town, I often bought some tea or butter as presents for the villagers. I also helped them as much as possible with farm work and housework, including threshing grains, roasting barley, spreading manure, milling grain, repairing electrical appliances, and so forth.

The original version of this report was written in Chinese, for Han readers inside China. For Western readers with a different background, the emphasis and attention will not be the same. The English version is a translation of selected parts of the Chinese.

Daily Life

Food: Tradition First

In Lara Village, food can be classified into three categories:

1. Traditional foods: *tsampa*, butter tea, yak meat, and so on, which are not only edible, but also culturally symbolic.
2. Adopted foods: noodles, rice, momo, and others; edible, but not culturally significant.
3. Supporting foods: potatoes, radishes, cabbage, and so on. Their significance depends on how they are cooked. They become indigenous if cooked in local ways.

Accordingly, traditional kitchen appliances are supposed to be basic. Every household has kitchenware such as the *dumo* (butter churn), the *tangu* (*tsampa*, or roasted barley, bag), the *qubo* (a large copper-made water container), *jo* (ladle), *jakhu* (leather tea bag), *marga* (a small butter box), and *khodir* and *mekho* (an old-style pottery pot and stove for preparing tea, now seldom used).

Electric stoves and pressure cookers are commonly used modern kitchen appliances. Villagers prefer pressure cookers simply because they feel the device helps cook food quickly, not because they want to raise the boiling point to 100°C, as some science-oriented outsiders have hypothesized. The use of pressure cookers does not significantly change traditional cooking habits, since nearly all the food cooked with traditional tools can also be cooked with pressure cookers, and vice versa.

The Irreplaceable Tsampa

As Food. The Lara villagers' principal daily food is tsampa, which is a kind of flour obtained by grinding roasted *ney* (highland barley).

Regardless of how it is prepared, tsampa is eaten in the traditional manner. First, butter tea (*ja*) is poured into a bowl, often wooden, until it is about one-third full. Tsampa is then added. Holding the bowl with the left hand, one pushes the floating tsampa down into the tea with the middle or ring finger of the right hand. Since the bowls are relatively small and tsampa is heaped high above the brim, the pushing must be skillful lest some grain fall out and be wasted. The next step, stirring, requires precision. With the bowl still in the left hand, one stirs and mixes the tsampa in it with all fingers except the thumb of the right hand. The bowl is rotated until the tsampa reaches a consistency that can be made into a ball to eat. This traditional way of preparing tsampa is a basic skill for everyone, and virtually a symbol of cultural recognition. Children learn and perfect it while still very young; I have often seen five- or six-year-olds relishing deftly revolving bowls.

Tsampa may be prepared in ways varying from the standard recipe of tsampa mixed with butter tea. For example, villagers often replace butter tea with clear tea—that is, without butter, which is regarded as a little lower grade. By contrast, if some milk residue is added to the tsampa, the grade is considered a little higher. Villagers often treated me by adding milk residue to show their friendship.

In villagers' eyes, one luxurious way to prepare tsampa is by adding sugar to the mixture. Strictly speaking, this kind of tsampa is too modern to be described as traditional. Some outsiders and young people like this kind of tsampa, but most older people cannot accept it, not because they do not like the sweet taste, but because they feel that the unique flavor of tsampa has been altered. In their view, there are countless choices of sweet food on earth, but tsampa is in a class by itself, with a flavor that is irreplaceable.

As Tradition. Tsampa is a special food, very easy to carry, store, and eat, unless one is without water. It is a food suitable for nomads, military personnel, and people who must travel over long distances. For settled agricultural people, such advantages as small volume and portability become less important, but even for them, factors like tsampa's easy storage and preparation remain meaningful.

Tsampa itself is only a staple, comparable to rice or bread in other cultures, but its uniqueness makes it much more meaningful. The villagers evince a profound sentiment toward it, regarding tsampa as a symbol of Tibetanness. Given the fact that few other ethnic groups eat tsampa, it becomes an important marker distinguishing Tibetans from others. Its significance is no less than those of blood and language. Hence, "tsampa-eating people" is synonymous with "Tibetan." Accordingly, whether one can or cannot eat tsampa has become a kind of touchstone of whether one is ready to accept Tibetan culture and meld into a Tibetan community.

The deep feeling of villagers for tsampa is shown by their adherence to the difficult way of preparing it. In fact, there is an easier way to prepare it: fold a piece of sheep skin into the shape of a *tangu* (tsampa bag), pour tsampa and buttered tea into it, hold the bag in one hand and knead it with the other. This is more convenient and efficient, and requires no special training. However, this efficient way has never been widely adopted. It seems too utilitarian, and is devoid of the distinction that symbolizes a specific ethnic culture. The hand and bowl way, on the contrary, is something that people cannot easily master: they must make some effort to learn. Therefore, traditional tsampa preparation has come to represent the culture. For villagers, the techniques reaffirm tradition, as well confirming their cultural identity.

Roasting Ney (Highland Barley)

Roasting ney is crucial to the process of making tsampa as well as a meaningful activity for every family after the harvest. In fact, it is not simply work, but a group activity.

Before being roasted, barley must be washed, normally in the stream near the village. There are several public stone stoves in the village for roasting barley. A special shrub called *shima* is used as fuel, since it makes a roaring fire. Barley is put in a type of jar called *drama,* which has an exit near the bottom. Boiled water is first poured from the top of the drama, heating the barley in it and leaking out through the exit. Clean sand is put in a pan and heated on the stove. Then the barley is poured into the hot sand and heated. A special wooden tool, called *gangba* (hammer-like, with a slot at the head that grips the rim of pans), is used to hold the pan and shake it up and down, helping to mix the sand and barley. Very soon, the barley pops and emits a fragrant odor. Then the mixture is poured into a sieve pan (a pan with many small holes larger than sand, but smaller than barley grains) above a normal pan. The sand falls down to the lower pan while the roasted barley is left in the sieve. The roasted barley has to be cooled down and collected into sacks. It usually takes two persons to roast barley. One roasts while the other adds fuel. Both need high skills to control the duration and heating. When a family roasts barley, neighbors and children like to come over to chat or help. Hence, the process of barley roasting often becomes a convenient opportunity for a social gathering.

The Water Mill. After being roasted, barley is sent to an old-style water mill (*qukhor*), two miles away from the village, to be ground into tsampa. Except for two months of the year, the water mill is always busy, and in fall and winter it typically runs twenty-four hours a day. In addition to paying a fee of 1.5 yuan per *ke* (14 kg) of barley, the customers must also have a person stay there and help the mill owner.

The water mill is an amazing device as well as a reminder of the old lifestyle. It sits on an aqueduct in the woods. The workshop and living rooms are dim, the air clouded with tsampa dust. The structure reverberates from the roaring rapids below and the rotation and friction of the stones. Stacks of barley sacks are piled around. A strong smell of wine fills the room as the mill owner drinks with some customers. The dogs are barking in the yard, announcing that someone is coming.

Butter: Tea and Lamp

Churning. Tibetan butter (*mar*), a type of fat extracted from milk, is the most important edible fat for villagers. Most families make butter themselves, using traditional methods. The major churning tool is the *shodong*, comprising two main parts: a cask about one meter tall and 20–30 centimeters in diameter, made of wooden bars fixed together with tightening hoops; and a piston-like puddler (*jalo*), which is a round wooden plate with gaps and a long handle. To extract butter, first pour milk (usually boiled) into a shodong until it is about half full; then insert the jalo into the shodong, moving it up and down repeatedly. The resulting pressure causes the milk to flow rapidly through the gaps between the piston and wall. After several minutes of such churning, one stops, waiting one to two hours before repeating the process again and again. After several rounds, a layer of yellowish fat, the butter, will float to the top. People do not normally harvest the butter immediately, stirring it for two to three days until the butter layer stops thickening. Then they pick it up with bare hands and put it into cold water to solidify the mass.

Usually only one person is involved in the process of butter churning, since villagers believe that more than one participant will negatively affect the output. When collecting butter from a shodong, people shape it like a bowl, with a small protruberance. After the butter has solidified in cold water, the small protuberance is removed and pasted on the wall, in the belief that this will guarantee a larger output next time.

Nowadays, some rich households in Lara Village buy butter from grocery stores or markets rather than making it themselves. Villagers feel that the quality of store-bought butter is inferior to that of the homemade product, but it is difficult for an outsider to be sure of this. Currently butter is sold at the price of 14–18 yuan per kilogram, which is rather expensive for average villagers.

Ja (Butter Tea). Butter is most heavily used for butter tea (*ja*), which is the villagers' most important drink. Whether resting, chatting, or working, villagers will drink butter tea at any moment. They make the beverage themselves, with no commercial inputs. To prepare it, a special tool called a *dumo*, or *jadong*, is used. It is one of the most basic pieces of kitchen equipment in Lara. A dumo has the same basic design as a shodong, but is a little thinner and taller. It is 15–25 cm in diameter and about one meter high. A strip of yak hide or canvas is attached to the dumo for ease of carrying. Like the shodong, a dumo consists of a barrel made of wooden bars with hoops, and a mixing piston.

To make butter tea, one first tears apart some brick tea and places it in an aluminum boiler or teapot, and boils it in salty water until the leaves have completely dissolved. The liquid is poured into a dumo through a small filter, so that all the tea solids are kept out. An appropriate amount of butter is then added to the dumo, and the piston moved to stir the mixture. The mixture is poured into a thermos or teapot, and the butter tea is ready to drink.

Butter and butter tea are closely associated with every aspect of the villagers' lives. Butter tea is a basic traditional drink in daily life, as well as the liquid for tsampa and an essential drink for guests. When guests arrive, butter tea must be served. The hosts fill the tea bowl to capacity and pass it to the guests with both hands. This politeness often makes guests feel obliged to the hosts for their hospitality. According to local custom, the hosts must refill the tea bowl immediately after the guests drink it. And the bowls are filled so full that the butter tea almost overflows. Villagers believe that this shows that their welcome and respect for the guests is at its height, with nothing more to be added. Although various modern drinks have made their way into local society, villagers still regard butter tea as the most natural and basic drink. The strong smell of butter tea accompanies villagers from their childhood to old age, and the customs related to butter tea constitute an important foundation of community life.

Qoeme (Butter Lamp). Besides food and drink, butter is also a basic material for religious rituals, especially for qoeme (butter lamps). The countless butter-burning lamps in Tibetan temples never go out. Most almsgivers give butter to the temples. Similarly, butter becomes a measure of value. A family's wealth can be gauged by how much butter it consumes.

Clothing: Adaptation and Change

In general, clothing in Lara is changing from the traditional Tibetan style to modern Western fashion. According to older residents, only Tibetan clothing was worn before 1959. After the democratic reforms were begun in that year, the use of traditional garb declined. Many men, and even some women, began to imitate revolutionary fashion, which Westerners call Mao suits. In the 1980s, the trend turned in two directions: traditional garb was resurrected at the same time that Western suits and other sorts of modern clothes became popular.

Men's Clothes

Most of the adult males in the village wear army-style uniforms, most of which are old and worn, being made at least a decade ago. A few wear relatively new but still well-worn Western suits. People do not care much about clothes and, because they work every day, cannot keep them clean. Several elders who held high social status before 1959 continue to wear traditional Tibetan robes. Modern clothes have begun to prevail among those who are under thirty, and children have even more choices.

Those who no longer normally wear traditional clothes have not necessarily abandoned them, but they are no longer part of their daily lives. Villagers all wear Tibetan clothes for such important activities as festivals, weddings, funerals, and other religious rituals. Family members all put on their best Tibetan dresses when they asked me to take photos for them to bring to their daughter, who is studying in eastern China. Villagers also wore Tibetan clothing when they held an open-air farewell party (*lingka*) for me. Almost every adult man owns one well-made, fully adorned Tibetan robe. Some of them are made of fur of marten or otter and are worth up to more than 10,000 yuan (the exchange rate was at that time one U.S. dollar to four yuan), so such robes are actually a key indicator of the wealth of the villagers' families.

Tibetan robes seem to have developed mainly for the requirements of the nomadic life. They are very loose and even longer than the height of a person, with the sleeves longer than the arms. A person needs help from others when putting on a robe. The part above the waistband is always kept very loose so that belongings or even a baby can be stored in it, and so that the lower part is not too long to walk about in. Usually people only wear one sleeve with another folded or just hung, so that they can put it on or off easily when they feel warmer or colder.

Because of Lara's mainly agricultural lifestyle, it is not very convenient to wear traditional Tibetan robes. There is a shorter Tibetan-style jacket, said to have been widely worn before Mao-style and Western suits were introduced. This partly explains why villagers accepted the Mao jacket so easily, since it was well suited to their requirements. However, neither the Tibetan jacket nor Mao-style or Western suits have replaced Tibetan robes for formal dress. In fact, male clothing can be classified into two categories: the culturally meaningful but seldom-worn Tibetan robes, and the common but informal Mao-style, Western suits, and Tibetan jackets.

Tradition-keeping Women's Clothes

In contrast to the diversity of male clothing, women's outfits completely keep or exactly restore traditional styles. A Tibetan female outfit has three components: a shirt made of thin cotton cloth or silk; a long, sleeveless coat; and, if the wearer is married, an apron (*bangden*) made of colorfully striped wool. Nearly all middle-aged women wear Tibetan dress, even while working in the fields. Interviews with female villagers indicated that they like traditional outfits, partly because they are suitable for the daily work and lifestyle and partly because they feel that traditional dresses better exemplify gender differences and femininity. Recently, some young married and single women have begun to give up Tibetan clothes in favor of new fashions. Pretty young women from wealthier families tend to be the first to wear modern clothes, while others hesitate to follow them.

Spiritual Life

Villagers' Knowledge of Buddhism

All the adult villagers I met described themselves as Buddhists. Although most people have some basic knowledge of Buddhism, they tend to remember its descriptive components rather than abstract principles.

Case 1: Knowledge of Buddhism (interview with a farmer and peddler, male, 33, noble descendant)

Religious Life of Villagers

Daily Worship

Every household has a place to enshrine figures of the Buddha. Some even have special rooms for their shrine. The shrine is made of wood and set on top of a traditional Tibetan cabinet. It is normally divided into several sections, one for each figure. In front of the shrine are copper or silver butter lamps and pure water bowls, seven in a set. In the past, the lamp wick was made from *haulm*, the stem of a local plant, but nowadays all are made from cotton. Most lamps and bowls are produced in factories rather than hand-made as before.

Every morning, the host (usually the hostess) of the family burns incense, changes the pure water before the Buddha figure, and prays for his blessing. In recent years, more and more villagers observe the daily prayer ritual. Older people and middle-aged women are the most conscientious. While younger people do not care very much about religion, they pay more attention to it as they age.

There is no strict norm about the arrangements of the figures and pictures of the Buddha. People like to attach many small pictures of Sakyamuni, the Dalai Lama, or the Panchen Lama to frames of pictures of the Buddha. Larger pictures are posted on the wall with yellow or white *khada,* or ceremonial scarves. Villagers like to put as many pictures as possible there, even if they are exactly the same ones.

Worshiping in Temples

Worshiping in temples mainly involves such activities as circling inside and outside the temple, turning prayer wheels, praying, and giving alms. In recent years, more and more families have returned to this tradition, normally in three ways:

1. Participation in festival activities. Most of the traditional festivals have connections with Buddhism, and the big monasteries, like Drebung, Sera, Ganden,

and Jokhang, hold religious activities such as the "Exhibition of Buddha" at the Shoton festival in Lhasa. Villagers like to go there with all their family members. "It makes me excited," villagers comment: "The more activities we participate in, the firmer our faith will become."

2. Visits and invitations to monks. Sometimes people go to temples and invite monks for services to solve practical problems, such as choosing the proper date for weddings, housebuilding, a long trip, a funeral, or expelling evil if something strange happens in the village, especially when people feel that the ghosts of some dead people cannot leave the village for *samsara*. The biggest ritual is a series of funeral services for the souls of the dead. The public will evaluate the performance of the monks in these events. Those they consider effective will have more invitations, while the others will have fewer.

3. Pilgrimages. People usually go to temples on the 8th, 15th, and 30th of each month in the Tibetan calendar. The nearest temple is in a valley three kilometers east of the village, where two monks reside. In addition, villagers go to bigger temples at least once a year. They are particularly attracted to the Jokhang in Lhasa as a place to worship, as well as to the "three big temples": Sera, Ganden, and Drebung.

There are basic norms of worshiping Buddha in a temple. When entering the main gate, worshipers must take off their hats and remain solemn and serious. In Gelugpa temples, people walk around the hall clockwise and bow their heads, touching their foreheads to the figures or shrines. The worshipers often bring alms, such as butter, tsampa, or cash. They can either give them to the monks or put the money in front of the Buddha figure. If they have only paper money of large value and do not want to donate so much to only one figure, they can put the large bill there and take some change back from the donations of others. Some villagers bring their own burning butter lamps, and pour the dissolved butter into the lamps in the temples.

After walking around once, which sometimes includes many small halls on different floors, people like to kowtow before leaving. After doing so, they walk backward to the gate. To turn their backs while exiting would be considered disrespectful to the Buddha and to the temple.

Other Beliefs

The general concept of *lha*, the spirit force that dominates mountains, rivers, forests, villages, and so forth, is important to villagers. Sometimes lha are very friendly to humans, but they also hurt people, depending on their attitudes and offerings. Some villagers believe that there is a differentiation between lha and Buddha. "Buddha is the highest result of self-cultivation. Buddha can bless us or not bless us, but it will never hurt us," said one villager. However, other villagers think Buddha is only a different name for lha.

Case 3: A Story About Lha (by a female villager, thirty-three years old)

The small hill behind the village is called Marbo. It came from Han areas, so its lha can speak Mandarin and looks like a Han. It is a good thing if the mountain lha is from other places, because a guest from afar can bring good luck to the village. There was once a woman in our village who could speak on behalf of that lha through a special ritual before 1959. But after 1959, she did not hold the ritual any more and became weaker and weaker. She finally died last year at the age of fifty-five. It is thought that she would not have died so early if she could have kept holding the rituals.

The stories of mountain lha are not always the same, and some have become confused with others.

Case 4: Another Version About the Small Hill

The mountain lha of the small hill behind the village is from India. The hill was originally located near the Quxu bridge southwest of Quxu Town, and fled to our village later. There were 108 temples, 108 springs, 108 beasts, and 108 Buddhas and their servants on it. It is believed that one can be healed of stomach illness if s/he walks around the hill once or kowtows continuously.

Some villagers believe that this tale is about another hill on the opposite side of the river, not the one behind the village.

Case 5: The Tale About This Mountain

This mountain is the one in charge of all the mountains surrounding Lhasa, called Shimoboli. It is located at the joint of Lhasa River and Yarlung River. Its lha is bad and was beaten by Daimdro. Otherwise it would have grown larger and larger, and blocked the rivers, causing flooding in the north of the river, including Lara.

In addition to lha, there is another supernatural existence that the villagers believe in. People always say: "If you do not respect lha, it will become as horrible as *soledongshin,*" meaning the ghosts of the dead who have not left for normal samsara but still stay around the villages.

These ghosts only show up at night and cannot be seen in daytime. "After movie time in the town every night [around 9 to 10 o'clock], when stars are shining in the sky, ghosts come out," say the villagers. It is said that ghosts usually walk around in the village or on the road, looking like a human from a distance, but like a skeleton from nearby. They call the people's names and ask them to follow. People can be led to the riverside or mountains and be killed. Some villagers said, "In daytime, ghosts are hidden in the forest or under the bridge"; others think that during the day ghosts are around, but that they dare not do anything until night.

Nearly all the ghost stories in the village are related to an old stone bridge over a river to the west of the village, just on the way to the county seat.

Case 6: A Widely Circulated Story (told by a woman, age forty-six)

One night before the democratic reforms, several noblemen were crossing the bridge when suddenly they saw many figures like small dogs around them. Red, black, and white in color, the figures blocked the way, so they could not pass.

Something unnamable appeared in front of them and became bigger and bigger until it was as wide as the road. Then suddenly it swooped down and killed several people. Villagers believe that they were ghosts that just came to kill these nobles.

Waiting for some adventure, I stayed up around that bridge after midnight and even later all through the night several times, but nothing strange happened.

Case 7: The Latest Ghost Story (narrated by a woman villager)

In 1988, a villager in his fifties passed away. In 1989, a young man called Phuntsok met the dead man on the bridge on the anniversary of his death. Phuntsok, then about twenty years old, knew the dead man well. He was on his way to the town with a tape recorder in hand when he suddenly saw a figure before him. He recognized it as the dead man, while the dead man also recognized Phuntsok and quickly started approaching him. Phuntsok was scared and felt he had to fight him. All of a sudden, the recorder began to make sounds by itself. During the fight, the recorder fell off the bridge, and Phuntsok saw the dead man leaving a white horse.

This story is very popular and has become the freshest evidence of ghosts, though some people consider it simply a case of robbery. It is said that the dead man had traded butter with Phuntsok before. He went riding two days before Ongkor Festival in 1988 when it was raining, and he fell off and died without any last words. His wife moved to Lhasa with her son (not the man's). Their house was sold to a single woman, who frequently complained that there were ghosts in the house so that she could not sleep well. She said that the door often opened automatically, and the dishes and plates on the table or in the cabinet often hit each other and made noises by themselves. The woman currently drinks a lot.

The villagers believe that ghosts fear light, fire, and noise. If someone walks with fire or shouts loudly at night, ghosts will not disturb him or her. But it is said that the fundamental way to deal with ghosts is by appealing to the power of Buddha. "If you are walking by yourself at night, you will be safe if you keep chanting the six syllables. If the ghosts disturb you frequently, you'd better go to the temple and ask the monks to drive them off. Ghosts fear monks," say the villagers. After the wife of the aforementioned dead man asked the monks in Lhasa for help, they wrote his name on a piece of paper and burned it while chanting the scriptures. The ghost didn't disturb anyone any more.

Although the villagers have a very solid belief in soledongshin and lha, Buddha (Sanggye) still occupies the dominant place in their minds. Buddha is regarded as the most powerful force in the universe, capable of controlling ghosts and other gods.

Festivals: Ritualization of Life

Some Local Traditions During the Tibetan New Year

Tibetan New Year's Day (Losa) is the first day of the first month in the Tibetan calendar, which is partly derived from that of the Han, but differs in the details of calculation, so that the two are not exactly consistent.

Before New Year's Day, all villagers need to thoroughly clean their houses. Since it is taboo to clean on New Year's Day, they sometimes need to work up through New Year's Eve to get the job done. Villagers must also prepare a kind of fried food called *kapse.* Kapse made on New Year's Eve can usually be consumed for four to five days. They are piled onto big plates in five to six layers that cross each other at right angles and are called *qakam.*

On New Year's Eve, villagers put a plate of kapse under the figure of Buddha as an offering. "It is not important whether Buddha eats it or not. We must show our faith with this offering," said one villager.

On the first day of the New Year, people usually get up very early, some even at four o'clock, put on their new clothes, and prepare food such as noodles, rice, butter, and sugar before daybreak. These must be eaten before sunrise.[5] The animals also need to be fed early. After eating, children visit neighbors with a "lucky box" known as *trashipude* or *shemapude,* calling out the traditional *trashi delek* greeting. The lucky box is wooden and contains highland barley grains and red- or blue-dyed barley heads called *losa medo* (New Year's flowers), and also a wooden bar with colorful butter flowers called *dzepjo.* After the children's greetings, all family members listen to the radio together for official New Year's greetings, and pray for the New Year, burning joss-sticks before the Buddha figure and changing its water.

As the morning advances, people come together, singing, dancing, or playing cards, mahjong, or a local game called *sho* (dice). It is a gambling game, though luck rather than skill or intelligence generally determines the winner. The components of the game include a wooden bowl, a leather pad, several shells, and coins. The shells are aligned and separated by coins. By turns, each player puts the dice in the bowl, shaking randomly, and then quickly turns the bowl upside down, slapping it strongly on the pad. The numbers on the dice will decide how many shells and coins the player can cross or reach.

Another important activity on New Year's Day is renewal of all the *tarjo* (prayer flags) on the roofs of houses, roadsides, and slopes of the hill behind the village. "When the sun rises to the top of the hill" (about 9 or 10 o'clock), said the villagers, "the kids will rush to climb the small hill and change the tarjo there. Everyone is willing to do it voluntarily." About the same time, each family also renews the tarjo on their own roof, and then all the family members sit on the roof with *qiang* (Tibetan barley wine) and other foods. Neighbors may also join for drinking and singing.

Some Customs in the Sagadawa Festival

The fifteenth day of the fourth month on the Tibetan calendar is believed to be the birthday of Sakyamuni, which is celebrated as the Sagadawa festival. The fourth month is also a time of fasting for Tibetans. In Lara, some villagers refrain from killing animals, drinking alcohol, or smoking. Those who are unable to fast for the entire month try their best to do so for at least eight days. Another significant activity in the fourth month is mountain circling (*rikhor*). Villagers walk around the hill behind Lara in a large circle, chanting the six syllables, often with prayer wheels in their hands. They try to walk in as large a circle as possible, so it often takes an entire day to circle once. Sick people need to circle once every seven or eight days and burn a kind of plant called *sang*.

Shoton Festival

The Shoton festival is limited to Lhasa and takes place at the end of the sixth and beginning of the seventh months. In administrative terms, Lara can be considered part of Greater Lhasa, but the villagers do not have sense of belonging to Lhasa. However, some villagers go to Lhasa to join the activities. People usually bring *qiang* (wine), butter tea, and food with them, and go to Norbu Linka (the summer palace) to watch Tibetan drama or to enjoy lingka.

Traditions During Ongkor Festival

Ongkor is one of the most important festivals in Lara Village. Literally meaning "circling the field," Ongkor starts around the end of July each year. The exact date depends on the harvest of barley and wheat, which varies somewhat from year to year. Before 1959, the date in each village was decided by the nobles. After the democratic reforms, the date was determined by village committees and local officials. During the Cultural Revolution, Ongkor was changed in form and even stopped for a time, but it was restored afterward. Currently, Ongkor always occurs around the same time as Army Day, which is August 1. People link the two, and usually amuse themselves for one month. The main activities include:

1. Circling the fields, the most important and traditional activity: Led by village committee members, Lara residents walk in a line around the fields with Buddha figures in their hands and scriptures on their backs, burning joss sticks, and praying for a good year and continuous harvests. It takes nearly a day to finish one circle.
2. Horse racing: Usually organized by the county-level administration; outstanding riders from all over the county will come together to compete.
3. Watching Tibetan drama: Every year, about 100 to 200 Tibetan drama actors and actresses are invited to perform in Quxu County for several days. People from all the villages can come and watch for free.
4. Lingka: The most popular activity in Ongkor is holding outdoor parties.

Traditions about "Gadanamju"

Gadanamju (festival), the 24th to 25th of the tenth month, is regarded as the anniversary of the day when Dzongkhapa, the founder of the Gelug Sect, met his

Parinirvana. For two days, the devout villagers intone the six syllables repeatedly and prepare good food as offerings. Rich families put thirty to forty oil lamps outside the houses from nine in the evening until midnight. These lamps are small bowls with rape oil and wicks in them, and are quite different from the butter lamps of the temples.

Marriage and Family

The Wedding as a Secular Custom

Young people in Lara usually do not begin to have girlfriends or boyfriends until they are fifteen years old, and will not formally marry until they are at least twenty.

Meeting the Parents

Before marriage, there is a relatively long period when young men and women can associate with each other freely and make their own choices. Parents do not interfere in the relationships. Even if parents favor one boy or girl and hope that their child will marry him or her, they only play the role of introducer without any coercion. Currently, even this introduction role is less common.

Parents are involved in the marriage at the time of the final decision. After the couple has known each other for a period of time, it is normally the girl who tells her parents about the boy and asks for their opinions. Usually, the mother's advice carries more weight. If the mother is not opposed, the girl will bring the boy to meet her parents. Assuming that the mother is pleased, she will ask the boy if he would like to stay with the girl for the rest of their lives. The boy should give a strongly affirmative reply.

At the meeting, the young people and their parents also need to discuss where the couple will live after marriage. There being no clear custom regulating this, the decision is based on discussion and factors specific to the individual situation. On average, more newly married couples live with the girl's family. Nowadays, as more and more boys refuse to move into the girl's home, the girl's parents tend to encourage the couple to set up their own household instead of joining the boy's family, in order to guarantee their daughters' freedom. In fact, if a girl is poorly treated by the boy's side after marriage, she can go back home or move out anytime. The married woman's parents have the right to intervene in these kinds of issues, and it will not cause serious disputes between the two families.

The Ceremony

The size of the wedding is decided according to the families' economic conditions. Wealthy families can have a big one, while some poor families may decide to forgo a ceremony. The *hukou* (system of residence registration throughout China) has not been completely established in the village, so there is no official administrative procedure for marriage. Folk weddings are fully recognized.

Villagers believe that their weddings are not as complicated as those of the Han. If the bridegroom moves to the bride's house, the bride will go to his home to meet him, and vice versa. Most of the time, tractors are used to pick up the newly-wed. Before going to the new home, the list of gifts and bride's dowry will be announced, and all the people will drink and sing to celebrate. The parents, or sisters or brothers, of the bride or bridegroom can accompany the newlyweds. When the bride or bridegroom arrives at her or his new home, relatives and friends will come to congratulate them. Ordinary friends bring only some qiang (barley wine) and khada (ceremonial scarves), while relatives will give such gifts as butter, barley, wheat, tea, soap, and eggs. Few give money or clothes directly. The gifts received by both families are first considered their property, and then delivered to the bride and bridegroom as gifts. The dowry of the bride should include a complete set of Tibetan dresses, enough food for one year, 300 to 400 yuan, and, if possible, some jewelry.

The wedding is held in the house of the new couple. The guests arrive and stand in one line, while the bride, bridegroom, and their parents stand in another line at a right angle to their guests. Positioned between them is a master of ceremonies, normally an important person such as a relative or the village leader. He will give a carefully prepared congratulatory speech that contains Buddhist precepts and prayers for Buddha's blessing. Then the guests give their gifts or khada in turn. They take the khada from inside the loose front of their Tibetan robes, open it, and holding the scarf in both hands, put it on the bride and bridegroom, with the traditional greeting of *trashi delek*. They also offer qiang to the bride, bridegroom, and their parents.

After the ceremony, the guests are treated to candies, butter tea, and cigarettes. Meanwhile, the bride offers each guest a big bowl of qiang with three or four pieces of butter on the rim. The bride sings when she hands over the bowl, and the guest must finish drinking by the time the song ends. If he fails, he will be "punished" by being made to drink more. This typically gets people drunk quickly. After offering wine, the newlyweds present khada to the guests. They can re-use the khada that the guests previously gave to them. People also burn joss sticks and cast tsampa for luck.

The dinner is served by the bride and bridegroom, including a special food called *marsa,* made of butter, tsampa, and milk. Round in shape with a sharp point at the top, it is cut into small pieces with a knife and shared. After dinner, some guests leave, while others remain and drink until dawn.

On the second day, the couple's friends continue to come and celebrate, but on the third day only their parents and relatives arrive. After that, there are no rules. Some families invite friends to a lingka that can last for seven to eight days. The expenses are shared by both families.

Customs

Some special aspects of the weddings of Lara villagers include:

1. The date of the wedding is decided by a monk or diviner.
2. It is regarded as very lucky if the team picking up the newlyweds accidentally encounters somebody carrying water. Since in reality the chance of doing so is very small, a person is normally chosen to wait by the road, carrying water. He or she offers khada and qiang, and burns joss as they pass by.
3. It is also considered very lucky if a *dregar*, a kind of roaming folk performer, visits during the wedding. Some times a dregar is invited to come, but these are considered to bring less luck than those who come by chance.

Among the taboos for the wedding are that people observing a period of mourning should avoid participation in the wedding. If a wedding and funeral must be held simultaneously in the village, the size of the wedding should be reduced. Overall, compared with funerals, weddings are mundane and on a completely different level.

Family: A Reasonable Arrangement

The Young and the Old

Case 8: Drengdui Family

Seventy-five-year-old Yangjin was originally the maid of a nobleman's daughter in Xigaze. Drengdui was the housekeeper in a big noble family in Gyangtze. They fell in love fifty years ago and eloped to Lara because their masters did not agree to their marriage. They had nine children, of whom one son and three daughters are alive now. The son is working in Nyingchi. The eldest daughter opened a teahouse in the town. The second daughter (46, a farmer) and her husband (48, a road worker) live together with them, with five grandchildren. The youngest daughter married a Han more than ten years ago, with their permission, and moved to Gansu Province with her husband, without their permission. They lost contact for two to three years.

The elderly people of the family are respected and supported, but have no dominant power. The daughter who lives with them performs not only all the housework, but also most of the field labor. Accordingly, she also takes the leading role in daily life. This reflects a general rule: in a family, once the elder members lose their ability to work, they also lose their power. Those who do most of the work, such as the daughter or daughter-in-law, inherit it.

The younger generation has an ethical responsibility to take care of the old, but the social pressure to do so is not very strong. If someone refuses to comply, there is no force that can compel them to do so. If such a situation occurs, neighbors will talk privately, but not in public. "Because the nature of bad children is bad, it is useless to say anything to them. And everything has its fate: retribution will come sooner or later," said a female villager. Here, religion plays a dual role: as both a defender of morality and as a mediator between the moral and the immoral. Given the fatalistic explanation and prediction on the outcome of improper conduct, "good guy" and "bad guy" are not absolute opposites. With the question of retribution put aside until the next life, they can get along with each other normally.

In most families, the older generation will choose at least one child to live with the parents after marriage. The meaning of living together with the parents is changing gradually from "the children do not leave the parents" to "the parents live in the children's home." As older people become weaker and more dependent on the younger generation, the center of power in the family shifts from the old to the young. Since those who live with the parents bear more of the burden of taking care of them than do their siblings, they also receive some preference in inheritance when the parents die. In return for their filial piety, they can continue to live in the house and inherit all their parents' furniture and land.

Binjia (Relatives)

Four generations on the father's side are classified as "relatives," the most important significance of which is to decide whether two persons can marry or not. In principle, people with the same ancestor should not get married, but this is compromised in practice. The children of sisters and brothers cannot get married. If love or a sexual relationship occurs, the two must be separated immediately. The grandchildren of sisters and brothers are also prohibited from marrying each other. But if a marriage occurs because no one had prior knowledge of the relationship, the couple need not divorce. The villagers attribute all marriage taboos to Buddhism. "According to the Buddha," said one villager seriously, "a marriage between close relatives will bring disaster to all the next eight generations of the whole village!"

Natural Children

Asked about children born out of wedlock, villagers reply that people older than eighteen have a right to sexual experience, as well as to take the responsibility of having babies. There is no discrimination against, or maltreatment of, natural children. They usually live with their mothers. In most cases, the villagers know who their fathers are. The fathers have the responsibility to help raise them by providing some clothing and food.

Divorce

Divorce is not stigmatized. Former spouses tend to maintain normal friendships with each other after divorce.

Case 9: Family of Phuntsok (from interview with Phuntsok)

Phuntsok, fifty-one, got married freely to an older woman thirty years ago. They have two sons. One is twenty-eight years old; the other is twenty-one. When the younger son was five or six years old, Phuntsok's wife's mother decided to move to Lhasa and his wife wanted to move with her. But Phuntsok refused, so they quarreled for a long time and finally got divorced. After the divorce, the ex-wife's mother unfortunately died and she stayed in Lara instead of going to Lhasa. Currently the elder son lives with Phuntsok and the younger with the ex-wife. The two families take care of each other. Phuntsok often helps his ex-wife with farming and they have a very friendly relationship.

When asked why they did not remarry, Phuntsok said he does not like his ex-wife: "She seldom talks, just like a dumb person. In addition, she is not at all good at housework."

The villagers get married without government administrative procedures, and divorce without them, too. If there are property disputes, they may be solved by grass-roots officials, without the involvement of the formal judicial system. Villagers can also remarry by themselves.

Partly because of the land system, a tendency toward intra-village marriage has emerged. However, marriages across social classes or positions are rejected, at least by some villagers. There seem to be complicated underlying psychological reasons for this.

Case 10: Divorce (narrated by a woman in the village, age twenty-four)

Two girls from Lara Village got married to workers in a nearby state-run farm and later got divorced. After marriage, their husbands could neither take care of the families nor help with the farming, so the two wives had to divorce them. Their farm has a responsibility system under which one's salary is paid as a loan in advance. If the harvest is not good, they will have to return the money. So the workers in the farm earn higher salaries, but at the same time bear certain risks, which are also risks for the whole family. Therefore, although the workers have a better social status and better working conditions (mechanized) than the villagers,' these preferential terms were not enough to convince the Lara girls to spend the rest of their lives with them.

Housing

Most of the houses in Lara are of the same Tibetan type, built with mud, stone, and wood, although there is considerable variation in the configuration and structure of individual homes. Only the village primary school is built mainly in the style of the coastal regions of China.

Room Allocation

Room allocation within a household depends mainly on how many rooms the family has; no strict rules govern it. Families with fewer rooms make fewer distinctions in the use of individual rooms. The same room can be the living room in daytime and the bedroom at night, and also the kitchen. An average family has a big room used as a living room, in which important possessions such as electric appliances, shrines, and beautiful Tibetan cabinets are proudly placed. Many families do not have a separate kitchen. Quite often, the kitchen is just a stove in one of the rooms, with all kinds of cookware around, while other things in that room, such as tables and beds, are similar to those in other rooms.

Some wealthier families set aside a separate room for shrines; this is usually an inner room of a complex at the end of the house. Besides shrines, the room has no other furniture. Some families store vegetables and fruit in the shrine room temporarily, but never put trash in it. When special guests visit, such as this author, or family members return from afar, they might be asked to stay in this room.

The allocation of rooms among family members is quite free and flexible, primarily based on family members' habits. Factors such as gender and age produce no fixed pattern. The arrangement can be changed at any time. As for non–family members, the guests mostly live in the main rooms, sometimes even in the shrine room, while the servants and casual laborers live in the side rooms, "kitchens," storerooms, or can even sleep under the veranda (*gebe*) if they do not mind.

Architecture

Outward Appearance

Villagers' houses are built in a traditional form. All the doors and windows of the houses are adorned with typical Tibetan black frames and mini-rafters painted with strong-color figures. The villagers believe that black frames prevent evil from coming in. The outside walls are painted white and the higher part near the roof dark red. There are many rough arc lines on the walls called *drugele*, created by scratching the mud with one's fingers when it is still wet.

There are *lhadzu* on the roof—mini-houses less than one meter high and wide, with miniature roofs on top and walls painted white and dark red like the real houses. Usually *lhadzu* are built on the corners of the roof, standing as bases on which the poles of *tarjo* (prayer flags) are erected. Some households also have white stones set on them. Most villagers have no idea about the origin of this practice or whether it has meaning beyond being a custom or "something that looks great with the white stones."

Interior: Daily Art

The area of the house is calculated as a unit not by "room" or "square meter," but by "pillar." There is at least one pillar in the center of each room. Each pillar has a space of approximately 15 to 20 square meters around it, which is considered to be "one pillar." In addition to their function in supporting the Tibetan-style architectural structure, pillars have considerable cultural and religious meaning, especially regarding lha and deities.

Most houses do not have ceilings, so the rough rafters and small covering branches of the roof remain visible from below. On the crossbeams, pillars, and the underlays, transfigurations of clouds, lotus, *badra* (lucky knot), and other traditional symbols are painted. Pictures, photos, and *thangga* (religious scroll paintings) are hung on it. The visible sides of the crossbeams and pillars are painted with very pure and neat colors of red, yellow, and green.

Average families do not paint their walls, although some wealthy families may do so. Three-color stripes are painted around the rooms about one meter above the ground. These are red, green, and blue, or red, yellow, and green. It seems that red is always necessary. At the top of the wall, realistic depictions of pleated curtains are painted: they show a row of rectangles under belts of red and yellow, each of which is painted as a spectrum from red in the upper parts to green in the lower parts, and darker on the left, shading to light on the right. This represents the image of the real curtains in the temples.

Most villagers tend to decorate living rooms rather than kitchens and storerooms. Even poor families who cannot afford color painting like to decorate their crossbeams, pillars, and walls in the main rooms by drawing some figures with chalk, such as *badra* (a geometric design pattern composed of small diamond shapes that make a larger one), eight-luckies, lotus flowers, and animals. Images of scorpions can often be seen on the wall near the stove.

Aesthetic Preferences

Some common characteristics in the design and decoration of the houses are:

1. The overall appearance of decorations is as similar as possible to that of the temples.
2. All the figures are derived from several basic elements:

   lotus: most flowers in paintings show some signs of the lotus; many decorative patterns are variations of the lotus;
   "卐": *yungdrong*, a symbol from ancient Asian civilizations, its image can always be found on the pillars and walls;
   badra: a pattern composed of six crossing connected lines;
   cloud: the shape and curve of clouds include several decorative patterns;
   fire: various permutations of the established image of fire in Tibetan Buddhism, some of which are similar to those of clouds;
   sun and moon: Tibetan designs of a sun above a moon are usually painted at the main gate of the yard; those used on the pillars and crossbeams need to be modified to fit the narrower width available.

3. In the composition of pictures, there seems to be a pattern of alternation of asymmetry and symmetry: if the details are asymmetrical, the whole

will be approximately symmetrical, and vice versa. This is a concept of neither absolute symmetry nor balance—for example, the figures of clouds on crossbeams of two sides of the pillar are drawn symmetrically from bigger to smaller, but the clouds on the two sides are not exactly the same. This is intentional, not the result of inaccuracy.

4. There is a predilection for the use of primary colors (red, yellow, and blue) and binary colors (orange and green) of very high purity. Complementary colors (red with green, orange with blue) tend to be juxtaposed. Backgrounds are usually in dark or cold colors, with the foregrounds in warm colors. Strong, contrasting, and conflicting colors are favorites. Possible reasons include both their high visibility in the thin plateau air and the relatively darkness of monasteries before modern illumination was introduced. Hence, a religious aesthetic developed and influenced the decorative tastes of the common people.

Some Conclusions from the Fieldwork

On "Backwardness"

Many phenomena found in this fieldwork will be seen as "backward" and the opposite of "modernization" by the mainstream elite, especially the folk beliefs with shamanic characteristics. But no evidence was found of direct conflict between local customs and modern social norms. To be sure, local customs will predispose villagers to deal with social change in different ways from other ethnic groups, but the customs do not lead them to simply resist modernization.

On "Mysteriousness"

"Mysteriousness" is one of the most widespread stereotypes of Tibet among both Han Chinese and those in the outside world.[6] It produces a sense of otherness that blocks communication between Tibetans and other peoples. This fieldwork does not support the impression of mysteriousness. The local people's faith in and reverence toward gods or Buddha is not so different from that of many other peoples on earth. Buddhism itself is not a religion of mysticism.[7] One of the reasons behind the mystification of Tibet is probably the richness of the visible or physical expression of Tibetan culture, including rock paintings, *tsha tsha* (miniature Buddhist images molded of clay), *tarjo*, stone carvings, as well as dress, adornment, manner, etiquette, and so forth. These expressions highlight, if not exaggerate, the "inexplicability" of Tibet.

Identity and Customs

Attitudes toward tradition within a given culture are simply a matter of different political stance, as the Han elite generally understands. But in inter-ethnic relationships, the minority group tends to construe them in terms of lack of respect or denial of the ethnic group as whole. Hence, the anti-traditionalist attitudes of most Han constitute a potential negative element in Han–minority relations. This fieldwork shows that Tibetan villagers are strongly attached to some traditions, such as traditional robes and tsampa, as symbols of their ethnic identity. At the same time, they have no problem in accepting certain elements of Han culture, such as food, kitchenware, language, and informal clothing. Any efforts by the Han to get Tibetans to abandon tradition in the name of modernization may be interpreted as efforts, if not as a conspiracy, to destroy their ethnicity as Tibetans.

The Function of Spiritual Beliefs

The Han elite has a strong tendency to regard religion as antithetical to modernization. Stemming from their secularized concept of "development," many members of the elite continue to criticize religion as spiritual opium.[8] But this fieldwork indicates that spiritual opium is not necessarily negative, especially in a rapidly changing society like that of China. In the absence of a mature religion such as Tibetan Buddhism, cults may arise to fill the spiritual vacuum and bring more social problems. In Tibet, scholars are already historically attuned to the possibility of a harmony between religion and the official ideology. This fieldwork shows that there is no hard evidence for an inevitable conflict between Buddhism and socialism in either final goals or personal self-cultivation.

For Policymaking

Every year the central government pours enormous financial subsidies into Tibet. This research can aid those who plan investment projects, in that it indicates that more consideration for local concerns, viewpoints, feelings, and aesthetics will reduce potential misunderstandings and strengthen the trust of the local people in the motives and outcomes of those investments.

Notes

The author would like to acknowledge all the relevant people for their direct and indirect help. During my fieldwork, local villagers and grass-roots officials provided necessary cooperation. Special thanks to Ms. Yuedren for her help with oral and written translation, and to the Qampa family for providing my accommodations.

1. The Han nationality, which makes up the overwhelming majority of the Chinese population, is itself a mixture and assimilation of the populations of many extant or dissolved ethnic groups who gave up, forgot, or ignored their original ethnic identities. The process of formation of the Han explains the fact that cultural diversity among the Han is often more than the average difference between "Han" and other ethnic cultures.

2. According to this theory, all human societies develop from primitive society, through slavery, feudal, capitalist, and socialist stages, finally entering communist society. Different

ethnic groups are currently simply in different stages of development; in communist society, these differences among ethnic groups will have disappeared.

3. For instance, in the 1950s and 1960s, both before and after the democratic reform, there were a lot of detailed descriptions of Tibetan customs in the large-scale survey organized by the Chinese government. Some Western Tibetologists have also conducted fieldwork in Tibetan communities outside China.

4. Strictly speaking, the duration of my fieldwork was shorter than that of typical anthropological research, which should be at least one year. Nonetheless, given that this research focused on "how to see Tibet," instead of "what is Tibet?" it is safe to say that the study was successfully completed.

5. Tibet is geographically in western China, which the government has decreed is a single time zone, so sunrise in Lara is two hours later than in Beijing.

6. The commercial campaign for tourism, which publicizes the notion of Tibet's mysteriousness as the area's best selling point, strengthens such impressions.

7. Even tantra, the most "mysterious" part to an outsider's eyes, is not regarded as particularly mysterious in Buddhist circles, but as merely a higher stage of conventional religious education. Tantra is actually not unique to Tibetan Buddhism. It was introduced and developed in other cultures, such as Han society, long ago. Similarly, the *bon* elements of Tibetan Buddhism are not very different from animism as it is practiced elsewhere in the world.

8. The term is a quote from Marx; it is not meant in a derogatory sense.

References

Fei Xiaotong, ed. 1999. *Zhonghua minzu duoyuan yiti geju* (The Pattern of Diversity in Unity of the Chinese Nation). Beijing: Central University of The Minorities Press.

Ma Rong. 2000. "One Definition of Minzu" 'Guanyu Minzu dingyi.' " *Yunnan Minzu Xueyuan Xuebao* (Journal of Yunnan Minorities University), no. 1: 5–13.

Yuan Fang, ed. 1999. *Shehuixue bainian* (One Hundred Years of Sociology). Beijing: Beijing Press.

PART IV

The International Dimension

13

The Tibet Question and the West

Issues of Sovereignty, Identity, and Representation

Dibyesh Anand

In the past two decades, the "Tibet cause," defined in opposition to the Chinese "occupation" of Tibet and "violations of human rights" of Tibetans, has gained widespread currency within the international media. This has as much, if not more, to do with changes within the West, as with what is perceived as Chinese intransigence and the Tibetan diaspora's strategy of internationalization. Within international politics, the Tibet Question is defined, somewhat simplistically, as the debate over the status of Tibet vis-à-vis China.[1] The West, as a political actor, is seen as a sympathetic outsider or an imperialist intruder. However, both the Chinese and the Tibetans ignore the fact that they are "prisoners of modernity," a modernity whose terms have been dictated by the West as a political actor as well as an ideational construct. Whether one likes it or not, the West is already within the Tibet Question, as the dominant vocabulary available to political communities derives mostly from Western ideas and language. This dominance of the West is demonstrated very clearly in the discussion of the Tibet Question, where instead of resisting the hegemony of Western ideas, arguments from all sides buy into them with a vengeance. Ironically, the Chinese state, which defies the West politically, does so without questioning its wholesale adoption of Western conceptions of statehood, sovereignty, and *realpolitik*. Similarly, the Tibetans, exoticized as products of a uniquely non-Western culture, argue for their independence using the same Western ideas that they considered as alien until mid-twentieth century.

All sides marshal an international legal terminology consisting of sovereignty, suzerainty, autonomy, self-determination, independence, and human rights, and make attempts to solve the problem within this limited framework. While this problem-solving approach is commendable, it often draws upon conventional conceptualizations within the study of international politics. Therefore it remains a faithful product of modernity, with its will to power masked in supposedly neutral terms of sovereignty, nation, and people—a modernity that has often been characterized by state-sanctioned violence in the name of progress, mass killings in the name of liberation, exploitation in the name of development, suppression in the name of democracy, imperialism in the name of liberalism, control in the name of order.

This chapter reflects pessimism about the problem-solving framing of the Tibet Question. What is required is a critical understanding that involves historicizing (different from the common strategy of deploying selective interpretations of history) the questions of status, sovereignty, and statehood. It is about identity and representation too—Tibet (or, for that matter, China or the West) is not some entity existing "out there" but constructed in the very process of debate. Thus the Tibet Question is as much about the discursive construction of Tibet and Tibetans as it is about the political status of these entities. The underlying argument is that instead of concentrating solely on political actors (who nevertheless remain important), we may critique the only vocabulary of political expression available to them and try to find spaces for *post-modern emancipatory, people-oriented, political communities* that challenge the statism of contemporary international order. Here the emphasis is on critique and on highlighting the crucial role played by the West, both at the level of theory and praxis, in the framing of the Tibet Question and limiting the vocabulary for possible answers. This does not deny the importance of the internal dynamics of the wider Tibetan society and the Chinese state, but productively complicates the picture to gain a better understanding.

Conventional study of world politics has operated on unquestioned assumptions of positivist social science. Theory is seen as a tool to explain, understand, interpret, and/or predict reality. What is ignored is the crucial role played by theory in constituting the very reality that it seeks to understand. Keeping in mind the constitutive and performative role of ideas, the contemporary discussions on the Tibet Question should not be seen in terms of Tibet vis-à-vis China, where the West is a disinterested onlooker, neutral arbiter, or interested intruder. While some see the Tibet Question as an internal matter of China, others see it as an international concern. What both sides in the argument ignore is the integral part played by the West in the very framing and shaping of the entire debate. The West, both as political actor and ideational construct, is part of the problem in the sense of being a primary actor in the problem construction.

The relationship between the West and the Tibet Question can be investigated at several overlapping levels through various themes. Here I shall concentrate on two such themes, which have been selected because they illustrate very clearly the constitutive role played by the West in framing the problem. They challenge the limitations of conventional accounts as afforded by dominant international political theories, and draw inspiration from emerging hybrid knowledge formations including critical international theories, post-colonialism, and cultural studies. These selected aspects also warn against nurturing any naive ideas about Tibetan exceptionalism and support arguments in favor of contextualizing the Tibet case within the predicaments faced by many in the post-colonial world.

The first theme involves the wider issue of European (British, in the case of Tibet) imperialism, the historical legacy in general, and the concept of sovereignty in particular. While history is used as a resource by both sides when Chinese sovereignty over Tibet is either affirmed or denied, the very concept of sovereignty is left unproblematized and unhistoricized. There is *no neutral historical "truth"* that can resolve whether Tibet was always an independent nation or an integral part of China. What is more important is to recognize historical developments that have contributed to the framing of the question in absolutist terms of sovereignty or independence, something that was alien to both the Chinese and the Tibetans before the twentieth century. Modernity, with its universalization of specific Western politico-legalistic ideas and concepts such as territoriality and sovereignty, has offered a highly problematic framing of the Tibet issue and legitimized colonial reifications of the region. As long as Western-modernity-universalized-as-Modernity is left out of the analysis, there is little hope for an adequate understanding of the Tibet Question. The second theme touched upon here is the complex relationship between Western representations and Tibetan identity—political as well as cultural. Particular emphasis is laid on the articulation of Tibetanness within the diaspora since the identity discourses prevalent here play a very important part in shaping international perceptions of the Tibet Question. A discursive approach, which sees identity in terms of process of identification, is adopted.

Historical and Political Status of Tibet

Within international politics, the Tibet Question is seen primarily in terms of the historical and political status of Tibet vis-à-vis China. Concepts deployed include sovereignty, suzerainty, independence, autonomy, vassalage, protectorate, overlordship, and colony. However, for the most part, it is sovereignty that is asserted and contested. On the one hand, the Chinese state marshals historical arguments buttressing its historical claim of sovereignty over Tibet; on the other, the Tibetan exiles and their supporters make counter-claims and assert that Tibet was for all practical purposes independent from China. The official Chinese position is reflected in the following statements: "for more than 700 years the central government of China has continuously exercised sovereignty over Tibet, and Tibet has never been an independent state. There was no such word as 'independence' in the Tibetan vocabulary at the beginning of the 20th century" (Information Office 1992). In contrast, the Tibetan claim is that historically Tibet has been independent and even now, "From a legal standpoint, Tibet has not lost its statehood. It is an independent state under illegal occupation. Neither China's military invasion nor the continuing occupation by the PLA has transferred the sovereignty of Tibet to China" (Government of Tibet in Exile 1996).

Thanks to the dominance of positivist ideas behind the realist as well as liberal international relations, there is historical amnesia on the part of various political actors; those involved in the Tibet Question are no exception. Both sides ignore the fact that the very idea of presenting one's case in terms of sovereignty or exclusive national jurisdiction is a feature of modernity—modernity where Western ideas have been more or less hegemonic. Ironically, the Chinese, who during the nineteenth century rejected the European mode of international relations as alien, have few qualms in exerting their control over Tibet using the absolutist European conception of sovereignty that had its origin in nineteenth-century Europe. Similarly, the Tibetans, who resisted the "modernization" that came under the guise of British imperialism, now try to draw upon the imperialist interpretations of Sino-Tibetan relations to buttress their claims. Some use the imperial archive to argue for their independence. Others who are willing to accept substantial autonomy under some kind of nominal Chinese control highlight the fact that even though the British Indian officials recognized Chinese suzerainty over Tibet, this was conditional upon Tibetan autonomy. As China refused to honor the commitment to autonomy, it has little legal and moral authority left.

Since 1905 China has consistently claimed that its position in Tibet is that of a sovereign and not suzerain. At the beginning of the twenty-first century, even though there is little space for suzerainty within international law and politics and all states recognize the Chinese claim of sovereignty over Tibet, the pro-Tibet lobby contests the assertion of sovereignty by highlighting the difference between suzerainty and sovereignty within international law. As Oppenheim had argued: "Suzerainty is by no means sovereignty. It is a kind of international guardianship, since the vassal state is either absolutely or mainly represented internationally by the suzerain state" (Van Praag 1987, 107). However, as debates within international studies have shown (Weber 1995; Bartelson 1995; Hoffman 1998; Biersteker and Weber 1996), instead of being caught within the confines of a reified usage of sovereignty, we need to historicize it.

Even though sovereignty has been a foundational concept in world politics, for a large part of the twentieth century, a reified and particularistic understanding of it was promoted as historically constant and universally valid. As Bartelson puts it, it is "essentially uncontested as the foundation of modern political discourse"; what is contested is the meaning of sovereignty within the same discourse (1995, 13–14). It is a modern European conceptualization of sovereignty, commonly seen as a product of the Westphalian order, that has shaped the current map of the world. It presumes clearly bounded political communities with internal and external sovereignty. Hinsley's definition, representing the conventional historical approach that underlines the link between the modern version of absolute statehood and sovereignty, is instructive: "a final and absolute political authority in the political community . . . and no final and absolute authority exists elsewhere" (Shinoda 2000, 3). This conceptualization is based on a jigsaw puzzle view of the world, where a proper map always shows a set of sharply bounded units that fit together with no overlap and no unclaimed territory (Lewis and Wigen 1997). There is no space for mutually inclusive and overlapping territorial jurisdiction of the kind that, for instance, characterized the traditional relationship of Tibet with external powers, including the Chinese empire.

Imperial China operated with its neighbors on bilateral relations of fealty and patronage. This sat very uncomfortably with the nineteenth–twentieth century European conceptualization of territoriality and governance. Even though this particular conceptualization has gained global acceptance within the post–World War II international system, recognition of its history leaves room for affirmation of its contingency and allows space for contesting sovereign statehood. Tibetans are only one among numerous communities of people that have become victims of the modern idea of sovereign statehood. Hegemony of this idea does not preclude struggle for different conceptions of sovereignty and statehood, that do not see both as necessarily interdependent (Hoffman 1998, 2–3).

The genealogy of the modern idea of sovereignty also reveals its close nexus with European imperialism. Until the first half of the twentieth century, the international community of states was based on a double standard. While the "civilized" world (read: Europe, and later the United States and Japan) had a right to sovereign statehood, the rest was open to various forms of imperial control. "[A] degree of civilization necessary to maintain international relations was considered as one of the conditions for statehood" (Hannum 1990, 16). The Westphalian system was confined to Europe. The Tibet situation is one of many examples where imperial efforts throughout the non-European world were empowered by the social construction of Western understandings of non-Western political communities and "states." In these cases, a lack of affirmative recognition of non-Western interstate relations was accompanied by an active de-legitimation of non-Western modes of sovereignty (Strang 1996, 24). This de-legitimation provided a basis for parlor statesmanship, as well as the restless activity of the colonial "*men* on the spot."[2] The European idea of sovereignty, which may be seen as a political entity's externally recognized right to exercise final authority over its affairs, has acquired global acceptance since the decolonization movements of the twentieth century. However, before this formal decolonization, the recognition involved in sovereignty was linked to specific cultural practices and embedded in a particular network of international political economy practices. Throughout the nineteenth and twentieth centuries, international or regional communities excluded cultural, ethnic, or racial "others" by denying them sovereign recognition. And even now, despite its recognition of formal equality for all sovereign states, "organized hypocrisy" (Krasner 1999) is the norm of the international system.

European imperialism, with its various modes of direct and indirect colonization, was in a certain sense similar to pre-modern international relations in Asia, where formal as well as informal hierarchy was the norm. Empires such as that of the Manchus in China and the Mughals in South Asia typically conceived inter-state relations in terms of the superiority and inferiority of states. However, European international and imperial relations had their own unique characteristics—sovereignty was tied up with statehood, only one type of inter-state relations was seen as legitimate, and states had to be territorially bound, leaving no room for fuzziness. It is within this context that during the turn of the nineteenth–twentieth century, traditional Sino-Tibetan relations were considered by the British as "irrational" and lacking legitimacy for not conforming to "modern" ideas of diplomacy. The failure of the British to understand the complex relation had as much to do with their heady faith in the superiority of European norms as with their conflicting interests in the region.

For a large part of the nineteenth century, to the British in India, Tibet was a "forbidden land" ruled by "strange lamas" under some form of Chinese control. While some, including Bogle, named the control as *sovereignty* (Markham 1876, 195), most used the terms *overlordship* or *suzerainty*. This was based on the presence of a Chinese *amban* in Lhasa, claims of the Manchu emperor, and refusal of the Tibetans to clarify the situation. Due to their own familiarity with feudalism and with the Chinese international system of tributary relations, it is not surprising that the British interpreted Sino-Tibetan relations in terms of suzerainty and protectorate. Political actors interpreted and understood their inter-state relations in terms familiar to them.[3] The same relations could have been understood by the Chinese imperial officials in terms of Confucian tributary relations and by the Tibetans as Buddhist *mchod-yon*.[4] This does not validate the primacy of either worldview, but reveals the complexity of the issue involved and militates against the recourse of international law to understand the Tibet Question. The Chinese did not need to force the Tibetans to accept their control in writing. Nor did the Tibetans need to assert their independence and disabuse the emperor of his belief in his sovereignty over Tibet. If the Tibetans did not declare their "independence," neither was there a "definite *de jure* surrender of any power of sovereignty on the part of Tibet" (Ghosh 1977, 205). If we take Krasner's (1999) typology of sovereignty—international legal, Westphalian, domestic, and finally, interdependence sovereignty—Tibetans exercised the last two types habitually and Westphalian sovereignty substantially until the Chinese assertion of control in 1951.

Grounding the relation in some absolutist universally accepted terms was unnecessary within the Chinese as well as Tibetan worldview. Personal, moral, and spiritual overtones were significant parts of relations; brutal takeover was not. The influence of the *amban* varied according to many factors, including the strength of the Dalai Lama. Even when China had "the upper hand" (Bataille 1992, 33), Tibet "enjoyed local autonomy over domestic matters" (Grunfeld 1987, 57), and more significantly, "on the basis of simple experienced reality, Tibetans considered themselves not as Chinese" (Barnett and Lehman 1998).

However, this traditional relationship was constructed as a "problem" when the sociocultural and political environment was altered, first by the arrival of Western colonial powers in Asia, and second by the transformation of the traditional Chinese Confucian-dominated polity toward a more European type of political system, which produced a republican China and the growth of Chinese nationalism

(Shakya 1999, xxiii). The Chinese "forward policy" (Song 1994) of the early twentieth century took its cue from the British invasion, asserted its case of sovereignty using international legal terminology, and embarked upon "a new activist, annexationist" route (Goldstein 1989, 46). The termination of Tibet's relations with China at the first available opportunity in the aftermath of the fall of the Qing empire reflected military inability as well as moral indignation with the change in Chinese policy (Norbu 1990, 39). And then Tibetans started taking faltering steps toward modernization of their own statehood and international relations. But due to the conservatism of the monastic elite and the ambiguous policy of the British, this project of modernization failed to take off both within Tibet and in its international relations. The Tibetans continued to resist Westernization of their statehood and international relations. For instance, they allowed both the British Mission and the Chinese mission to exist in Lhasa. But from their point of view, neither had any legal status; they were allowed to remain only to avoid giving offense (Goldstein 1989, 330). After the Simla Convention of 1914, the only serious step toward asserting independence and gaining international recognition was made with the trade mission of the late 1940s. Both the Simla Convention and the Trade Mission revealed the ambiguous and hypocritical attitude of Western states toward Tibet: they were willing to deal directly with Tibetans without recognizing their independence (Goldstein 1997, 37). This double standard was a legacy of British imperialism and its perceived interests during the turn of the century.

As many scholars have argued, the exercise of interpreting Sino-Tibetan relations in the late nineteenth and early twentieth centuries in terms of suzerainty and autonomy was linked to the dynamics of British imperialism. British policy in the case of Tibet was shaped by conflicting dynamics, including the infeasibility of direct colonization, Tibet's strategic location as a buffer state in Central Asia, commercial interests in the Chinese empire, and so on. These conflicting interests dictated an ambiguous policy, where Tibet's relation with the Chinese empire was seen in terms of Chinese suzerainty and Tibetan autonomy from the very beginning of the twentieth century (see Norbu 1990). Despite the political compulsions of the so-called Great Game (a euphemism for Anglo-Russian rivalry in the Central Asian region) being the primary motive behind the British forcible "opening" of Tibet, the imagery of wealth was never very far off (see Carrington 2003). As one of the participants in the Younghusband expedition writes: "In fact the visible riches and treasures of Lhasa fairly made our mouths water. The Tibetans however would not sell, and to our honor be it said; although Lhasa was a fair object to loot, and lay in our power, not a farthing's worth was *forcibly* (adds this word in pen) taken from it" (Iggulden undated, 6). The invasion, as well as later activities of men on the spot, were also colored by a spirit of adventure—something that had been aggravated by the forbiddenness of Tibet and its refusal to conduct normal international relations with the British. In the true spirit of imperialism, the British blamed everyone except themselves for the invasion and forcible opening of Tibet to the outside world: the obstinate, conservative lamaist hierarchy (Landon 1905,

27); the suspicious feelings of smaller Himalayan countries (Cammann 1951, vii); Chinese suspicion of foreigners (Woodcock 1971, 25); the Gorkha invasion of 1792; and at most, the arrogant bullying and frequent deceit of various explorers and adventurers (Richardson 1988, 28). However, Norbu argues that Tibet's closed-door policy during the nineteenth century can be explained most convincingly in terms of Tibetans' fear of a British takeover. There was a direct correlation between British expansionism in the Himalayan region and the Tibetan authorities' decision to close Tibet's door to Westerners (Norbu 1990, 30–32).

As numerous treaties signed between Britain and China in the nineteenth century show, the British accepted Chinese suzerainty and sought to operationalize their interest within Tibet through China. However, the Tibetans refused to comply with these. The British tolerated this situation until they perceived a serious threat to their security and the Indian empire during the Great Game. Fearing an increase in Russian influence over the "roof of the world," the British perception of Tibet took a geopolitical turn under the viceroyalty of Curzon; it was now viewed as an important buffer state. It was with this idea of a buffer zone in mind that attempts were made to make Tibet subservient to British India. At the same time, British commercial interests in China and the European balance of power made it expedient to maintain the pretense of Chinese suzerainty.

After playing with the idea of influencing Tibetans through the Chinese, by the beginning of the twentieth century, British Indian officials decided to take matters into their own hands (Verrier 1991). A cavalier attitude was adopted toward Chinese suzerainty. Emphasizing the need for direct communication, Curzon in his January 8, 1903, dispatch to the secretary of state in London stated: "We regard the so-called suzerainty of China over Tibet as a constitutional fiction, as a political affectation which has been maintained because of its convenience to both parties" (Ghosh 1977, 43). However, soon after the 1903–1904 expedition, Britain reverted to its old stance when it signed a treaty with China in 1906 confirming the Lhasa convention of 1904. China's exclusive rights in Tibet (apart from special rights to be enjoyed by Britain) were recognized without naming those rights as sovereignty or suzerainty (Dreyer 1989, 9). However, it was in a treaty between Britain and Russia, two Western powers, that Sino-Tibetan relations were first referred to in writing as the "suzerainty" (of China). Article II of the Anglo-Russian Convention of 1907 lays down: "In conformity with the admitted principle of the suzerainty of China over Thibet" (Ghosh 1977, 81). This reflects how non-Western people and communities were "written over" by the Western powers in their own terms and then the victims were forced to use the language of the powerful. Through a memorandum on August 17, 1912, the British government clarified its stance that "while recognizing the Chinese suzerainty, they were not prepared to admit the right of China to interfere in the internal administration of Tibet . . ." (Foreign Office 1920, 41). Thus, "Outer Tibet would become an autonomous state under Chinese suzerainty and British protectorate" (1920, 43). Britain's position remained more or less the same for most of the century.

The consequences of the new Anglo-Tibetan encounter that began with the Younghusband invasion have contemporary ramifications too. The Tibet Question as a problem of world politics today is influenced to a significant extent by the legacy of this encounter. For the first time, it forced the Tibetans to confront the differing perceptions of nation and state identity held by traditional and modern societies (McKay 1997, 16). To serve as a proper buffer state, the British needed Tibet to be a stronger, more clearly defined entity on the nation-state model. They encouraged this especially during the second and third decades. The most concrete step taken was in the Simla Convention, where the McMahon line was set out to demarcate the Indo-Tibetan border. As McKay argues, this was not about the separation of pre-existing states, but the creation of mutually exclusive states (1997, 198). This encounter (along with Western influence within mainland China) also had an impact on the way the Chinese elite conducted their intercourse regarding Tibet in relation to the external world. After 1904, the traditional conception of Sino-Tibetan relations was transformed into the political language of nationalism through a new generation of Chinese officials with Western educations and a series of negotiations whose frame was dictated by the British as the greater power (Norbu 1990, 51). As the Chinese learned modern diplomatic language, from 1905 they began to assert their relationship in terms of sovereignty. Tibetans, on the other hand, were late in adjusting to the modern world and continued to refuse to comply with any treaties between British India and China concerning it. Thus, out of the legal Europeanization arose the contemporary Chinese claim that Tibet is an integral part of China. Contemporary critics of China often ignore the fact that it was a "forceful interpretation of Sino-Tibetan relations in terms of European international law and the *praxis* of (British) imperialism" (Norbu 1990, 67) that lies at the genesis of the Tibet Question, not some intractable nationalist and historical conflict between the Chinese and the Tibetans. The Westernization of international relations made it inevitable that when China gained control over Tibet in 1951, it was no more the traditional symbolic relationship, but an absolute rule. For the first time in its history, through the Seventeen Point Agreement, Tibet acknowledged Chinese sovereignty (there was no space left for an ambiguous term like suzerainty) in writing. However, the Tibet Question reemerged on an international plane after the Dalai Lama fled Tibet in 1959, denounced the 1951 Agreement, and established a government-in-exile in India.

The inability and lack of desire of British Indian officials to appreciate the subtleties involved in traditional Sino-Tibetan relations should be seen in this wider context of European imperialism and its practice. Use of the discourse of suzerainty and sovereignty, which had highly specific resonance within the European world, was problematic since it sought to extrapolate European ideas in a situation where people operated on a *different* (which is not the same as inferior) worldview. The Westernization of Sino-Tibetan relations has had serious ramifications, mainly for the Tibetans, for they were late in catching up with the modern world, where Western ideas ruled. Chinese rule in Tibet found justification in a realist interpretation of the concept of sovereignty. This illustrates how a conventional under-standing of international relations concepts has facilitated victimization of some communities. So, instead of referring back to some hoary past, a nuanced discus-sion of the Tibet Question in the contemporary world may begin by appreciating the context of Western (British) imperialism under which it acquired its formative shape. Rather than treating the concept of sovereignty as sacrosanct, a historicization and deconstruction of the concept can provide a better understanding of how the Tibet Question as a problem of international politics came to be framed in the first place. It is here that the constitutive part played by Western ideas and concepts is bared and rendered open to contestation. In the words of Hannum (1990, 5):

> Sovereignty, self-determination, and human rights are the philosophical under-pinnings claimed by one group or the other (or both), and such legal totems are the primary grounds of appeals for outside support. State and non-state groups define themselves as peoples or nations, not because these terms are necessarily descriptive or because they will contribute to a better understanding of a given situation, but rather because certain legal consequences are thought to flow from such designations.

Social constructionist understandings of sovereignty make space available for imagining alternative conceptions of sovereignty and political communities that place a premium on human dignity instead of national integrity and state authority. As Weber points out, sovereignty is "embedded in the web of practices of states and non-state actors in international relations" (Shinoda 2000, 6). Tibetans cannot be expected to readily accept heavily circumscribed autonomy as a part of China and give up the demand for a state of their own in the prevailing international environment. As Hoffman argues, it is impossible to deny nations a right to statist forms of self-determination as long as sovereign statehood remains an organizing principle of international relations (Hoffman 1998, 98). People can only be per-suaded to accept political forms of self-determination that are not themselves stat-ist in character in a world in which the principle of statehood itself is openly and explicitly challenged. From its current emphasis on how to balance the Chinese state's right to territorial integrity with the Tibetan right to self-determination, the focus should shift to combating the realist conception of sovereign statehood and exploring alternative imaginings.

The Poetics of Representation and the Cultural Politics of Identity

As pointed out earlier, it is mainly since the middle of the twentieth century that the Chinese as well as the Tibetan elite in exile (and their Western supporters and detractors) have competed to legitimize their own representations of Tibetan his-tory and current events. These "confrontations of representations" (Goldstein 1997, 56) are about history and political status; at the same time they are intimately connected to cultural representations and identity discourses. It is not possible to speak of Tibet or Tibetans without taking into account the constitution of these categories within representational practices and identity discourses. The Tibet Question is as much a political issue as it is connected to the cultural politics of the modern world. The very idea of Tibet and what it means to be Tibetan is constructed and contested within the matrix of identity and representation discourses, thus making it an integral part of the Tibet Question.

The placing of the West *within,* rather than outside, the discourses on the Tibet Question can also be examined by looking at the theme of Western representations of Tibet and their interface with Tibetan (trans)national identity. It could be argued that the Tibetan elite, especially in the diaspora, have adopted a Western representation of what "Tibetanness" is as their own self-image. From the outset, it should be qualified that in most cases our discussion of "Tibetanness" here is based on discourses circulating within the Tibetan diaspora. This qualification, however, does not imply that representational practices do not have a significant effect on Tibetans living within Tibet. As various studies of cultural and religious revival (Goldstein and Kapstein 1998), Lhasa protest movements (Barnett and Akiner 1996; Schwartz 1996; Mills 2002), and identity articulations by Lhasa-Tibetans (Adams 1996, 1998) have shown, political and cultural expressions by Tibetans here negotiate within the dominant vocabulary offered by Western, as well as Chinese, representations.

While recognizing the peculiarities of the Tibetan situation, one may also look at the question in the wider context of orientalism (Said 1979), commodification of culture, asymmetrical power structures, and reflexive identity discourses.[5] Tibet is not an exception, since "due to relative powerlessness, anti-imperialist struggles often are compelled to utilize Western media in order to mobilize crucial world support" (Bishop 2000, 645). All Third World resistance groups have to "negotiate both the post–cold war reframing of global politics and the lingering traces of Western post-colonial fantasies about their country and culture" (Bishop 1998, 123). As the works of post-colonial scholars have emphasized, Western representational practices affect and have an effect on the identity of the represented (Hall 1997), in this case the Tibetans in exile. The representational regimes have *truth effects* on the Tibetan identity politics. While the poetics of representation (the question of "how" the Tibetans are represented) is an important area of investigation (Bishop 1989, 1993; Norbu 1998; Lopez 1998; Schell 2000), for our purpose we have to move beyond to consider the politics of representation (the impact of representational practices on the people involved). It should be emphasized that it is not only the Westerners who have exoticized Tibet and the Tibetans; the Tibetans living in the diaspora too have invested heavily in such (neo)orientalist representation strategies for their own tactical purposes.

Geographically and culturally, Tibet's peripheral place gave permission for many Europeans and Americans to use it as an imaginative escape, as a sort of time-out, a relaxation from rigid, rational censorship of their own society (Bishop 1989, 7). This explains the unease of many Westerners with the "modernization" of Tibet under the aegis of the Chinese state. Hence writings about Tibet are sometimes "conservative protests against modernism, the masses, and the changing world order" (Bishop 1989, 15) and at other times "counter to the globalising tendencies" of modernization (Neilson 2000). The presence of opposites and contradictions within Western imaginings of Tibet is not new. Since the beginning of the twentieth century, there has been "a play of opposites: the pristine and the polluted, the authentic and the derivative, the holy and the demonic, the good and the bad" (Lopez 1998, 10). While some held disparaging views about Tibet, others extolled it. For instance, for Grenard, Tibet was a hard and miserly land "destined only to serve as a refuge for some race wanting in ordinary intelligence; and, in fact, the Tibetan people have never achieved more than an indifferent culture, a pale reflection of the civilizations of China and Hindustan" (1904, 221). On the other hand, while discussing the potential contribution of his translation of the *Bardo Thodol,* Evans-Wentz observed that it might aid to "awaken the Occident to the extreme dangers into which it has been led, in large measure by a medical science ignorant for the most part of the Art of Dying" and thus further "the prayers of the lamas by helping to dissipate that Darkness of Ignorance which, as the Buddha realized, enshrouds the world" (1949, xii–xiii). In the aftermath of the Younghusband invasion, sentiment was expressed to the effect that something sacrosanct had been violated and hence the aura of Lhasa was lost forever. Holdich opined that the fascination of Lhasa and Tibetan travel might die as the invasion had exposed the sham and dirt of the city (1906). This could not be further from the mark. As numerous twentieth-century works of fiction and nonfiction (especially travel writings) show, Lhasa and Tibet continue to excite the imaginations of Westerners. McCue's sentiments about Tibet being a land of contrasts and superlatives and Lhasa retaining its aura of hidden splendor are reflective of the whole genre of recent Western writings about Tibet that continue in the tradition of exoticism (McCue 1999). The strategies of essentialism, reductionism, and stereotyping are common to both the positive as well as the negative representations. Debasement and exoticization are part of the same representational regime. (For a discussion on rhetorical tropes common to Western representations of the non-West see Spurr 1993.) Both sides flatten Tibet's complexities and competing histories into a stereotype that operates through adjectives. These then become innate qualities immune from history (Lopez 1998, 10).

This exotic Tibet (henceforth used as a shorthand for the exoticized—both positive and negative—representation of Tibet) was not confined to the cultural sphere. It influenced and was in turn influenced by political processes at work. Accounts of British Indian officials like Bell and Richardson show that their "more prosaic view did not destroy this exotic representation but tacitly encouraged it" (McKay 1997, 207). They too used metaphors of remote space, isolation, and timelessness to maintain the implicit sense that Tibet was exotic. In a similar vein, CIA operations during the sixties and seventies were influenced by some romanticism too, as sometimes Tibet was designated as a "final retreat (Shangri-La) to which peace-loving people could flee when atomic war breaks, for Tibet is too remote to be of significance in any war" (quoted from a War Department Memorandum by Knaus 1999, 26). It should therefore come as no surprise that during the Younghusband invasion, most British writings spoke of a despicable state of affairs within Tibet; with the American rapprochement with China in the seventies, little was heard about destruction of traditional life within Tibet that peaked during the Cultural Revolution; but a lot of attention was paid to the Tibet Question when other communist regimes fell in Eastern Europe and the discourse of human rights emerged on the international plane. This linkage of the Tibet Question with the West's political interests may be unsurprising, but it nevertheless underlines the need to move beyond conventional international politics with its emphasis on *realpolitik* and narrowly defined national interest if we seek to address the Tibet issue.

While recognizing the political factors behind the relative popularity of the Tibet Question internationally, we should not ignore that there are various nonpolitical (political in the conventional sense of the term) forces that contribute more significantly to the international understanding of the issue. These range from counter-cultural New Age movements to transnational nongovernmental and intergovernmental groups. While pursuit of the exotic is rife among many of the constituents of the pro-Tibet movement, there is no necessary correlation between positive exoticism and support for Tibetan independence. Alexandra David-Neel, the famous admirer of Tibetan mysticism, for instance, believed that the "Tibetans have never formed a true nation" and therefore Chinese domination was inevitable and unassailable (Foster and Foster 1987, 303–304).

Exotica Tibet is more about the West's self-image than about Tibet. While charting different phases in the West's encounter with Tibet at the level of the imagination, Bishop argues how in each of these images of Tibet is also mirrored an image of the West (Bishop 1993, 15). Throughout the pre-twentieth century, the most common imagery was one that emphasized the similarity between the Tibet of the time and the held interpretation of the European Middle Ages. For many Tibetophiles today, the idea of Tibet is of something that the West has lost or should strive toward. And a lot of what is behind the support for Tibetans today may not be actual support for the Tibetans, but unconscious support for Western ideas of what is right for the Tibetans (Barnett 1991, 281). The exotic Tibet is also connected with the Western imagination of China. Some see it as an antidote to Chinese communism (for example, see Riencourt 1950, 238), while others contrast "peaceful" Tibet with the perceived violence and xenophobia of the traditional Chinese mentality ("Frontline" 1998). Yet as long as support for Tibet is connected to anti-Chinese sentiment (Schell 2000, 269), no serious appreciation of the Tibet Question is possible.

The importance of exotic Tibet in our understanding of the Tibet Question lies in the impact it has on the very construction and contestation of categories of Tibet and Tibetans. For the language of stereotype about Tibet "not only creates knowledge about Tibet, in many ways it creates Tibet, a Tibet that Tibetans in exile have come to appropriate and deploy in an effort to gain both standing in exile and independence for their country" (Lopez 1998, 10). Interaction with a Western audience is a very important dynamic shaping Tibetan identity/Tibetanness in the diaspora. This is an area that has received substantial attention from scholars only since the last decade of the twentieth century (Anand 2002; Klieger 1994; Korom 1997a, 1997b; Mountcastle 1997; Harris 1999). Rather than painting Tibetans as mere victims, it is now recognized that they have been active in the appropriation and internalization of Western representations, and in the creation and presentation of their own cultural, political, and religious identity. This has been possible due to the influence of new developments in social and cultural theories: adoption of a discursive approach that, instead of taking identity as an ontological imperative, considers identity as a process as well as a product. Rather than seeing the identity question as one of simple historical investigation, the question is dealt with in terms of deployment of the resources of history, language, and culture in the *process of becoming rather than being.* Such an approach to identity helps us appreciate subtleties and cultural dimensions of the Tibet Question.

The domestic as well as international politics followed by the Tibetan elite in the diaspora too has been influenced by an interaction with a Western audience. Recognizing the dominance of nationalism as a source of legitimacy in contemporary international politics, Dharamsala has molded its expositions on Tibetan identity accordingly. Though "Old Tibet" had elements of *natio* (Lopez 1998, 197–198), proto-nationalism (Dreyfus 1994), and what Anthony Smith calls *ethnie* (Anand 2000, 273–274), a modern sense of nationhood was absent (Ekvall 1960, 382). Tibet as a nation is not a historical reality but a product of post-exile imagination. In their search for outside support, the Tibetan elite has been learning the language of international politics dominated by the Western powers (Kolas 1996). The Western influence can also be seen in the evolving political structure of the government-in-exile. In fact, the Dharamsala establishment has been moving toward democratization in order to gain legitimacy in the West. These developments may be explained in terms of an image-building exercise, steps taken toward keeping up with the times, response to pressures from within the refugee community, and finally, the Dalai Lama's personal initiative.

Apart from nationalism, Tibetan activists have also taken up transnational ideas for political expression. Democracy, human rights, peace, development, and environmental protection are some such ideas. Transnational social movements, New Age orientalism, international Buddhist fora—all have been quite influential in shaping the Tibetan identity claims in terms of universalist discourses of world peace, environmentalism, global indigenous sovereignty, and spiritual haven. Western representations and diaspora conditions have also contributed to a shifting of emphasis from ethnicity (Tibetans as *tsampa* eaters) to religion (the "modern" version of Tibetan Buddhism) as the basis of Tibetanness (Lopez 1998, 198).[6]

Soliciting international support has been one of the main strategies of the Tibetan diaspora elite. The Dalai Lama's high profile and frequent trips to various countries is a significant part of this strategy of raising the profile of the Tibetan cause in the international media and mobilizing public opinion in Western states. Conspicuous avoidance of the Tibet Question in the conventional forums of international relations (for instance, lack of recognition of Tibetan statehood by any existing state) has forced the Tibetans to seek support through nonconventional means; cultural politics is a part of this. The ultimate goal behind the transnational mobilization remains the acceptance of the right of self-determination. In a poem of dedication at the beginning of his book, Gyatso reflects a sentiment common to most Tibetans, a hope that international support might help them realize their goal of independence: "And to all of you who inhabit the world who also believe in the virtues of truth, justice and decency.... Help to deliver us. Help us to be free, to be independent, to be able to do what we choose—in our own country" (Gyatso 1997). While the awareness-raising campaign in the West frequently translates into activism on the part of individuals and groups, to what extent this gains substantive political support from the governing elite is open to disturbing questions. In fact, the existing support for the Tibetan cause is based on particular representations of Tibetans as inherently spiritual and peaceful people. This restricts the alternatives available to those Tibetans (see Shakya 1991; Lazar 1998) who might be disillusioned with the Dalai Lama's insistence on nonviolence and giving up of the demand for independence.

Support in the form of Free Tibet movements is often based on the image of "Tibet as a defenseless underdog, a spiritual society that was minding its own business only to get crushed under the jackboot of an aggressive, materialist overlord" (Schell 2000, 206). However, even the cultivation of this victimization paradigm reflects the agency of Tibetans. Though the Tibetan global publicity campaign consciously portrays Tibetans as victims of Chinese oppression, this does not deny them their subjectivity. They have made conscious and extensive use of Western discourses, such as psychology, philosophy, physics, personal growth, and holistic health, in their attempts both to communicate with Westerners and to reconstitute themselves in conditions of exile. Tibetans have also colluded with, as well as contested, various Western images of Tibet (Bishop 1997, 67). Though many Westerners may like to overrate their own importance in nurturing Tibetan resistance to the Chinese state, the fact of the matter remains that resistance to domination exists in all societies (Bass 1990, 218).[7] Western (and Chinese[8]) cultural and political ideas dictate the precise forms that the resistance takes. In the diaspora, it is preservation of traditional culture and nationalism that are the main dynamic behind the politics of resistance. Within Tibet it ranges from protest movements demanding independence to forces demanding the accommodation of special rights within the Chinese state structure; in either case, this reveals their political agency (Barnett in this volume; Adams 1996, 1998).

Conclusion

The West as a material-discursive construct has played a constitutive role in the framing of the Tibet Question. This is about conscious actions and rhetoric as well as latent cultural imperialism. Historically, the debate over the sovereignty of Tibet is a legacy of extrapolation of Western ideas to an alien territory and exigencies of British imperialism. In contemporary times, the poetics of Western representation of Tibet and Tibetans play a constitutive and performative role in the politics of Tibetan identity. Without giving up the search for some solution to the Tibet Question within the existing international system, we also need to move beyond the confines of the empirical, positivist idea of theorization and adopt a critically self-reflexive, historicized, and cross-disciplinary approach that allows space for alternative imagining of political communities. It is only then that we may begin to address the Tibet Question in a holistic manner.

Notes

1. According to Goldstein, the Tibet Question—the long-standing conflict over the political status of Tibet in relation to China—is a conflict about nationalism, an emotion-laden debate over whether political units should directly parallel ethnic units. He calls for examining the "anatomy of the Tibet Question" in "a balanced fashion using a *realpolitik* framework to focus on the strategies of the actors" (Goldstein 1997, ix, x). As the ensuing discussion reveals, not only are cultural forces behind the existence of a "Tibet Question" on the international plane important (Sautman and Lo 1995, 1), they also play a constitutive part in the question.

2. In the case of Tibet, often there was a disjuncture between activities of the "men on the spot" and policymakers in Britain. This was evident very clearly during and after the Younghusband invasion of Tibet when the "forward" policy of the expedition sat uncomfortably with the nonconfrontational attitude of the British policymaking circle. See McKay (1997).

3. This type of international relations based on diffused and fuzzy sovereignty was connected to practices of statehood in the Tibetan region. Tibet did not fit very clearly within the conventional definition of state. But this is not surprising, for neither did states in most of Asia and Africa. For a discussion of statehood in Tibet, see Samuel (1982 and 1993). He argues that fluidity within Tibetan categories corresponds to a similar fluidity within social institutions (Samuel 1993, 141)—an image of Tibet that also provides a critique of the dominant view of Tibetan society as essentially stagnant and closed. In a similar vein, Goldstein argues that religion, though a homogeneous force in Tibetan politics in one sense, was also a fragmenting and conflicting force (1989, 37). Van Spengen draws upon Rudolph's idea of ritualized sovereignty and Stein's theory of the ecclesiastical state to caution against the use of standard conceptions of the "state" as developed on the basis of European analogues (2000, 25–26).

4. While some have argued that *mchod-yon*, patron–priest relations, was the main characteristic of the Sino-Tibetan world (see Klieger 1994), others have clarified that this was more about a personal relationship between rulers and not about statehood (Barnett and Lehman 1998). Shakya points out that the concept indicates that the Tibetans viewed the Chinese emperor only as a secular institution, but that is far from the case; the Manchu emperors, for instance, were often referred to as Jampeyang Gongma, the incarnation of Manjushri (1999, xxiii).

5. There is, however, a significant difference between Western representations of Tibet and those of China or India: instead of being idealized first and then despised, Tibet was first seen as a wretched land of feudal barons and serfs and only later romanticized (Kierbab 1995, 180).

6. On the complex relation between nationalism and religion inside Tibet see Goldstein and Kapstein (1998); Schwartz (1996); Mills (2002).

7. Contrary to commonly held assumptions on all sides, even in the theocratic, conservative, and "feudal" society of "Old Tibet," resistance to authority was never completely absent. For instance, Bell recalls theater performances in Lhasa in which actors did not hesitate to ridicule certain aspects of their religion, and even less so of their officials (Bell undated, 11). He further mentions a "Sun body" play by Kyor-mo Lung-nga troupe in which there was an explicit anti-Chinese political allusion, with "a kick for the Emperor of China" (Ibid., 18–19). Going back even earlier, Aris talks of an eighteenth-century writing by a Tibetan in which a positive sympathy can be detected for the undefeated Marathas and their long stand against both the Mughals and the British (Aris 1994, 12). All of this goes on to challenge the view of a passive Tibetan society.

8. Chinese policies too are supported by representational practices. Chinese representation of Tibetans as essentially backward, primitive, and barbaric is witnessed not only at the popular level, but more dangerously within state discourse too (see Wei 1998; Sautman and Yan 2000; Kolas 1998). Development under the aegis of the Chinese state is thus seen as a part of a civilizing mission.

References

Adams, Vincanne. 1996. "Karaoke as Modern Lhasa, Tibet: Western Encounters with Cultural Politics." *Cultural Anthropology* 11, no. 4: 510–546.

———. 1998. "Suffering the Winds of Lhasa: Politicized Bodies, Human Rights, Cultural Difference, and Humanism in Tibet." *Medical Anthropology* 12, no. 1: 74–102.

Anand, Dibyesh. 2000. "(Re)imagining Nationalism: Identity and Representation in the Tibetan Diaspora of South Asia." *Contemporary South Asia* 9, no. 3: 271–288.

———. 2002. "A Guide to Little Lhasa in India: The Role of Symbolic Geography of Dharamsala in Constituting Tibetan Diasporic Identity." In *Tibet, Self, and the Tibetan Diaspora: Voices of Difference*, ed. P. Christiaan Klieger, 11–36. Leiden: Brill Academic.

Aris, Michael. 1994. "India and the British According to a Tibetan Text of the Later Eighteenth Century." In *Tibetan Studies: Proceedings of the 6th Seminar of the International Association for Tibetan Studies, Fagernes 1992*, ed. Per Kvaerne, 7–15. Oslo: Institute for Comparative Research in Human Culture.

Barnett, Robbie. 1991. "The Effectiveness of Parliamentary Initiatives." In *The Anguish of Tibet*, ed. Petra K. Kelly, Gert Bastian, and Pat Aiello. Berkeley: Parallax Press.

Barnett, Robert, and Shirin Akiner, eds. 1996. *Resistance and Reform in Tibet*. Delhi: Motilal Banarsidass.

Barnett, Robbie, and Steve Lehman. 1998. *The Tibetans: Struggle to Survive*. New York: Umbrage.

Bartelson, Jens. 1995. *Genealogy of Sovereignty*. Cambridge: Cambridge University Press.

Bass, Catriona. 1990. *Inside the Treasure House: A Time in Tibet*. London: Victor Gollancz.

Bataille, Georges. 1992. "Lamaism: The Unarmed Society." *Lungta* 6: 33–40.

Bell, Charles. Undated. "Type Copy of Book III 'Tibetan Sketches,' 196 folios." MSS EUR F 80/219 NEG 11088. *Oriental and India Office Collections*. London: British Library.

Biersteker, Thomas J., and Cynthia Weber, eds. 1996. *State Sovereignty as Social Construct*. Cambridge: Cambridge University Press.

Bishop, Peter. 1989. *The Myth of Shangri-la: Tibet, Travel Writing and the Western Creation of a Sacred Landscape*. Berkeley and London: University of California Press.

———. 1993. *Dreams of Power: Tibetan Buddhism and the Western Imagination*. London: Athlone.

———. 1997. "A Landscape for Dying: The *Bardo Thodol* and Western Fantasy." In *Con-

structing Tibetan Culture: Contemporary Perspectives, ed. Frank J. Korom. Quebec: World Heritage Press.

——. 1998. "To Raise the Tibetan Flag? The Dalai Lama as News." *Australian Journal of Communication* 25, no. 1: 111–125.

——. 2000. "Caught in the Cross-Fire: Tibet, Media and Promotional Culture." *Media, Culture & Society* 22: 645–664.

Cammann, Schuyler. 1951. *Trade Through the Himalayas: The Early British Attempts to Open Tibet*. Princeton, NJ: Princeton University Press.

Carrington, Michael. 2003. "Officers, Gentlemen and Thieves: The Looting of Monasteries During the 1903/4 Younghusband Mission to Tibet." *Modern Asian Studies* 37, no. 1: 81–109.

Dreyer, June Teufel. 1989. "Recent Unrest in Tibet." In *Tibet: Past and Present*, ed. Hungdah Chiu and June Teufel Dreyer, 1–25. Occasional Papers/Reprints Series in Contemporary Asian Studies, no. 1 (93). Baltimore: School of Law, University of Maryland.

Dreyfus, Georges. 1994. "Proto-Nationalism in Tibet." In *Tibetan Studies: Proceedings of the 6th Seminar of the International Association for Tibetan Studies, Fagernes 1992*, ed. Per Kvaerne, 205–218. Oslo: Institute for Comparative Research in Human Culture.

Ekvall, Robert B. 1960. "The Tibetan Self-Image." *Pacific Affairs* 32, no. 4: 375–381.

Evans-Wentz, W.Y. 1949. *The Tibetan Book of the Dead or the After-Death Experiences of the 'Bardo' Plane, According to Lama Kazi Dawa-Samdup's English Rendering*. London: Geoffrey Cumberlege, Oxford University Press.

Feigon, Lee. 1996. *Demystifying Tibet: Unlocking the Secrets of the Land of the Snows*. Chicago: Ivan R. Dee.

Foreign Office. 1920. *Tibet (Number 70)*. London: H.M. Stationary Office.

Foster, Barbara M., and Michael Foster. 1987. *Forbidden Journey: The Life of Alexandra David-Neel*. San Francisco: Harper and Row.

"Frontline." 1998. "Dreams of Tibet: A Troubled Country and Its Enduring Fascination; Interview with Martin Scorsese." Available at www.pbs.org/wgbh/pages/frontline/shows/tibet/interviews/scorsese.html. Accessed on October 15, 2003.

Ghosh, Suchita. 1977. *Tibet in Sino-Indian Relations 1899–1914*. New Delhi: Sterling.

Goldstein, Melvyn C. (with Gelek Rimpoche). 1989. *A History of Modern Tibet, 1913–1951: The Demise of the Lamaist State*. Berkeley: University of California Press.

Goldstein, Melvyn C. 1997. *The Snow Lion and the Dragon: China, Tibet, and the Dalai Lama*. Berkeley: University of California Press.

Goldstein, Melvyn C., and Matthew T. Kapstein, eds. 1998. *Buddhism in Contemporary Tibet*. Berkeley: University of California Press.

Government of Tibet in Exile. 1996. "The Status of Tibet." Available at www.tibet.com/Status/statuslaw.html. Accessed on April 12, 2001.

Grenard, F. 1904. *Tibet: The Country and Its Inhabitants*. London: Hutchinson.

Grunfeld, Tom A. 1987. *The Making of Modern Tibet*. London: Zed Books.

Gyatso, Palden (with Tsering Shakya). 1997. *The Autobiography of a Tibetan Monk*. New York: Grove Press.

Hall, Stuart, ed. 1997. *Representation: Cultural Representations and Signifying Practices*. London: Sage.

Hannum, Hurst. 1990. *Autonomy, Sovereignty, and Self-Determination: The Accommodation of Conflicting Rights*. Rev. ed. Philadelphia: University of Pennsylvania Press.

Harris, Clare. 1999. *In the Image of Tibet: Tibetan Painting After 1959*. London: Reaktion Books.

Hoffman, John. 1998. *Sovereignty*. Minneapolis: University of Minnesota Press.

Holdich, Thomas. 1906. *Tibet, the Mysterious*. London: Alston Rivers.

Iggulden, Colonel. "An Undated Account of Lhasa and Its Inhabitants by Brigadier-General Herbert Augustus Iggulden (1861–1937), Chief Staff Officer Tibet Mission

Escort, 1903–04." MSS EUR C 270 FL2/E/1/144, 15 folios. *Oriental and India Office Collections.* London: British Library.

Information Office of the State Council of the People's Republic of China. 1992. "Tibet—Its Ownership and Human Rights Situation," September, Beijing. Available at www.china.org.cn/e-white/tibet/. Accessed on April 12, 2001.

Kierbab, Victor. 1995. *The Lords of Human Kind: European Attitudes to Other Cultures in the Imperial Age.* London: Serif.

Klieger, P. Christiaan. 1994. *Tibetan Nationalism: The Role of Patronage in the Accomplishment of a National Identity.* Meerut: Archana.

Knaus, John Kenneth. 1999. *Orphans of the Cold War: America and the Tibetan Struggle for Survival.* New York: PublicAffairs.

Kolas, Ashild. 1996. "Tibetan Nationalism: The Politics of Religion." *Journal of Peace Research* 33, no. 1: 51–66.

———. 1998. "Chinese Media Discourses on Tibet: The Language of Inequality." *Tibet Journal* 23, no. 3: 69–77.

Korom, Frank J., ed. 1997a. *Constructing Tibetan Culture: Contemporary Perspectives.* Quebec: World Heritage Press.

———, Frank J., ed. 1997b. *Tibetan Culture in the Diaspora.* Vienna: Verlag der Österreichischen Akademie der Wissenschaften.

Krasner, Stephen D. 1999. *Sovereignty: Organized Hypocrisy.* Princeton, NJ: Princeton University Press.

Landon, Perceval. 1905. *Lhasa: An Account of the Country and People of Central Tibet and of the Progress of the Mission Sent There by the English Government in the Year 1903–04.* London: Hurst and Blackett.

Lazar, Edward, ed. 1998. *Tibet: The Issue Is Independence.* Delhi: Full Circle.

Lewis, Martin W., and Karen E. Wigen. 1997. *The Myth of Continents: A Critique of Metageography.* Berkeley: University of California Press.

Lopez, Donald S. Jr. 1998. *Prisoners of Shangri-La: Tibetan Buddhism and the West.* Chicago: University of Chicago Press.

McCue, Gary. 1999. *Trekking in Tibet: A Traveller's Guide.* 2d ed. Seattle: The Mountaineers.

McKay, Alex. 1997. *Tibet and the British Raj: The Frontier Cadre 1907–1947.* Richmond: Curzon Press.

Markham, Clements R. 1876. *Narratives of the Mission of George Bogle to Tibet and of the Journey of Thoman Manning to Lhasa.* London: Trubner and Co.

Mills, Martin A. 2002. *Identity, Ritual and State in Tibetan Buddhism.* London: Curzon Press.

Mountcastle, Amy. 1997. "Tibetans in Exile: The Construction of Global Identities." Ph.D. dissertation, Rutgers University.

Neilson, Brett. 2000. "Inside Shangri-La/Outside Globalisation: Remapping Orientalist Visions of Tibet." *Communal/Plural* 8, no. 1: 95–112.

Norbu, Dawa. 1990. "The Europeanization of Sino-Tibetan Relations, 1775–1907: The Genesis of Chinese 'Suzerainty' and Tibetan 'Autonomy.'" *Tibet Journal* 15, no. 4: 28–74.

Norbu, Jamyang. 1998. "Dances with Yaks: Tibet in Film, Fiction and Fantasy of the West." *Tibetan Review* (January): 18–23.

Richardson, Hugh E. 1988. "Tibetan Lamas in Western Eyes." *Bulletin of Tibetology*, no. 1: 21–33.

Riencourt, Amaury De. 1950. *Roof of the World: Tibet, Key to Asia.* New York: Rinehart.

Said, Edward. 1979. *Orientalism: Western Conceptions of the Orient.* New York: Penguin.

Samuel, Geoffrey. 1982. "Tibet as a Stateless Society and Some Islamic Parallels." *Journal of Asian Studies* 41, no. 2: 215–229.

———. 1993. *Civilized Shamans: Buddhism in Tibetan Societies.* Washington, DC: Smithsonian Institution Press.

————. 1994. "Tibet and the Southeast Asian Highlands: Rethinking the Intellectual Context of Tibetan Studies." In *Tibetan Studies: Proceedings of the 6th Seminar of the International Association for Tibetan Studies, Fagernes 1992*, ed. Per Kvaerne, 696–710. Oslo: Institute for Comparative Research in Human Culture.

Sautman, Barry, and Shiu-hing Lo. 1995. *The Tibet Question and the Hong Kong Experience*. Occasional Papers/Reprints Series in Contemporary Asian Studies, no. 2 (127). Baltimore: School of Law, University of Maryland.

Sautman, Barry, and Yan Hairong. 2000. "China's Ethnic Minorities: From Self-Determination to Self-Representation." Paper presented at the eighteenth World Congress of the International Political Science Association, Quebec City, August.

Schell, Orville. 2000. *Virtual Tibet: Searching for Shangri-La from the Himalayas to Hollywood*. New York: Metropolitan Books, Henry Holt.

Schwartz, Ronald D. 1996. *Circle of Protest: Political Ritual in the Tibetan Uprising*. Delhi: Motilal Banarsidass.

Shakya, Tsering. 1991. "The Myth of Shangri-la." *Lungta* (April): 21–28.

————. 1999. *The Dragon in the Land of Snows: A History of Modern Tibet Since 1947*. London: Pimlico.

Shinoda, Hideaki. 2000. *Re-Examining Sovereignty: From Classical Theory to the Global Age*. London: Macmillan.

Song, Liming. 1994. "The Younghusband Expedition and China's Policy Towards Tibet, 1903–1904." In *Tibetan Studies: Proceedings of the 6th Seminar of the International Association on Tibetan Studies, Fagernes 1992*, ed. Per Kvaerne, 789–800. Oslo: Institute for Comparative Research in Human Culture.

Spurr, David. 1993. *Rhetoric of Empire: Colonial Discourse in Journalism, Travel Writing, and Imperial Administration*. London: Duke University Press.

Strang, David, 1996. "Contested Sovereignty: The Social Construction of Colonial Imperialism." In *State Sovereignty as Social Construct*, ed. Thomas J. Biersteker and Cynthia Weber. Cambridge: Cambridge University Press.

Van Praag, Michael C. van Walt. 1987. *The Status of Tibet: History, Rights, and Prospects in International Law*. London: Wisdom.

Van Spengen, Wim. 2000. *Tibetan Border Worlds: A Geohistorical Analysis of Trade and Traders*. London: Kegan Paul International.

Verrier, Anthony. 1991. *Francis Younghusband and the Great Game*. London: Jonathan Cape.

Wei, Jingsheng. 1998. "A Letter to Deng Xiaoping." In *Tibet Through Dissident Chinese Eyes: Essays on Self-Determination*, ed. Cao Chang-ching and James D. Seymour, 75–89. Armonk, NY: M.E. Sharpe.

Weber, Cynthia. 1995. *Simulating Sovereignty: Intervention, the State and Symbolic Exchange*. Cambridge: Cambridge University Press.

Woodcock, George. 1971. *Into Tibet: The Early British Explorers*. London: Faber and Faber.

14

The Tibet Question

A New Cold War

Xu Mingxu and Yuan Feng

A steadily growing economy in the world's most populous nation has drawn attention to China in regard to the role that it will be able to play in international affairs. Since the 1990s, especially after the collapse of the Soviet Union, the Western powers headed by the United States have adjusted their strategies in managing their relationships with China. While it seems to be plausible for them to encourage the creation of a Western-style democratic China, the size of this nation, with its potential influence on the global economy and world affairs, has been viewed as a threat to the existing world order by some who have dominated it. Concerns of this kind can be seen in the writings of Brzezinski (1997) and Huntington (1996). A new Cold War has been launched by the Western powers against China. The old stories of the Tibet Question have been rewritten to create a scene.

The Tibet Question in essence concerns whether the Chinese central governments of dynastic courts and republican and Communist regimes must allow Tibet to split from China and become an independent nation as has been desired by the Thirteenth and the Fourteenth Dalai Lamas. History witnesses that the Tibet Question has roots in British expansion in Asia (Wang, Xiraonima, and Tang 1995). It remains a question in the international arena as a result of Western intervention. In the first half of the twentieth century, the United Kingdom played a major role in influencing the Thirteenth Dalai Lama. Determined to maintain its predominant position in world affairs since World War II, the United States has become the most influential in the pursuit of Tibetan independence. A variety of strategies, including military intervention with guerrillas, economic containment, and Cold War–style accusations of human rights abuses in Tibet, have been applied to "discipline" China.

The Double Standard on Human Rights and Sovereignty

It is not incomprehensible that the bombing of Yugoslavia by NATO with an excuse of "human rights over national sovereignty" has encouraged the Tibet independence movement in recent years. The presupposition might be that the United States would intervene with its military might so that the Dalai Lama and the Tibetans would be able to have independence. The activists for Tibet independence and their supporters have increased the frequency and the volume of their requests for the U.S. government to make China behave.

As pointed out by a number of developing countries, the Western powers have held self-contradictory double standards on international affairs, including issues of human rights, self-determination, and sovereignty (UN General Assembly 1999; Xu 1999). In its declaration on the granting of independence to colonial countries and peoples, says the United Nations General Assembly (1960), "All peoples have the right to self-determination; by virtue of that right they freely determine their political status and freely pursue their economic, social and cultural development." In the same document, it states that "Any attempt aimed at the partial or total disruption of the national unity and the territorial integrity of a country is incompatible with the purposes and principles of the Charter of the United Nations."

The Western powers have applied each of the above two principles based on their respective "national interests" at different times. An American-led NATO operation bombed Yugoslavia allegedly to halt the ethnic cleansing of Kosovo. The killings and destruction by NATO and the intensified ethnic strife in that area after the bombing were nothing but a human rights disaster. During the same period of time, Turkey was mercilessly suppressing the Kurdish independence movement. The United States/NATO did not bomb Turkey, but instead helped Turkey kidnap Ocalan, the leader of the Kurdish independence movement. India has been suppressing the Kashmir independence movement. The United States has not taken any military action to punish India. Instead, it has been trying to stop Pakistan from providing support to the Kashmiris.

Albanians in Kosovo are now persecuting the Serbs who have lived on the same land. Ninety percent of the Serbs in Kosovo were driven away from their homes and became new war refugees. Hundreds of them were killed. This human rights disaster was a direct result of NATO's military involvement in the Balkans. NATO did not take any effective procedures to protect the Serbs, who have the same human rights as do the Albanians in Kosovo. NATO has not charged any Albanians with killing, but it charged Yugoslavia's president with war crimes. NATO had the "right" to bomb Yugoslavia because NATO had military might. Yugoslav cities and villages, which are part of the European and world civilizations, were destroyed because the people there did not bow to the Western powers and did not, unfortunately, have the ability to keep the bombs away from their homes.

The Western powers have a history of applying double standards on issues of sovereignty. They do not allow the Serbs in Bosnia to exercise self-determination.

They do not permit the Turks of Cyprus to become independent. The federal government of the United States will never honor the claim for Hawaii independence. Northern Ireland must be under the sovereignty of the United Kingdom. Corsica will have no chance to break away from France. The Basques of Spain have no way to become an independent country. Canada has not agreed to the emergence of an independent Quebec. The newly independent Ukraine does not tolerate the idea of letting Crimea reunite with Russia. In contrast, the Western powers have ardently supported the Tibetan independence movement. In its Resolution 1723, the UN General Assembly (1961), which had been manipulated by the Western powers, says that it "solemnly renews its call for the cessation of practices that deprive the Tibetan people of their fundamental human rights and freedoms, including their right of self-determination."

On the wall of the Lincoln Memorial are engraved the words, "In this temple as in the hearts of the people for whom he saved the union, the memory of Abraham Lincoln is enshrined forever." The United States is forever grateful for its president who suppressed resolutely the rebellious South that dared to claim independence. Will other nations have the same right to protect the union of their own nations? The glory of President Lincoln as the protector of the union, ironically, puts a check on the morality of the U.S. policy of sovereignty in international relations.

The Origin and Development of the Tibet Question

The causes of the Tibet Question are much more complicated than those that have been propagandized by the Dalai Lama, the Chinese government, and the Western powers. Since the end of the nineteenth century, political, economic, cultural, and religious forces of international and domestic backgrounds have interacted to contribute to the Tibet complex. As a chessman on the grand chessboard, the Fourteenth Dalai Lama has willingly become a pawn for the Western powers wanting to split China.

The Dalai Lama has been telling the world that the cultural and religious differences between Tibetans and Han Chinese are the major cause of the Sino-Tibetan conflict, which has pushed the Tibetans to pursue independence (Dalai Lama 1990). It is inevitable and understandable that cultural differences, including religious differences, have been the psychological background of the conflicts in Tibet. However, cultural differences alone were not, and will not be, the only condition to create or split a nation. Otherwise, other multi-ethnic countries, including the United States, the United Kingdom, Canada, Switzerland, and India could not have existed as nations. The Thirteenth Dalai Lama, the immediate predecessor of the Fourteenth Dalai Lama, sought support from Britain against the Manchu emperor of the Qing dynasty who was a Buddhist and shared the same religion with the Dalai Lama. None of the British kings or queens had ever believed in Buddhism. The Dalai Lama turned to the British to seek support for his own political and economic interests. The ethnic, religious, and cultural differences were not a barrier in his alliance with the then superpower.

The Tibet Question emerged as a direct result of the British expansion in Asia and its aggression into Tibet (Wang, Xiraonima, and Tang 1995). In the early years of the twentieth century, the British colonialists founded a pro-British clique in the Tibetan hierarchy by invasion and bribery. That pro-British clique launched the Tibetan independence movement. The Thirteenth Dalai Lama wished that Britain would help him to become independent from China. In 1914, the representative of the Thirteenth Dalai Lama, Thubten Gyatso, and the representative of British India, Sir Henry McMahon, signed the infamous Simla Treaty and two other agreements (Goldstein 1991). According to those agreements, British India annexed 90,000 square kilometers of Chinese territory. In addition to grabbing land, British Indians had the privilege of exemption from customs duty and other taxation in Tibet. During that period, British India controlled many trading ports and stationed troops in Tibet. Consequentially, Tibet became a de facto British colony. During different periods of history, the Chinese governments rebuffed all these treaties and agreements (Yang 1992).

After the Chinese People's Liberation Army advanced to Chamdo in 1950, the Kashag, which claimed to represent an independent country, appealed to the United Nations to prevent a Chinese invasion, but the UN refused to discuss the appeal. The United States, Britain, and India all refused to respond to the request. Having no other way out, the Fourteenth Dalai Lama accepted the Seventeen-Point Agreement proposed by the central government of the newly established People's Republic of China under Chairman Mao Zedong. The Dalai Lama expressed his formal acceptance of the Agreement with a telegram to Mao Zedong in late October 1951, and thus recognized Chinese sovereignty over Tibet (Goldstein 1991).

During the Cold War era, the Tibet Question was a front-line for the United States to confront the Chinese Communist Party (CCP) (Wise 1973). Nepal had been used as the base by the United States to train guerrillas selected from exiled Tibetans to raid China (Knaus 1999). In order to play the China card to contain the Soviet Union, the United States lessened its support of the Dalai Lama after President Nixon's historic visit to China in 1972. At the request of the Chinese government, the Nepali army wiped out the Tibetan guerrillas. The Nixon administration rejected a visa application by the Dalai Lama for a private visit to the United States in 1973. During the Cultural Revolution (1966–1976), human rights in Tibet, as in other areas of China, were severely violated. Yet, rights violations were seldom mentioned by the U.S. government during that period. In September 1979, the Dalai Lama obtained a tourist visa and visited the United States. Throughout his visit, no government officials, neither those in the administration nor the Congress, met with him. The State Department did not even allow him to visit NASA (Zhiyunbianji 1997). The inhuman behavior and brutality of the CCP in Tibet and other areas of China were tolerated because China was then an "ally" of the United States against the Soviet Union.

The strategic importance of China for the Western powers began to diminish in 1986 when Mikhail Gorbachev patronized political reform in the Soviet Union and initiated a pro-West policy in international affairs. On June 18, 1987, the U.S. House set a precedent of Western parliamentary interference in the Tibet Question by passing "A Bill Concerning Human Rights Violations in Tibet by the People's Republic of China" (U.S. Congress 1987a). Later that year, the Dalai Lama was invited for the first time to give a talk to the U.S. Congressional Human Rights Caucus. During his speech, he proposed a "Five Point Peace Plan for Tibet" (Dalai Lama 1992). It was applauded by the Congress but criticized by the State Department for its veiled independence agenda. A columnist noted, "The Dalai Lama's proposal was hailed by leading lawmakers as a historic peacemaking gesture and attacked by the State Department as an inappropriate political message. The Administration takes the position that Tibet is an integral part of China" (Sciolino 1987).

It is clear that the United States holds a double standard when measuring human rights in China, switching sides freely to meet the needs of its national interests. Nevertheless, the U.S. government seems to have verbally been able to stay with its recognition that Tibet is an integral part of China. President Bill Clinton reiterated on June 27, 1998, in Beijing that, "First, I agree that Tibet is a part of China, an autonomous region of China. And I can understand why the acknowledgment of that would be a precondition of dialogue with the Dalai Lama" (Clinton 1998). The Chinese government has rejected negotiations with the Dalai Lama because the latter has not accepted that Tibet is an indivisible part of China, though he sometimes says he would be willing to have autonomy instead of independence (Xu 1999).

In action, the U.S. Congress has supported the Tibetan independence movement. The main points of that "Bill Concerning Human Rights Violations in Tibet by the People's Republic of China" were posted on the streets in Lhasa, which caused a series of riots there in the late 1980s (Donnet 1994). The Dalai Lama was awarded the Nobel Peace Prize in 1989. Yet the Nobel Prize Committee did not make laureates of the pro-democracy Chinese student leaders. It seemed that the Committee was more interested in splitting than democratizing China. Some disappointed participants of the Chinese pro-democracy movement, who had denounced the CCP and had been longing for U.S.-style democracy, began to question Western sincerity in promoting democracy in China. They also began to question the real intention of the Western powers that had been playing the card of human rights in international relations.

On April 16, 1991, President George H.W. Bush had a "private" meeting with the Dalai Lama in the White House. After Bush, the heads of the Western powers have met the Dalai Lama one by one almost annually (Goldstein 1997). These meetings were reported as "private" or "unofficial." This is a gesture of support to the activists of Tibetan independence.

On May 21, 1991, the U.S. Senate passed Resolution 41 condemning the Chinese "occupation of Tibet." This Resolution reads, "Tibet, including those areas incorporated into the Chinese provinces of Sichuan, Yunnan, Gansu, and Qinghai, is an occupied country under the established principles of international law; Tibet's true representatives are the Dalai Lama and the Tibetan Government in exile as recognized by the Tibetan people" (U.S. Congress 1991). This was a great leap on the part of the United States on the Tibet Question from concerns for human rights in Tibet to challenging China's sovereignty over Tibet and to openly advocating the splitting of China. In a number of its official documents such as the above resolution, the U.S. Congress has continuously condemned China for human rights violations in Tibet. These accusations have not gone beyond repeating "China killed over one million Tibetans," and "demolish[ed] the Tibetan culture and religion" (U.S. Congress 1987a).

The Congress believes that "[o]ver 1,000,000 Tibetans perished from 1959 to 1979 as a direct result of the political instability, executions, imprisonment, and wide-scale famine engendered by the policies of the People's Republic of China in Tibet" (U.S. Congress 1987a). These are repetitions of irresponsible exaggerations and propaganda by the Dalai Lama (Dalai Lama 1990). They can be easily turned around with information from documents published by the Dalai Lama and his administration. The Kashag, the local Tibetan government that announced independence in 1950, wrote to the UN that the Tibetans were "a weak and peace loving people, hardly exceeding 3 million" (Kashag 1950). The Dalai Lama said on September 21, 1987, in his speech to the U.S. Congress Human Rights Caucus that there were 6 million Tibetans (Dalai Lama 1992). This would mean that the Tibetan population doubled in the first thirty-seven years of the CCP administration. During the same period, the Chinese population composed of Han and other ethnic groups doubled, too. If the CCP had killed more than 1 million Tibetans from 1959 to 1979, there would have been fewer than 2 million left. An increase from 2 million to 6 million in 1987 would indicate that the Tibetan population had tripled in thirty-seven years under CCP governance. It would also mean that the Tibetan population had increased by 200 percent while the population of other Chinese people had increased by 100 percent in the same period of time. The tale of the Tibetan population sounds like a biological wonder, if not a medical marvel, and could only convince those who live by fairy tales.

Openly, the U.S. State Department has not agreed with all the denouncements of the Chinese government by the U.S. Congress. A report by the State Department to the Congress on the treatment of minorities in China says: "Since 1980, the Chinese Government had made a conscious effort to ease tensions and begin economic and other changes. Beijing has stressed its commitment to preserve Tibet's unique cultural, linguistic and religious traditions" ("Beijing Is Backed" 1987). The State Department, which knew well the U.S. national interests, characterized the accusation of mass Chinese immigration to Tibet as inaccurate, incomplete, and misleading. The Senate and the House were faulted for failing to recognize significant changes in China's policies that had led to improvement of human rights conditions in Tibet. In addition, the State Department acknowledged that China has carried out a policy of promoting greater cultural and religious tolerance in Tibet since the early 1980s (Southerland 1992).

The Welfare Policy of the Chinese Government

Mao Zedong wanted to eradicate serfdom and to replace Tibetan society with communism, as he did in other areas of China. This caused many grievances, especially among upper-class monks and aristocrats who did not want to lose their inherited power and privileges in the hierarchy established and protected by the Tibetan theocracy. Monks and aristocrats rose up in March 1959 and were quickly suppressed by the People's Liberation Army. Many of them followed the Dalai Lama to exile in India.

As was recognized by the Dalai Lama (1962), Tibetan serfdom was an out-of-date, feudal system. Mao Zedong intended, by exterminating serfdom, to liberate the serfs and slaves so that they would enjoy a basic human right—personal freedom. However, he did a wrongful thing to force the Tibetans to accept a socialist revolution that was guided by atheism and communism. From 1959 to 1976, many Tibetans were killed or persecuted, many Tibetan monasteries and nunneries destroyed. This tragedy intensified tensions between Tibetans and Han Chinese.

The situation of human rights in Tibet, as recognized by the U.S. State Department, improved substantially from the 1980s during the Deng Xiaoping administration and after the implementation of a conciliatory welfare policy (Committee for the CCP-TAR 1995). Authorized by the Chinese central government, the Tibet Autonomous Region (TAR) government has redressed mishandled cases in Tibet caused by political and religious factors from the 1950s to the 1970s, including grievances dating from the Cultural Revolution. Those who were family members of the Tibetan hierarchy have been granted high positions, high salaries, and other kinds of privileges.

The welfare policy has uplifted the living standards of common Tibetans. The Chinese central government has provided enormous financial support and technology to improve the living conditions in the Tibetan highlands. All farmland and livestock of the people's communes in Tibet were redistributed to Tibetan farmers and nomads in the 1980s. All Tibetans have enjoyed tax exemptions, free medical care, and free education (Redi 1991). These benefits have not been provided to any Han Chinese peasants. Besides tuition exemption, Tibetan students have been provided stipends, free books, free clothing, free board, and free supply of other school necessities. No other Chinese ethnic group has enjoyed such high-level social welfare benefits (Information Office of the State Council 1992).

Since the 1990s, many non-Tibetan cadres and other government employees have been transferred back to China proper (Committee for the CCP-TAR 1995; Bureau of Statistics 1998). Many Tibetans have been promoted to leadership positions in the TAR governments. In the 1990s, 85 percent of TAR government officials were Tibetans ("Solang Luobu Says" 1992; G. Wu 1995). Tibetans have been granted affirmative action considerations for college admission and employment (Ma 1996).

Religious freedom has been restored and respected. Even the Dalai Lama has acknowledged that the "Tibetans are allowed to visit temples and to pray" (Dalai Lama 1995). The central government funded the reconstruction of 1,787 monasteries and nunneries around Tibet, and has paid stipends to 46,380 monks and nuns who have free medical care provided by the government. Their theological schools are subsidized by the government (Information Office of the State Council 1998). Uniquely in Tibet, the government finances ecclesiastical professionals to pursue their religious freedom.

The TAR government, guided and supported by the central government, has adopted a Tibetan-*putonghua* (common speech or Mandarin) bilingual language policy. The Tibetan language has been taught and used in all Tibetan schools. TAR government agencies, radio and TV stations, newspapers, and other media carry out their tasks bilingually (D. Wu 1995).

After twenty years of implementation of the welfare policy, "material life has been improved tremendously in both Lhasa and in the countryside. . . . So long as Lhasans did not engage in political dissidence, they were free to go where they wished, meet with friends, invite monks for religious services, and have parties and so forth" (Goldstein 1997, 75, 93).

The Catch-22 Strategy of the U.S. Government

New accusations by the U.S. Congress have been launched to combat the above conciliation efforts by the Chinese central government. The Congress finds that "Tibet's economy and education, health, and human services remain far below those of the People's Republic of China as a whole," and that "the People's Republic of China has encouraged a large influx of Han-Chinese into Tibet, thereby undermining the political and cultural traditions of the Tibetan people" (U.S. Congress 1987b).

Standing alone, each of these two allegations sounds believable, but they are in fact baseless. It is true that the economy, education, medical, and other social services in Tibet have been far behind those in other areas of China. That is why the Chinese central government has sent many scientists, engineers, medical workers, teachers, artists, and other professionals to Tibet. Most of these professionals are Han Chinese. They have built power plants, television stations, hospitals, schools, hotels, airports, department stores, cinemas and theaters, gymnasiums, apartment buildings, waterworks, and so forth. Han Chinese teachers have taught science, mathematics, and foreign languages such as English to Tibetan students. These actions have greatly improved Tibet's economy, education, health, and human services.

Instead of being acknowledged, these efforts by the Chinese government to promote cultural reconciliation and economic development have been criticized by the U.S. Congress as Chinese plans of mass migration to Tibet and the elimination of the political and cultural traditions of Tibet. Should, or should not, the Chinese government provide the above support to the Tibetan people? If the Chinese government did not do so, the Congress would condemn it for leaving Tibet behind in poverty. Applying such double standards has been the standard behavior of the Congress in its policies toward China since the late 1980s. The Chinese government has fallen into a Catch-22 on the Tibet Question and can never make the U.S. Congress happy.

It would be impossible for the Chinese government to avoid furious, continuing condemnation by the U.S. Congress unless the Chinese government could find an Aladdin's lamp for each Tibetan. There would be no need for Han Chinese professionals to work in Tibet if power plants, television stations, hospitals, schools, hotels, airports, department stores, cinemas and theaters, gymnasiums, apartment buildings, waterworks, and so forth, appeared by themselves on the Tibetan highland in a puff. But China has no magical solutions. As the richest, most advanced nation in science and technology that cares most for human rights, could the United States produce the magic lamps and provide them to the Tibetans in Tibet?

The U.S. government is often self-contradictory in its remarks on, as well as its attitudes toward, the Tibet Question. The U.S. Department of State (1998) says in its "1997 Report on Tibet Human Rights," "The central government and other provinces of China heavily subsidize the Tibetan economy, which has grown by an average annual rate of 10.5 percent during 1989–1996. Over 90 percent of Tibet's budget income comes from outside sources. Tibet also benefits from a wide variety of favorable economic and tax policies. . . . Overall, government development policies have helped raise the economic living standards of many ethnic Tibetans." These words seem to have acknowledged that the Chinese government has done good things for the Tibetan people. Yet the same document criticizes that "China's economic development policies, fueled in Tibet by central government subsidies, are modernizing parts of Tibetan society and changing traditional Tibetan ways of life," and "risk undermining Tibet's unique cultural, religious, and linguistic heritage."

The "risk" noticed by the State Department reflects the reality that the Tibetans in Tibet are changing (Liu 1994; Ma 1994; Ma 1996). They are now using electric lights as a substitute for butter lamps. They are cooking with gas instead of yak chips. They travel by buses, cars, motorcycles, planes, and bicycles to schools, hospitals, friends' houses, and places outside of Tibet. They are enjoying other basic conveniences of modern times, such as telephones, movies, television, and running water. Over 94 percent of the Tibetan families in cities have television sets (Information Office of the State Council 1998). Computers and the Internet are entering Tibetan schools, businesses, government offices, and social services. Children, middle-aged, and even old Tibetans like to watch TV at home. They visit temples less frequently than they did in the past, making the monks and nuns feel cold-shouldered.

Tibetan youths, especially those in the cities, prefer going to bars, cafeterias, restaurants, ballrooms, cinemas, and billiard rooms to prostrating themselves in monasteries. They wear blue jeans and Western suits more often than the traditional Tibetan costume. They like disco more than Tibetan folk dance. They like Coca-Cola and beer more than *chang* (Tibetan barley wine). They like chocolate cake more than *tsampa* (roasted barley flour). They do not want to return to the age of butter lamps and yak chips. They do not want to spin prayer wheels and prostrate themselves before the Buddhist statues everyday. They seek promotion to higher positions in the government, compete to possess apartments in concrete buildings with electricity, running water, and toilets. They are eager to learn Chinese and English rather than the Tibetan language because they want to participate in the national and global socioeconomic life. These changes have been witnessed by the authors and their Han and Tibetan friends and former colleagues in Tibet who have been communicating with each other.

The above sketch of contemporary Tibetans shows that they are learning to live the way other peoples live in modern societies. In "The Declaration on the Right to Development," the United Nations General Assembly (1986) confirms that "the right to development is an inalienable human right." Conventionally, the economy is the first and most important measure of development. The development of an economy is always marked by material conveniences brought with the advancement of science, technology, and education. Modern material conveniences, should the Tibetans pursue them, influence values and reshape lives. Like most Americans, most Tibetans like material conveniences and want to make money and play. They worship money as much as, if not more than, Americans and other peoples around the world. Should this trend in Tibet be reversed, if it could? The Chinese government would be blamed for denying the Tibetan people the right to development if it had not provided astronomical figures of financial aid and technological support to start the modernization in Tibet.

The Hollywood movie *Seven Years in Tibet* tells the story of the young Dalai Lama. The privileged young Dalai Lama had a car, a film projector, a telescope, a gramophone, magazines, and so on, in his Potala and Summer Palaces. At that time, the Dalai Lama was the only Tibetan who enjoyed electricity and drove a car in Tibet. These things did not belong to the traditional Tibetan culture. They were imported from the United Kingdom for him. Applying the logic used by the U.S. State Department in the above report, it was the Dalai Lama who took the lead to modernize Tibetan society, change its traditional ways of living, and thus destroy its cultural heritage.

The Chinese government is also accused of wiping out the Tibetan language by using the Chinese language as the medium of instruction in Tibetan schools. Here the Dalai Lama and the Chinese government face the same difficulty: the Tibetan language does not have enough vocabulary and terms to carry numerous concepts of science and technology. The Dalai Lama himself studied English hard. English has been used to teach mathematics and science in the Tibetan schools of India

(Grunfeld 1996). Should the Dalai Lama be denounced as the primary person diminishing the Tibetan language?

Religious freedom in China, especially in Tibet, has been measured by a double standard. In the same official document the "1997 Report on Tibet Human Rights" (U.S. Department of State 1998), first the Department is pleased: "The authorities permit many traditional religious practices, and public manifestations of belief." Then it attacks: "It does not tolerate religious manifestations that advocate Tibetan independence or any expression of 'splittism.'" The authors of this report do not seem to be willing to distinguish between political and religious activities in this case. Advocating Tibetan independence is a political not a religious action. Separation of church and state is a principle established and followed by all Western democracies. After all, would the United States tolerate any intention or action to split its union for any religious or political reason?

The Unexpected Results of the New Cold War

Henry Kissinger (1998) has warned it is folly to try to bring China to collapse with another Cold War as was done to the Soviet Union. It is a pity his voice does not seem to be as loudly heard as it once was, though his warning has proved correct. The effect of the new Cold War has been the opposite.

The United States does not seem to understand the Chinese people and Chinese society. In China, there are about 6 million Tibetans and 6 million Uyghur people. The number of Han people is 100 times that of Tibetans and Uyghurs, or 1.3 billion. It has been and will be fruitless for the United States to encourage nationalism and ethnic separation among Tibetans and Turkestans because their populations are too small to enable them to split from China with pieces of land as their territories. An unexpected result is that this new Cold War has stimulated nationalism among the Han Chinese and antagonized them toward the United States for its hostile attitude and behavior toward China. It is pushing them to stand behind the CCP government, which can uphold the unity of the country and shield their interests.

In 1997, when President Jiang Zemin visited Harvard University, about 1,000 pro–Tibet independence activists demonstrated against him. Over 4,000 Chinese gathered in the streets and welcomed him. One Chinese graduate student at Harvard said, "There would not be so many Chinese to come and welcome Jiang Zemin if there were not so many Americans to support Tibet independence." When Premier Zhu Rongji of China visited the Massachusetts Institute of Technology in 1998, over 500 pro–Tibet independence activists rallied against him, while over 2,000 Chinese cheered him. After NATO's bombing of the Chinese Embassy in Yugoslavia, millions of Chinese held indignation meetings. Many Chinese students demonstrated to vent their anguish outside the U.S. and U.K. embassies in Beijing.

Among those who welcomed Jiang Zemin and Zhu Rongji in Cambridge, Massachusetts, were participants in the 1989 pro-democratic student movement at Tiananmen Square. Those students who threw rocks and eggs at the walls of the

U.S. Embassy in Beijing after the bombing of the Chinese Embassy by NATO would probably have gone to Tiananmen and taken part in pro-democracy rallies had they been college students ten years earlier. If any were asked today whether they wanted democracy in China, the answer would still be a definite "yes." So why have they changed their attitude to support the Chinese Communist Party? Can they see the virtue of human rights ideals through the behavior of the Western powers? Will U.S.–style democracy be the only model able to offer all peoples a promise of peace, equality, and prosperity? As noted by some prominent historians, this young generation of Chinese will not take it for granted that the Western powers know exactly the right method by which the Chinese should organize themselves (Kissinger 1999).

What the United States has done on issues of the Tibet Question is an insult to the Chinese people, especially to the Han Chinese. The Han make up over 90 percent of the Chinese population and their ethnicity has developed out of merged ethnic groups in history. The more hostile the U.S. attitude is toward China in propaganda, trade, and international relations, the more antagonistic Han Chinese become toward the United States. To protect their own national interests, they will stand fast behind the CCP government, which has proved itself to have the ability to uphold the union and to confront unfriendly foreign powers. This support for the CCP will only strengthen its leadership. In other words, the more the Western powers want to use the Tibet Question to constrain and split China, the stronger the union of China will be. When the Party shares people's interests and can take action on these interests, it will win over the people and grow roots among them. When the Party becomes more controlling, the democratic process in China will be slowed. From this point of view, the United States and the Dalai Lama are true supporters of the CCP maintaining power. The double-standard approach to the Tibet Question by the Western powers has done nothing good, but has instead blocked China's path to democracy.

Playing double standards in international affairs seems to have become a tradition of the Western powers in their communication with China and other developing countries. To halt China's social development, the Cold War–minded Western policymakers cannot see any other alternative but stimulating nationalism among the Tibetans, Inner Mongolians, and Uyghurs. Ironically, the more the Western powers encourage such splitting, the stronger the union of China becomes. This is an unexpected Catch-22 they have created for themselves.

If the United States wishes to overthrow the CCP and promote democracy in China, it would be wise to stop encouraging and fueling the Tibet and the East Turkestan independence movements. To animate nationalism among the Han Chinese, the Tibetans or the Uyghurs will not help create democracy or peace in the Eastern hemisphere. Stirring up ethnic hostility will produce nothing but an ethnic war that could be 300 times worse than the Bosnian war. It will victimize at a minimum the innocent people in China, and the "Yellow Peril" will have to escape to the Western hemisphere. Because of China's size, it will be too costly to silence its 1.3 billion people.

References

"Beijing Is Backed by Administration on Unrest in Tibet." 1987. *New York Times*, October 7, A1, A9.

Brzezinski, Z.K. 1997. *The Grand Chessboard: American Primacy and Its Geostrategic Imperatives*. New York: Basic Books.

Bureau of Statistics of Tibet Autonomous Region. 1998. *Yearbook of Tibet Statistics 1998*. Beijing: Statistics Publishing House of China.

Clinton, W.J. 1998. *A Speech at the Western Hall of the Great Hall of the People*. Beijing, China, June 27. Washington, DC: Office of the Press Secretary of the White House.

Committee for the CCP-TAR—Committee for the History of the Chinese Communist Party in Tibet Autonomous Region. 1995. *Events in the History of CCP-TAR 1949–1994*. Lhasa: Tibetan People's Publishing House.

Dalai Lama. 1962. *My Land and My People*. New York: McGraw-Hill.

———. 1990. *Freedom in Exile*. New York: HarperCollins.

———. 1992. "Address to the U.S. Congressional Human Rights Caucus on September 21, 1987—Five Point Peace Plan for Tibet." In *Congressional Ceremony to Welcome His Holiness the Dalai Lama of Tibet*, 80–85. Washington, DC: U.S. Government Printing Office.

———. 1995. "Statement on his September 1995 Visit to the U.S." *Tibet Press Watch* 7, no. 5: 4.

Donnet, P. 1994. *Tibet: Survival in Question [Tibet mort ou vif]*. Translated by Tica Broch. London: Zed Books.

Goldstein, M.C. 1991. *A History of Modern Tibet 1913–1951*. Berkeley: University of California Press.

———. 1997. *The Snow Lion and the Dragon*. Berkeley: University of California Press.

Grunfeld, A.T. 1996. *The Making of Modern Tibet*. Armonk, NY: M.E. Sharpe.

Huntington, S.P. 1996. *The Clash of Civilizations and the Remaking of World Order*. New York: Simon & Schuster.

Information Office of the State Council of the People's Republic of China. 1992. *Tibet: Its Sovereignty and Human Rights Conditions*. Beijing: Information Office of the State Council of the People's Republic of China.

———. 1998. *New Progress in Human Rights in the Tibet Autonomous Region*. Beijing: Information Office of the State Council of the People's Republic of China.

Kashag. 1950. *Tibetan Appeal* [English]. FO 371/84455, Copy of UN file A/1658, December 11.

Kissinger, H. 1998. "No Room for Nostalgia." *Newsweek*, June 29, 50–52.

———. 1999. Boston University Commencement Address. May 23, Boston: *BU Bridge*, 1–2.

Knaus, J.K. 1999. *Orphans of the Cold War: America and the Tibetan Struggle for Survival*. New York: PublicAffairs.

Liu, W. 1994. *Steps of Tibet*. Lhasa: Tibetan People's Publishing House.

Ma, L. 1994. *Crossing Tibet*. Beijing: Writers Press.

Ma., R. 1996. *The Tibetan Population and the Tibetan Society*. Beijing: Tongxin Publishing House.

Redi. 1991. "A New Epoch in Tibetan History." *China Tibetology*, no. 2: 3–12.

Sciolino, E. 1987. "U.S. Official Defends Stance on Turmoil in Tibet." *New York Times*, October 15, A18.

"Solang Luobu Says the Tibetan People Enjoy Human Rights." 1992. *People's Daily* (overseas edition), March 30.

Southerland, D. 1992. "U.S. Policy on Tibet Assailed at Hearing." *Washington Post*, July 29, A18.

United Nations General Assembly. 1960. *Declaration on the Granting of Independence to Colonial Countries and Peoples. Resolution 1514 (XV)* (December). New York: UN General Assembly.

―――. 1961. *Resolution 1723 (XVI)*. New York: UN General Assembly.

―――. 1986. *Resolution 41/128* (December 4). New York: UN General Assembly.

―――. 1999. *Hearing Held for the Region of the Economic and Social Commission for Western Asia*, May 23–24. Beirut: UN General Assembly.

U.S. Congress. 1987a. *House Concurrent Resolution 2476: A Bill Concerning Human Rights Violations in Tibet by the People's Republic of China* (June 18).

―――. 1987b. "Human Rights Violations in Tibet by the People's Republic of China." *United States Public Law 100–204, Foreign Relations Authorization Act, Fiscal Years 1988 and 1989*, SEC 1243 (December 22).

―――. 1991. *Senate Concurrent Resolution 41—Relative to the Occupation of Tibet* (May 21).

U.S. Department of State. 1998. "1997 Report on Tibet Human Rights." *Tibet Press Watch* 10, no. 1: 6–8.

Wang, G., Xiraonima, Tang, J. 1995. *Comments on the Historical Status of Tibet*. Beijing: Minzu Publishing House.

Wise, D. 1973. *The Politics of Lying: Government Deception, Secrecy, Power.* New York: Random House.

Wu, D. 1995. *A Study on the Educational Reform and Development in Tibet.* Kunming: Yunnan Educational Publishing House.

Wu, G. 1995. "The Number of Tibetan Cadres Is Increasing in the Tibet Autonomous Region." *People's Daily* (overseas edition), August 7.

Xu, M. 1999. *Intrigues and Devoutness: The Origin and the Development of the Tibet Riots.* Canada: Mirror Books.

Yang, G. 1992. *A History of China's Resistance to Foreign Invasion and Interference in Tibet.* Beijing: China Tibetology Press.

Zhiyunbianji. 1997. *The Life of the Dalai Lama: A Splittist in Exile.* Haikou: Hainan Publishing House.

15

Tibet and the United States

A. Tom Grunfeld

More than fifteen years ago I observed that for all of Tibet's political associations, "understanding the U.S.–Tibetan relationship is most crucial for understanding the history of Tibet" in the last half of the twentieth century. To be sure, the Tibetan relationship with China was, and remains, the most consequential, but the shadow of the United States looms large over this region and as a consequence it was regrettable, I lamented, that this association was "to be the most elusive to understand."[1] Sadly, nothing has transpired since then to allow me to think otherwise, for although we now have access to more information than we had fifteen years ago, the bulk of the documents we need to understand these historical events remain classified and inaccessible.[2]

Early Encounters

America's first quasi-encounter with Tibet came in the middle of the nineteenth century when the former U.S. ambassador to China, Anson Burlingame, quit his diplomatic post to represent the Chinese state in an effort to urge the foreign powers, including the United States, not to act in any way to jeopardize the territorial integrity of the Manchu empire, which included Tibet. Then, early in the twentieth century, explorer, scholar, author, and ambassador to China William Woodville Rockhill began wandering through areas populated by ethnic Tibetans.[3] In 1908 he met with the Thirteenth Dalai Lama in Shaanxi Province and spent the rest of his life championing the Tibetan cause. "We are greatly pleased," wrote the Dalai Lama to Rockhill in 1911, "having learnt from your letter that you exert yourself for the sake of Tibet. The relations between our Tibet Government and [the United States] are untroubled as before." For his part, Rockhill advised the Dalai Lama that Tibet "is and must remain a portion of the [Chinese] Empire for its own good

... [and] because the Great Powers of the world deem it necessary for the prosperity of its own peoples."[4] Nothing ever came of this contact.

For the next several decades U.S.–Tibet contacts were limited. To the best of my knowledge the only Americans to reach Tibet proper were Mr. and Mrs. Suydam Cutting and Arthur Vernay on trips sponsored by the American Museum of Natural History, and Theos Bernard, a converted Buddhist monk—all in the 1930s.[5] A handful of other Americans reached the ethnic Tibetan areas outside of Tibet proper. Leonard Clark was ostensibly climbing mountains but probably gathering intelligence.[6] And there were missionaries, several in the eastern Tibetan city of Batang for the Foreign Christian Missionary Society (later, United Christian Missionary Society) and the Robert Ekvall family farther north.[7]

World War II led to the first official Washington contacts with the Lhasa government. In May 1942 Chinese forces under the command of American General Joseph "Vinegar Joe" Stilwell were defeated by the Japanese in Burma, thereby cutting off the major supply route ("Burma Road") to the Chinese Nationalist (Kuomintang—KMT) government in Chongqing (Chungking). To compensate, the United States began flying supplies from India into China over the Himalayan mountains (the "Hump"). One of these flights crashed some 96 kilometers (60 miles) outside Lhasa. All five crewmen survived and were rescued by the Tibetans, treated with utmost hospitality, and escorted safely back to India.[8]

The air route was efficient but unable to provide sufficient war matériel. One possible alternative was a land route north from the Indian plains, over the Himalayan passes into Tibet and then eastward across more formidable passes onto the plains of Sichuan Province (or Xikang Province as the western part of Sichuan was then known; Kham to the Tibetans). With this route in mind, the American Office of Strategic Services (OSS, forerunner to the Central Intelligence Agency [CIA]) assigned Captain Ilia Tolstoy and First Lieutenant Brooke Dolan to undertake a mission to, ostensibly, ascertain the viability of such a route. The men were in Lhasa from December 1942 to March 1943.

While their mission produced nothing of substance, they were the first officially sanctioned American mission to Tibet, even bringing presents from President Franklin Delano Roosevelt to the seven-year-old Fourteenth Dalai Lama.[9] In addition, the Tibetans asked for and received three fully equipped long-range radio transmitters "for use for broadcasting within Tibet."[10]

Some sixty years on, questions about this mission persist. What was its real purpose? Aerial reconnaissance, or discussions with British officials in Lhasa, could have shown that a new route of the magnitude required was untenable. There already was a commercial trade route of sorts from India to Lhasa and another from Lhasa to Kham/Xikang Province that, at its peak, could carry up to 3,000 tons of goods each year. In contrast, the U.S. Army Air Corps was flying 3,000 tons of supplies each month over the Hump. Moreover, since Republic of China leader Chiang Kai-shek scoffed at the idea of an independent Tibet, why would the United States risk alienating an important wartime ally by dealing directly with the Tibetans and thereby implying some form of autonomy for the latter? Although CIA officials assured me in the mid-1980s that OSS records were then completely declassified, newly released OSS documents continue to appear, the latest as recently as June 2000.

After World War II some Tibetan officials understood they were at a crossroads. The victorious struggle for Indian independence just to the south and the civil war raging in China to their east and north convinced many, but not all, Tibetan government officials that their historic isolation from the rest of the world might no longer be tenable.

Tibet did not take part in the war, but in an attempt to break out of its isolation, a "goodwill" mission was dispatched in 1946 to congratulate the British and the Americans on their decisive victories. Because the two nations were allied to the KMT, visas for the delegation were denied and the delegates never got farther than India. The Dalai Lama's letters to President Harry S Truman were presented at the U.S. Embassy in New Delhi as was a letter complaining that the gasoline generators sent in 1943 to run the radio transmitters were ineffectual in Tibet's rarefied air. The U.S. Army was instructed to procure three diesel generators and in December 1946 they were sent from Calcutta to Kalimpong, where they were handed over to the Tibetans.[11]

To American policymakers, the new generators were seen as token gifts—of limited expense and readily available technology—that could easily be shrugged off if the Chinese complained. But to the Tibetans—for whom electricity had only recently been introduced, and then only in Lhasa for a few hours a day—these gifts had symbolic value far surpassing their technological worth. They were seen as further symbols of American concern and support for the government of the child Dalai Lama in Lhasa.

In reality America had little interest in Tibet. Its Nationalist ally (the Guomindang) considered Tibet a historical part of China that would, after the war, be duly reunited with China proper and the United States agreed with that view. In 1943 Washington, for the first time, declared its official position on Tibet.

> For its part, the Government of the United States has borne in mind the fact that the Chinese Government has long claimed suzerainty over Tibet and the Chinese Constitution lists Tibet among areas constituting the territory of the Republic of China. This Government has at no time raised a question regarding either of these claims.[12]

American indifference changed with the advent of the Cold War. Because of Tibet's potential as a venue for anti-Communist activity, Washington began to engage Tibetan officials in a dialogue, and later a guerrilla war, that would last for years. Unfortunately the two sides had very different objectives and this divide would, ultimately, deceive and harm those Tibetans struggling to become free of Chinese rule.

The first hint of a change in U.S. policy came in January 1947 when the chargé d'affaires of the U.S. embassy in New Delhi, George R. Merrell, sent a lengthy cable to Washington expressing his view that the truncated 1946 Tibetan Goodwill Mission should be reactivated by a mission to Lhasa, for "Tibet is in a position of inestimable strategic importance both ideologically and geographically." As a result, he continued, it would be in an excellent position to act as a buffer against Soviet influence. Moreover, Merrell believed, there was a real possibility that hostile governments might come to power in India, China, Burma, and/or Indochina. In such an event, Tibet and its highly conservative people could act as "a bulwark against the spread of Communism throughout Asia . . . an island of conservatism in a sea of political turmoil . . . [and, moreover,] in an age of rocket warfare might prove to be the most important territory in all Asia." Anticipating Washington's hesitancy to antagonize the KMT, Merrell concluded by arguing that the benefits from such a gesture of friendship toward Lhasa would easily outweigh any political difficulties it might cause with Chiang Kai-shek.[13]

Merrell's views were not shared by his superiors in Washington. Acting Secretary of State Dean Acheson replied that the U.S. Army's assessment was that Tibet would not be a suitable launching pad for rockets and that a visit at this time would be of no use. But, he continued, it might be useful to continue contacts with Lhasa so Washington would be "disposed to regard with favor" trips to Tibet by Foreign Service officers if these trips could be kept "unobtrusive and unofficial."[14]

The Lhasa government's next gesture came in 1947 when it sent a "Tibetan Trade Mission" to India, Britain, the United States, China, and several other countries.[15] While trade was a vital component of Tibet's economy and, indeed, there were now considerable difficulties that had an adverse impact on the Tibetan economy,[16] the trade mission was not all it seemed to be. Tsepon W.D. Shakabpa, the leader of the delegation, claimed that the mission was designed to ease Indian restrictions on Tibetan trade, to expand Tibetan trade—especially with the United States—to purchase gold bullion to back up the Tibetan currency, and "to demonstrate Tibet's independence and sovereign status."[17] Arthur J. Hopkinson, British/ Indian Political Officer for Sikkim from 1945 to 1948, believed that the sole purpose of the mission was to buy gold and silver, a feat Shakabpa had been attempting to accomplish for over a year—mainly "for the joy of the chase." New Delhi informed Washington that in its opinion the main purpose of this mission was to enrich the participants.[18]

The trade delegation traveled on the first officially produced Tibetan passports. However, visas were issued, for the most part, in special circumstances that allowed admission to certain countries without, at the same time, according recognition to the passports. For example, the U.S. Department of State informed the U.S. embassy in New Delhi that if the delegation arrived without Chinese passports, then visas were to be issued on Form 257, "standard procedure [in] cases where applicant presents passport of [a] Government [the] United States *does not recognize*."[19] Moreover, the U.S. embassy in Nanjing was instructed to inform the Chinese government that there should be "no reason whatsoever to believe issuance of visas indicated any change in American policy on [the] question of sovereignty over Tibet."[20] Ultimately the mission failed to enhance Tibet's trade, failed to end Tibet's isolation, failed to bring international recognition, and failed to win many adherents to the cause of independence.

Lhasa also tried inviting American journalists to visit the once forbidden land. As early as 1944, Arch T. Steele, a foreign correspondent for the *Chicago Daily News,* spent three weeks in Tibet and became enamored of it.[21] In autumn 1949 the politically connected American journalist, explorer, author, and broadcaster Lowell Thomas and his son traveled to Lhasa. When the Thomases returned to the United States they held an airport news conference calling for American aid against the Communists in China, U.S. advice on guerrilla warfare for the Tibetans, and the immediate dispatch of an American mission to Lhasa. They also carried a personal letter from the Dalai Lama to President Truman, whom they briefed along with Secretary of State Dean Acheson.[22]

But ultimately, it was the Chinese who were responsible for ending Tibet's isolation. On October 1, 1949, Mao Zedong proclaimed victory in the Chinese civil war and the establishment of the People's Republic of China and promised that the "liberation" of Tibet from Western "imperialism" was imminent.

Earlier that year, with a Chinese Communist victory almost certain, U.S. officials had begun a reappraisal of their policies toward the region. Ruth E. Bacon of the Office of Far Eastern Affairs, Department of State, argued that a Communist expropriation of Tibet would grant the region "ideological and strategic importance" so that in the event of a Communist victory in the Chinese civil war, the United States should no longer consider Tibet under Chinese authority. She urged establishing a covert relationship by sending American officials to Lhasa immediately but "inconspicuously," cautioning against "giving rise to speculation that" the United States might "have designs upon Tibet."

U.S. Ambassador to India Loy Henderson, an ardent and vociferous cold warrior, agreed, expressing his fear of Communist rule in Tibet and urging haste in sending a covert mission to Lhasa as well as leaving some Americans there for an indefinite period. U.S. Ambassador to China Leighton Stuart concurred on the urgency of the matter.

The Department of State conceded, informing its ambassadors in the region on July 28, 1949, that it was "considering . . . [a] . . . covert mission." Nonetheless, it appears the plan was never implemented. Henderson had discovered that a British attempt at a similar mission a year earlier had been discouraged by the Indian government. Indian concurrence was considered essential, since India, in Henderson's words, had a "practical monopoly on Tibet's foreign relations."[23]

On November 19, 1949, American diplomats in New Delhi met with Tibetan officials who told them America was the "greatest and most powerful country" and Tibet's only hope.[24] Ambassador Henderson was instructed to tell the Tibetans that the United States was sympathetic to their predicament although it could not publicly demonstrate any concern or involvement. Secret talks between the Americans and the Tibetans continued throughout 1950 and 1951, often with British missionary George Patterson acting as the liaison.[25] The currently available documentation gives no hint of aid actually being provided at this time.

Nevertheless, Henderson's urging of U.S. support for the Tibetans began to be heard with more sympathy back home as the Cold War intensified. In the summer of 1950, after the outbreak of the Korean War, the Office of Policy Coordination (OPC), the bureaucratic arm officially in charge of covert operations, began "to initiate psychological warfare and paramilitary operations against the Chinese Communist regime" resulting in an "explosion" of covert anti-Communist actions, according to Franklin Lindsay, chief of operations for the OPC.[26] The purpose—in the words of a National Security Council memo of a year later—was to "foster and support anticommunist elements both outside and within China with a view to developing and expanding resistance in China to the Peiping [Beijing] regime's control, particularly in South China."[27] Also, as succinctly expressed by an American involved in the clandestine Tibetan operation: "the theory was that by creating chaos in China's rear we could blunt Chinese aggression elsewhere."[28]

At the same time as covert operations against China were being initiated, an unusual pamphlet surfaced in India. Entitled *Armed Forces Talk No. 348: Tibet—Roof of the World*, it was published by the U.S. Department of Defense and "intended as a lesson plan for military unit commanders or their representatives to use in conducting troop education and information programs," and was "part of a continuing program on international awareness." The appearance of this publication no doubt contributed to the new Chinese government's growing apprehension about U.S. intentions in the region. All documentation concerning the pamphlet has either been lost or destroyed, if the Department of Defense is to be believed.[29]

The Korean War hardened U.S. Cold War policies designed to "contain" China. Immediately after the outbreak of the war, Acheson cabled that the "Department [was] now in [a] position [to] give assurances [to the] Tibetans re U.S. aid to Tibet." The plan called for Henderson to tell the Tibetans that the United States was "ready to assist procurement and financing." There was a catch, however—a stipulation that India had to agree to the plan first. If India refused to aid the Tibetans, Washington instructed the Tibetans to ask New Delhi for permission to transport aid across India from a third party (the United Sates). Shakabpa, when informed of these plans, asked for clarification on the type of aid to be expected. Were they getting American troops and planes, he wanted to know. No, the Tibetans should expect only "war materials and finance."[30]

At the urging of the United States the Tibetans also turned to the United Nations with the help of a public relations firm and the services of Ernest Gross, a former deputy U.S. representative to the UN and personal counsel to two UN secretaries general who had been introduced to the Tibetans by the U.S. government. Washington apparently footed the bill for all these services. The United States tried pressuring India and other nations to support the Tibetans, promising that they would follow suit; however, in the end, only El Salvador would sponsor the UN resolution.

All to no avail, as on November 24, 1950, the UN voted unanimously to indefinitely postpone the vote. Henderson was now instructed to continue to work for a British–U.S.–Indian joint effort to aid the Tibetans. As late as June 1951, and perhaps later, Fraser Wilkins, the First Secretary of the U.S. Embassy in New Delhi, continued to meet with prominent Tibetans in India on such issues as the further release of gold by the United States and the continued purchase of Tibetan wool. George Patterson was often the liaison and translator.[31]

For all of its efforts on behalf of the Tibetans, the main concern of U.S. policymakers was never Tibetan independence. "Historically, the United States Government has recognized a continuing claim by the Government of China to suzerainty over Tibet," according to one U.S. government report. Yet at the same time, "the United States Government believes that Tibet should not be compelled by duress to accept violation of its autonomy and that the Tibetan people should enjoy the rights of self-determination . . . ."[32] The obvious contradiction in this policy was never clarified because Tibetan independence was always secondary to other goals. Besides, U.S. commitments to the KMT government of Taiwan, which agreed with Beijing that Tibet is an inalienable part of China, foreclosed any U.S. official commitment to true Tibetan independence. In fact, U.S. officials were more interested in using the Tibet issue to harass China militarily and to castigate the Communist government in the international media and at fora such as the UN. Even more important to Washington was the use of the Tibet issue to convince Prime Minister Jawaharlal Nehru that China, and communism in general, was such a threat that he should disavow Indian neutrality in the Cold War. Acheson thought this latter objective was of particular importance.[33]

When the Communist People's Liberation Army (PLA) reached the Tibetan border around the city of Qamdo, a battle of several days' duration ensued in which the Chinese handily overcame the much weaker Tibetan resistance. Several weeks later the Dalai Lama fled Lhasa for the Tibetan town of Yadong, just north of the Indian border. India told the United States that it expected the Chinese to have no trouble gaining control over Tibet and that the Dalai Lama was welcome in exile, although he would not be permitted to live near the Tibetan frontier.

After the Tibetan leader fled Lhasa for Yadong, American diplomatic officials tried to lure him across the Indian frontier. Loy Henderson was particularly committed to encouraging the Dalai Lama to flee Tibet. Some Tibetan leaders were less than cooperative because they were "unable to counterbalance the tremendous weight of superstition and selfish officialdom, including delegates from monasteries, oracles of incredible influence, and the misguided wish of the Lhasa Government itself . . . to preserve the religious integrity of Tibetan life as personified and symbolized by the Dalai Lama," in the words of an American diplomat indignant at Tibetans having the audacity to put their own cultural and political interests above Washington's worldwide anti-Communist crusade.

Ultimately the Dalai Lama rejected the American entreaties and returned to Lhasa. Washington continued to pursue him, laying out its terms in a secret 1951 letter composed by Henderson. To begin with, he would have to "disavow" his formal agreement with Beijing and appeal for aid from the United Nations and the United States. The United States would then publicly support him and arrange for his exile in Thailand, India, Ceylon, or the United States. The United States would also promise to organize and supply a resistance movement against Chinese rule, being "prepared to send . . . light arms through India" and money directly to him. Lastly, arrangements would be made to have Thubten Norbu, one of his older brothers, travel to the United States.[34]

On his way to the United States Norbu stopped in Kalimpong to meet secretly with the Americans to discuss the terms they had offered. He was told that the question of military aid would be left to discussions with the Dalai Lama when he arrived in India, where he would be expected to first ask India for aid and then, if turned down, ask for permission to approach another nation. Norbu promptly flew to the United States under the auspices of the American Committee for Free Asia, a CIA-funded anti-Communist organization.[35] While the negotiations with the United States were in progress, another of the Dalai Lama's older brothers, Gyalo Thondup, began conferring with KMT officials in Taiwan.

Serious U.S.–Tibet talks in India lasted until 1952, using such intermediaries as George Patterson, Heinrich Harrer, Surkhang Rimshi, and especially Tsepon Shakabpa, of whom the Americans were wary. After that date U.S. officials (from both the State Department and the CIA) met periodically with Gyalo Thondup, who had traveled from Taiwan to Lhasa in 1952, from where he fled, after only a few months, into Indian exile.

The Dalai Lama's voluntary return to Lhasa led to negotiations with Beijing resulting in the "Agreement of the Central People's Government and the Local Government of Tibet," commonly referred to as the Seventeen-Point Agreement.[36] This treaty was the legal document that incorporated Tibet into the People's Republic of China. Ironically, the Chinese insistence on such a pact demonstrated that even Beijing understood that Tibet was not a province of China but an entity outside of China's boundaries that required some form of official incorporation.

The Central Intelligence Agency

No aspect of Tibetan–U.S. relations is more controversial than the role of the Central Intelligence Agency.[37] So sensitive was this issue that for years the Dalai Lama and his followers denied that the U.S.–Tibet relationship even existed. When China accused the rebels of receiving help from the outside, the Dalai Lama retorted that the reports were "completely baseless."[38] In 1961 he was quoted as saying that "the only weapons that the rebels possess are those they've managed to capture from the Chinese. They have guns but they've even been using slingshots, spears, knives, and swords."[39] In 1974 he was quite unequivocal: "The accusation of CIA aid has no truth behind it. My flight [in 1959] was conditioned by circumstances developing in Lhasa because of Chinese atrocities. . . ."[40]

When the Dalai's brother, Thubten Norbu, was asked by *US News and World Report* in 1959, "Are you getting any weapons to resist the Chinese?" he replied, "There is nothing at all coming in from the outside."[41] In fact, Gyalo Thondup had been receiving arms from the KMT on Taiwan as early as 1952.[42] The CIA pipeline began to produce weapons in 1956, although he had been conferring regularly with U.S. officials in India since 1952.[43]

The impetus for CIA involvement came directly from Secretary of State John Foster Dulles and his undersecretary, Herbert Hoover, Jr. Their goal was not an independent Tibet but rather ". . . to keep the Communists off balance in Asia." As a consequence, the "Far East Division of the CIA was ready to undertake a full program of support if the initial teams [of trained Tibetans clandestinely dropped into Tibet] found it warranted by the situation on the ground and the capabilities of their comrades."[44]

However, the CIA's involvement in the region did not begin in the 1950s but a decade earlier. The story of the very first CIA operation in that region remains to be fully told as the agency continues to refuse declassification of the appropriate papers. Douglas S. Mackiernan was a thirty-five-year-old meteorologic and cryptologic expert who spoke several languages, including some Russian, Mongolian, and Kazakh, when he arrived at the U.S. Consulate in the Xinjiang capital of Urumqi (then called Tihwa) in the far west of China in 1947 for his lowly duties as a U.S. consulate clerk. But clerking was not what Mackiernan was there for; in truth he worked for the CIA. We can't be sure, but it is believed that Mackiernan was engaged in multiple intelligence operations. He was probably spying on the Soviet nuclear program (their first atomic bomb was tested in Central Asia on August 29, 1949). He was also, probably, spying on Soviet activities in Xinjiang: tracking their access to its sources of uranium, gold, and petroleum, and their aid to the Chinese Communist Party (CCP), then battling the U.S.-supported KMT for control of China. And, most likely, he was aiding dissident ethnic groups in the region, such as the Kazakhs, against the Chinese Communists. There have been hints that he may have also been assisting dissident Tibetans as well.

When Chinese troops reached the former U.S. Consulate in Urumqi they claimed to have found an arsenal of weapons. When Mackiernan was attacked in the Chinese press as "an American imperialistic agent" the U.S. government dismissed the charge as "the usual tripe."

Days after the Soviet bomb test, and only days before the arrival of the PLA, Mackiernan, along with three White Russians and an American Fulbright scholar named Frank Bessac, who just happened to be in Urumqi and was, in all likelihood, also employed by the CIA, fled southward toward Tibet and India. Mackiernan and two of the Russians were shot and killed on April 29, 1950 at the Tibetan border by Tibetan guards who had not yet received orders from Lhasa to allow the travelers to pass unhindered. Consequently, Mackiernan became the first CIA officer to be killed in the line of duty. The two survivors eventually made it safely to the United States. Mackiernan's activities remain so secret to this day that he is still not acknowledged by name at the memorial for fallen officers at CIA headquarters.[45]

Beijing has insisted that it had to attack Tibet to prevent it from being seized by "imperialist forces." Although China has never provided any evidence for this claim, nor is there evidence from any other sources, I have argued elsewhere that there were several episodes that could have led Chinese leaders to believe this was so.[46] It is highly probable that Mackiernan's activities contributed to convincing Chinese leaders that the United States had designs on Tibet. However, until the Chinese archives become available we will not know for sure.

By 1956 Chinese policies in the Tibetan areas of western Sichuan (Kham) had led to such severe alienation of the local population that a major revolt broke out against Chinese rule. The CIA saw the revolt as a golden opportunity by which it could escalate its covert harassment of the People's Republic of China.

Gyalo Thondup became the Tibetan liaison to the CIA, arranging the first CIA training missions. Selected Tibetans were taken on a five-hour flight to Saipan where they were joined by Thubten Norbu. Their training lasted four months and consisted of learning how to read maps and use radio transmitters, parachutes, and weapons. They were then dropped back into Tibet in the autumn of 1957, from a plane flown by an American pilot. They each carried a pistol, a small machine gun, an old Japanese radio that had to be wound by hand, US$132 worth of Tibetan currency, and two small vials of poison to swallow if captured. Their mission was to contact rebel forces and to urge the Dalai Lama to publicly appeal for U.S. assistance.

Upon landing back in their homeland they contacted Gompo Tashi Andrugstang, the Tibetan rebel leader. In January 1958 they approached the Dalai Lama's chamberlain, Thubten Woyden Phala, who offered no help, telling the rebels that half the cabinet preferred working with the Chinese. Moreover, he felt the Dalai Lama could not morally support a movement dedicated to violence. He advised them that rebellion was useless. But Andrugstang was not one to be deterred. He appealed to Washington for further assistance, only to be told that such help would be provided only if the Dalai Lama requested it directly.[47]

Phala's role in these events remains murky. Supporters of the guerrillas have argued that he played a negative role by protecting the Dalai Lama and discouraging the revolt. However, John Kenneth Knaus, the CIA official in charge of the Tibet operation for many years, argues that Phala did indeed support the revolt while keeping the Dalai Lama uninformed.[48]

There is no doubt that there was a split within the Tibetan ranks. The guerrillas were anxious to mobilize Tibetans against the Chinese and to encourage maximum U.S. aid. Many in the Lhasan bureaucracy, on the other hand, were more intent on preserving their privileged lifestyles through compromise with the Chinese. Within Tibet proper the Chinese government had promised that the traditional Tibetan society would be kept intact and, to a large degree, it kept that promise until March 1959.

Despite their inability to get the Dalai Lama to join their cause, the CIA went ahead with plans to encourage, train, and equip those Tibetans willing to revolt against Chinese rule. The CIA's proprietary airline, Civil Air Transport, began flying over Tibet from its base in Takli, just north of Bangkok, Thailand, using Polish and Czech mercenaries as pilots with "smoke jumpers" (forest fire fighters) from Montana as parachute dispatch officers. Some 25–30 missions dropped some 250–400 tons of equipment into Tibet from 1957 to 1961: arms, ammunition, radios, medical supplies, hand-operated printing presses, and more.[49]

By 1958 the United States had established a training base at Camp Hale, Colorado, and over the next six years some 170 guerrillas were trained there.[50] In March 1959, the Dalai Lama fled Lhasa in a revolt whose origins remain unknown. The Dalai Lama and his supporters claim that the revolt was entirely spontaneous. I have argued that the *circumstantial* evidence points to a planned uprising by either the CIA or the guerrillas, or both.[51] Here again, the absence of documentation prevents this incident from being satisfactorily explained.

The revolt and the Dalai Lama's flight to India were "a windfall for the U.S.," according to President Eisenhower's Operations Coordinating Board, which also urged that the United States "keep the rebellion going as long as possible. . . ."[52] Be that as it may, the resistance effort inside Tibet was not going well. By 1961 the last of the guerrillas were dropped into Tibet. Of 49 men who had infiltrated since 1957, only 10 made it back out of Tibet; one surrendered, one was captured, and the remaining 37 were killed.[53]

It was just as well for Eisenhower that he had ordered all clandestine operations—including the flights over Tibet—to come to a temporary halt after the downing of an American U-2 spy plane piloted by Francis Gary Powers over the Soviet Union in May 1960. According to some sources, the CIA officers involved in the Tibetan operation were "very bitter" about this turn of events, feeling that the crisis with the Soviet Union had nothing to do with their activities.[54] The suspension of flights, however, did not affect the planning for a new phase in the CIA operation: the establishment of a guerrilla base in Mustang, a small semi-autonomous feudal principality on Nepal's northern frontier—in effect, a peninsula jutting into Tibet.

The United States also took advantage of the Dalai Lama's having left Tibet by having the CIA revive up its Cold War propaganda machine, creating supposedly popular organizations such as the American Emergency Committee for Tibetan Refugees, prodding its clandestinely funded Cold War "human rights" organizations such as the International Commission of Jurists to prepare propagandistic reports attacking China and arranging for press interviews with Thubten Norbu.[55] Secretary of State Christian Herter even went so far as to lie to the Dalai Lama when he wrote to him that "it has been the historical position of the United States to consider Tibet as an autonomous *country* under the suzerainty of China."[56]

At this point the Indian government enlisted in the clandestine operation by establishing, with U.S. support, a Tibetan military unit called the Special Frontier Force. Eventually 12,000 Tibetans were trained by U.S. Special Forces (Green Berets) and partly funded by the United States to operate from bases along the Kashmir frontier, where they crossed the border into Tibet planting electronic listening devices.[57]

The Kennedy administration, which took office in January 1961, was divided over whether to continue support for the Tibetans. The strongest opponent of the policy was the ambassador to India, John Kenneth Galbraith, who wrote, "the reasons for this operation, which in my view were never sufficient, have diminished in value and now depend in part . . . on the fact that men have been trained, action is under way and now must be continued. . . ."[58] After a brief pause, U.S. aid—and the guerrilla war—continued.

By early 1964 the Indian and American governments had initiated a Combined Operations Center, also funded by Washington, to oversee the Mustang operation. The U.S. supplied matériel and aid, the Tibetans manpower, and India "controlled the territory and thereby the operations."[59] From 1964 to 1967, twenty-five teams were sent into Tibet with little success as they found few Tibetans willing to support them.[60] Their activities were confined to ambushes of Chinese military convoys, sabotage of communication lines, and the mining of roads and bridges.

By 1969, with very little to show for years of operations, the CIA decided to wind down the Mustang operation. That deadline was extended briefly, but Henry Kissinger's secret visit to Beijing in 1971 would mark a sudden shift in U.S. policy toward China and, as a consequence, the end of all covert operations in that theater. After almost fifteen years the guerrillas had been unable to create a sustainable, independent military force, nor a beachhead inside Tibet. When the U.S. prop was pulled out, the whole operation collapsed. The Tibetans in Mustang were left to fend for themselves.

In December 1973 Mao Zedong told visiting Nepali king Birendra that the guerrillas were a major obstacle to better Sino-Nepali relations. In March 1974 a prominent rebel was arrested and an ultimatum was presented to the Tibetans giving them until July to surrender or face the consequences.[61] Most did, and by February 1975 the few who had refused were slain by the Royal Nepalese Army just as they were about to cross into India.

While the clandestine military operation was the major focus of the CIA's Tibet undertaking, it was not its sole endeavor. The "CIA paid for Tibetan delegations to travel to Geneva to press their case before international organizations. Some of the Tibetan aid groups were CIA-created fronts. Others were legitimate organizations that had been penetrated by CIA agents, who eagerly pushed the Tibetan human rights cause."[62] They also subsidized various activities such as the establishment of offices in Geneva and New York to allegedly promote Tibetan handicrafts and to publicize the Tibetan cause, but really to establish quasi-diplomatic offices for the Dalai Lama. This was also true for the Tibet House in New Delhi. In conjunction with Cornell University, the CIA sponsored (at a cost of $45,000 a year) several

Tibetans as students to prepare them for bureaucratic careers in Dharamsala, the seat of the Dalai Lama's administration in India. There were also direct subsidies to the Dalai Lama himself. From 1959 to 1974 he was receiving funds for his personal use to the tune of US$180,000 a year.[63]

The revelation that the Dalai Lama had been getting $180,000 a year from the CIA somewhat diminished his public stature. His spokesperson claimed "categorically that there was no direct connection between the CIA and His Holiness the Dalai Lama" and, moreover, the $180,000 "was spent on financing the setting up of Offices of Tibet in Geneva and New York and other international lobby activities."[64]

Maybe no one told the Dalai Lama *directly* that the CIA was involved. U.S. presidents have been known to practice "plausible deniability" whereby they are not told the details of a particularly odious action being taken by their government although it is correctly assumed they know, and approve of, what is being done in their name. It stretches credulity to believe that the Dalai Lama did not know that his two older brothers were working with the CIA for almost twenty years, or that the entire guerrilla movement was CIA-funded, or that he didn't know where his stipend was coming from. His disclaimer notwithstanding, U.S. diplomatic documents indicate that there was money put aside (with $75,000 for the first six months of operations alone) for the establishment of those offices in Geneva and New York—money that was in addition to the Dalai Lama's subsidy.[65]

The CIA officers who worked with the Tibetans became enamored of both the Tibetans and their cause. "In the simplistic ethos of the operational world of that era," recalled one CIA operative, "the CIA men viewed their Tibetan pupils as Oriental versions of the self-reliant, straight-shooting American frontiersmen who were under attack and seeking only the means to fight for their own way of life."[66] This was not a view shared in the corridors of power in Washington, DC, for in the end, the first phase of the U.S.–Tibetan relationship ended in a betrayal of the dissident Tibetans. There was never any intention of supporting a military force sufficient to achieve Tibetan independence, a salient fact that was, apparently, never conveyed to the Tibetans themselves. They were led to believe that the Americans were with them for the long haul.

What these men (both the CIA men in the field and the Tibetans) did not understand until much later was how insignificant Tibet was to United States foreign policy interests. For example, President John F. Kennedy came to office in January 1961, only twenty-two months after the abortive Lhasa uprising. China was then in the throes of a food shortage as a result of the Great Leap Forward. A debate ensued within the administration and Congress over supplying food to China, regardless of the events in Tibet. Supporters of better relations with China and of supplying aid carried the day only to have Beijing reject the offer. A poll at the time found that 48 percent of Americans supported aid if the Chinese asked for it, while 43 percent were opposed and 9 percent were without an opinion. This group did not end its efforts to better ties with China until the Sino-Indian war of 1962. Significantly, events in Tibet were never a major factor in this debate.[67]

Recent Times

Meanwhile, momentous changes were occurring inside China. After the revolt in 1959 Beijing considered the special status of Tibet to have ended and socialist transformation was quickly introduced. The commencement of the Cultural Revolution seven years later led to disaster in Tibet as almost every religious building was destroyed, indigenous culture was attacked, and countless Tibetans died. However, in 1971 a split in the leadership emerged, culminating in the mysterious death of Lin Biao, Mao Zedong's designated heir apparent. Lin's death led to, or coincided with, changes in government policies throughout the mainland, including Tibet. In 1976 Mao Zedong died, a leadership group dubbed "the Gang of Four" was arrested, and government policies were further moderated.

To Tibetans the changes were welcome. Beijing publicly admitted its past policies to have been harmful; a handful of tourists were allowed to visit, Tibetans were appointed to positions with at least a modicum of power, and refugees were permitted to visit families in Tibet. Furthermore, in February 1978, the Panchen Lama, second only in stature to the Dalai Lama in the Tibetan Buddhist hierarchy, was released from fourteen years of house arrest and prison.

The Dalai Lama responded to these changes by calling for the authorities to open Tibet to more visitors, which the Beijing government almost immediately did.[68] The Dalai Lama reacted favorably, tempering his speeches by speaking less of his hopes for achieving Tibetan independence and more about the economic well-being of Tibetans: "if the six million Tibetans in Tibet are really happy and prosperous as never before," he declared in 1978, "there is no reason for us to argue otherwise."[69] He also began to speak publicly of reconciling Buddhism with socialism. Without international support the Dalai Lama understood that he had to deal directly with Beijing, and since total independence seemed out of the question, some compromise was worth exploring.

In December 1978 the Beijing authorities stepped up their overtures by directly contacting the Dalai Lama's brother, Gyalo Thondup, who had been waiting in Hong Kong for just such an invitation at the advice of the CIA,[70] and a new round of Dalai Lama–Beijing contacts immediately began,[71] resulting in an agreement to send an investigative delegation to Tibet in August 1979, the first such visit since the events of 1959. The Dalai Lama also began to travel around the world more to gain visibility for his cause, visiting in 1979 the Soviet Union, Mongolia, and the United States, all for the first time. The trip to the United States was significant since he had been denied a visa for ten years on the grounds that it was "inconvenient."[72]

Although visas were officially issued to the Dalai Lama as a religious figure, Beijing was publicly upset over the Tibetan's trips to the United States and the Soviet Union, then in conflict with China. Yet the negotiations were not derailed, and in 1979 and 1980 the Dalai Lama sent three fact-finding delegations to Tibet. A fourth trip was not permitted until July 1985 and its movements were restricted. They were not permitted to visit Tibet proper.

Also in 1980 Chinese Communist Party leader Hu Yaobang traveled to Tibet and found conditions so appalling he immediately ordered dramatic changes.[73] These changes (only partially implemented), and the acknowledgment that there were serious problems in Tibet, continued to set a climate for compromise. In April 1982 the Dalai Lama sent another delegation to Beijing, where it was agreed that he would return to Lhasa in 1985 after an advance party prepared for the trip sometime in 1984.[74] He even publicly announced his imminent return home.

Sadly, an accommodation was not at hand as the talks broke down. The details remain secret, although we can surmise that the Dalai Lama wanted the freedom to travel, to speak openly, to live in Lhasa, and gain a very large measure of autonomy for Tibet while the Chinese probably wanted him to live in Beijing, to be able to regulate his movements, and to have him accept limited autonomy.

As long as the Dalai Lama was talking to Beijing, looking for third-party support was deemed unnecessary. The Dalai Lama traveled[75] as a religious figure, and while he took every opportunity to meet local officials and present his case to politicians, the major focus of these trips was indeed nonpolitical, if for nothing else not to embarrass the governments that had, only begrudgingly, issued him visas.[76] When talks stalled in the latter half of the 1980s the Dalai Lama had to rethink his options.

This rethinking led to a bold new program. The plan called for increasing awareness of Tibet by building popular support on moral grounds (independence, religious freedom, environment, etc.) and then using the resulting popular protest to compel governments to line up behind the Dalai Lama by pressuring Beijing to be more flexible at the bargaining table. This strategy called for: (1) the Dalai Lama to travel more and be openly political, (2) support groups to be established around the world, especially in the United States, to lobby their governments on the Dalai Lama's behalf, (3) members of parliaments of major nations to be recruited with the eventual goal being support from the governments of these nations, (4) peaceful civil disobedience to be encouraged inside Tibet, and (5) the Dalai Lama to continue to plead for talks offering flexible terms to Beijing.[77] While not all these proposed groups and activities were coordinated from a single office in Dharamsala, and some groups were only loosely connected to this campaign, together they constituted a major new effort on behalf of self-determination for Tibet.

During late 1986 and early 1987 the Tibetans convened meetings in London, New York, and Washington, DC, to establish what came to be known, colloquially, as the Tibet Lobby. The internationalization of the Tibet issue had begun in earnest. The Dalai Lama traveled widely, visiting Latin America, the United States (frequently), Europe, and the Soviet Union, meeting with heads of state, parliamentary members, the Pope—anyone who would see him, including Austrian president Kurt Waldheim twice, when Waldheim was subject to an international boycott by world leaders for his earlier Nazi affiliations.[78] The Tibetans initiated a political campaign in the United States aided by the powerful Washington, DC law firm of Wilmer, Cutler and Pickering. Known for its ability to lobby the U.S. Congress and the White House, the firm registered on July 5, 1985, with the U.S. Justice Department as agents for the "Government of Tibet in Exile."[79]

Parallel with the efforts to win governmental approval, similar efforts were made to win broad popular support. Conferences were held in India, Germany, Denmark, and London to coordinate international efforts to publicize the Tibetan cause. Support groups were established around the world both among the general public and among parliamentarians in the United States, England, German, Canada, Norway, Italy, and elsewhere.[80] The Dalai Lama announced 1990 to be the "Year of Tibet" with a "treasures of Tibet" art exhibit, cultural performances, "debating monks" (Tibetan Buddhist monks traditionally debate religious issues), and such. Also announced was the establishment of a major cultural center in New York City to be dubbed "Tibet House."[81] In addition, the cause was aided immeasurably when Tibetan Buddhism became fashionable among Hollywood film stars, which added luster and money to the internationalization efforts.[82]

In March 1988 the International Campaign for Tibet was founded in Washington, DC, where it registered with the Justice Department as a foreign agent for "His Holiness the Dalai Lama" and began a publication called *Tibet Press Watch,* a compilation of news stories on Tibet. The group's activities included the sponsoring of visits by congressional aides to Tibetan settlements in India and Nepal.[83] The Campaign also launched *Tibet Forum,* a Chinese-language publication aimed at the exile Chinese dissident community and written by expatriate Tibetan students who had been educated in China.[84]

All of these efforts began to bear fruit, especially in the U.S. Congress, where some congressional members were already angry at China over various issues such as the trade imbalance, human rights in general, military sales, export of goods produced by prison labor, and so on. One of the Tibet Lobby's earliest successes was a June 1987 U.S. House of Representatives amendment to the Foreign Relations Authorization Act denouncing "human rights violations" in Tibet and asserting that Tibet is forcibly occupied by China.[85]

In 1987 the Dalai Lama addressed the U.S. Congressional Human Rights Caucus and outlined a plan calling for: (1) Tibet to be a zone of peace, (2) an abandonment of ethnic Chinese migration to Tibet, (3) respect for human rights and democratic freedoms, (4) respect for the environment, and (5) negotiations on the future status of Tibet. Both the specifics and the forum were meant to convey a message to Beijing that the Dalai Lama had U.S. backing for his efforts to resume talks.

While the Dalai Lama was in the United States, on September 24 the authorities in Lhasa held a public trial, executing two Tibetans accused of being common criminals. Tibetan exiles claimed the men were political prisoners. Whatever the truth, three days later Lhasa saw its first public demonstrations in twenty-eight years. More disturbances followed on October 1—China's National Day—which led to bloodshed.

These events in Tibet were triggered by deepening hostilities in the Tibetan-

Chinese relationship, continued restrictions on religious practices, anger at the executions, agitation by visitors (both Western and Tibetan), and the knowledge that the Dalai Lama was at that moment in Washington, DC. It is probable that foreign visitors played some role in instigating the protests.[86]

Five days later, in response to the activities in Lhasa, the U.S. Senate unanimously passed a resolution similar to the earlier House bill, adding provisions that tied future military sales to the resolution of human rights abuses. For these sales to continue, according to the bill, the U.S. president would have to affirm that China was "acting in good faith and in a timely manner" in correcting human rights abuses in Tibet. In December, President Ronald Reagan signed the bill.[87]

But congressional resolutions do not represent the official view of the United States. Deputy Assistant Secretary of State for East Asian and Pacific Affairs J. Stapleton Roy testified to Congress that "the United States Government considers Tibet to be a part of China and does not in any way recognize the Tibetan government in exile that the Dalai Lama claims to head." Moreover, the United States rejected his Five Point Plan because it was "a political program advanced by a man who is the head of a government in exile" that no government recognizes.[88]

When the Dalai Lama returned to India he held a news conference and although questioned repeatedly he refused to say that he still favored independence, thereby demonstrating his continued hopes for reconciliation with Beijing.[89]

In Tibet things remained quiet until March 5, 1988, when Lhasa saw its biggest demonstration ever (March 10 is the day Tibetans commemorate the 1959 uprising). Several thousand Tibetans took part and the police used tear gas and electric cattle prods to restore order. The Dalai Lama had hoped that a little civil disobedience in Lhasa and the internationalization of the Tibet Question would help prod Beijing toward further compromise. The plan was backfiring, for unrest in a sensitive border area with a history of rebellion, coupled with Western interference at a time when Beijing might have been willing to deal with the Dalai Lama, only served to buttress the arguments of those opposing compromise. U.S. refusal to acknowledge its covert hand in the contemporary history of Tibet only diminished the force of its pious pronouncements on human rights abuses in the region.[90]

Nonetheless, the Dalai Lama took a bold initiative. Speaking in front of the European Parliament in Strasbourg, France (to again highlight his international support), on June 15, 1988, he reiterated much of his earlier Five Point Plan and went one big step further, saying, for the first time publicly, that he would be willing to return to a Tibet that was less than independent. He proposed a Tibetan political entity "in association" with China. That is, Beijing would be responsible for foreign affairs and defense while the Tibetans would maintain relations with other nations in the "fields of religion, commerce, education, culture, tourism, science, sports and other non-political activities."[91] And, since the Chinese government had repeatedly said it would be willing to meet the Dalai Lama, or his representative, anywhere, anytime, to discuss anything except independence, the Dalai Lama proceeded to name a six-member delegation, with two aides and a legal adviser who, he declared, would be in Geneva in January 1989 waiting for their Chinese counterparts.

The speech called the Chinese bluff, for the Dalai Lama had agreed to the one condition China had always placed on the talks. "The Dalai Lama's concession landed like a bombshell here and the authorities still do not know how to respond," observed one Chinese official.[92] At first there was even some conciliatory language. Agence France-Presse quoted a Chinese official, Mo Zhaoping, as saying that although "partial independence is not acceptable . . . we think there is a change in tone."[93] But in the end Beijing rejected the outstretched hand.

Meanwhile unrest continued in Tibet, and Chinese officials who supported fewer freedoms, more repression, and no compromise with the Dalai Lama were becoming more vocal. "We must deal resolute, accurate and rapid blows against the serious crimes of a small number of separatists," read an editorial in *Xizang Ribao* (Tibet Daily), on March 13, 1988; "[they] are the cause of this earthquake and a cancer cell in society."[94] The head of the public security apparatus, Qiao Shi, called for "the government [to] adopt a policy of merciless repression toward all rebels."[95]

The battle among Chinese officialdom over policy toward Tibet was joined. "There are people who think it necessary to strike down the lamas and destroy the monasteries," the Panchen Lama said on March 29, 1988. "We must not fall back to the errors of the past . . . I must seriously warn against people who have the idea of 'dealing merciless blows at the lamas and closing all the temples.'"[96] Premier Zhao Ziyang was quoted as saying that while some of the unrest may be due to "splittists in foreign countries," there is the problem of "long-standing leftist policies in Tibet . . . [for example] a serious degree of sectarianism existed among Tibetan leaders. The work of addressing the wrongs were advanced very slowly. The Tibetan people's autonomous rights, the Tibetan language and the customs and habits of this nationality were neglected and such mistakes were not properly and quickly corrected."[97]

Despite, or perhaps because of, the liberalized policies, demonstrations continued and in March 1988 a political rally culminating months of marches and protests led to a declaration of martial law in Lhasa and its environs. It was to last until May 1990.

Hu Yaobang had initiated a decade-long liberalization of policies in Tibet. The 1980s had seen an increase in the use of the Tibetan language, the rebuilding of religious structures, and a strengthening of Tibetan culture. The goal was to bring stability to Tibet and in the pursuit of that goal come to some accommodation with the Dalai Lama. With the sudden death of the Panchen Lama in January 1989, these moderate officials reached out to the Dalai Lama by inviting him to attend funerary rites for the Panchen Lama in Beijing while letting him know that there would also be political discussions. This is what he had been hoping for—direct talks with the top Chinese officials. But his advisers were reluctant to accept: he would not be allowed to visit Lhasa; what would he do if he were treated badly;

besides, the international Tibet campaign was flourishing, so going later would give him more international support.[98]

Turning down the invitation was probably the Dalai Lama's greatest political blunder. In China the moderates were discredited; their policies had resulted in riots in Lhasa and the Dalai Lama had refused to visit Beijing. Now it was the turn of the hard-liners, who justified more repressive policies by pointing to the unrest in Tibet and the interference of foreigners in China's internal affairs—both powerful arguments in a country long worried about such matters. Each time the U.S. Congress held a hearing attacking and threatening China, each time a Free Tibet concert publicly ridiculed China, the hard-liners' position was strengthened.

For most of the next decade Chinese policy was devised and carried out by Chen Kuiyuan, the CCP Party secretary in Tibet. Chen was adamantly opposed to negotiating with the Dalai Lama, believing that when the spiritual leader died the international campaign would dissolve. Inside Tibet, Chen's goal was to win the hearts, minds, and loyalties of Tibetans through their stomachs. Economic development, Chen believed, would make Tibetans forget about the Dalai Lama, so to that end he encouraged Chinese migration and substantial investment in the region. Coupled with that were a strict ban on photographs of the Dalai Lama and restrictions on religious institutions, cultural activities, and, of course, any political activities no matter how benign. While economic investment and tourism have brought material benefit to some Tibetans, the migration of perhaps hundreds of thousands of Chinese into Tibet threatens the continued practice of Tibetan culture. By the time Chen was reassigned, his policies had done more to increase ethnic tensions than to ameliorate them.[99]

Martial law in Lhasa received very little international coverage, but the events in Tiananmen Square in the spring of 1989 were seen live on the world's television sets. The power of those images seriously eroded Beijing's reputation, proportionally enhancing the Dalai Lama's, especially in the West. The most immediate consequence was the awarding of the Nobel Peace Prize. Newspaper accounts indicated that the decision had more to do with anti-Chinese sentiment than the activities of the Tibetan prelate. As the *New York Times* reported, people close to the Norwegian Nobel Committee said their choice of the Dalai Lama "was an attempt both to influence events in China and recognize the efforts of the student leaders of the democracy movement."[100]

In Washington the efforts of the Tibet Lobby continued to succeed. Both houses of Congress kept pressure on the White House to do something on Tibet while passing bills with such provisions as a $500,000 grant to Tibetan refugees, thirty U.S. college scholarships (for $1,000,000) for exiled Tibetans, a prohibition on the export of defense goods to China, a bill urging the United States to impose trade sanctions against China, and Tibetan language radio broadcasts on the Voice of America (which began in spring 1991). In 1996 Congress authorized the creation of the federally funded Cold War–style era, Radio Free Asia, to broadcast Washington's version of the news into countries of East Asia where governments were seen as hostile to U.S. interests, including Tibet. In 1997, bowing to public and congressional pressure, President Bill Clinton created the post of Special Coordinator for Tibetan Affairs. This part-time Department of State position could have no influence over Tibetan affairs and was meant to be nothing more than a political sop to Clinton's critics. The appointment is symbolic of U.S. support for the Tibetan exiles: feel-good gestures but no serious policy initiatives that could bring about concrete results or any change in U.S. policy on the issue.

Indeed, the official policy of the U.S. government has always been, and remains today, one of support for China's contention that Tibet is a part of China, that Tibet has never been fully independent and should not be seeking independence. Moreover, no government, including the United States, has ever recognized the Dalai Lama's self-styled government-in-exile. The United States supports talks between the Dalai Lama and Beijing and the attainment of autonomy for an undefined Tibetan region. However, public and congressional pressure have forced successive administrations into activities that have enough symbolic value to appease those applying the pressure while not actually altering official foreign policy.

For example, in April 1991 the Dalai Lama met with members of both houses of Congress (not in the congressional chambers but in a hallway) and, afterward, with President Bush and National Security Advisor Brent Scowcroft in the White House (but not in the Oval Office). He subsequently met with President Bill Clinton and Vice-President Al Gore, as well as President George W. Bush and Vice-President Dick Cheney. Each time, U.S. officials insisted that the visits were private, that the Dalai Lama was invited as a spiritual leader and despite several visits to the White House, the Dalai Lama has never been formally invited to, nor allowed to sit in, rooms where state visitors are received. These actions please the Tibet Lobby, ease pressure from Congress and the public, don't change U.S. policy that Tibet is part of China, and anger the Chinese. In the end the administrations gain domestic political benefit, the Dalai Lama gets more publicity, but it only angers the Chinese, encourages mistrust, and makes a peaceful solution harder to achieve. Ultimately the millions of Tibetans in China are the losers.

Another example of these failed policies are congressional resolutions concerning Tibet that have no formal standing, represent only a "sense of Congress," and are not binding on the government.[101] For example, on October 28, 1991, President Bush signed a State Department Authorization Act that included the following paragraph, of no consequence to U.S. foreign policy but greeted with joy by exile Tibetans:

> That it is the sense of Congress that Tibet, including those areas incorporated into the Chinese provinces of Sichuan, Yunnan, Gansu, and Qinghai [areas of greater Tibetan inhabitation], is an occupied country under established principles of international law whose true representatives are the Dalai Lama and the Tibetan Government-in-Exile as recognized by the Tibetan people.[102]

Back in Asia the talks broke down completely, with China blaming the Dalai Lama's intransigence on the independence issue and arguing that "we have never changed our eagerness to hold negotiations,"[103] and the Dalai Lama insisting that he was searching for a middle way: "I am not demanding complete independence from China," he declared at a press conference on August 1, 1990, for that demand would be "a little unrealistic."[104]

Whoever was at fault, the Dalai Lama withdrew his Strasbourg plan in September 1991, offering in its stead a somewhat less comprehensive proposition asking Beijing to allow him to visit his homeland on a mission of peace, allow him the right to travel freely, to speak freely, and to allow the world press to accompany him.[105] The Chinese response this time was swift and unequivocal: the Dalai Lama cannot go home until he renounces independence.[106] Earlier renunciations were deemed insufficient.

China charged that the Dalai Lama was plotting to restore the old society: "it seems obvious that what he wishes to bring back is the privileges of a few estate holders enslaving the bulk of the Tibetan people."[107] They see unrest in Tibet as solely the result of agitation by outsiders and a "handful of splittists."[108] In November 1991, Beijing issued a sixty-two-page rebuttal of charges concerning human rights abuses throughout the country.[109]

While the Chinese claims are nonsense, Chinese leaders' worst nightmare is that the Dalai Lama's efforts will contribute to the breakup of China or damage the Chinese economy through the elimination of trade concessions or boycotts. But for all the clamor on human rights, there has been no effect on foreign investment in China and the Chinese economy has continued to grow at a healthy pace. Indeed, in November 2001 China was admitted into the World Trade Organization.

Nevertheless, China has been psychologically hurt by all the attention and pressure, and its response has been to organize think tanks and university centers devoted exclusively to the study of Tibet, to try to win over Western scholars to their way of thinking,[110] and to launch a wide-ranging media blitz. The attention given to Tibet inside the People's Republic of China is nothing short of astonishing. No other ethnic minority gets anywhere near this amount of attention. There is a deluge of TV and radio programs, magazines, articles, conferences, and such, all because of the international success of the Tibet Lobby. Since very little of the Tibet Lobby's materials reach a Chinese audience (publications are banned, websites blocked), why Beijing feels the need to respond, and with such magnitude, remains a mystery. Even more curious is that the 150,000 foreign tourists who visit Tibet each year and who have been subjected to the Tibet Lobby's message find no Chinese counter-propaganda in their own languages in the hotels and shops of Lhasa.

The official Chinese view of Tibet is universally accepted within the country. Chinese have been subjected to decades of articles in the press emphasizing obscure historical points to prove that Tibet has always been a part of China, stressing the dismal conditions of the past, and arguing that things have improved so much that outsiders are using the wrong measures to judge conditions today. However, outside the country Chinese propaganda has been stunningly incompetent because of its stilted and ungrammatical language, the use of obscure historical anecdotes that have no meaning to non-Chinese, and because of China's unwavering attacks on the Dalai Lama, who enjoys enormous popularity. In short, the arguments being made are not believable and do not ring true to the ears of non-Chinese. However able China is to compete economically and technologically in the world, it seems to have a tin ear when trying to influence foreign cultures. The Chinese government has employed several public relations firms in the United States, including, for a short time, the most notorious and most effective Hill and Knowlton, to represent it on a host of issues including Tibet.[111] On Tibet at least, they have failed miserably.

In April 1992, at the request of the Chinese government, the Dalai Lama's brother, Gyalo Thondup, resumed talks in Beijing for the first time since martial law was declared in Lhasa four years earlier.[112] The talks continued for a short time in Beijing and with the Chinese ambassador in New Delhi but produced no concrete results.[113] Informal ties continued until 1998 and, after a two-year hiatus, Gyalo Thondup was back in Beijing in October 2000.[114] From all outward signs, none of these talks seems to have produced any concrete results.

Then, quite suddenly, in July 2002, the seventy-three-year-old Gyalo Thondup turned up in Beijing again, perhaps not coincidently, on the fifth anniversary of the Chinese reclamation of Hong Kong, which was predicated on a "one country, two systems" formula. More significantly, perhaps, he was allowed to visit Tibet for the first time since he had fled to India in 1952. His public statements about his reception were exceedingly laudatory. Two months later, in September, an official delegation from the Dalai Lama was welcomed in Beijing and permitted to travel to Tibet. In May 2003 the same delegation returned to Beijing—apparently undeterred by the SARS epidemic—and was escorted on visits to Tibetan-inhabited regions outside the TAR.

It is unclear to those of us without access to the private negotiations what these meetings mean. China has said little publicly, while every statement from the delegates and the Dalai Lama have been positive and hopeful. Is this an attempt at better public relations in the run-up to China's hosting of the Olympic Games in 2008? Or is this a serious attempt to solve the Tibet issue by the new leadership in China led by Hu Jintao? At this point we simply don't know.

However hopeless the situation has seemed, a solution was, and is, possible. What China wants most in Tibet is stability and economic development. The Dalai Lama has the same objectives, along with a reasonable measure of local autonomy so that he can work to preserve and advance Tibetan culture. These are not mutually exclusive objectives, and the two sides are closer together than it may seem. But more than twenty years of failed talks have engendered considerable distrust on both sides. The internationalization of the issue has made Beijing defensive and has contributed to the curbing of the power of officials most willing to negotiate with the Dalai Lama. A settlement would greatly benefit both sides: the Dalai Lama would get to go home and preserve his culture and the Chinese government's international image would be considerably enhanced. Moreover, the Dalai Lama would attract considerable foreign investment, easing Beijing's huge subsidies to the region.

For the United States, Tibet has no political, economic, or strategic importance. Washington pays lip-service to moral values but rarely acts on them. Up until September 11, 2001, there was a debate raging within foreign policy circles over U.S. policy toward China. No more. Now China is a vital ally in the furtherance of U.S. foreign policy interests: in the battle against terrorism, in its efforts to disarm North Korea's nuclear program, at international fora such as the World Trade Organization, and so on. Moreover, China's veto in the UN, which it has never used against the United States, gives it enormous leverage. And then there is always the issue of trade and the PRC's huge potential market. As Washington's and Beijing's interests continue to converge, the Tibet issue will slide further and further into obscurity.

As the second phase of the U.S.–Tibet relationship winds down, it is apparent that once again the United States has done more to betray the exile Tibetan community than to help it. Just as the CIA purported to support the same goals as the Tibetans they were aiding, only to turn its back on them when they no longer served U.S. foreign policy interests, so America's most prominent China-bashers have supported the Tibet Lobby only because it was useful in the campaign against the Chinese Communists. As U.S. interests shift, so will Tibet's "friends." As for Americans in general, Tibet is a fad and like all fads will soon recede and be replaced with something else. However, there will be one important remnant, and that is the growth of Tibetan studies within academia; this, I predict, will continue to grow long after the Tibet groupies have allowed their "Free Tibet" bumper stickers to fade. As for the exile Tibetans, they will likely carry on their struggle long after the groupies and the current Dalai Lama are gone.

In the meantime, a decade of American belligerence has not produced much tangible benefit to the majority of Tibetans in exile, except for those on Washington's payroll. And for the vast majority of Tibetans—those in China—American belligerence has done the opposite of what was intended, strengthening the power of hard-line officials whose policies have resulted in a serious long-term threat to Tibetan culture.

Indisputably, the Dalai Lama's major success has been his ability to create interest and fascination with himself, his cause, and his religion around the world. This fascination has led—not for the first time, but never so widespread and with such intensity—to an infatuation with a romanticized and idealized Tibet, a land of peace and gentility where nonviolence is universally practiced and monks are omniscient. Fascination with this fantasy Tibet has propelled the international campaign to heights unimagined by its originators; Hollywood movies, rock concerts, and celebrities practicing Buddhism have all combined to make the Dalai Lama and Tibet household words.

There is a similar phenomenon going on in China, where the government's attention to Tibet has resulted in a different sort of a fad; an infatuation with things Tibetan, at times portraying Tibetans as "noble savages" with curious ways. Tibetan traditional medicine has become very popular while some young Chinese are "dropping out" by leading "hippy" lives in Lhasa.[115]

At first glance all the attention in the United States and the West appears to be good for the Tibetan cause. But in reality it may be a Pyrrhic victory, for American groupies feel far more about Tibet than they know. Indeed, they would be deeply disillusioned by the real Tibet. Moreover, the creation of this "virtual" (Orville Schell's word) Tibet as an icon has made it, like so much else in American popular culture, a temporary fashion whose time will run out as something else becomes fashionable. Tibetans—real people, with a real history and a real struggle—will have been cartoonized by American (and Chinese) popular culture. It could be the third betrayal.[116]

Notes

1. A. Tom Grunfeld, *The Making of Modern Tibet* (London: Zed Books, 1987), 79. Revised edition published by M.E. Sharpe, Inc., 1996.

2. There is very little of real substance from China. In the United States the Central Intelligence Agency (CIA) is the worst offender. In the 1958–1960 volume of the *Foreign Relations of the United States*, which is the "official documentary historical record of major foreign policy decisions and significant diplomatic activity," the State Department historian notes that because of CIA intransigence "the compilation on Tibet in this volume falls short of the standards of thoroughness and accuracy mandated" by U.S. law. *Foreign Relations of the United States, 1958–1960. Vol. 29. China* (Washington, DC: U.S. Government Printing Office, 1996), iii, x. In a later volume, even though the CIA continued to withhold materials, the historian claimed that this chronicle "provides an accurate account of U.S. policy towards . . . Tibet." There is no mention of the declassification of documents needed for the previous volume. *Foreign Relations of the United States, 1964–1968. Vol. 30. China* (Washington, DC: U.S. Government Printing Office, 1998), viii. (Hereafter *FRUS 1964–1968*.)

3. Frederick Wells Williams, *Anson Burlingame and the First Chinese Mission to Foreign Powers* (New York: Scribner's, 1912), 112–113, 134–139. William Woodville Rockhill, *Diary of a Journey Through Mongolia and Tibet in 1891 and 1892* (Washington, DC: Smithsonian Institution, 1894). Despite the title, Rockhill never reached Tibet proper. Karl E. Meyer and Shareen Blair Brysac, *Tournament of Shadows: The Great Game and the Race for Empire in Central Asia* (New York: Counterpoint Press, 1999), 397–424.

4. First quotation cited in Meyer and Brysac, *Tournament of Shadows*, 422. Second cited in John Kenneth Knaus, "Official Policies and Covert Programs: The U.S. State Department, the CIA, and the Tibetan Resistance," *Journal of Cold War Studies* 5, no. 3 (Summer 2003): 54.

5. Suydam Cutting, *The Fire Ox and Other Years* (New York: Charles Scribner's Sons, 1947). There has been some speculation, although no proof, that Cutting may have been engaged in some intelligence gathering as well. Theos Bernard, *Penthouse of the Gods* (New York: Charles Scribner's Sons, 1939).

6. Leonard Clark, *The Marching Wind* (New York: Funk and Wagnalls, 1954).

7. Albert L. Shelton, *Pioneering in Tibet* (New York: Fleming H. Revell, 1921); Flora Beal Shelton, *Shelton of Tibet* (New York: George H. Doran, 1923); Zenas Loftus, *A Message from Batang* (New York: Fleming H. Revell, Co., 1911); Marion H. Duncan, *The*

Mountain of Silver Snow (Cincinnati: Powell & White, c. 1929); Robert B. Ekvall, *Tibetan Sky Lines* (New York: Farrar, Straus and Young, 1952).

8. "So This Is Shangri-la," *Newsweek*, January 31, 1944, 24–25; William Boyd Sinclair, *Jump to the Land of God: The Adventures of a United States Air Force Crew in Tibet* (Caldwell, OH: Caxton Printers, 1965).

9. OSS, "Outline of Journey and Observation Made by Ilia Tolstoy, Captain, AUS and Brooke Dolan, First Lt., AC," September 1943, Central Intelligence Agency, Roslyn, VA, 1–2; Rosemary Jones Tung, *A Portrait of Lost Tibet* (New York: Holt, Rinehart and Winston, 1980); R. Harris Smith, *OSS: The Secret History of America's First Central Intelligence Agency* (Berkeley, Los Angeles, and London: University of California Press, 1972), 254–255; Ilia Tolstoy, "Across Tibet from India to China," *National Geographic* 90, no. 2 (August 1946): 169–222; Meyer and Brysac, *Tournament of Shadows*, 546–553.

10. *Foreign Relations of the United States, 1943. China* (Washington, DC: U.S. Government Printing Office, 1967), 624. (Hereafter *FRUS 1943*.)

11. Office of Intelligence Research, "Tibet," No. 4731, July 19, 1948, National Archives, Diplomatic Branch, Washington, DC. (Hereafter OIR "Tibet.") George Merrell to Secretary of State, New Delhi, December 9, 1946; Main Decimal File (1945–49) Box 7024, 893.00 Tibet/12–946, National Archives, Diplomatic Branch, Washington, DC.

12. *FRUS 1943*, 630; Charles F. Romanus and Riley Sunderland, *United States Army in World War II. China-Burma-Indian Theater. Stilwell's Mission to China* (Washington, DC: Office of the Chief of Military History, Department of the Army, 1953), 287.

13. *Foreign Relations of the United States, 1947. Vol. 7, The Far East: China* (Washington, DC: U.S. Government Printing Office, 1972), 588–592. (Hereafter *FRUS 1947*.)

14. Ibid., 595–596, 599.

15. Tsepon W. Shakabpa, *Tibet: A Political History* (New Haven, CT and London: Yale University Press, 1967), 294; Shakabpa claims the decision to send the mission was made in October, but as early as August American and Indian officials were discussing the proposed trip. *FRUS, 1947*, 598–600. Amaury de Riencourt recalled that when he was in Lhasa during the summer of 1947 Shakabpa was already planning an overseas trip. Amaury de Riencourt, *Roof of the World: Tibet, Key to Asia* (New York: Rinehart, 1950), 130.

16. See details of Tibetan trade in Grunfeld, *The Making of Modern Tibet* (rev. ed., 1996), 88–91. Also OSS, "Outline of Journey," no page numbers, see chapter titled "Economic Report."

17. Shakabpa, *Tibet*, 295.

18. *FRUS 1947*, 598–600. Shakabpa was not universally liked or trusted; see George N. Patterson, *Requiem for Tibet* (London: Aurum Press, 1990), 103. *Foreign Relations of the United States, 1948. Vol. 7. The Far East* (Washington, DC: U.S. Government Printing Office, 1973), 757–758. (Hereafter *FRUS 1948*.)

19. Emphasis added. *FRUS 1947*, 604. Shakabpa was repeatedly told that the issuance of visas did not denote any recognition of Tibet as a separate entity from China. Yet he misrepresented this in his history of Tibet and historians have followed his lead on this issue almost without exception.

20. *FRUS 1948*, 760–761.

21. A.T. Steele in the *Chicago Daily News* in a seven-part series in the Pictorial Section; November 18, 25, December 2, 9, 16, 23, 30, 1944. A.T. Steele, "The Boy Ruler of Shangri-La," *Saturday Evening Post*, April 13, 1946, 14.

22. Lowell Thomas, Jr., *The Silent War in Tibet* (Garden City, NY: Doubleday, 1959), 21; "Lowell Thomas Back from Tibet," *New York Times*, October 17, 1949, 25; Albert Siegfried Willner, "The Eisenhower Administration and Tibet, 1953–1961: Influence and the Making of US Foreign Policy" (Ph.D. dissertation, University of Virginia, 1995), 29.

23. *Foreign Relations of the United States, 1949. Vol. 9. The Far East: China* (Washington, DC: U.S. Government Printing Office, 1974), 1065–1080.

24. Ibid., 1980–1982.

25. Memo of conversation in Kalimpong, June 7, 1951, between one of the Pangdatsang brothers, Rev. G. Tharchin (a converted Christian Tibetan and editor of *Tibet Mirror*, the only Tibetan-language newspaper of that time), George Patterson, and Fraser Wilkins, First Secretary, U.S. Embassy, New Delhi, #3030, June 14, 1951, declassified to author. "Department [of State] would not wish Tibetans misinterpret our failure [to] accede [to] their requests as disinterest or lack [of] sympathy [for] their predicaments or difficulties." *Foreign Relations of the United States, 1950. Vol. 6, East Asia and the Pacific* (Washington, DC: U.S. Government Printing Office, 1976), 272–273, 275–276, 330–331. (Hereafter *FRUS 1950.*)

26. Harry Rositzke, *The CIA's Secret Operations: Espionage, Counterespionage, and Covert Action* (New York: Reader's Digest Press, 1977), 173. Lindsay quoted in Knaus, "Official Polices and Covert Programs," 55.

27. "Brother of the Dalai Lama Arrives Here to Study," *New York Times*, July 9, 1951, 8; Steve Weissman, "Last Tangle in Tibet," *Pacific Research and World Empire Telegram* 4, no. 5 (July–August 1973): 5.

28. Quoted in T.D. Allman, "A Half Forgotten Conflict," *Far Eastern Economic Review*, February 11, 1974, 27. For a discussion of CIA operations against China, see A. Tom Grunfeld, "'God We Had Fun': The CIA in China and Sino-American Relations," *Critical Asian Studies* 35, no. 1 (2003): 113–138.

29. Copy of pamphlet in author's possession. Letter to author from J.S. Evans, Capt. USN, Chief, Directorate for Print Media, Department of Defense, Washington, DC, July 3, 1979.

30. *FRUS 1950*, 376, 378–618.

31. John Kenneth Knaus, *Orphans of the Cold War: America and the Tibetan Struggle for Survival* (New York: PublicAffairs, 1999), 201, 204. Fraser Wilkins to Secretary of State, New Delhi, June 7, 1961 and June 14, 1951. Declassified to author.

32. "United States Policy Concerning the Legal Status of Tibet, 1942–1956," Research Project No. 403, November 1957, Box 3949, Decimal File 611.793B, National Archives, 18.

33. U.S. Department of State, *Foreign Relations of the United States, 1955–1957, Vol. 8* (Washington, DC: U.S. Government Printing Office, 1987), 36. For a detailed analysis of Eisenhower-era policies toward Tibet, see Willner, *The Eisenhower Administration and Tibet, 1953–1961*.

34. Public Records Office, Kew Gardens, UK (hereafter PRO) FO 371/84468 FT 1621/ 2; PRO FO 371/84450 FT 1015/44; PRO FO 371/84450 FT 1015/19; PRO FO 371/92997; PRO FO 371/92998 FT 10310/79. Considerable cable traffic went between the U.S. Department of State and the U.S. Embassy in New Delhi on this subject. See 793B.00/7–2151. For plans see 7936.00/7–7151. National Archives, Diplomatic Branch, Washington, DC; B.N. Mullik, *My Years with Nehru: The Chinese Betrayal* (Bombay: Allied Publishers, 1971), 80–81.

35. Weissman, "Last Tangle," 1–18; Steve Weissman and John Shock, "CIAsia Foundation," *Pacific Research and World Empire Telegram* 3, no. 6 (September–October 1972): 3–4; David W. Conde, *CIA–Core of the Cancer* (New Delhi: Entente Private, 1979), 111–115.

36. Tsering Shakya, *The Dragon in the Land of Snows: A History of Modern Tibet Since 1947* (New York: Columbia University Press, 1999), 61–71, 89–91.

37. Knaus, *Orphans of the Cold War*, 147, 154–155. The most thorough and scholarly, but still incomplete, account of CIA activities in Tibet is by John Kenneth Knaus. For the most details about the operations, see Kenneth Conboy and James Morrison, *The CIA's Secret War in Tibet* (Lawrence: University Press of Kansas, 2002). One other CIA participant has written a book that is deeply flawed and a little bizarre ("The Dalai Lama, an openly declared admirer and advocate of Marxist socialism"); Roger E. McCarthy, *Tears of*

the Lotus: Accounts of Tibetan Resistance to the Chinese Invasion, 1950–1962 (Jefferson, NC: McFarland, 1997), 3. For CIA operations in the Tibetan region in the late 1940s see Thomas Laird, Into Tibet: The CIA's First Atomic Spy and His Secret Expedition to Lhasa (New York: Grove Press, 2002).

38. Asian Recorder, 61, no. 30 (1959): 2785–2786.

39. "The Red Terror in Tibet: Interview with the Dalai Lama," US News and World Report, April 24, 1961, 79.

40. "Diplomacy and the Dalai Lama," Far Eastern Economic Review, March 18, 1974, 32.

41. "Interview with the Dalai Lama's Brother—'Holy War' in Tibet—What Is It All About?" US News and World Report, April 13, 1959, 48.

42. Knaus, Orphans of the Cold War, 136.

43. Ibid., 138. John F. Avedon, In Exile from the Land of Snows: The First Full Account of the Dalai Lama and Tibet Since the Chinese Conquest (New York: Alfred A. Knopf, 1984), 47; David Allan Mayers, Cracking the Monolith: U.S. Policy Against the Sino-Soviet Alliance, 1949–1955 (Baton Rouge and London: Louisiana State University Press, 1986), 78–87, 95.

44. Knaus, Orphans of the Cold War, 139, 140. The Eisenhower administration created a body called the 5412 Group, which acted as an intermediary between the CIA and the president, thereby giving Ike "plausible deniability" when it came to approving CIA operations. Willner, The Eisenhower Administration and Tibet, 1953–1961, 90–102.

45. The most complete account is Laird, Into Tibet. Also, Ted Gup, The Book of Honor: Covert Lives and Classified Deaths at the CIA (New York: Doubleday, 2000), 9–42; Ted Gup, "Star Agents," Washington Post Magazine, September 7, 1997, 6–13, 22–28; "Log of Mr. Frank Bessac's Journey From Tihwa, Sinkiang," Department of State, 793b.00/9–2150, September 21, 1950.

46. Grunfeld, The Making of Modern Tibet (1996), 99–106.

47. Chris Mullin, "The CIA: Tibetan Conspiracy," Far Eastern Economic Review, September 5, 1989, 30–34; Dalai Lama (Tenzin Gyatso), Freedom in Exile: The Autobiography of the Dalai Lama (New York: HarperCollins, 1990), 126–127; Evan Thomas, The Very Best Men. Four Who Dared: The Early Years of the CIA (New York: Simon & Schuster, 1995), 276; Kraus, Orphans of the Cold War, 137–140.

48. Knaus, Orphans of the Cold War, 145; Gompo Tashi Andrugtsang, Four Rivers, Six Ranges: Reminiscences of the Resistance Movement in Tibet (Dharamsala, India: Information and Publicity Office of H.H. the Dalai Lama, 1973), 50–51; Michel Peissel, The Secret War in Tibet (Boston, MA: Little Brown, 1972), 94.

49. Conboy and Morrison, The CIA's Secret War in Tibet; Knaus, Orphans of the Cold War, 147, 154–155; Mullin, "The CIA," 33; T.D. Allman, "Cold Wind of Change," Guardian, December 19, 1973, 11; William M. Leary, "Secret Mission to Tibet," Air & Space 12, no. 5 (December 1997–January 1998): 71.

50. David Wise, The Politics of Lying: Government Deception, Secrecy and Power (New York: Vintage Books, 1973), 239–261; Knaus, Orphans of the Cold War, 216–222.

51. Grunfeld, The Making of Modern Tibet (1996), 134–139, 141–145, 155–157; A. Tom Grunfeld, "Reexamining the 1959 Lhasa Revolt," unpublished paper presented at "Tibet: The Ecology of a Culture," Yale University, October 24, 1992. An article in Jeune Afrique, widely reproduced in the Chinese press, claimed that the United States promised to train 400 Indian scientists in nuclear technology in return for giving asylum to the Dalai Lama. No evidence is provided although it may have come from William R. Corson. Andre Lewin, "Nehru, la bombe et le dalai-lama," Jeune Afrique, October 5–11, 1999, 74.

The late William R. Corson, a Chinese-speaking former marine lieutenant colonel and CIA operative, claimed he was engaged in planning the Dalai Lama's escape before the

March 1959 revolt. Corson spoke at the "Nuclear Weapons in Asia Conference," sponsored by National Security News Service, Washington DC, August 9, 1999.

52. Knaus, *Orphans of the Cold War*, 181.

53. Ibid., 233.

54. L. Fletcher Prouty, *The Secret Team: The CIA and its Allies in Control of the United States and the World* (Englewood Cliffs, NJ: Prentice-Hall, 1973), 21, 37–82; Evans, personal correspondence.

55. Grunfeld, *The Making of Modern Tibet* (1996), 146–149, 151–152, 195–198.

56. Emphasis added. "U.S. Affirms Belief in the Principle of Self-Determination for Tibet," *Department of State Bulletin* 42, no. 1082 (March 21, 1960): 443–444.

57. Knaus, *Orphans of the Cold War*, 271–276; Conboy and Morrison, *The CIA's Secret War in Tibet*.

58. *Foreign Relations of the United States, 1961–1963. Vol. 22. Northeast Asia* (Washington, DC: U.S. Government Printing Office, 1996), 170–172; John B. Roberts II, "The Secret War over Tibet. A Story of Cold War Heroism—and Kennedy administration Cowardice and Betrayal." *American Spectator*, December 1997. Roberts attacks the Kennedy administration for briefly withholding aid in 1961 but says nothing of the far greater betrayal of the Tibetans by the Nixon administration and Kissinger.

59. Kraus, *Orphans of the Cold War*, 276.

60. Ibid., 281.

61. Dawa Norbu, "China Behind Khampa Disarmament," *Tibetan Review* (hereafter *TR*) 10, no. 1 (January 1975): 3–4.

62. Roberts, "The Secret War." The author offers no documentary evidence, but does say "officials at the Central Intelligence Agency were unusually helpful in the research for this article."

63. Knaus, *Orphans of the Cold War*, 275, 282, 284–285, 287, 310; *FRUS 1964–1968*, 731–744.

64. "Tibetan Government Press Release," T.C. Teething, Department of Information and International Relations, Central Tibetan Administration, Dharamsala, October 10, 1998.

65. *FRUS 1964–1968*, Document No. 337, January 9, 1964.

66. Knaus, *Orphans of the Cold War*, 216.

67. Victor S. Kaufman, "A Response to Chaos: The United States, the Great Leap Forward, and the Cultural Revolution, 1961–1968," *Journal of American–East Asian Relations* 7, nos. 1–2 (Spring–Summer 1998): 73–92.

68. Dalai Lama, *Freedom in Exile*, 222–223.

69. His Holiness the Dalai Lama, *Collected Statements, Interviews and Articles* (Dharamsala, India: The Information Office of His Holiness the Dalai Lama, 1982), 51.

70. Dawa Norbu, "China's Dialogue with the Dalai Lama 1978–1990: Prenegotiation Stage or Dead End?" *Pacific Affairs* 64, no. 3 (Fall 1991): 369.

71. Dalai Lama, *Freedom in Exile*, 223.

72. *TR* 14:6 (June 1979): 8–9; *TR* 14:12 (December 1979): 14. The exile Tibetans' first effort at lobbying in the United States was unorganized but successful nevertheless. Their goals were to obtain a visa for the Dalai Lama and to get the Department of State to use the designation "Tibet" as a birthplace on the passports of newly naturalized Tibetan-Americans. Dongdong Tian, "The Tibet Issue in Sino-American Relations: United States Policy Making Since Rapproachment" (Ph.D. dissertation, Brandeis University, 1995), 56–69.

73. Norbu, "China's Dialogue with the Dalai Lama," 353; Wang Lixiong, "The 'Tibetan Question': Nation and Religion," unpublished ms.

74. Dalai Lama, *Freedom in Exile*, 240.

75. For a complete list of countries visited, see Rogers Hicks and Ngakpa Chogyam, *Great Ocean* (Longmead, UK: Element Books, 1984), 198–199.

76. *TR* 19:5 (May 1984): 6; *TR* 19:10 (October 1984): 5; *TR* 19:12 (December 1984): 7–8; *TR* 21:2 (February 1985): 5; *Tibetan Bulletin* (hereafter *TB*) 15:5 (December 1984–January 1985): 2–3, 16; *TB* 16:1 (April–May 1985): 12.

77. Melvyn C. Goldstein, "The Dragon and the Snow Lion: The Tibet Question in the 20th Century," in *China Briefing 1990*, ed. Anthony J. Kane (Boulder, CO: Westview Press, 1990), 150; Melvyn C. Goldstein, *The Snow Lion and the Dragon: China, Tibet, and the Dalai Lama* (Berkeley: University of California Press, 1997), 75–76.

78. Not only did the Dalai Lama meet Waldheim but he seems to have a propensity for meeting former and current Nazis. His relationship with Heinrich Harrer, who served in both the Nazi SA (storm troops) and the SS (black shirts) in the 1930s is well known. Bernard Weinraub, "Film's Hero was a Nazi," *New York Times*, June 21, 1997. Also, Li Jianhua, "The Dalai Lama's Teacher—a Nazi?" *China Today* 46, no. 12 (December 1997): 34. On one visit to Austria he met and was photographed with Bruno Berger, who had been convicted of killing Jews at Auschwitz. Meyer and Brysac, *Tournament of Shadows*, 526–527. On a visit to Chile in June 1992 the Dalai Lama was met at the airport by, among others, the leader of Chile's Nazi party, Miguel Serrano, who told reporters he had met the Dalai Lama while he was Chile's ambassador to India and that the two "are friends." "Dalai Lama Greeted by Tense Climate in Chile," Reuters, June 16, 1992. *TR* 21:6 (June 1986): 6–7; *TR* 21:9–10 (September–October 1986): 4, 5; *TR* 22:4 (April 1987): 7–8; *TB* 17:2 (June–July 1986): 2–3.

79. *TB* 16:3 (August–September 1985): 13. Papers filed with the U.S. Justice Department's Foreign Agents Registration Unit say that Wilmer, Cutler & Pickering will "provide legal advice . . . on a pro-bono basis." Registration No. 3355, July 5, 1985.

80. *TR* 25:4 (April 1990): 10–11. Originally the conference in India was to be called the International Contact Conference of Tibet Supporters. When Indian officials expressed reservations about the title it was renamed the International Friends of Tibet, which also received Indian disapproval.

The issue of Tibetan independence was a very delicate one in India. At the time, Prime Minister Rajiv Gandhi had signed a protocol in Beijing with Chinese premier Li Peng reiterating India's long-held belief that "Tibet is an autonomous region of China and anti-China political activities by Tibetan elements are not permitted on Indian soil." Barbara Crossette, "Indo-China Statement Angers Tibetans," *New York Times*, January 3, 1989, A11. *TR* 25:8 (August 1990): 6–7. *TR* 28:1 (January 1993): 6. *TR* 24:9 (September 1989): 7. *TB* 20:2 (June–July 1989): 1–2, 12. *TR* 24:6 (June 1989): 5. *TR* 24:12 (December 1989): 5.

81. Douglas C. McGill, "Dalai Lama Promoted an Exhibition," *New York Times*, September 28, 1987, C23; *TB*, March–April 1992, 34.

82. For example, Richard Gere raised $525,000 to buy a $825,000 brownstone in New York City for the Dalai Lama's political headquarters in the United States. Some of the groups headquartered in the new building were: the Office of Tibet, the U.S.-Tibet Committee, the Tibetan Woman's Association, the Tibetan Youth Association, Potala Publications, Eco-Tibet, TibetNet, Tibetan Association, Tibet Fund, and the Tibetan-U.S. Resettlement Project.

Some of the more prominent adherents to Tibetan Buddhism are Richard Gere, John Cleese, Harrison Ford, and Danielle Mittérrand, the late French president's wife. Tim McGirk, "Stars Get High on Spiritual Picnic," *The Independent on Sunday* (London), August 23, 1993, 12.

83. *TR* 23:11 (November 1988): 4; *TR* 20:1 (April–May 1989): 7.

84. *News Tibet* 22:4 (September–October 1988): 9, *TB*, March–April 1991, 5.

85. One researcher has argued that the members of Congress who supported the Tibet Lobby could be broken down into three categories: those truly interested in the Tibet issue, those who were interested in human rights in general, and the vehement anti-Communists. Tian, "The Tibet Issue in Sino-American Relations," 103–107.

86. Shakya, *The Dragon In the Land of Snows*, 417.

87. *TR* 22:8 (August 1987): 77–79; *TR* 22:11 (November 1987): 11; *TR* 23:1 (January 1988): 5.

88. "Human Rights Situation of the Tibetan People," *Department of State Bulletin* 87, no. 2129 (December 1987): 50; Elaine Sciolino, "US Official Defends Stance on Turmoil in Tibet," *New York Times*, October 15, 1987, A18.

89. Sanjoy Hazorika, "Dalai Lama Urges Peaceful Protest," *New York Times*, October 8, 1987, A8.

90. A. Tom Grunfeld, "Letter to the Editor," *New York Times*, March 23, 1988, A26. Elaine Sciolino, "Beijing Is Backed by Administration on Unrest in Tibet," *New York Times*, October 7, 1987, A1.

91. Address to Members of the European Parliament by His Holiness the Dalai Lama, Strasbourg, June 15, 1988.

92. Agence France-Presse (hereafter AFP), July 28, 1988, in Foreign Broadcast Information Service (hereafter FBIS)-CHI-88–145, July 28, 1988, 44.

93. FBIS-CHI-88–121, June 23, 1988, 42.

94. British Broadcasting Corporation, Summary of World Broadcasts (hereafter SWB), Part III, Far East, March 16, 1988.

95. Quoted in the *South China Morning Post*, July 20, 1988.

96. FBIS-CHI-88–060, March 29, 1988; FBIS-CHI-88–066, April 6, 1988. The sudden and unexpected death of the Panchen Lama at the age of fifty in Shigatse in January 1989 removed from the scene an important player who could have contributed greatly to the solution of the Tibet problem. A. Tom Grunfeld, "Enigmatic Buddha Who Works from Within," *The Guardian* (London), October 8, 1988, 8.

97. Quoted in *Ming Pao*, June 2, 1988, in SWB, Part III, Far East, FE/0169–B2/1, June 4, 1988. For a good description of events inside Tibet during the 1980s see Tseten Wangchuk Sharlho, "China's Reforms in Tibet: Issues and Dilemmas," *Journal of Contemporary China* 1, no. 1 (Fall 1992): 34–60.

98. Goldstein, *The Snow Lion and the Dragon*, 90. A. Tom Grunfeld, "The Question of Tibet," *Current History* 98, no. 629 (September 1999): 294.

99. For an excellent review of Chen's policies, see Robert Barnett, "The Chinese Frontiersman and the Winter Worm—Chen Kuiyuan in the T.A.R., 1992–2000," paper delivered at the History of Tibet Conference, University of St. Andrews, 2001.

100. Sheila Rule, "How, and Why, the Dalai Lama Won the Peace Prize," *New York Times*, October 13, 1989, A14.

101. Gwen Ifill, "Lawmakers Cheer Tibetan in Capitol Rotunda," *New York Times*, April 19, 1991, A7; *TB*, May–June 1991, 16; *TR* 26:5 (May 1991): 6. Author's interviews with State Department officials on the China Desk, March 9, 1992.

102. *TB*, November–December 1991, 22. *News Tibet*, January–February 1992, 4.

103. Fan Cheuk-wan, "Dalai Lama 'Accused' of Blocking Talks," *South China Morning Post*, May 9, 1990, 6.

104. "Dalai Lama to End Institution, Independence Goal," AFP, August 1, 1990, in FBIS-CHI-90–148, 11. See also, "Dalai Lama Calls for Sino-Tibetan Confederation," AFP, December 13, 1990, in FBIS-CHI-90–241, 23.

105. Ari L. Goldman, "Dalai Lama Appeals for Help in Going Home," *New York Times*, October 10, 1991, A17; Gerald Renner, "Dalai Lama: Genial Manner, Serious Mission," *Hartford Courant*, October 10, 1991, A15.

106. "China Rejects Dalai Lama's Offer to End Exile," AFP, October 10, 1991.

107. Zhang Chunjian and Xeirab Nyima, "Human Rights in Tibet: Past and Present," *Beijing Review* 35, no. 8 (February 24–March 1, 1992): 27.

108. Graham Hutchings, "China's Fury at Major's Talk with God-King," *Daily Telegraph*, December 6, 1991, 12.

109. Nicholas D. Kristof, "China Issues Rebuttal to Human Rights Critics," *New York Times*, November 3, 1991, A12.

110. Zhao Qizheng, "Tibet—Related External Propaganda and Tibetology Work in the New Era," statement at the meeting on national research in Tibetology and external propaganda on Tibet, June 12, 2000. See the full Chinese, and a shortened English, version at www.savetibet.org/about/pressreleases/PRC_Tibet_propagandadocument.html.

111. For a $5,000 a month retainer, plus expenses, Hill & Knowlton promised to monitor Congress, provide public relations advice, monitor the media, "build support to avoid negative effects on China–US relations," "improve China's overall image," "recruit and organize third party allies," and "respond to urgent criticism." U.S. Department of Justice, Foreign Agents Registration Unit, Registration No. 3301, May 10, 1992.

112. "Dalai Lama Calls for Mutual Trust Between Tibet and China," AFP, July 24, 1992.

113. On the Gyalo Thondup visit, Kyodo News Service, July 22, 1992 and a knowledgeable anonymous source confirmed this to me; on the talks in New Delhi see press release from "Cabinet of the Tibetan Government in Exile," September 24, 1992. The Dalai Lama quoted the Chinese ambassador to India as saying that Chinese policy in the past had been "conservative" and was now more "flexible" if the Tibetans can be "realistic." Dalai Lama, "Statement on the 34th Anniversary of the Tibetan National Uprising Day, March 10, 1993," *TR* 28:4 (April 1993): 9.

114. Giles Hewitt, "Dalai Lama Celebrates 50 Years, Announces Fresh Contacts with Beijing," AFP, December 4, 2000.

115. Philip P. Pan, "China's Hippies Find Their Berkeley," *Washington Post*, September 22, 2003.

116. Orville Schell, *Virtual Tibet: Searching for Shangri-la from the Himalayas to Hollywood* (New York: Metropolitan Books, 2000); Patrick French, "Dalai Lama Lite," *New York Times*, September 19, 2003, A27. Also, Barbara Stewart, "In Current Films on Tibet, Hold the Shangri-La," *New York Times*, March 19, 2000. For a series of articles critical of the exile Tibetan view of Tibet see: http://members.tripod.com/~journeyeast/tibet.html.

The Editors And Contributors

The Editors

June Teufel Dreyer is professor of political science at the University of Miami and a commissioner of the U.S.–China Economic and Security Commission established by the United States Congress.

Barry Sautman is associate professor in the Division of Social Sciences at the Hong Kong University of Science and Technology.

The Contributors

Dibyesh Anand is a lecturer in the Department of Economics and International Development at the University of Bath, U.K.

Robert Barnett is program coordinator and lecturer in Modern Tibet Studies at the East Asian Institute of Columbia University.

Cynthia M. Beall is the S. Idell Pyle Professor of Anthropology and co-director of the Center for Research on Tibet at Case Western Reserve University.

Melvyn C. Goldstein is professor of anthropology at Case Western Reserve University.

A. Tom Grunfeld is professor of history at Empire State College in New York City.

He Baogang is Chair in International Studies in the School of Politics and International Studies at Deakin University, Australia.

Hu Xiaojiang received her Ph.D. in sociology from Harvard University and is currently a post-doctoral fellow at the Center for Chinese Studies of the University of California at Berkeley.

Ben Jiao is a research scientist at the Tibet Academy of Social Sciences in Lhasa, Tibet.

P. Christiaan Klieger is senior curator of history at the Oakland Museum of California.

Amy Mountcastle is an associate professor of anthropology at the State University of New York in Plattsburgh.

Dawa Norbu is professor of Central Asian Studies at Jawaharlal Nehru University in New Delhi.

Miguel A. Salazar is a Ph.D. candidate in sociology at Harvard University. His work concentrates on issues of international migration.

Phuntsog Tsering is the former president of the Tibet Academy of Social Sciences.

Wang Lixiong is an independent scholar in Beijing.

Xu Mingxu and Yuan Feng are independent scholars in Cambridge, Massachusetts.

Yu Changjiang is professor of sociology at Beijing University.

Index